Mastering Adobe Photoshop 2024

Discover the smart way to polish your digital imagery skills by editing professional looking photos

Gary Bradley

<packt>

BIRMINGHAM—MUMBAI

Mastering Adobe Photoshop 2024

Group Product Manager: Rohit Rajkumar
Publishing Product Manager: Nitin Nainani
Book Project Manager: Sonam Pandey
Senior Content Development Editor: Feza Shaikh
Technical Editor: Simran Udasi
Copy Editor: Safis Editing
Proofreader: Safis Editing
Indexer: Manju Arasan
Production Designer: Jyoti Kadam
DevRel Marketing Coordinator: Namita Velgekar and Nivedita Pandey

First edition: January 2024

Production reference: 1151223

Published by Packt Publishing Ltd.
Grosvenor House
11 St Paul's Square
Birmingham
B3 1RB, UK

ISBN 978-1-83882-201-9

`www.packtpub.com`

For Sarah.

Your love, strength, and patience help me become the person I've always wanted to be.

Contributors

About the author

Gary Bradley is an award-winning designer and Adobe Certified Expert based in Sheffield, England. With over 25 years of industry experience delivering projects for clients such as Virgin Atlantic and the London Science Museum, Gary has worked across several disciplines, including illustration, 3D visualization, printing, and web design. In 2009, he launched a creativity consultancy to support design teams in nurturing their in-house capabilities and achieving Adobe Specialist status. Gary also teaches graphic design and illustration at the Sheffield College.

About the reviewers

Mayank Verma is a seasoned online graphic designer specializing in broadcast and digital media. With a distinguished career spanning over a decade, he has excelled in illustrating concepts and creating visually compelling layouts. His journey includes contributions to leading firms such as Sit-Down, Australia; NDTV; and Republic TV. His expertise spans 3D modeling, lighting, rendering, and client relationship management. Notably, he played a key role in establishing virtual studios for live broadcasts of major events. His ability to blend technical acumen with creative ingenuity sets him apart as a dynamic professional.

Matthew Gibbon (ASCP) is an Apple Certified professional with over 33 years of experience in the advertising industry.

The **Apple Certified Support Professional** (**ACSP**) certification is designed for help desk professionals, technical coordinators, and power users who support macOS users, manage networks, or provide macOS technical support. ACSP certification verifies an understanding of macOS core functions and that the following functions can be carried out:

- Configure key services
- Perform basic troubleshooting
- Support multiple Mac users

Having started as a photo-typesetter, Matthew has worked with leading global brands for South African ad agencies, corporate clients, and smaller companies.

Matthew also teaches corporates and private individuals in South Africa and offers online support to clients all over the world.

Contact him at: `matthew@cardilogix.co.za`.

Table of Contents

5

6

7

Creating Animated GIFs and Videos 207

Part 3: Building Visual Components

8

Bringing Typography to Life with Effects and Styling 249

9

Creating Textures, Patterns, and Backdrops 291

10

Creating and Applying Brushes 317

Part 4: World Building

11

Blending and Collaging Images 349

Preface

Mastering Adobe Photoshop 2024 will guide you step by step through the in-demand skills required by the industry. This book will build on your existing Photoshop knowledge, helping you become a more productive image editor and improve the quality of your work. It will teach you about essential resources for graphic designers or marketers looking for transformative career growth.

As a digital content creator, whether you're working on projects for print, screen, or social media, having a solid understanding of Adobe Photoshop is essential. This powerful application can take your designs to new heights, allowing you to create captivating visuals that leave a lasting impression on your audience. So, if you are ready to elevate your skills and expand your capabilities, *Mastering Adobe Photoshop 2024* is the book you've been waiting for.

This book takes a step-by-step approach, breaking down each technique into easily understandable terms, making it accessible even to those who are new to advanced editing. The jargon-busting approach ensures that you can grasp the concepts without feeling overwhelmed. Then, through a series of hands-on exercises, you'll have the opportunity to practice your newfound knowledge, learning about each tool's strengths and limitations.

In the book's final section, you'll bring everything together and learn how to produce your digital media projects from start to finish. From project planning and organization to final delivery, this book provides a comprehensive framework to streamline your workflow and achieve remarkable results.

From creating captivating visuals for social media to mastering retouching and compositing, this book equips you with the knowledge and skills needed to excel in digital imagery. Embrace this opportunity to unlock your creative potential and propel your career forward.

Who this book is for

This book is for people with a basic working knowledge of Adobe Photoshop who are determined to enhance their skills to a professional standard with proven industry techniques and workflows. Understanding digital media file types will be an advantage to help you gain the most value from this book.

If you're a designer or marketer looking to build upon a basic working knowledge of Adobe Photoshop, gain invaluable insights into professional editing techniques, and take your career to the next step, this book is for you.

What this book covers

Chapter 1, Making Photoshop Work Harder and Smarter, provides you with new ways of working with familiar tools that will build upon and enhance your basic knowledge of Adobe Photoshop.

Chapter 2, Non-Destructive Healing, and Retouching, teaches you how to hide unwanted content from images and apply essential color and tonal edits non-destructively, meaning that your edits can be edited multiple times without losing quality. This will first require quick and accurate selections with a variety of tools.

Chapter 3, Masking and Cutouts, delves into one of the must-have Photoshop skills and showcases powerful tools for concealing and revealing layer content without permanent deletion. These skills enable you to extract intricate details such as hair from backgrounds and create montages.

Chapter 4, Building Brand Mock-Ups and Prototypes, teaches you how to bring ideas and concepts to life by creating realistic mockups. You will learn how to apply graphics to a series of surfaces, such as walls, device screens, t-shirts, and cushions, using smart workflows that allow you to re-edit your assets without losing quality.

Chapter 5, Creating Printed Marketing Collateral, provides an in-depth look at how to prepare new documents for print output for flyers, posters, and business cards, and how to create grid systems and print characteristics such as bleed to expertly manage content such as text layers, branding, and photos.

Chapter 6, From Pixels to Post: Images for Social Media, takes you through a streamlined process for creating social media images. You will learn how to use artboards to manage multiple images in a single document, protect text and logos in smart object layers, and text styles for rapid type formatting. Then, you will see how to export your branded images with ease to multiple file formats and sizes, ready for posting online.

Chapter 7, Creating Animated GIFs and Videos, looks at how to create and edit video and animated GIFs in Photoshop. We will be using familiar tools to import video clips, add transitions and audio to a simple yet powerful timeline, and export animated GIFs or render video to common file formats ready for posting online or on platforms such as YouTube.

Chapter 8, Bringing Typography to Life with Effects and Styling, takes you through a series of typographic effects to make your text stand out. We will use editable layer effects to create paper folds, slices, dripping paint, graffiti art, and embossed paper, all while keeping your text layers editable. You will learn how to change characters, words, font families, and font size without compromising your final designs.

Chapter 9, Creating Textures, Patterns, and Backdrops, provides you with a set of invaluable skills to create your own backdrops, from realistic textures to geometric gradients, pop art, and science fiction space scenes. All will be created from scratch without any source images so you can build visually captivating backdrops anytime.

Chapter 10, Creating and Applying Brushes, introduces you to the immense power and flexibility of Photoshop brushes. You will learn how to create your own brush tip shapes, from a flock of birds and snowflakes to sampled paint strokes and facial hair for retouching.

Chapter 11, Blending and Collaging Images, combines many of the professional-grade techniques in this book to successfully create image montages, seamless panoramas, collage self-portraits, double-exposure effects, and beautifully lit scenes using high dynamic range images that blend the lighting data of multiple shots.

Chapter 12, Creating Surrealist Artwork, challenges you and your new skills with two breath-taking art projects. You will draw upon the techniques covered throughout this book to produce visually captivating surreal artwork.

To get the most out of this book

Software/hardware covered in the book	Operating system requirements
Adobe Photoshop Adobe Bridge Adobe Express	Windows, macOS, or Linux

To get the best quality of images, please refer to the free copy of ebook version of this book.

Download the example code files

You can download the example code files for this book from GitHub at `https://github.com/PacktPublishing/Mastering-Adobe-Photoshop-2024`. If there's an update to the code, it will be updated in the GitHub repository.

We also have other code bundles from our rich catalog of books and videos available at `https://github.com/PacktPublishing/`. Check them out!

Conventions used

There are a number of text conventions used throughout this book.

`Code in text`: Indicates code words in text, database table names, folder names, filenames, file extensions, pathnames, dummy URLs, user input, and Twitter handles. Here is an example: "Left-click on the Shadows layer group and repeat the same technique to import `Paint-02.jpg` from the `11-Collage` folder."

Bold: Indicates a new term, an important word, or words that you see onscreen. For instance, words in menus or dialog boxes appear in **bold**. Here is an example: "Go to **File** → **Save** and close the document."

Tips or important notes
Appear like this.

Get in touch

Feedback from our readers is always welcome.

General feedback: If you have questions about any aspect of this book, email us at `customercare@packtpub.com` and mention the book title in the subject of your message.

Errata: Although we have taken every care to ensure the accuracy of our content, mistakes do happen. If you have found a mistake in this book, we would be grateful if you would report this to us. Please visit `www.packtpub.com/support/errata` and fill in the form.

Piracy: If you come across any illegal copies of our works in any form on the internet, we would be grateful if you would provide us with the location address or website name. Please contact us at `copyright@packtpub.com` with a link to the material.

If you are interested in becoming an author: If there is a topic that you have expertise in and you are interested in either writing or contributing to a book, please visit `authors.packtpub.com`.

Share Your Thoughts

Once you've read, we'd love to hear your thoughts! Scan the QR code below to go straight to the Amazon review page for this book and share your feedback.

`https://packt.link/r/1838822011`

Your review is important to us and the tech community and will help us make sure we're delivering excellent quality content.

Download a free PDF copy of this book

Thanks for purchasing this book!

Do you like to read on the go but are unable to carry your print books everywhere?

Is your eBook purchase not compatible with the device of your choice?

Don't worry, now with every Packt book you get a DRM-free PDF version of that book at no cost.

Read anywhere, any place, on any device. Search, copy, and paste code from your favorite technical books directly into your application.

The perks don't stop there, you can get exclusive access to discounts, newsletters, and great free content in your inbox daily

Follow these simple steps to get the benefits:

1. Scan the QR code or visit the link below

`https://packt.link/free-ebook/9781838822019`

2. Submit your proof of purchase
3. That's it! We'll send your free PDF and other benefits to your email directly

Part 1: Raising Your Photoshop Game

We all discover Photoshop differently, often learning about tools and features that are relevant to our working needs. However, this can lead to knowledge gaps that may hold us back. *Part 1* of this book will focus on essential skills and how to build upon them, starting with *Chapter 1*, which establishes a streamlined interface and tools setup.

This part has the following chapters:

1

Making Photoshop Work Harder and Smarter

We all discover **Photoshop** differently, often learning about tools and features that are relevant to our needs. However, this can lead to knowledge gaps that may hold your skills back. *Part 1* of this book, *Raising Your Photoshop Game*, will focus on essential skills and building upon them, starting with *Chapter 1*, which establishes a streamlined interface and tools setup.

First, we'll look at significant updates and new features to arrive in recent versions of Photoshop. Easy to miss, updates can pass you by, often installed automatically without being discovered. You could be missing out on valuable time-saving enhancements to your workflow. From sharing files on the cloud to edit along with others and receiving feedback on live projects to the web browser version of Photoshop (beta) and restoration filters, you can get a feel for the latest changes.

Then, we'll customize the interface, modifying panels and tools so that they're easier to locate, putting the most effective features front and center in your interface while keeping less frequently used features just a mouse click away. We'll reorder the **Tools** panel, stripping away redundant tools in place for your favored go-to, high-impact tools, and set up keyboard shortcuts that make little-known features easy to activate or modify a tool with ease.

Then, we'll finish with a little digital imaging 101 to ensure you've got a clear understanding of key industry terminology. Having an appreciation of how images are composed will make the process of deconstructing them and enhancing them easier to comprehend while avoiding common mistakes.

As with many concepts in this book, the first chapter focuses on attaining the best possible quality from the outset while leveraging time-saving techniques whenever possible, essential for today's busy digital image editors. In this chapter, we'll cover the following topics:

- Updates and new features
- Creating a bespoke workspace

- Modifying preferences
- Quality-first approach

Technical requirements

The project files for this chapter can be found at: `https://github.com/PacktPublishing/Mastering-Adobe-Photoshop-2024/tree/main/Chapter01`

Updates and new features

2023 marks a decade since Adobe released Creative Cloud, replacing the older Creative Suite in June 2013. Much has changed in that time. Arguably, Adobe's most significant advances have been digital connectivity between its flagship desktop apps such as Photoshop, and online technology that allows for greater collaboration.

Thanks to a constantly connected workplace, today's Creative Cloud updates are more of a trickle than a deluge. Outside of Adobe's annual creativity festival, *Adobe MAX*, new updates can be installed automatically with little to no fanfare. With this in mind, I've summarized the most significant changes to Adobe Photoshop in recent months, just in case they passed you by!

Contextual Task Bar

To reduce the amount of time you spend navigating the interface for tools and features, Photoshop now includes the contextual task bar. Its aim is to predict your next logical step and put those options close to your cursor. The default position of the contextual task bar is often at the bottom of the image window. If, however, you have a text layer active, the contextual task bar will move to the underside of the text frame in the active layer. You can hide, reset, or pin (lock) the position of the contextual task bar by clicking on the **More Options** icon (shown as *A* in *Figure 1.1*) to reveal the options:

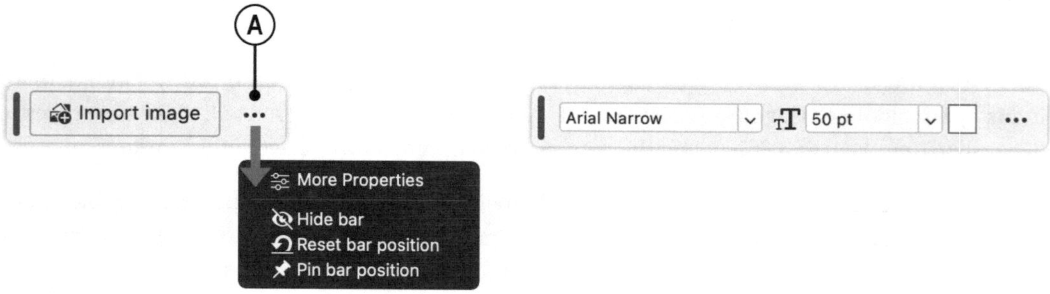

Figure 1.1: The Contextual Task Bar

Depending on the kind of layer you have active or the tool you have selected, the options in the contextual task bar will vary. For example, when you create a new document, the contextual task bar displays a button for importing an image, or under the **More Options** icon, you can reveal the **Properties** panel.

When you open an existing document containing only a background layer, the contextual task bar will display the **Select subject**, **Remove background**, **Transform image** (shown as *B* in *Figure 1.2*), and **Create new adjustment layer** (*C*) icons. Clicking on **Select subject** results in a selection of a prominent region in your image, providing one can be detected, while **Remove background** goes one step further and conceals the region of the image around your subject with a layer mask.

If an unlocked layer is active, the contextual task bar and the **Transform image** icon will become available. When you left-click on the **Transform image** icon, the contextual task bar changes to display **Flip Horizontal** (*D*) and **Flip Vertical** (*E*) icons. You can subsequently apply or abort your transform edits by clicking on **Done** or **Cancel** respectively:

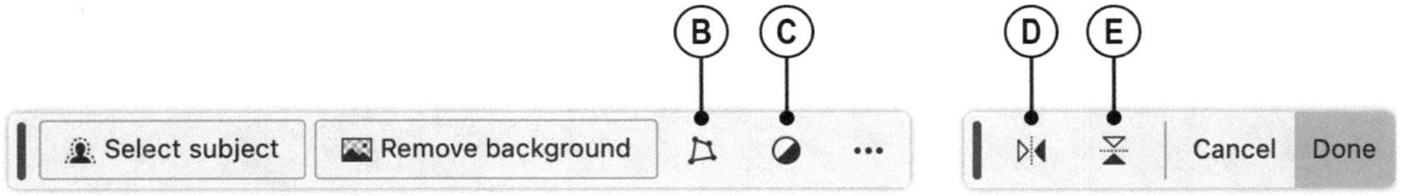

Figure 1.2: Transform and adjustment layer options in the Contextual Task Bar

With a selection active, the contextual task bar displays options to modify your selection (shown as *F* in *Figure 1.3*), invert a selection (*H*), create a layer mask from the selection (*G*), or fill the selection (*I*). In addition, you can deselect an existing selection and fill a region with pixels using **Generative Fill**:

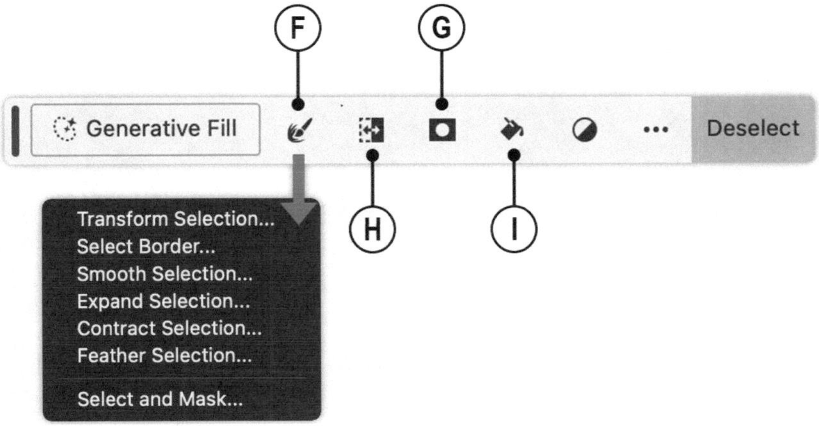

Figure 1.3: Selection options in the Contextual Task Bar

Some of the best time-saving features to be found in the contextual task bar relate to the task of editing layer masks, a process that will be covered in greater depth in *Chapter 3* of this book. With a layer active and containing a layer mask, you can now press the **Subtract from mask** button, which switches you to the **Brush** tool and sets the foreground color in the **Tools** panel to black. Then, simply click and drag across parts of your layer to reveal pixel content. You can also achieve the opposite result by clicking on the **Add to mask** button, which sets the foreground color to white. You can click on the **Modify mask feather and density** icon (shown as *J* in *Figure 1.4*) to reveal a popup. You can also launch the **Select and mask** workspace to access the full suite of mask refinement features from the same popup. The final two icons are for **Hide mask** (*Figure 1.4, K*) and **Change mask view** (*Figure 1.4, L*):

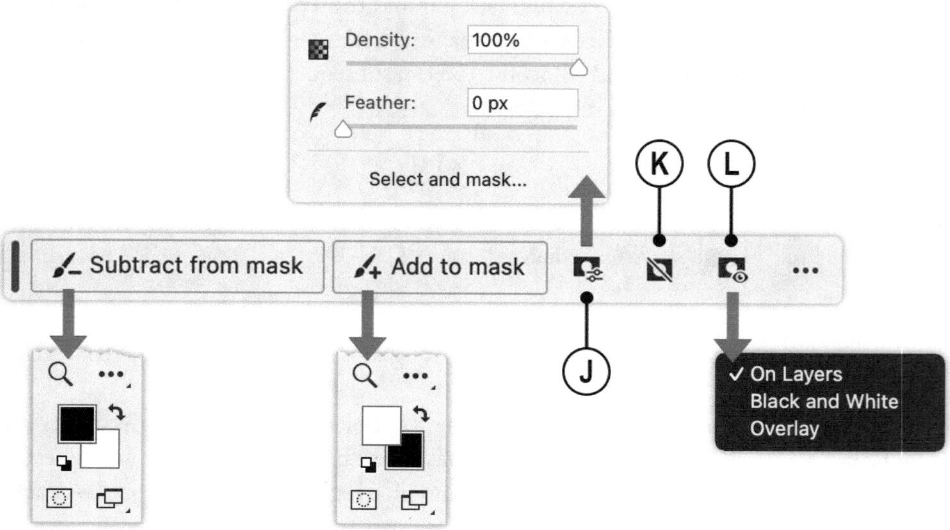

Figure 1.4: Masking options in the Contextual Task Bar

Adobe Firefly

In recent years, there has been growing interest in the practical use of **artificial intelligence** (**AI**) in creative industries. AI-driven technology has featured in Photoshop for many years since the arrival of **Content-Aware Fill**. However, the emergence of imagery that is generated from a text prompt represents a seismic shift in digital image creation.

Adobe Photoshop 2024 includes its own text-to-image AI in the form of Adobe Firefly, allowing you to add content to an existing image using two methods: **Generative Fill** and **Generative Expand**. **Generative Fill** uses an active selection to remove unwanted content or add new pixels via a text prompt, while **Generative Expand** extends your existing canvas, creating new pixels in the expanded region.

In the example shown in *Figure 1.5*, the image contained a rickety old chair, which I felt could benefit from a subject to enhance visual interest. I created a basic selection with the **Rectangular Marquee** tool around the region where I wanted the subject. With the selection in place, the contextual task bar then displayed the **Generative text prompt field**, into which I typed `Seagull` and pressed the **Generate** button:

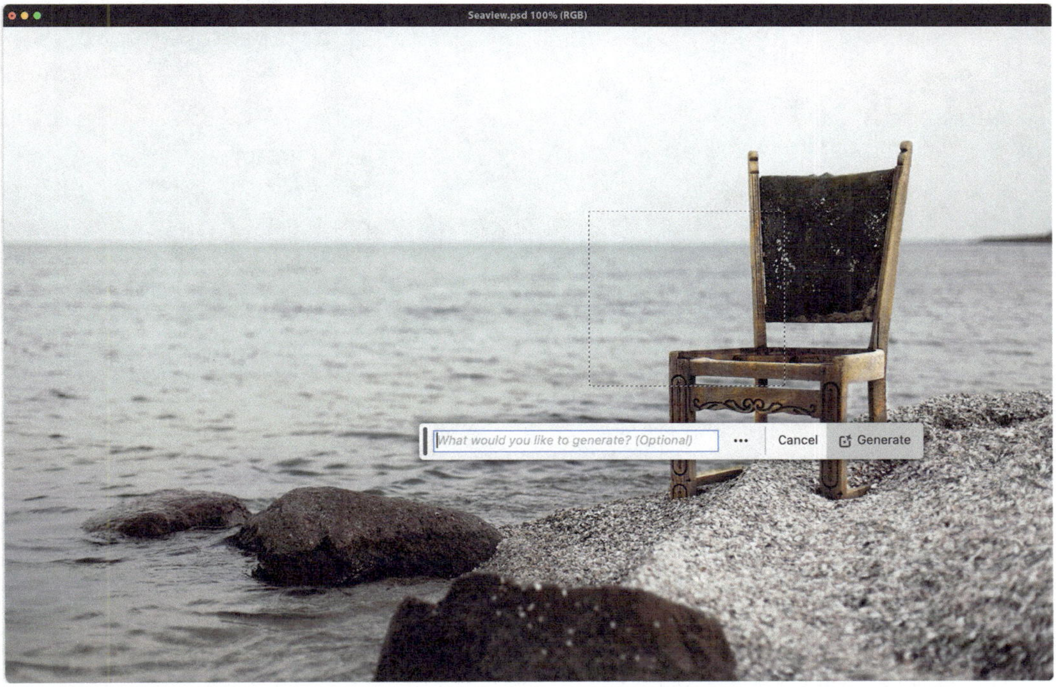

Figure 1.5: Generative Fill options in the Contextual Task Bar

After a few seconds, Photoshop displayed a seagull in a new generative layer. The contextual task bar then changed to display one of three possible results from my text prompt. You can use the **Previous** and **Next** buttons to cycle through each version. The **Properties** panel also displays your text prompt and thumbnails of the three results.

In this scenario, the results Photoshop delivered were impressive, even down to minor details such as the position of the birds' feet on top of the chair frame. In addition, Photoshop has also matched the light and shade of the original image as well as the angle with a high degree of accuracy. For the best results, try using descriptive nouns and adjectives in your **Generative Fill** prompts instead of instructive prompts such as "*create a landscape*."

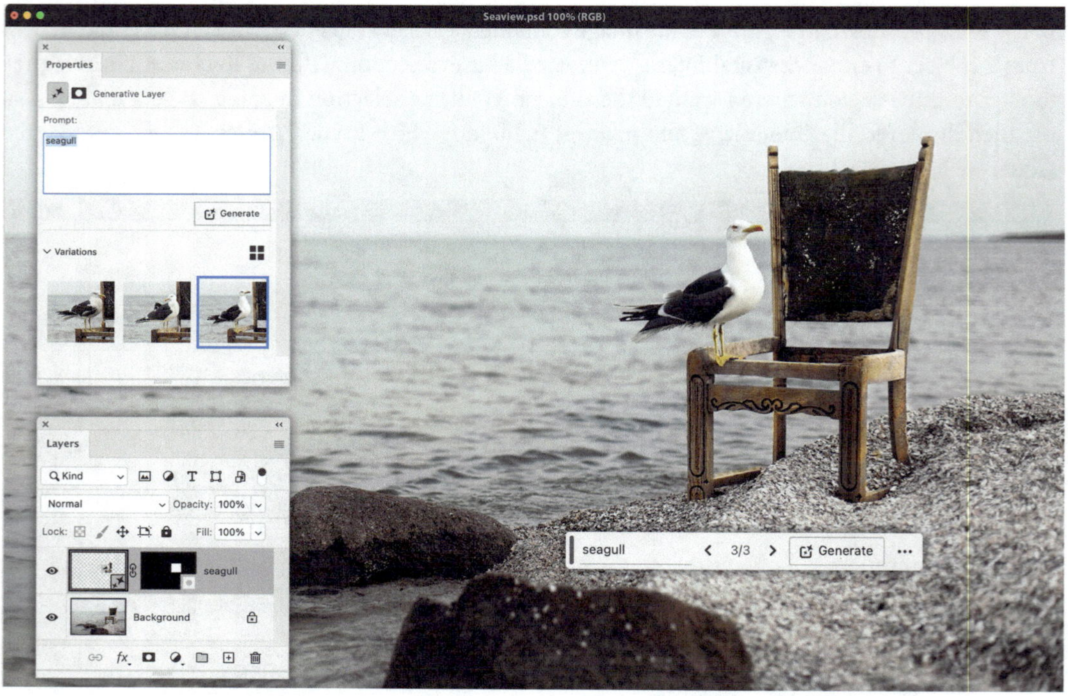

Figure 1.6: Generative Fill used to add a seagull to the image

As with most features, there are limitations. You'll need an internet connection to use **Generative Fill**. At the time of writing, shortly after *Adobe MAX* in October 2023, the maximum resolution **Generative Fill** can render is 1024 pixels. If you're trying to fill a large region in a high-quality image, larger than 1024, the results might appear a little blurred.

Creative Cloud users on an **All Apps** package have 1,000 generative credits included with their monthly subscription. Each text prompt you generate in Photoshop uses one credit. You can monitor your credit usage by logging in to your Creative Cloud account. Adobe's reason for rationing the use of **Generative Fill** is that it requires significant computational resources. At the time of writing, you can purchase additional credits for $4.99 (USD) per month for an additional 100 credits.

The Remove tool

For many years, I've resorted to using the **Spot Healing Brush** tool to remove unwanted content from an image. In general, the **Spot Healing Brush** tool has provided good results, albeit occasionally, it would add back unwanted pixels and require a little finessing. With the addition of the **Remove** tool in May 2023, the process has become simpler thanks to a simplified workflow when compared to other healing and retouching tools.

Firstly, you don't have to concern yourself with a full set of brush tip settings, just the brush tip size. This can also be changed by pressing the open (*[*) and closed (*]*) bracket keys respectively to make the brush size smaller or larger. Then, click and drag the cursor across the region you wish to remove. Once you release the left mouse button, leave Photoshop to repurpose the surrounding pixels and replace unwanted pixels.

The affected region will be highlighted by a translucent color as you drag across it. You can change this from the **Options** bar to improve legibility depending on the content within your image. To do so, click on the cog icon in the **Options** bar to define one of thirteen different highlight colors and the opacity of the color.

Another advantage of the **Remove** tool is that you can choose to make several brush stroke marks before applying an edit. To do this, turn off the **Remove after each stroke** checkbox in the **Options** bar. Then, when you're ready to apply the edits, click on the **Commit** button in the **Options** bar.

You can also use a nifty, hidden feature that is built into the **Remove** tool, allowing you to paint around the perimeter (shown as *B* in *Figure 1.7*) of the region you wish to remove instead of having to paint the entire area (*Figure 1.7*, *A*). This technique can be used with or without the **Remove after each stroke** feature being active. The inset image (*Figure 1.7*, *C*) demonstrates the completed edits:

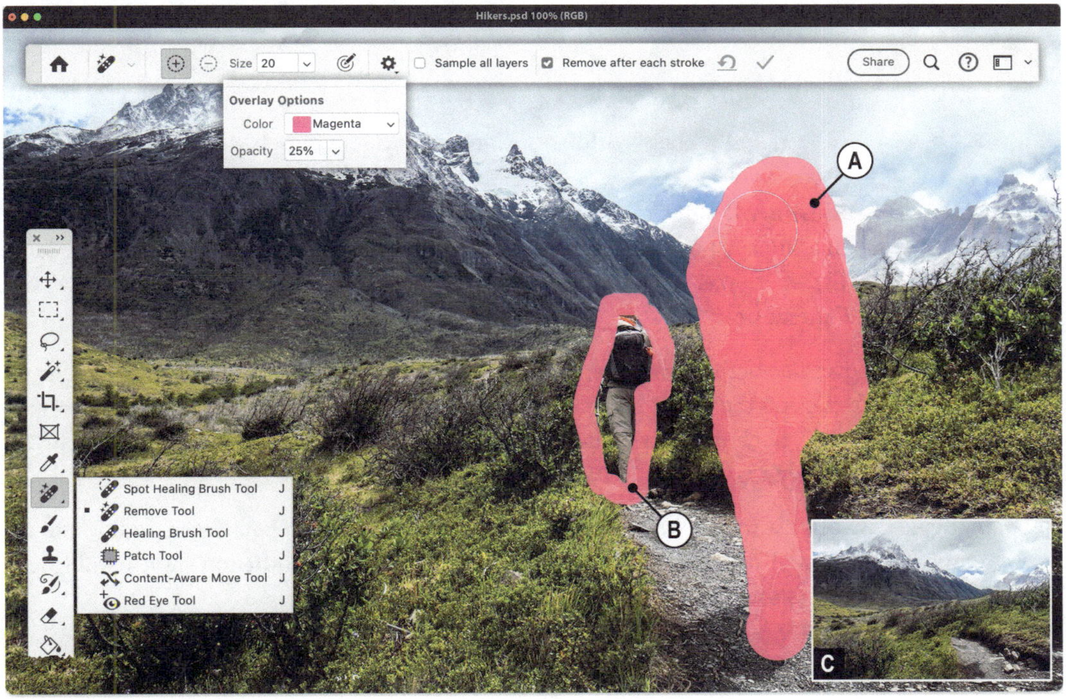

Figure 1.7: The Remove tool and related settings

Adjustment presets

The **Adjustments** panel now includes a library of presets that allow you to quickly preview how they will appear on your image before adding them to your document. These range from classic black and white for portraiture to split-tone effects:

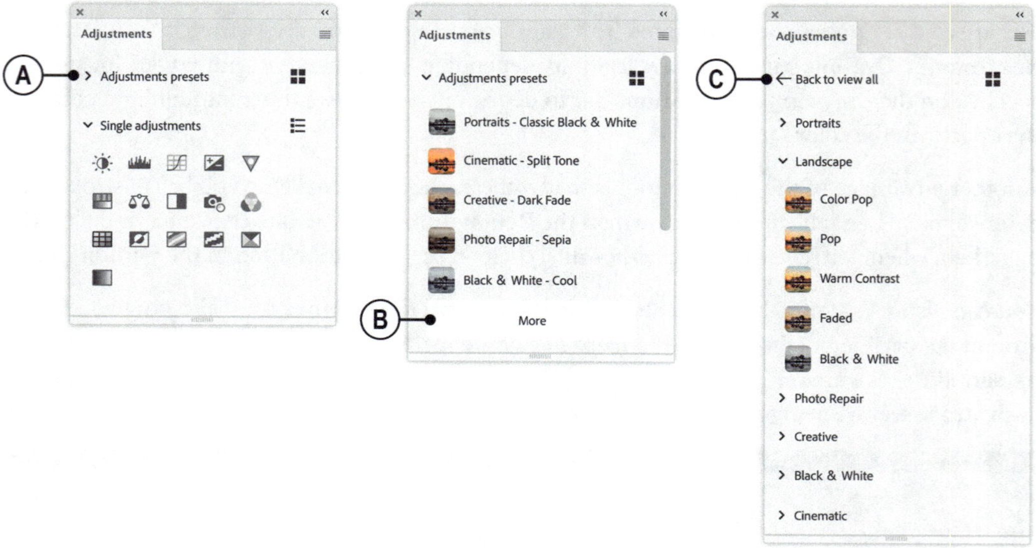

Figure 1.8: The Adjustments panel now includes presets

Go to **Window** → **Adjustments** and click on the toggle adjacent to **Adjustment presets** (shown as *A* in *Figure 1.8*) to open a short list of sample presets. To explore additional presets, click on the **More** button (*Figure 1.8, B*), where you will be presented with a list of categories that include **Portraits**, **Photo Repair**, and **Cinematic**.

Hover your cursor over one of the presets to preview how it will affect your active document. To apply a preset, simply left-click on the preset name. To exit the library of presets, click on the **Back to view all** toggle (*Figure 1.8, C*). Each preset typically consists of two adjustment layers with accompanying layer masks that are neatly organized into layer groups.

You can toggle between list mode, which shows a small thumbnail of each preset in addition to the preset name, or thumbnail-only mode by clicking on the icon located at the top right-hand side of the **Adjustments** panel (shown as *D* in *Figure 1.9*):

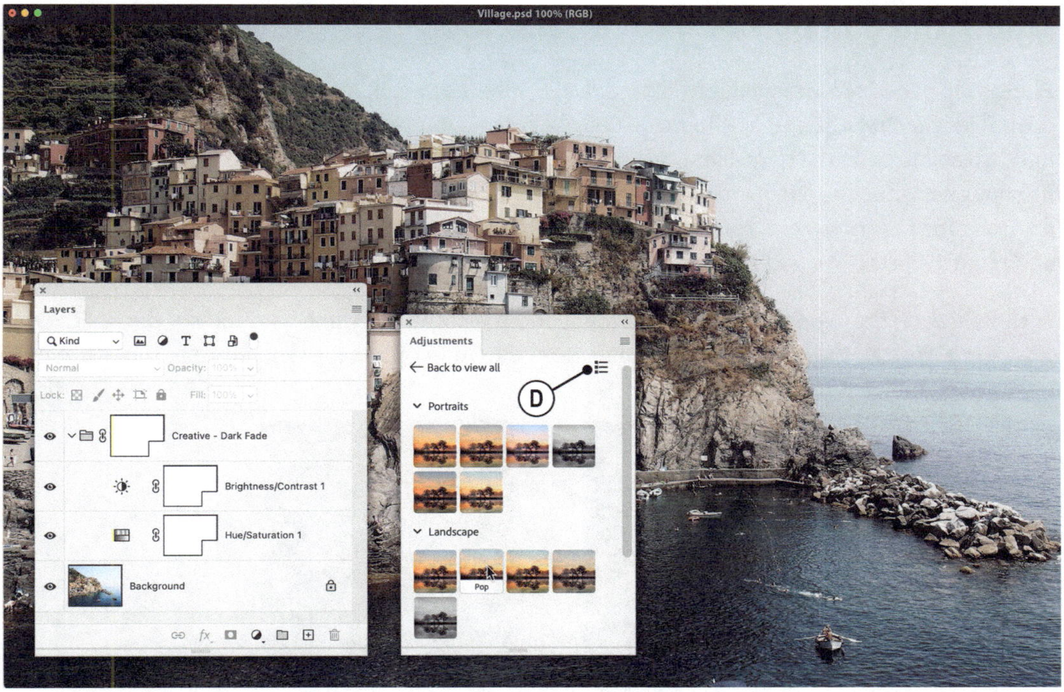

Figure 1.9: Each adjustment preset is organized and added via a layer group

Creating a bespoke workspace

It's one thing to know your Photoshop tools and features, but quite another to make them more accessible. Delving into a rabbit hole of sub-menus to find a time-saving tool burns valuable time, diminishing its effectiveness. At first, the extra mouse clicks might seem inconsequential, but over the course of a year, that could amount to dozens of hours wasted when you could have been meeting deadlines faster. I would suggest thinking about which tools and panels you use most frequently and prioritizing your screen real estate.

In the following exercises, we'll look at customizing panels, tools, and shortcuts. You can adjust these techniques to suit your individual workflow.

Modifying panels

Photoshop panels are arranged into "workspaces," with the default, called **Essentials**, active when you open it for the first time, an option that Adobe believes is important to all Photoshop users. Arranged into two columns on the right-hand side of the interface, the right-hand column is expanded for high-use options, while the left-hand column is collapsed into a thin set of icons for less frequently used features. The **Layers** panel is core to almost everything we do in Photoshop, therefore it's omnipresent and requires space. We will arrange other panels around it. Here's how to do this:

1. Click on the **Workspace Switcher** menu located at the top-right-hand side of the interface (*A* in *Figure 1.10*) and choose **Essentials** from the list of options. Then, return to the same menu and choose **Reset Essentials**:

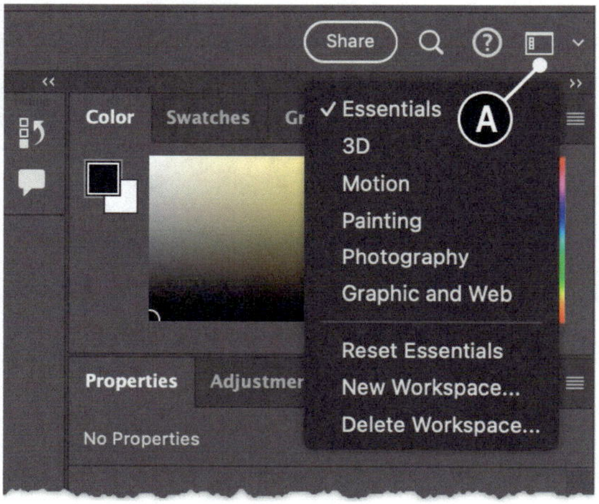

Figure 1.10: The Workspace Switcher menu

2. Click on the **Color Panel** tab to make it active, then click on its **Panel** fly-out menu in the top-right corner. From the list of options, choose **Color wheel**. This can make the process of visualizing new colors easier. If you need to create a specific color value, you can simply left-click on the foreground icon located at the top of the **Color** panel.
3. Next, hover your cursor over the **Libraries Panel** tab and drag it over to the image window to undock it. This panel often requires lots of height to browse through assets, and the best place I've found for it is in the left-hand column, collapsed into icons with the **History** and **Comments** panels. To add the **Libraries** panel to this column, drag the **Libraries Panel** tab above the icon for the **History** panel, at which point you will see a pale blue line appear. Release the mouse to dock it at the top of the column (*B* in *Figure 1.11*).

4. The **Libraries** panel now appears in icon mode, left-click on it to expand it. Hover your cursor over its bottom edge to reveal the scaling symbol, a double-headed arrow, and drag the panel edge downward to extend its height so that more content will be visible when needed. Then, left-click on the **Libraries Panel** icon to minimize. Use the same technique to expand the height of the other panels in the column to reduce the amount of scrolling that is required with small panels:

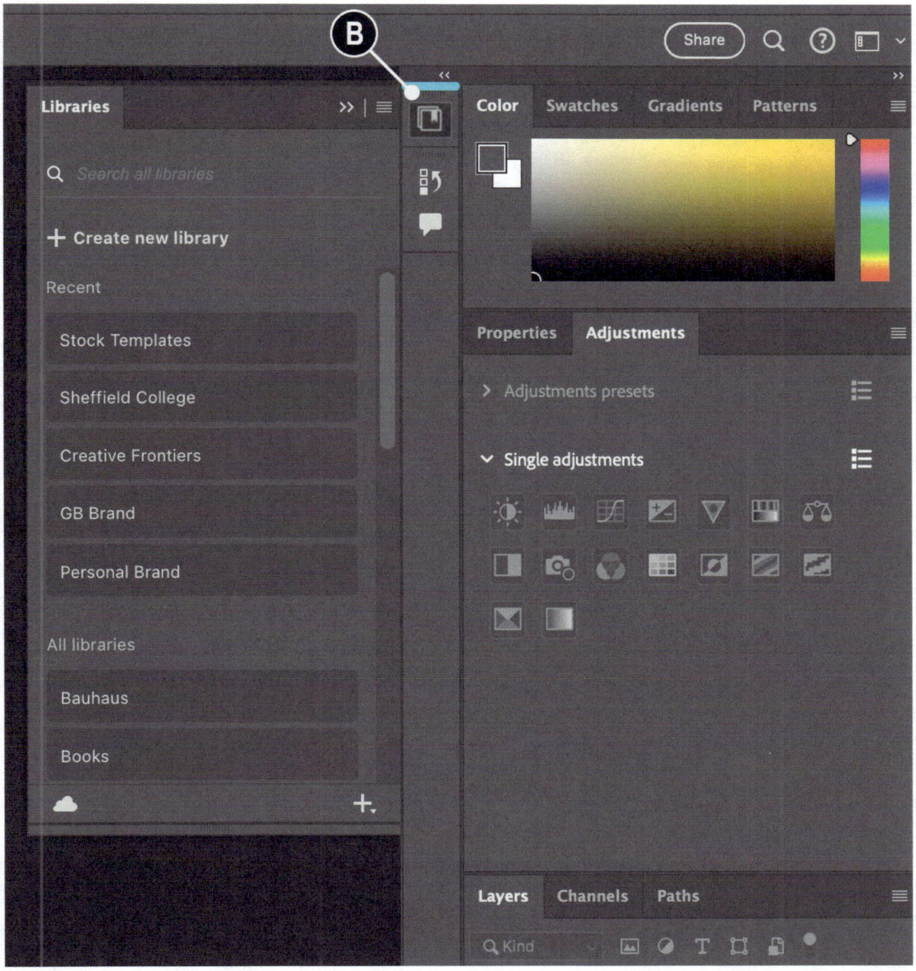

Figure 1.11: Repositioning the Libraries panel above the History panel

5. Within the collapsed column, I also added the **Brushes** panel, which also appears with the **Brush Settings** panel (**Window → Brushes**). Both are handy. Using the same technique, you can add any other infrequently used panels to the collapsed column. In the example shown, and my personal preference, I also dragged the **Patterns** and **Gradient** panels, originally adjacent to the **Color** panel into the collapsed column, along with the **Shapes** panel and **Styles** panel, found under the **Window** menu:

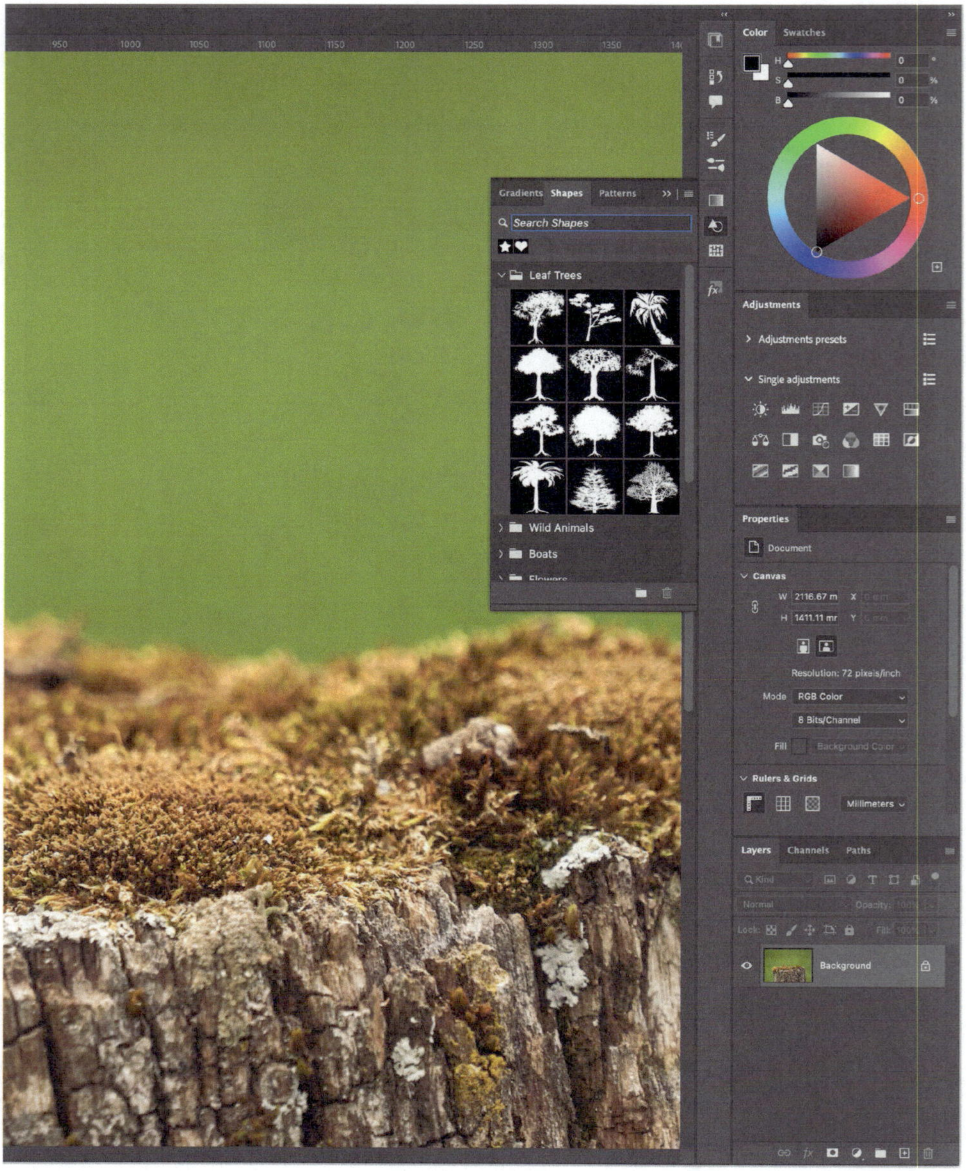

Figure 1.12: The workspace after reconfiguration

Customizing the Tools panel

The Photoshop **Tools** panel contains in excess of 70 tools; only 21 are visible at any one time, and the majority are hidden. This is another of those scenarios where Adobe can make a best guess as to the tools appropriate to your workflow, but never exactly. This leaves room for improvement and a little simplification. You can start by modifying the default set of tools or you can create a fresh tool panel with just a handful of specialist tools; the choice is yours. We'll start with the former:

1. Click and hold down on the **Edit Toolbar** button in the lower section of the **Tools** panel, (shown as three dots). From the pop-out menu that appears, click on the only option, also called **Edit Toolbar**.

   This opens the **Customize Toolbar** dialog, where you'll be presented with two columns. The left-hand column, named **Tools Panel**, lists tools included in the **Tools** panel, and there is an **Extra Tools** column on the right-hand side for tools you wish to hide. It's likely there will be no tools listed on the right at this point.

   The list of tools on the left is grouped; each group represents a "slot" on the **Tools** panel. Take the second group down in the list, starting with the **Rectangular Marquee** tool, currently visible in the **Tools** panel in the second slot down, under the first slot of tools that include the **Move** tool. The remaining three selection tools in the group, **Elliptical Marquee**, **Single Row**, and **Single Column**, are hidden under it.

2. Start by dragging the **Single Row** and **Single Column** selection tools to the right-hand column. I can honestly say I've used them twice in the last 20 years. Repeat the same step for the **Slice** tool and the **Slice Selection** tool.
3. As the **Frame** tool behaves like a clipping mask within which you can place images, it can be associated with the crop tools. Drag the icon for the **Frame** tool under the **Perspective Crop** tool to add it to the same group of tools.
4. Focusing on the next group down, drag the **3D Material Eyedropper**, **Ruler**, **Notes**, and **Count** tools to the right-hand column.
5. Hover your cursor over the edge of the tool group containing the eraser tools. This will allow you to drag the entire group across to the right-hand column.
6. Drag the **Red Eye**, **Color Replacement**, **3D Material Drop**, **Vertical Type Mask**, and **Horizontal Type Mask** tools to the right-hand column.
7. Although not entirely necessary, you can combine all of the brush tools by dragging the **History Brush** and **Art History Brush** tools into the same group as the **Brush** tool.
8. Having removed what I would call redundant tools, you may wish to click on the **Save Preset** button, give your new **Tools** panel a name, and save it in the folder presented to you by Photoshop. Then, click **Done**.

Naturally, this is how I alter the **Tools** panel, but you may need to adjust this layout to better suit your own needs by using the same techniques covered in the exercise:

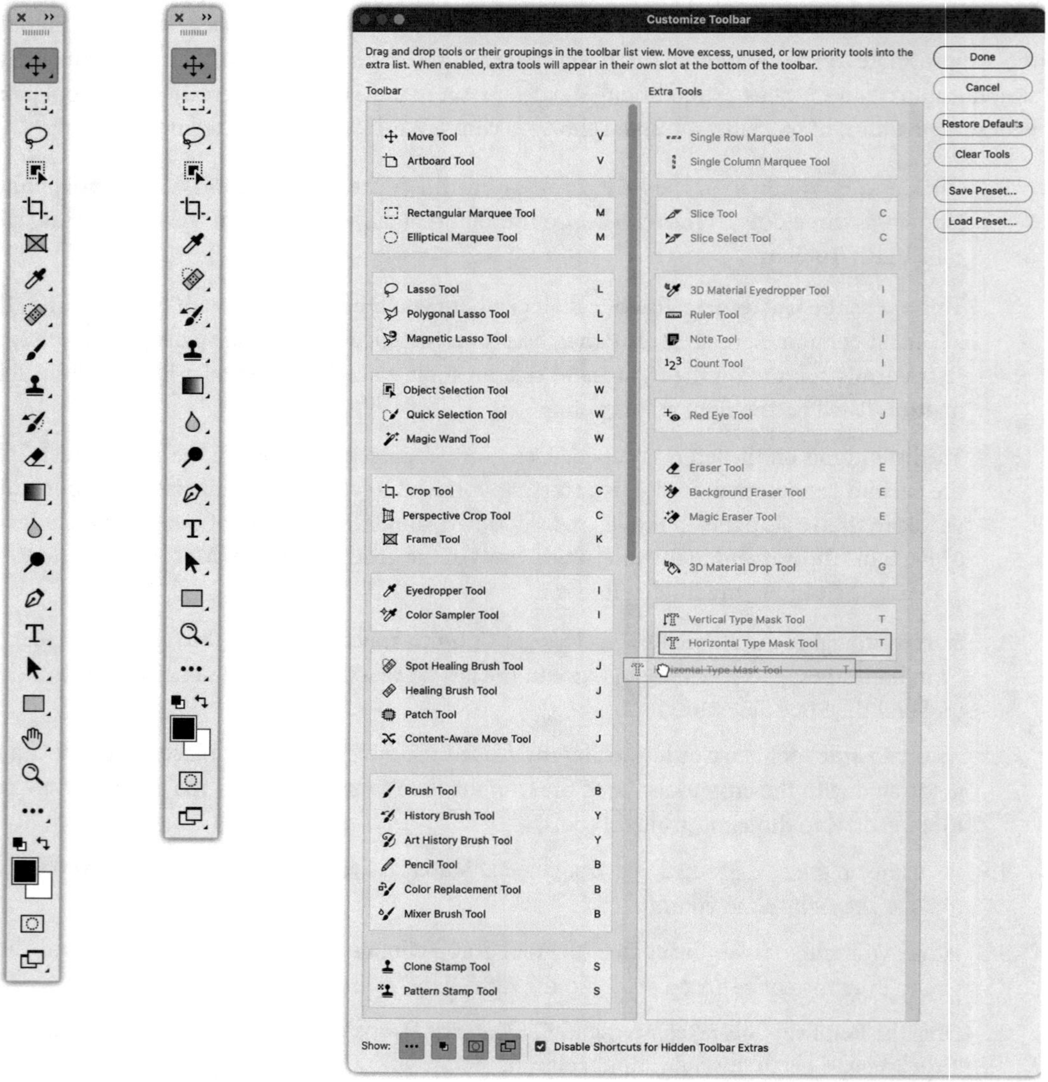

Figure 1.13: The customized Toolbar dialog alongside the edited Tools panel

Saving a custom workspace

Now that we've created a streamlined version of the interface, it's time to save it. This will achieve two things: firstly, the layout of panels will be captured for future use, and secondly, you can reset a saved workspace back to its original state if you find panels have been moved around on screen. Let's get started:

1. Head up to the top right-hand side of the Photoshop interface and click on the **Workspace Switcher** menu. From the list of options provided, click on **New Workspace**. Despite its misleading name, the command won't undo any of your hard work arranging panels; it simply saves the current state of the interface.
2. From the **New Workspace** dialog that will now appear, enter a name for your workspace. I entered `Pro` in this example, but you can choose your own name. Just make sure it's short and snappy so that it fits neatly into the **Workspace Switcher** drop-down menu.

   By default, panel locations are saved with every new workspace, but you can also capture alterations to the **Tools** panel, keyboard shortcuts, and menu items. The latter two will be explored in the next exercise. I prefer to keep the **Tools** panel consistent no matter the task I'm performing. You can update an existing workspace anytime and choose to include changes to the **Tools** panel, keyboard shortcuts, and menu items. Just enter the same name as the existing workspace to update it.
3. In this example, we'll capture just the panel locations. As such, leave the checkboxes unchecked and click **Save** to complete the process. You will now find that your new workspace is located at the top of the **Workspace Switcher** drop-down menu, while Adobe's supplied workspaces are listed lower down in the dropdown:

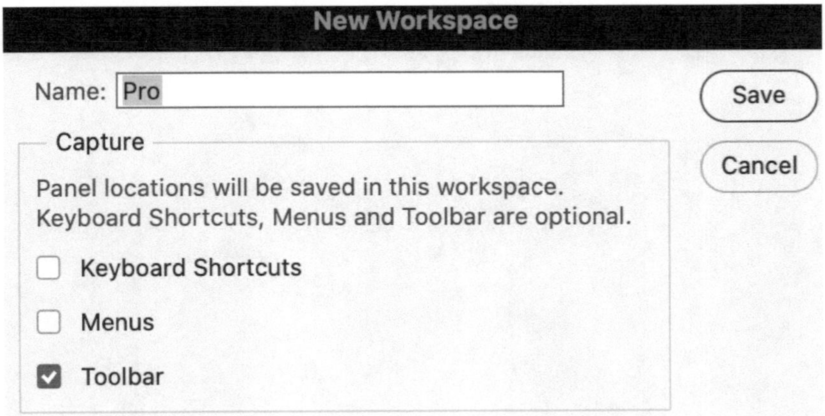

Figure 1.14: The New Workspace dialog captures panel locations, shortcuts, and menus

Modifying keyboard shortcuts and menus

Keyboard shortcuts can save you invaluable time and help avoid navigating through convoluted sub-menus, from more rudimentary tasks such as copying to applying warps. You can also hide redundant menu commands, found from the application dropdowns at the top of the screen. In this exercise, you will explore techniques for assigning a custom shortcut and hiding a menu option:

1. Go to **Edit** → **Keyboard Shortcuts and Menus**. Ensure the **Shortcuts For** drop-down menu is set to **Application Menus** (*Figure 1.15, A*). Scroll down the list to **Window** and expand the toggle to reveal the sub-categories.
2. Under the right-hand column, labeled **Shortcut**, click in the empty space adjacent to **2-up Vertical** (*Figure 1.15, B*) to open the type entry field. Type into the field `Ctrl+Alt+1` (Windows) or `Cmd+Option+1` (macOS). If the shortcut is already assigned elsewhere, click on the **Accept** button in the upper right-hand side of the dialog.
3. Once you have all other remaining shortcuts, click on the **Create New Set** button (*Figure 1.15, C*). Enter a name for the set of shortcuts and click **Save**.
4. Then, click on the **Menus** tab (*Figure 1.15, D*), scroll down the list until you reach **Image**, and click on the toggle to expand and open a list of sub-categories. Turn off the visibility icons for **Auto Tone**, **Auto Contrast**, and **Auto Color** (*Figure 1.15, E*). This will hide those destructive editing options in the **Image** menu.

   Once you have altered the visibility settings of all other menus of your choosing, click on the **Create New Set** button (*Figure 1.15, F*). Enter a name for the set of menus and click **Save**. Then, click on **OK** to close the **Keyboard Shortcut and Menus** dialog. Click on the **Image** menu, and you'll notice the items have been hidden. To temporarily reveal them, you can click on the **Show Menu** items at the bottom of the list:

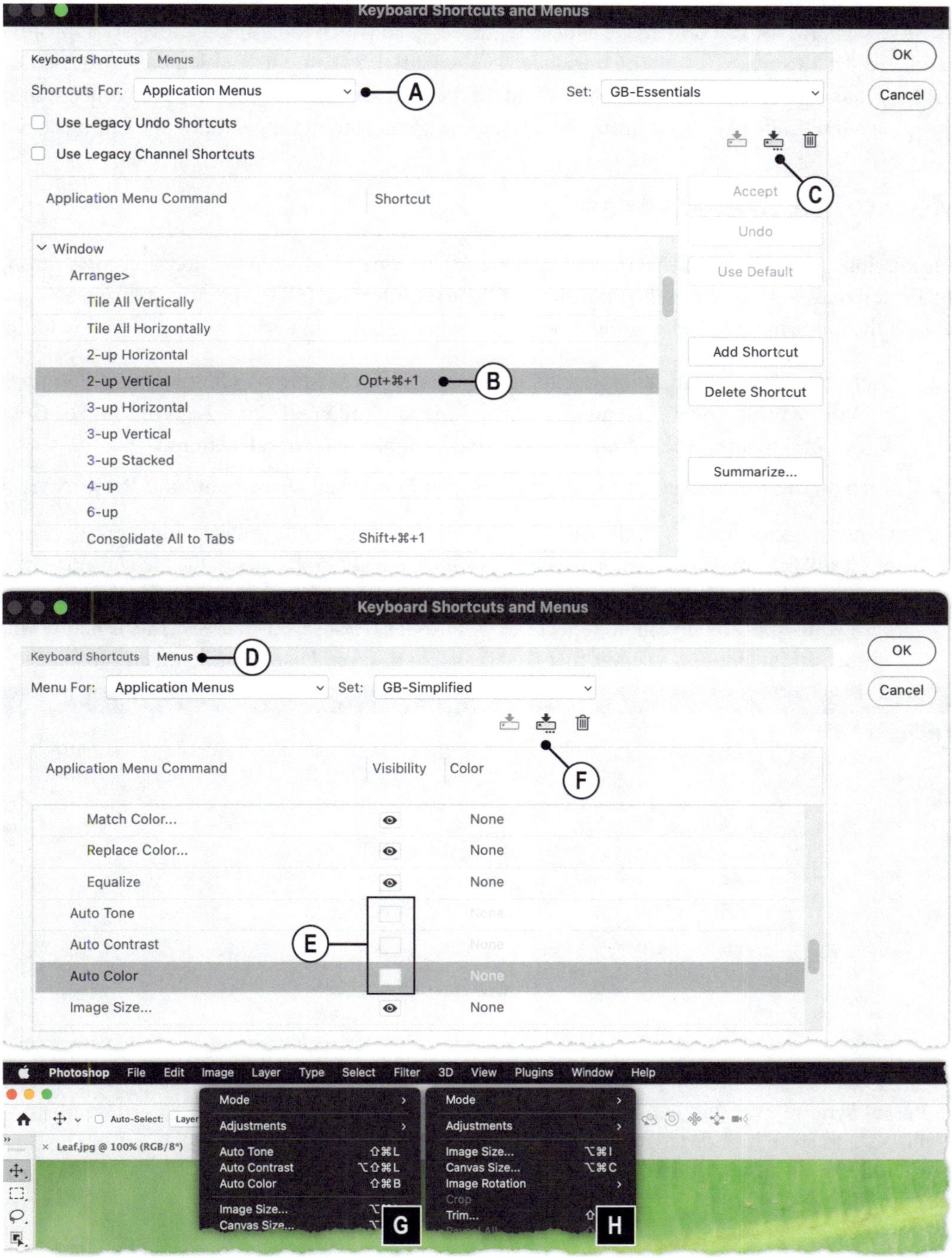

Figure 1.15: You can edit keyboard shortcuts and hide menu items; default (G) and with the three Auto Tone, Auto Contrast, and Auto Color commands hidden (H)

As we've seen, Adobe can only make educated guesses as to which tools and features are appropriate to our needs. As such, refining the interface is an essential first step to making day-to-day editing faster by making the tools we need easy to find. In the next section, we'll modify preference settings, changing a multitude of options, from the interface brightness to the appearance of painting cursors.

Modifying preferences

It is possible to modify the behavior and appearance of some Photoshop features and tools through the **Preferences** settings, from the brightness of the **user interface** (**UI**) to painting cursors and auto-save. In the following steps, I'll highlight settings that could offer high value to your editing workflow:

1. Preferences can be found on macOS via **Photoshop** → **Settings** → **General**, or on Windows, via **Edit** → **Preferences** → **General**. Alternatively, you can press *Ctrl* + *K* (Windows) or *Cmd* + *K* (macOS) to launch the **Preferences** settings and reveal **General** settings.
2. Turn on the checkboxes for **Auto-Update Open File-based Documents** and **Preset Syncing**.

   Contrary to the option's name, **Auto-Update** won't automatically update your active document, but it will inform you that someone else has edited and saved changes to the file you are working on. Photoshop will then give you the option to keep editing your active version or dispense with your edits and update to reflect the other user's latest saved changes. This is handy when editing project files on a server that are accessible to several users simultaneously:

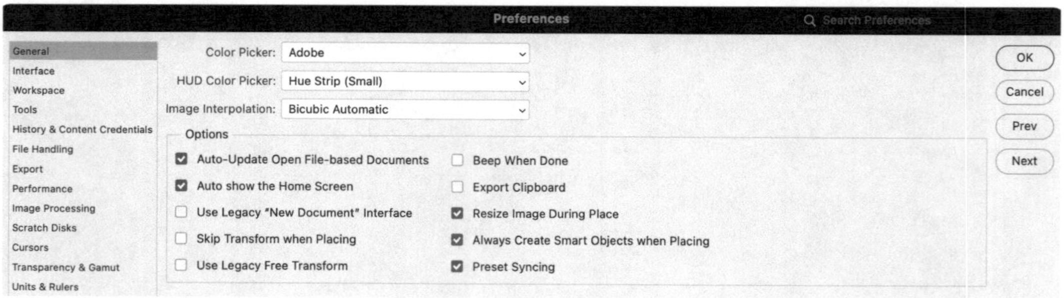

Figure 1.16: General preferences

> **Syncing presets**
>
> **Preset Syncing** was introduced in February 2021 and uploads your brush, pattern, gradient, shape, and swatch libraries to Creative Cloud. So, wherever you log in with your Adobe ID and use Photoshop in the future, your library assets download from the cloud and become available to use.

3. Next, click on **Interface** from the list on the left-hand side. You can change the **UI Color Theme** option from the default of **Medium Dark** to three other variations. You can also alter the style of the image border shown in the image window as well as the background color that surrounds your images.

   I find that if the UI brightness is high, this often contributes to eye strain. As such, I tend to set the UI theme to **Dark** or leave it set to **Medium Dark** to compensate. Turning on the **Neutral Color Mode** checkbox removes distracting color from interface buttons and icons. I don't find lines or shadows around images' edges helpful; these I set to **None**. You may wish to alter the brightness of the image window background to **Black**, **Dark**, **Medium**, **Light Gray**, or a **Custom** color of your choice. I prefer the less distracting **Default** of mid-tone gray:

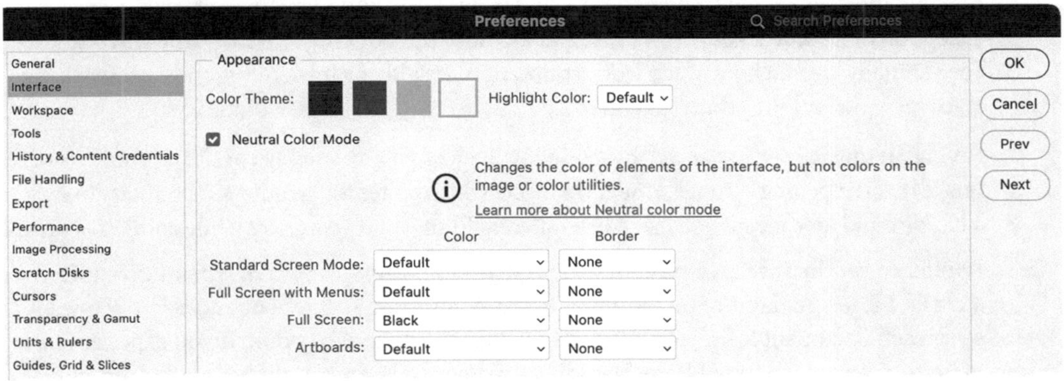

Figure 1.17: Interface preferences

4. Click on **Tools** from the list on the left-hand side. With the exception of **Show Rich Tooltips**, you can turn on all checkboxes in this section:

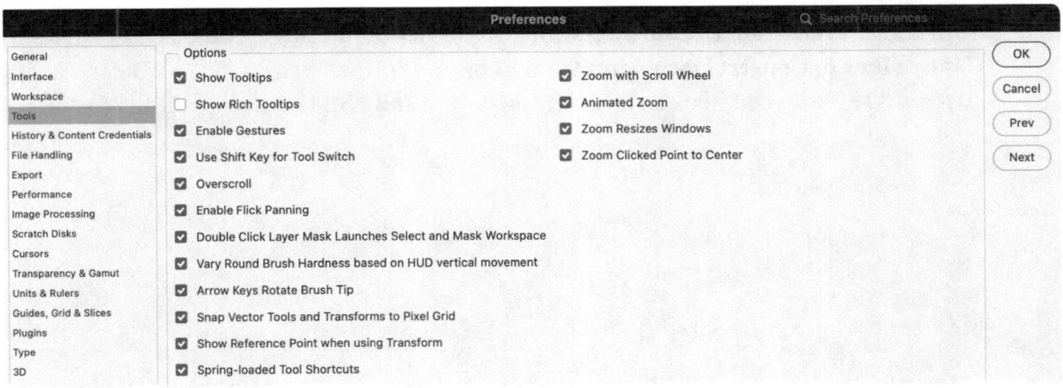

Figure 1.18: Tools preferences

Tool preferences

Rich Tooltips is the animated video explainer that appears every time you hover your cursor over a tool in the **Tools** panel, which can become tedious very quickly. Other features in this section generally enhance the usability of a tool or the ease with which you accomplish tasks. **Zoom with Scroll Wheel** allows you to avoid activating the **Zoom** tool altogether, while **Animated Zoom** and **Flicked Panning** make the motion of panning and zooming less jarring on the eye. **Overscroll** allows you to position the edges of an image anywhere in the image window, making edge editing easier to accomplish.

5. Click on **File Handling** from the list on the left-hand side. Under **File Saving Options**, I would recommend that **Image Previews** is set to **Always Save**, and turn on all checkboxes with the exception of **Enable legacy "Save As"** and **Do not append "copy" to filename when saving a copy**. Finally, decide how much work you want to risk losing by defining the **Automatic Save Recovery** interval dropdown to either `5, 10, 15, 30, or 60` minutes.

   Saving an image preview and a thumbnail will allow you to quickly check the contents of an image before opening through Finder on macOS or Explorer on Windows. The ability to save as a background task means you can edit a different Photoshop document while another is saving.

   I prefer to set the save recovery increment to every 5 minutes so that when I do experience a crash, I lose a maximum of 5 minutes' work. Photoshop will reboot and ask if you want to open each document from your previous session at its last saved point. If you experience a lag in performance each time Photoshop saves a recovery file, you might have to balance the pros and cons of setting the interval to 10 minutes.

   I still prefer to save my Photoshop documents in a dedicated network folder along with related project assets. However, you can set the default save location to Creative Cloud. There are many benefits to saving on Creative Cloud, which include a file history and, not least, a backup of your file. The option to save to Creative Cloud is also available each time you save a document.

6. Turn on the **Prefer Adobe Camera Raw for Supported Raw Files** checkbox and **Use Adobe Camera Raw to Convert Documents from 32 bit to 16/8 bit**. Turn on the **Ask Before Saving Layered TIFF Files** checkbox and set **Maximize PSD and PSB File Compatibility** to **Always**:

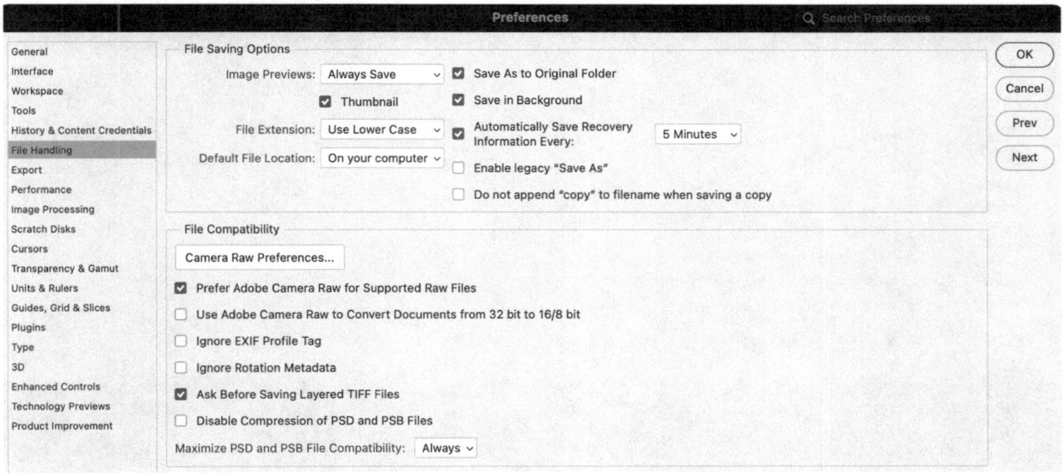

Figure 1.19: File Handling preferences

Camera Raw

Adobe Camera Raw offers fantastic tools and features for editing digital negatives; as such, I would recommend utilizing it for such tasks rather than Photoshop. Maximizing the compatibility of your **Photoshop Document** (**PSD**) files means that when you share files with colleagues who have older versions of Photoshop, they will be able to open and edit them.

7. Click on **Cursors** from the list on the left-hand side. Set **Painting Cursors** to **Normal Brush Tip** and turn on the **Show Crosshair in Brush Tip** checkbox. Set the **Other Cursors** option to **Precise**. Preview images in the dialog update accordingly to visualize changes to brush tips and icons:

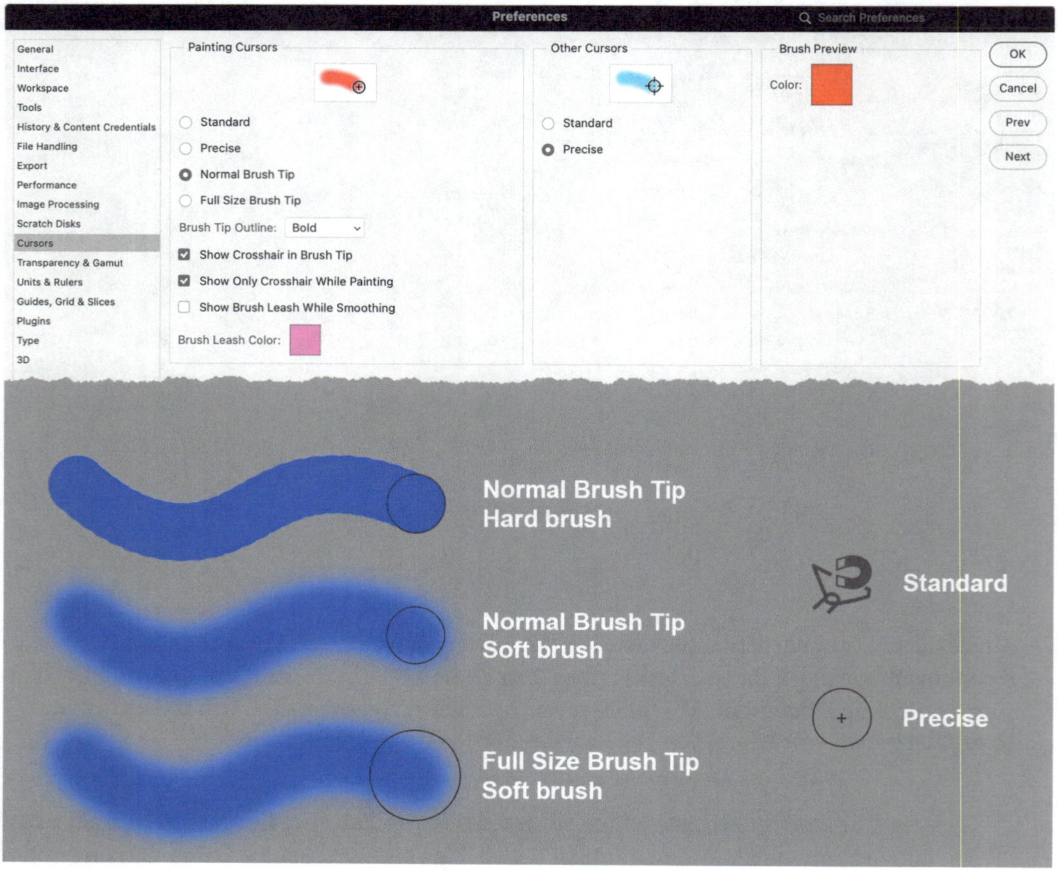

Figure 1.20: Cursors preferences

Painting tools

Painting cursors are integral to editing in Photoshop, so it's important to understand how each of the cursor appearances might affect the way you use them. The size of a brush tip is indicated by an outline, shown in the preferences as a circle for simplicity, with a red paint stroke. A normal brush tip indicates only the area that receives a full coverage of red, while a full-size brush tip indicates full coverage of red and soft brush marks. I find the normal brush tip size more intuitive to work with. The crosshair inside a brush tip is mainly used for alignment. The section labeled **Other Cursors** includes selection tools. **Standard** will make the cursor appear as the icon of the tool itself, while the far more intuitive precise version includes features that make the **Magic Wand** selection tool far easier to use.

8. Click on **Type** from the list on the left-hand side. Turn off all checkboxes apart from **Show Font Names in English** and **Use ESC key to commit text**.

Smart Quotes look terrible and resemble inch marks. I would highly recommend that you deactivate Smart Quotes.

Photoshop now automatically replaces missing fonts or glyph characters with the most suitable match available on your computer. The trouble is that you might not notice this. By turning off **Glyph Protection**, this issue should highlight missing characters, allowing you to manually correct the issue with a font of your choice:

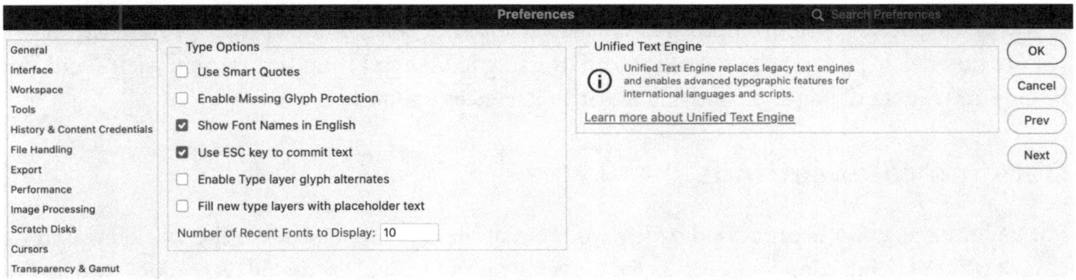

Figure 1.21: Type preferences

You can now exit type editing mode in Photoshop by pressing the *Esc* key, matching the behavior of Illustrator and InDesign.

Photoshop will now highlight alternative characters when editing text; however, the pop-out tooltip to use this feature appears on the text frame and can make editing smaller text frames frustrating. For this reason, I deactivate it and go to the **Glyphs** panel instead (**Window** → **Glyphs**).

When you create new text frames in Photoshop, it fills it with copy using the last known type settings. I find this a hindrance and deactivate it.

9. Finally, click on **Technology Previews** from the list on the left-hand side. I would suggest that you turn on all checkboxes.

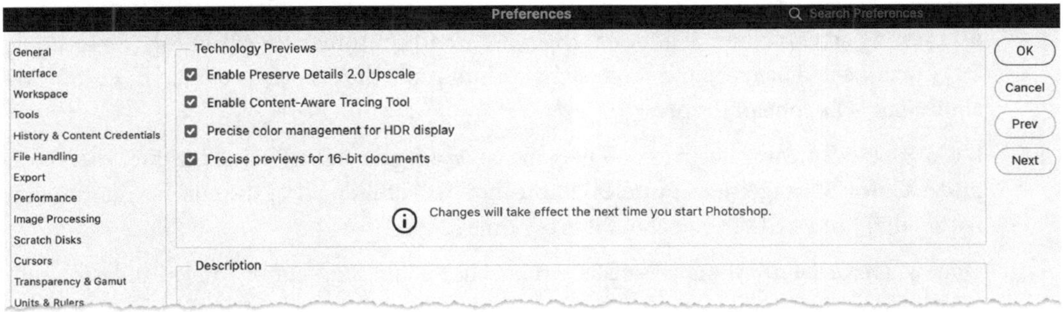

Figure 1.22: Technology preferences

I have found all of the features in this section enhance my experience of Photoshop. **Preserve Details 2.0 Upscale** allows for better-quality enlargements of images. The **Content-Aware Tracing** tool detects edges when creating a path; this can save valuable time rather than creating a vector path manually with the **Pen** tool.

Preference settings are only saved when you close Photoshop, so as soon as you complete your preference changes, close Photoshop and launch it once more.

If you experience persistent Photoshop crashes, it could be related to a corrupt preference file. To resolve this, delete preferences and redo them by going to **General** from the list on the left-hand side of the **Preferences** dialog and choosing **Reset Preferences on Quit**.

Defining color settings

For us humans, color is processed by the wonders of biology as we observe the world around us, almost without being conscious of it. Sadly, the same cannot be said for digital technology, where data is captured on **digital single-lens reflex cameras** (**DSLRs**) and smartphones and then passed from one application to another before ultimately being viewed in print and on screen.

To ensure that each device and application recreates color consistently, we need a method by which our technology talks the same language of color. Rather like traveling to a country where language differs, we communicate in the same tongue to understand one another. And so, we use color management to achieve this. It's relatively simple to set up, can be synchronized across all Adobe Creative Cloud desktops, and only takes a few moments – a small price to pay for relatively consistent color across our projects. Here's how to do it:

1. You define a color management policy for your artwork by going to **Edit → Color Settings**. Click on the **Settings** drop-down menu in the upper left-hand corner of the dialog. Depending on which region of the world you're based, the default setting displayed will differ.
2. If you are based in the US, choose **North American Prepress 2**, which is often recommended for creating artwork intended for onscreen, web, and consumer-level printing (for example, a USB-connected printer) and professional printing at a third-party provider. In Europe, the equivalent is **European Prepress 3**.
3. If you want to avoid warning messages popping up on a regular basis, turn off the three checkboxes under **Color Management Policies**. Photoshop will still do all of the color synchronizing required; it just won't tell you about it every time it does!
4. Once you have defined the appropriate settings, click on the **Save** button located at the top right of the dialog. You should be prompted to save the file in the `Settings` folder presented to you. This is where Adobe looks for the settings file (CSF). Enter a filename of `MyColor` and click on the **Save** button.

A message in the middle of the **Color Settings** dialog reads **Not synchronised**. This indicates that your other Adobe applications are not using the same settings. We will resolve this in the next step. Click **OK** to exit. You will need to install Adobe Bridge from the Creative Cloud desktop application to complete the final stage.

5. To sync the color settings across Creative Cloud desktop apps, we need to open Adobe Bridge. In Photoshop, go to **File** → **Browse in Bridge**. Once Bridge opens, go to **Edit** → **Color** Settings. Select **MyColor** from the list of available color settings and click on **Apply**. Bridge will apply the same settings across any desktop applications you have already installed:

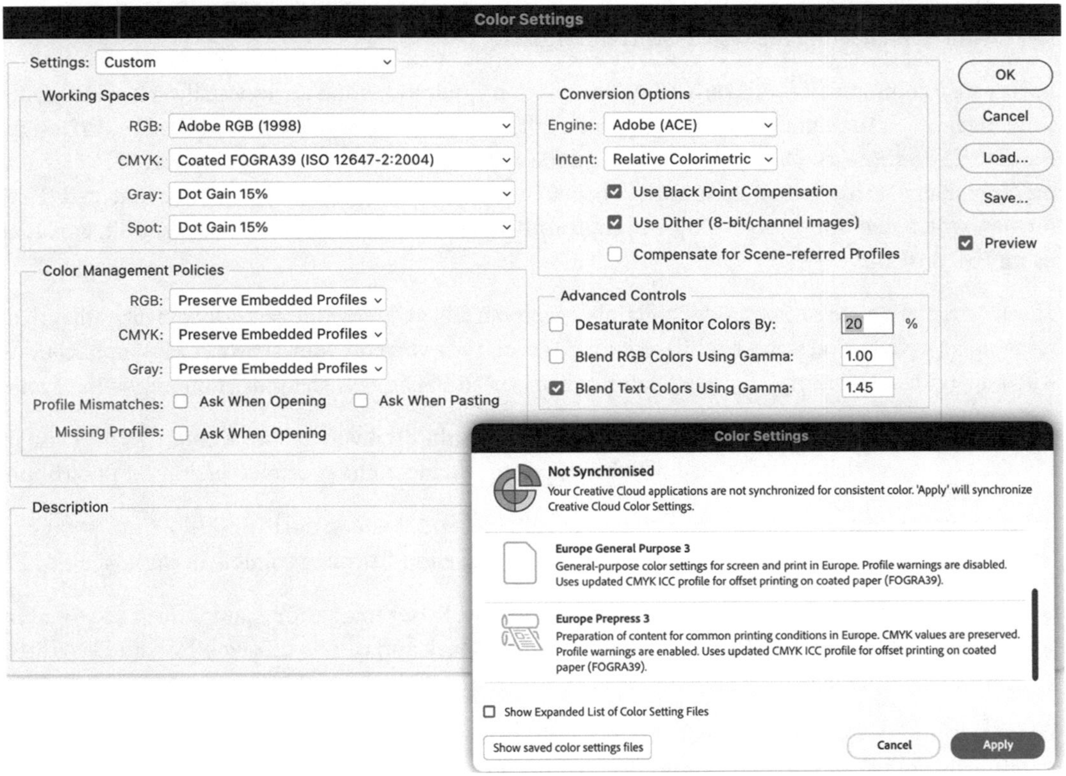

Figure 1.23: Color settings, defined in Photoshop and synchronized in Adobe Bridge

In this section, we've modified preference settings and color management. As the heading suggests, some edits are simply down to your personal preference, such as the interface brightness. However, some tools will now become more intuitive to use, simply by modifying the cursor appearance when active. Color management helps ensure color consistency across Creative Cloud applications. The final part of the chapter explores the building blocks of digital images. The better we understand how images are composed, the easier it will be to deconstruct them and attain the best possible quality.

Quality-first approach

You've probably heard of the saying, "garbage in, garbage out." Well, this holds true in Photoshop as well. Just because an image looks fantastic on screen, it doesn't guarantee it will when printed. Trust me – the last thing you want to experience is the horror of unboxing thousands of prints containing pixelated or blurred images.

PSD is by far the most powerful image format, offering tremendous flexibility within the application. The PSD format supports up to 250,000 layers in a single document, allowing you to scale, rotate, or reposition each component of your design with ease. Or, if you prefer, you can hide or even delete a layer without it affecting the rest of the composition.

Layers are a common facet of nearly all Adobe desktop applications and are especially critical to saving time. Because of the tight integration between other Adobe products, such as Illustrator, InDesign, Premiere, After Effects, Dreamweaver, and Adobe XD, you can directly import layered PSD files and preserve many of the Photoshop features. So, before you save your project artwork in a flattened JPEG format, which can only store a single background layer and no transparent background, consider using PSD instead.

This is a critical step to saving production time as you can edit and reuse the same document, rather than resaving an updated version in a different format each time you edit your artwork. Most applications will auto-update or prompt you to update your imported PSD rather than insist on importing again.

When saving a PSD and setting it to maximize file compatibility, it will include a composite version of a layered image so that it can be read by other applications, including previous versions of Photoshop.

Layered image files mean your text layers stay editable, and if you export from Illustrator, you can choose to create a layered PSD and keep text frames made in Illustrator editable in Photoshop too.

Common edits that you make to the color or brightness of your image, for example, can be stored in adjustment layers. They affect any layer below it in the stack and can be turned off/on and re-edited at any point by double left-clicking on the layer's adjustment icon thumbnail in the **Layers** panel.

You can apply layer effects to specific layers to add a drop shadow or glow. Then, re-edit the effect at any time by double left-clicking on the effect name. If you wish to move the effect to a different layer, you can simply drag it from the source layer and onto the destination layer. Or, you could even create a duplicate by holding down the *Alt/Option* key as you drag and drop a layer effect.

Image quality

All digital photos are mosaics composed of tiles called pixels, an amalgamation of two words: *picture* and *element*. These tiny squares each contain just a single color. If you magnify an image in Photoshop beyond a zoom factor of 500%, those pixels become more apparent. But at first glance, at 100% magnification, they are indistinguishable, and our brains resolve those tiny patterns of color into a seamless representation of what the camera captured.

Resolution

Resolution has long been established and leveraged by artists over the centuries. Monet painted with short brush strokes known as daubs to create small clusters of colors. Standing close to the canvas, they have no apparent structure, but walk further back, and our eyes resolve these paint marks to create an image. Therefore, the distance and the size of the color marks are significant. This is as true for pixels as it is for paint.

Pixels per inch (PPI)

In industry, we refer to our formula as **pixels per inch** (**PPI**), a method for calculating image size in relation to the number of pixels in a given region, such as an inch. Magazines, read at a distance of 18 inches, require images with 300 pixels vertically and horizontally within every inch. A billboard ad viewed from several meters away requires only 30 PPI, while web graphics require in the region of 72 to 144 PPI to attain the appropriate quality.

Vector graphics

As with photographs, vector graphics are used in abundance in print, online, and on screen. When you see a logo, a road sign, or wayfinding graphics in a supermarket, those are almost certainly made from vector graphics. Unlike digital photographs, vectors typically contain a dozen or so colors and are composed of anchor points and segments that form shapes, not pixels. This means vector graphics are resolution-independent and capable of being used at any size capable of being printed and manufactured without losing quality.

Digital text is a form of vector art, but it could be simple shapes such as circles, rectangles, and lines. Photoshop provides a set of vector-editing tools and several shape libraries that can retain their vector quality. By storing vector art in its own shape layer, Photoshop can preserve the quality of the graphics, allowing them to be modified without losing quality:

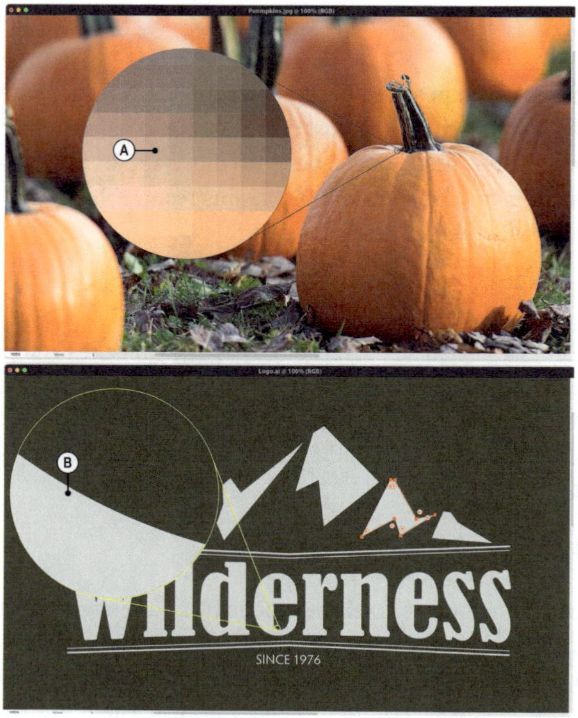

Figure 1.24: A comparison between pixel-based images (A) and vector graphics (B)

Calculating PPI in Photoshop

Image Size isn't the most exciting Photoshop feature, but essential to determine the maximum size an image can be in print and on screen. Here's how to use it:

1. Go to **Image** → **Image Size**. When the dialog appears, set the **Width** and **Height** units to **Millimeters** (or whichever unit of measurement you are accustomed to) by clicking on the drop-down menu.
2. Then, turn off the **Resample** checkbox (*A*) to create a link between not only the width and height of the image but also the resolution.

3. It is normal that when you download an image from a stock site or your digital camera, it will possess a large width and height – for example, 2116 mm x 1411 mm – but a very low resolution of 72 PPI. With a link between the size of the image and the resolution, you can now simply enter the desired PPI into the **Resolution** setting. For professional print, this is 300 PPI. Click **OK** when done:

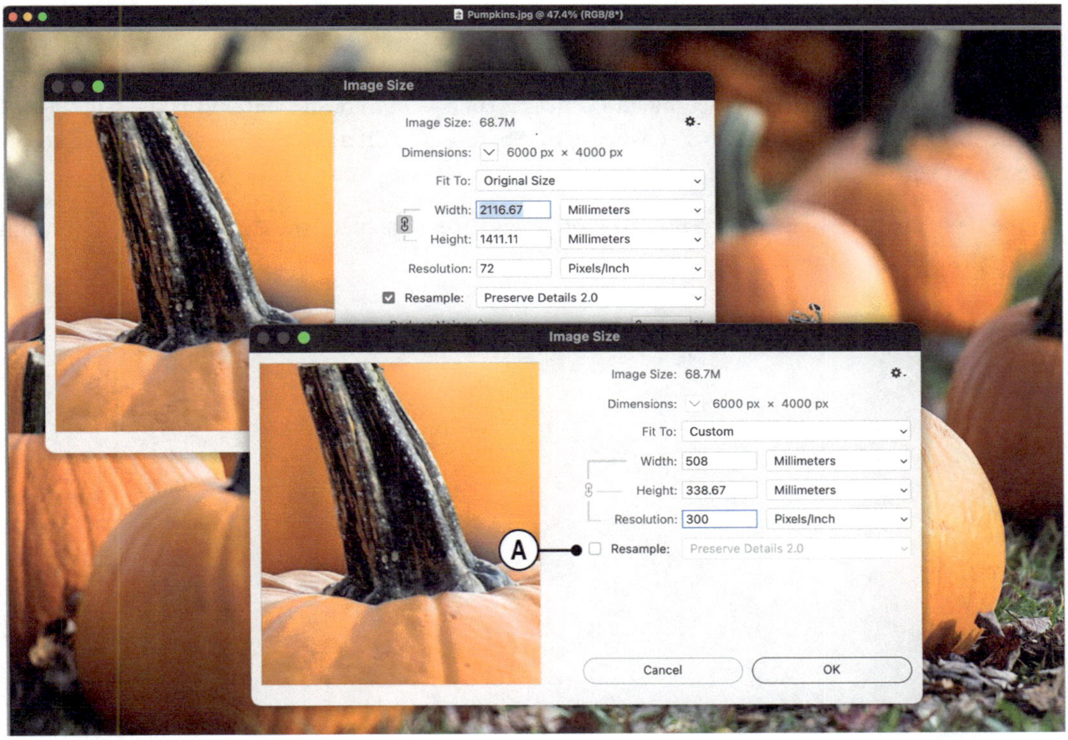

Figure 1.25: The Image Size dialog

In this section, we have learned the importance of defining quality from the outset by measuring the resolution of pixel-based images.

Summary

In this chapter, we have reviewed some of the standout new features and updates to appear in Photoshop, essential client feedback tools, and collaboration features that can make visualizing artwork and concepts easier.

We've customized the Photoshop interface to better suit our needs, simplifying how panels are arranged on screen to make finding tools easier to access while providing lots of space for images to take center stage. We've customized the **Tools** panel, hiding redundant tools and making popular tools easier to locate. We've seen how keyboard shortcuts can make features more accessible and hide nonessential menu options, all of this captured in a workspace that can be saved for future use.

We've seen how preference settings can make a significant impact on the way we interact with cursors and the behavior of tools in general.

Finally, we looked at crucial image-quality concepts such as PPI and resolution that help define the quality of pixel-generated artwork, ensuring that before we edit a file, it has been supplied in the appropriate quality.

In the next chapter, we will learn how to crop images, remove blemishes, and correct colors with nondestructive workflows.

2
Non-Destructive Healing and Retouching

The size and quality of source images can vary greatly, and they often end up being integrated into compositions that bear no resemblance to the original artwork. This process starts by removing unwanted content. This involves trimming peripheral details, fixing imperfections, and correcting tone and colors to ensure our source imagery is in good shape for further editing or integration elsewhere.

In this chapter, we'll focus on cropping techniques, which allow you to trim unwanted edge details precisely and correct crooked photos. We'll extend the canvas using techniques that allow you to transform image orientation while seamlessly filling new regions with image content.

Blemishes, or unwanted content, which are often captured in the original photo, can be removed with a combination of retouching tools. We'll look at scenarios in which each of these tools provides quick, high-quality results with a combination of precise selections, painting cursors, and dedicated retouching workspaces.

With blemishes concealed, we'll then move on to color and tonal edits. This will include simple edits to alter image brightness and contrast, through to detailed color matching. We'll achieve all this without permanently changing the course image by using non-destructive adjustment layers.

In this chapter, we'll cover the following topics:

- Cropping and straightening the images and extending the canvas
- Working with the healing and spot healing tools and content-aware technology
- Color and tone editing with adjustment layers

Technical requirements

The project files for this chapter can be found at: `https://github.com/PacktPublishing/Mastering-Adobe-Photoshop-2024/tree/main/Chapter02`

Cropping and straightening images and extending the canvas

In *Chapter 1*, we established that the first task when working with new images is to verify their maximum output size and quality. The next step is to review the composition. Does the image appear level and are the subjects framed appropriately? Cropping is ideal for addressing this issue.

Straightening a crooked image

Crooked images are commonplace. Even mounting a camera on a tripod to capture a photo won't guarantee that the horizon line is level. Fortunately, the crop tool comes with a straightening feature that makes removing a crooked horizon a breeze. Let's take a look:

1. Go to **File** → **Open**, browse to the `02-Retouch` folder, and select `Horizon.jpg`. Ensure that the entire canvas is visible in the image window by going to **View** → **Fit on Screen** and then zoom out slightly so that you can see the region beyond the edge of the canvas.
2. Switch to the **Crop** tool by pressing the *C* key to activate the correct group of tools. Then, left-click and hold down the left mouse button on the active tool in the **Tools** panel. From the pop-out menu, left-click on the **Crop** tool to make it active.
3. From the **Options** bar, ensure the **Delete Cropped Pixels** checkbox is turned on. Then, left-click on the **Straighten** tool to make it active. Hover your cursor over the far-left edge of the horizon in the photo, click and hold the left mouse button down, and drag to the far right-hand side of the horizon in the image. Release the mouse button.
4. Photoshop will now display a crop frame and rotate the image so that it matches the angle of the **Straighten** tool, set between the start and end point you dragged with the mouse. If you accurately matched the horizon line in the photo, it should appear level. **Apply** the straightened edit; Photoshop will now delete the region of the image that falls outside of the crop frame (the shaded region), leaving you with a straightened photo. With the edits now applied, go to **File** → **Save** and then go to **File** → **Close**:

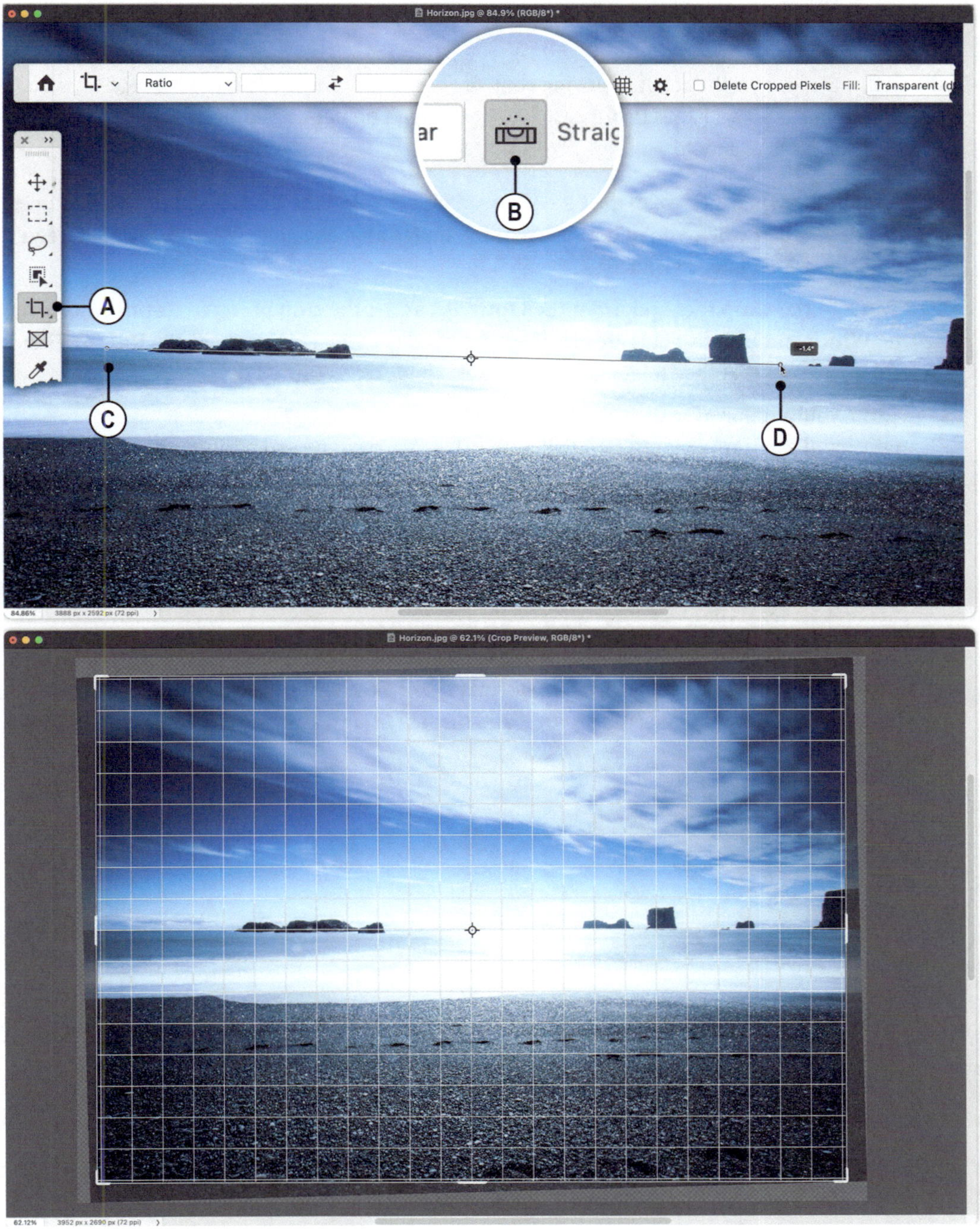

Figure 2.1: Using the Straighten tool to correct crooked images

Cropping images

Traditionally, cropping is the act of removing content from one or more edges of an image. This image requires the subjects – two ladies in our case – to be cropped tighter and conform to a compositional rule of thirds. Let's take a look:

1. Go to **File** → **Open**, browse to the `02-Retouch` folder, select the `Shoreline.jpg` document, and click **Open** when you're done. When the image appears, go to **View** → **Fit on Screen** to make the whole image visible.
2. Switch to the **Crop** tool and, from the **Options** bar, set the crop preset to **Ratio**, ensure both the **Width** and **Height** fields are blank, set the overlay menu (*Figure 2.2,* **A**) to **Rule of Thirds**, and make sure that the **Delete Cropped Pixels** checkbox is turned off.
3. Hover your cursor over the top-left point on the crop frame (*Figure 2.2,* **B**) and drag to the right-hand side. As you drag, you will notice that a grid composed of nine squares will appear in the crop frame. Drag the crop frame until the left dividing line of the grid, which marks a third of the width, is positioned between the ladies (*Figure 2.2,* **C**).
4. Click on the **Commit** button in the **Options** bar to apply the crop. This will crop the image but not delete the region outside of the crop frame. To reveal the region in the future, go to **Image** → **Reveal All**.
5. With the edits now complete, go to **File** → **Save As**, keeping the filename the same. However, you will need to save the document in PSD format to keep the cropped region of the photo within the file (JPG format flattens the artwork and dispenses with any content outside the canvas):

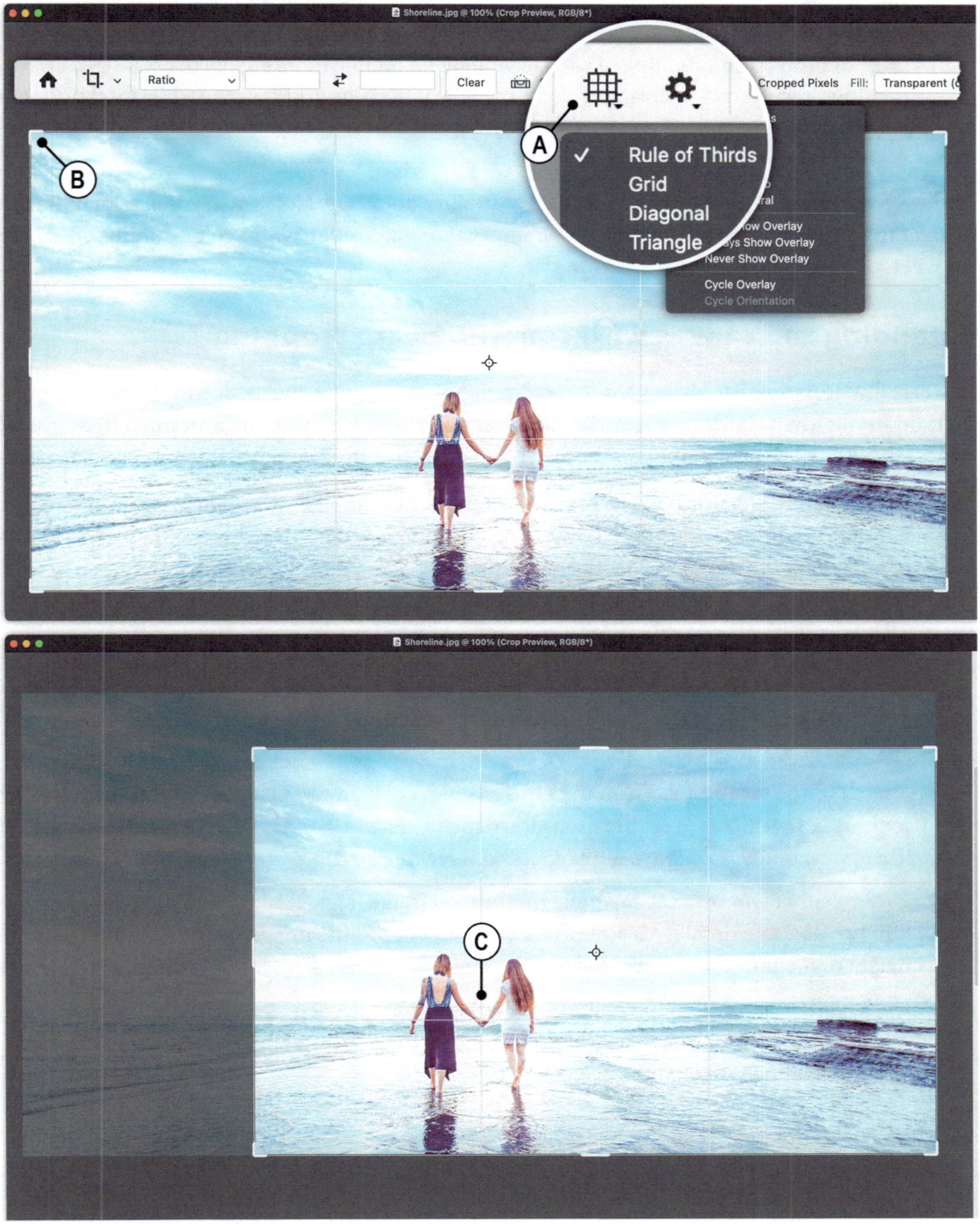

Figure 2.2: Using the rule of thirds grid to create more visually interesting compositions

Rule of thirds

The rule of thirds is commonly used as a technique for adding more energy to create dynamic compositions, with content arranged along any one of the nine grid squares, while focal points or subjects are placed on intersecting lines.

In this section, we saw how to use cropping features in Photoshop. Not only can you trim unwanted content from image edges, but you can also improve the composition with a rule-of-thirds grid. Next, we will look at ways to extend the canvas.

Extending the canvas with content-aware cropping

Historically, cropping has always led to a reduction in image size, partly due to the once-popular method of "digitizing" print images via a scanner and trimming away the unwanted background. However, with the advances of Photoshop's AI-enhanced features, we can also extend the canvas.

The process is almost identical to the previous exercise, but instead, we will drag one or more crop frame handles beyond the edge of the canvas. In addition, content-aware technology uses existing image content to build onto the artwork and fill the new region for us. This is especially handy when you need to alter the orientation of an image or extend its width to create an extra-wide web banner for social media. Let's get started:

1. Go to **File** → **Open** and select `Waves.jpg` from the `02-Retouch` folder. Click **Open** when you're done. This image calls for an extension to the canvas to convert its ratio from square to portrait.
2. Switch to the **Crop** tool. From the **Options** bar, click on the **Overlay** button menu, which appears as a grid, to reveal the drop-down menu (*Figure 2.3*, **A**). Choose **Grid** from the list. Then, turn on the **Content-Aware** checkbox (*Figure 2.3*, **B**).
3. Hover your cursor over the top point on the crop frame (*Figure 2.3*, **C**) and drag upwards until you reveal approximately `5` additional grid rows above the image. These should extend the height of the image to `3000` pixels, as shown in the tooltip adjacent to your cursor.
4. Click on the **Commit** button in the **Options** bar. This will extend the canvas to the point where you dragged the frame handles. Photoshop will fill in the new region using parts of the existing image, blending it in with the original pixels.

5. With the edits now complete, go to **File** → **Save**. Save the image in the `02-Retouch` folder as a PSD file, then close the document:

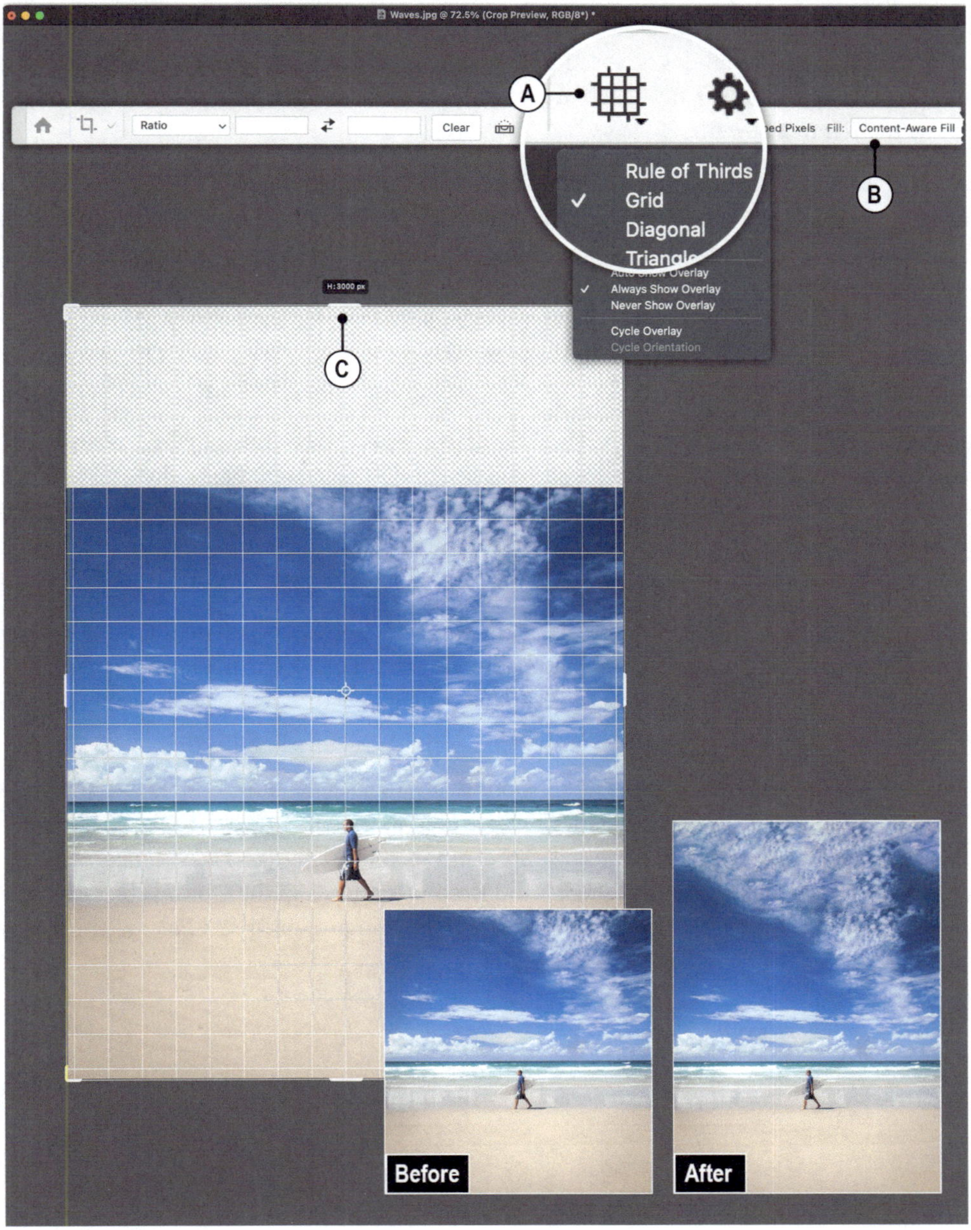

Figure 2.3: Using the Crop tool to extend the canvas and fill new regions with repurposed pixels

Quickly cropping tips

Buried away in a Photoshop sub-menu is an auto-cropping feature that was once intended for extracting photos from scanned backgrounds. However, auto-crop is brilliant for extracting thumbnail images or logos from a plain background. With your image open, go to **File** → **Automate** → **Crop & Straighten Photos**. Photoshop will detect any items surrounded by a plain background, and then copy, straighten, and paste them into a new file.

There may be occasions when, after cropping, you notice unwanted rows and columns of pixels along the edges of an image. By default, the crop tool snaps to the edge of the canvas, making cropping a few pixels a tedious task. Instead, zoom above 500% zoom level so that you can see the pixels grid appear and estimate the number of rogue pixels. Then, go to **Image** → **Canvas Size**. Set the units to pixels, then set a negative value for the pixels you wish to remove (`-7`, for example). Anchor the canvas at the opposite side from the one you are trying to remove pixels from. Then, click **OK** to remove those troublesome pixels.

If you need to crop away transparent pixels or contrast colored pixels from any edge of an image, you can use **Image** → **Trim**. By default, Photoshop will search for transparent pixels along all four edges of an image and crop them away. You can change this behavior, and instead search for any pixel color that matches that of top-left pixel color or bottom-right pixel color, and crop those away from each edge. You can also choose which edge is trimmed by turning off one or more of the **Trim Away** checkboxes.

You can avoid the **Crop** tool altogether by using the selection tool. Create a selection using any method or tool you prefer. Then, with your selection active, go to **Image** → **Crop**. Photoshop will crop the image down to the four edges of your selection, leaving you with a rectangular region. Any pixels outside of your original selection will be deleted.

It is possible to crop one image to the dimensions of another. Open both images in Photoshop and ensure that the image you wish to reference the size of is active. Then, switch to the **Crop** tool. From the **Options** bar, click on the **Crop Preset** drop-down menu and choose **Front Image** from the list. Photoshop will populate the **Width**, **Height**, and **Resolution** fields in the **Options** bar with sampled canvas data. Click on the tab of the document that requires cropping and press *Enter* to apply cropping to the image:

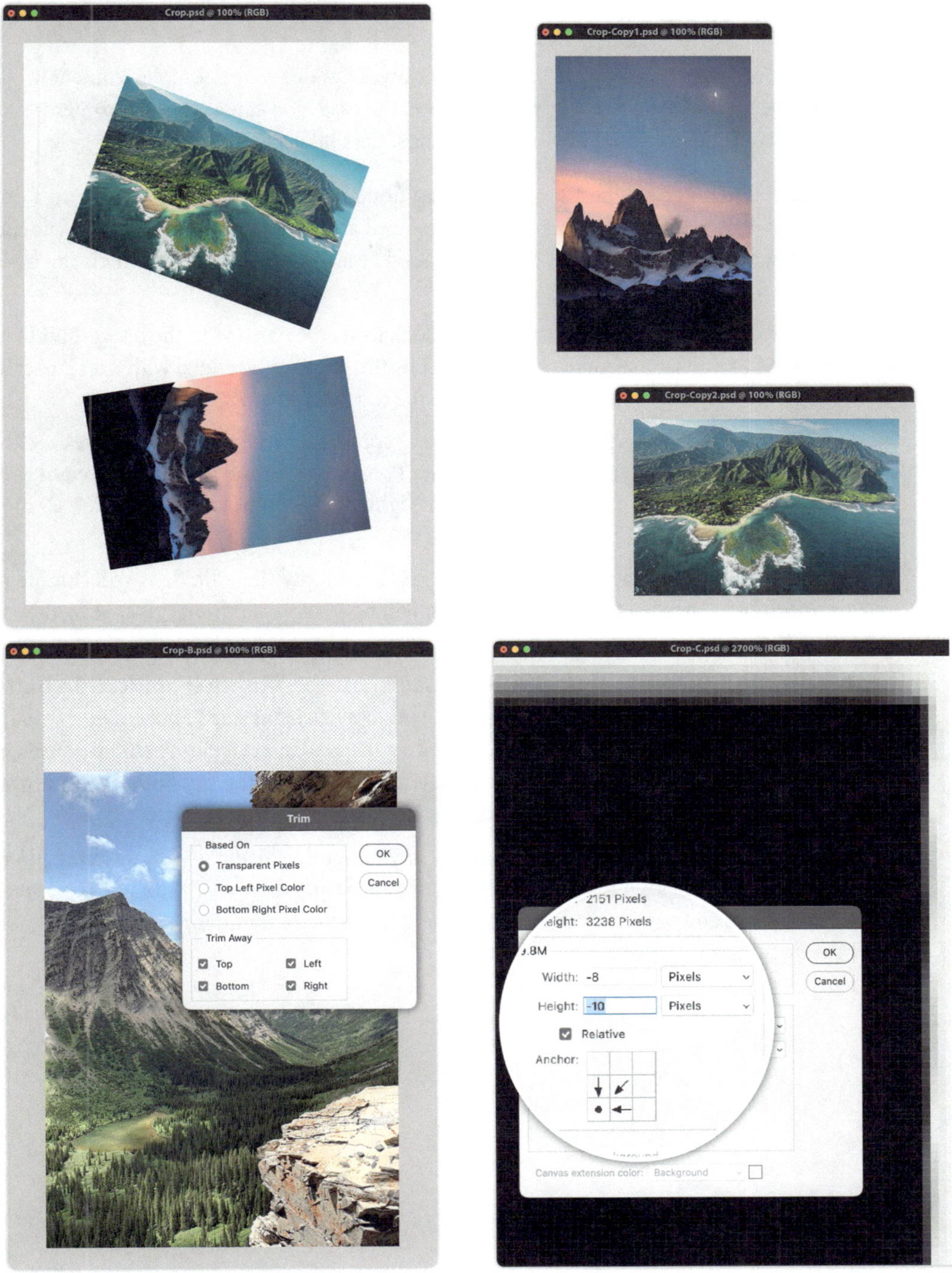

Figure 2.4: Cropping and straightening photos (top), trimming (bottom left), and canvas size (bottom right)

Content-aware scale

There may be occasions when you need to extend your canvas but due to the complex content in your image, you cannot use content-aware cropping. If this is the case, you can always try content-aware scaling to stretch your image without obvious distortions. Let's take a look:

1. Go to **File** → **Open** and select the `Boats.jpg` document from the `02-Retouch` folder. Click **Open** when you're done. This image is required as a web banner and must be widened. However, the challenge here is that the background contains lots of details, which can be too complicated for content-aware cropping.
2. Go to the **Layers** panel and left-click on the padlock icon associated with the background layer (*Figure 2.5*, **A**) to unlock the content. This will allow the photo to be edited with a feature called **Content-Aware Scale** in a follow-up step. Rename the layer `Panorama`.
3. Next, go to **Image** → **Canvas Size**. When the dialog appears, ensure that the **Relative** checkbox is turned off. Then, set the unit of measurement to **Percentage** for the **Width** and **Height** drop-down menus (*Figure 2.5*, **B**). Click on the center-right anchor point icon (*Figure 2.5*, **C**) in the **Anchors** section of the dialog.
4. Enter `150` into the **Width** field and then click **OK** to apply the edit. This will double the canvas' width but crucially, the extended region will be transparent (empty), as shown by the checkered region.
5. Next, go to **Edit** → **Content-Aware Scale**. Turn off the **Link Aspect Ration** button (*Figure 2.5*, **D**) in the **Options** bar. Then, grab the middle left-hand side handle of the bounding box (*Figure 2.5*, **E**) that resides over the layer and drag it across to the left until all the transparent canvas is concealed. This will distort low-detailed areas such as the sky but leave important detailed areas untouched. Click on the **Commit** button to apply the changes.
6. Take a quick look at the image to see if there are any noticeable distortions by switching to the **Zoom** tool and left-clicking to a magnification of at least 100%. With all edits now complete, go to **File** → **Save** and save the document in the `02-Retouch` folder as a PSD file. Finally, close the document:

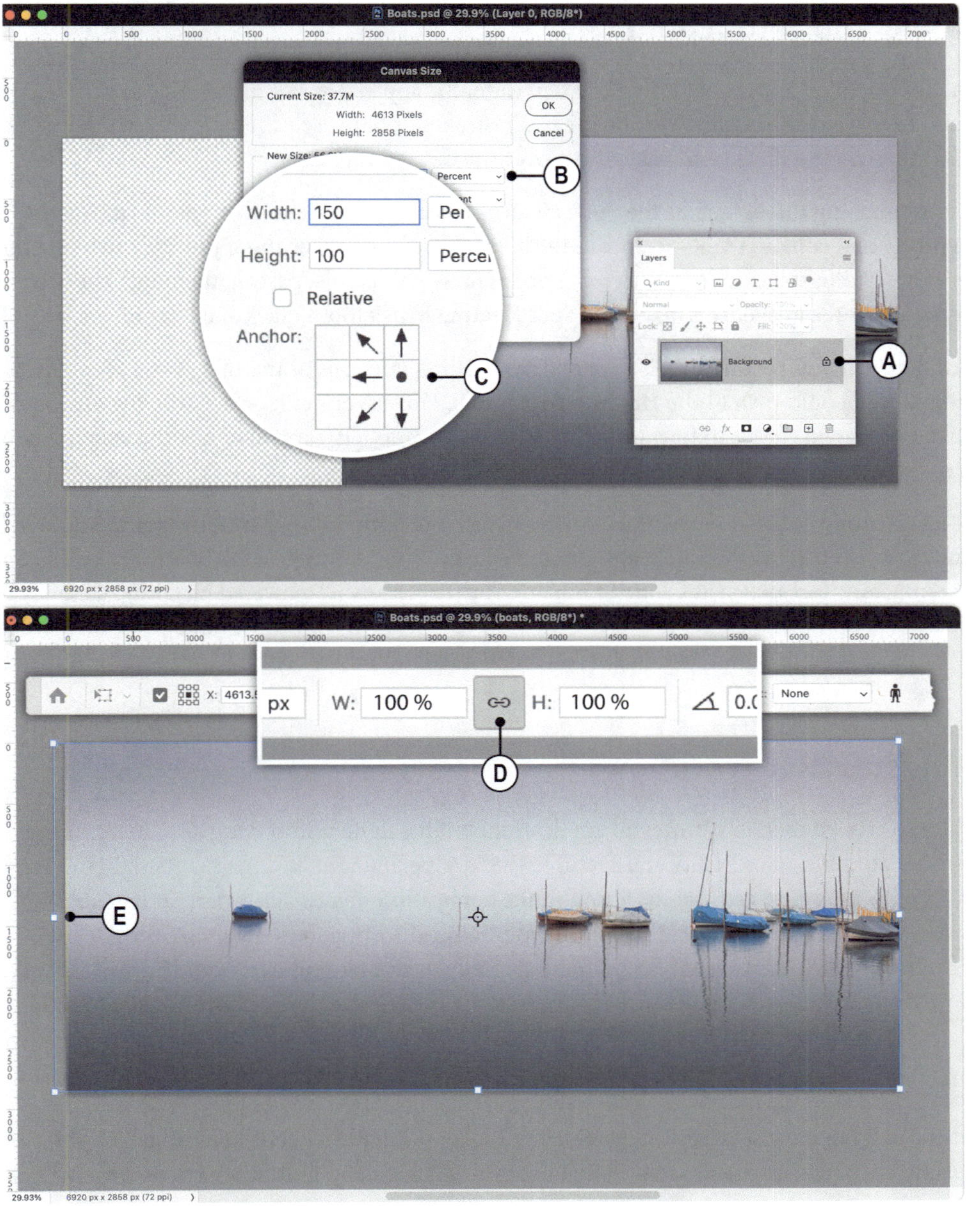

Figure 2.5: Extending the canvas (top) before extending the photo with Content-Aware Scale (bottom) to distort low-detail areas such as the water while protecting the boats

In this section, we saw how Photoshop's suite of cropping tools can be used to extend the canvas and repurpose the original pixels in the image to add AI-generated content. Next, we will take a look at healing and retouching techniques.

Healing and retouching

In the following exercises, we'll explore two different approaches to removing unwanted content, referred to as blemishes, either by applying brush strokes or filling selections. Both techniques replicate parts of the existing image and paste them over the desired region.

Newer retouching tools, such as the **Spot Healing Brush** tool, carefully sample "blemish-free" parts of an image that contain similar colors as the blemish and repurpose them precisely to blend them in seamlessly. Photoshop decides which parts of the image to sample, pasting them into the brush tip as you drag across the image. This makes the **Spot Healing Brush** tool a quick and relatively reliable choice.

Alternatively, if you require precise control over which portions of the image you want Photoshop to sample, you could turn to the **Healing Brush** tool. Hover your cursor over the region you wish to sample, hold down *Alt* (Windows) or *Option* (macOS), and left-click to define the starting point for your sample. Head to the blemished pixels and drag across them.

The **Spot Healing brush** tool and the **Healing Brush** tool both utilize **Content-Aware**, powered by AI technology. This can result in smudged or blurred details on the edge of the brush stroke. In contrast, older retouching tools, such as **Clone Stamp**, don't perform any AI-powered blending. It simply copies and pastes sampled pixels into the brush tip. This can be used to your advantage on highly detailed images, such as landscapes. This helps you avoid small details becoming smudged or blurred. The challenge here is to modify the brush tip so that it does the blending for you.

Nondestructive workflows

Photoshop is a wonderfully powerful application, but it can be unforgiving as a linear image editor. Wherever possible, avoid edits and features that are permanent and incapable of being removed, reset, or edited. Several commands found in the application menus apply permanent edits, but there are two features related to layers that have revolutionized editing in Photoshop over the last 20 years: **Smart Objects** and **Adjustment layers**. Both techniques will be explored extensively in the following section. Both are relatively quick and simple to use and can save hours of precious production time.

Remove cables from a photo

Great-looking images can be ruined by cables and other unsightly content, some of which at the time of capturing the image might not seem all that noticeable. Let's take a look at how to remove such objects:

1. Go to **File** → **Open**, browse to the `02-Retouch` folder, select `Sunset.jpg`, and click **Open** when you're done. The cable runs across this image, ruining the view of the sunset; the industrial-type buildings to the right of the image also need to be removed. Left-click on the **New Layer** icon (shown as **A** in *Figure 2.6*) at the bottom of the **Layers** panel and name the new empty layer `retouch`. Ensure the new layer is active.

2. Press the *J* key and hold down the left mouse button on the active tool in the **Tools** panel. From the pop-out menu, left-click on the **Spot Healing Brush** tool (*Figure 2.6*, **B**). In the **Options** bar, set the brush tip's (*Figure 2.6*, **C**) **Size** to `70` px, **Mode** to **Normal**, and **Type** to **Content-Aware**. Then, turn on the **Sample All Layers** checkbox.
3. Hover your cursor over the left edge of the cable and then hold the left mouse button down as you drag across the cable to the right-hand side. This will remove the cable once you release the left mouse button.
4. Then, with the **Spot Healing Brush** tool still active, click and drag over the pole from top to bottom. You can run your cursor through the greenery to ensure all of it has been removed:

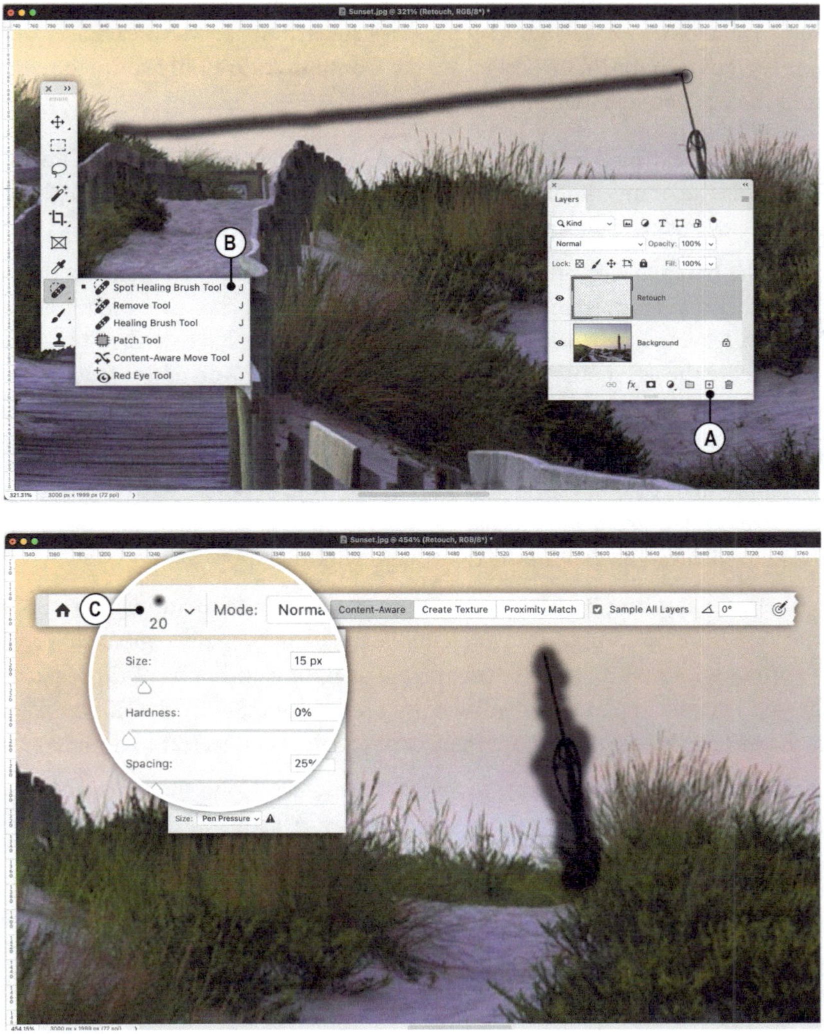

Figure 2.6: Left-clicking and dragging across blemishes with the Spot Healing Brush tool to conceal them

Painting straight lines

Although dragging Photoshop's painting tools across an image to apply edits feels natural, you can also paint in straight lines. Left-click in the region where you wish to start your straight paint mark and release the left mouse button. Then, hover your cursor over the region where you wish to end the straight line, hold down *Shift*, and then left-click again. Release the mouse button and the *Shift* key. This technique can be used for a variety of painting and retouching tools, such as the **Spot Healing Brush**.

Removing large blemishes with Content-Aware Fill

The brush tools are handy for small edits such as the cables in the previous exercise. However, when there are large regions to retouch, it's best to use the **Content-Aware Fill** feature to remove the small structure from the horizon. Let's take a look:

1. With the **Spot Healing Brush** tool still active, click and drag over the small details labeled **D** to **G**, such as the orange light and the mast on top of the tower. These small details are best removed before using **Content-Aware Fill** to ensure they are not sampled.
2. Switch to the **Lasso** tool by pressing *L*. Set the selection **Mode** to **New** and set the **Feather** value to `0`. Left-click and drag around the tower with the masts attached to it and the adjacent building to the right, leaving a generous region around it. Once you have reached the place where you started, release the left mouse button. If necessary, you can **Add** or **Subtract** from the original selection by changing the selection **Mode** and then using the same click-drag technique.
3. Go to **Edit** → **Content-Aware Fill** to enter the dedicated workspace. Photoshop will use the green highlighted region in the left half of the editor to denote the regions of the image it will sample pixel content from and replace the original content with matching pixels, the previewed results for which can be seen in the right-hand window.
4. Switch to the **Sampling Brush** tool and then change **Mode** to **Subtract** from **Overlay Area** and increase the brush size to `180` px. If necessary, paint over any regions that are not suitable, such as the lighthouse, to remove them from sampling and prevent those parts from being duplicated. Once complete, you will see the preview update. Click **OK** when you're done to apply the edits and close the dialog. Then, choose **Select** → **Deselect** to deactivate the selection.
5. Once all the edits are complete, go to **Select** → **Deselect**. Go to **File** → **Save As**, browse to the `02-Retouch` folder, and name the file `Sunset.psd`. Close the document when you're done:

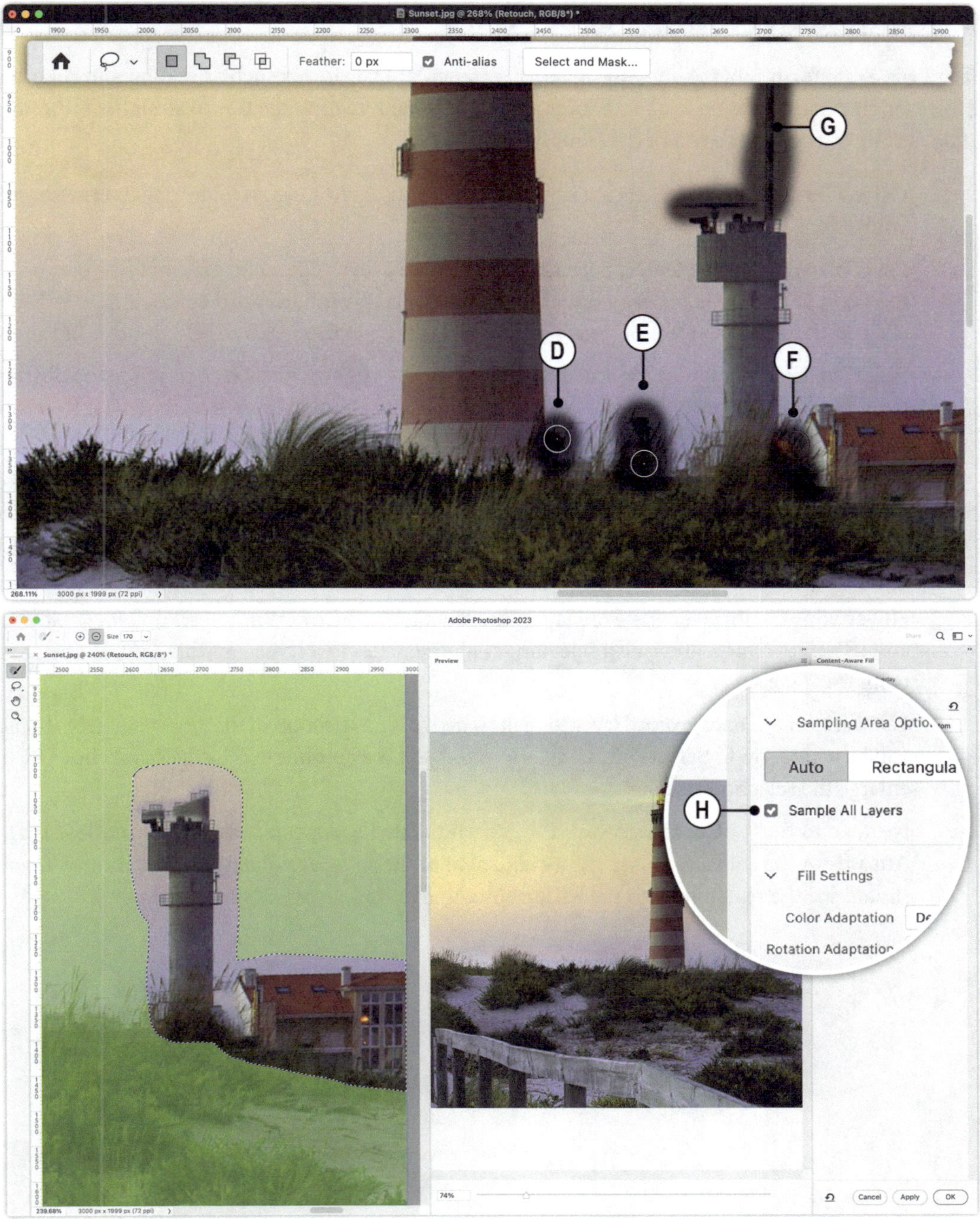

Figure 2.7: Removing minor details with the Spot Healing Brush tool before using the Content-Aware Fill feature to avoid unwanted details being replicated

Bending subjects with Puppet Warp

The **Free Transform** tool is handy for making rectangular transforms such as scaling and rotating. However, in this case, we need a more "organic" way of manipulating the tree to straighten it so that it doesn't distract from the rest of the composition:

1. Go to **File** → **Open** and select `Palm.jpg` from the `02-Retouch` folder. Click **Open** when you're done.
2. Press *W* to activate the **Object Selection** tool (*Figure 2.8,* **A**). Click and long-hold on the visible tool icon in the **Tools** panel to reveal the pop-out and ensure the correct tool is active. Then, click on the **Subject Select** button (*Figure 2.8,* **B**) in the **Options** bar to select both palm trees.
3. Switch to the **Rectangular Marquee** tool by pressing *M*. Change the selection **mode** to **Subtract** from the **Options** bar. Create a selection around the smaller palm tree to remove it from the current selection.
4. Next, press *Ctrl* + *J* (Windows) or *Cmd* + *J* (macOS) to copy and paste the selected pixels onto a new layer. Double left-click on the layer name and rename it `Tree`. Hover your cursor over the layer's name and right-click to reveal the context menu. Choose **Convert to Smart Object** to protect the content of the layer and make **Puppet Warp** re-editable.
5. Hover your cursor over the **Tree** layer thumbnail, press *Ctrl* (Windows) or *Cmd* (macOS), and left-click. This will create a selection of all the pixels in a layer – in this case, all the large palm tree pixels.
6. Left-click on the **Background** layer to make it active. The selection of the large palm tree should still be active. Go to **Select** → **Modify** → **Expand**. Set the amount to `20` pixels and click **OK** to enlarge the selection size.
7. Next, go to **Edit** → **Content-Aware Fill**. When the dialog appears, ensure that **mode** is set to **Auto** from the settings on the right-hand side of the interface dialog. After a moment, you should see the selection with the background image content of the sky and sea:

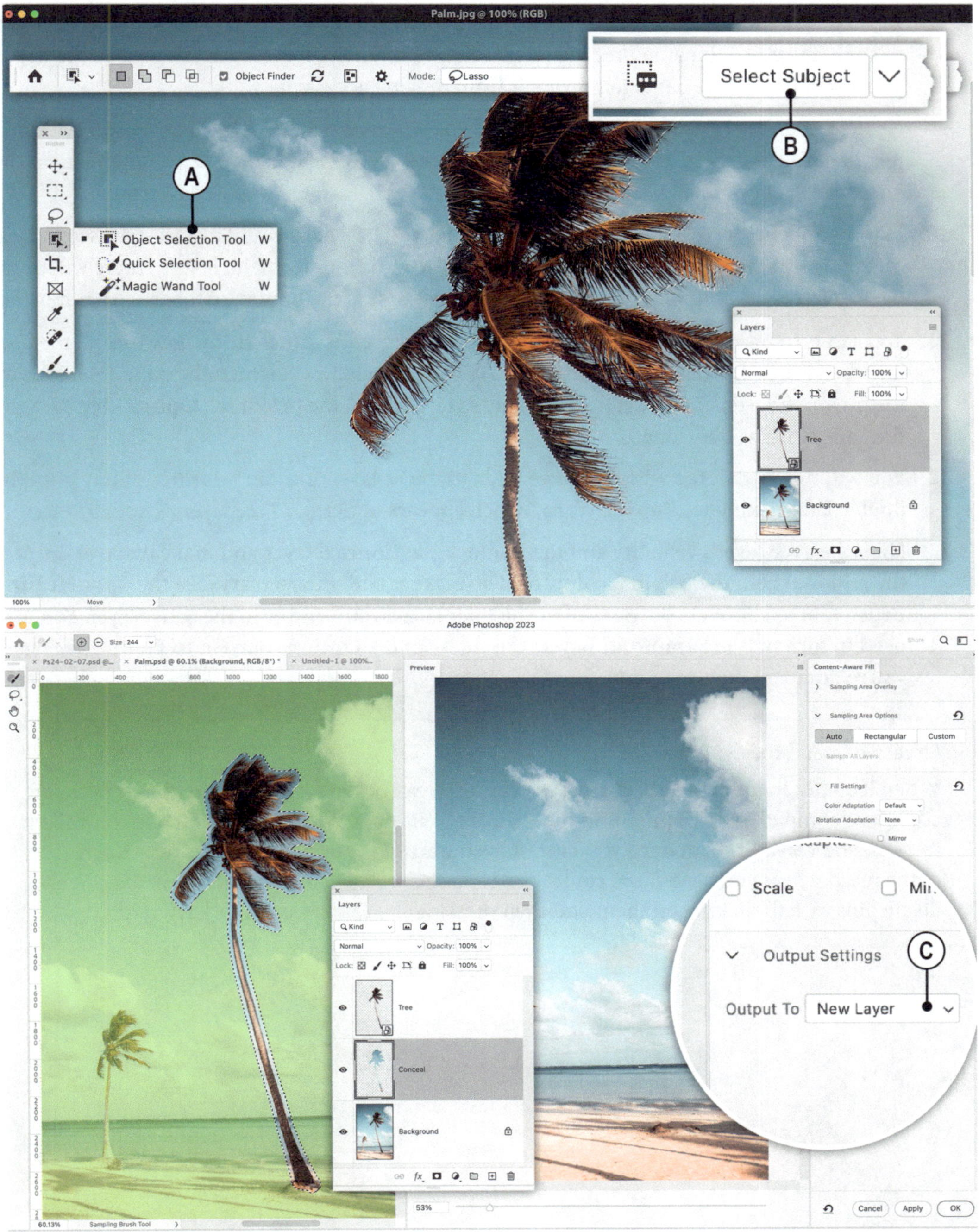

Figure 2.8: Concealing the original palm tree with Content-Aware Fill

8. Ensure the **Output to** dropdown is set to **New Layer** (*Figure 2.8*, **C**) and then click on **OK** to apply the edits. Rename the new layer `Conceal`. Click on the **Lock All** icon in the upper portion of the **Layers** panel to prevent it from moving accidentally.
9. Next, go to **Edit** → **Puppet Warp**. When the options appear at the top of the screen, set **Mode** to **Normal**, **Density** to **More Points**, leave **Expand** set to the default of 2 px, and turn on the **Show Mesh** checkbox.
10. Hover your cursor over the base of the tree trunk and left-click to add a pin. Add a second pin on the trunk where it bends, and a third pin in the middle of the palm leaves. There will be no need to move the bottom pin – we're only adding it to stop the bottom of the tree from moving.
11. You can turn off the **Show Mesh** checkbox to see your edits more clearly now that all the pins have been added. Drag the top pin to the right-hand side to straighten the palm tree. Modify the pin on the trunk accordingly to straighten it. Click on the tick in the **Options** bar to apply the edits when you're done.
12. You will notice that the edits have been added to the layer and can be edited at any point by double left-clicking on **Puppet Warp**, which appears under the **Tree** layer as a smart filter.
13. Hide the **Tree** layer's visibility and then unlock the **Conceal** layer and make it active. Inspect the region where the original palm tree leaves were and, if necessary, use the **Spot Healing Brush** tool to eliminate portions of the old palm leaves still visible in the active layer. You may need to turn on the **Sample all Layers** checkbox in the **Options** bar. Go to **File** → **Save** when you're done:

Creative Cloud mesh advice

When it comes to mesh objects of any type within Creative Cloud, it is best to start simple and add more complexity as required. In the case of the **Puppet Warp** mesh, which is controlled by pins, you can add them once you have started warping your pixels. Hover over the region of the mesh where you need more control and left-click to add an additional pin. You can also delete pins by left-clicking on them and then pressing the *Del* key on your keyboard.

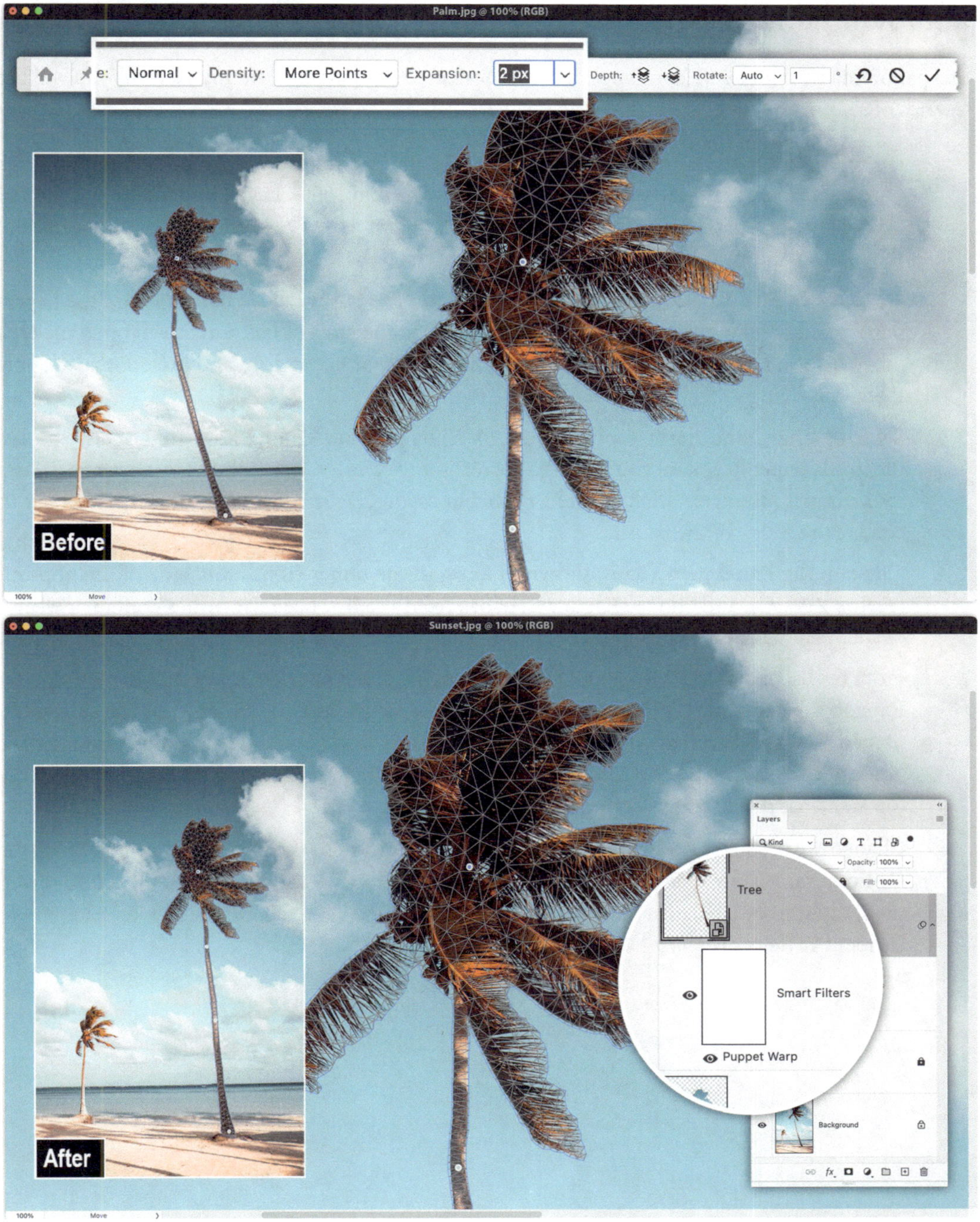

Figure 2.9: Puppet Warp can be used to bend pixels into a different position

Removing unwanted content with the Clone Stamp tool

The panorama will not be without imperfections or distracting elements. In this exercise, you will use a series of retouching tools to enhance the image:

1. Go to **File** → **Open** and select `BeachPano-01.jpg` from the `02-Retouch` folder. Click **Open** when you're done. Zoom into the image to around 100%, navigating to the sign located on the far right-hand side of the panorama so that you have a clear view of it in the center of the image window.
2. Go to the **Layers** panel and left-click on the **Create New Layer** icon at the bottom of the **Layers** panel to add a new empty layer. Double left-click on the current layer's name to open the type entry field in the layer in the stack, enter a new name of `Retouch`, and press *Enter* to apply the name change.
3. Switch to the **Clone Stamp** tool (*Figure 2.10,* **A**) by pressing *S*. Long-hold on the active tool in the **Tools** panel to ensure you have the correct tool active – **Clone Stamp** and **Pattern Stamp** look almost identical. Click on the **Brush Tip** menu (*Figure 2.10,* **B**) in the **Options** bar to change the shape of the brush.
4. Click on the **Panel** menu icon, shown as a cog in the upper right-hand side of the pop-out (*Figure 2.10,* **C**), and choose **Legacy Brushes** from the list. Legacy brushes contain a wealth of shapes and styles; some are especially effective when retouching organic content in photos.
5. From the list of brush tips listed in the pop-out, a new folder named **Legacy Brushes** will appear. Expand it by clicking on the toggle adjacent to the folder and do the same for the sub-folder named **General**. Scroll down the list until you find a brush named **Chalk 60** (*Figure 2.10,* **D**). You can change the view options of the brush tip presets by clicking on the panel menu at the top right-hand side and selecting **Small List View**.
6. Change the brush tip size to `150` px, then press *Enter* to close the brush tip pop-out. From the **Options** bar, ensure that **Mode** is set to **Normal** and **Opacity** and **Flow** are set to `100%`. From the sampling settings, turn on the **Aligned** checkbox and set the **Sample** drop-down menu to **Current & Below** (*Figure 2.10,* **E**):

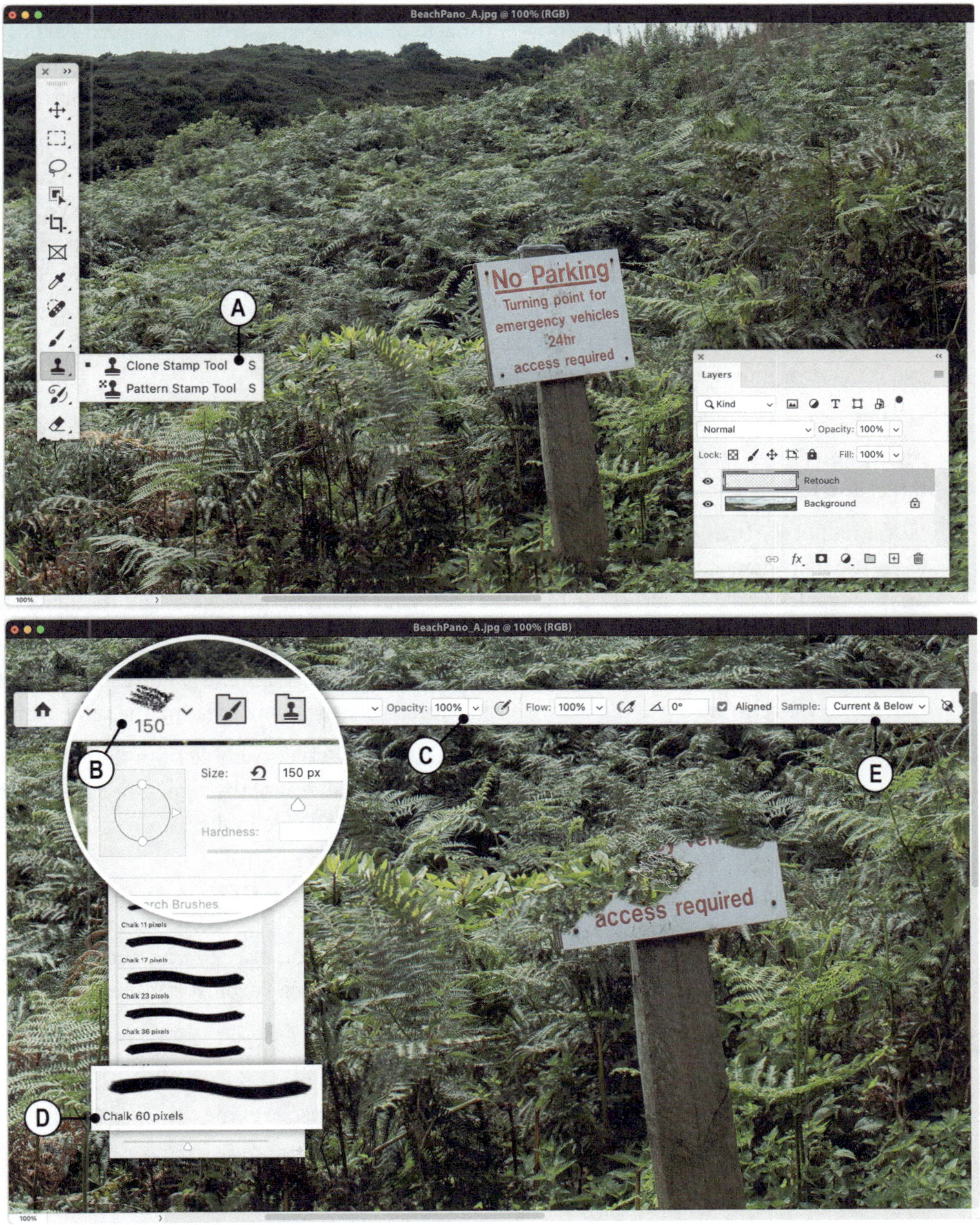

Figure 2.10: The Clone Stamp tool acts as a copy-and-paste brush to hide unwanted details

7. The photo contains a foreground that contains the sign, nettles, and stalks of the bracken. The mid-ground contains the tops of the bracken, while the background shows the hills and sky. You will need to sample content from the foreground and mid-ground to hide the sign.

The **Clone Stamp** tool acts like a copy-and-paste brush, copying from a sampled part of the image and then pasting it into your cursor as you perform brush strokes. You can sample by pressing *Alt* (Windows) or *Option* (macOS) as you simultaneously left-click, and then release the key and the left mouse button.

The sample, shown as a small target, will be visible as you apply a cloned brush mark and always starts at the point where you sampled. The sample target moves in perfect synchrony with your brush tip. Avoid sampling close to the edge of the canvas as Photoshop may run out of images to sample if the target runs off the edge of the canvas. It is also worth thinking about how long your brush strokes will be and ensuring that your sample target doesn't pick up unwanted content. I would also recommend resampling before each new brush stroke to avoid patterns emerging in your artwork.

8. With the **Clone Stamp** tool active, hover your cursor over a portion of bracken located slightly higher and to the left of the sign. Hold *Alt* (Windows) or *Option* (macOS) to reveal the sample target and left-click to define the sample start point. Release the key and the left mouse button.
9. Hover half of the brush tip over the top-left edge of the sign and the other half over the bracken to ensure that when you apply a brush stroke, the entire top section of the sign will be concealed. Then, left-click and drag across the top edge until your brush tip passes beyond the sign's right edge. Once you've done this, release the left mouse button.
10. Repeat the same technique to remove the white part of the sign. Sample a slightly different patch of bracken from the mid-ground before each brush stroke to avoid repeating the same content.
11. To conceal the upright post of the sign, you would be well served to ample from the foreground, using a mixture of the nettles and bracken stalks to hide the rest of the sign. Once the sign has been concealed, go to **File** → **Save**. Save the document as a PSD file in the `02-Retouch` folder.

Adding smiles to portraits with Face-Aware Liquify

It can be frustrating to capture the image you have been looking for, only to find someone wasn't smiling. But thanks to Photoshop's liquify tools, you can now change facial expressions. Let's take a look:

1. Go to **File** → **Open**, browse to the `02-Retouch` folder, select the file named `Smile.jpg`, and click **Open** when you're done. Right-click on the **Background** layer in the **Layers** panel and choose **Convert to Smart Object** from the list of options. Rename the layer `Smile`.
2. Then, go to **Filter** → **Liquify**. Activate the **Face** tool (*Figure 2.11*, **A**). Then, from the **Face-Aware Liquify** settings on the right-hand side, choose a face to edit. Photoshop will detect all human faces. It will start on the left, which is **Face #1**, to **Face #2** in the middle, and then **Face #3** on the right.
3. From the **Mouth** sliders and settings found on the right-hand side, you will see the **Smile** slider (*Figure 2.11*, **C**). Like all the others, the slider is set to the center at a neutral value of zero. Dragging to the left will apply a negative effect, which is frowning in this case, while dragging to the right will increase the smile effect.

4. If you want to create a more convincing smile effect, try reducing the value of the **Mouth Height** slider (*Figure 2.11*, **D**). It can make the lips appear pursed like a real smile would tend to appear.
5. Left-click on the **Face** tool located to the left of the interface (*Figure 2.11*, **A**). This will allow you to hover over and left-click on each of the three faces to identify whether they are **Face #1**, **Face #2**, or **Face #3**. You have the choice of altering the sliders on the right of the interface or dragging the on-image annotators (*Figure 2.11*, **E**) to make edits.
6. Once you have finished, click **OK** to exit the **Liquify** dialog. Save the file in `02-Retouch` folder as a PSD file with the same name:

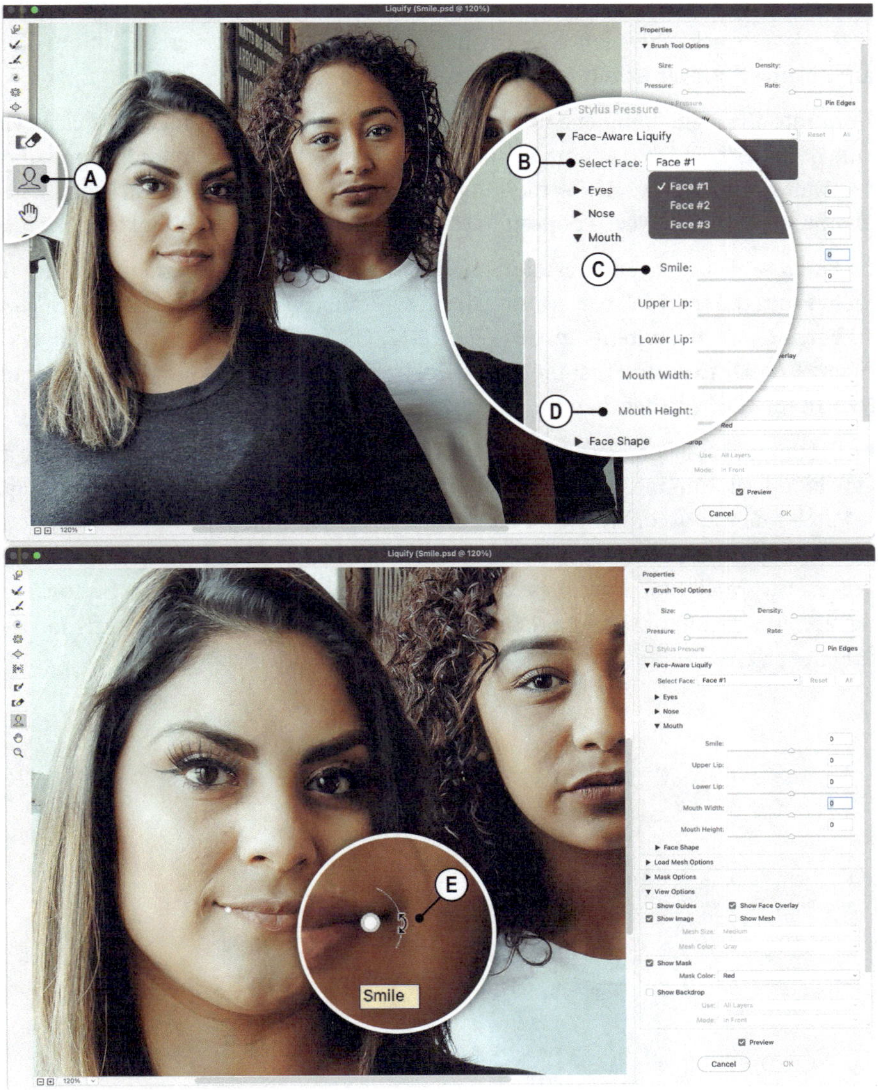

Figure 2.11: Liquify detects human facial features that can be altered, such as mouths

Portrait retouching

The patch and healing brush tools excel at editing skin tones and textures, softly blending in edits automatically with their surrounding pixels for a more natural finish. We'll take a closer look at them in this section:

1. Go to **File** → **Open** and select `Snowboarder.jpg` from the `02-Retouch` folder. Click **Open** when you're done. The photo requires some edits to be made to the man's face and clothing with the use of retouching tools.
2. Go to the **Layers** panel and left-click on the layer named **Snowboarder**, which should be at the top of the stack. Then, left-click on the **Create New Layer** icon at the bottom of the **Layers** panel. Name the layer `Heal` and make sure it is active.
3. Zoom into the right-hand eye to around `600%` so that you can take up a clear view of the white of the eye, which contains a blood vessel. Switch to the **Patch** tool by pressing the *J* key to activate one of the retouching tools in the **Tools** panel, and then left-click and hold down the left mouse button to reveal a pop-out menu. Left-click on the **Patch** tool to make it active (**A**).
4. The **Patch** tool allows you to create a lasso tool-style selection around the pixels you wish to repair. From the **Options** bar, set the selection **Mode** (*Figure 2.12,* **A**) to **New** (*Figure 2.12,* **B**) and **Patch** mode to **Content-Aware** (*Figure 2.12,* **C**). Turn on the **Sample All Layers** checkbox (*Figure 2.12,* **D**) to ensure that the **Patch** tool has pixel content to sample from the underlying layers in the stack, rather than the empty new layer you just created.
5. The **Patch** tool has a lasso selection mode built into it. You can use this tool to create a selection of the blood vessel in the right-hand eye or use a different selection tool. In the example shown, the **Patch** tool was used. With the **Patch** tool active, click and hold down the left mouse button and create a tight selection around the blood vessel. Then, hover your cursor inside the selection to reveal the **Patch** tool symbol. Left-click and hold down the left mouse button and drag the selection to a region of white in the eye immediately above. Release the left mouse button to apply the patch:

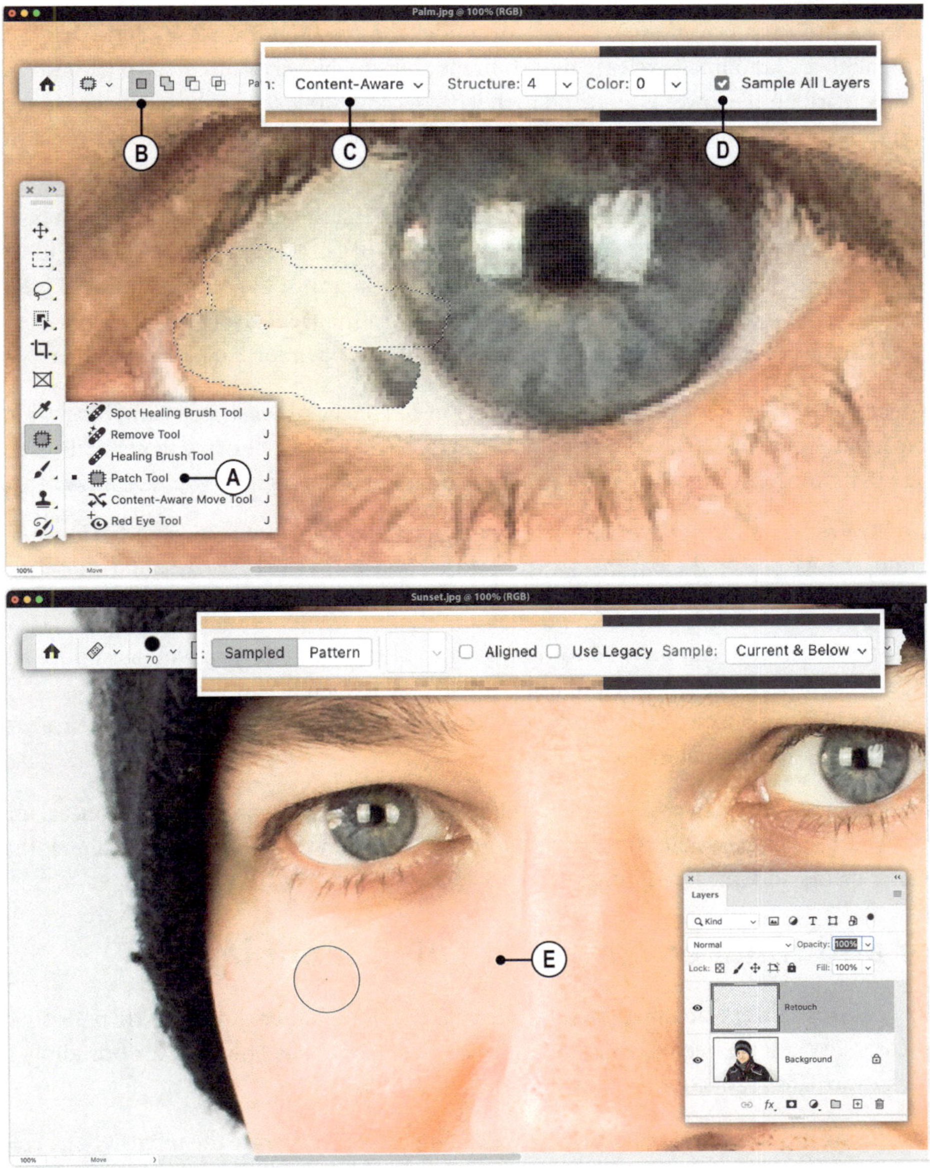

Figure 2.12: The Healing Brush tool and the Patch tool are well suited to portrait retouching

6. Go to **Select→ Deselect**. Then, switch to the **Healing Brush** tool by holding the left mouse button down on the **Patch** tool icon in the **Tools** panel to reveal it in the pop-out menu. Set the brush tip's size to `80` px. Ensure that **Mode** is set to **Normal**, **Source** is set to **Sampled**, the **Aligned** checkbox is on, **Sample** is set to **Current & Below**, and **Diffusion** is set to `4`.

7. Hover the cursor over a portion of skin under the eye (*Figure 2.12,* **E**), left-click to sample, then release, and finally release the left mouse button. Hover your cursor over one end of the dark mark on the lower eyelid, and then left-click and drag across the blemishes to remove it. Photoshop will automatically blend your edits with the surrounding pixels. Repeat the same technique for the other eye.
8. To finish off the retouching work, switch to the **Spot Healing Brush** tool, which can be found in the same set of sub-tools in the **Tools** panel. Set the brush size to `70` px, set **Mode** to **Content-Aware**, and turn on **Sample All Layers**. Left-click on any of the pimples in the skin or pieces of white fluff on the clothing to remove them. Turn the **Heal** layer's visibility back on and go to **File** → **Save** when you're done. Keep the document open for the next set of exercises.

In this section, we explored techniques that allow us to conceal undesirable content and blemishes captured in the original shot. The **Spot Healing Brush** tool has become one of the most popular retouching tools due to its simplicity, requiring you to simply drag across an image to replace unwanted pixels.

Content-Aware Fill is ideal for replacing larger regions of an image. Starting with a loose selection of a region, the AI-powered **Content-Aware** feature hand-picks the best parts of the existing image to remove subjects from their background.

The **Healing Brush** tool can be used to remove skin blemishes, allowing you to choose a healthy part of the image to sample from before using the sample to blend away unwanted pixels. Next, we'll correct colors and tones with nondestructive adjustment layers that can be edited, hidden, or removed without harming the original image.

In this section, we utilized an array of healing and retouching tools, in many cases to conceal unwanted content, but also to enhance the appearance of the image. Next, we will focus on techniques that allow you to alter colors and image brightness.

Color and tonal editing with adjustment layers

The term **color** is self-explanatory, if not a little vague. After all, there are more than 18 quadrillion known colors. When we need to reference a specific color, such as one used for branding, there is usually an exact CMYK or RGB formula that describes it visually.

As far as editing in Photoshop is concerned, we can increase or decrease the intensity of a color with saturation or boost just low-intensity colors with something called vibrance. A hue is a pure pigment, unaltered by white to create a tint or a shade that darkens a hue by adding black.

Tone is a less commonly used term that means light. Photoshop commonly characterizes light in 256 grayscale steps from pure black to pure white. Regarding RGB, black has a value of 0 (red 0, green 0, blue 0), while white is defined as 255 (red 255, green 255, blue 255). It's important to be aware of these numbers because Photoshop's selection tools use them as a method for selecting colors, including the **Magic Wand** tool and the **Color Range** dialog, both of which will be covered in this chapter.

How adjustment layers work

Adjustment layers have been around for decades in Photoshop and remain one of the most popular features because of their ability to edit color and tone non-destructively. Believe it or not, these kinds of edits had to be applied permanently to pixel layers, making the editing process far more tedious, not to mention frustrating.

Photoshop offers 16 color and tonal editing adjustments that can be added to a document layer stack, within which all the edits are stored. This means their visibility can be turned off, or the opacity altered like all of layer types. Adjustments only affect the appearance of layers lower down in the stack. It's typical to see two or three adjustments in a document, and you can add as many adjustments as necessary, although any more than a dozen can become confusing.

To re-edit an adjustment layer, double left-click on the adjustment layer thumbnail in the **Layers** panel. The settings for altering adjustment layers can be found in the **Properties** panel, which appears automatically when a new adjustment is added or re-edited. Adjustment layers come equipped with a layer mask by default to control which parts of a composition it affects.

Quick tonal editing with adjustment layers and blend modes

The simplest adjustments within Photoshop allow you to make edits with just a couple of sliders. This is ideal when all you need is to achieve a quick, effective edit without any fuss. In this exercise, you will boost the contrast in an image to give it more impact:

1. Go to **File** → **Open** and select `Forest.jpg` from the `02-Retouch` folder. This image could benefit from a boost in contrast. Click on the **Brightness/Contrast** icon (*Figure 2.13,* **A**), which is located in the top-left corner of the **Adjustments** panel.
2. The **Properties** panel will display two sliders – one to control **Brightness** and another to alter **Contrast**. Left-click on the **Auto** button in the top right-hand side of the panel; Photoshop will attempt to improve the image. I scaled back the edits by lowering the **Brightness** slider to `6` and the **Contrast** slider to `46`. You can show/hide the layer adjustment visibility by clicking the visibility icon at the bottom of the **Properties** panel.
3. Increasing image contrast will usually intensify colors. If you show/hide the adjustment layer, you will notice that the autumnal reds and oranges of the tree tops have been intensified. With the adjustment layer still active, click on the **Blend Mode** drop-down menu in the top left-hand side of the **Layers** panel (*Figure 2.13,* B) and choose **Luminance** from the list. This will ensure that only the brightness levels, referred to as tone, are altered and not the colors.

4. Go to **File** → **Save As**. Save the document as a PSD file in the `02-Retouch` folder and then close the document:

> **Blend modes**
>
> You can think of blend modes as transparency effects between the layer you edit and the layers behind it in the composition, or lower down in the layer stack. Divided into six sections, blend modes are set to **Normal** by default and perform no blending. Other blending groups hint toward their purpose by the name of the first mode in each group, such as **Darken** and **Lighten**. **Overlay** provides contrast, while **Difference** inverts the colors in overlapping layers. As you work down each item in a blend group, the result tends to become more pronounced.

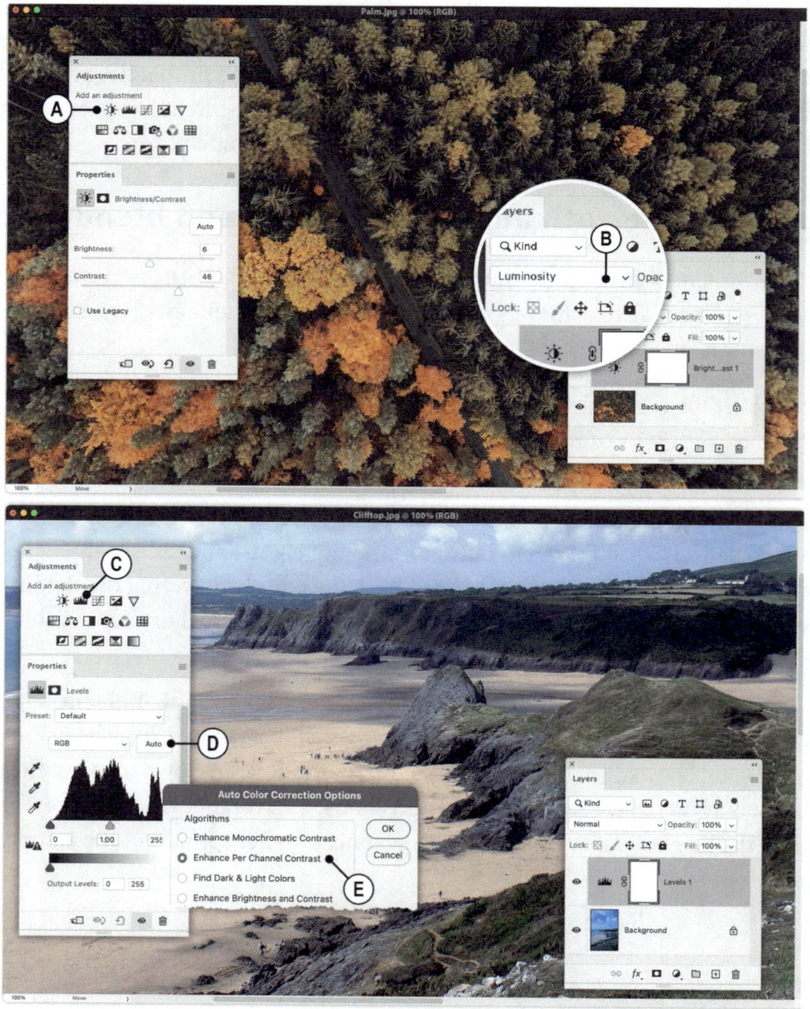

Figure 2.13: The Brightness adjustment (top) and the Levels adjustment (bottom)

Removing color casts

A color cast is an unwanted wash of color that affects an image. Certain types of light can cause digital cameras to capture a color cast. Outdoor images are prone to blue color casts, while in indoor images, yellow is often captured due to artificial lighting. Let's take a look:

1. Go to **File** → **Open** and select `Clifftop.jpg` from the `02-Retouch` folder. Click **Open** when you're done. This image of the coast contains a blue color cast.
2. Go to the **Adjustments** panel and left-click on the **Levels** adjustment icon (*Figure 2.13*, **C**) to add a new adjustment layer to the **Layers** panel and display the **Levels** settings in the **Properties** panel.
3. Then, press *Alt* (Windows) or *Option* (macOS) and then left-click on the **Auto** button (*Figure 2.13*, **D**) to open the **Auto Color Correction Options** dialog. Click on the **Enhance Per Channel Contrast** radio button (*Figure 2.13*, **E**). This will edit the red, green, and blue channel data, enhancing the contrast and the blue color cast.
4. Experiment with each of the different algorithms to see how they affect the image. **Enhance Monochromatic Contrast** will preserve the existing colors in the image while making the shadows darker and the highlights whiter. **Find Dark & Light Colors** samples the average lightest and darkest pixels in the image, enhancing contrast and helping prevent the shadow and highlight details from being clipped.
5. Toggle the visibility of the **Levels** adjustment layer to compare the results. Then, go to **File** → **Save**. Save the image as a PSD file in the `02-Retouch` folder and then close the document.

How Photoshop removes a color cast

In Photoshop, color casts exist when there is an imbalance or loss of the red, green, or blue values that make up an image. Photoshop knows that a healthy image should have an even distribution of data for all three colors, from the darkest shadows to the brightest highlights. Stretching the data for all three channels of color along the entire histogram creates balance and neutralizes the color cast.

Altering the hue of multiple subjects

The **Magic Wand** tool selects by color, which is handy for images where, for example, the same color is found throughout, and you want to avoid selecting 100 flowers individually. Let's take a closer look:

1. Go to **File** → **Open** and select `Tulips.jpg` from the `02-Retouch` folder. Click **Open** when you're done. This image contains dozens of red tulips that need recoloring.
2. Switch to the **Magic Wand** tool by pressing *W*, then long-hold on the active tool in the **Tools** panel to reveal the pop-out and select the **Magic Wand** tool (*Figure 2.14,* **A**).
3. From the **Options** bar, set the selection **Mode** to **New** (*Figure 2.14,* **B**), **Sample Size** to **Point Sample**, and **Tolerance** to `160` (*Figure 2.14,* **C**). Ensure the **Anti-alias** checkbox is active and then turn off the **Contiguous** checkbox (*Figure 2.14,* **D**) so that you can select all the red tulips in the image rather than just the one you click on.
4. Hover your cursor over one of the red tulips in the center of the image (*Figure 2.14,* **E**). Try to ensure that your cursor hovers over a mid-range red rather than a very bright or very dark red in the tulip – this will provide you with a better chance of selecting all the reds in the image. Left-click to make your selection.
5. Click on the **Hue/Saturation** icon (*Figure 2.14,* **F**) in the **Adjustments** panel. Drag the **Hue** slider (*Figure 2.14,* **G**) to the left until the red tulips appear more magenta. In the following example, the **Hue** slider was set to `-37`.
6. Change the blend mode (*Figure 2.14,* **H**) of the **Adjustment** layer to **Hue** to make the color edits appear more natural. With the edits complete, go to **File** → **Save As**. Save the document as a PSD file in the `02-Retouch` folder. Then, close the document:

Magic Wand insider tips

The **Tolerance** value controls how similar a selected color should be to the original pixel you click on. The higher the value, the broader the range of similar colors you'll select. Try doubling or halving the **Tolerance** value to find the appropriate selection quickly. When **Contiguous** is active, Photoshop searches for similar colors from the point where you click with the **Magic Wand** tool, but when inactive, Photoshop searches the entire image for similar colors.

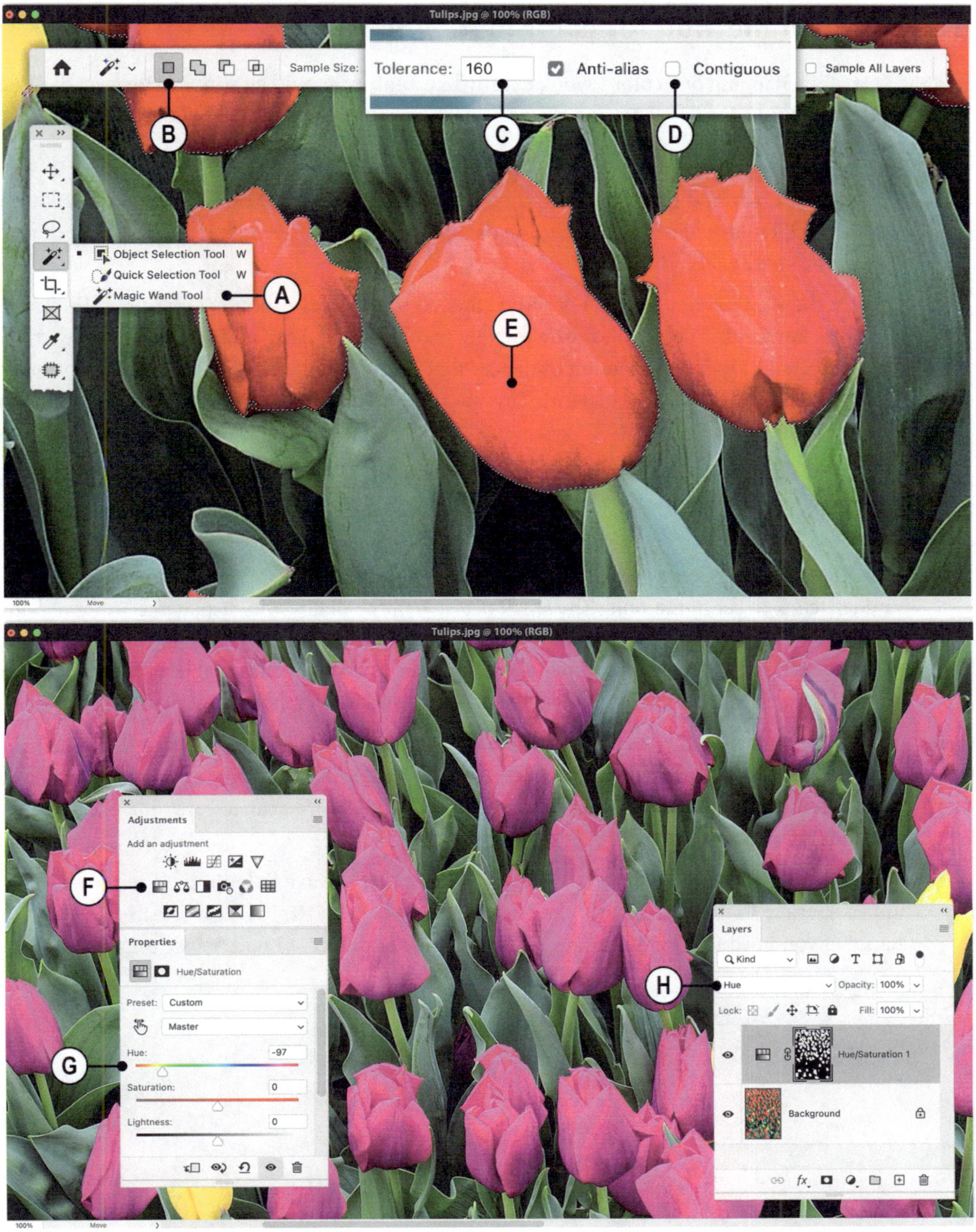

Figure 2.14: Using a combination of the Magic Wand tool and Hue/Saturation to alter colors

The simplest method for color matching

On the face of it, changing one color to look exactly like another should be simple. However, it often proves to be the opposite. Avoid getting bogged down by a bewildering array of adjustment layers, and instead try this technique:

1. Go to **File** → **Open** and select `Respray.jpg` and `Porche_Blue.jpg` from the `02-Retouch` folder. Click **Open** when you're done. The paintwork of this car needs to be altered from orange to a client-specified blue.
2. Ensure the `Respray.jpg` file is active. Switch to the **Lasso** tool by pressing *L*. From the **Options** bar, set the selection **mode** to **New** and leave the **Anti-alias** checkbox turned on. Then, create a very loose selection of the car that includes the orange paintwork but excludes details such as the tires and ground. This should help make the next stage of the selection process more accurate.
3. With the selection in place, go to **Select** → **Color Range**. When the dialog appears, ensure that the **Invert** checkbox is inactive and the selection preview is set to **None** from the drop-down menu at the bottom of the dialog (*Figure 2.15,* **A**).
4. Hover your cursor over a mid-range orange in the paintwork of the car in the image window and left-click to set the sample. The small preview in the dialog will display the white regions that have been selected. Switch to the **Add to Sample** tool (*Figure 2.15,* **B**). Hover your cursor over the rear end of the car in a patch of orange paintwork, then click and drag through only a variety of oranges in the car. As you do, the preview window will show the selected regions grow.
5. When you are happy that a large portion of the orange has been selected, drag the **Fuzziness** slider (*Figure 2.15,* **C**) to increase or decrease the number of similar colors you have selected. When almost all of the oranges have been selected, click **OK**. You can always refine the missing portions later.
6. With your enhanced selection still active, go to **Select** → **Save Selection**. When the dialog appears, enter `Paintwork` into the **Name** field and click **OK**. Saving a selection can prove handy if you need to reload it in the future by going to **Select** → **Load Selection**:

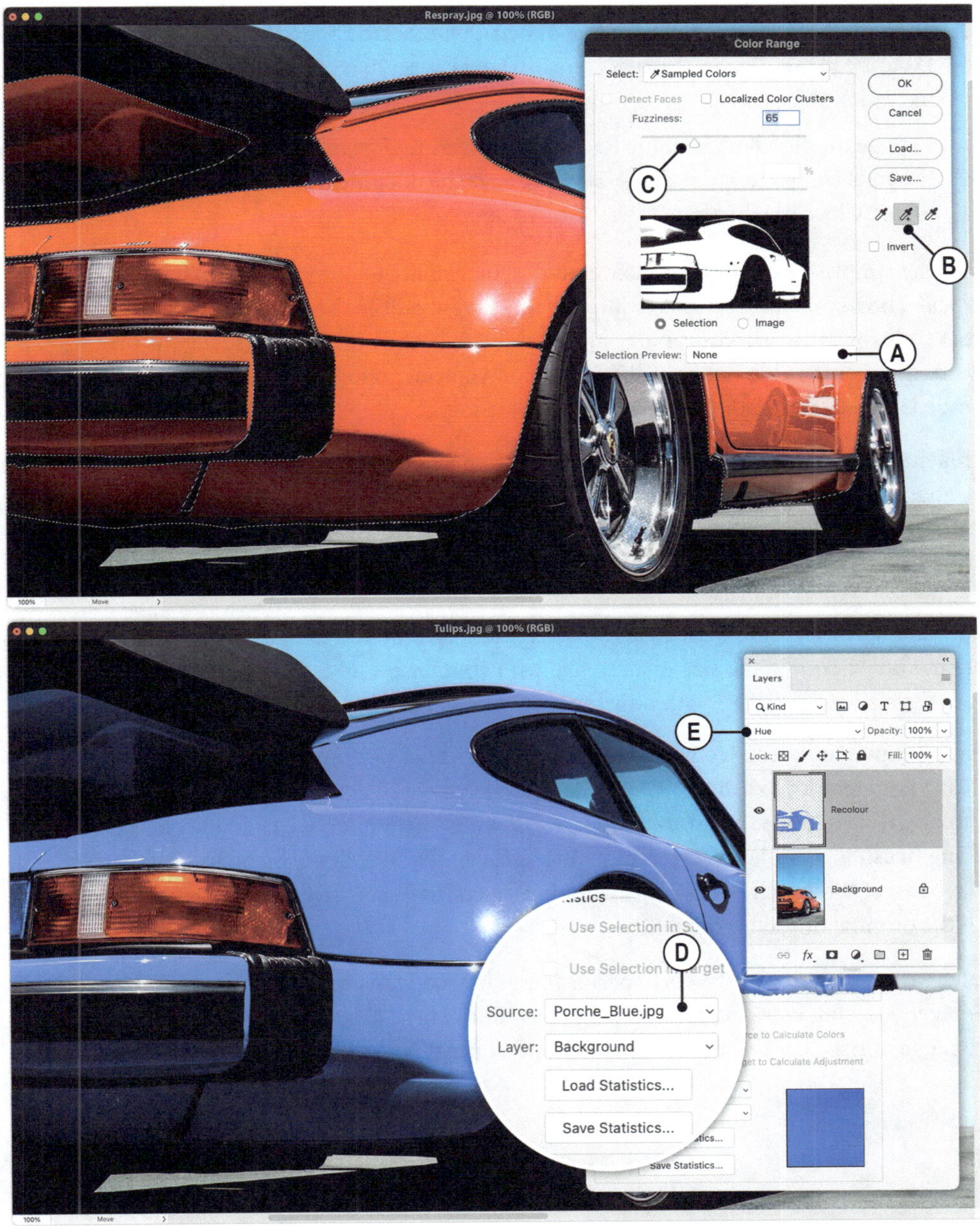

Figure 2.15: Match Color is simple to use yet highly effective for altering contrasting highlights, mid-tones, and shadows in colors

7. Next, create a copy of the selected pixels and paste them into a new layer. To do this, ensure the **Background** layer is active, then press *Ctrl* + *J* (Windows) or *Cmd* + *J* (macOS). The new layer will appear in the **Layers** panel. Rename it `Recolor`.

8. Then, go to **Image** → **Adjustments** → **Match Color**. Set the **Source** drop-down menu (*Figure 2.15*, **D**) to `Porche_Blue.jpg` and ensure **Layer** is set to reference the background of that same file. Click **OK**.
9. Change the blend mode of the **Recolor** layer to **Hue** (*Figure 2.15*, **E**) to complete the effect. With the edits complete, go to **File** → **Save As**. Save the document as a PSD file in the `02-Retouch` folder. Close the document when you're done.

This is the simplest method I've discovered for color matching in Photoshop. It does come with one downside, however, and that is it requires a permanent edit in the form of the **Match Color** feature. **Match Color** won't work with smart objects, and this is one of the reasons why the original selection was saved. If you need to match a different color, you can go to **Select** → **Load Selection** and choose the saved selection from the **Channel** drop-down menu.

In this final section, we used adjustment layers, smart objects, and precise selections to accurately alter image colors, remove color casts, and enhance image tonality.

Summary

In this chapter, we edited the canvas by straightening crooked images, trimming away unwanted content, and extending the size of an image with content-aware technology. This is a crucial step to reduce file size and progress with only the content you need.

Then, we explored several techniques to conceal blemishes or unwanted content in photos with tools such as **Spot Healing Brush** and **Clone Stamp**. Both are well equiped to conceal smaller details such as cables. We also looked at **Content-Aware Fill** when the regions we need to conceal are larger. The **Healing Brush** tool is adept at repairing skin blemishes that seamlessly blend in with their surrounding pixels. Most of these techniques utilize multiple layers, with new layers being created to separate edits from the original image for flexibility.

Finally, we used adjustment layers to perform nondestructive color and tonal edits such as brightening an image, boosting contrast, and altering hues. In the next chapter, we will become familiar with a wide range of masking techniques to reveal and conceal layers rather than delete them.

3

Masking and Cutouts

Photoshop is an incredibly versatile application. However, it can be unforgiving if you fail to protect pixel-based content. In this chapter, we'll explore masking techniques to reveal and conceal layer content, rather than deleting it. Masks can be applied to almost any layer type in Photoshop and are commonly used when applying adjustment layers to control the parts of an image the adjustment affects.

We'll start by removing a background from an image and then place the "masked" subject into a new background. This will allow you to experience how an accurate selection is used as the basis for a layer mask that is intended to conceal the background while revealing the subject.

Using this masking technique, we'll then apply it in the context of an adjustment layer to create a black-and-white isolation, with the subject in color and the background in grayscale. Then you'll have the opportunity to edit the layer mask with painting tools to fine-tune the accuracy of the mask.

Masks can also be used to blend the best parts of two or more images together, which is ideal when you have a group photo and one person is looking the wrong way or has their eyes closed. You'll create the complete masked version combining each source image.

After accomplishing these fundamental masking techniques, you'll then learn how to extract hair from a background with the help of a dedicated masking workspace, enhancing fine details and removing rogue background colors to create a high-quality cutout.

Technical requirements

The project files for this chapter can be found at: `https://github.com/PacktPublishing/Mastering-Adobe-Photoshop-2024/tree/main/Chapter03`

We'll then experiment with different applications of layer masks, including using text as a mask, layer effects that use luminance to conceal parts of an image, and masks composed of vector shapes. In this chapter, we'll cover the following topics:

- Applying and editing a basic layer mask
- Unlinking images and masks
- Masking hair
- Working with vector masks

Applying and editing a basic layer mask

Masks come in various forms, from standard layer masks to clipping masks, vector masks, and **Blend If** masks. They control the visibility of one or more layers in Photoshop and can be applied to almost any type of layer. The purpose of a mask is to avoid deleting image content; this allows for re-editing at any stage of the production process.

Once assigned, a layer mask denotes concealed regions in black and revealed portions of a layer in white; as such, they are commonly composed of pixels and can be edited with any number of painting tools. Layer masks can be deactivated or removed without harming image content if necessary.

Clipping masks are based on the presence of layer pixels that vary in transparency. For example, you can use an editable text layer as a clipping mask, position a photo above the layer stack, and "clip" the photo to the text layer. The photo would only be visible where there is text present in the underlying layer. This allows for text to be edited and the photo to be repositioned relatively easily.

Blend If is a type of mask that is applied from the effects dialog box. It analyzes the active source layer and determines which part of that layer to display, based on whether the underlying pixels in other layers in the stack are darker than those in the source layer. As a scenario, you could use a blend on an active layer containing a logo that is black with a layer below it in the layer stack that contains a photo of clouds. By altering a **Blend If** slider, you can make lighter portions of the cloud show through the logo to give the impression that the logo is in the sky.

As you can see, the variety of masks is vast and offers incredible flexibility to the editing process. Documents saved in PSD format can be imported into applications such as Adobe InDesign, which can detect the presence of a layer mask to apply features such as text wrap. You will find the ability to mask in almost any Adobe application, and the principles remain similar.

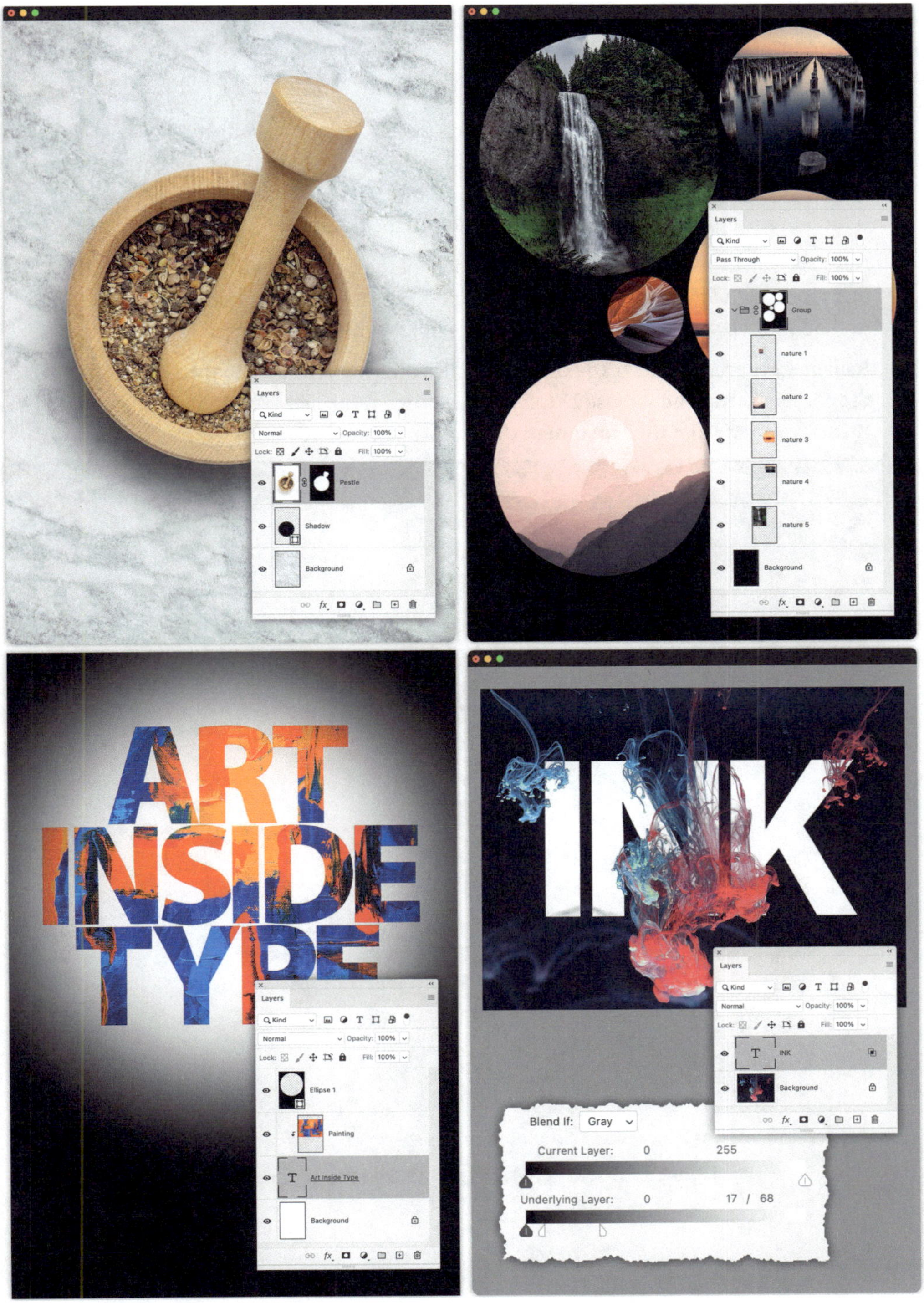

Figure 3.1: Examples of different mask types that can be used in Photoshop

Using masks to cut out image backgrounds

In this first exercise, you will create an accurate selection of a subject in a photo and then hide the region beyond the selection with a mask:

1. Go to **File** → **Open**, and select `Pestle.jpg` and `Marble.jpg` from the `Info` folder. Ensure the image of the pestle is active. Switch to the **Object Selection** tool. Click on the **Select Subject** button in the options bar to create a selection of the pestle.
2. Next, click on the **Add a Mask** icon at the bottom of the **Layers** panel to hide the white background that is not part of the current selection. The mask will now appear adjacent to the layer thumbnail in the **Layers** panel. Black regions conceal, while white regions reveal image content.
3. Rename the layer `Pestle` and then right-click on the layer name in the **Layers** panel to reveal the context menu and choose **Duplicate Layer** from the list. When the dialog appears, select `Marble.jpg` from the **Document** drop-down menu, and click **OK**.

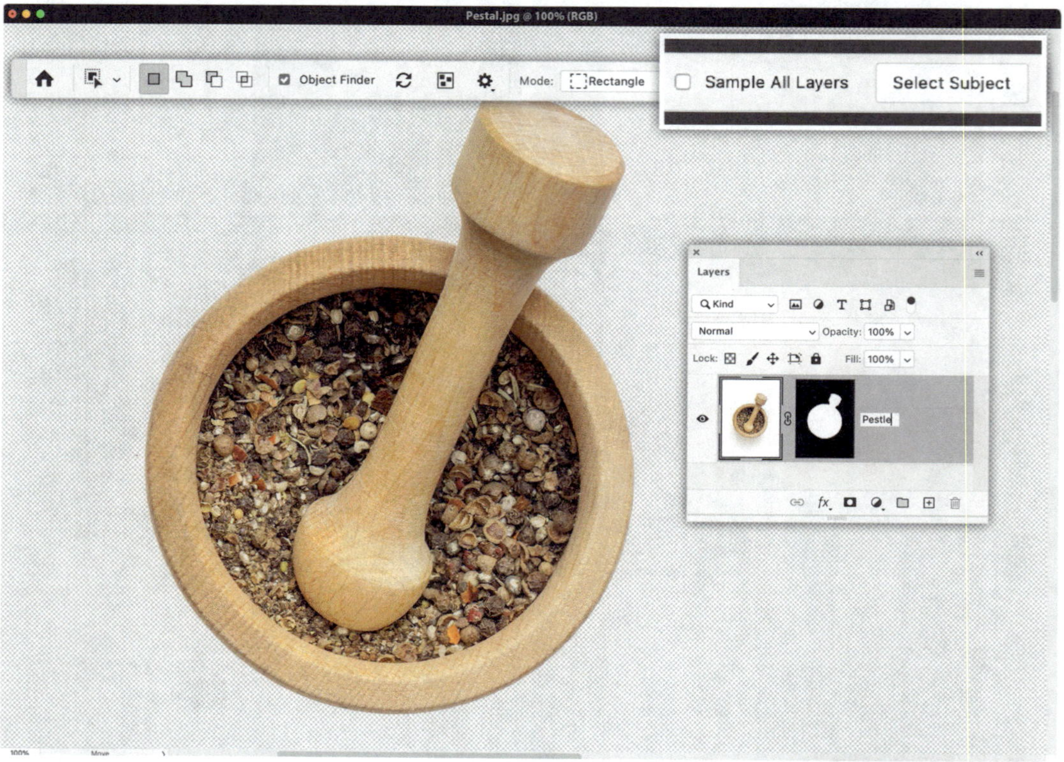

Figure 3.2: The original image with the layer mask added

4. Click on **Tab** for the `Marble.jpg` document and switch to the **Move** tool. Reposition the **Pestle** layer centrally.
5. Left-click on the background layer in the **Layers** panel to make it active. Next, select the **Ellipse** tool from the **Tools** panel by pressing the *U* key and then long-hold on the active tool icon to reveal the popout. Click on the **Ellipse** tool.
6. From the options bar, set **Mode** to **Shape**, click on the **Fill** icon, and set the color to black (`red 0, green 0, blue 0`). Click on the **Stroke** icon and choose **None** from the pop-out menu.
7. Hover your cursor over the top-left edge of the pestle bowl, click and hold down the left mouse button, and drag down to the left-hand side of the pestle bowl, matching its overall width and height before releasing the left mouse button. Change the new shape layer name to `Shadow`.

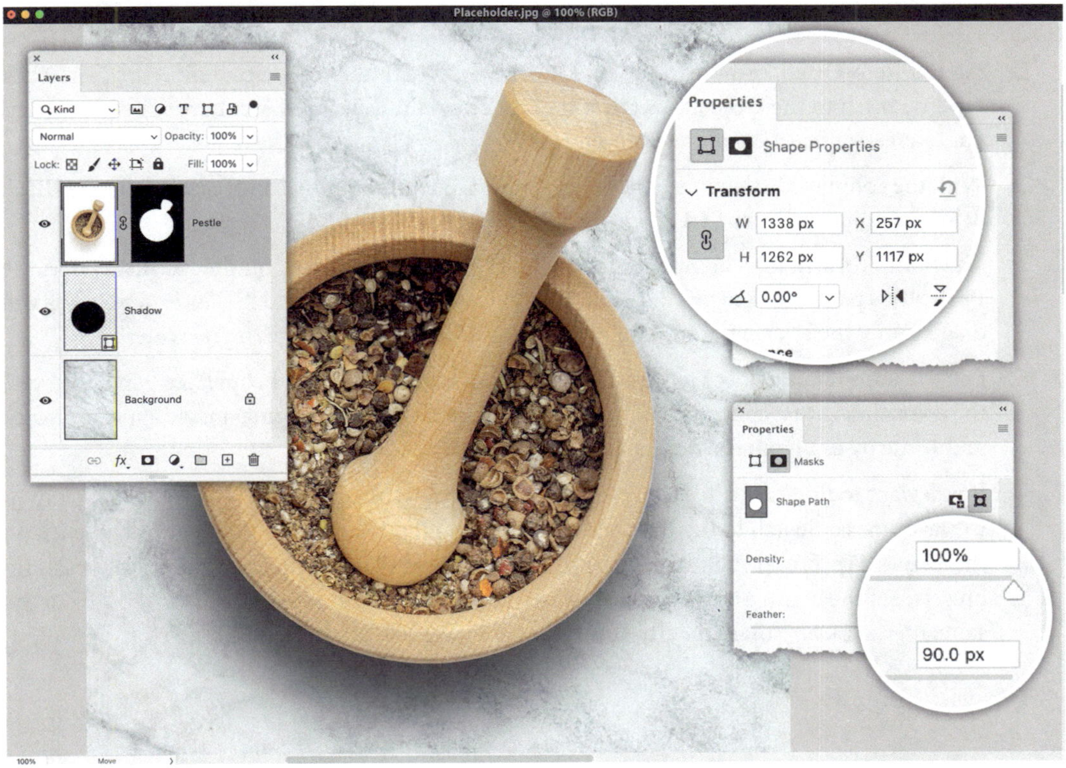

Figure 3.3: The completed image cutout shown on a new backdrop

8. Switch to the **Move** tool and reposition the black elliptical shape to the lower left-hand side of the bowl. Go to the **Properties** panel and click on the **Mask Properties** icon to reveal the settings. Increase the **Feather** amount to `90 px`.
9. Finally, change the **Shadow** layer blend mode to **Multiply** from the **Blend Mode** menu in the **Layers** panel. Reduce the layer's **Opacity** value to around `70%`. Go to **File → Save**, and name the file `Food-A` as a PSD file in the working folder. Close both documents when done; there is no need to save the `Pestle.jpg` image.

Applying masks to adjustment layers

In this masking exercise, you will use a selection of the pumpkin as the basis for a black-and-white effect that is controlled by a layer mask:

1. Go to **File → Open**, browse to the `03-Masking` folder, select `Pumpkins.jpg`, and click **Open**. Switch to the **Object Selection** tool. Click on the **Select Subject** button in the options bar to create a selection of the pumpkin.
2. With the completed selection in place, go to the **Adjustments** panel and left-click on the **Black & White** adjustment icon (**A** in *Figure 3.4*) to add a new adjustment layer.
3. The pumpkin will now appear in grayscale. However, if you click on the **Masks** icon in the **Properties** panel (**B** in *Figure 3.4*), and then click on the **Invert** button (**C** in *Figure 3.4*), it will display only the selected pumpkin in color and the rest of the image in grayscale.
4. Left-click on the **Black & White** adjustment icon at the top of the **Properties** panel to reveal the color sliders that control how dark or light those parts of the original image appear in black and white by dragging the sliders.
5. If you want to fine-tune the layer mask to add or remove the grayscale effect, you can paint in the layer mask. Switch to the **Brush** tool by pressing the *B* key. From the options bar, click on the **Brush Tip Preset** menu and choose the **Soft Round** brush tip from the list of brush tip presets. Set the brush **Size** value to between `15px` and `30px`. Set **Hardness** to `90%` from the same menu. Ensure that **Opacity** and **Flow** (in *Figure 3.4*) are both set to `100%`.

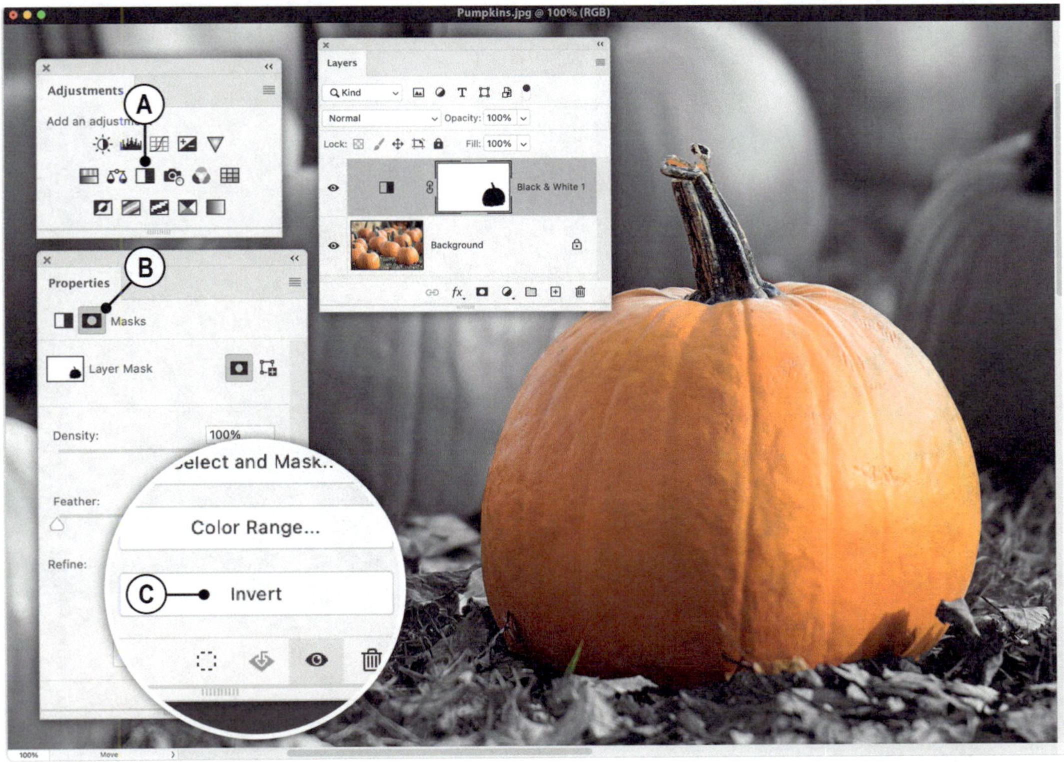

Figure 3.4: The assigned layer mask controls where the grayscale effect appears

6. Then, press the *D* key to reset the default colors and set black as the active color. Paint with white to reveal the grayscale effect or black to conceal the effect. You can press the *X* key to switch the foreground color. Regions that will most likely require attention will be around the stem of the pumpkin.
7. Once complete, you can go to **File** → **Save**, browse to the `03-Masking` folder, and name the document `Pumpkins.psd`. Close the document.

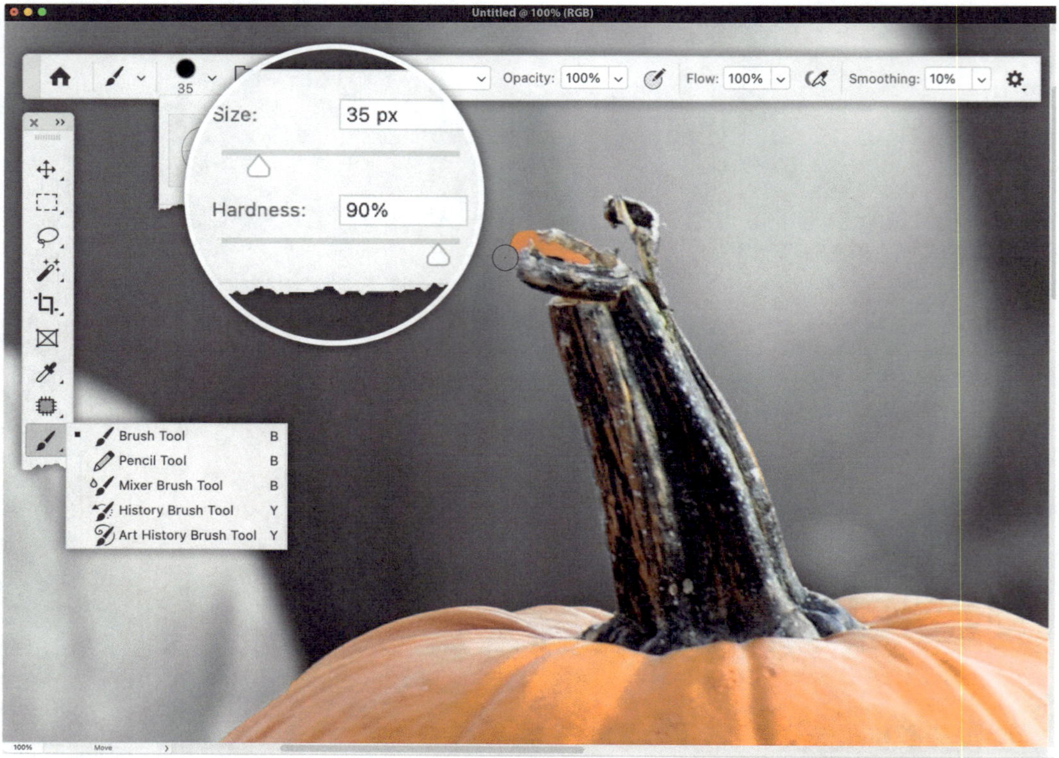

Figure 3.5: Use the Brush tool to edit the mask

Blending multiple images with a layer mask

Imagine the scenario: you take a photo, only to realize later that someone had their eyes closed or someone else is in the shot that you want to remove. By combining two images, you can pick the best of both with layer masks:

1. Go to **File** → **Scripts** → **Load Files into Stack....** When the dialog appears, click on **Browse** and go to the `03-Masking` folder. Select `Portrit-A.jpg` and `Portrit-B.jpg`. Turn on the **Attempt to Automatically Align Source Images** checkbox and then click **OK** when done. The **Layers** panel will now be populated with the two original photos.
2. Left-click on the `Portrit-B.jpg` layer's **Visibility** icon in the **Layers** panel to hide it. The transparent edges need trimming away.

3. Left-click on the **Crop** tool, then drag the bottom-left corner of the crop frame toward the center of the canvas until all the transparency is outside the crop frame.

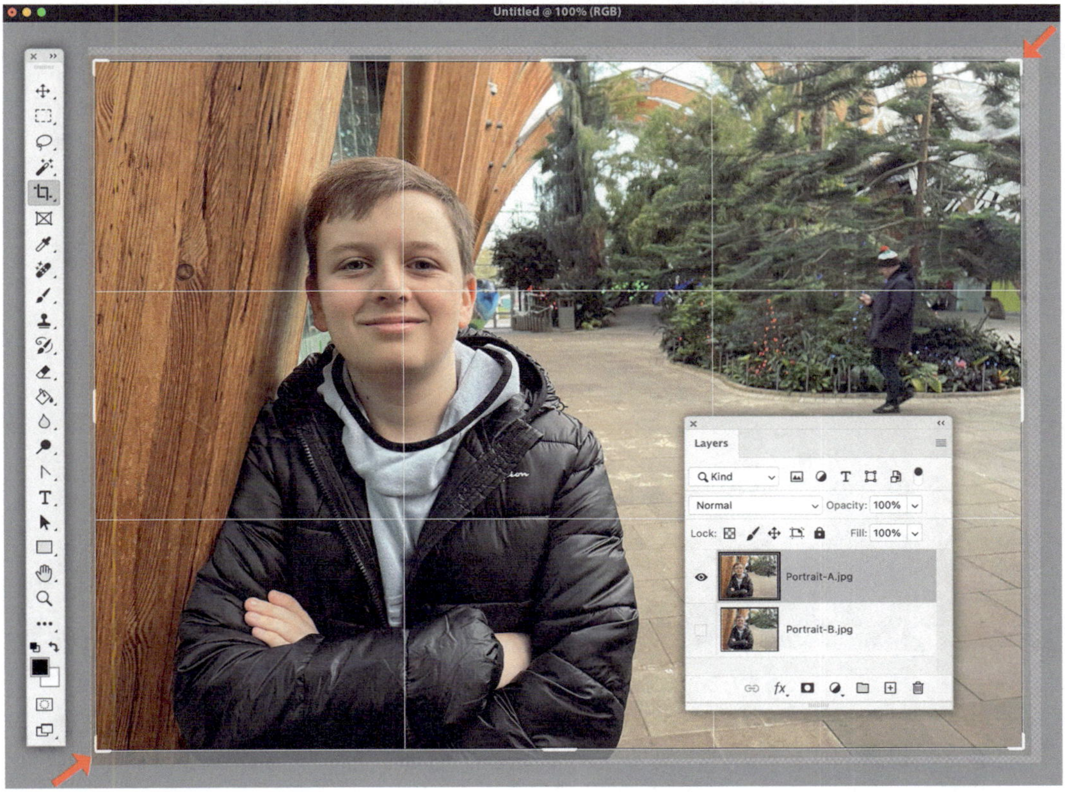

Figure 3.6: Both images aligned in a single document

4. Repeat the same step for the top-right corner of the crop frame. All transparent pixels should be outside of the crop frame. Click on the **Commit** icon in the options bar to apply the edits.
5. Turn on the visibility of the `Portrit-B.jpg` layer and left-click on the `Portrit-A.jpg` layer to make sure it is active. Click on the **Add Layer Mask** icon at the bottom of the **Layers** panel. When you add a layer mask with no selection active, a white layer mask is added, revealing all content in that layer, which permits you to conceal parts of the layer.
6. Press the *B* key to switch to the **Brush** tool. From the options bar, click on the brush tip preset menu. Set the brush **Size** value to `300 px`, **Hardness** to `0%`, and **Opacity** to `100%` (**A** in *Figure 3.7*).
7. Then, press the *D* key to reset the default colors and set black as the active color, and then press the *X* key to set black as the foreground color. Painting black in the layer mask will conceal parts of the image in that layer and, in turn, reveal parts of the layer below in the layer stack.

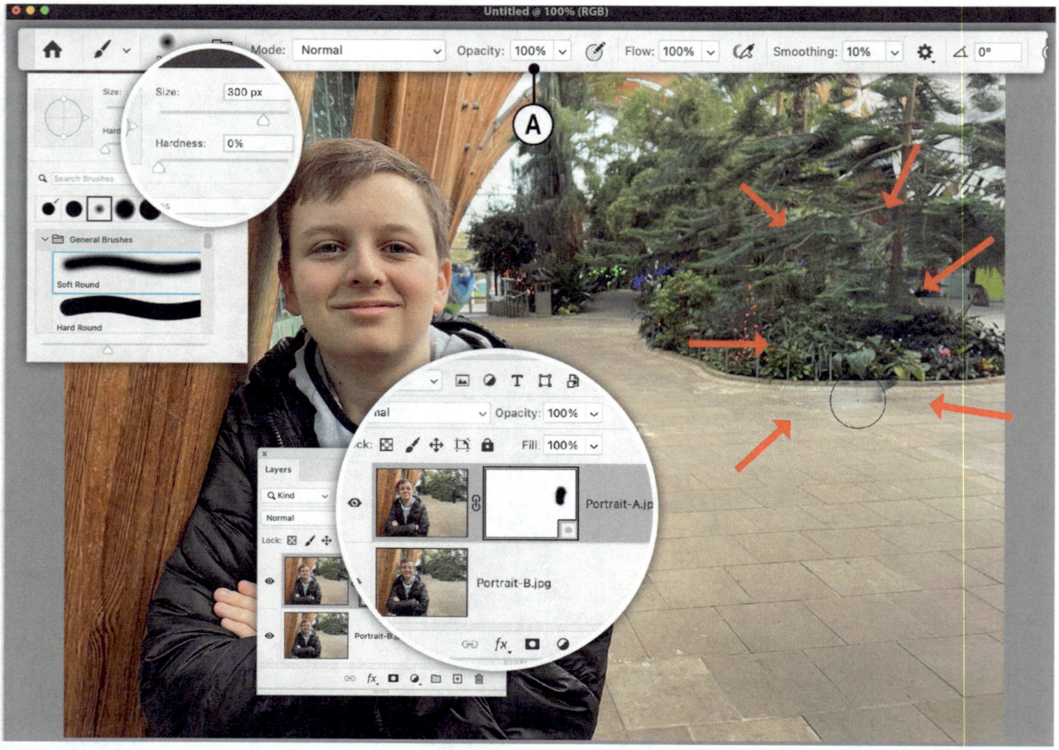

Figure 3.7: Both photos merged with the help of layer masks

8. Hover the **Brush** tool cursor over the person on the far right-hand side of the image. Left-click and drag over that region to conceal the person. This will reveal the **Background** layer below it, which contains no people in that part of the image, making the person in the background disappear.
9. Go to **File** → **Save** and browse to the `03-Masking` folder. Name the file `Merge-Portrait`, click **Save** when done, and close the document.

Masking with Blend If

Blend If settings are one of those mysterious, hidden features that can offer incredible value. When used correctly, they can perform highly detailed masking without the need for a single selection or layer mask:

1. Go to **File** → **Open** and navigate to the `03-Masking` folder. Select `InkDive.psd` and click **Open** when done.
2. Hover your cursor over the text layer named **INK** and double-left-click on the empty space to the right of the layer name (**A** in *Figure. 3.8*) to open the **Layer Style** blending options. **Blend If** settings can be found at the bottom.

3. The two grayscale strips allow you to hide part of the active layer based on the luminance of the current layer compared to **Underlying Layer** or **This Layer**. Reduce the **Underlying Layer** slider to `17` (**B** in *Figure. 3.8*). This means that any pixels in the background photo that are lighter than a luminance level of `17` will make the text disappear.

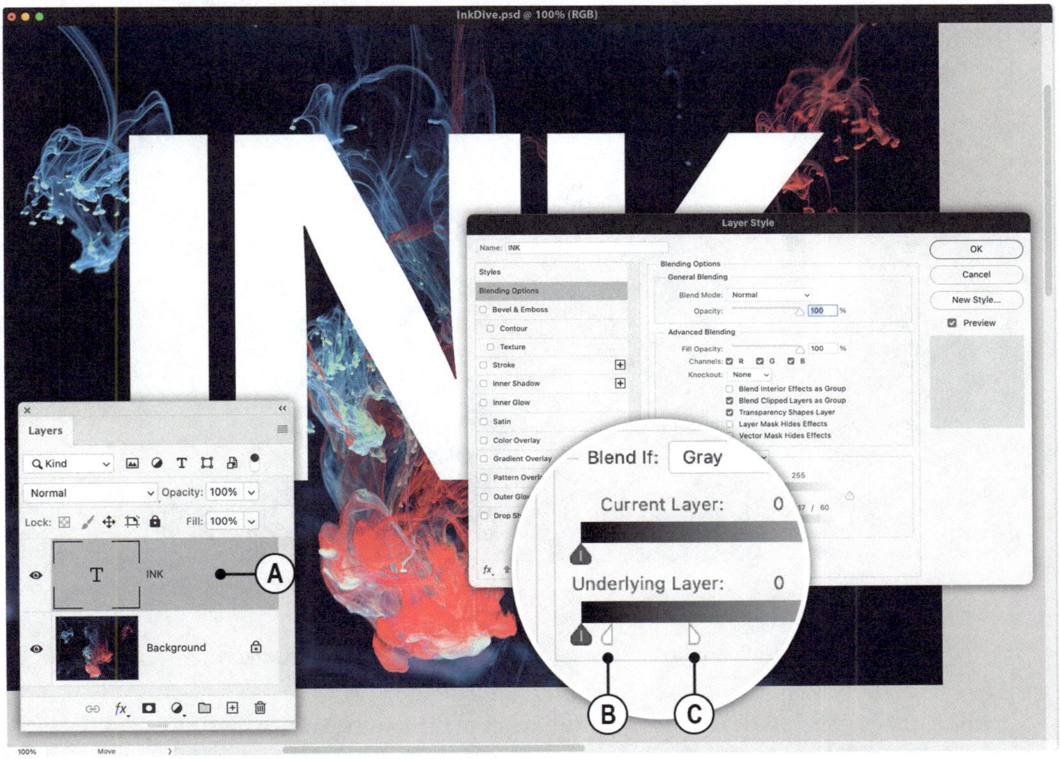

Figure 3.8: Blend If layer style settings can create intricate masks based on luminance

4. To eliminate the hard transition around the ink, hold your cursor over the white point slider, and hold down *Alt* (Windows) or *Option* (macOS) as you drag the right half of the slider, splitting the slider to create a fall-off. Stop when you reach a value of `68` (**C** in *Figure. 3.8*). This will create a softer transition between pixels that are visible and those that have been hidden by the **Blend If** settings. Click **OK** when done to apply the edits.

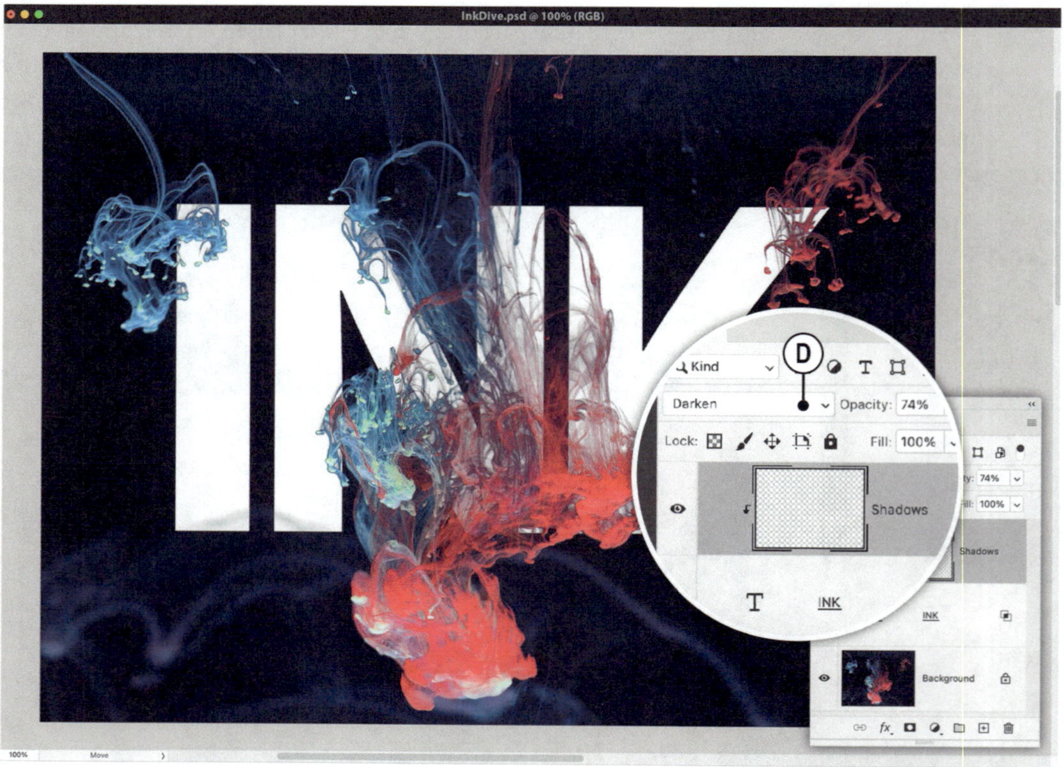

Figure 3.9: Add a new layer and change Blend Mode to Darken

5. Click on the **Create new layer** icon at the bottom of the **Layers** panel, name the layer `Shadows`, and change **Blend Mode** to **Darken** (**D** in *Figure 3.9*). Right-click on the `Shadows` layer name in the **Layers** panel and again choose **Create Clipping Mask** to make it affect only the text layer.
6. Switch to the **Brush** tool by pressing the *B* key. Choose a **Soft Round** brush tip from the **Brush Tip** preset menu. Set **Size** to `500 px`. Then lower **Opacity** to `10%` and set black as the foreground color.
7. Apply brush strokes over the regions where the ink appears in front of the text to make it appear as though it is casting a faint shadow across the text. Once you have added soft shadows across the text as required, go to **File** → **Save** and close the document.

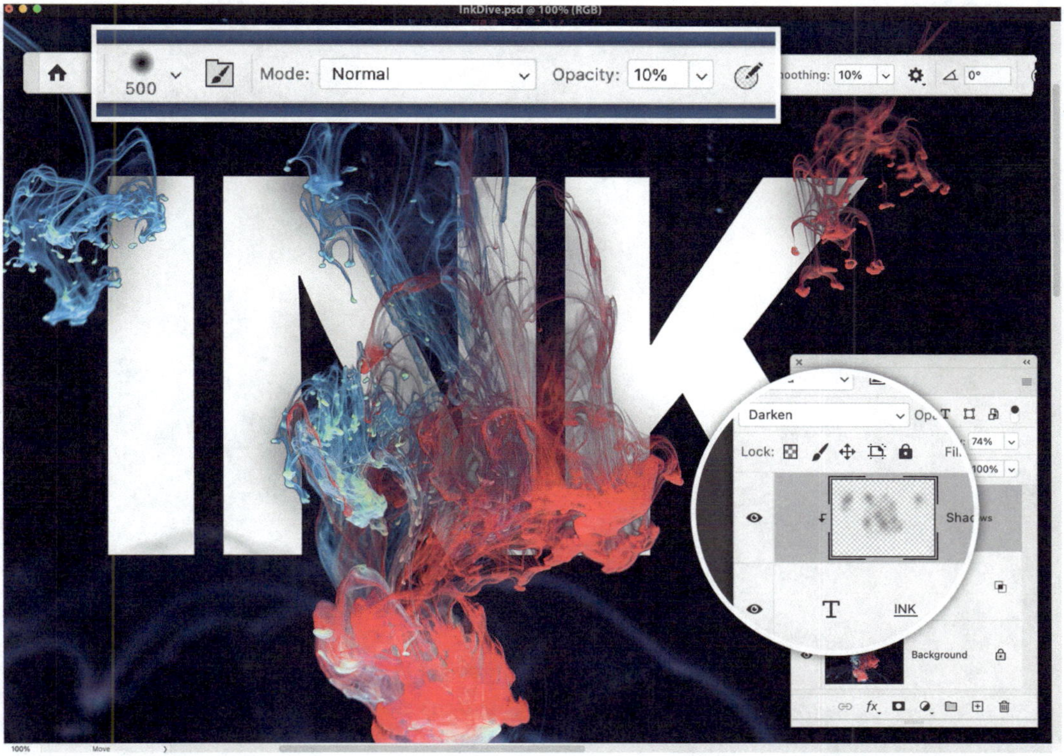

Figure 3.10: Add shadow effects by painting black with the Brush tool

Creating distressed photo edges

The **Select & Mask** workspace settings can be manipulated to create an interesting frame around your images:

1. Go to **File** → **Open**. Browse to the `03-Masking` folder and select the document named `Edges.jpg`. Ensure that you can see all the photos within the image window.
2. Create a selection of the entire canvas by going to **Select** → **All**. Then you will need to shrink the selection area by going to **Select** → **Modify** → **Contract**. When the dialog appears, enter `200` into the **Contract By** field. Turn on the **Apply effect at canvas bounds** checkbox and click **OK**.

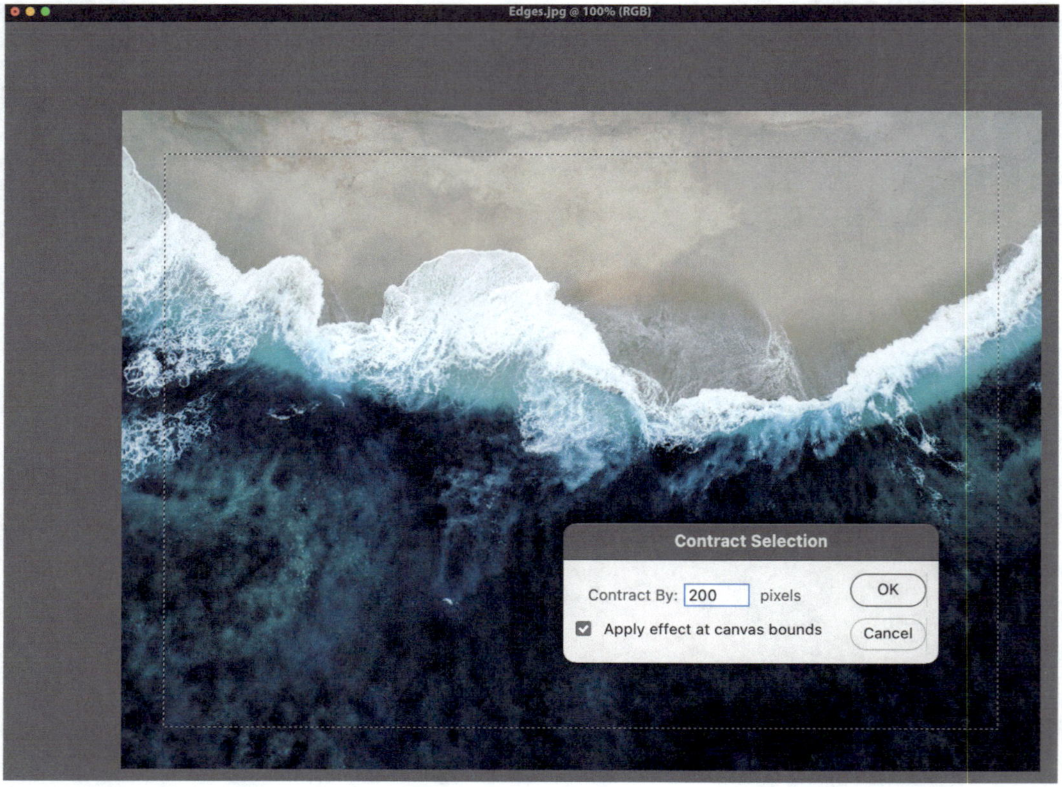

Figure 3.11: Select the image and contract the selection to set the border frame size

3. Soften the selection by going to **Select** → **Modify** → **Feather**. Enter `20` into the **Feather Radius** field and click **OK**. This will not only soften the edges of the selection, allowing it to be distressed in the next step, but also round the corners of the selection.
4. Click on the **Select and Mask** button in the options bar, which will be visible whenever one of the selection tools is active. When the dialog appears, change the **View** drop-down thumbnail to **On Layers** to set the artwork against a transparent background.
5. Set the **Radius** slider to `71` pixels, under the **Edge Detection** settings. Then, from the sliders lower down in the workspace, change **Contrast** to `60%` and **Shift Edge** to `+70%`. Set the **Output To** drop-down menu to **New Layer with Layer Mask** and click **OK**. Rename the new layer `Frame edges`, and then left-click on the background layer in the **Layers** panel to make it active.

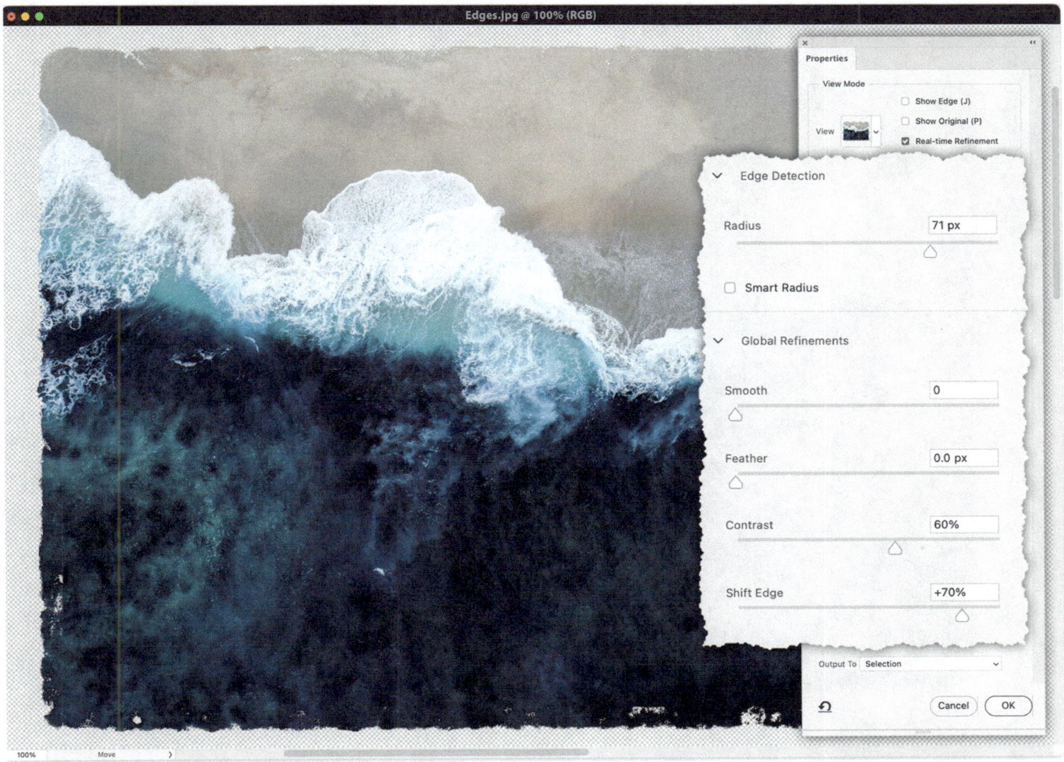

Figure 3.12: Using the content in the photo, you can use Refine Edge to create the roughened edge effect of the image edges

6. Click on the **Create new fill or adjustment layer** button at the bottom of the **Layers** panel to create a new layer containing a single color. Set **Color** to white and click **OK** when done to generate the layer. With the edits now complete, go to **File** → **Save As** and save the document in the `03-Masking` folder with the same name as a PSD. Then go to **File** → **Close**.

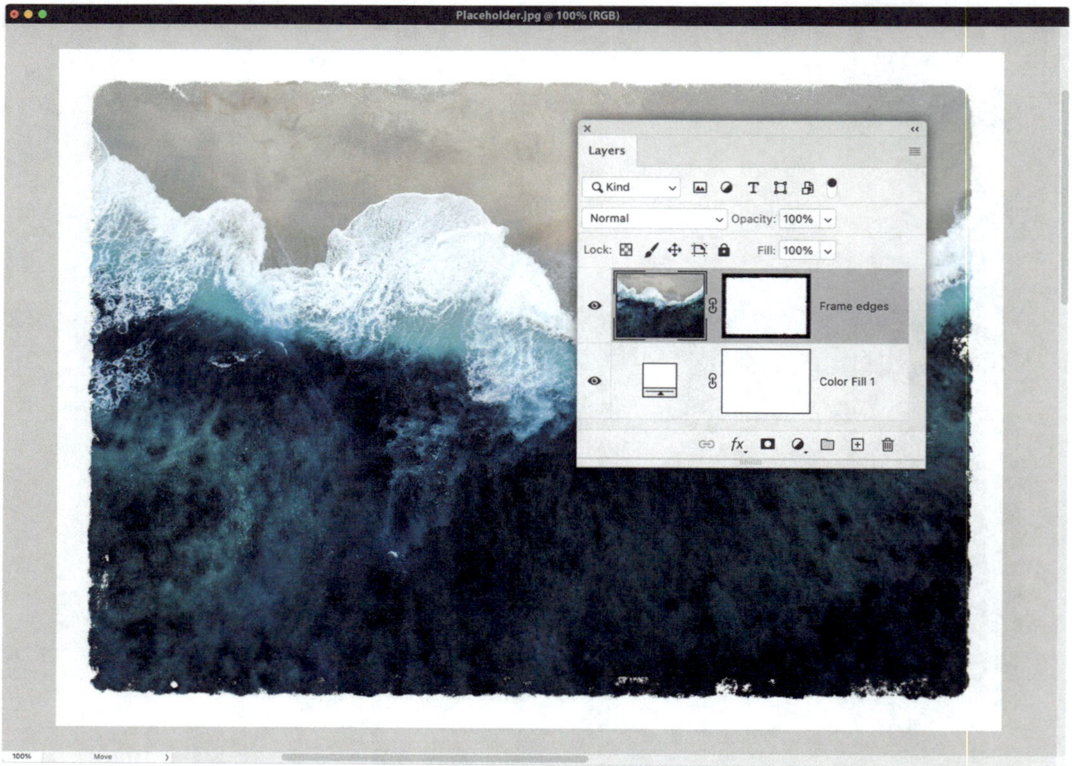

Figure 3.13: The finished photo frame effect

In this section, we have looked at a range of scenarios where two or more layers require blending together to achieve a desired outcome. Hiding unwanted parts of one layer to reveal another underlaying layer, or, in the case of the ink image, we used a form of masking that uses the luminance levels of one layer to hide portions of our text in a separate layer. Next, we will look at masking hair.

Masking hair

One of the more challenging aspects of masking is being confronted with fine details such as hair, which require Photoshop's powerful mask refinement tools:

1. Go to **File** → **Open** and navigate to the `03-Masking` folder. Select `Cutout.jpg` and click **Open** when done.

2. Switch to the **Object Selection** tool. Click on the **Select Subject** button in the options bar to create a selection of the woman. Then click on the **Select and Mask** button in the options bar (*Figure 3.14*, **A**).

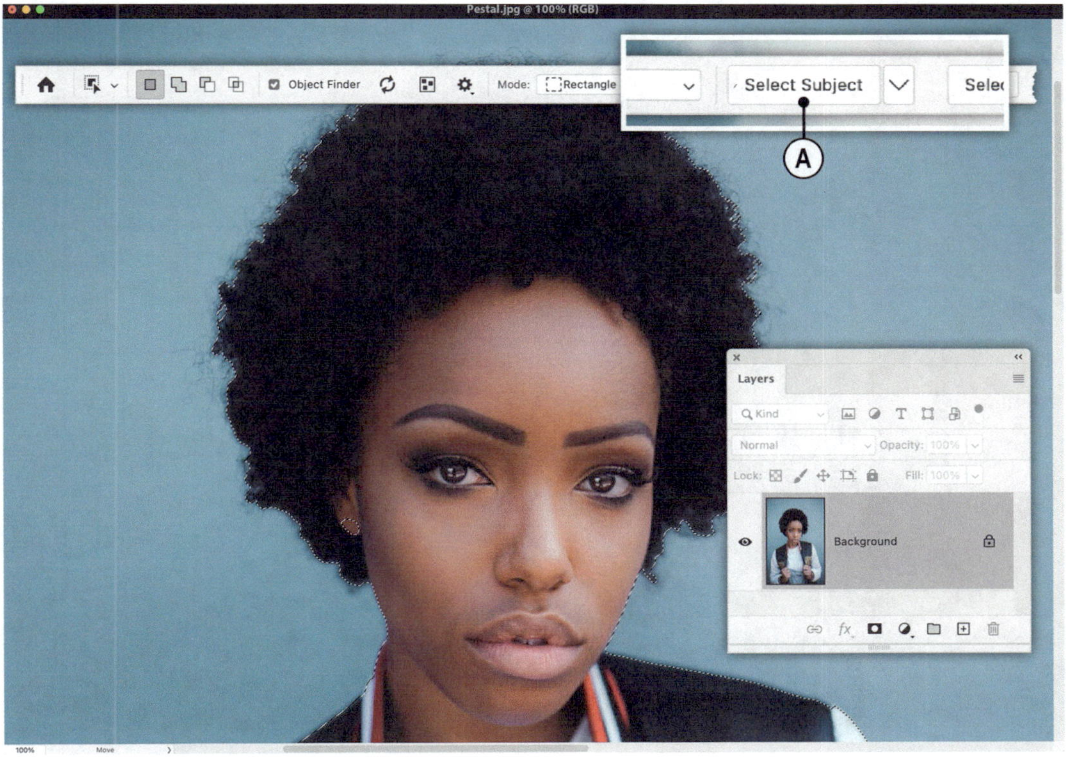

Figure 3.14: Use the Select Subject feature to make your base selection

3. When the dialog appears, change the **View** drop-down thumbnail (*Figure 3.15*, **A**) to **Overlay**. This will allow you to preview the region outside of your selection in a temporary color of your choosing.
4. You will need to change the overlay color to one that contrasts with the hair and the original background of the photo. Click on the color picker (**E**), choose a bright green color, and click **OK**. Set the **Opacity** slider to `100%`. Turn on the **Smart Radius** checkbox and set **Radius** to `2 px`, under the **Edge Detection** settings.

It is worth noting that the **Radius** value will need to be adjusted from image to image to achieve the desired result. Provided that you zoom in close to the edge of the selection in the **Refine Edge** dialog, you will be able to clearly see how increasing or decreasing the **Radius** value affects the selection edge.

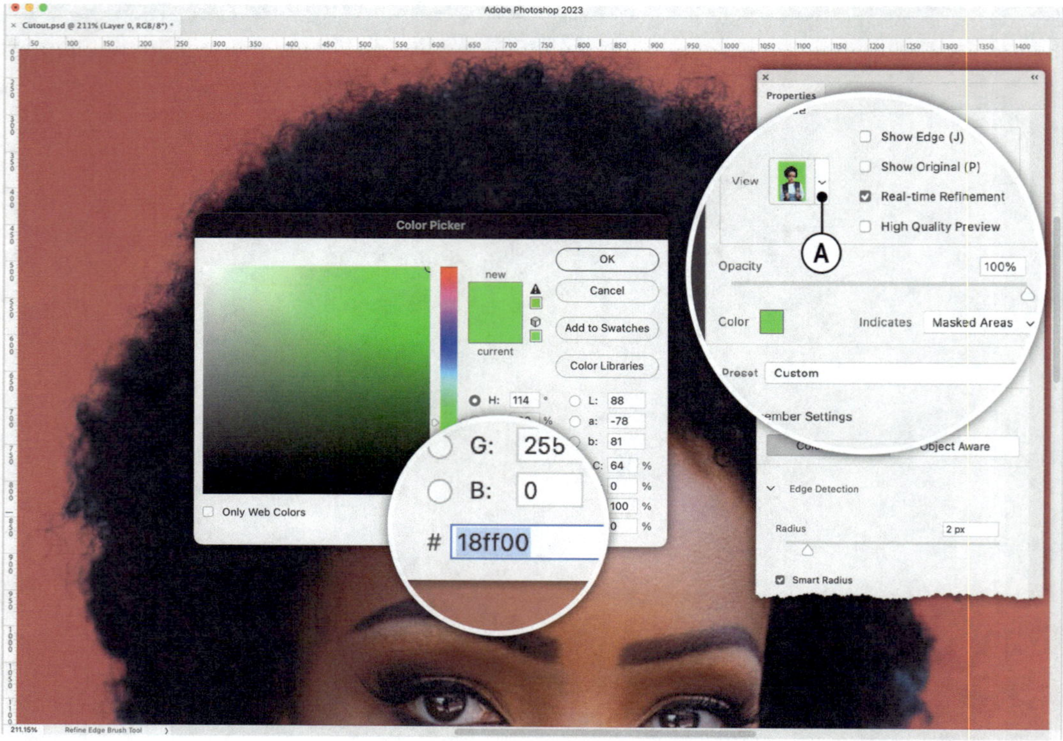

Figure 3.15: Choose an overlay color that contrasts from the background

1. Click on the **Refine Radius** brush, located in the **Select and Mask Tools** panel. Set the brush **Size** value to `90 px` from the left-hand side of the **Options Bar**.
2. Click and drag the brush from the recolored background toward the visible pixels of the hair until you overlap a very small portion of visible hair. On releasing the left mouse button, the brush will reveal colors similar to those of the hair but will hide the background colors.
3. Paint along the edges where the hair meets the background. You should avoid using the **Refine Radius** brush along hard edges such as the skin and clothing as this tends to make those regions transparent.

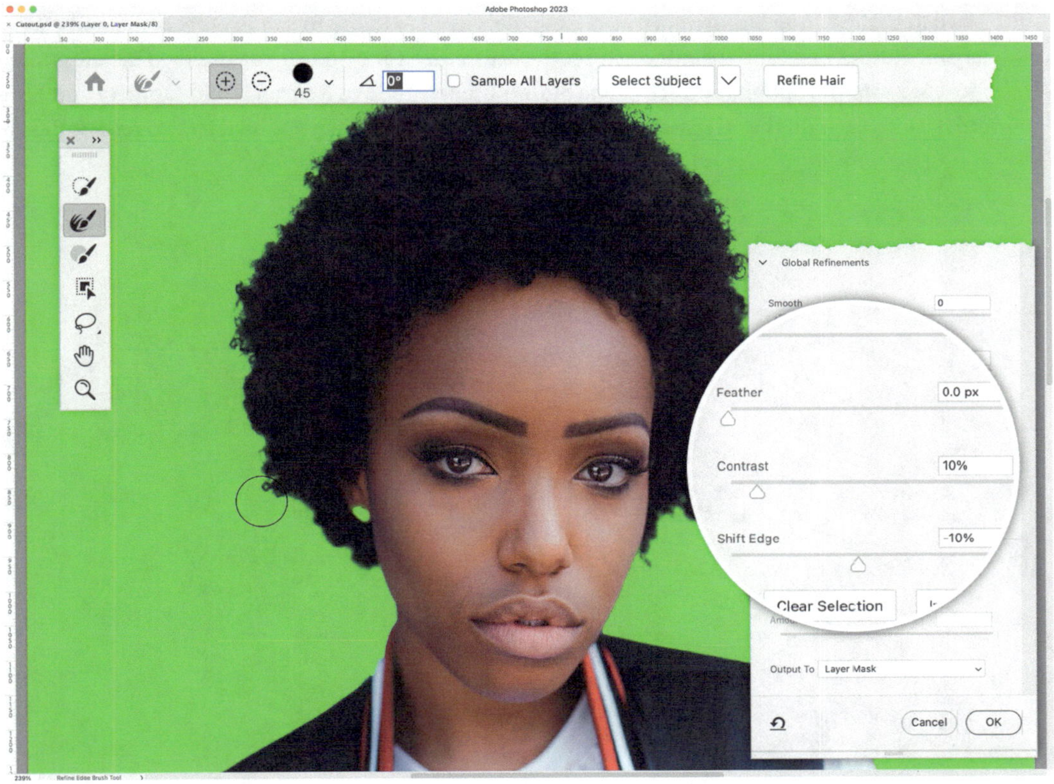

Figure 3.16: Edit the Global Refinement settings

4. As a final step, head over to the right-hand side of the workspace, where you will find **Global Refinements**; alter **Contrast** to `10%` and **Shift Edge** to `-10%` to shrink the overall selection edge and help hide any random colors from the background of the photo. Ensure the **Output To** menu is set to **Layer Mask**. Then click **OK** to apply the changes.
5. Ensure that the background layer is active in the **Layers** panel and click on the **Add a Mask** button at the bottom of the **Layers** panel to hide the original blue background. Rename the layer `Subject`.
6. Click on the **Create new fill or adjustment layer** button at the bottom of the **Layers** panel to create a new layer containing a single color. Enter a new color from the **Hexadecimal field** of `cac816` and click **OK**. Drag the new layer to the bottom of the **Layers** stack so that it appears behind the other layer in the image.
7. Ensure that the **Subject** layer is active in the **Layers** panel, then click on the **Create a new layer** icon at the bottom of the **Layers** panel. Name the new layer `Hair`. Change the `Hair` layer **Blend Mode** setting to **Darken** from the **Blend Mode** menu. Go to the **Layers** panel fly-out menu and choose **Create Clipping Mask** to make sure any edits only appear where there are pixels in the **Subject** layer below it.

8. Switch to the **Clone Stamp** tool by pressing the *S* key. Go to the **Brush Presets** menu and choose a **Soft Round** brush tip from the list. Set the brush **Size** value to `80 px` and the **Hardness** value to `0%`. From the options bar, set **Clone Stamp Blend Mode** to `Normal`, and **Opacity** and **Flow** to `100%`. Turn on the **Aligned** checkbox and set the **Sample** dropdown to **Current & Below**.

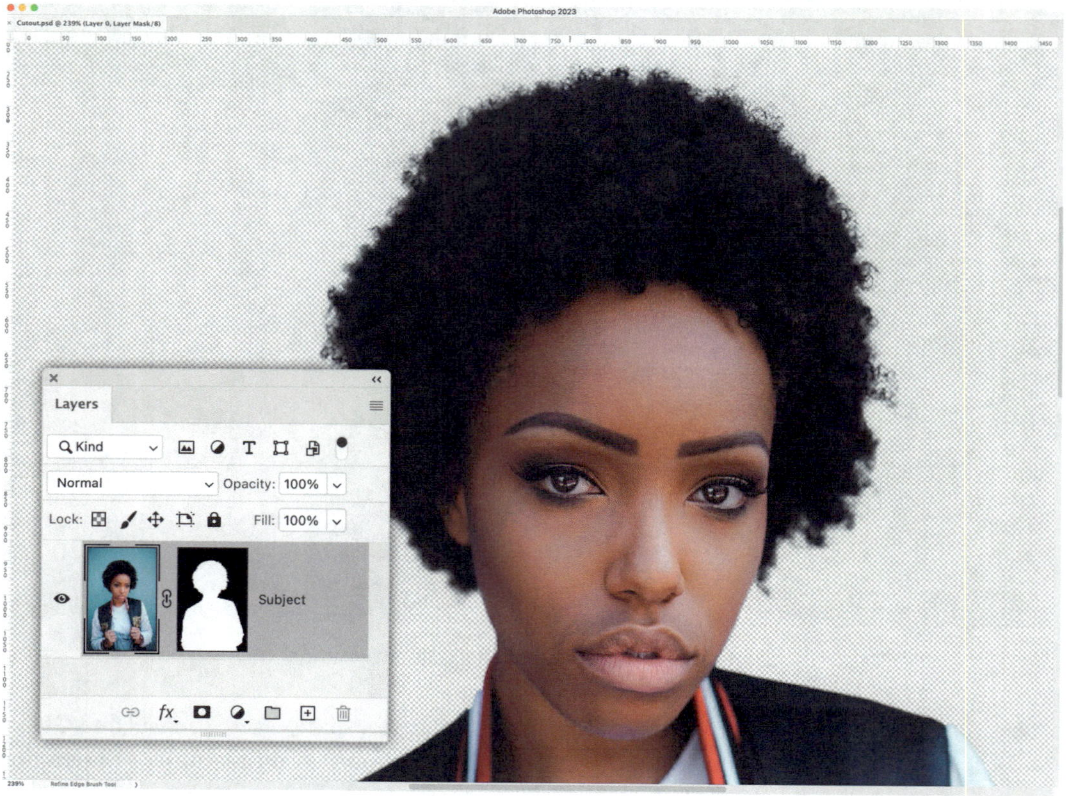

Figure 3.17: The masked image

9. Hide the **Color Fill** layer for the next steps. Ensure that the **Hair** layer is active in the **Layers** panel, then hover your cursor over a region of hair in the subject and hold *Alt* (Windows) or *Option* (macOS) as you left-click to sample a region of black hair in the center of the head. Stay away from the edges of the hair as you need solid hair texture.
10. With the sample now captured, hover the **Clone Stamp** tool cursor over a region of fine hair strands and drag across them to remove the blue fringe pixels. Work in small clusters and remember to resample new hair textures before cloning a new region of hair. Once complete, you can turn the **Color Fill** layer visibility back on.

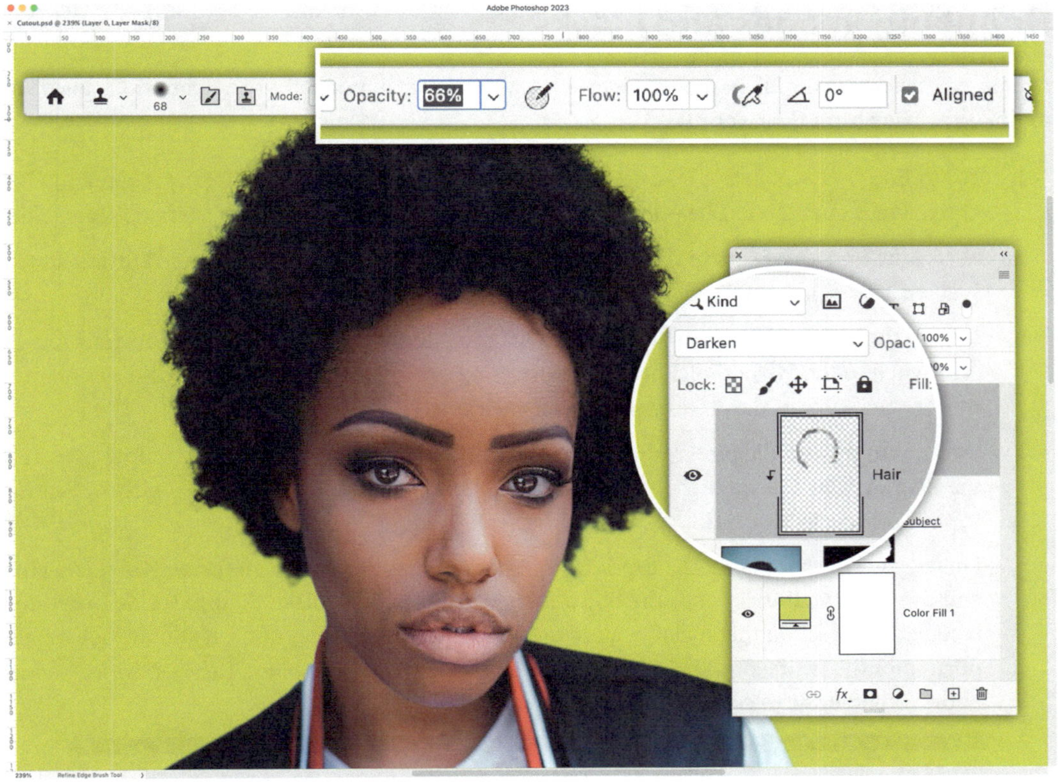

Figure 3.18: Fine details such as hair can be preserved in a layer mask

11. You can adjust any patches of the original layer mask by switching to the **Brush** tool. Click on the first brush tip preset, **Soft Round**, in the **Brush Tip** preset menu. Set **Size** to `80 px` and set **Hardness** to `0%`. Change the **Brush** tool's **Blend Mode** to **Overlay** in the options bar.
12. Left-click on the **Mask** thumbnail in the **Layers** panel. To expand regions of hair and make them more visible, set the **Foreground** color to white, and left-click and drag the **Brush** tool over the edges of the hair. The overlay blend mode will intensify the contrast of white pixels only and leave very dark gray and black pixels unaffected. You can set black as the foreground to achieve the opposite result.
13. Go to **File** → **Save** to save the image with the same name as in the `03-Masking` folder.

In this section, we have worked with the **Select and Mask** workspace and the **Refine Radius** brush to extract fine details such as hair from a background. Next, we'll focus on how separating an image from its corresponding layer mask can be advantageous.

Unlinking images and masks

In this exercise, you will fill an empty picture frame to create a mockup of an exhibition space and unlink the image from the layer mask:

1. Go to **File** → **Open**. Select `PictureFrame.jpg` from the `03-Masking` folder and click **Open**. Once open, go to **File** → **Place Embedded** and select `Ravine.jpg` from the same folder.
2. When the image appears in the canvas, go to the options bar and change the **Width** field to a scale of `17%`. Click on the tick in the options bar to apply the edits when done.
3. Reduce the `Ravine` layer by changing the **Opacity** value to `70%` in the **Layers** panel (*Figure 3.19*, **A**). Switch to the **Move** tool, hover your cursor over the **Ravine** image in the canvas, and drag it over the center of the largest, empty picture frame.
4. Zoom into the middle picture frame so that it occupies most of the image window. Switch to the **Rectangular Marquee** tool by pressing the *M* key. Set the selection mode to **New**, **Feather** to `0`, and **Style** to **Normal**.
5. Hover your cursor inside the top-left edge of the plain black picture frame. Then left-click and drag diagonally down to the bottom-right corner of the black picture frame to create a rectangular selection that includes all of the white space inside the frame. If you include a small portion of the inside of the black picture frame, this is not a problem. Release the left mouse button when done to complete the selection.

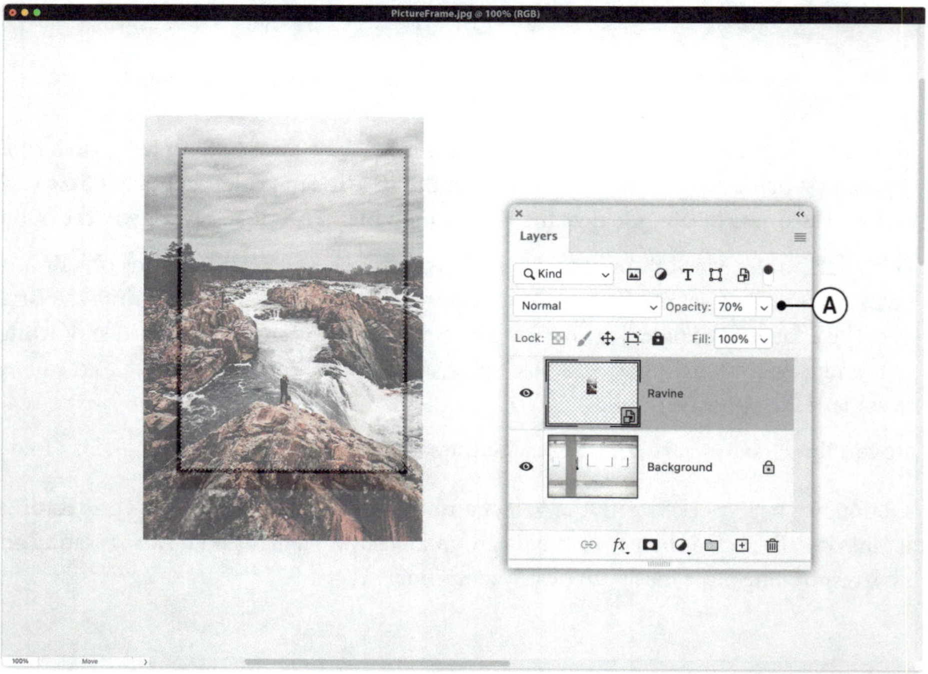

Figure 3.19: Position the photo over the frame

6. Left-click on the `Ravine` layer in the **Layers** panel once to make sure that it is active. Then click on the **Add a Mask** button at the bottom of the **Layers** panel. The region outside of your selection will now be concealed, leaving only the part of the photo inside your selection area visible. This will be shown in a new thumbnail in the **Layers** panel. A visual representation of your selection, where black conceals and white reveals.
7. Left-click on the link between the image and the layer mask thumbnail (*Figure 3.20*, **B**). Then left-click on the image thumbnail to make it active. You can now reposition or scale the ravine photo by dragging it around the image window while keeping the layer mask static. To complete the effect, change the **Blend Mode** setting of the `Ravine` layer to **Multiply** (*Figure 3.20*, **C**). This will make the shadow behind the photo visible and help make the effect more convincing.
8. Once you have positioned the photo in the picture frame to your liking, link the image and the layer mask once more by left-clicking in the empty space between both thumbnails in the **Layers** panel.

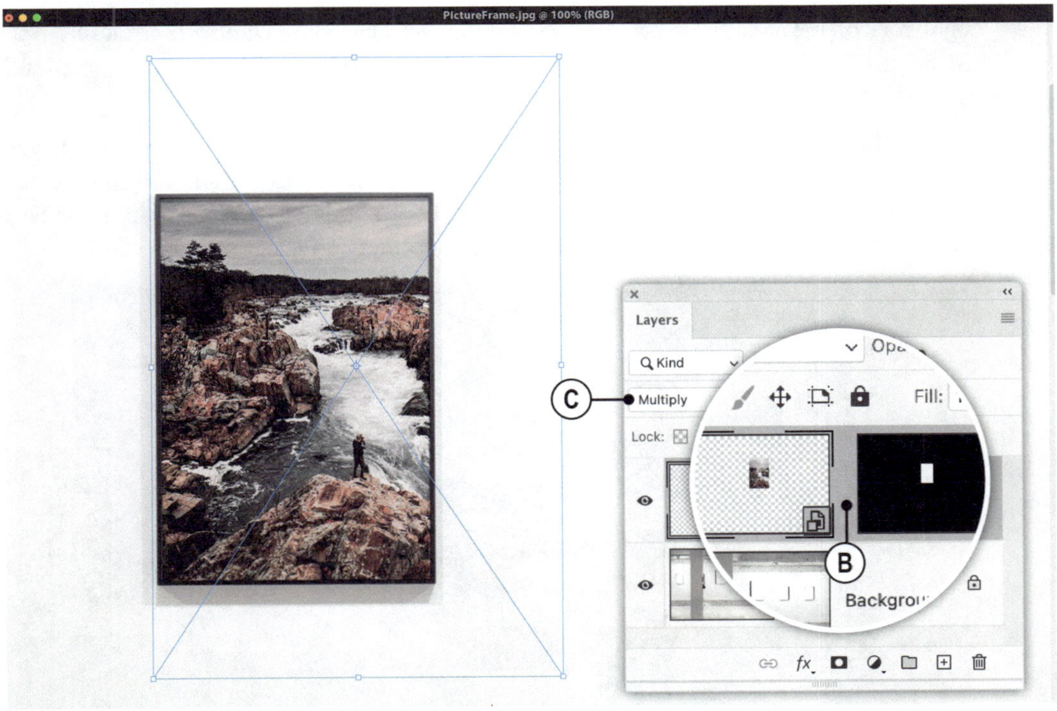

Figure 3.20: Unlinking the layer mask from the image

9. Go to **File** → **Save As**, browse to the `03-Masking` folder, name the file `PictureFrame.psd`, and close the document when done.

Masking layer groups

Copying and arranging images into a grid can be time-consuming but there are some sneaky scripts, cropping features, and group masking techniques that you can use to save time:

1. Go to **File** → **Open**, select `Poster_A4_01.psd` from the `03-Masking` folder, and click **Open** when done.
2. Go to **File** → **Scripts** → **Load Files into Stack...** and click on **Browse** when the dialog appears. Navigate to the `03-Masking` folder, select the 14 images from `Trek_01.jpg` to `Trek_14.jpg`, and click **Open** when done to add them. Ensure both checkboxes at the bottom of the dialog are deactivated, then click **OK**.
3. Photoshop will now copy all 14 images into a new document. Go to **Select** → **All Layers**. Then press *Ctrl* + *G* (Windows) or *Cmd* + *G* (macOS) to group all the active layers. Rename the layer group `Images`.
4. Right-click on the layer group name in the **Layers** panel and choose **Duplicate Group** from the list. Set the **Destination** dropdown to **Poster_A4_01.psd** and click **OK** when done. Left-click on the `Poster_A4_01.psd` document tab to make it active.
5. Expand the layer group by clicking on the **Toggle** adjacent to the layer group in the **Layers** panel. Switch to the **Move** tool. Left-click on the layer named **Trek_01** and drag it down the canvas so that it aligns centrally with the empty grid cell adjacent to the logo. Repeat the same technique to reposition all 14 images into each of the empty grid cells.

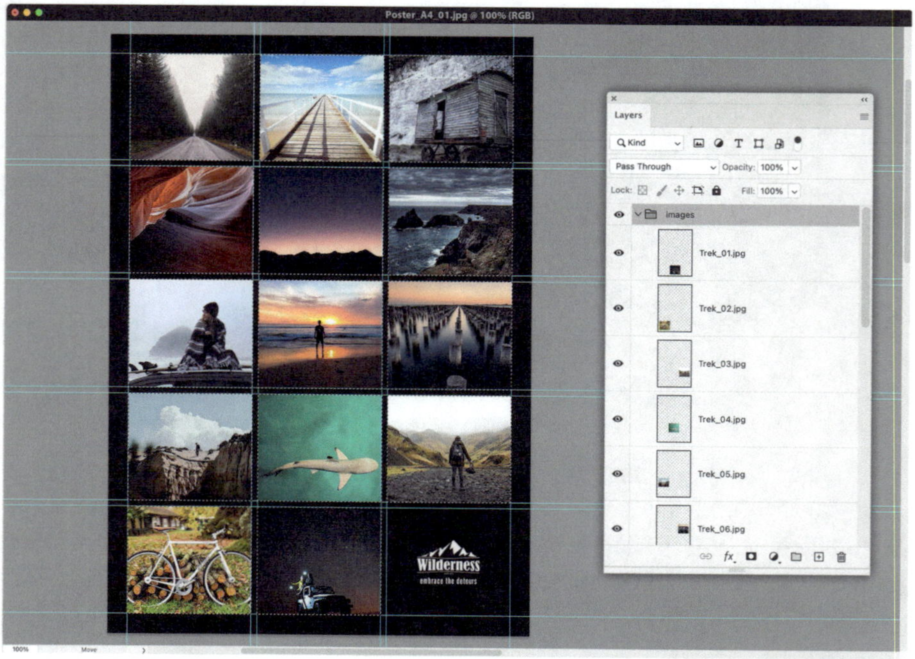

Figure 3.21: Merge multiple photos into a new document using scripts

6. Press the *M* key, then long hold on the active tool in the **Tools** panel to reveal the popout. Left-click on the **Rectangular Marquee** tool. Set **Selection Mode** to **Add to Selection** from the options bar. Ensure that **View** → **Snap to Guides** is active. Create a selection of each of the 14 grid squares that contain images.
7. Double-check that the `Photos` layer group is active in the **Layers** panel and then click on the **Add a Mask** button at the bottom of the **Layers** panel to hide the regions that appear in the margin and gutter of the grid. If necessary, reposition individual layers in the `Photos` layer group.
8. Go to **File** → **Save** and close the document when done. You can close the `Untitled` file without saving changes as it is no longer required.

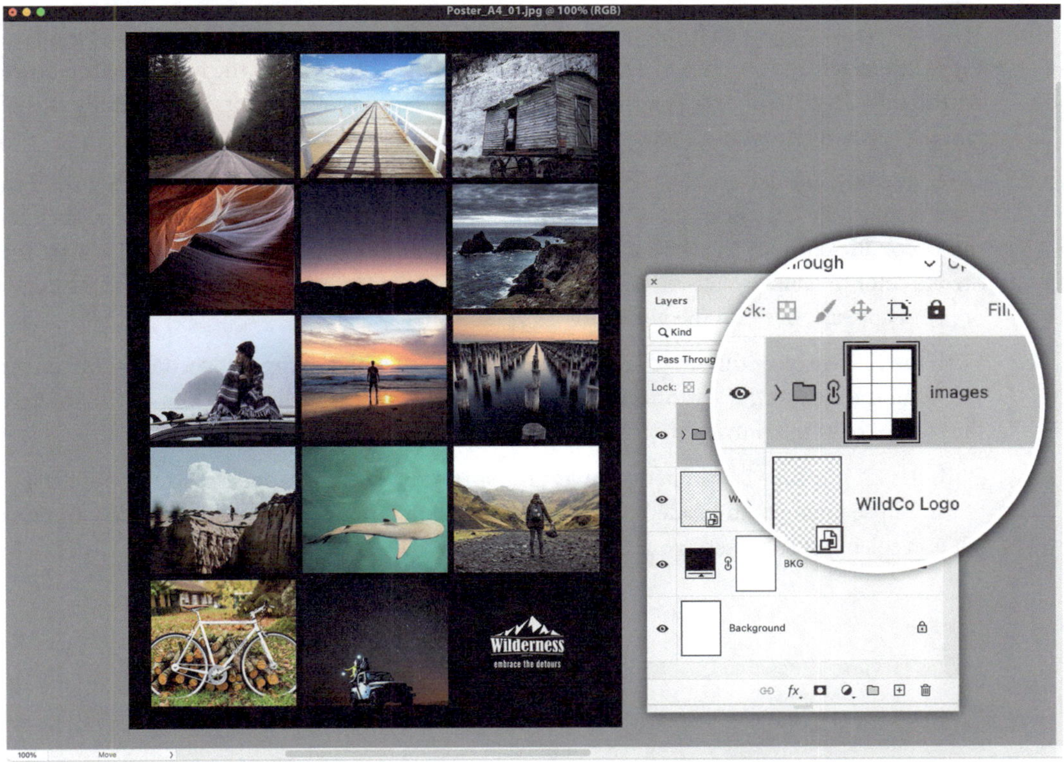

Figure 3.22: Masks can also be applied to layer groups that affect any layer stored within it

In this section, we have looked at techniques for unlinking layer masks to provide more flexibility. Firstly, a photo can be scaled and repositioned without affecting the mask. Secondly, we've seen a similar technique with the mask applied to a layer group. This allows each layer within the group to be repositioned and edited as required while keeping the mask unaffected. Next, we'll look at using vector content as the basis for a mask.

Working with vector masks

So far in this chapter, we've seen how pixel-based masks can be used to good effect, but they aren't the only kind of mask available to us in Photoshop. Vector masks can be used to create pin-sharp edges with shapes or even text.

Creating an editable vignette with a vector mask

Vignettes can be used to create an atmospheric darkened edge around an image or to add a focal point. In this exercise, you'll use a vector shape as the basis for this effect, combined with feathering of its mask properties:

1. With `Ravine.jpg` open from the `03-Masking` folder, switch to the **Ellipse** tool by pressing the *U* key to activate the correct group of tools, then left-click and hold the mouse button down on the active tool icon to reveal the sub-list of tools. Hover your cursor over the **Ellipse** tool and left-click on it to make it active.
2. Go to the options bar and ensure the **Mode** drop-down menu is set to **Shape**. Set the **Fill** color to black by left-clicking on the **Fill** icon. When the **Swatches** pop-out appears, click on the **Color Picker** icon. Set the **Red**, **Green**, and **Blue** fields to `0`, then press **OK**. Then set the **Stroke** color to **None** by left-clicking on the **Stroke** icon in the options bar. When the **Swatches** pop-out appears, click on the **No Color** button.
3. With the **Ellipse** tool still active, hover your cursor level with the top-left corner of the canvas and drag it down to the bottom right-hand corner to create an ellipse that is approximately the same size as the canvas.
4. With the `Ellipse 1` layer active, invert the shape so that black appears around the outside of the ellipse rather than inside by clicking on the **Path Operations** dropdown in the options bar and selecting **Subtract Front Shape**.

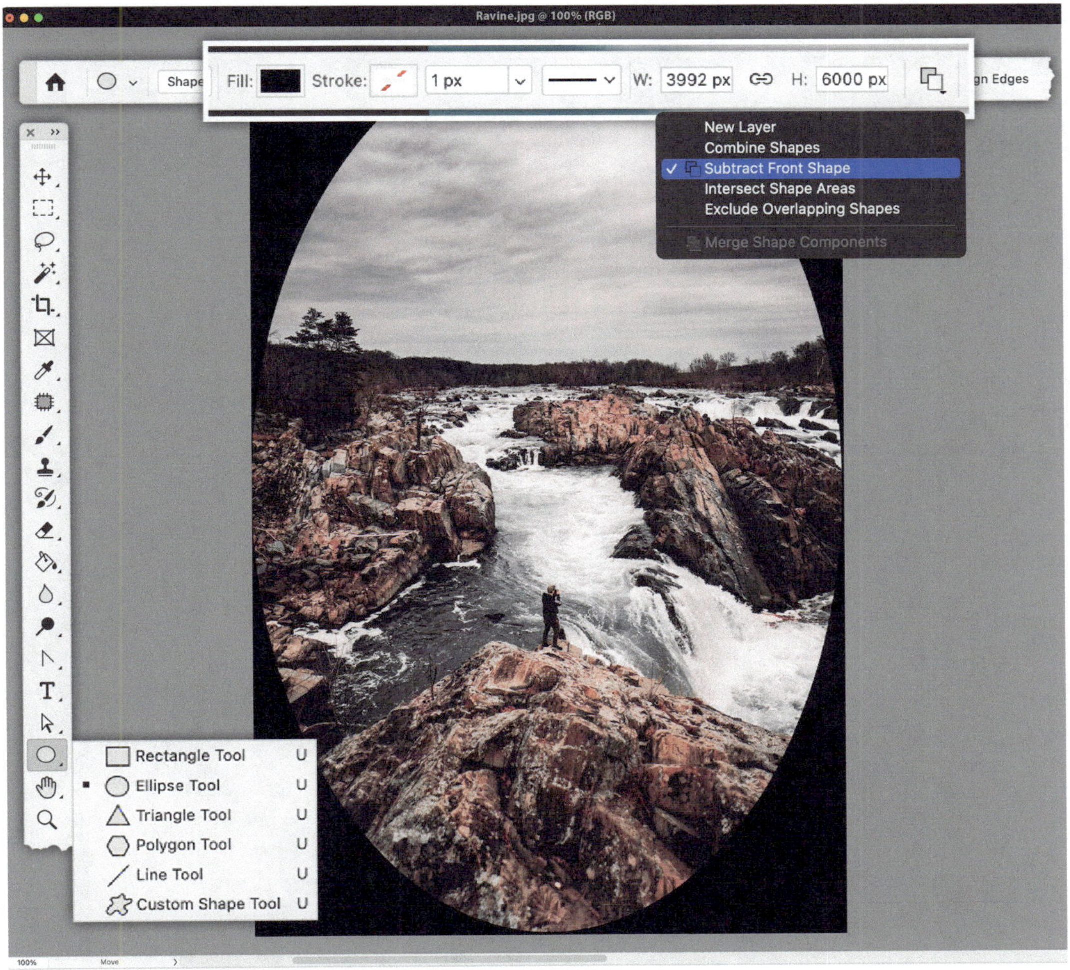

Figure 3.23: Create an elliptical shape with the Ellipse tool

5. Click on the **Mask** icon at the top of the **Properties** panel to reveal the masking options in the same panel. Change the **Feather** slider to `275` to soften the ellipse and create the vignette. Change the **Blend Mode** setting of the `Ellipse 1` layer to **Multiply** in the **Blend Mode** dropdown, then set **Opacity** to `60%`.

6. Go to **File** → **Save As**, saving the file as `Ravine.psd`. Then go to **File** → **Close** when done.

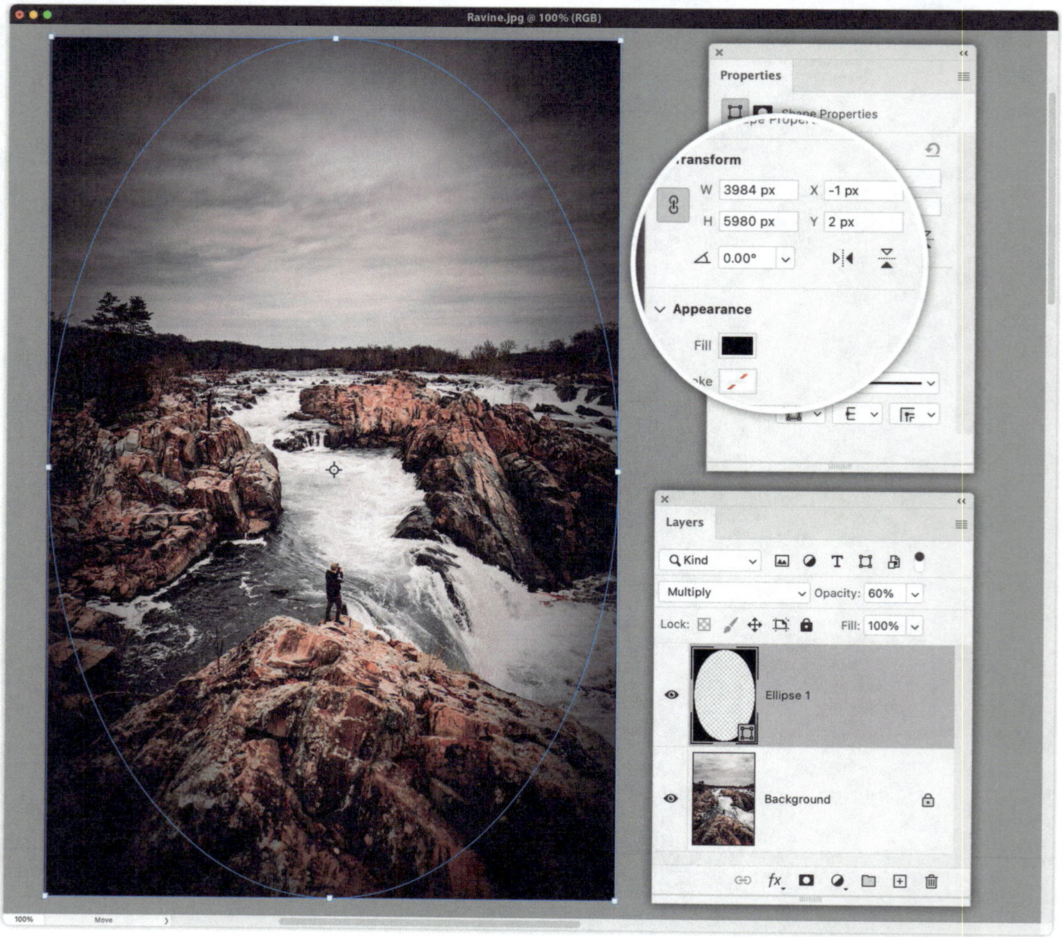

Figure 3.24: The vignette effect, created by using the feather value

Creating a typographic mask effect

Clipping masks offer a flexible method for masking underlying layers such as photos, and can be edited with ease, especially when composed of editable text:

1. Go to **File** → **Open**, and select the `ParagraphClipping.jpg` document from the `03-Masking` folder. To ensure that you can see the whole of the image and some of the region beyond the canvas, go to **View** → **Zoom Out**.

2. Go to the **Layers** panel and left-click once on the padlock located on the right-hand side of the **Background** layer (*Figure 3.25,* **A**). Double-left-click on **Layer Name** to edit the layer name and enter a new name of `Left`. Press *Return* or *Enter* when done to apply the name change.

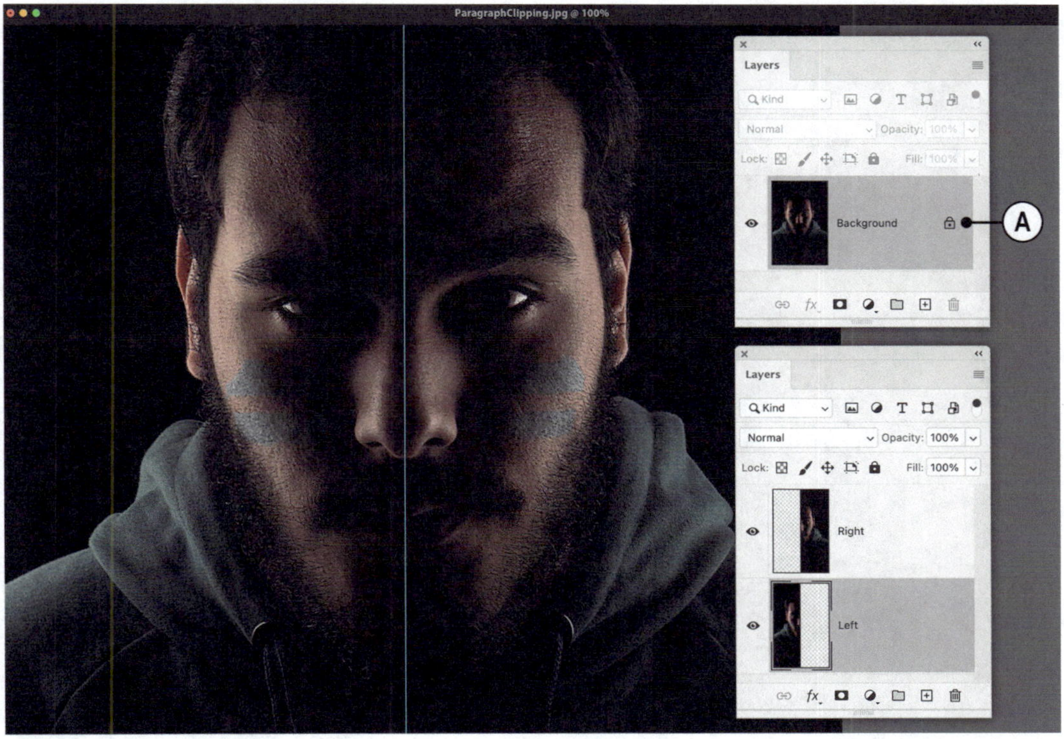

Figure 3.25: Split the face in half

3. Next, click on the **Create New Fill or Adjustment Layer** icon at the bottom of the **Layers** panel and select **Solid Color** from the top of the list. When the layer is generated, enter `5` into the **Red**, **Green,** and **Blue** fields to match the dark backdrop in the photo, then click **OK**. Then drag the newly added layer in the **Layers** panel under the photo of the subject.
4. If you do not see any guides visible in the document, go to **View** → **Show Guides**. You should now see a guide in the center of the canvas.
5. Switch to the **Rectangular Marquee** tool by pressing the *M* key to activate the correct group of tools, and then hold the left mouse button down on the active tool icon to reveal the list of hidden tools. Left-click on the **Rectangular Marquee** tool icon to make it active (*Figure 3.25,* **A**).
6. Hover your cursor outside the top-right corner of the canvas. Then, left-click and drag down to the bottom of the canvas, and along to the left until your cursor reaches the guide in the center of the canvas. Release the mouse to generate the selection.

7. Ensure that the layer named `Face Left` is active, and then go to **Layer → New → Layer via Cut** to cut and paste the selected content into a new layer. Double-left-click on the new layer name to edit it, type `Right`, and press *Enter* or *Return* to accept the name change.

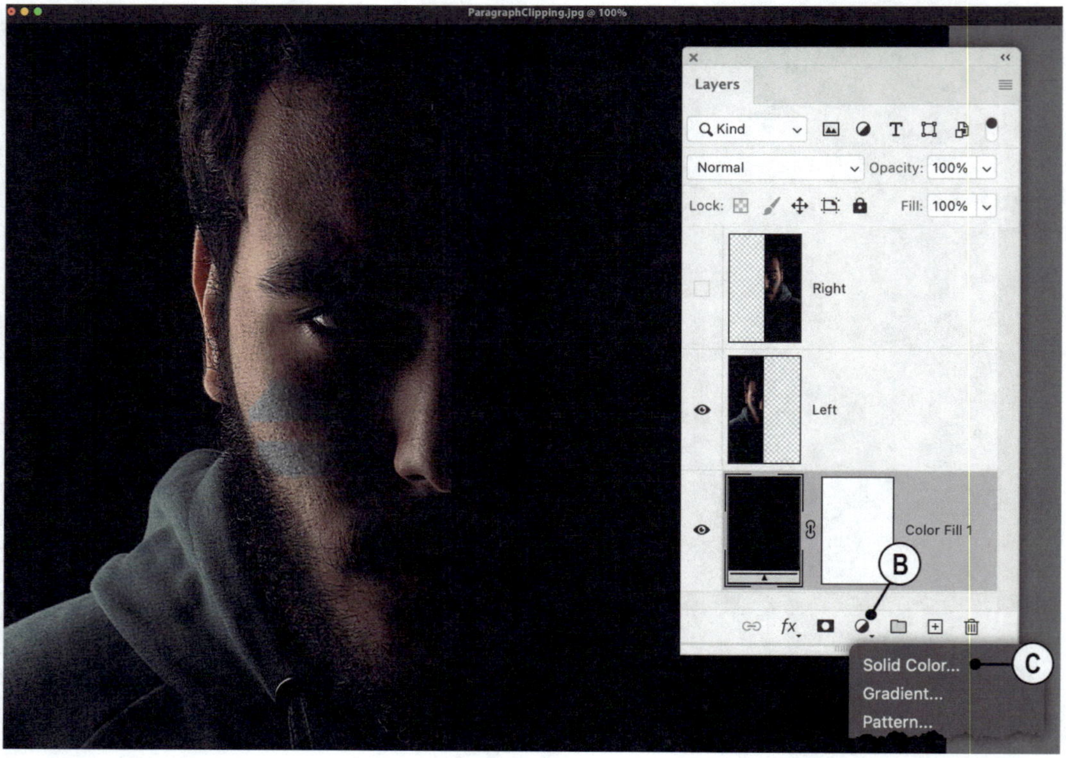

Figure 3.26: Add a black Solid Color fill layer

8. You will need to add text to the document. Fortunately, this has been prepared in advance. Go to **File → Open**, and select the document named `Text.psd` from the `03-Masking` folder. Once open, left-click on the only layer in that document, the text layer, and right-click on the layer name in the **Layers** panel to reveal the context menu. Choose **Duplicate Layer** from the list of commands. Set the document **Destination** dropdown to `ParagraphClipping.jpg` and then click **OK**. Close the `Text.psd` document when done.

9. The text layer should now appear on the canvas and in the **Layers** panel, just above the `Face Left` layer. Turn off layer visibility for the `Face Right` layer by clicking on its **Visibility** icon. Switch to the **Move** tool and drag the left edge of the text artwork to the guide in the middle of the canvas, leaving a roughly equal gap at the top and bottom of the text layer.

10. Turn on **Layer Visibility** for `Face Right` and left-click once on the layer in the **Layers** panel to make it active. Then, go to the **Layers** panel fly-out menu and choose **Create Clipping Mask** from the list of commands. This will make any visible content in the text layer act as a mask and hide portions of the `Face Right` layer where there is no text in that layer. Go to **File** → **Save As** and save the document in the `03-Masking` folder as `ParagraphClipping.psd`.

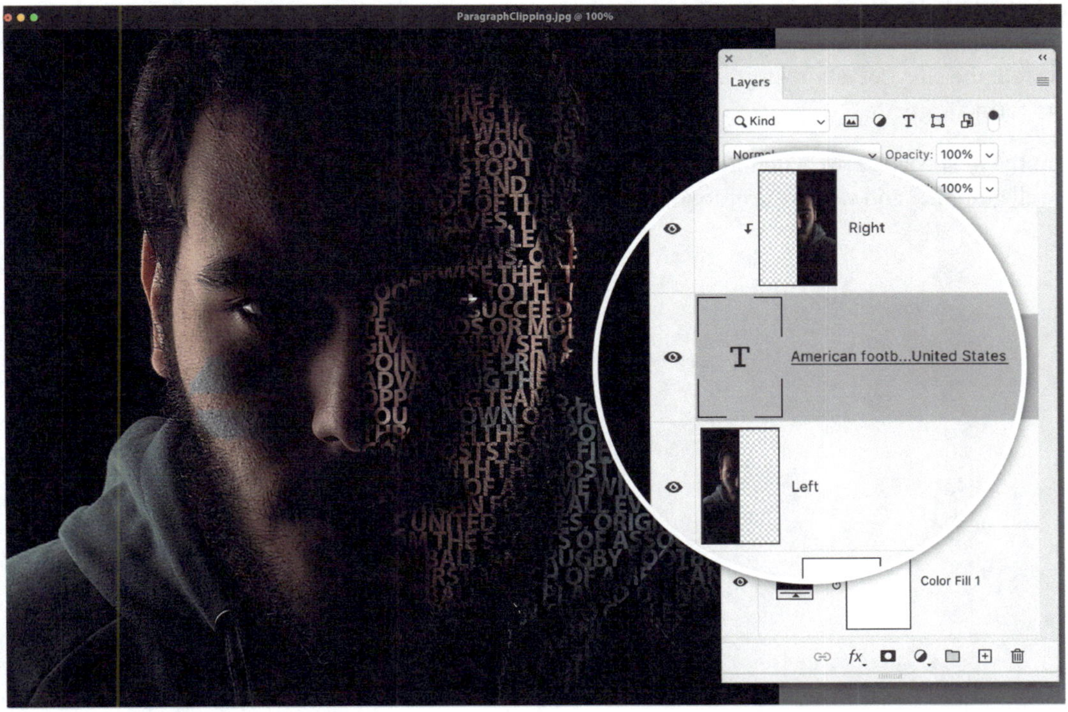

Figure 3.27: Editable text can be used as a clipping mask that affects the underlying layer

Although the principles of masking are central to effective editing in Photoshop, they don't always require a pixel-based layer mask. Vector masks and clipping masks are just two examples covered in this section that are highly effective masking techniques that don't require a pixel-based layer mask.

Summary

In this chapter, we have seen how masking plays a fundamental role in controlling the visibility of layers: firstly, to remove an unwanted background while keeping a subject visible and combining it with a new backdrop; and secondly, in conjunction with a black-and-white adjustment layer, excluding the subject from the effect to maintain its color. We then used the **Brush** tool to edit the mask, painting black in the mask to conceal the adjustment layer and white to reveal it.

We have seen how masks provide a unique method for extracting hair from a background using specialist masking tools that detect image colors to hide background details and preserve a subject's hair.

In contrast to the previous techniques, we have also seen how disconnecting a mask from image content has advantages. It allows images to be scaled or rotated independently of a mask to juxtapose the photo better without affecting the mask itself.

Finally, we leveraged vector tools as the basis for a mask, using editable text as a clipping layer to create the effect of a typographic portrait and then using basic shapes and their masking properties to form a vignette.

In the next chapter, we will build branded prototypes in a variety of scenarios such as clothing, vinyl wall graphics, and website prototypes on device screens.

Part 2: Bringing Brands Front and Center

All brands exist to be seen in print, onscreen, and on the web. The process of bringing brands to life is iterative and often calls for mock-ups of logos, websites, and products, and feeding the constant demands of social media. In *Part 2* of this book, you will create realistic mockups, print assest such as flyers and posters, and social media templates for images, posts, videos, and animated GIFs.

This part has the following chapters:

- *Chapter 4, Building Brand Mock-Ups and Prototypes*
- *Chapter 5, Creating Printed Marketing Collateral*
- *Chapter 6, From Pixels to Post: Images for Social Media*
- *Chapter 7, Creating Animated GIFs and Videos*

4

Building Brand Mock-Ups and Prototypes

All brands exist to be seen in print, onscreen, and on the web. This process is iterative and often calls for mock-ups of logos, websites, and products before committing to the final product while aiming to reduce costs attributed to manufacturing the actual product. This is especially pertinent as we should also endeavor to reduce our carbon footprint and consider the use of natural materials.

In this chapter, you will create mock-ups for a range of scenarios, from devices such as iPads and smartphones to bottles, T-shirts, and murals. The vast majority of these can be edited through the power of smart objects, group masks, and linked assets.

We'll start by reviewing the key characteristics of source images and the environment within which your mock-ups will be brought to life. We will scrutinize aspects such as angles, depth of field, and content that obscures the focal point of a mock-up.

Then, we'll look at placing artwork into a perspective grid, either to place a logo on a product or to prototype large-format graphics such as murals in real-world environments.

After, we'll use transforms and warps to distort artwork into a composition, with the additional benefit of being able to edit or replace the prototype artwork, when necessary, without starting from scratch. Many of the techniques in this chapter aim to create a "surface" within which artwork is stored.

Finally, we'll cover the most challenging form of mock-ups – irregular surfaces where artwork needs to conform to the folds, creases, and indentation of products such as cushions and T-shirts using displacement maps and an organic editor called **Liquify**.

In this chapter, we'll cover the following topics:

- Applying branding to perspective
- Wrapping artwork around curved surfaces

- Replacing device screens with your own artwork
- Creating clothing and soft furnishing mock-ups

Technical requirements

The project files for this chapter can be found at: `https://github.com/PacktPublishing/Mastering-Adobe-Photoshop-2024/tree/main/Chapter04`

Applying branding to perspective

There are two popular methods for adding artwork to perspective in Photoshop: using a transform and using the **Vanishing Point** filter effect. Transforms can be applied to smart objects, which makes them ideal for repeat editing, but the mesh points that control a transform can be challenging at times.

Vanishing Point has been around for decades, providing a relatively simple method for not only adding artwork to a perspective grid but also healing and retouching in perspective to good effect. The downside to **Vanishing Point** is that it can't be applied to smart objects and the workflow needs modernization.

In this chapter, we'll look at both techniques so that you can experiment with each workflow for yourself and judge their strengths and weaknesses.

When you're sourcing photos of walls, devices, and other surfaces to apply your design onto, there are a few factors to consider. You'll want your designs to look convincing and authentic, but most importantly, legible. So, wherever possible, avoid acute angles. Anything that obscures your design will add to its authenticity but will probably require masking. So, take a moment to think about how time-consuming it will be to mask those regions before purchasing stock content.

As an Adobe Creative Cloud subscriber, you also have access to over 70,000 free assets, including ready-made mock-ups. If you need to save time and money, these can be a valuable resource, and the techniques covered in this chapter will allow you to edit them with confidence or become an official Adobe stock contributor so that you can sell your mock-ups. Head to `https://stock.adobe.com/uk/free` to access free stock assets.

Depth of field can be a highly effective facet to make mock-ups look authentic, but motion blur is challenging to mask and time-consuming. Equally so, having a pedestrian walking in front of your bus shelter advert mock-up, for example, might seem like an authentic visual addition, but think about how you would go about masking the individual that obscures the region where your mock-up will appear. You'll want to avoid surfaces that are out of focus as your pin-sharp artwork will either need to be blurred, and become illegible as a result, or stand out like a proverbial sore thumb.

The colors of the source image play a significant role. From my experience, white tends to be more forgiving as a backdrop to apply logos or other types of artworks onto than dark backgrounds, but it's all about context:

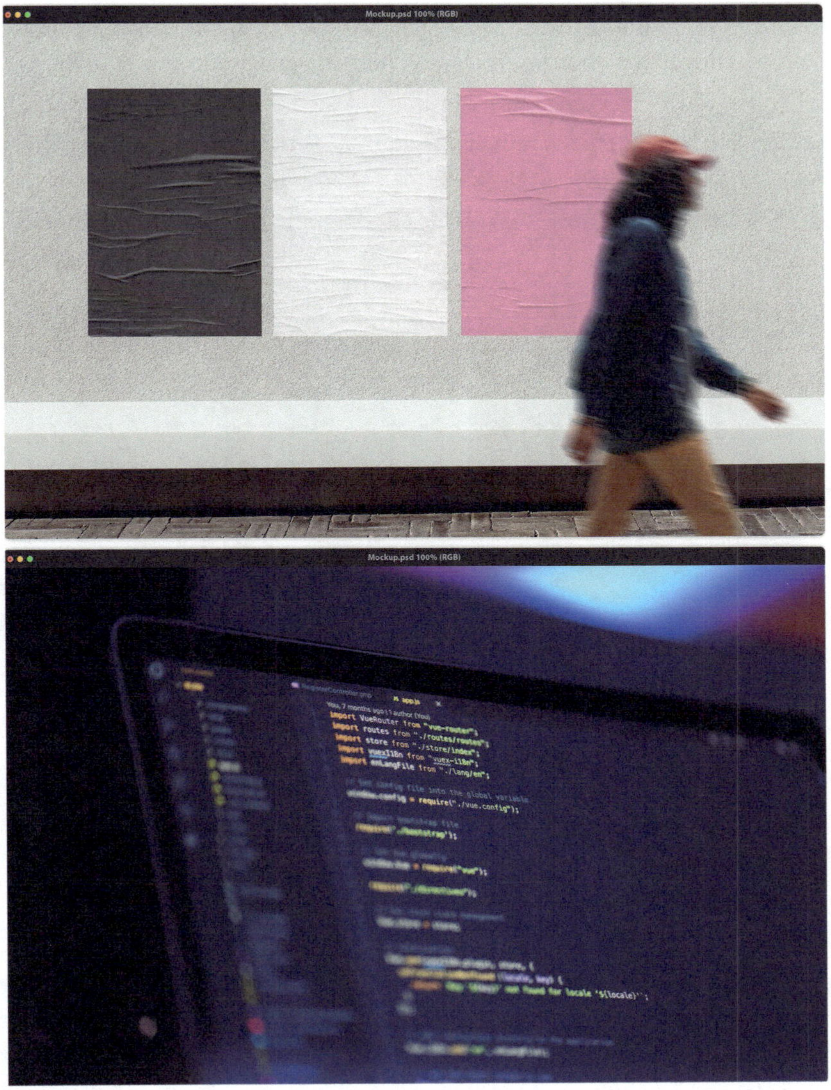

Figure 4.1: If possible, avoid obstructions and shallow depth of field in your source images

Adding a logo to a bag in perspective

In this example of perspective editing, you will take an original logo made in Adobe Illustrator and place it in a photo to create a realistic mock-up. After, you'll match the perspective of the bag using **Vanishing Point** and a blend mode:

1. Go to **File** → **Open** and select `ShoppingBag.jpg` from the `04-Mockup` folder. Click **Open** when you're done.

2. Go to **File** → **Place Embedded**, browse to the `04-Mockup` folder, select the `WildCo_Logo.ai` file, and click **Place** when you're done. When the image appears, drag the placed artwork over the front of the bag.

3. Ensure the link between the **Width** and **Height** fields is active before setting the scale to `40%`. Click on the **Commit** button in the **Options** bar to complete the import process:

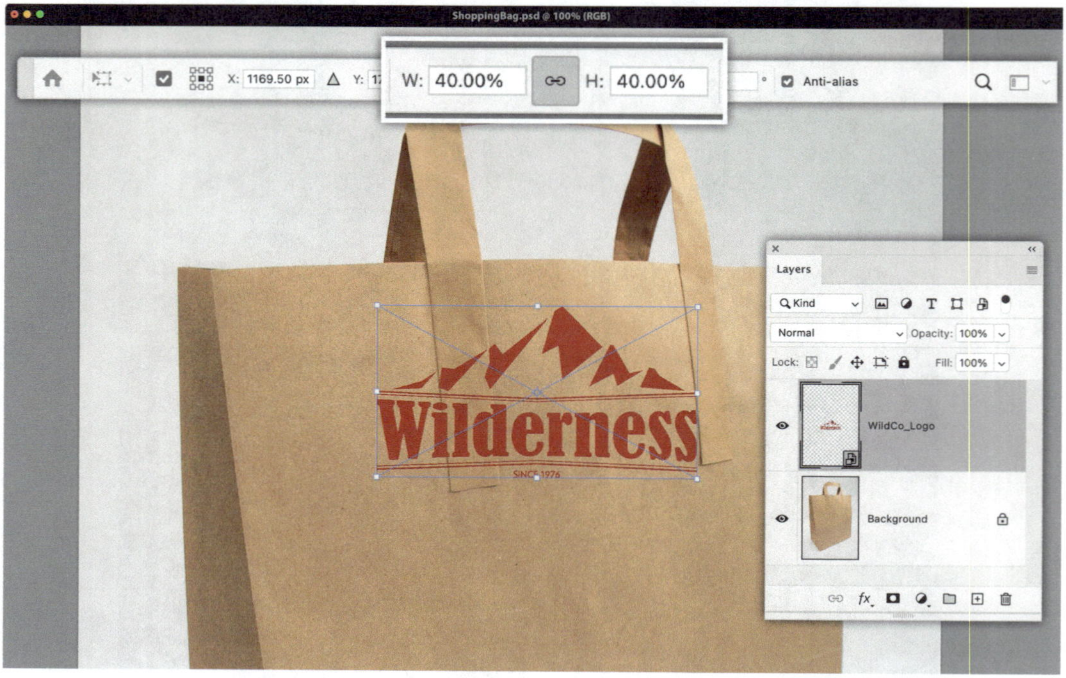

Figure 4.2: The imported logo, shown here at 40% of its original size

4. As we have seen in previous chapters, imported artwork, especially those from Adobe Illustrator, automatically becomes smart objects in the **Layers** panel. However, smart objects cannot be imported into the **Vanishing Point** editor. Therefore, you will need to hover your cursor over the imported layer name in the **Layers** panel, right-click, and choose **Rasterize Layer** from the list of options.

5. Next, double left-click on the current layer name to open the type entry field, rename it `Logo`, and press *Enter*:

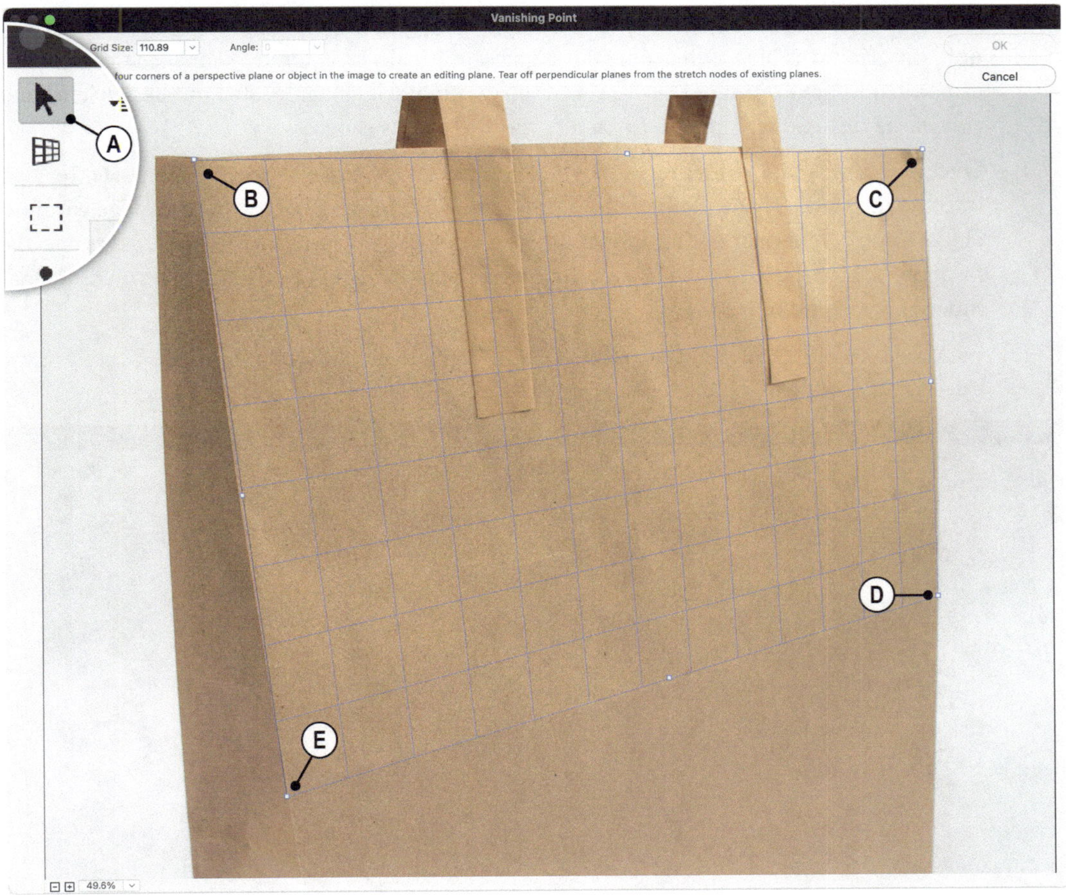

Figure 4.3: The Vanishing Point dialog showing the perspective grid

6. Select the **Logo** layer from the **Layers** panel by left-clicking on it once. Then, go to **Select → All** and choose **Edit → Cut**.
7. To launch the **Vanishing Point** interface, go to **Filter → Vanishing Point**. The **Create Plane** tool, which you'll need to use here, is already active when you enter **Vanishing Point**. Photoshop needs to work with a perspective plane, one that you will create and usually trace from the image that appears in the **Vanishing Point** image window.
8. Hover your cursor over the front top-left corner of the bag (*Figure 4.3, B*) and left-click to add the first grid point. Then, hover your cursor over the top right-hand side of the bag (*Figure 4.3, C*) and click to add a second grid point. Place a third grid point at the bottom right-hand side of the bag (*Figure 4.3, D*) and a last grid point at the bottom-left corner of the bag (*Figure 4.3, E*). The grid should now appear and will be one of three colors: red (unhealthy grid), yellow (requires improvement), or blue (healthy grid).

9. If your grid is not blue, it will require editing; try dragging each of the corner points slightly until the grid turns blue. Often, only the slightest of tweaks is required to enhance the grid. You can switch to the **Zoom** tool or the **Hand** tool, both of which are located on the top left-hand side of the dialog, if zooming into each of the grid points is necessary.
10. Once you have a blue grid, press *Ctrl* + *V* (Windows) or *Cmd* + *V* (macOS) to paste the logo into the interface. This will always appear in the top left-hand corner of the image window. Hover your cursor over the middle of the logo and drag it down into the grid, central to the front of the bag; the logo will conform to the grid's perspective. Click **OK** when you have fine-tuned the position of the logo.
11. Finally, go to **File** → **Save** and save the file as a PSD file named `ShoppingBag.psd` in the `04-Mockup` folder. Then, choose **File** → **Close**:

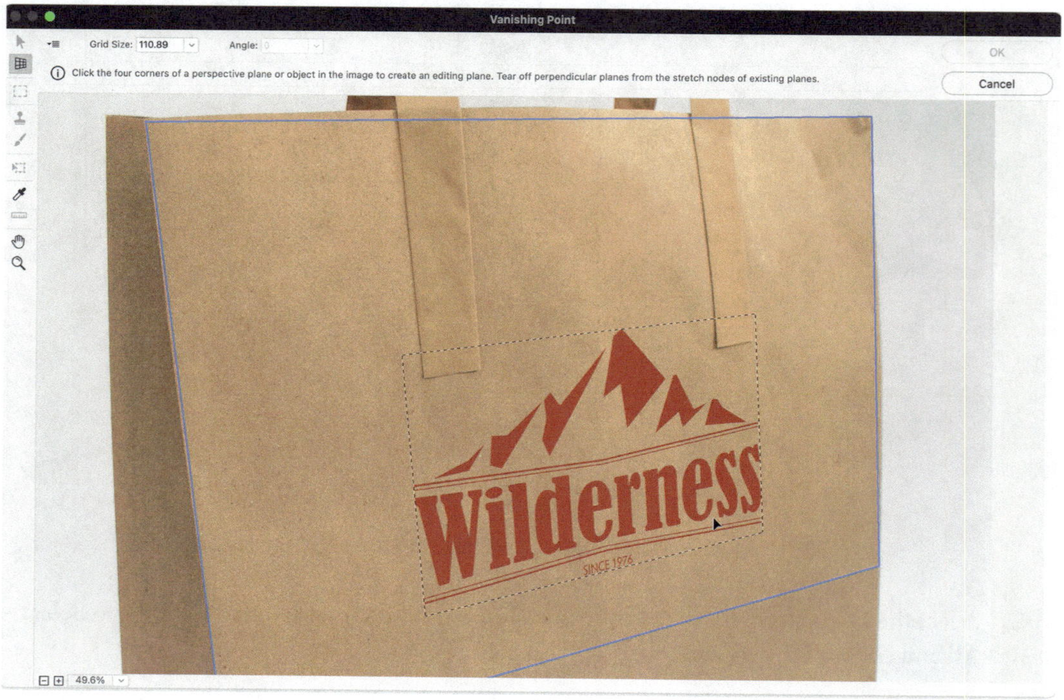

Figure 4.4: The Vanishing Point dialog showing the artwork that was applied within the grid

The limitations of Vanishing Point

As useful as the **Vanishing Point** feature is, sadly, it doesn't accept smart objects and you can't repeat edit a raster layer using this feature in the same way you can with a layer effect such as **Drop Shadow**. If you are looking for a more flexible workflow for perspective editing, I would recommend transform warps, which will also be covered in this chapter.

Creating a mural mock-up

One of the hidden gems of the **Vanishing Point** feature is its ability to wrap artwork around corners. This is ideal for creating murals as you can use a single image and let **Vanishing Point** do the rest of the work:

1. Go to **File** → **Open**. Browse to the `04-Mockup` folder, select `Walls.jpg` and `Mural-A.jpg`, and click **Open** when you're done. Ensure the `Mural-A.jpg` document is active, then go to **Select** → **All**. Then, go to **Edit** → **Copy** and close the document as it is no longer needed.
2. With `Walls.jpg` open and active, go to the bottom of the **Layers** panel and click on the **Create a New Layer** icon. Name it `Mural Art` and ensure it is targeted.
3. Go to **Filter** → **Vanishing Point**. When the dialog appears, the **Create Plane** tool will already be active. You're going to create a perspective grid that covers the far right-hand side wall and the wall behind the cushions only.
4. Start by left-clicking in the top-left corner of the right-hand side wall in the room (*Figure 4.5* **A**). Then, hover your cursor over the top-right edge of the wall where it meets the ceiling and the edge of the image and left-click to add a second plane point (*Figure 4.5* **B**). Add a third point where the right-hand wall meets the wooden skirting along the right edge of the image (*Figure 4.5* **C**). Add a fourth point approximately where the corner of the wall would finish behind the cushions. Finally, click on the point you first added to complete the plane.
5. Fine-tune the position of each point by zooming into them in turn and dragging them to match the four corners of the wall. It is better to make the vanish point plane larger than the walls as they can be masked later; you won't end up with a region of the wall devoid of mural art because the grid didn't cover the entire area:

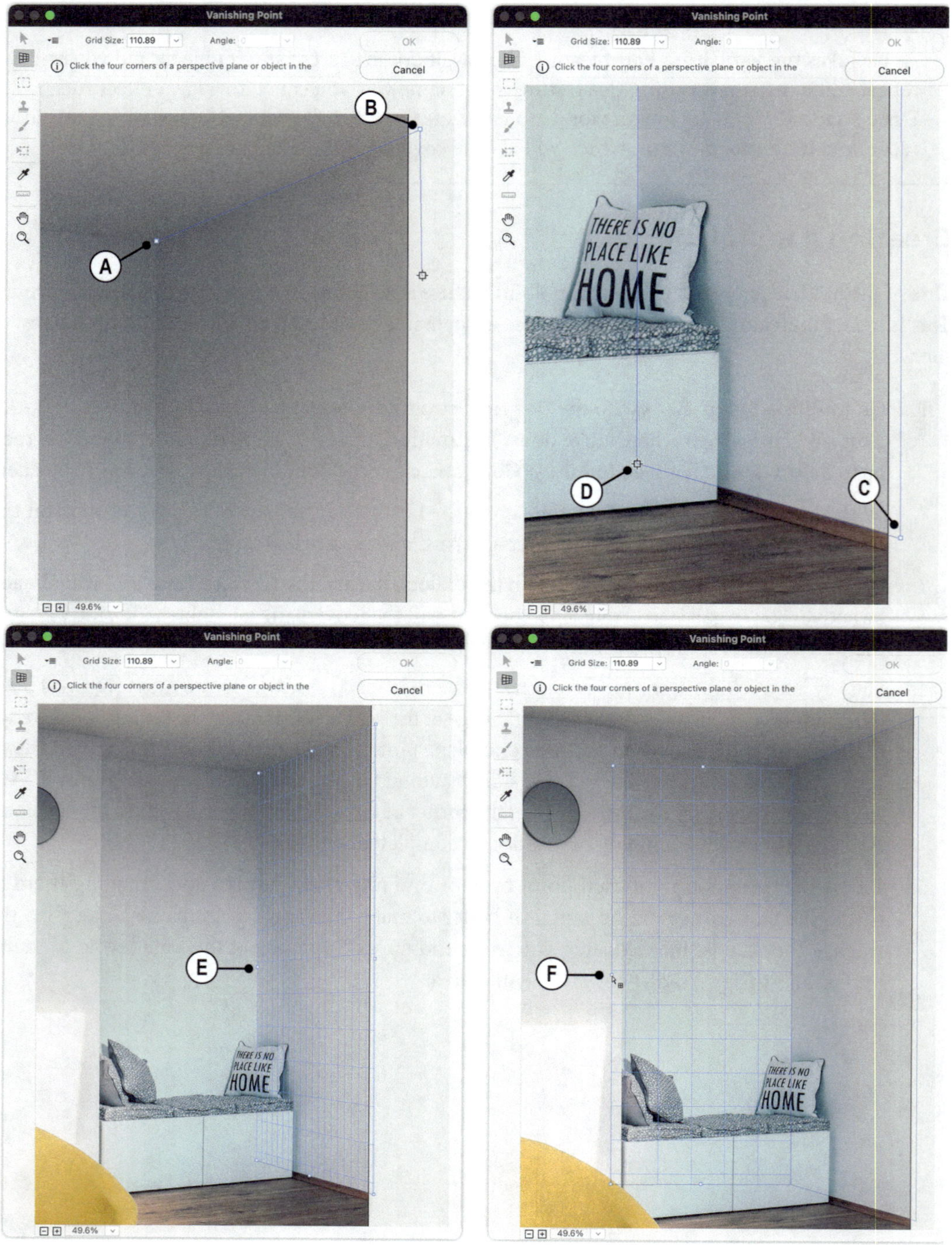

Figure 4.5: The Vanishing Point grid, created as a corner to match the walls

5. With the grid fine-tuned, hover your cursor over the center-left handle of the grid. Then, hold *Ctrl* (Windows) or *Cmd* (macOS) as you drag the handle to the left-hand side and across the other wall that runs behind the cushions until you reach slightly further than the edge of that wall. Once you've done that, release the left mouse button and the key on the keyboard. This will create a perspective corner that the artwork will wrap around:

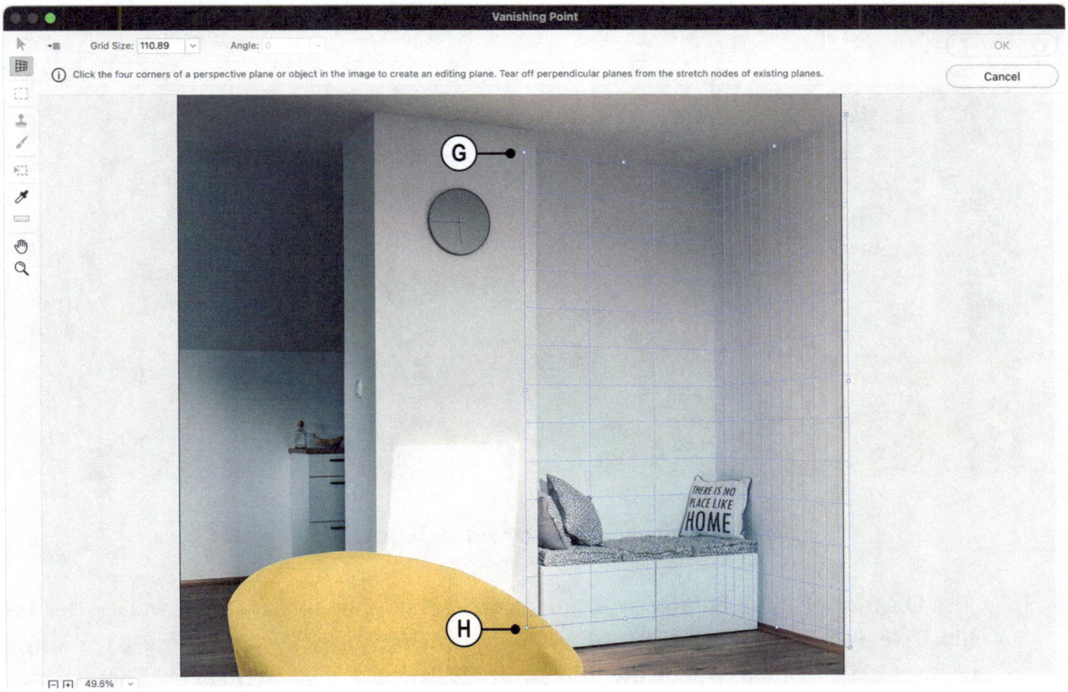

Figure 4.6: Some fine-tuning of the grid will be necessary

6. The second plane will no doubt require adjusting. Drag the top-left and bottom-right handles to match the wall, ensuring the grid runs down to the floor. This cannot be seen, but a rough estimate will be sufficient.

7. With the perspective grid in place, press *Ctrl* + *V* (Windows) or *Cmd* + *V* (macOS) to paste the mural art that you copied from the `Mural-A.jpg` file earlier in this exercise. Hover your cursor over the middle of the artwork and drag it into the grid. It has been sized slightly larger than the grid. All you will need to do is ensure that both walls are covered with artwork:

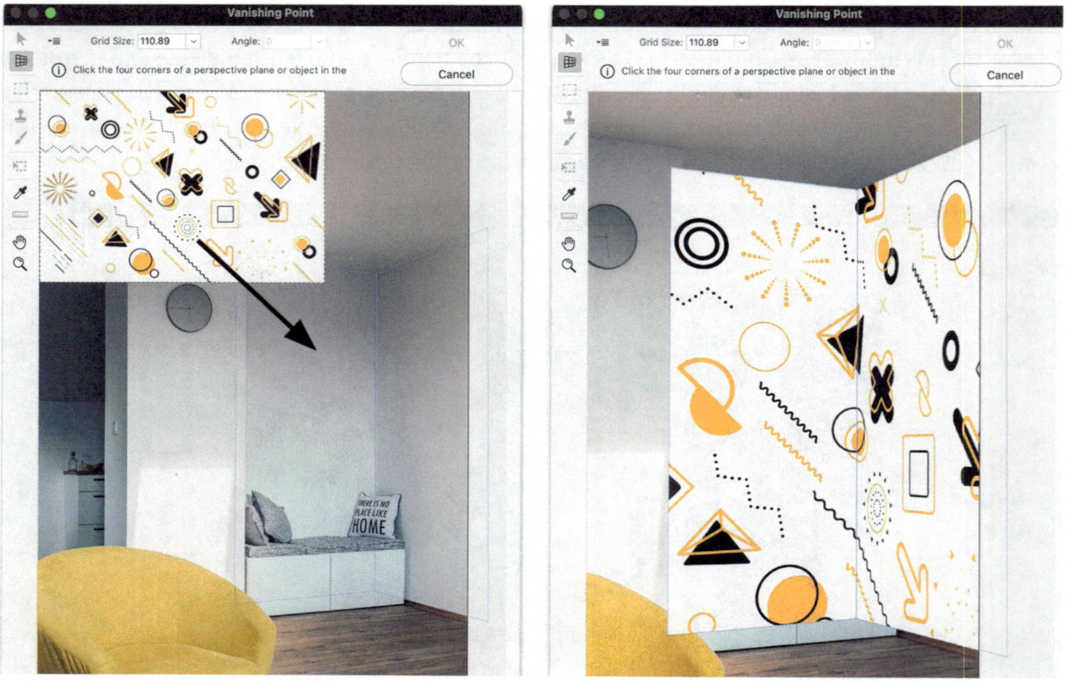

Figure 4.7: The mural artwork added to the perspective grid

8. Click **OK** to apply the edits and return to the main Photoshop interface. You will see that the edits have been applied to the **Mural Art** layer, which requires masking. Ensure the **Mural Art** layer is active, then click on the **Add Layer Mask** icon at the bottom of the **Layers** panel.
9. Switch to the **Brush** tool by pressing the *B* key. From the **Options** bar, click on the **Brush Tip Preset** menu and choose the **Hard Round Brush** tip from the list of brush tip presets. Set the brush's **Size** to approximately `50` px. Set **Hardness** to `95%` from the same menu and ensure that **Opacity** and **Flow** are both set to `100%`.
10. Then, press the *D* key to reset the default colors and set black as the active color. Paint with black to conceal parts of the mural that extend beyond the two walls or overlap the cabinet and cushions. You can press the *X* key to switch the foreground color:

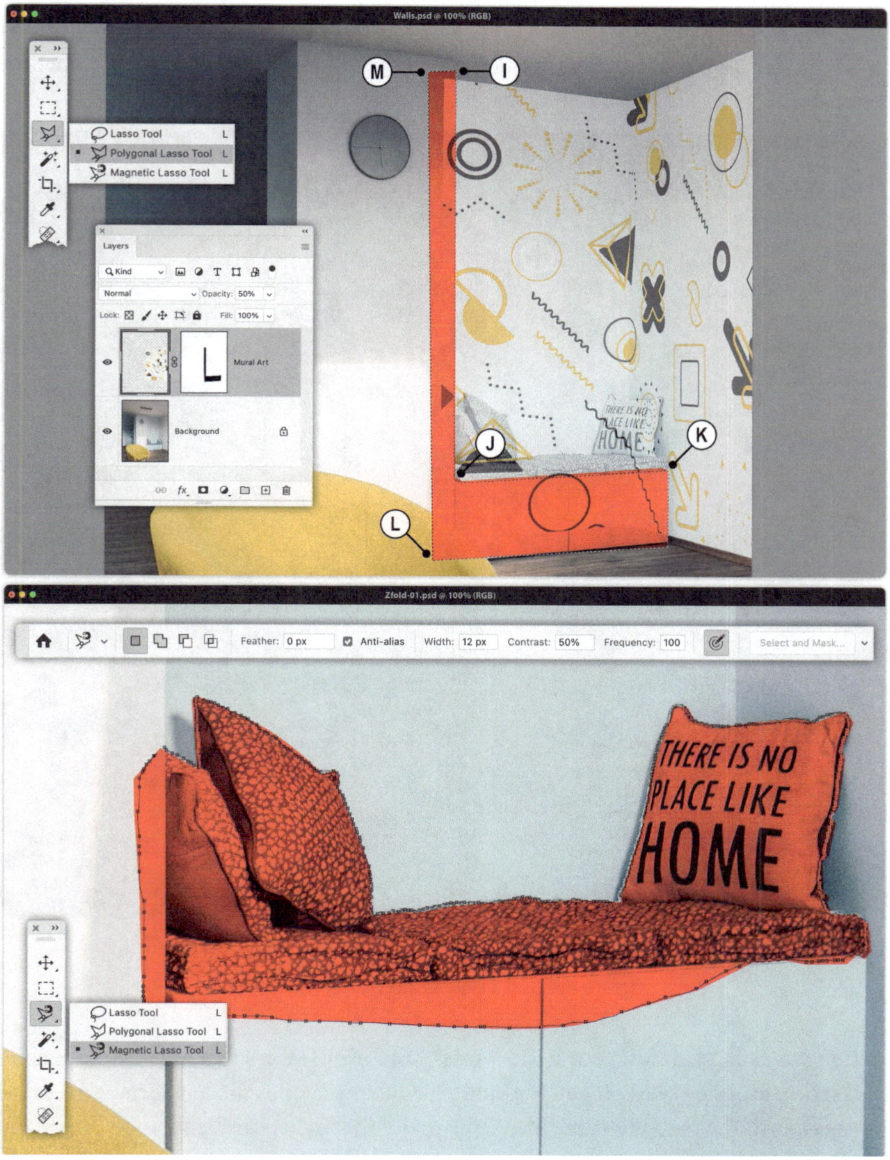

Figure 4.8: The red regions denote the selections you will make for a layer mask

11. Change the **Mural Art** layer's blend mode to **Color Burn** from the **Blend Mode** drop-down menu. If you wish to desaturate the colors of the mural or alter the color scheme, you can go to the **Adjustments** panel and add a **Hue/Saturation** adjustment layer above the **Mural Art** layer in the stack. Ensure the adjustment layer is clipped to the mural by right-clicking on the adjustment layer's name in the **Layers** panel and choosing **Create Clipping Layer** from the list of options.

12. Once you have altered the mural colors and saturation to your liking, go to **File → Save As**, browse to the `04-Mockup` folder, name the file `Mural.psd`, and close the document when you're done:

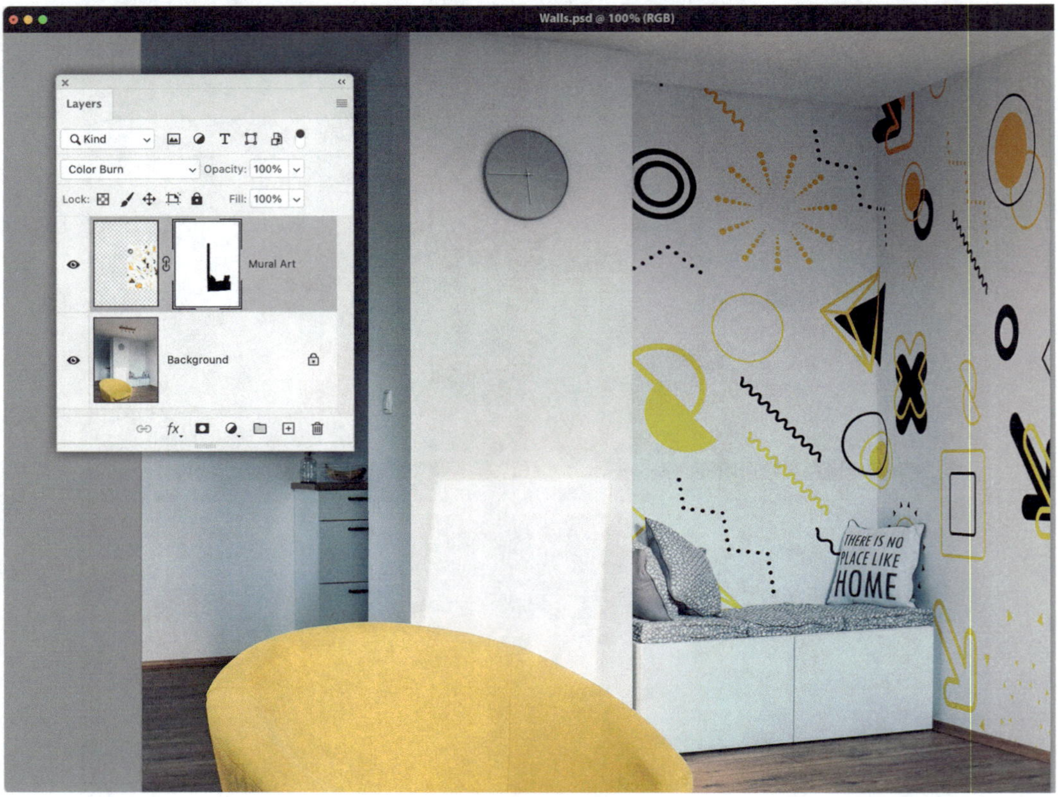

Figure 4.9: The completed mural mock-up

In this section, we looked at how to use the **Vanishing Point** feature to add artwork to a perspective grid. This is a process that relies on you to draw a grid that matches the flat surface accurately before pasting artwork into the perspective grid. We also saw that grids can be formed of one or multiple planes where required. In the case of the mural, we wrapped artwork along two walls by extending the first grid. The drawback of **Vanishing Point** is its lack of editability. We will explore more sophisticated forms of warping and distorting in this chapter.

Wrapping artwork around curved surfaces

In the following two exercises, you will apply 2D artwork to a bottle and a page within a book. In doing so, you will match the surface of both products.

Applying a cylinder warp

The warp transforms features in Photoshop provide effective techniques for skewing and distorting artwork. In this section, you will utilize a recently added feature to specifically warp cylindrical shapes:

1. Go to **File** → **Open** and select the `Bottle.jpg` document from the `04-Mockup` folder. This photo contains an unbranded bottle onto which we will add a logo.
2. Then, go to **File** → **Place Linked**, browse to the `04-Mockup` folder, and select `Bottle-Label.jpg`. Click **Open** when you're done to import the artwork.
3. The logo will appear in a **Transform** box in the center of the canvas. Link the **Width** and **Height** fields before setting the scale to `115%`. Click on the **Commit** button in the **Options** bar to complete the import process. Switch to the **Move** tool and drag the label down the bottle, aligning the bottom edge of the label with the bottom edge of the bottle edge.
4. Right-click on the imported **Bottle-Label** layer and choose **Convert to Smart Object** from the list of commands.
5. Then, go to **Edit** → **Transform** → **Warp**. The warp settings will then appear in the **Options** bar. Click on the **Warp** drop-down menu and choose **Cylinder**:

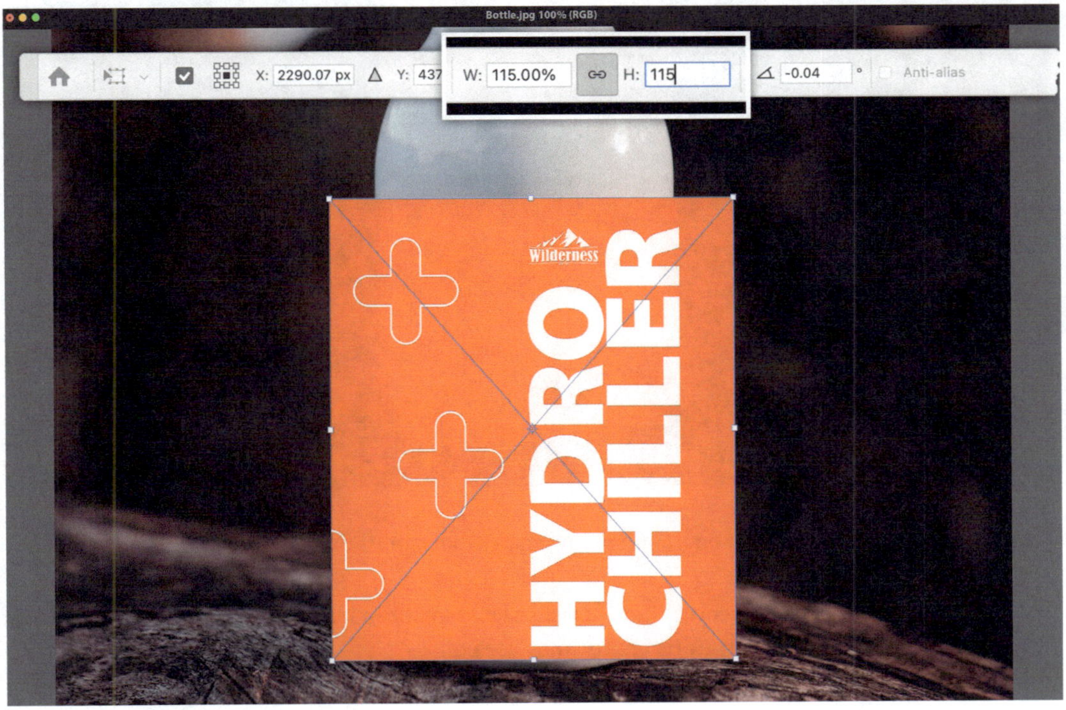

Figure 4.10: The imported label art, ready to be scaled and warped

6. When the cylinder warp becomes active, the artwork will distort considerably, requiring you to pull the design back toward the bottle in the photograph. Start by dragging the bottom-left corner of the warp grid (*Figure 4.11, A*) to the bottom-left corner of the bottle, above the lip of the bottle.
7. Next, drag the top-right corner of the warp grid (*Figure 4.11, B*), to the top-right edge of the bottle at the point before the bottle tapers inward. This will set a rough size for the warp grid.
8. Now, you will need to alter the top edge curve (*Figure 4.11, C*) so that it matches the curve of the bottle; it should have a slight downward curve. Then, drag the bottom edge curve upward so that it matches the lower lip of the bottle. The photo contains a slight distortion. As such, you will find placing the label so that it matches the bottle exactly challenging, but this will be addressed later. For now, just ensure the warp matches the bottle as closely as possible:

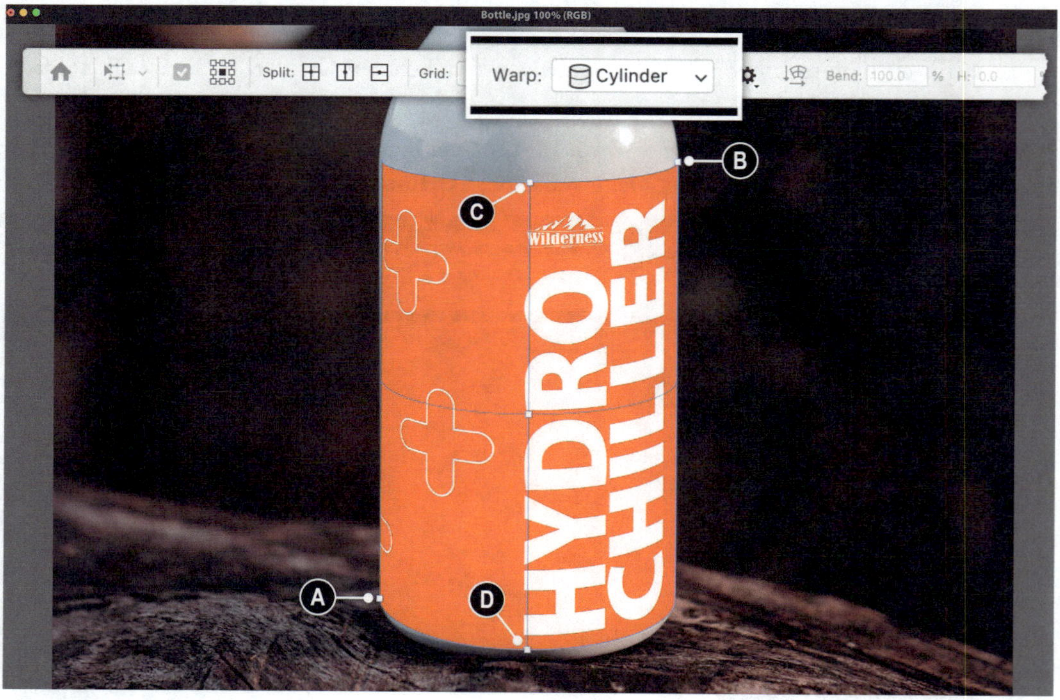

Figure 4.11: The cylinder warp mode creates the impression of curved artwork

9. Once all of the cylinder's corners and curved edges have been repositioned, click on the **Commit changes** button in the **Options** bar to apply the edits.
10. Then, go to **Edit** → **Transform** → **Distort**. When the distort frame appears, zoom in close to each corner and drag the corner points as close to the edge of the bottle as possible. It will be better to make the artwork slightly larger than the bottle so that you can hide any white edges of the bottle; these will stand out if the label doesn't cover them. Once the points have been repositioned, click on the **Commit changes** button in the **Options** bar to apply the edits.

11. To help blend the artwork into the bottle, change the blend mode to **Color Burn** from the **Blend Mode** menu in the **Layers** panel.
12. Go to **File** → **Save As**, browse to the `04-Mockup` folder, and name the file `Bottle.psd`. Close the document when you're done:

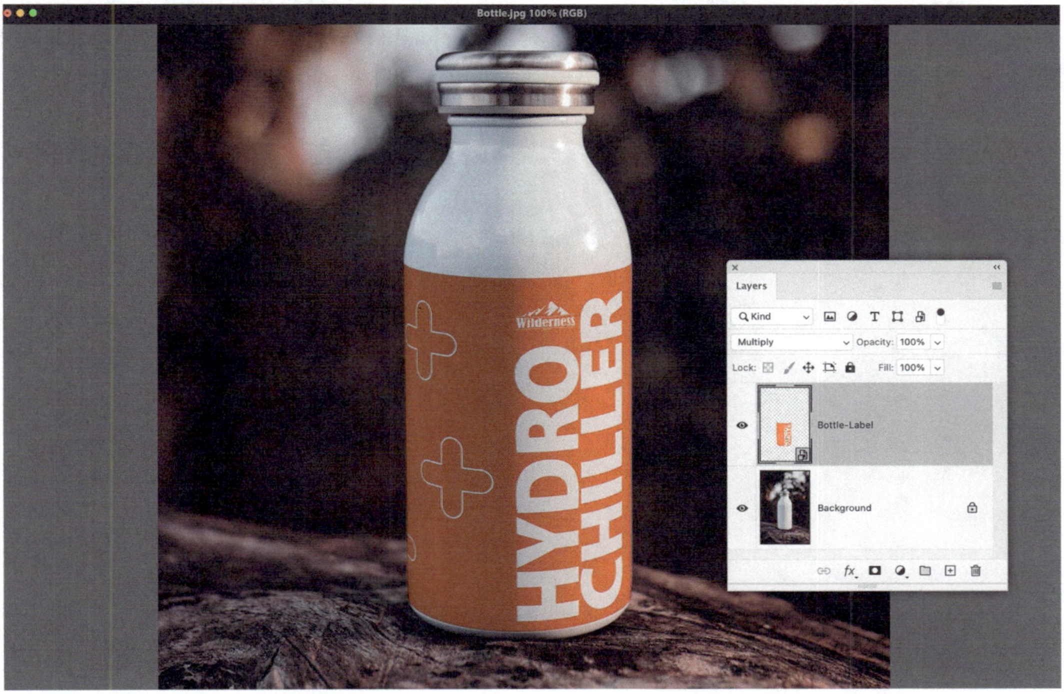

Figure 4.12: The completed bottle mock-up

Warping artwork across book designs

The warp transforms features in Photoshop provide effective techniques for skewing and distorting artwork. In the form of a rectangular grid, you can use mesh points to pull, morph, and stretch the contents into almost any appearance you wish. Let's take a look:

1. Go to **File** → **Open** and select the `Book.jpg` document from the `04-Mockup` folder. The pages of this book are blank and require artwork to be added to them.
2. Go to **File** → **Place Linked**, browse to the `04-Mockup` folder, and select the Photoshop document named `Page-Left.psd`. Click **Open** when you're done to import the artwork onto the canvas.

3. The artwork will appear in a **Transform** box in the center of the canvas. Move the top-left corner of the grid in the imported artwork so that it aligns with the top-left corner of the left-hand side page in the photo.
4. Go to **Edit** → **Free Transform**. Click on the checkbox in the **Options** bar to activate the **Reference Point** grid and click on the top-left corner point in the **Reference Point** grid. Increase **Scale** to `104.5%` and set **Rotation** to `41.6°`. This should align the left edge of the imported grid with the left edge of the page. Click on the **Commit changes** button in the **Options** bar when you're done:

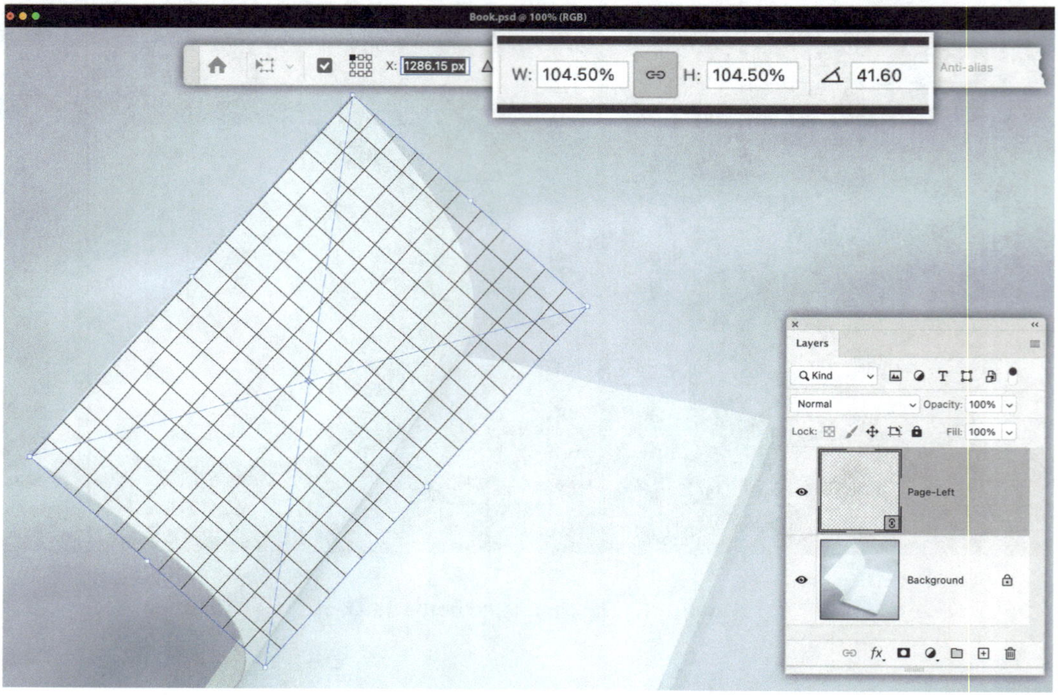

Figure 4.13: The imported grid has been aligned to the left-hand page

5. Go to **Edit** → **Transform** → **Warp**. When the settings appear in the **Options** bar, click on the **Grid** drop-down menu and choose **Custom** from the list. When the **Custom Grid** dialog appears, change **Column** and **Row** to `1` and click **OK** when you're done.
6. Click on the cog icon to reveal the **Guide Options** popout; click on the **Never Show Guides** radio button to hide them. As we have our own grid, hiding these guides will simplify things a little onscreen:

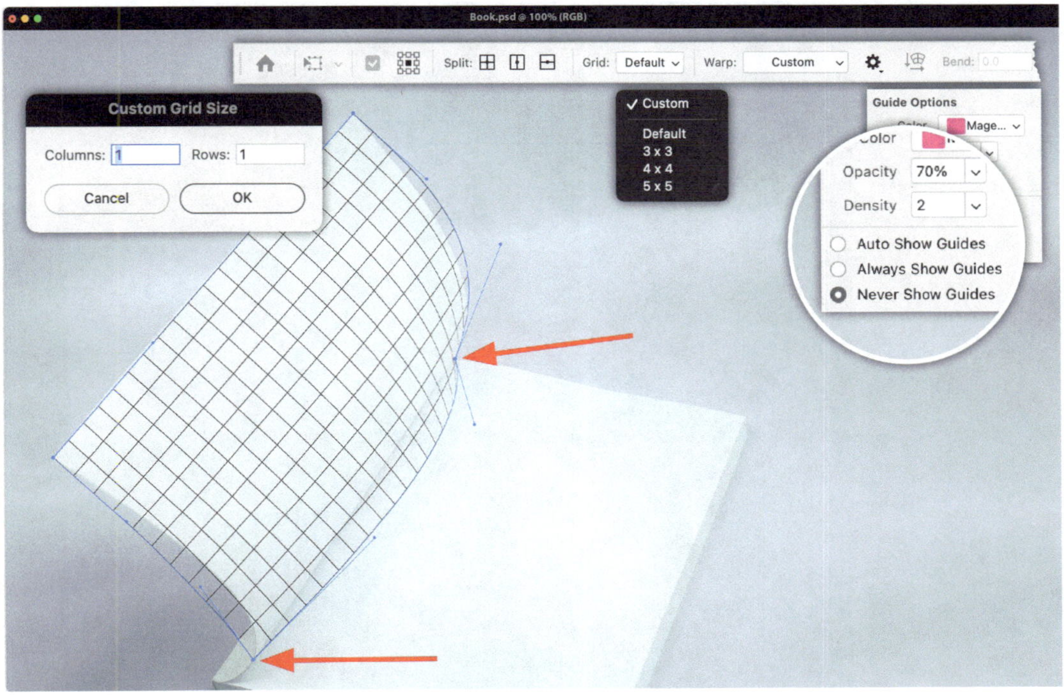

Figure 4.14: Use the corner handles to curve the edges of the grid to match the book

7. With the warp grid visible around our artwork, drag the bottom-right corner of the grid to the lowest visible portion of the page turn. Then, drag the top-right corner of the warp grid to the highest right-hand portion of the page turn.
8. Next, you will need to drag the handles of the top-right and bottom-right grid points so that they match the angle of the page edges. To do this, I often refer to the angle of these handles as hands around a clock face. Odd, I know, but if you think of the grid point as the center of a clock face, then the handles that emanate from it act like the hands on a clock that point to numbers 1 to 12.
9. Starting with the bottom-right corner of the warp grid, hover your cursor over the right-hand side handle end (*Figure 4.15, A*) and drag it to the right edge of the page so that it points to a 2 o'clock position. The handle should also point to the top right-hand corner of the grid now:

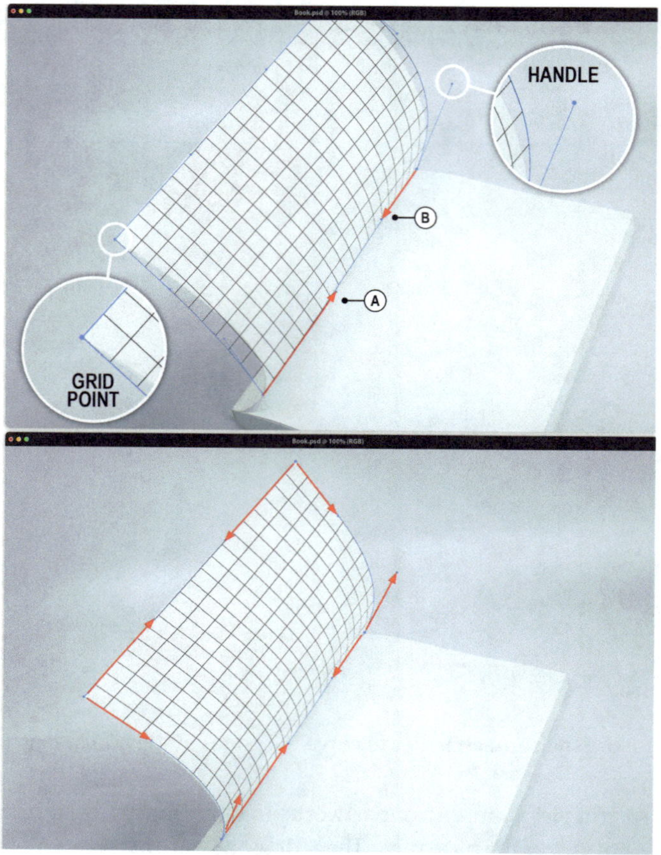

Figure 4.15: The grid corners, each with two handles, matching the angle of the page edges

10. Next, focus on the top-right grid point (*Figure 4.15*, *B*) and drag the lower left-hand handle down so that it points to a 7 o'clock position. This should also result in the handle pointing to the bottom right-hand side of the grid.
11. Use the same technique to drag each of the remaining six handles so that they match the diagram in *Figure 4.15*, where the angle and length of each handle are shown as a red arrow. Once all the handles have been repositioned, click on the **Commit changes** button in the **Options** bar to apply the edits.
12. Now that the grid artwork has been suitably matched to the curves of the page, it's time to reveal the magazine design. Hover your cursor over the **Page Left** layer thumbnail in the **Layers** panel and double left-click on it to open the file.

13. When the document opens, turn off the layer visibility of the **Grid Left** layer, and then turn on layer visibility for the **Page Left** layer. Go to **File** → **Save** and close the document. The edits will now be updated in the book mock-up:

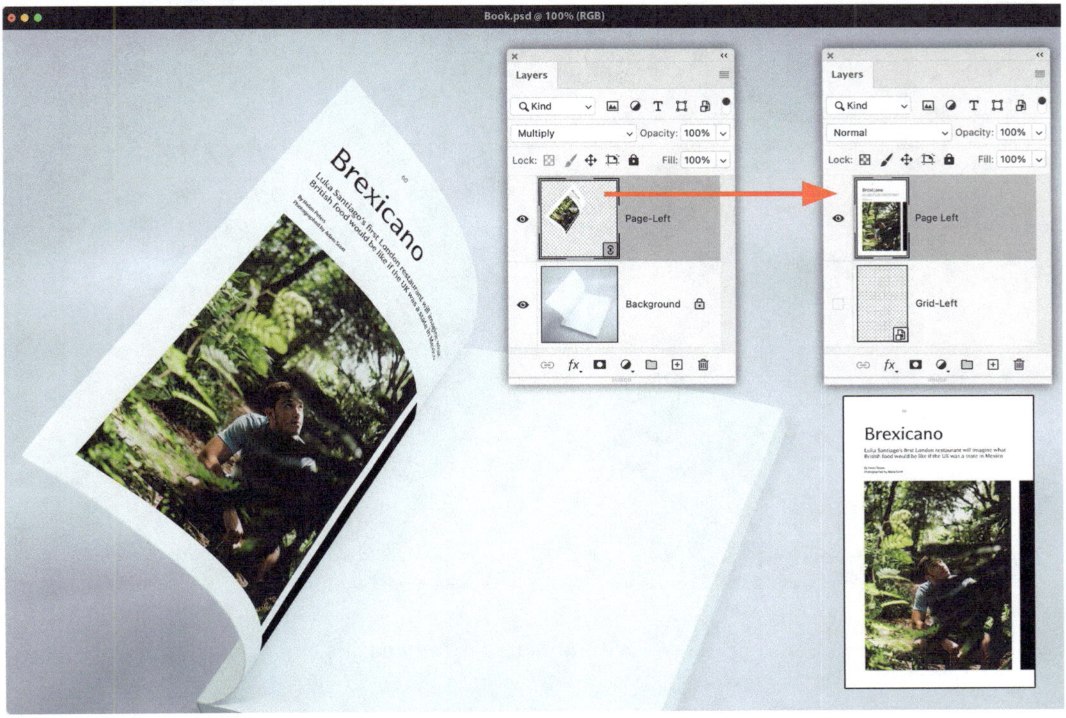

Figure 4.16: The imported page design is now visible over the photo

14. To help blend the artwork into the page, change **Blend Mode** to **Multiply** from the **Layers** panel.
15. Now that we have made significant edits to this document, go to **File** → **Save**, browse to the `04-Mockup` folder, and name the file `Book.psd`. Next, we need to add the right-hand page artwork.
16. Go to **File** → **Place Linked**, browse to the `04-Mockup` folder, and select the Photoshop document named `Page-Right.psd`. Click **Open** when you're done to import the artwork onto the canvas:

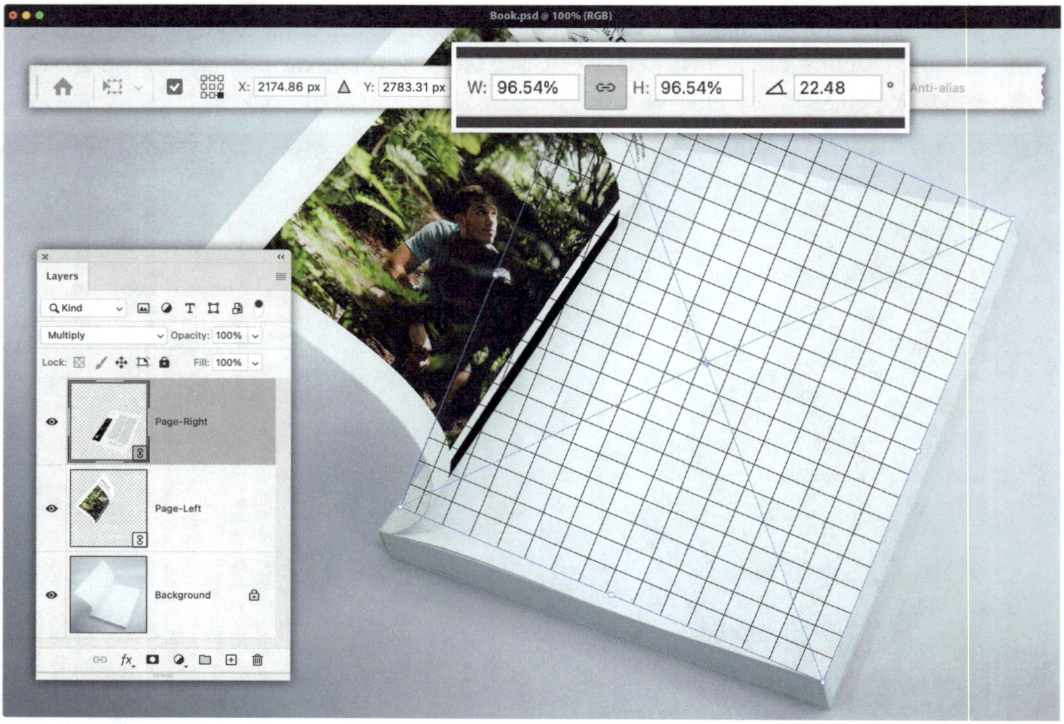

Figure 4.17: The imported right-hand grid

17. The artwork will appear in a **Transform** box in the center of the canvas. Move the bottom-right corner of the grid in the imported artwork so that it aligns with the bottom-right corner of the right-hand side page in the photo.
18. Go to **Edit** → **Free Transform**. Click on the checkbox in the **Options** bar to activate the **Reference Point** grid and click on the bottom-right corner point in the **Reference Point** grid. Increase **Scale** to `96.5%` and set **Rotation** to `22.4°`. This should align the right edge of the imported grid with the right edge of the page. Click on the **Commit changes** button in the **Options** bar when you're done to apply the edits.
19. Go to **Edit** → **Transform** → **Warp**. When the settings appear in the **Options** bar, click on the **Grid** drop-down menu and choose **Custom** from the list. When the **Custom Grid** dialog appears, change **Column** and **Row** to `2` and click **OK**. This imported grid requires an additional warp point in the center to match the curve along the top edge of the page.
20. Repeat the same technique you used in the previous steps to move the warp grid points into each corner of the right-hand side page of the photo, and then adjust each of the handles so that they match the curve of the page. Click on the **Commit changes** button to apply the edits:

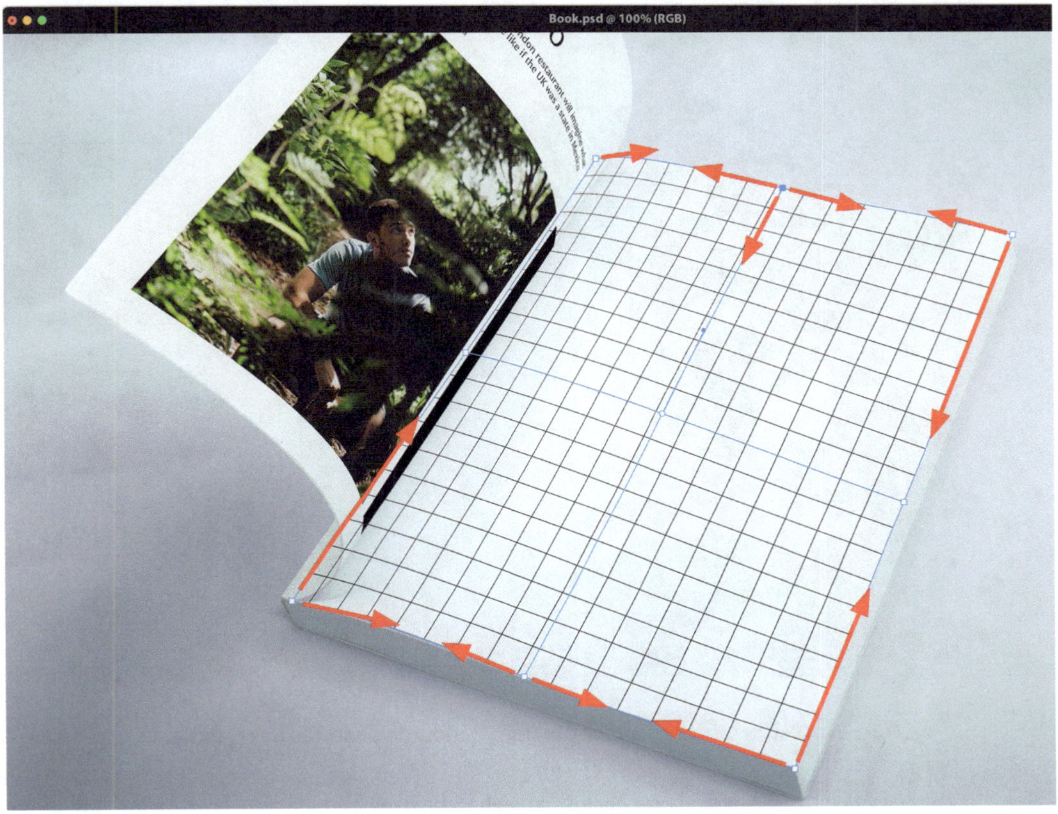

Figure 4.18: The grid points and handles have been edited to match the curve of the page

21. Next, hover your cursor over the **Page Left** thumbnail, then press *Ctrl* (Windows) or *Cmd* (macOS) as you left-click to turn the content in that layer into a selection.

22. Next, switch to the **Polygonal Lasso** tool from the **Tools** panel. Set the selection **Mode** to **Add to Selection** and set **Feather** to `0` px. Create a selection around the small portion of the book cover that can be seen in the lower left-hand side of the photo. Then, go to **Select → Inverse**.

23. With the selections combined, and the **Page Right** layer active, click on the **Add a mask** icon at the bottom of the **Layers** panel to apply the mask. Change the **Page Right** layer's **Blend Mode** to **Multiply**:

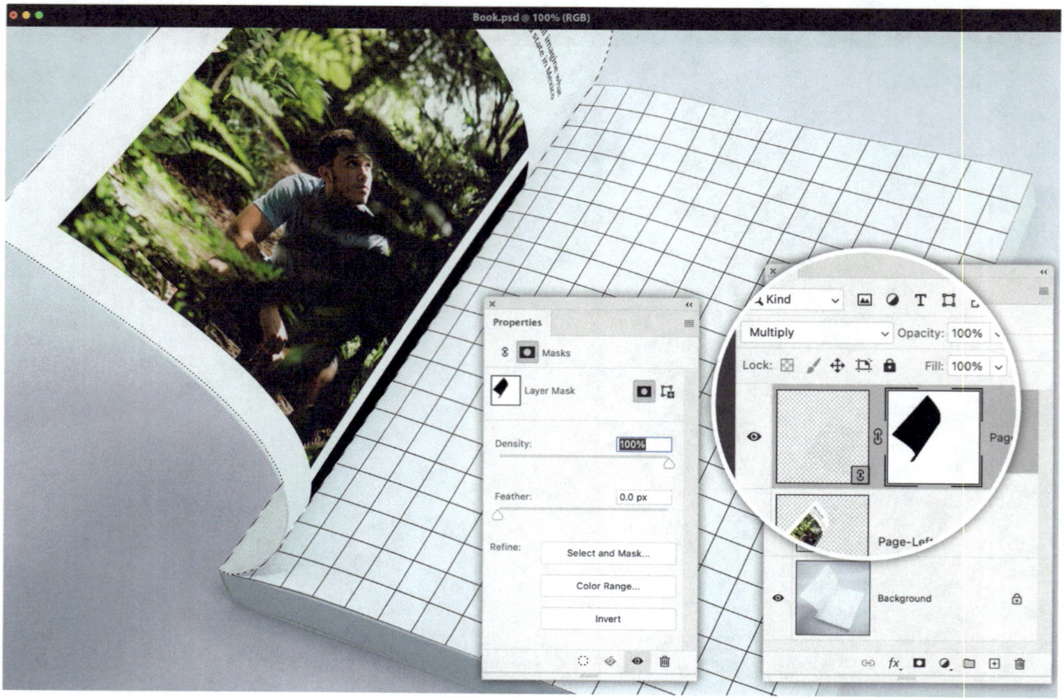

Figure 4.19: The grid artwork for the right-hand side page has been masked

24. With the grid artwork masked and curling to match the page in the photo, hover your cursor over the **Page Right** layer thumbnail in the **Layers** panel and double left-click on it to open the file.
25. When the document opens, turn off the layer visibility of the **Grid Right** layer, and then turn on the layer visibility for the **Page Right** layer. Go to **File** → **Save** and close the document. The edits will now be updated in the book mock-up.

26. Go to **File** → **Save** and close the document when you're done:

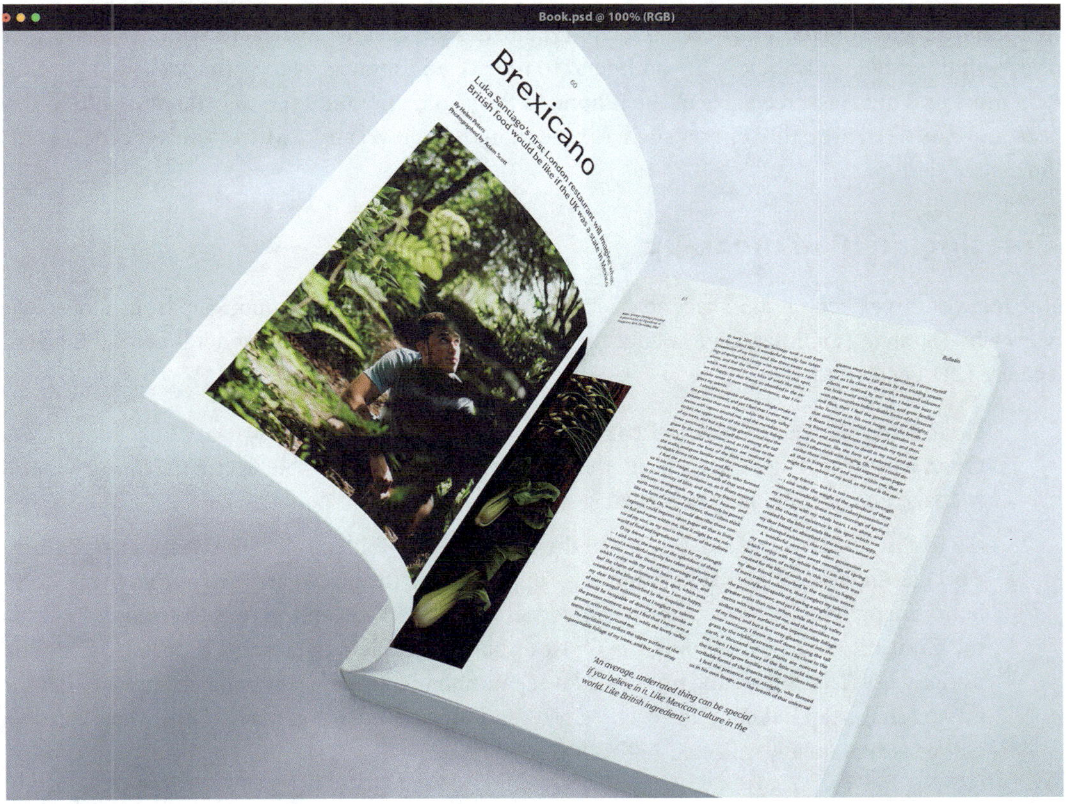

Figure 4.20: The completed book mock-up

In this section, we used Photoshop's perspective editor, **Vanishing Point**, to create a perspective grid within which our artwork was placed to match a surface within an existing photograph, such as the front of a bag and a wall. We then refined the result with combinations of masking and blend modes. We also used transform warps and distortion tools to curve our designs, giving the impression they were applied to a bottle and a page. In the following exercises, we will replace device screens with our own artwork and blend the designs with the original photograph.

Replacing device screens with your own artwork

It is important to note that all good mock-ups require designs that have been created to fit the content they will be added to. Therefore, if you intend to replace an iPhone screen with a website mock-up, you must find out the screen size of the iPhone in the photo and build the website mock-up to that size and ratio. High-quality effects such as reflections, shadows, and textures cannot hide a badly formatted design.

Creating an iPad mock-up

The focus of this exercise is to replace an existing iPad display with a website mock-up from a top-down view while applying an inner shadow effect to make the design appear as though it is behind the glass screen. Let's get started:

1. Go to **File** → **Open** and pick the `Tablet.jpg` document from the `04-Mockup` folder. Click **Open** when you're done and ensure the entirety of the image is visible within the image window to make positioning the new screen easier.
2. Go to **File** → **Place Linked**, browse to the `04-Mockup` folder, select the `Website_iPad.psd` file, and click **Place**. When the image appears, drag the placed artwork so that the bottom-left corner aligns with the bottom-left corner of the iPad screen in the background. Click on the **Commit changes** button in the **Options** bar to complete the import process. You should notice a link icon inside the imported layer thumbnail in the **Layers** panel indicating that the artwork has been linked to the original PSD and that any edits you make to the website design will be automatically reflected in this file.
3. Next, go to **Edit** → **Free Transform**. In the **Options** bar, pin the bottom-left **Reference Point** grid, which can be found on the far left-hand side. Then, enter a rotation value of `-23.6°` to match the iPad screen angle. After, click on the **Maintain Aspect Ratio** button. Change the **Width** field to a scale of `95%` to make the new screen fit appropriately to the iPad screen. Click on the **Commit changes** button in the **Options** bar to apply the edits:

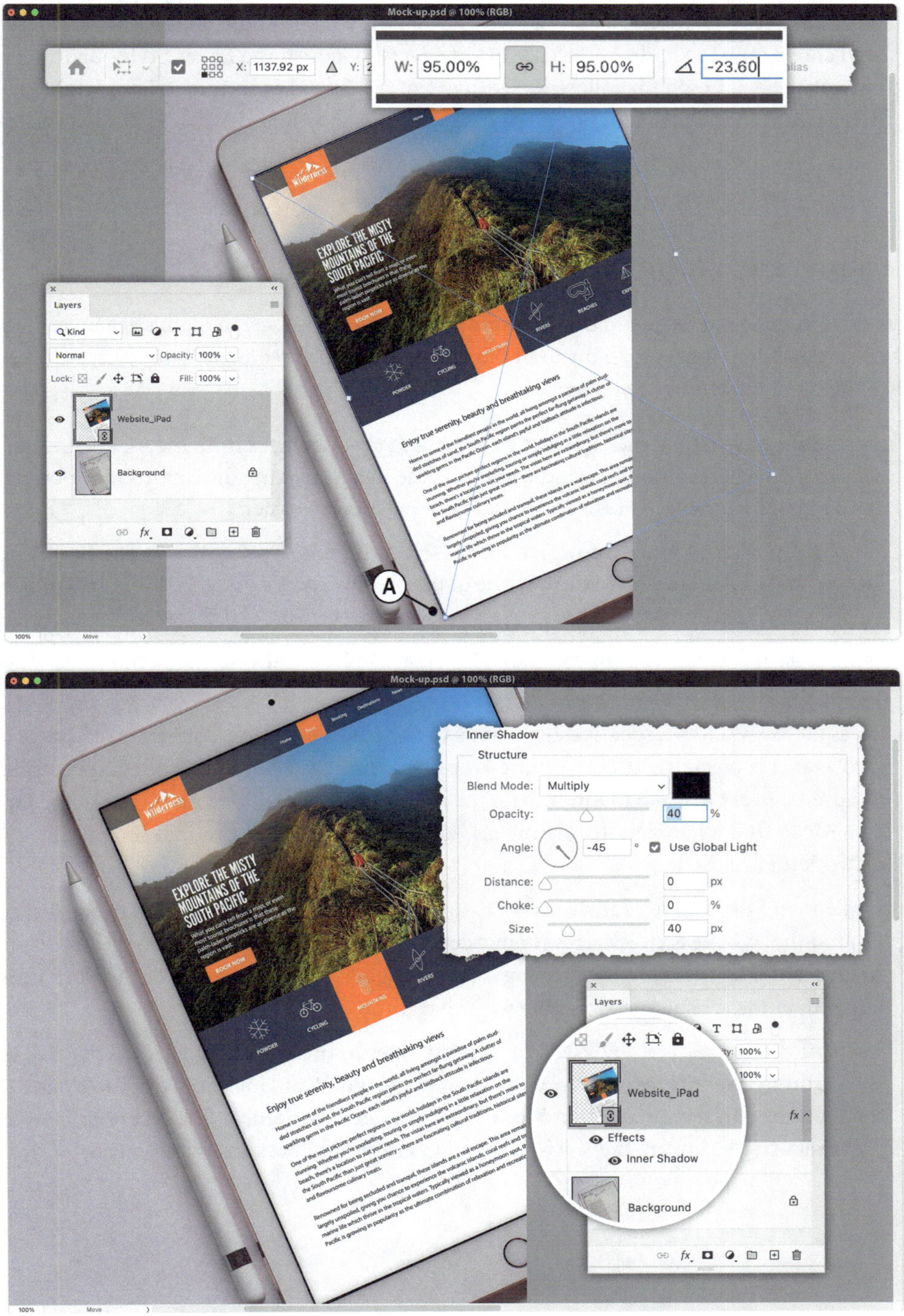

Figure 4.21: Scale and rotate the placed artwork to match the screen

4. With the **Website_iPad** layer still active, click on the **Fx** icon at the bottom of the **Layers** panel and choose **Inner Shadow** from the list of effects to launch the **Layer Styles** dialog. To fine-tune the effect, I used the following settings, but feel free to experiment. I set **Angle** to `-45°`, **Distance** to `0` px, **Spread** to `0%`, **Size** to `46` px, and **Opacity** to `33%`. Click **OK** when you're done.
5. Go to **File** → **Save As**, browse to the `03-Masking` folder, name the file `Device.psd`, and close the document.

Creating a smartphone mock-up

The previous exercise only required a flat, top-down view of a device screen. In this example, the screen display is angled and requires masking to fit the screen. It will also require you to re-create reflections to make the mock-up look convincing:

1. Go to **File** → **Open** and pick the `Smartphone.jpg` document from the `04-Mockup` folder. Click **Open** when you're done and zoom into the image, making the smartphone occupy most of the image window to make positioning the new screen easier.
2. Go to **File** → **Place Linked**, browse to the `04-Mockup` folder, select the `Website_iPhone.ai` file, and click **Place**. Increase the scale of the placed artwork to `136%` from the **Options** bar.
3. Drag the placed artwork so that the top-right corner aligns roughly with the top-right corner of the smartphone's screen in the photo. Click on the **Commit changes** button in the **Options** bar to complete the import process.
4. To apply skew and perspective distortions to the placed artwork, you will need to convert it into a smart object. Right-click on the **Website_iPhone** layer's name in the **Layers** panel and choose **Convert to Smart Object** from the list of commands. Then, lower the layer's **Opacity** to `25%` so that when you distort the artwork, you can see the original screen through the artwork for accuracy.
5. Next, go to **Edit** → **Free Transform** → **Distort**, at which point the transform frame will appear around the website artwork. Hover your cursor over each of the corner bounding box points in turn and drag them to the outer edges of the original screen, ensuring the artwork is slightly larger than the screen to conceal the white backdrop.
6. Turn off the visibility of the **Website_iPhone** layer in the **Layers** panel and left-click on the **Background** layer to make it active. Switch to the **Magic Wand** tool from the **Tools** panel. From the **Options** bar, set the selection **Mode** to **New Selection**, **Sample Size** to **Point Sample**, and **Tolerance** to `50`. Ensure the **Anti-alias** and **Contiguous** checkboxes are active:

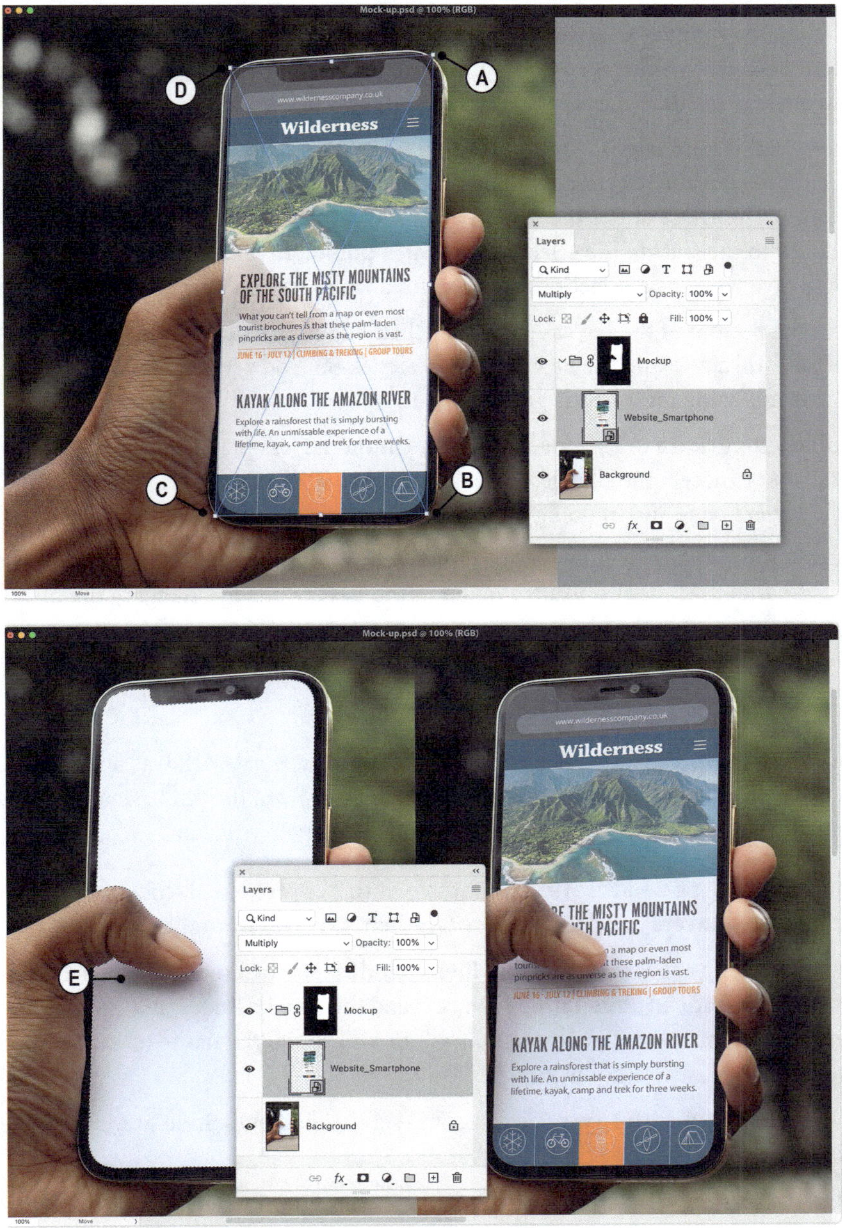

Figure 4.22: The website's design applied to the screen with a warp transform

7. Hover your cursor over the white region of the original phone screen toward the upper half and left-click to select that region. Then, change the selection **Mode** to **Add to Selection** and click on the white screen regions under the thumb to add them to the current selection. This will add portions of the thumb as well, but this can be corrected. Zoom in closer to the thumb first.

8. Switch to the **Magnetic Lasso** tool from the **Tools** panel. Then, from the **Options** bar, set the selection **Mode** to **Subtract Selection**, **Width** to `20`, **Contrast** to `10`, and **Frequency** to `100`. Ensure the **Anti-alias** checkboxes are active.
9. Hover your cursor over the top of the thumb where it meets the left edge of the phone and left-click to start the selection. Glide the cursor along the top edge of the thumb in a clockwise direction. Continue under the thumb until you reach the joint, then hover across the thumb and back to the start of the selection, at which point left-click to complete the selection. This should give you a neat selection of the original white screen.
10. Go to the bottom of the **Layers** panel and click on the **Create a New Group** button. With the selection still active and the new layer group, click on **Add a Mask** at the bottom of the **Layers** panel to apply the mask to the group.
11. Double left-click on the layer group's name in the **Layers** panel, change it to `Mockup`, then press *Enter* to accept the change. Drag the **Website_iPhone** layer into the **Mockup** layer group in the **Layers** pane and in doing so, mask the corners of the artwork to fit the screen.
12. Increase the **Website_iPhone** layer's **Opacity** to `100%` and change **Blend Mode** to **Multiply** from the **Blend Mode** drop-down menu in the **Layers** panel. Changing the blend mode will reveal the shadow in the photo. Keep the document open.

Adding screen reflections

In the example we covered in the previous exercise, prototype artwork was applied to an original smartphone screen. However, this often conceals highlights from the photo, making the result look less than convincing. Let's look at some techniques that can help with this:

1. With the `Website_iPhone` layer active in the **Layers** panel, click on the **Fx** icon at the bottom of the **Layers** panel and choose **Gradient Overlay** from the list of effects.
2. When the dialog appears, ensure that **Blend Mode** is set to **Screen** and enter `50%` for **Opacity**. Click on the **Gradient Preset** dropdown, expand the `Basic` folder, and click on the thumbnail named **Foreground to Transparent**. Tooltips will reveal the name of each preset when you hover over them with the cursor.
3. Turn on the **Align with Layer** checkbox and set the gradient's **Style** to **Linear**, **Angle** to `-77`, and **Scale** to `100%`.
4. To fine-tune the appearance of the gradient, you will need to left-click on **Gradient Preview** in the **Layer Styles** dialog (*Figure 4.23* **F**), which is shown as a thin, horizontal strip.
5. When the **Gradient Editor** area appears, click on the bottom-left color stop (*Figure 4.23* **G**) and change it to white by clicking on the color picker (*Figure 4.23* **H**) in the large square of color (this is referred to as **Saturation and Brightness**). Then, click in the top-left corner or enter `255` into each of the **Red**, **Green**, and **Blue** numerical fields. Repeat the same step for the right-hand color stop (**I**).

6. Finally, change the top-right transparency stop's (*Figure 4.23* **J**) **Location** to `20%`. This should create the appearance of a white highlight that starts at the top-left corner of the website artwork and slowly disappears a quarter of the way down the screen:

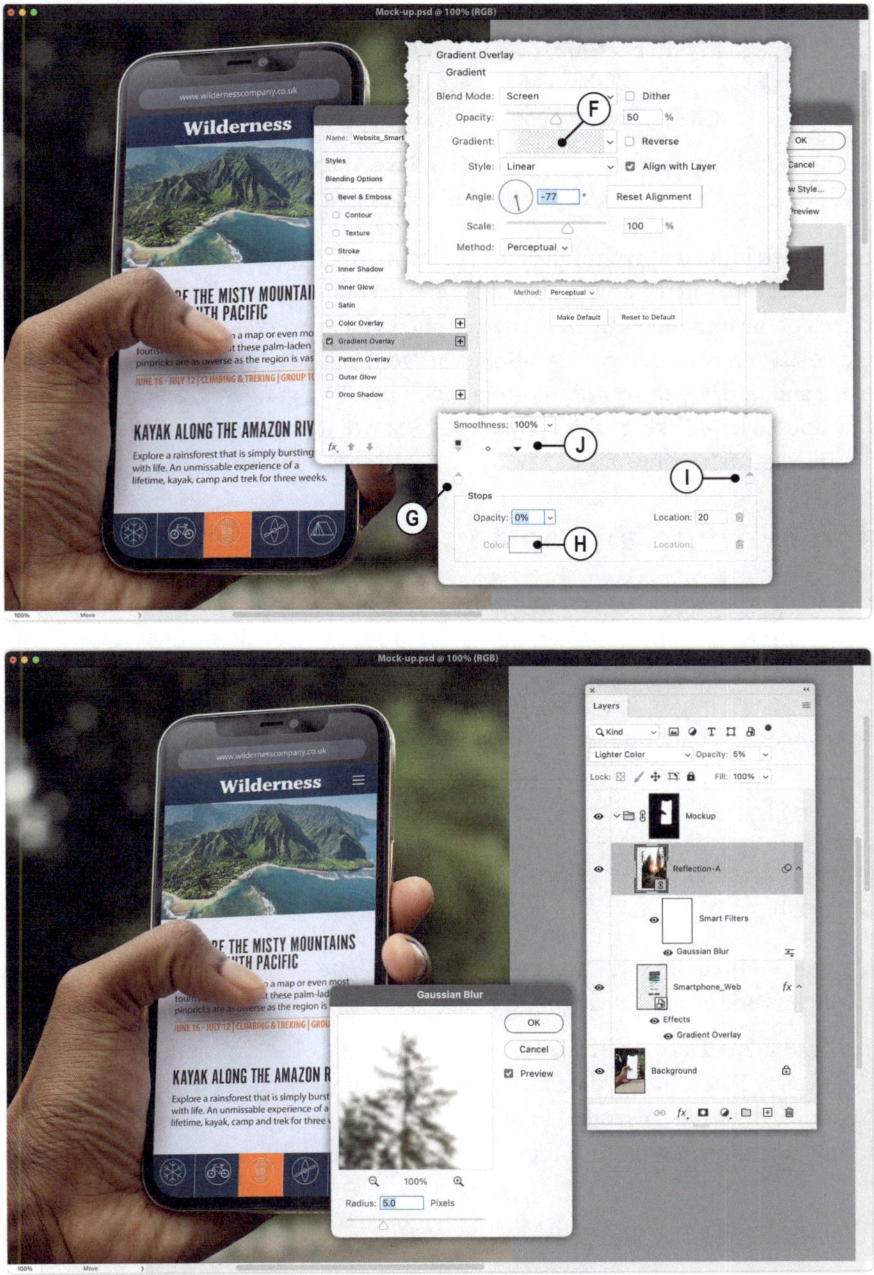

Figure 4.23: Gradient highlights and a Gaussian blur help make the mock-up more realistic

7. Next, go to **File** → **Place Linked**, browse to the `04-Mockup` folder, select the `Reflection-A.jpg` file, and click **Place**. Increase the scale of the placed artwork to `130%` from the **Options** bar. Then, press *Enter* to complete the import.
8. Change **Blend Mode** to **Lighter Color** and reduce the layer's **Opacity** to `5%` from the **Layers** panel. Then, go to **Filter** → **Blur** → **Gaussian Blur**. When the dialog appears, adjust **Radius** so that it blurs the trees where they can be seen over the website's artwork. In this example, **Radius** was set to `5.0`. Click **OK** when you're done to apply the settings.
9. With all the edits now complete, go to **File** → **Save As**, browse to the `04-Mockup` folder, name the file `Smartphone.psd`, and close the document.

In this section, we looked at techniques for replacing device screens that account for the angle, obstructions, and glass, where necessary re-creating reflections and highlights to create a more realistic mock-up. Each of the techniques we have covered allows for every component to be edited or replaced without the need for recomposition. Live-linked artwork can be edited in the original PSD or Adobe Illustrator file and updated in your Photoshop mock-ups. The gradients, reflections, and effects can be edited by double left-clicking with the mouse. Next, we will apply designs across fabric surfaces, such as clothing and soft furnishings.

Creating clothing and soft furnishing mock-ups

As we have already seen in this chapter, applying designs to flat or even curved regular surfaces presents numerous challenges. When it comes to applying designs to fabric with irregular surfaces, this presents numerous challenges. Firstly, how can we match our designs to the curved, rippled, or distorted surface of the fabric? But most importantly, how can we do this without committing to abortive work when we need to change or update a design? In the following exercises, we will master both.

Applying original designs to a T-shirt

In this section, you will import original designs onto a photo of a T-shirt using displacement maps that match the fabric:

1. Go to **File** → **Open**, select `T-Shirt.jpg` from the `04-Mockup` folder, and click **Open**. This file contains one layer: a background image of a T-shirt ready for a logo or motif placement.
2. Next, go to **File** → **Place Embedded**. Then, browse to the `04-Mockup` folder, select `LogoType.ai`, and click **Place**. When the **Place PDF** dialog appears, click **OK** to place the artwork. The artwork will be sized correctly and does not require scaling, so click on the **Commit changes** button in the **Options** bar to complete the placing process:

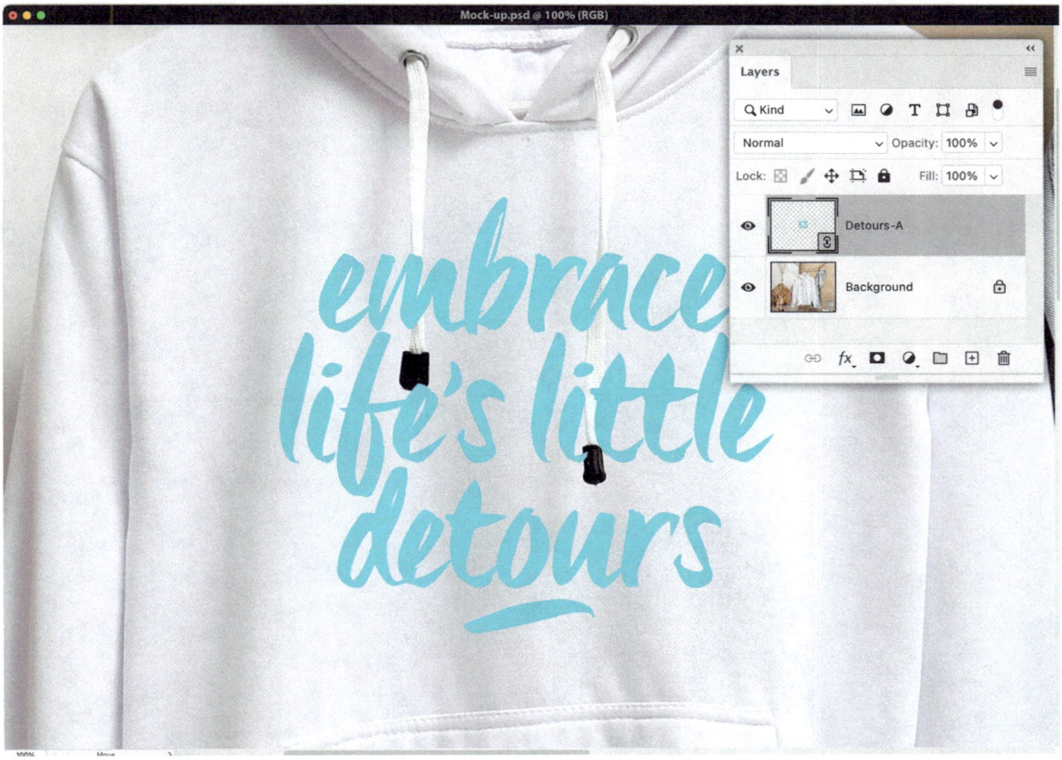

Figure 4.24: Import and position the logo

3. Switch to the **Move** tool and center the motif over the center of the T-shirt. Then, go to **Filter** → **Distort** → **Displace**. When the dialog appears, accept the default options as they tend to be a good starting point. Click **OK**.
4. Then, browse to the `04-Mockup` folder, select `T-Shirt-Displace.psd`, and click **Open**. This image contains a black and white version of the T-shirt image, with the ripples in the T-shirt exaggerated. Black regions denote low or no raised regions, while white denotes the raised regions.
5. With the **Detours-A** layer still active, click on the **Add a Mask** icon at the bottom of the **Layers** panel. Zoom into the logo type at a magnification level of around `350%`. Switch to the **Brush** tool and set the foreground color to black. From the **Options** bar, click on the **Brush Preset Picker** tool and select the **Soft Round** brush tip. Set its **Size** to `15` px and **Hardness** to `95` px:

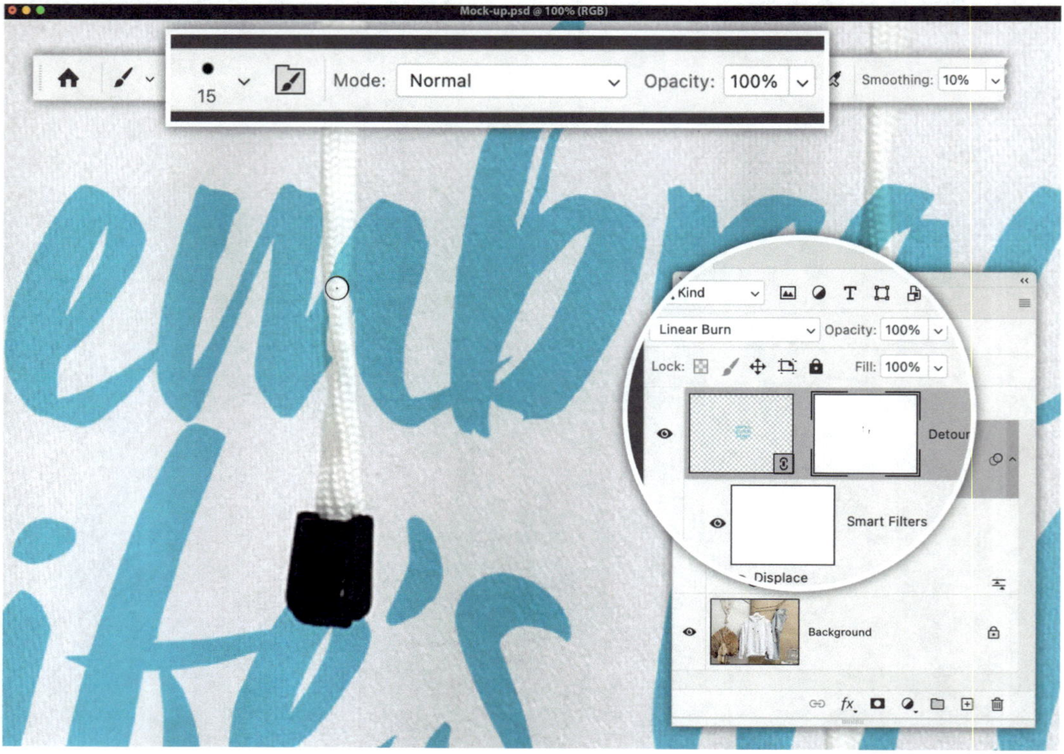

Figure 4.25: Hide the logo with a layer mask where it overlaps the jumper ties

6. Paint black in the layer mask where the pull-strings of the sweater hood overlap the region where the **Detours-A** layer appears, concealing the design.
7. Switch to the **Rectangular Marquee** tool and left-click on the **Background** layer in the **Layers** panel to make it active. From the **Options** bar, set the selection **Mode** to **New Selection**, **Feather** to `0` px, and **Style** to **Normal**:

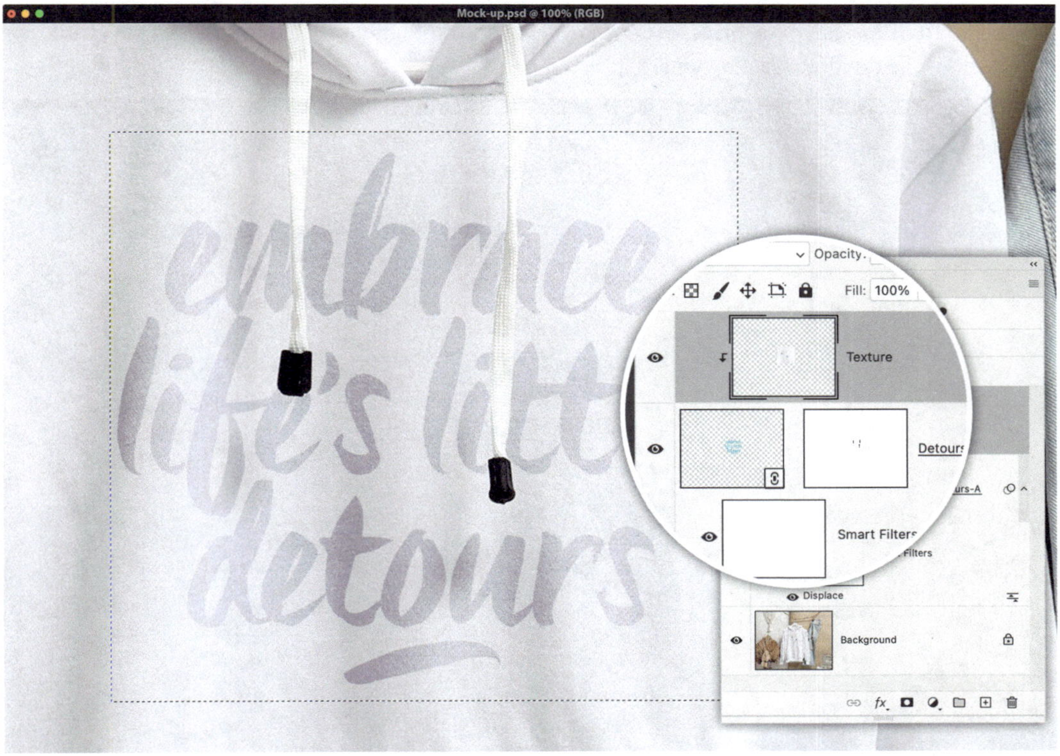

Figure 4.26: Copying a section of the sweater photo into a new layer at the top of the stack

8. Create a selection of the sweater that is slightly larger than the region the type design occupies. With the selection in place, go to **Layer** → **New** → **Layer via Copy**. Drag the new layer to the top of the layer stack, then change **Blend Mode** to **Multiply**.
9. Change the layer's name to `Texture`, then right-click on the layer's name and choose **Create Clipping Mask** from the list of options. This will apply the texture of the sweater to the logo type to make it look more convincing.
10. The final step is to help blend the motif into the T-shirt. With the **Detours-A** layer still active in the **Layers** panel, change the blending mode to **Linear Burn** from the **Blend Mode** drop-down menu.

11. Go to **File** → **Save As**, browse to the `04-Mockup` folder, name the file `T-Shirt.psd`, and close the document when you're done:

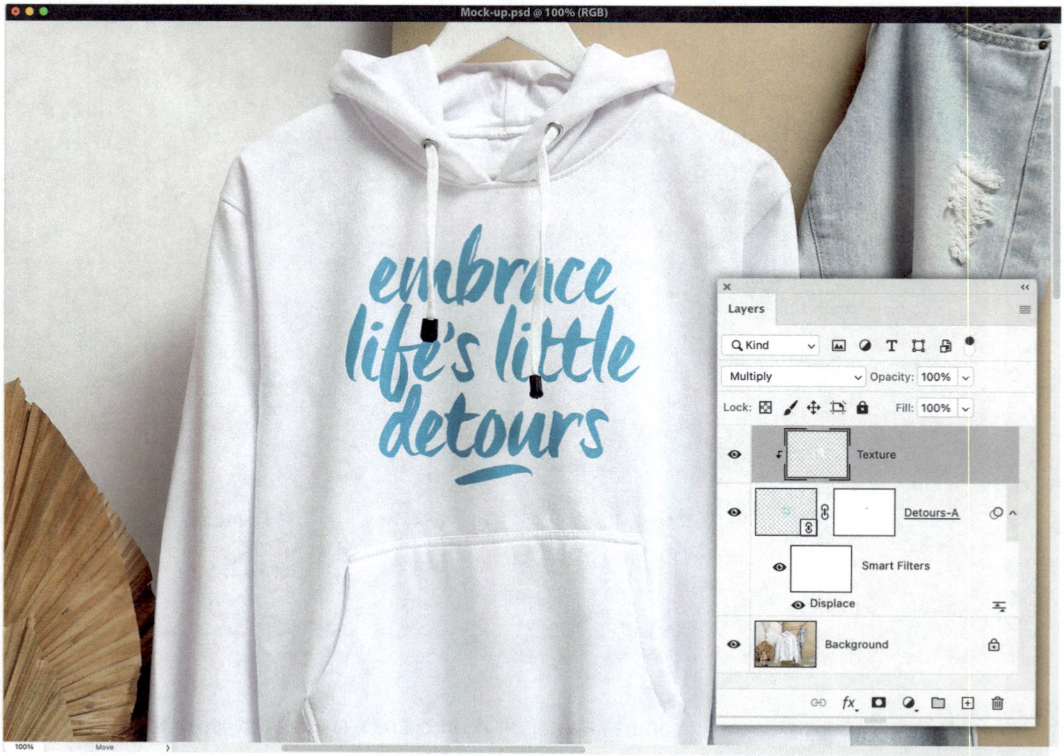

Figure 4.27: A displacement map creates the effect of rippled or uneven surfaces

Adding pattern designs to a cushion

In this section, you will import original designs onto a photo of a cushion, once again using displacement maps that match the fabric. However, on this occasion, not only will you create the displacement map, but you will also finesse the design so that it matches the contours of the cushion with the **Liquify** dialog.

Creating the cushion displacement map

Follow these steps:

1. Go to **File** → **Open**, select `Cushion.jpg` from the `04-Mockup` folder, and click **Open**. This file contains one layer: a background image of a white cushion on a sofa for a soft furnishings mock-up.
2. Before we start applying the pattern design to the photo, we need to create a displacement map. Go to **Image** → **Duplicate**. When the dialog appears, name the duplicate `Cushion-Displace` and click **OK**.
3. Go to **Filter** → **Convert for Smart Filters**. When the dialog appears informing you that the selected layer will be converted into a smart object, click **OK**. Rename the layer `Photo` in the **Layers** panel.
4. Next, go to **Filter** → **Blur** → **Surface Blur**. This type of blur maintains edge details but smoothens surfaces and similar color regions, such as the texture of a cushion. This will help prevent tiny details from distorting the appearance of the artwork once they're applied to a cushion while maintaining the large creases and folds. Set **Radius** to `10` px and **Threshold** to `15` px.
5. Then, go to the **Adjustments** panel and add a **Levels** adjustment. When the **Properties** panel displays the **Levels** settings, enter `33` in the **black point** field, `0.75` in the **mid-tone** field, and `237` in the **white point** field at the bottom of the **Properties** panel.
6. Next, add a **Black & White** adjustment from the **Adjustments** panel. When the settings appear in the **Properties** panel, select **Maximum Black** from the **Preset** drop-down menu.
7. With both adjustment layers now added to the **Layers** stack, change the blend mode of the **Black & White** adjustment layer to **Color** and the **Levels** adjustment layer to **Luminosity**.
8. Go to **File** → **Save As**, browse to the `04-Mockup` folder, and name the file `Cushion-Displace.psd`. Leave the file open for now in case any further edits are required:

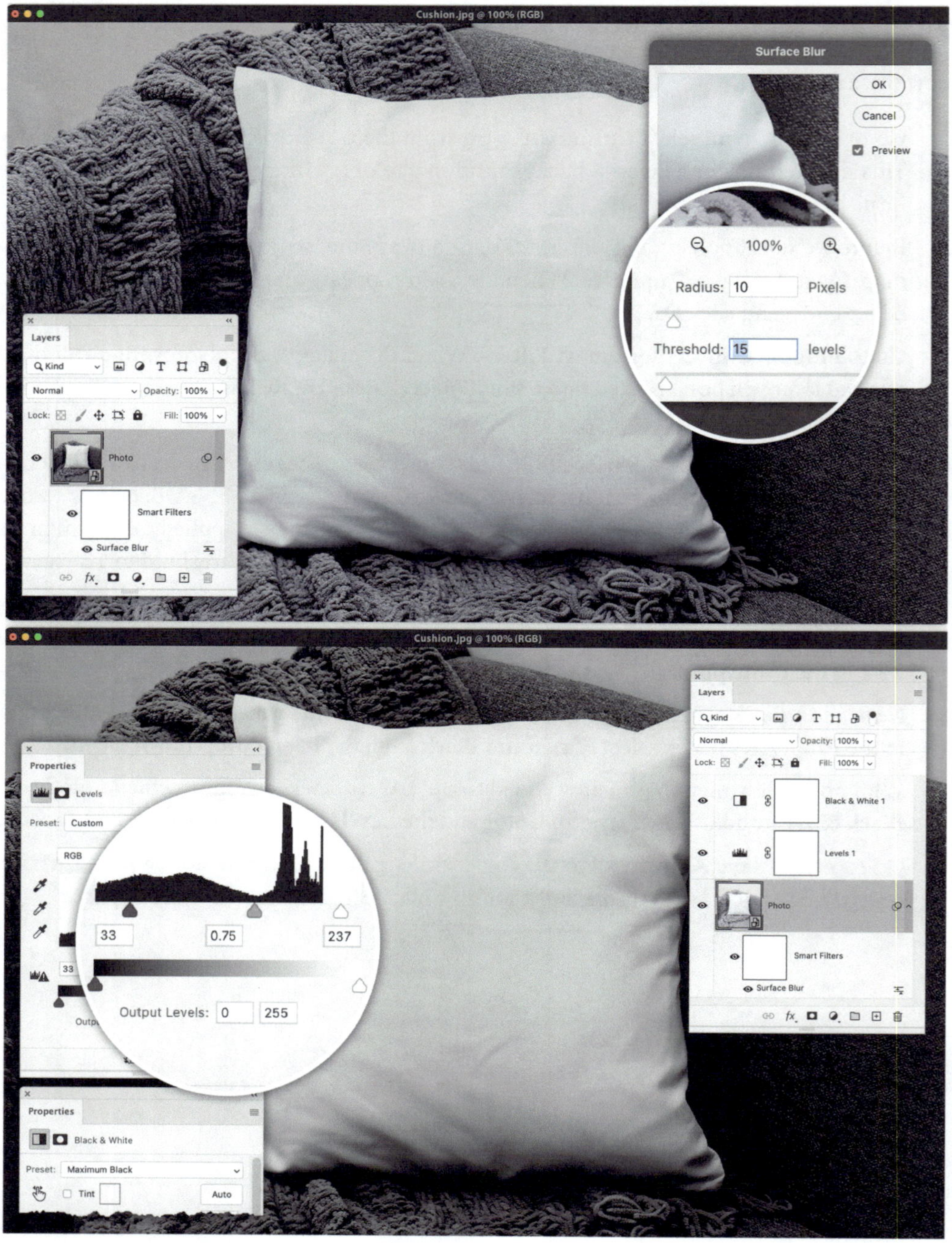

Figure 4.28: Enhancing the shadows of the cushion with adjustment layers

Applying the pattern artwork

With the displacement map now generated and saved, you can focus on the pattern artwork and apply it to the cushion in the photo:

1. Switch to the **Document** tab for the `Cushion.jpg` file. Go to **File** → **Place Linked**. Then, browse to the `04-Mockup` folder, select `Pattern-A.ai`, and click **Place**. When the **Place PDF** dialog appears, click **OK** to place the artwork.
2. Change the pattern's **Scale** to `90%` from the **Options** bar and then click on the **Commit changes** button to complete the placing process.
3. Switch to the **Move** tool and move the pattern artwork to the center of the cushion. Turn off the visibility of the pattern layer in the **Layers** panel and click on the **Background** layer to make it active.
4. Switch to the **Magnetic Lasso** tool from the **Tools** panel. From the **Options** bar, set the selection **Mode** to **New Selection**, **Feather** to `0`, the **Anti-alias** checkbox on, **Width** to `30` px, **Contrast** to `10%`, and **Frequency** to `100`.
5. Hover your cursor over the top-left edge of the cushion in the photo and left-click to start the selection. Guide the cursor around all the cushion's edges until you return to the selection start point, then left-click to complete the selection.
6. Go to the bottom of the **Layers** panel and click on the **Create a New Group** button. With the selection still active and the new layer group targeted, click on **Add a Mask** at the bottom of the **Layers** panel to apply the mask to the group. Name the group `Design`.
7. With the **Pattern-A** layer still active in the **Layers** panel, change the blending mode to **Linear Burn** from the **Blend Mode** drop-down menu. This will help show the shadow and highlight details throughout the design:

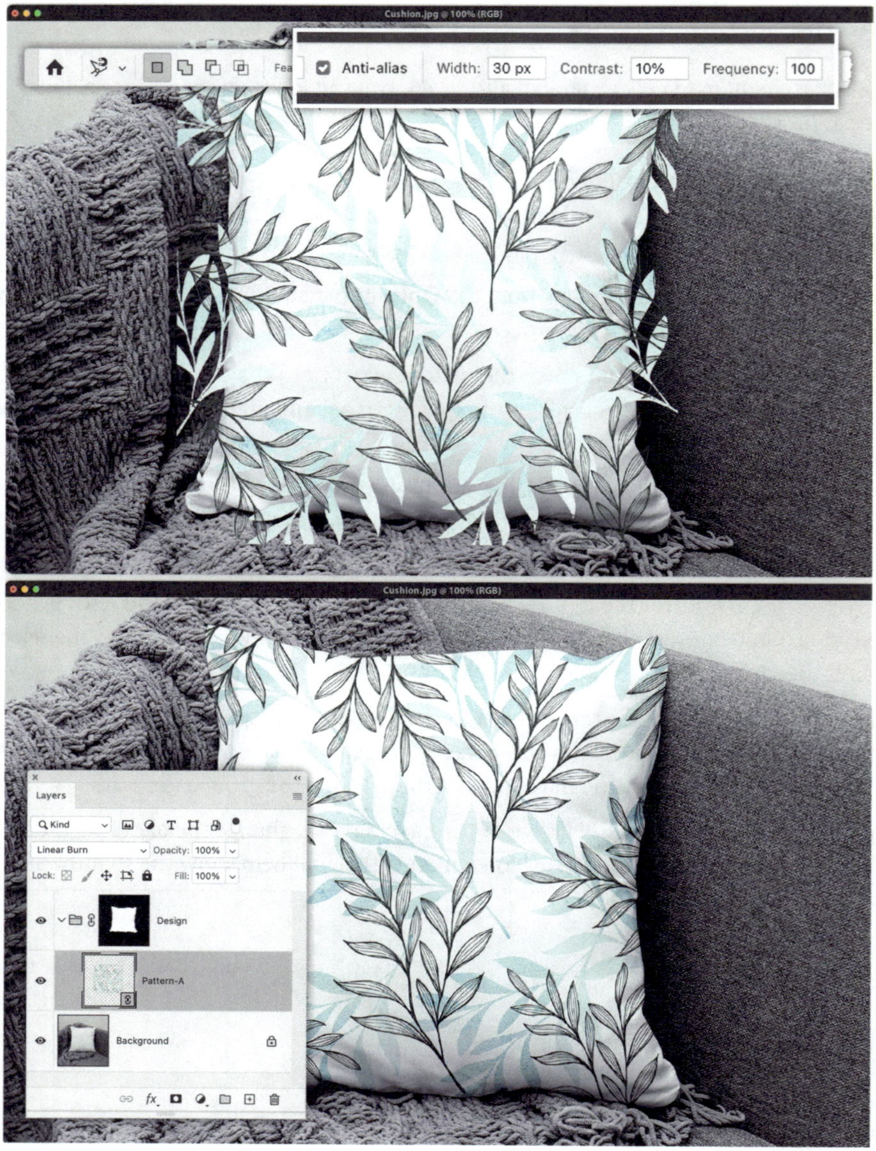

Figure 4.29: Applying a layer mask to the cushion design

Finessing the rippled surface details

As we have already witnessed, displacement maps provide a subtle yet effective level of detail to irregular surfaces. However, when a more aggressive form of distortion is required, **Liquify** is ideal:

1. Drag the **Pattern-A** layer into the layer group to apply the mask to it. Then, go to **Filter** → **Distort** → **Displace**. When the dialog appears, accept the default options as they tend to be a good starting point. Then, click **OK**.
2. Then, browse to the `04-Mockup` folder, select `Cushion-Displace.psd`, and click **Open**. You will notice that the pattern design matches the contours of the creases in the cushion.
3. Ensure that the **Pattern-A** layer is active and visible in the **Layers** panel. Then, go to **Filter** → **Liquify** to launch the dedicated editor.
4. When the dialog appears, expand the **View Options** section on the right-hand side and turn on the **Show Image** checkbox. Lower down in the same set of options, turn on the **Show Mask** checkbox, and set **Mask Color** to **Red**. Turn on the **Show Backdrop** checkbox and set the **Use** mode to **Background**, **Mode** to **Behind**, and **Opacity** to `100`.
5. The next stage involves "freezing" sections of the pattern artwork so that they are unaffected by **Liquify** and work in fold details. Switch to the **Freeze Mask** tool by pressing the *F* key. Hover your cursor over the **Liquify** image window to reveal the circular brush tip. To increase/decrease its size, you can change the **Size** slider on the top right-hand side of the interface.
6. Paint along the left edge of the fold located in the top-left corner of the cushion where a long fold can be seen. You will need to freeze that portion from the fold to the edge of the cushion by painting over it.

7. Then, switch to the **Forwards Warp** tool, located at the top left-hand side set of tools, by pressing the *W* key. You will need to make the brush size considerably larger than you might first expect. In this case, start by setting the **Size** slider to `400` px:

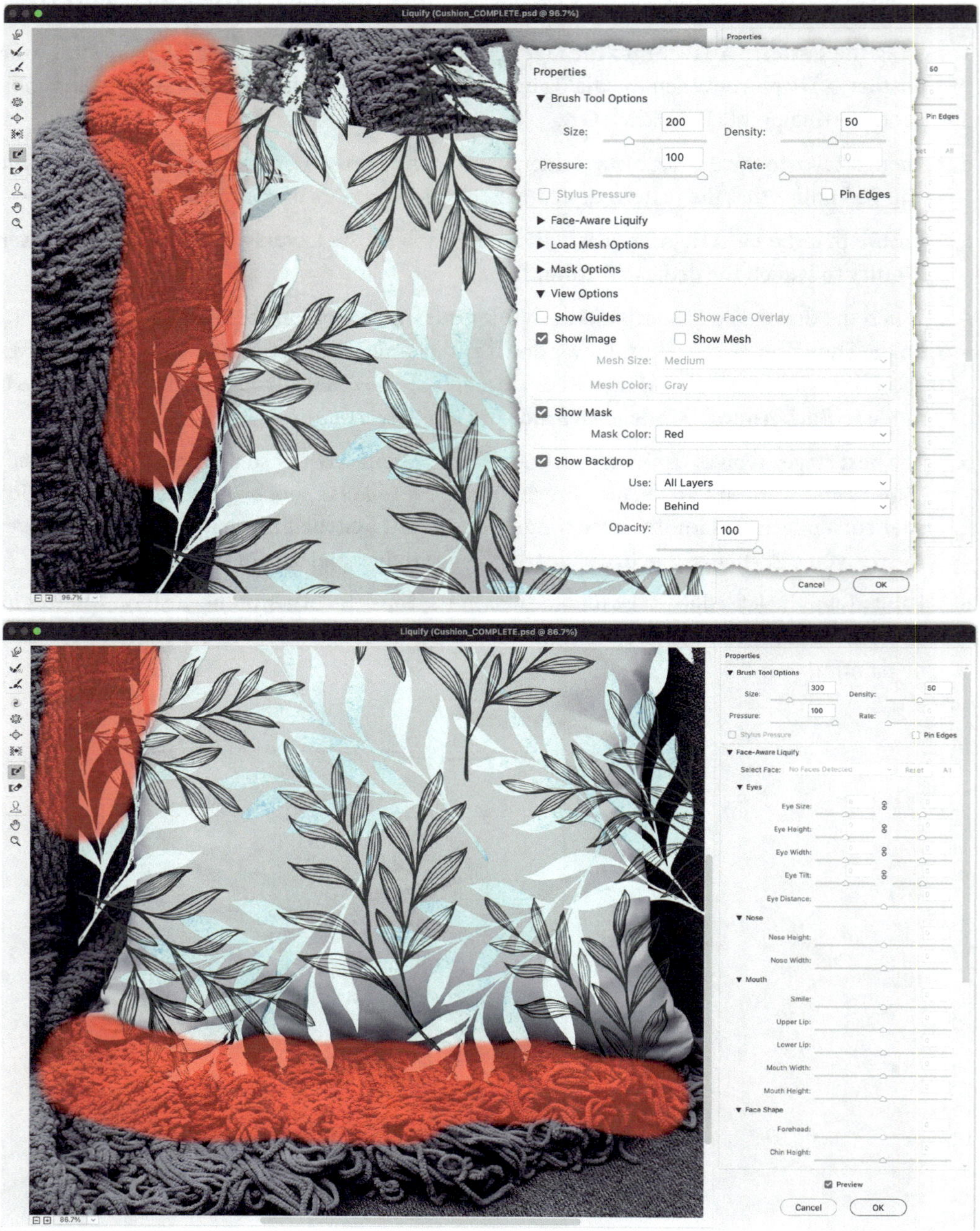

Figure 4.30: The red regions in Liquify freeze the artwork, preventing it from being affected

8. Then, hover your cursor over the right-hand side of the fold you just froze. Very gently, click and drag toward the fold on the left to create the impression that some of the pattern has disappeared behind the fold.
9. Repeat the same technique with other significant folds on the cushion where you feel it will provide value. Freeze one side of a fold, then warp the other. In places where the indentation changes, you can also distort the pattern so that it matches the changes in the cushion's surface.
10. Click **OK** when you're done to apply the changes and exit the **Liquify** dialog. Notice that the edits have been added to the **Pattern** layer's smart filters in the **Layers** panel. You can edit the **Liquify** edits whenever necessary.
11. Go to **File** → **Save As**, browse to the `04-Mockup` folder, name the file `Cushion.psd`, and close the document:

Freezing and thawing a Liquify mask

The masking tools in **Liquify** allow you to dictate which portions of an image can be affected or protected from warping edits. The **Freeze Mask** tool protects image areas, while the **Thaw Mask** tool removes masked regions. This is similar to painting black or white in a regular Photoshop layer mask.

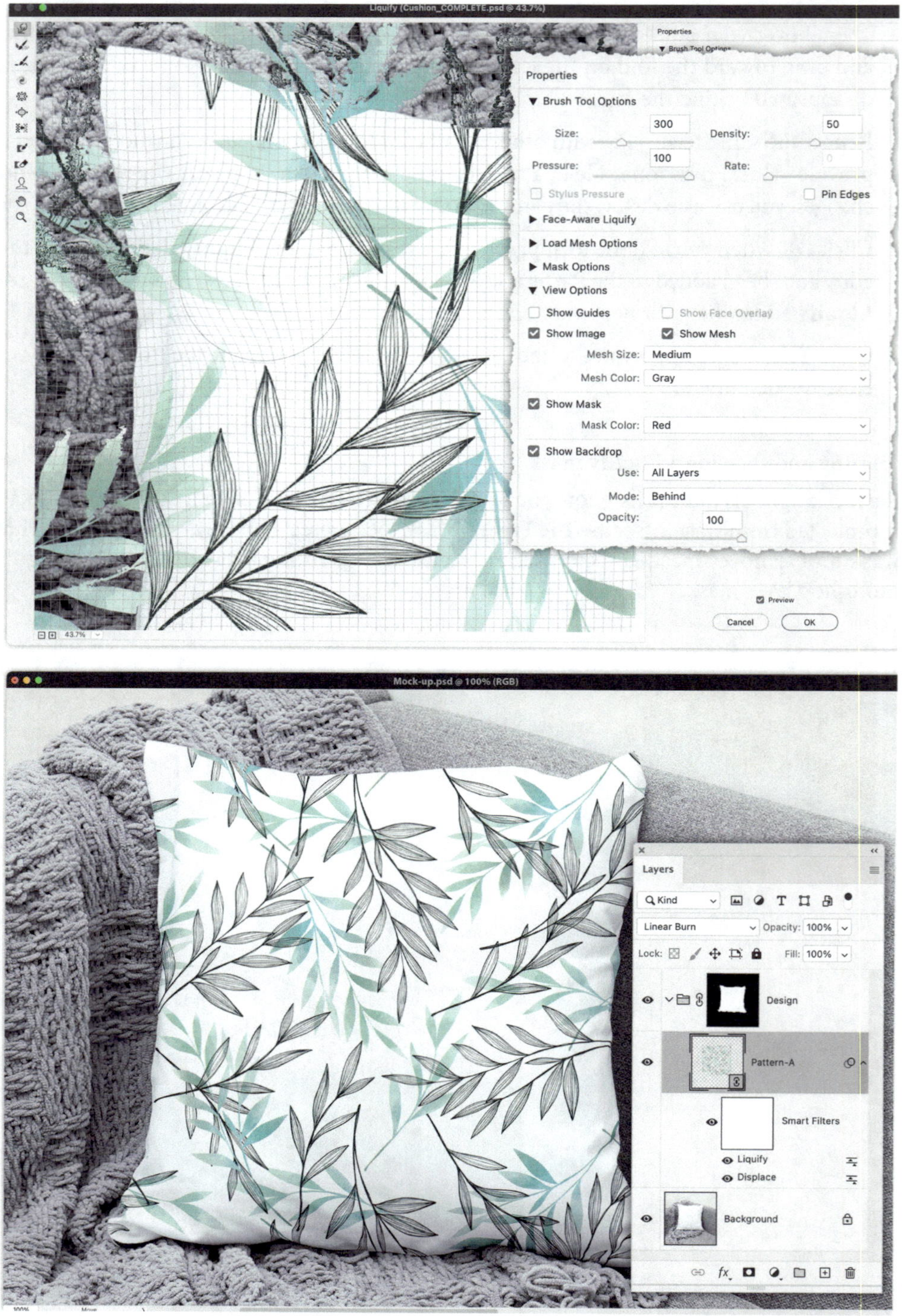

Figure 4.31: The Forward Warp tool morphs pixels to enhance the rippled effect

Replacing pattern artwork

Whenever you change pattern artwork with surface details applied to it such as displacement maps and liquify distortion, those edits remain intact. This makes mock-ups of this nature incredibly flexible. To replace the pattern layer artwork, simply right-click on the layer name of the pattern or placed artwork and choose **Replace Contents** from the context menu.

In this section, we applied original designs to fabric such as T-shirts, and in doing so, we matched the irregular contours of the material to make the mock-up look convincing enough that it can be used for marketing or as a tool to drive further design decision-making.

Summary

In this chapter, we looked at the multi-faceted challenges of creating branded mock-ups that have to look convincing and legible for either marketing purposes or to further inform decision-making during the design process. In some cases, the mock-up may only need to convey a look or approximation of the final product, but there may also be occasions when the visuals need to feel real and convincing.

To accomplish these challenges, we identified the characteristics that make a suitable source photograph, as well as the scene or scenario within which our prototype will appear.

Then, we applied the methods that are required to match a surface, whether it be a wall, a bottle, or a fabric such as a T-shirt, using **Vanishing Point**, transforms and warps, and displacement maps. Apart from **Vanishing Point**, which doesn't accommodate smart object layers, each technique could be edited, or the source artwork replaced with ease.

Finally, we looked at techniques for re-creating reflections and highlights or leveraging existing glass properties through the use of blend modes.

In the next chapter, we will continue with the theme of mock-ups and prototypes by creating print collateral such as business cards and flyers.

5

Creating Printed Marketing Collateral

Applications such as InDesign are adept at creating multi-page publications; however, this doesn't mean that you can't create single-page or front-and-back designs for print within Adobe Photoshop. In this chapter, you will create common print collateral such as flyers and posters that can be used internally or sent to a professional print provider for mass production.

We'll start by defining new document characteristics that are appropriate for print, ensuring PPI and color modes have been considered. Then we'll look at how to add bleed to a print file to ensure our projects are printed edge-to-edge on the destination paper stock using **Canvas Size**.

Guides will play an important role in setting up our print files, both to indicate the edges where our artwork will be trimmed and to identify a safe zone where type and other important content are kept clear from the paper edges when printed.

Photoshop isn't regarded as an application for editing vast amounts of text; however, the features and control it offers for a one- or two-page project are incredibly powerful, matching the granular control of its sister applications InDesign and Illustrator for basic character formatting.

It is possible to export to a range of file formats for print when working in Photoshop. These include JPG, TIFF, and Adobe PDF. We will carefully review each to ensure our projects are sent in the best possible quality for professional print output. In this chapter, we will explore the following topics:

- Creating new print documents
- Setting up a Photoshop grid system
- Importing artwork and formatting types
- Exporting documents for professional print

Technical requirements

The project files for this chapter can be found at: `https://github.com/PacktPublishing/Mastering-Adobe-Photoshop-2024/tree/main/Chapter05`

Creating new print projects

Unlike images intended for screen or use on the web, print projects require additional steps for managing the process from a digital desktop to ink and paper on a multitude of stock types. Mistakes in print can be costly; you don't have the luxury of simply replacing a print image as you would with a web graphic.

Color

It is common for artwork to be composed of **red**, **green**, and **blue** (**RGB**) pixels displayed on a backlit RGB display. When your RGB document is printed, those pixels are printed as tiny dots of ink using combinations of cyan, magenta, yellow, and black. These are the four inks used by a commercial print bureau on a standard print run. This process can cause a shift in the appearance of color as they are converted, so it is important to manage this process with screen and printed proofs. Photoshop can simulate printed colors onscreen (soft proof), providing an approximation of what your RGB colors could look like when printed. However, the best form of approximating print colors is to print them on a locally connected print device (hard proof). In addition, the print provider should supply a hard proof of their own before the final print run.

Printers' marks

Playing an essential role within the world of print, printers' marks are required for almost every print project. They help the print provider understand what should be done with the document (see *Figure 5.1)*.

Crop marks are thin lines placed on the corners of a print design that indicate where the paper should be cut to make it the correct size after printing. Crop marks are essential for any artwork, but especially if the design is to be printed to the edge of the trimmed paper.

Bleed is used when the printed publication is required to extend to the edges of the finished document. Bleed is typically extended 3 mm/0.125 inches or more beyond the edge of your media and is commonly used for materials that you would hold at a typical reading distance, such as magazines. Large-format print projects, such as pop-up stands and banners, will typically require a bleed of 10 mm or more. This will ensure that the finished, trimmed product is printed edge to edge. Without bleed, the likelihood of there being white, unprinted strips along one or more edges increases significantly.

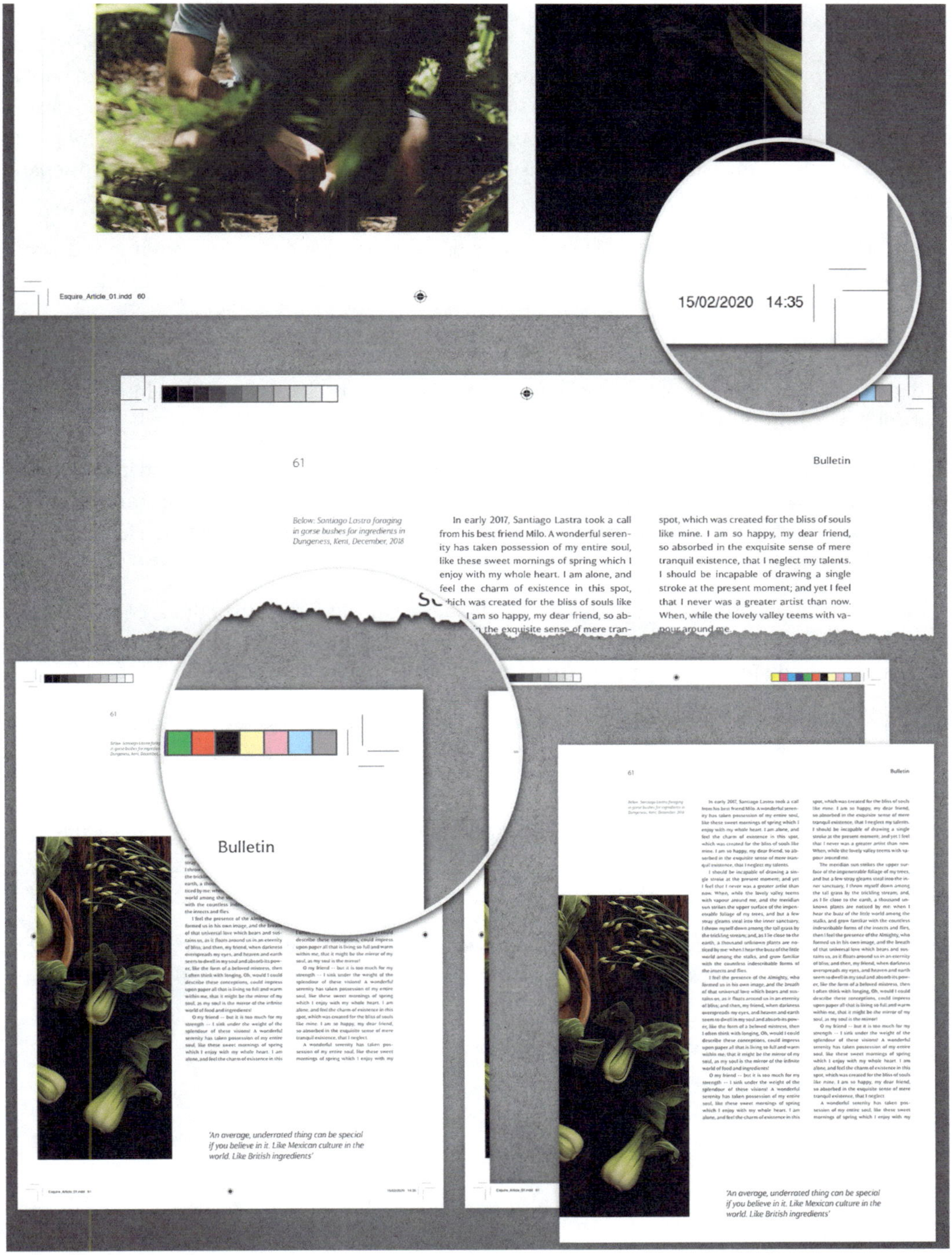

Figure 5.1: The printers' marks used to create professional print collateral

Folds

If your print project is an ambitious multi-page publication such as a brochure or a bound booklet, these would be better served by applications such as InDesign. By its very nature, Photoshop can only manage a single page of artwork in each document, stored within the canvas. This is ideal for printed posters where only one side needs to be visible, or perhaps a postcard composed of two separate documents, one for each side.

It is possible, however, to create short multi-page publications that contain no binding and instead incorporate folds (see *Figure 5.2)*. This would allow for two separate Photoshop documents to be created for the front and back of the print product.

One of the most common folds will no doubt be those used for greetings cards. A tent-fold is simply folded in half horizontally to create four pages: the front cover, back cover, and two internal pages. A tent-fold can be produced in portrait or landscape formats.

A tri-fold brochure is a perfect example of a common format used in print collateral, and it is economical to print, as it usually conforms to a standard A4 or letter size. Oddly, its name is misleading as it contains just two folds, not three. The result is a three-panel design printed on both sides, providing a total of six pages.

Tri-fold brochures feature one page that is slightly shorter in width than the others, enabling it to be tucked inside the other two. In an A4 format, two pages would measure 99 mm x 210 mm, whilst the shorter page would measure 97 mm x 210 mm.

A z-fold features two creases, forming six pages that are identical in width and height. For A4, that's 99 mm x 210 mm. The pages do not fold into one another but form a Z shape when opened out, making it look like an accordion.

An open gate-fold is creased twice to give six pages but contains a center page that is twice the size of the left and right page panels. This is ideal for adding arresting imagery to the inside center page. As the smaller panels are opened, they provide a dramatic reveal of the inner pages.

A roll fold features three creases that form eight pages. As the first page is opened, rather like a book, the inner pages that are tucked inside fold out in the opposite direction to the right-hand side, creating a rolling motion.

As we have already seen, Photoshop isn't intended to be used for large multi-page projects. However, multi-page designs can be generated from just two image files in Photoshop and combined with a combination of folds to form an interesting print product.

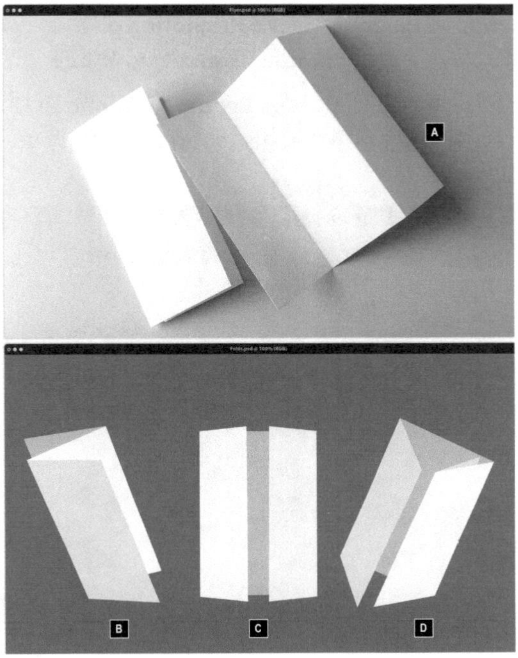

Figure 5.2: (A) Tri-fold, (B) z-fold, (C) open gate-fold, and (D) roll fold brochure types

In this section, we have examined a range of print terms and explored considerations for creating and managing print projects, from printers' marks to the types of documents suited to managing in Photoshop. In addition, we have also reviewed the challenges involved in working with RGB screen colors, which will ultimately be converted to CMYK ink. Next, we will create print templates furnished with grid systems.

Setting up a Photoshop grid system

Not every project starts with a digital photograph. There are occasions when it is prudent to start with a blank canvas and ensure that you are working to the target output size with all the correct quality settings in place from the get-go, including a grid system and bleed.

Building a new A4 poster document

In this first exercise, we will define document characteristics for a relatively simple, one-page print file that includes bleed, trim guides, and a safe zone for your copy:

1. Go to **File** → **New**. When the **New Document** dialogue appears, click on the **Print** tab at the top of the dialogue to display a series of page thumbnail presets. Click on the **A4** thumbnail. The word `Untitled` will be highlighted within the **Name** field on the right-hand side of the dialogue. This will become the file name when saved. Change the name to `A4-Poster-01`.

2. Change the **Orientation** to **Portrait**, enter a **Resolution** of `300 ppi`, and set the **Color Mode** to **RGB Color, 8-bit**. Change **Background Contents** to **White**.
3. In **Advanced Options**, change the **Color Profile** to **Adobe RGB (1998)**. Creating artwork in RGB and then converting to CMYK before print, when necessary, is the recommended workflow. Click **OK** when done.

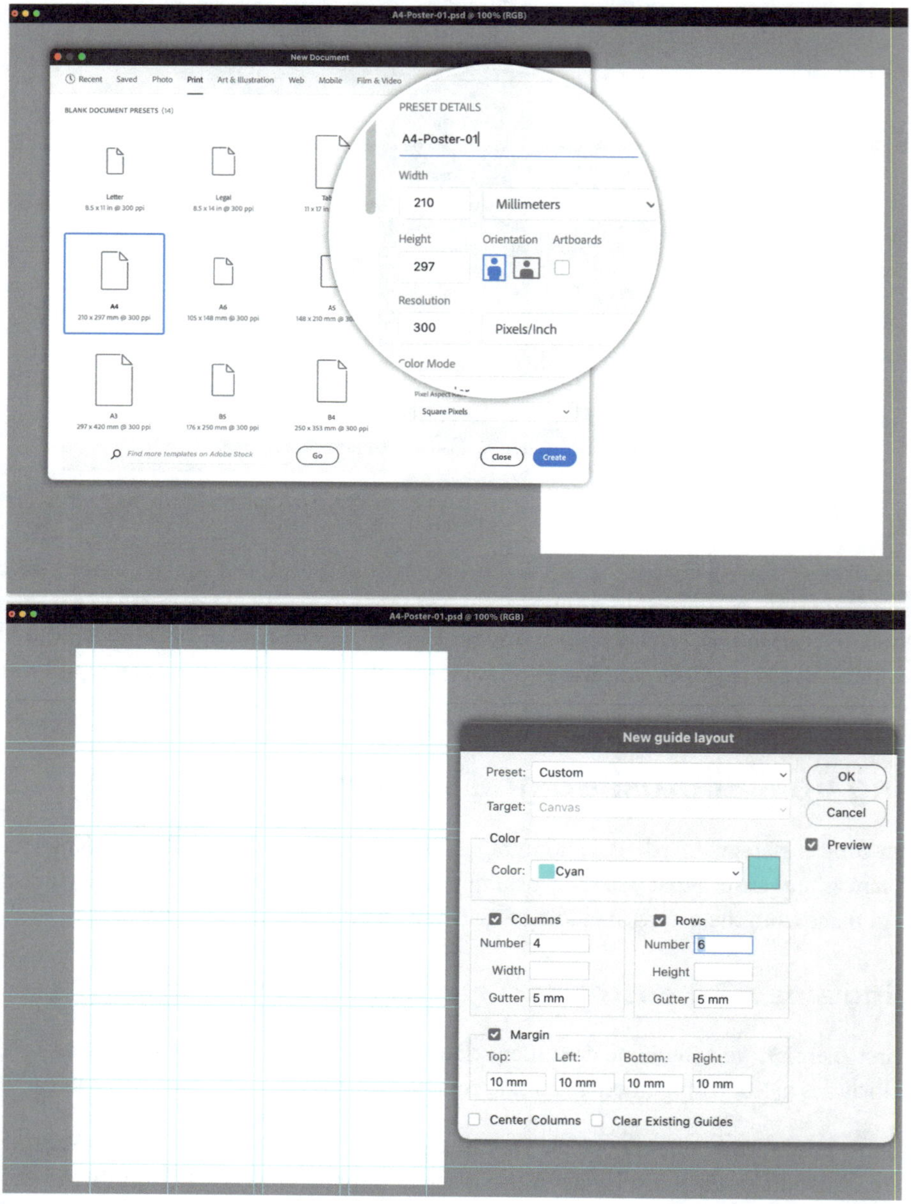

Figure 5.3: Custom document grids can be created in the New guide layout window

4. With the new document now open and active, ensure that the units are set to millimeters by going to **View** → **Rulers**. If a tick can be seen adjacent to the **Rulers** command in the menu this means they are active and visible in the **Image Window**, if not, click on the command to activate them. Then, right-click on either the vertical or horizontal ruler found around the edge of the **Image Window** and left-click on **millimeters** from the list.

5. Next, go to **View** → **Guides** → **New Guide Layout**. Set the guide **Color** to **Cyan** from the drop-down menu. Turn on the **Columns** checkbox and enter `4` into the **Number** field, leave the **Width** blank, and set the **Gutter** to `5 mm`. Turn on the **Rows** checkbox and enter `6` into the **Number** field, leave the **Height** blank, and set the **Gutter** to `5 mm`. Turn on the **Margin** checkbox and enter `10 mm` into the **Top**, **Left**, **Bottom**, and **Right** fields. Click **OK** when done.

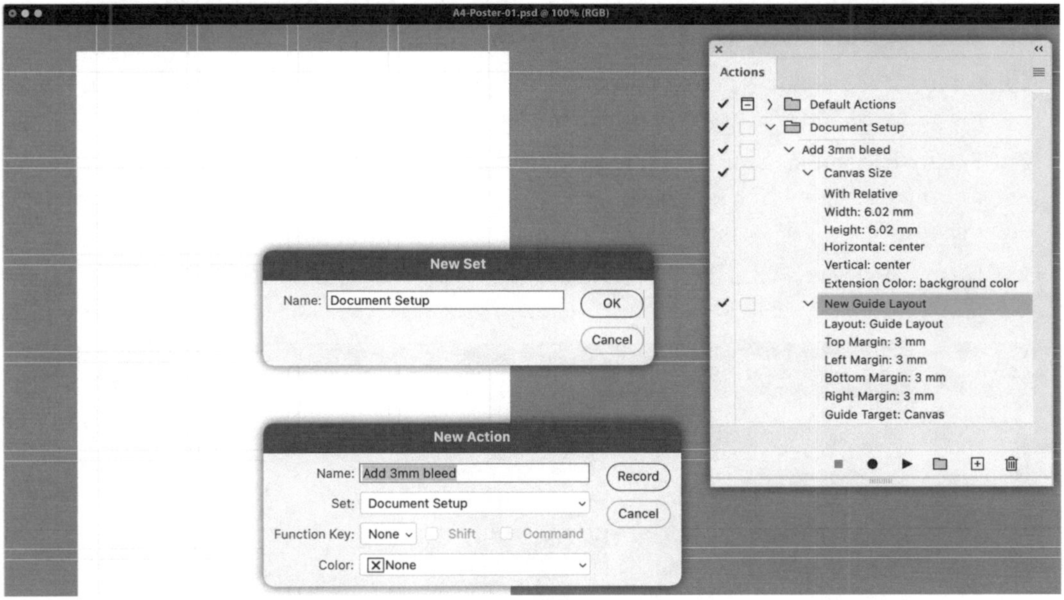

Figure 5.4: The Actions panel can record your Photoshop edits, such as adding bleed

6. Most print files created in Photoshop will require identical bleed settings, which can be recorded and used on any document in the future. Go to **Window** → **Actions**. When the panel appears, click on the folder icon at the bottom of the panel to create a **New Action Set**. Name it `Document Setup` and click **OK**.

7. Next, click on the **Create New Action** icon at the bottom of the **Actions** panel, shown as a circle symbol. **Name** the action `Add 3mm bleed`, ensure the action **Set** is defined as `Document Setup`, and click **Record**. Every edit you make will now be recorded—even clicking on different layers.

8. Go to **Image** → **Canvas Size**. Turn on the **Relative** checkbox found in the middle of the dialogue. This will set the **Width** and **Height** amounts to zero. Before you enter any values into the fields, ensure the **Units** are still set to **millimeters** from the drop-down menu. Enter `6` in both the **Width** and **Height** fields. This will add three millimeters of additional canvas on each edge of the current document, a standard bleed size for most print files that can be held in the hand at reading distance. Then, click **OK** when done to apply the edits.
9. Now that the bleed region has been added we need to add trim lines to visualize where the document will be trimmed down to after printing. Go to **View** → **Guides** → **New Guide Layout**. Set the guide **Color** to **Red** from the drop-down menu. Turn off the **Columns** and **Rows** checkboxes to deactivate them. Turn on the **Margin** checkbox and enter `3 mm` in the **Top**, **Left**, **Bottom**, and **Right** fields. Ensure that both the **Center Columns** and **Clear Existing Guides** checkboxes are deactivated before clicking **OK**.
10. Go to **View** → **Guide** → **Lock Guides**. This will prevent you from unintentionally repositioning the guides as you make edits to the document, which is easily done.
11. Finally, click on the **Stop Recording** icon at the bottom of the **Actions Panel**, which appears as a square symbol. You now have a quick way of adding bleed and trim lines to a print file in the future.
12. Go to **File** → **Save**. When the **Save As** dialogue appears, browse to the `05-Print` folder. Ensure that the format is set to `Photoshop (PSD)`, click **Save** when done, and close the document:

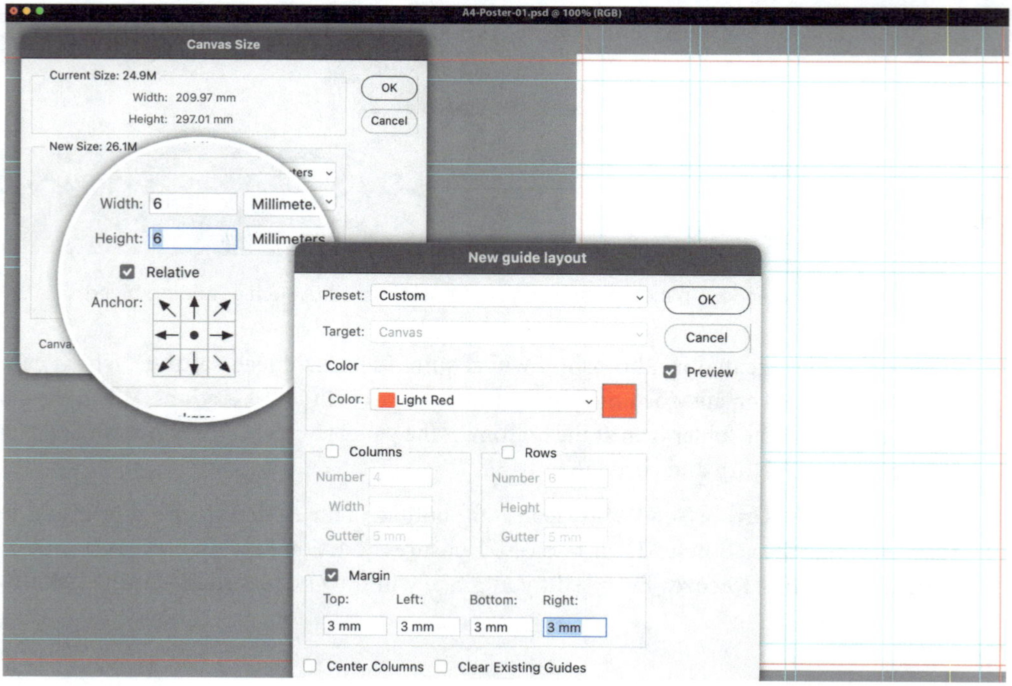

Figure 5.5: Add bleed marks

Creating a new business card template

In the previous exercise, we saw how a relatively simple A4 poster could be set up, accounting for bleed, trim lines, and a document grid. In this exercise, you will create a single document intended for creating a front and back design for a business card, but this time using layers to combine both designs:

1. Go to **File** → **New**. When the **New Document** dialogue appears, click on the **Print** tab, and then click on the **A4** preset thumbnail. Change the **Name** to `BizCards-01`.
2. Change the document **Width** to `85 mm` and the **Height** to `55 mm`. Set the **Orientation** to **Landscaped**, enter a **Resolution** of `300 ppi`, and set the **Color Mode** to **RGB Color, 8-bit**. Change **Background Contents** to **White**. Set the **Color Profile** to **Adobe RGB (1998)** and click **OK**.

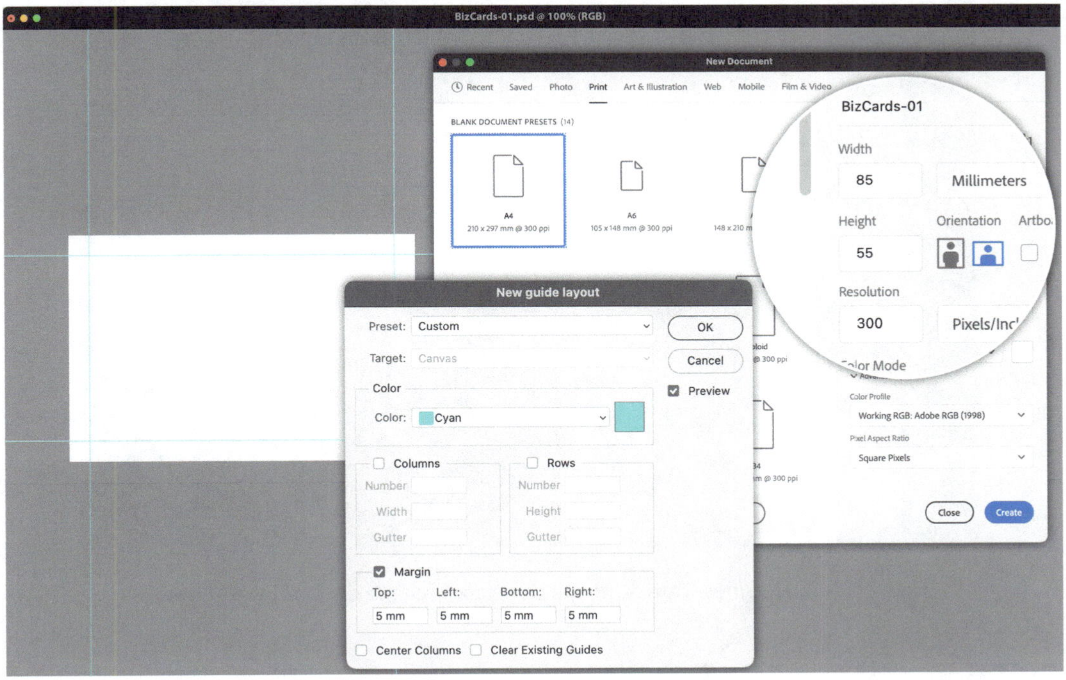

Figure 5.6: Add margins to the business card

3. As per the previous exercise, we need to denote a safe zone with guides. Go to **View** → **Guides** → **New Guide Layout**. Set the guide **Color** to **Cyan** from the drop-down menu. Turn off the **Columns** and **Rows** checkboxes to deactivate them. Turn on the **Margin** checkbox and enter `5 mm` into the **Top**, **Left**, **Bottom**, and **Right** fields. Click **OK** when done.
4. Now you will play the action created in the previous exercise. Go to **Window** → **Actions**. When the panel appears, left-click on the **Add 3mm bleed** action in the **Actions** panel. Then click on the **Play Action** icon at the bottom of the panel to apply the edits to the file.

5. Go to the **Layers** panel and click on the **New Group** icon at the bottom of the panel. When the group appears in the layer stack, change the name to `Reverse` and press *Enter*. Hover your cursor over the layer group visibility icon and right-click to reveal the context menu of color labels. Choose **Yellow** from the list. Repeat the same technique to create a second folder, but this time name it `Front` and set the group color to **Blue**.
6. Go to **File** → **Save**. When the **Save As** dialogue appears, browse to the `05-Print` folder. Ensure that the format is set to `Photoshop (PSD)` and click **Save** when done and close the document.

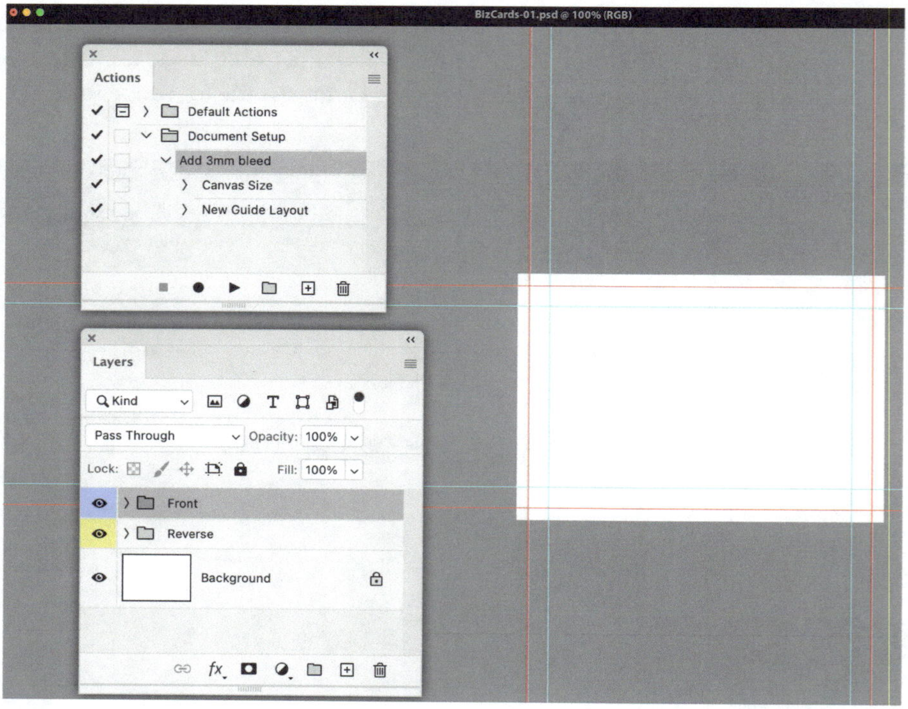

Figure 5.7: The business card template can store multiple designs in layer groups

Building a new z-fold brochure

In the last of our document-building exercises, we will set up a z-fold brochure template. This example will follow similar steps to the previous files, except we need to account for two folds within our grid system:

1. Go to **File** → **New**. When the **New Document** dialogue appears, click on the **Print** tab, and then click on the **A4** preset thumbnail. Change the **Name** to `Zfold-01`.
2. Change the **Orientation** to **Landscaped**, enter a **Resolution** of `300 ppi`, and set **Color Mode** to **RGB Color, 8-bit**. Change **Background Contents** to **White** and **Color Profile** to **Adobe RGB (1998)**. Click **OK** when done.

3. Go to **View** → **Guides** → **New Guide**. Add a `Vertical` guide at `99 mm`, set the guide **Color** to **Magenta** from the drop-down menu, and then click **OK**.
4. Repeat the same step, adding a second **Magenta** guides at `198 mm`. These guides will both indicate folds.
5. More guides! Add four **Cyan** guides at `94 mm`, `104 mm`, `193 mm`, and `203 mm`. These guides will indicate the inside margins for each of the three panels.
6. Go to **View** → **Guides** → **New Guide Layout**. Set the guide **Color** to **Cyan** from the drop-down menu. Turn on the **Margin** checkbox and enter `5 mm` into the **Top**, **Left**, **Bottom**, and **Right** fields. Click **OK** when done.
7. Go to **Window** → **Actions**. When the panel appears, left-click on the **Add 3mm bleed** action in the **Actions** panel. Then, click on the **Play Action** icon at the bottom of the panel to apply the edits to the tri-fold document.
8. Go to **File** → **Save**. When the **Save As** dialogue appears, browse to the `05-Print` folder. Ensure that the format is set to **Photoshop (PSD)** and click **Save** when done. Close the document when done.

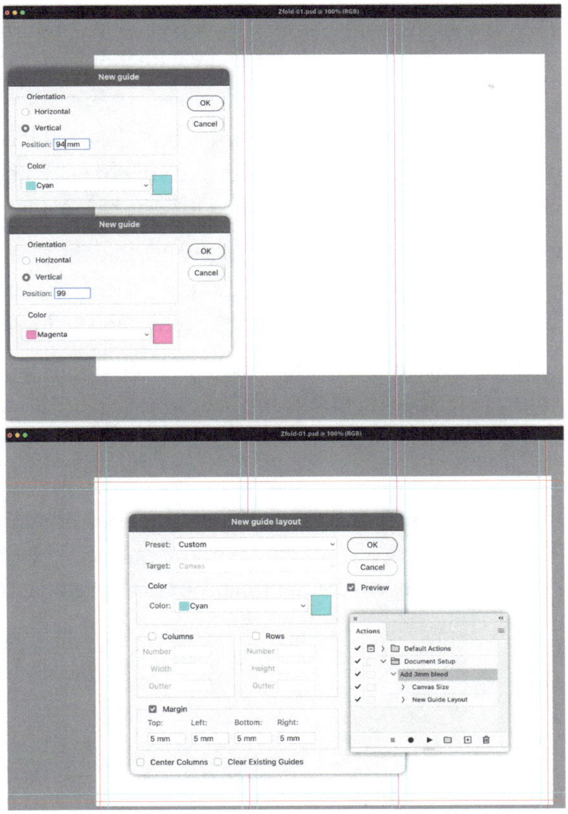

Figure 5.8: The z-fold brochure template and grid system

In this section, we have used a variety of tools for adding guides to a print file to indicate safe zones, trim lines, and bleed. Guides that can be added with millimeter precision and layout grids that form columns and rows allow for more broad methods of measuring the width and height of assets and assist in juxtaposing content. In the next section, we will add images, logos, and text to these templates.

Importing artwork and formatting types

We now have three print projects fully furnished with grid systems and other appropriate print settings. They just need arresting imagery and text, which is simple! There are good and better ways of importing assets, many of which we will address in the following exercises.

Creating a business card design using only vector assets

Follow the given steps below:

1. Go to **File** → **Open** and browse to the `05-Print` folder. Ensure that the format is set to `BizCards-01` and click **Open** when done.
2. Left-click on the layer group named `Front` to make it active. Then go to **File** → **Place Linked**, browse to the `05-Print` folder, and select the file named `WildCo_Logo.ai`. Click **Place** when done.
3. When the **Open as smart object** dialogue appears, accept the default options to import the first page of artwork by pressing **OK**. Ensure the **Width** and **Height** fields are linked before setting the scale to `11%`. Click on the **Commit** button in the **Options** bar to complete the import process.
4. Switch to **Move Tool** from the top of the **Tools** panel and drag the placed artwork to the top-left corner of the cyan-colored guides that denote the safe zone. If the imported artwork was not added into the `Front` layer group, drag it into the folder in the **Layers Panel**.
5. Photoshop doesn't allow you to import text from a saved document, so unfortunately, you will need to use your operating system file browser to locate the `BizCard-Copy.txt` file in the `05-Print` folder and open it. When the document opens, copy the text and return to Photoshop.
6. Switch to the **Horizontal Type Tool** from the **Tools** panel by pressing the *T* key. Hover your cursor level with the left-hand set of cyan guides in the canvas, under the imported logo. Then left-click and drag the cursor across to the right-hand set of cyan guides to create a new text frame.

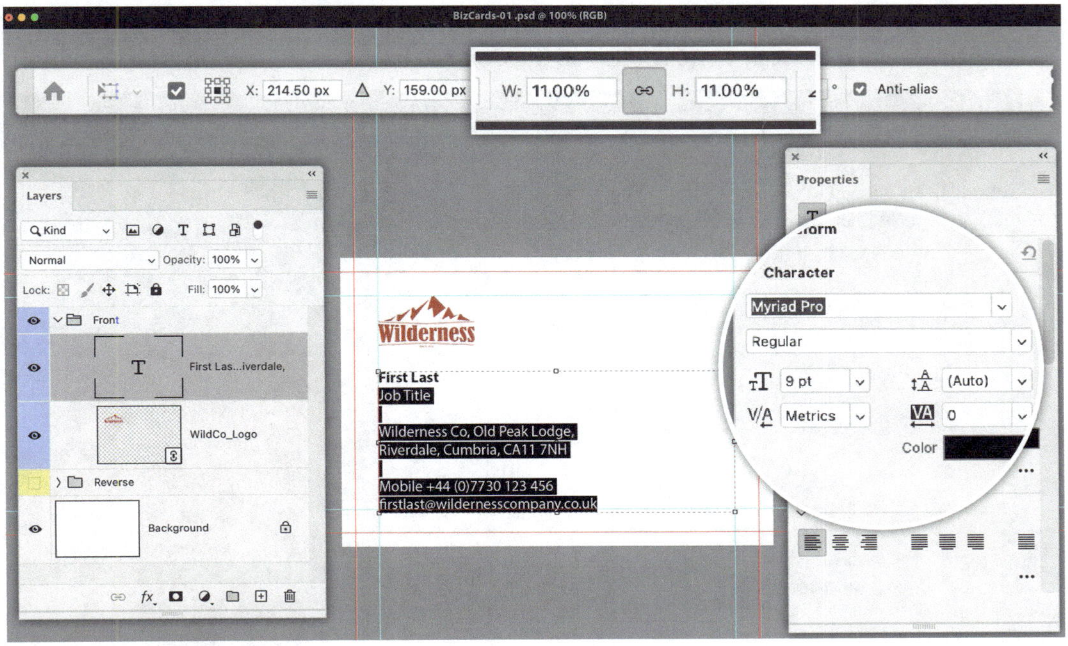

Figure 5.9: The completed front side of the business card design

7. With the text frame active, go to **Edit** → **Paste** to add the copy into the frame.
8. Highlight all text in the frame to make it active. Then, from the **Properties** panel, change the **Font** to **Myriad Pro**, set the **Size** to `9 pts`, and set the Paragraph option to **left align text**. Click on the **Set Text Color box**, also in the **Properties** panel, and enter `0` into the **Red**, **Green**, and **Blue** fields before making the text black. Click **OK** when done.
9. As a final touch, highlight the characters `First Last` within the text frame and change the **Font Style** to **Bold**. With the text edits now complete, press *Esc* to exit type editing mode and apply all edits to the text layer.
10. Right-click on the layer named `WildCo_Logo` in the **Layers** panel and choose **Duplicate Layer** from the list of commands. When the dialogue appears, change the layer name to `WildCo_Logo LARGE` from the **As field** and ensure **Destination** is set to the current document, `BizCard-01.psd`. Then click **OK**.
11. Drag the `WildCo_Logo LARGE` layer into the `Reverse` layer group folder in the **Layers** panel. Then turn off the `Front` layer group visibility.

12. Go to **Edit → Free Transform**. Ensure the link between the **Width** and **Height** fields is linked before setting the scale to `20%`. Click on the **Commit** button in the **Options Bar**.

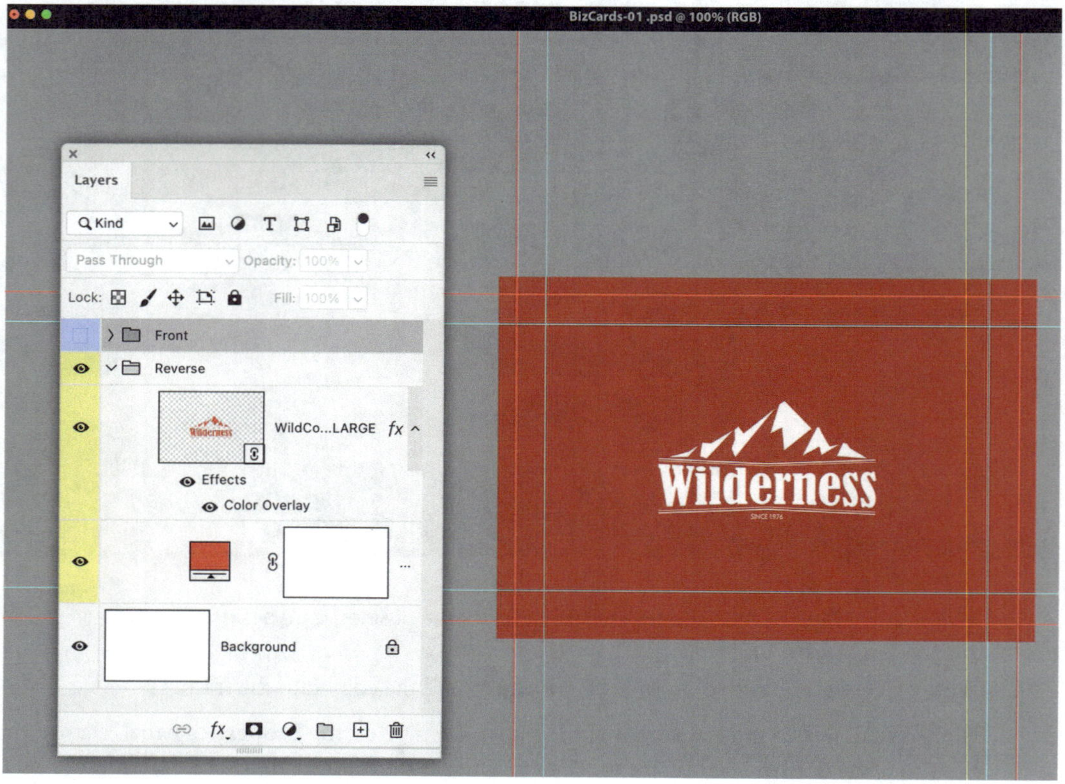

Figure 5.10: The completed reverse side of the business card design

13. Next, hold down *Shift* and left-click on the `Background layer` in the **Layers** panel to target (highlight) both layers in the stack. You should now see alignment options appear in the **Options** bar. Click on the **Align Horizontal Centres** and **Align Vertical Centers** icons to center the logo on the canvas.
14. Click on the `Background layer` in the **Layers** panel and click on the **Create new fill or adjustment Layer** icon at the bottom of the same panel to reveal the list of options. Choose **Solid Color** from the top of the list.
15. When the **Color Picker dialogue** appears, hover your cursor over the logo in the **Image** window and left-click to sample the red color of the logo. Click **OK** to add the **Fill Color** layer. This will make the logo disappear briefly, but we will correct that next.
16. Left-click on the `WildCo_Logo LARGE` layer in the **Layers** panel to make it active. Then click on the **Add a layer style** icon at the bottom of the same panel and choose **Color Overlay** from the list of options.

17. When the dialogue appears, click on the **Set color of overlay** square, adjacent to the **Blend Mode** menu, to open the **Color Picker**. Set the **Red**, **Green**, and **Blue** fields to `255`, making the color white, then click **OK**.
18. Go to **File** → **Save** to capture all edits. Then close the document.

In these layer groups, you now have the ability to generate designs for the front and back of the business card in a single document. Make each visible as necessary when they need to be exported for print.

Synchronizing fonts from Creative Cloud

Included with your monthly subscription to Creative Cloud is access to approximately 20,000 fonts. You sync them at any time to automatically install them. Here's how to synchronize fonts from Creative Cloud:

1. You can navigate to Adobe Fonts from the **Font Family** drop-down menu within Photoshop, from the Creative Cloud desktop app, or by heading to the website at `www.fonts.adobe.com`.
2. In the following exercises, you will need to sync two fonts, **Amatic Bold** and **Flood Std**. Ensure that you have signed into your Creative Cloud account by clicking on the account icon in the top-right of the web page.
3. Use the search field in the upper-right side of the site to find the fonts **Amatic Bold** and **Flood Std**. Once you reach the corresponding font page, scroll down the list of available font styles and click on the **Activate Font** button on the right side (see *Figure 5.11*). After a moment, the font will download, install, and become available to use in Photoshop.

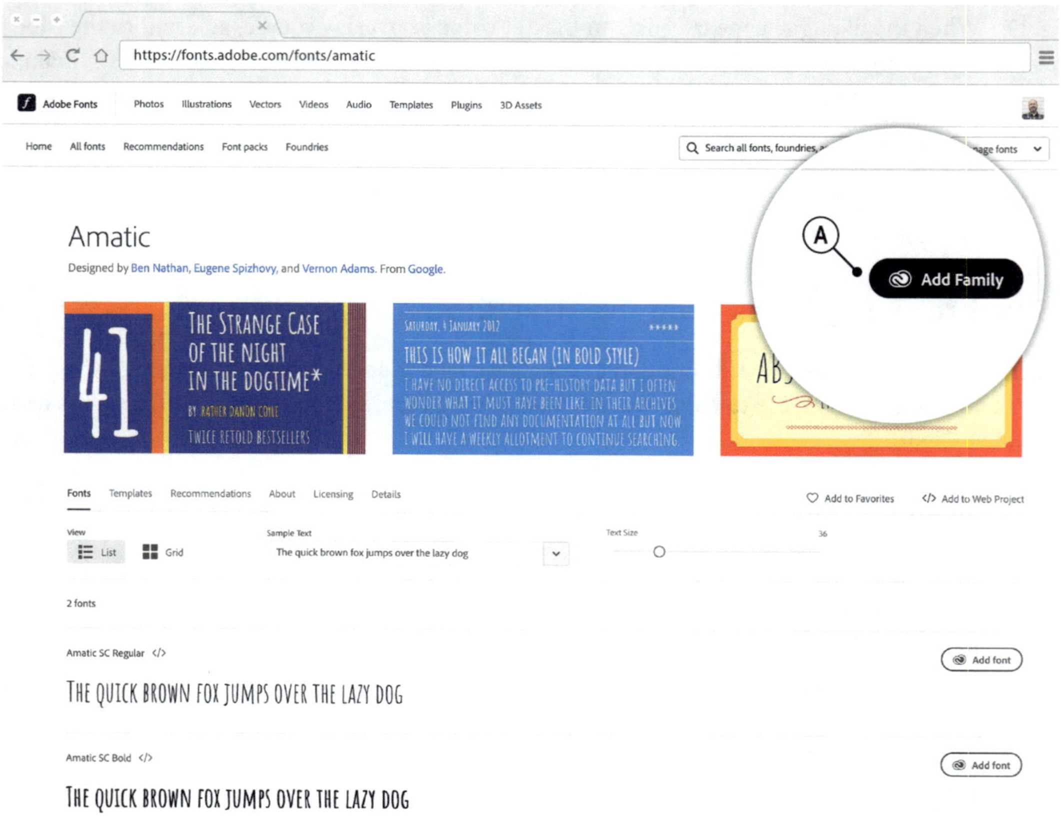

Figure 5.11: Sync fonts on the Adobe website by clicking on the Add Family button (A)

Adding a type to the z-fold brochure

Having experimented with importing types and branded images in the previous exercise, it's now time to take on a more challenging project and complete the z-fold brochure. You will edit a progressed version of the brochure to the one we created:

1. Go to **File** → **Open**, browse to the `05-Print` folder, and select `Zfold-Inner-01.psd`. Click **Open** when done.
2. Using the same technique in the previous exercise, use your file browser to locate the `ZFold-Copy-A.txt` file in the `05-Print` folder and open it. When the document opens, copy the text and return to Photoshop.

3. Switch to the **Horizontal Type Tool** from the **Tools** panel by pressing the *T* key. Hover your cursor over the center panel design in the middle of the canvas, level with the top cyan guides. Then, left-click and drag the cursor across to the right-hand cyan guides of the center panel design to create a new text frame. Then go to **Edit** → **Paste** to insert the text you copied.
4. Highlight all text in the frame to make it active. From the **Properties** panel, change the **Font** to `Myriad Pro` and set the **Size** to `9 pts`. Click on the **Set Text Color** box in the **Properties** panel and enter `255` into the **Red**, **Green**, and **Blue** fields to set the color to white. Click **OK** when done.
5. From the **Paragraph** options, set the alignment to **Justify last left**. This will force the text to use the full width of the text frame, creating a stronger regular region of text whilst keeping the last line of the paragraph left-aligned to avoid unsightly spaces between words.
6. Increase **Space After Paragraph** to `12 pts` to help indicate to the reader where new paragraphs start and finish.
7. Highlight all text in the first line of the text frame. From the **Properties** panel, change the **Font** to **Amatic SC** and **Bold** and set the **Size** to `24 pts`. Click on **Set Text Color** in **Properties** and enter `238` into the **Red** field, `200` into the **Green** field, and `50` into the **Blue** field to set the color to yellow. Click **OK** when done. Click on the **Commit** button under **Options** to apply the text edits.
8. Before finishing the type edits, ensure the text frame itself is the same size as the region within the cyan guides in the center panel. You can resize a text frame by hovering over one of the corner bounding box points of the frame and dragging them to the desired position. Press the *Esc* key to exit type editing mode and apply all edits to the text layer.
9. Go to **File** → **Open**, browse to the `05-Print` folder and select `Zfold-Outer-01.psd`. Click **Open** when done.
10. Switch to the **Horizontal Type Tool** from the **Tools** panel by pressing the *T* key. Create a new text frame in the center of the canvas. Type `Patagonia` into the text frame.
11. Highlight all text in the frame to make it active. From **Properties**, change the **Font** to **Flood Std** and set the **Size** to `52 pts`. Click on **Set Text Color** under **Properties** and enter `238` into the **Red** field, `200` into the **Green** field, and `50` into the **Blue** field to set the color to yellow. Click **OK** when done. Click on the **Commit** button under **Options** to apply the text edits.
12. Then go to **Edit** → **Free Transform**. Enter `-90` into the **Angle** field under **Options** to rotate the text so that the letter `P` is at the bottom and the letter `A` is at the top of the frame. Press *Enter* when done to apply the edits.
13. Switch to **Move Tool** from the top of **Tools**. Drag the `Patagonia` text frame across to the right-hand side of the canvas so that it is centered underneath the logo.

14. With the text layer still active, click on the **Fx** icon at the bottom of **Layers** and choose **Inner Shadow** from the list of effects to launch the **Layer Styles** dialogue. Set the **Angle** to `125°`, **Distance** to `8 px`, **Choke** to `0%`, **Size** to `6 px`, and **Opacity** to `75%`. Click **OK** when done.
15. Go to **File** → **Save** to capture all edits and keep both documents open for the next exercise.

Creating and applying paragraph styles

If there is one task that is repetitive and tedious, it's formatting text time and again with the same settings. Thankfully, paragraph styles allow you to capture type formatting and apply it elsewhere in your Photoshop document:

1. With the `Zfold-Inner-01.psd` open and active, go to **Window** → **Paragraph Styles**. Switch to the **Horizontal Type Tool** by pressing the *T* key. Then, double left-click on the text frame you added in the center panel of the flyer containing the titles and paragraphs of the copy. Ensure the type cursor is active in the first line of text, which contains the title.
2. Then click on the **Create New Paragraph Style** icon at the bottom of **Paragraph Styles** to add a new style, which will appear higher up in the same panel, named `Paragraph Style 1`. This style will need to be renamed by left-clicking on **Paragraph Styles** and going to the **Panel fly-out** menu located in the top-right of the panel.
3. Choose **Style Options** from the list. When the dialogue appears change the name to `Subhead` and click **OK**.
4. Repeat the same technique to create a new paragraph style, but this time select all the paragraphs of white text lower down in the text frame first. Once the style has been created, rename it by going to the **Panel fly-out menu** and enter `Body` into the **Style Name** field. Click **OK** when done.
5. Go to **File** → **Open**, browse to the `05-Print` folder, and select `Zfold-Outer-01.psd`. Click **Open** when done.
6. Next, you will apply this style to the new copy. Using your file browser, open the `ZFold-Copy-B.txt` file in the `05-Print` folder with any text editor you prefer. When the document opens, copy the text and then return to Photoshop.

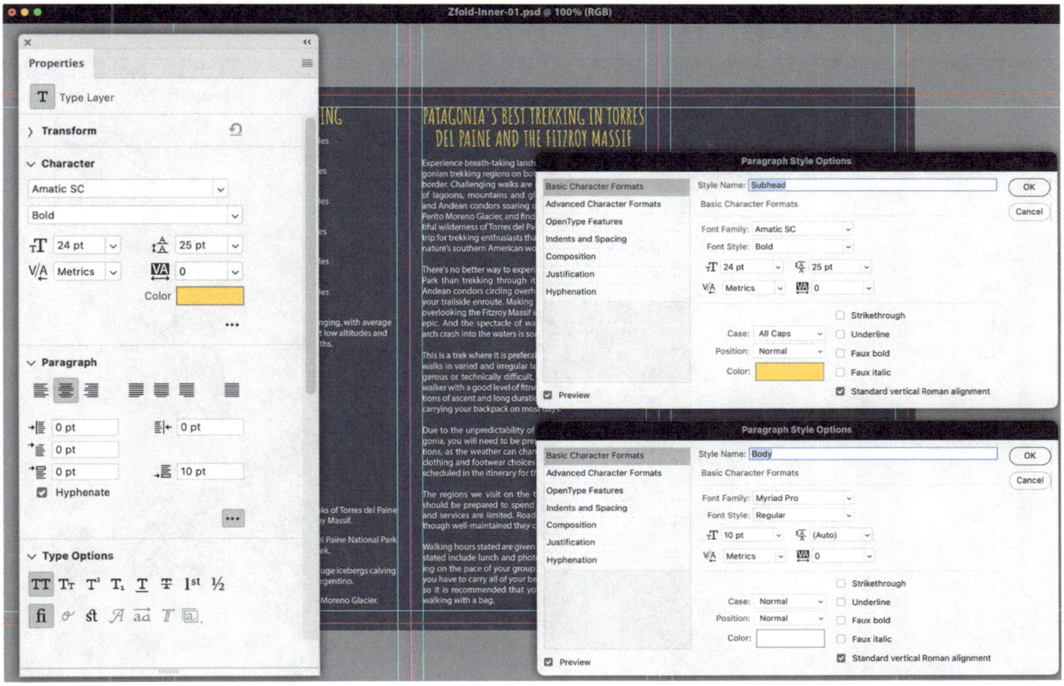

Figure 5.12: Create paragraph styles for the heading and body

7. Switch to the **Horizontal Type Tool** under **Tools** by pressing the *T* key. Create a new text frame in the center panel that is the same size as the previous one you made. Then go to **Edit** → **Paste** to insert the copied text.
8. Select all text in the frame to make it active and then left-click on the `Body` paragraph style located in the **Paragraph Styles** panel. You should now see that the formatting matches that of the first text frame you edited. Then, select all text in the first paragraph and left-click on the `Subhead` style to apply it to the selected text. Press the *Esc* key to exit type editing mode and apply all edits to the text layer.

9. Save both documents before moving on to the next exercise.

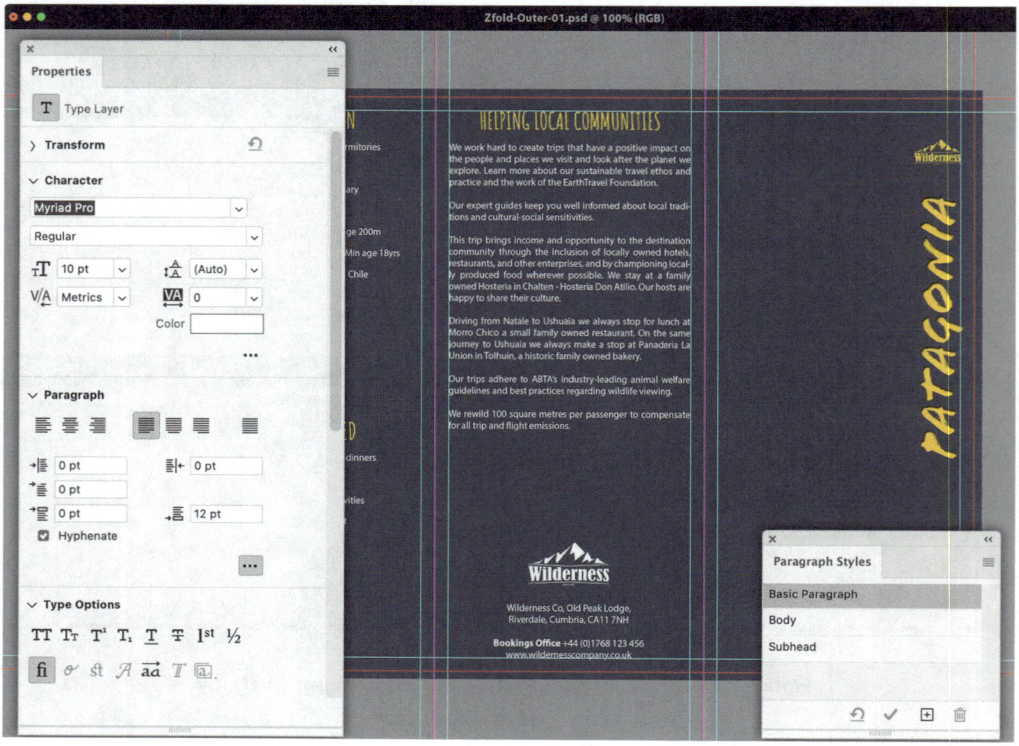

Figure 5.13: The completed type formatting for the internal z-fold brochure

About paragraph styles and character styles

To save time, Photoshop styles can be used to capture the appearance of existing later content. In the case of type, Photoshop can capture the type formatting of an active text layer or highlighted paragraph to create a paragraph style. The style can then be applied to other text layers, matching the original formatting. If you need to apply a style to just a single word or sequence of characters, then character styles can be used in the same way. To both capture and apply a character style, the desired text must be highlighted with the type tool.

Adding artwork to the brochure

With the text edits now complete, you can add the finishing touches to the outer flyer design in the form of new artwork:

1. With the `Zfold-Outer-01.psd` open, left-click on the layer group named `Front` in the **Layers** panel to make it active. Then go to **File** → **Place Linked**, browse to the `05-Print` folder, and select the file named `Paint.ai`. Click **Place** when done.

2. When artwork appears on the canvas, ensure the **Width** and **Height** fields are linked before setting the scale to `100%`. Drag the paint marks to the right-hand side so that half of the artwork is hidden off the edge of the canvas and it is centered vertically to the canvas. Click on the **Commit** button under **Options** to complete the import process.
3. Then go back to **File** → **Place Linked**, browse to the `05-Print` folder, and select the file named `Hiker.jpg`. Click **Place** when done.
4. When artwork appears on the canvas, ensure the **Width** and **Height** fields are linked before setting the scale to `14%`. Then drag the image of the hiker into a position directly in front of the paint marks on the right side of the canvas. Click on **Commit** under **Options** when done.

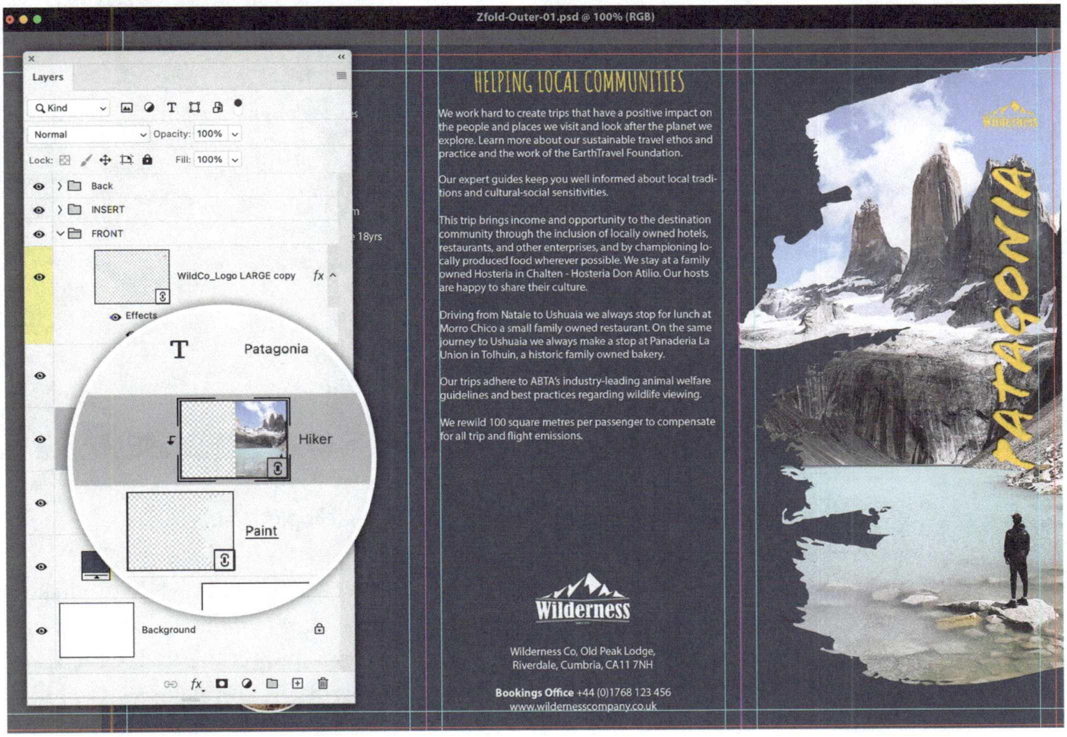

Figure 5.14: Create a clipping mask using the paint layer

5. Right-click on the layer name `Hiker.jpg` and choose `Create Clipping Mask` from the list of options. This will use the paint layer immediately underneath the photo as a mask. Reposition the photo so that all of the hiker is visible and no grey paint strokes can be seen.
6. Make the `Zfold-Inner-01.psd` active. Expand the layer group named `Inside Left` under **Layers** and left-click on one of the text frame layers in the group to make it active.
7. Switch to the **Ellipse Tool** under **Tools** by pressing the *U* key, then click and hold the active tool to reveal the popup. Left-click on the **Ellipse Tool** icon.

8. Hover your cursor over the left panel of the brochure, where the empty space appears between the two text frames, and left-click to launch the **Create Ellipse** dialogue. Enter a **Width** and **Height** of `30 mm` and then click **OK**.

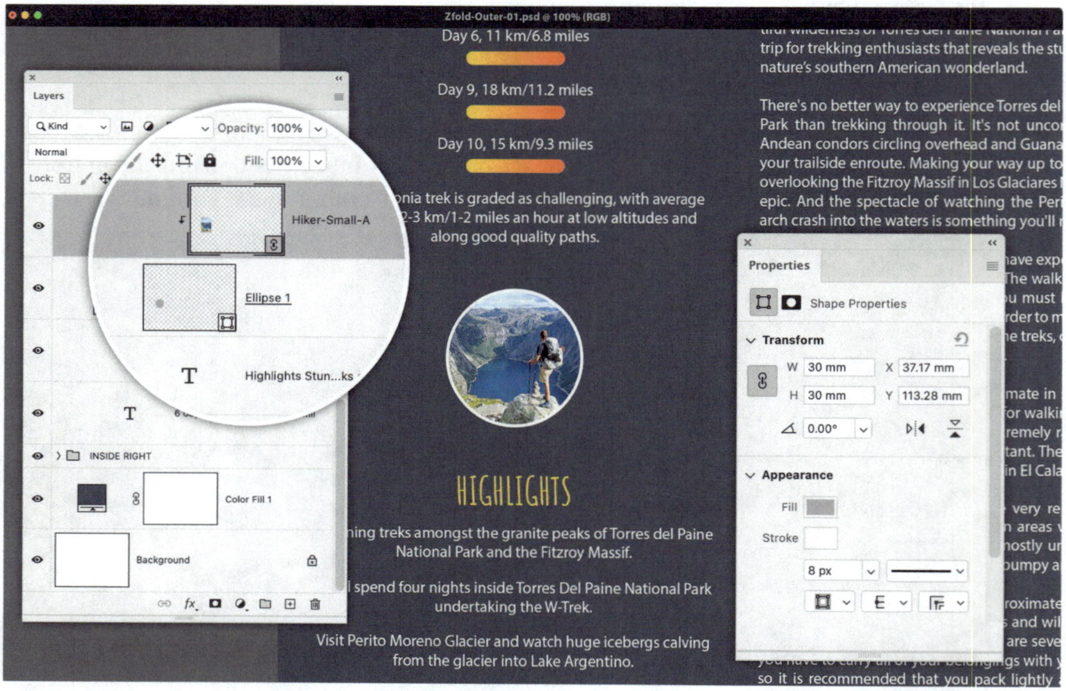

Figure 5.15: Add the hiker image to the circle using a clipping mask

9. When the shape appears, go to the **Properties** panel and set the stroke to white by clicking on the **Set Shape Stroke Type** icon adjacent to the word **Stroke**. When the dialogue appears, click on the **Color Picker** icons located in the top-right corner and set the **Red**, **Green**, and **Blue** values to `255`, then click **OK**. Enter `8 pts` into the **Stroke Width** field. Set the **Fill** of the circle to anything you wish; it will be hidden shortly, but a fill color is required.

10. Switch to the **Move Tool** and reposition the ellipse in the center of the empty space between the two text frames, and horizontally central to the text.

11. Go to **File → Place Linked**, browse to the `05-Print` folder, select the file named `Hiker-Small-A.jpg`, and click **Place** when done. Right-click on the layer name `Hiker-Small-A.jpg` and choose **Create Clipping Mask** from the list of options. This will use the fill of the circle as a mask but keep the white of the stroke.

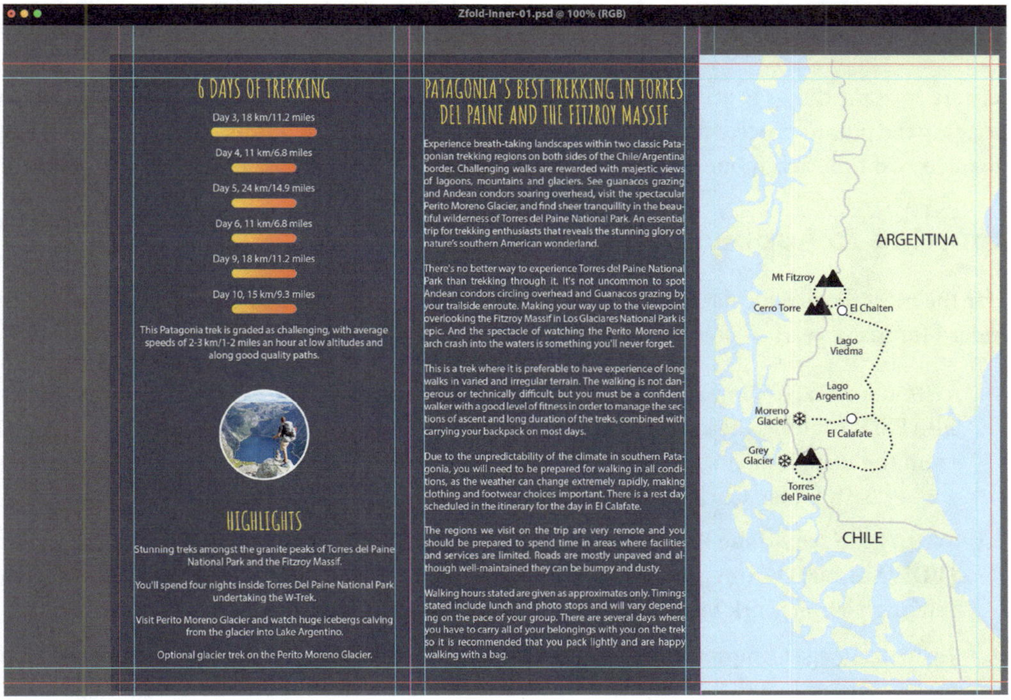

Figure 5.16: The completed z-fold brochure inner design

12. When artwork appears on the canvas, ensure the **Width** and **Height** fields are linked before setting the scale to `52%`. Drag the photo to appear in the same place as the circle you just made. Click on the **Commit** button under **Options** to complete the import process.
13. Left-click on the layer group named `Inside Right` under **Layers** to make it active. Go to **File** → **Place Linked**, browse to the `05-Print` folder, select the file named `Map.ai`, and click **Place** when done.
14. When artwork appears on the canvas, ensure the link between the **Width** and **Height** fields are linked before setting the scale to `100%`. Drag the map to the right-hand edge of the canvas, central to the canvas. Click on the **Commit** button under **Options** to complete the import process.
15. Go to **File** → **Save** when done and then close the document.

In this section, we have utilized techniques that allow for greater flexibility when editing project assets. We have seen how logos created in Adobe Illustrator can be placed into a Photoshop document and linked live to the source file. This means that any edits to the logo in Illustrator will be reflected in the Photoshop file. Text that can be edited at any point by double left-clicking to go into type editing mode, where all type of editing features remain available despite adding layer styles and effects to text. Color overlays and color fill layers that match brand colors accurately can also be edited by double-left-clicking the layer thumnail in the **Layers** panel. In the next section, we will export artwork in a variety of formats for professional print.

Exporting documents for professional print

There are so many things to account for when outputting your artwork for hand-off to a print bureau. Managing the output process for this option is far more critical than output to the web, as mistakes here often cost time and money.

Exporting to Adobe PDF

By far the most flexible format to pass onto a third-party print provider, PDF has been the industry standard for many years. It preserves vector shapes and text layers:

1. With the `Zfold-Inner-01.psd` document open, go to **File** → **Save** to ensure the master file **(PSD)** captures the latest edits. Then go to **File** → **Save a Copy** and choose **Photoshop PDF** from the format menu. Change the file name to `Trifold-ProPRINT` and browse to the `05-Print` folder. Click **Save**.
2. When the **Save Adobe PDF** dialogue box appears on screen, change the Adobe PDF preset to **[PDF/X-4:2001]** from the drop-down menu. This is the recommended option to pick when sending your artwork to a print bureau. Turn on the **View PDF after Saving** checkbox.
3. Go to the **Image Compression** heading on the left to reveal the options. Set **Bicubic Downsampling** to `300` and ensure that **Image Quality** is set to **Maximum**.
4. Go to **Output** from the list on the left-hand side and ensure that **Color Conversion** is set to **Convert to Destination**. Your document CMYK should be set to the **Destination** of `Coated FOGRA39` (or whatever is appropriate for your region), which is taken from Photoshop's color settings, as defined in *Chapter 1*.
5. Click on the **Save PDF** button when done. Your PDF will shortly launch for you to review. If you have not installed Acrobat Pro or Acrobat Reader, the PDF may launch in an alternative third-party application. Review the exported document and print a hard copy to a locally connected printer to evaluate any color shifts that may have occurred.

Export to the Tag Image File Format

The **Tag Image File Format** (**TIFF**) is still accepted by many print providers, especially magazines for supplying images for an ads section. Like the PDF format, TIFF can preserve all of the same things PSD can, including layers:

1. With the `Trifold-01` document open, go to **File** → **Save a Copy** and choose **TIFF** from the format menu. Change the file name to `Trifold-ProPRINT` and turn off the **Layers** checkbox. Browse to the `05-Print` folder, and click **Save**.
2. When the **TIFF Options** dialogue appears, set **Image Compression** to `None`. This will avoid issues with compatibility when opened on other devices. Turn off the **Image Pyramid** checkbox and leave **Pixel Order** as the default setting of **Interleave**. **Byte Order** can be set to either **IBM**

PC or **Macintosh** to address a historical issue with sharing files between different platforms. If you didn't turn off the **Layers** checkbox in the previous dialogue, choose **Discard Layers and Save a Copy** from the **Layer Compression** settings. Click **OK** when done.

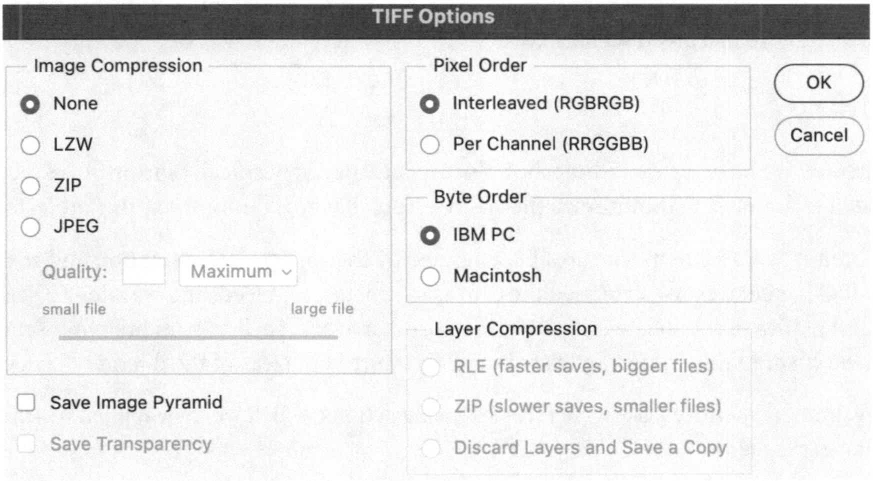

Figure 5.17: The TIIF options dialogue box

Saving as a JPG

The JPG format is incredibly flexible for continuous tone images, such as photos with millions of colors. The truth is that the human eye cannot detect the subtle differences between a printed PSD, TIFF, or JPG. If you are printing a high-end photographic project where fine quality is of paramount importance, then I would suggest avoiding JPG and instead using PDF or TIFF. But for many other use cases, JPG is a suitable alternative to PDF and TIFF:

1. With the `Trifold-01` document open, go to **File** → **Save a Copy**, choose **JPG** from the format menu. Change the file name to `Trifold-ProPRINT`, browse to the `05-Print` folder, and click **Save**.
2. When the **JPEG Options** dialogue appears, ensure **Quality** is set to **Maximum**. You can ignore the **Format Options** as they relate to web and screen output. Click **OK** when done.

> **File formats that should be avoided when printing**
>
> If there is one file format that I've seen used wrongly for print projects over the years, it must be **portable network graphic** (**PNG**) format. It was created as a free alternative to GIF and is only intended for screen and web output. Like the GIF format, it is most effective when saving images that possess 256 colors or less. For similar reasons, GIFs should also be avoided when dealing with print.

In the final section of this chapter, we have reviewed techniques for exporting artwork from Photoshop to pass onto a print provider, ensuring that all of our diligent work to build files fit for print are not undermined by choosing an inappropriate file format. Where necessary, we have also discussed the strengths and the limitations of those image formats so that you can make informed choices about which format to use in a given scenario.

Summary

In this chapter, we have created Photoshop documents made specifically for print. We've utilized a multitude of techniques that minimize the costly errors that are common in print projects.

We have built new documents that are characterized by the appropriate resolution and size to match common ISO paper sizes. We extended the canvas to account for bleed, and we added a series of grid systems and guides that indicate critical parts of print artwork, such as trim lines and safe zones. In doing so, we ensured that important visuals and text were kept clear of the document edges.

Time-consuming, repetitive tasks were recorded using actions, which we then applied in other projects at lightning-fast speeds.

We built flexibility into each project, from logos that were linked to an original Illustrator document to text that could be edited at any point. We also applied color overlays that allow for a single logo to contain different brand colors that can be turned on or off at the click of a mouse.

These techniques will be built upon in the next chapter, as we will create a set of social media templates.

6

From Pixels to Post: Images for Social Media

According to Statistica's data analysts, there are approximately 4.89 billion social media users worldwide, estimated to rise to 6 billion by 2027. On average, an online user will spend 144 minutes daily on social media platforms. With that kind of reach, you can understand the attraction for brands to engage online with their audience.

Businesses often pay a consultancy to manage their social media accounts. Given that over 30 platforms boast 100 million active users monthly, you can understand why. Where do you begin? If you've had to manage content for merely a small business with a modest customer base, you'll appreciate that it is a monumental task.

Over the years, I've worked with in-house design teams managing brand accounts. In that time, I've realized this type of work must respond to changing events within minutes rather than hours to be effective. Your artwork must be simple to edit with as little repetition of tasks as possible and adapt to a plethora of output sizes for each platform.

There are several features built into Photoshop that, when combined, provide a highly efficient workflow for creating and exporting visuals for the web and social media. These are tools that, although not initially intended for generating social media images, have proven essential to my Photoshop workflow.

This chapter will aim to address the challenges of creating social media content, focusing on the following topics:

- Creating new documents for screen and web
- Working with artboards
- Duplicating artboards
- Exporting and scheduling posts

Technical requirements

The project files for this chapter can be found at: `https://github.com/PacktPublishing/Mastering-Adobe-Photoshop-2024/tree/main/Chapter06`

Creating new documents for screen and web

In the previous chapter, we looked at the challenges involved in managing print projects. Whilst we don't have to furnish our web projects with bleed, trim, and other print characteristics, we are required to manage a sizable number of images, each with specific sizes for a multitude of platforms. The challenge here is the impact of repetition. The same artwork you use for Twitter, recently rebranded as 'X', will need to be adapted for LinkedIn, Pinterest, Facebook, and so on. What might seem like a minor text edit in a single file for print now becomes a time-consuming ripple effect across dozens of graphics. This calls for an organized approach and smart workflows.

Historically, Photoshop was only capable of producing a single page of artwork in each document, limited by its canvas. But with the release of CC2015, Adobe introduced artboards, allowing for multiple pages. Initially, artboards were intended to address the growing number of screen sizes available in a growing smartphone and tablet market. However, they can be adapted for social media campaigns. Each artboard is labeled to distinguish it (*Fig 6.1, C*), and the process of adding or duplicating artboards is made simple with widgets (*Fig 6.1, D*). Create an additional blank artboard by left-clicking a Widget or *ALT (Windows) or Option (macOS)* to duplicate the artboard along with its corresponding artwork.

Imported images will be protected as smart objects and include gradient effects to make text legible (*Fig 6.1, A*). Gradient effects can be edited from the **Layers** panel and adapted to suit the specific image and text colors. Imported logos will have multiple color overlays (*Fig 6.1, A*) applied, making it easier to switch brand colors by revealing and concealing the appropriate overlay rather than having to reimport artwork. Text in each of our social posts will be linked to the original files as smart objects. This means that when we make changes to the text, they update wherever we need them to, reducing the amount of repetitive work.

When it comes to creating the final image file for posting online, we'll avoid having to save each artboard by using scripts that are built into Photoshop to automate this process. There are predetermined file names, file types, and compression settings. Don't be put off by the term scripts; you'll be interacting with them via dialogue that looks like any other in Photoshop.

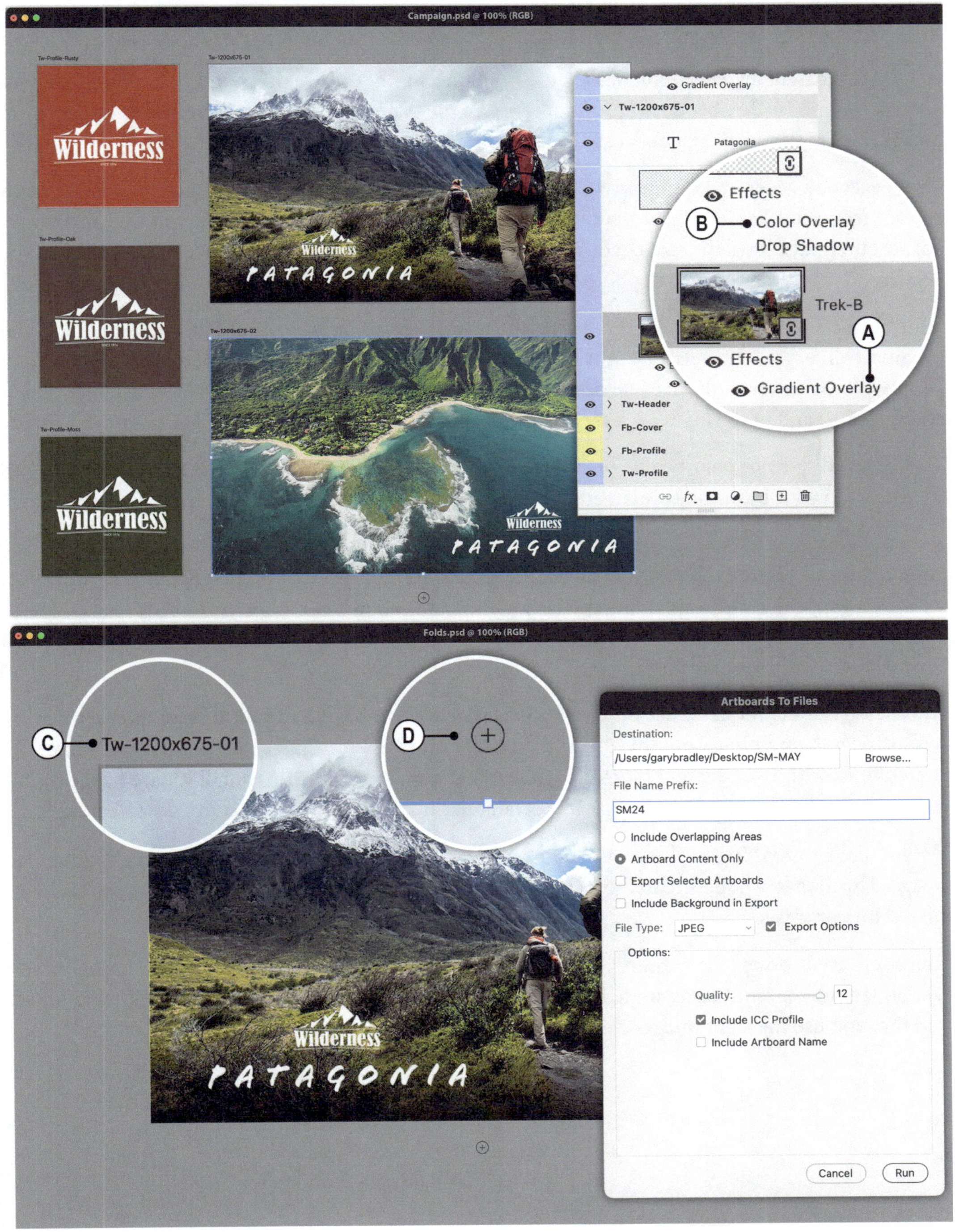

Figure 6.1: Photoshop artboards managed through the Layers panel

Creating artwork for Facebook

According to Statista, Facebook has over 2.7 billion monthly active users and is the world's largest social network. In October 2020, 13.1% of users on the platform were women between the ages of 25 and 34, and male users aged between 25 and 34 accounted for 19.3%.

Your Facebook cover photo (*Figure 6.2, A*) will only appear on your Facebook timeline, and like many social media sites, it's far bigger than your profile picture at 820 x 312 pixels. If you upload artwork smaller than this, it will be stretched. Your profile picture is an appropriate place for a picture of you or a brand logo. Use your cover photo to post something that encapsulates your brand or mission.

Your business profile photo (*Figure 6.2, B*) is the primary image representing you, your brand, or your organization across the network. It will be seen across the platform in several places by numerous people, so, as I'm sure you have guessed by now… ensure that your artwork is free from clutter, easily recognizable, and of the highest quality possible!

The largest display of your profile picture can be found on your homepage, where it can be viewed by visitors to your business page. In addition, a smaller version of your profile image will appear in a follower's stream every time you post (*Figure 6.2, C*).

A shared image (*Figure 6.2, D*) is one of the most common forms of posting on Facebook. Your posts will always appear on your timeline, and they should be seen by your followers in their feeds. As with most social platforms, the more people engage with your post, the more likely your followers and their followers will also see it.

Another great technique to use on Facebook is sharing a link (shared link image). It's very similar to posting a shared photo, but this method provides more opportunities to add data. You can create shared links with two different types of layout styles: a shared link with a small square image on the left and your copy on the right or a larger rectangular image on top with text underneath.

Do you have something to shout out about? You can also celebrate a milestone with a highlighted image. This image will be situated on your personal timeline, but it will occupy more space than a shared link or image.

Facebook Event posts help capture users' attention and rise above the Facebook chatter. Reminders will be sent to your audience, so make sure your post has adequate space for an eye-catching image and that you use the right image size for a Facebook Event cover photo.

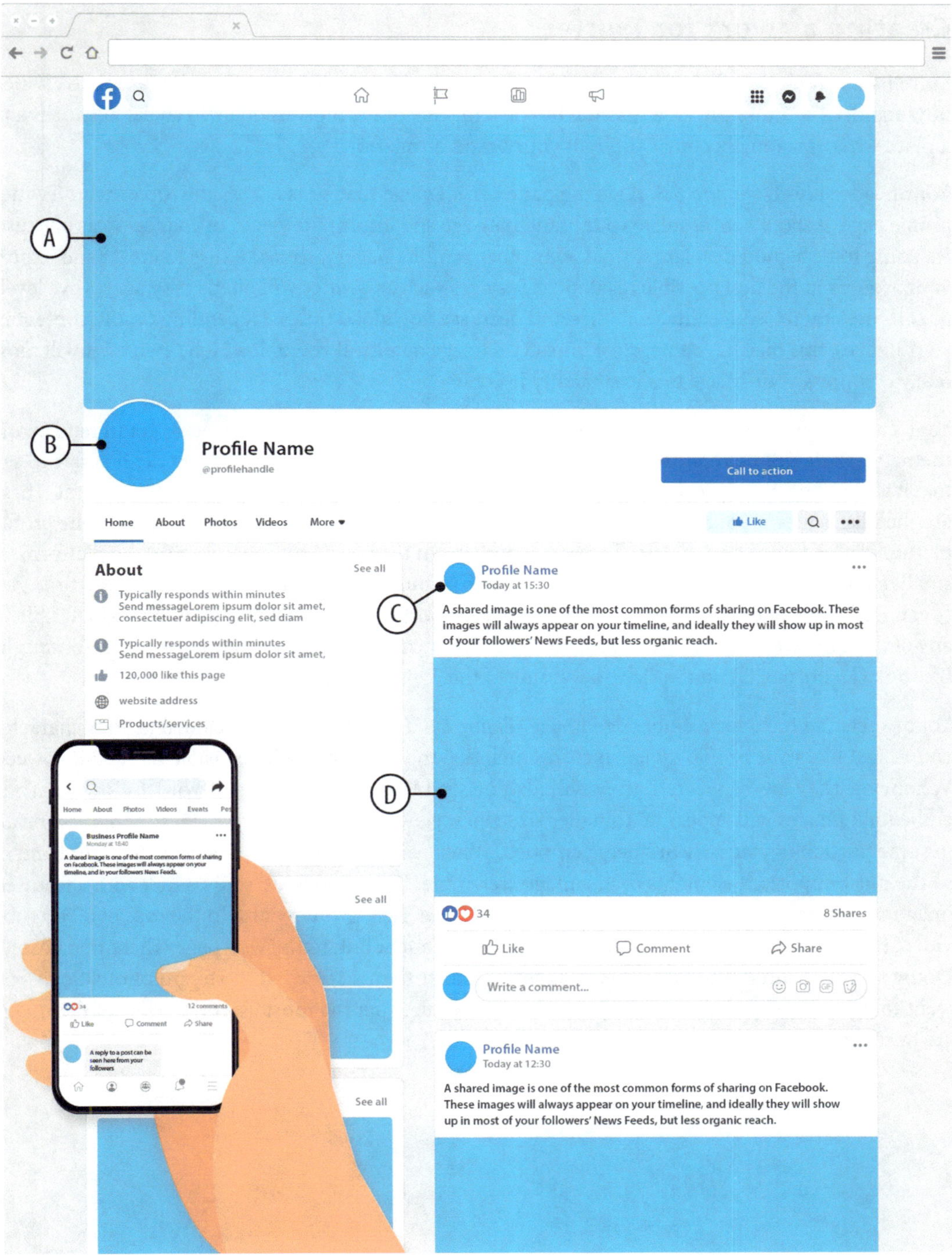

Figure 6.2: A Facebook profile page and the accompanying mobile app

Creating artwork for Twitter

Since its inception in July 2006, Twitter has witnessed a surge in its active monthly user base, which now stands at 415 million. As a result, it has become one of the most frequented social networks and a place where customers converse about your brand or mission.

Your header photo (*Figure 6.3, A*) is the panoramic image that runs across the top of your Twitter profile page. It should encapsulate your brand message and inform the visitor of your services or cause. It's going to be a good deal larger than your other profile imagery, so make sure to create and export your artwork at the best possible resolution. Services such as Twitter will often apply aggressive levels of compression to reduce image file size and decrease download times. Depending on the content in your images, this may have a negative impact on image quality. If you upload it to Twitter, it will most likely compress your image to a low-quality JPG file.

Your Twitter profile photo (*Figure 6.3, B*) is the primary image that represents you or your brand across the network. It will be replicated throughout the site and seen by numerous people. It is fair to say that it will be one of the most important pieces of artwork you will use, so quality is paramount. These are the places where your profile photo will be visible on the site. The largest display of your profile picture can be found on your profile page, where it can be viewed by anyone using the platform. A smaller version of your profile picture will appear in your followers' Twitter streams every time you tweet. Each time one of your followers retweets your posts, your profile picture will also be visible to any of their followers. Your profile picture could also be next to a link to your page in the **You might like** box (*Figure 6.3, C*) on the right-hand side of the Twitter interface.

Your tweets can include an embedded image (*Figure 6.3, D*) without being included in your character count. Just like your profile image, pictures included in your posts will be visible to your followers. Whenever they are retweeted, they will also be visible to the followers of your followers. Your embedded images will appear at a smaller size when viewed in the users' home feed. This will result in some portion of your artwork being cropped. Whenever possible, horizontally center your content so the most important elements of the image are visible. If you choose to share a link with a featured image on Twitter, you can display the image as part of a 'rich' Twitter Card, in the case of a YouTube video, the audience will see a thumbnail of the video, and a link to the web page where it is hosted. Doing so will result in the image being slightly smaller than a standard in-stream photo. So, if you want to optimize that featured image for Twitter, be sure that the most essential parts of the image are horizontally centered.

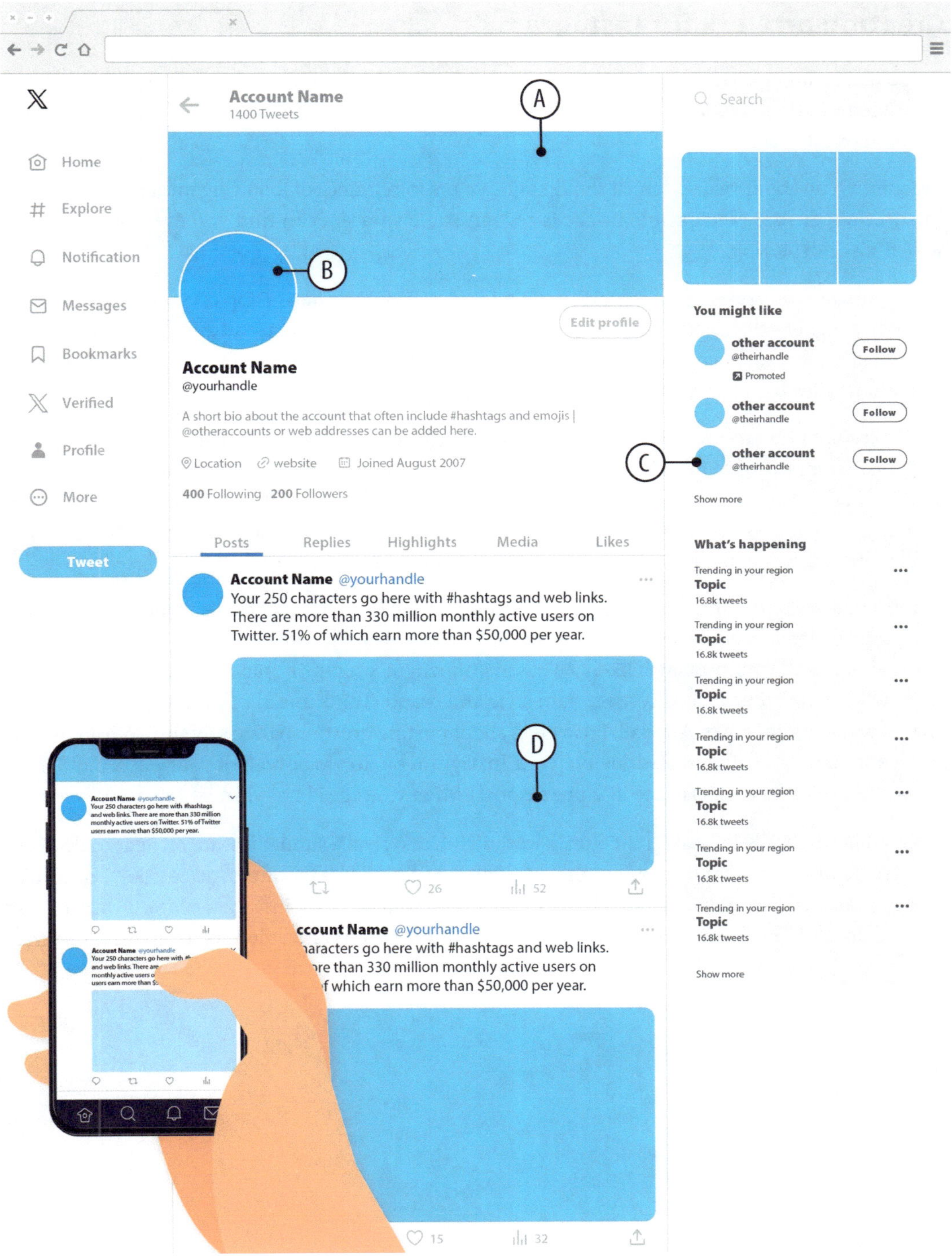

Fig 6.3: Twitter profile page and the accompanying mobile app

Creating artwork for Instagram

Instagram, commonly called IG or Insta, is a Facebook-owned, photo-sharing social network. Instagram launched in 2010, attracting a million users in its first two months. In September 2020, it reached two billion monthly users.

Instagram is all about visuals, which should indicate the importance of following image size guidelines. In addition, ensure your profile image is recognizable so users can find you even quicker when searching or exploring.

When posting to Instagram, it is worth trying to do so from the native app on your smartphone to generate a higher-resolution photo. The resolution will be lower if you upload an image or video from any other device, such as a desktop. Unlike Facebook and Twitter, which rely on text and pictures, Instagram relies solely on sharing unique and engaging visuals with its audience.

Whilst it might be acceptable to share numerous images on Facebook, you need to be ruthless with your Instagram posts. Why? Firstly, posting once a day is typical for an Instagram account, so hold off a bulk posting once a week and instead post daily. Be selective about how many images you post on a single event or post. Instagram isn't the kind of platform where you post several photos that look similar. Be ruthless and only post your best images and focus on quality.

It is essential to keep your Instagram feed consistent. This can often be more challenging when managing a personal or freelancer account, as the topics can be broad and go off-topic. But when it comes to a business account, your posts will likely be based on a singular topic or brand; you should make every effort to keep your image feed consistent in style and brand. Think ahead of time and plan how your images will work together. After all, it isn't just about posting great disparate visuals that lead to sales. Still, your audience will also be drawn to your Instagram bio to see how all of your posts build into a mosaic image gallery (referred to as a puzzle post) when viewed side by side.

Released in August 2016, Instagram Stories was intended to rival a similar feature on Snapchat. Stories allow users to post sequential content that can only be accessed by followers for 24 hours. According to Instagram, stories let you "share all the moments of your day, not just the ones you want to keep on your profile". The feature enables you to share multiple photos and videos in a "slideshow format".

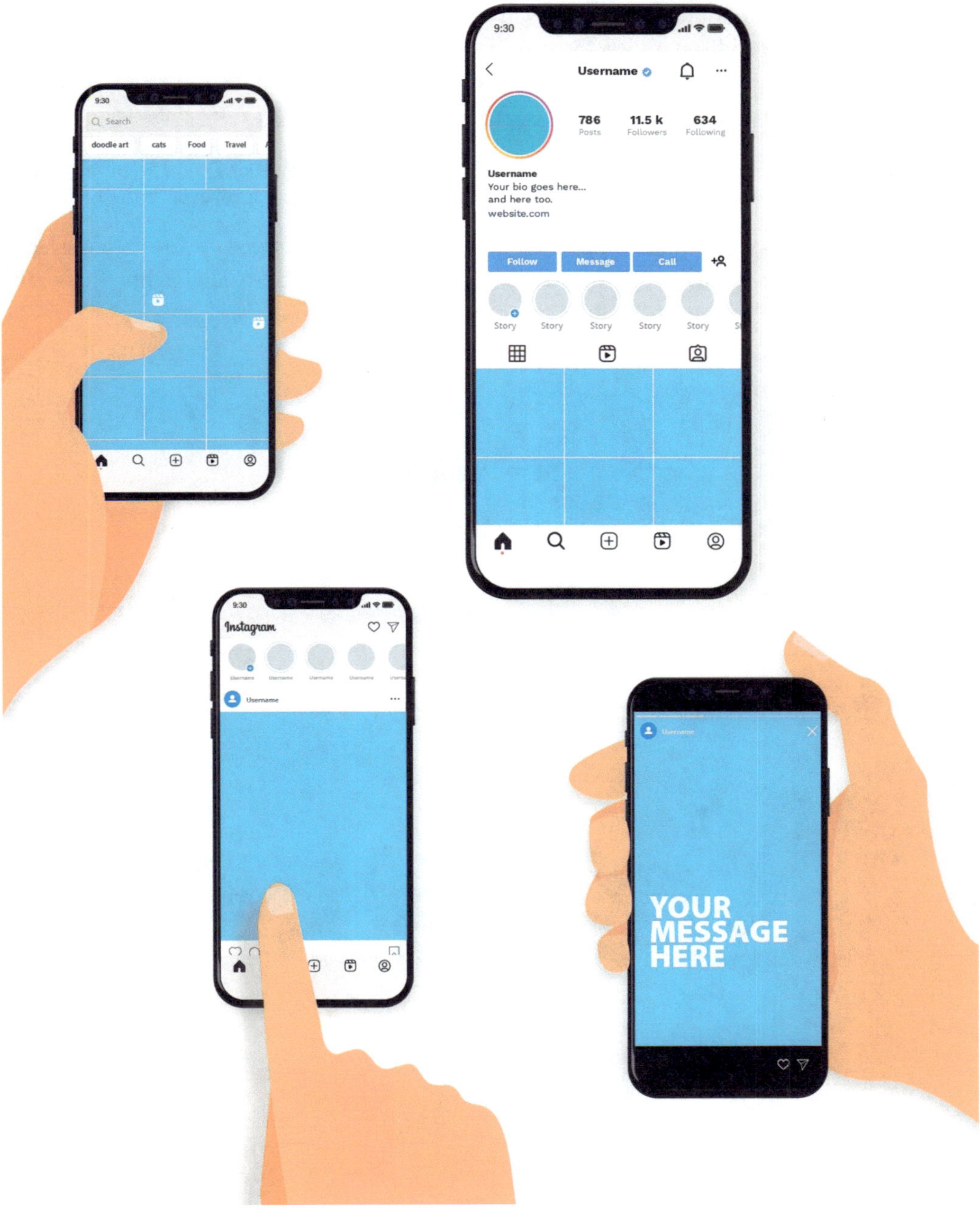

Figure 6.4: Instagram shown in its various modes via the mobile app

They are often used to create more informal or candid posts. Some brands leverage them to create a series of behind-the-scenes videos for an upcoming product release to build anticipation.

Adding effects such as doodles, text, stickers, live face filters, and geostickers to your story is also possible. You can also add songs directly to your stories. Facebook signed deals with all the major record labels to secure various songs, with more being added each day. But check before you post to avoid copyright infringement.

With your own story playing, you can swipe up to see who's watched each photo and video. If you prefer, you can hide your entire story from anyone you don't want to show it to, even if they follow you.

Your Instagram stories won't appear on your profile grid or in someone's feed by default; however, you can save Instagram stories to your profile where they can be added to Story Highlights. These can be sorted into collections and given a custom cover image.

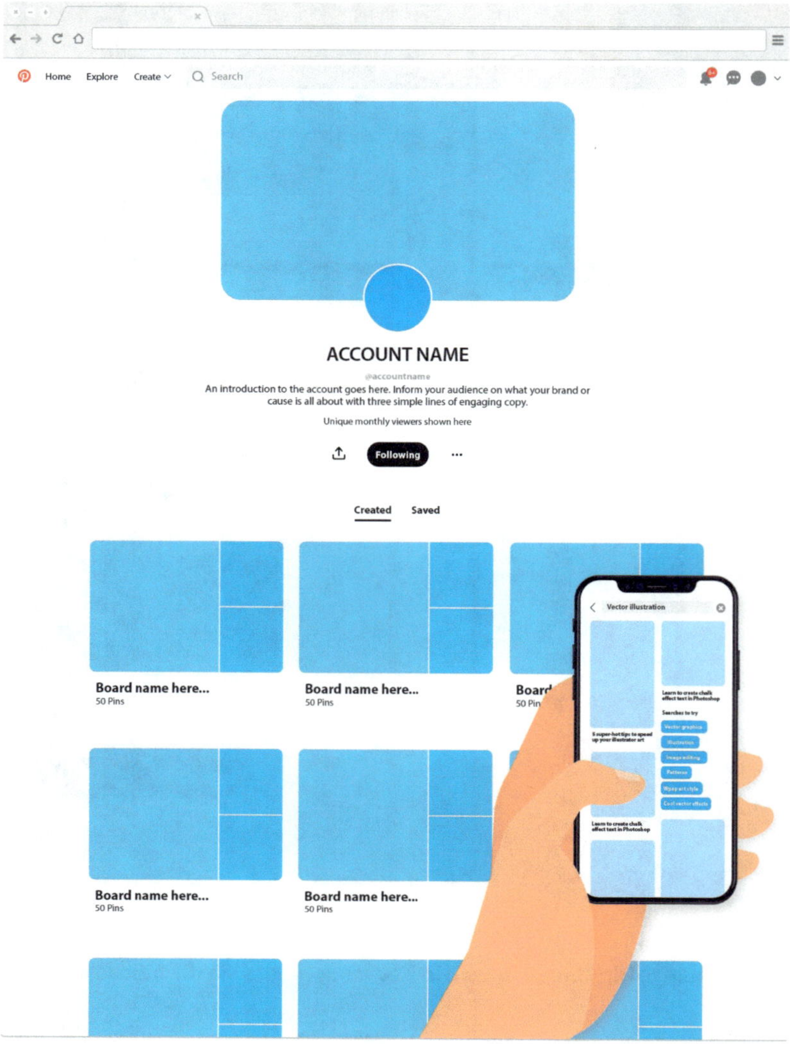

Fig 6.5: A Pinterest profile page and the accompanying mobile app

Creating artwork for Pinterest

Pinterest has 445 million monthly active users, but it was only the 14th most-used social platform in 2022, according to the Hootsuite 2022 digital trend report. Pinterest is popular with women—especially mothers. Eight in every ten mothers are on the platform, and more than two-thirds of Pinterest's user base is female.

Pinterest is the web's only "visual search engine", which should not be underestimated since 62% of Gen Z and Millennials say they'd like to be able to search by image, according to the company.

Your profile image (*Figure 6.5, A*) should be square (1:1 ratio). The larger, the better, but it is recommended to be at least 165 x 165 pixels. Pinterest will resize it to fit proportionally. Like other social sites, your profile picture should be closely tied to your brand or service.

Pinterest is a vertically oriented browsing experience, meaning that you are limited to the width of your image pins but not the height. This allows you to add a photo that's square (*Figure 6.5, B*) or one that will scale to be even taller (*Figure 6.5, C*), but if a photo is of a ratio larger than 2:3, your pin will be scaled to fit a width of 236 pixels or possibly truncated, which can affect the performance of your pin.

Long infographics pins have been popular on Pinterest for many years. The almost limitless height of a pin has allowed for rich visuals, but this is changing. Pinterest has a name for sprawling pins that the platform deems too high: giraffe pins. From June 2018, Pinterest's algorithm started to favor pins that are approximately 2:3 in proportion. If you deviate far from that golden ratio, you may struggle to get traction. The maximum size your pin can be posted at without being cropped is 1000 x 2100.

Creating Pinterest boards is one of the most important things you can do on the platform. It's essential to ensure you're using an image that fits the size criteria perfectly. Large thumbnail images (*Figure 6.5, D*) should be 222 x 150 pixels, and small board thumbnails should be 55 x 55.

Use your pins to help people become familiar with your brand and convince them to buy your product and service. Showcase images that are authentic and that bring your brand to life. Clearly show how someone might use your product. A 2019 survey found that 97% of all searches on Pinterest were unbranded, which means that users can discover new brands, products, and services.

Creating artwork for LinkedIn

With 722 million monthly active users, LinkedIn is not only the place to go grow your professional network but also an effective means of raising brand awareness and marketing your goods and services. Users can follow your company page to keep up to date with news and events you post, which can be seen on a user's home feed.

LinkedIn company pages feature a company logo and a slim cover image that runs the top of the page. There's also space for a brief company mission statement and geographical location, as well as a number of employees. It will also highlight any followers that are part of a user's own network that follow the company.

Due to the slimline size of 1128 x 191, it can be challenging to juxtapose a prominent subject within the company cover and still provide context to the page visitor. Some companies instead use a pattern or abstract art in this space. For example, Adobe uses its own logo as a pattern, while Apple uses an aerial shot of its headquarters, Apple Park, in California.

Along the header of a company page are quick links where a user can explore further information by navigating to **About** or **Jobs** pages. It also provides a **Life** section, where visitors can learn more about the company culture and staff success stories. This presents another opportunity to add artwork, and at 1128 x 376 pixels, you have more space to work with than the company cover.

When it comes to posting on LinkedIn, you are spoilt for choice by supported file types, from the standard JPG, GIF, and PNG formats to multi-page presentations such as PowerPoint, Word, and PDF. All of these are accommodated well with simple navigational icons to click through each page, rather like slides. A PDF is best suited to this format, with an aspect ratio of 1:1 and a size of 1080 x 1080 or a 16:9 ratio and a size of 1920 x 1080 tall. PDFs are limited to 300 pages in length and cannot exceed 100 MB.

Native videos up to 4K in resolution and in portrait or landscape orientations are also supported on LinkedIn. Unlike videos posted to LinkedIn via a link and hosted on YouTube, videos uploaded directly to the LinkedIn platform play automatically in a user's feed, making them more engaging. A native video is limited to 10 minutes in length and 200 MB.

Event posts, such as a demonstration, a how-to, or a product launch, are great ways of attracting engagement. You can broadcast live on LinkedIn, where viewers can post questions in chat. You can create event pages where users can find further details and register. Event pages are branded with a banner of 1600 x 900 pixels in size.

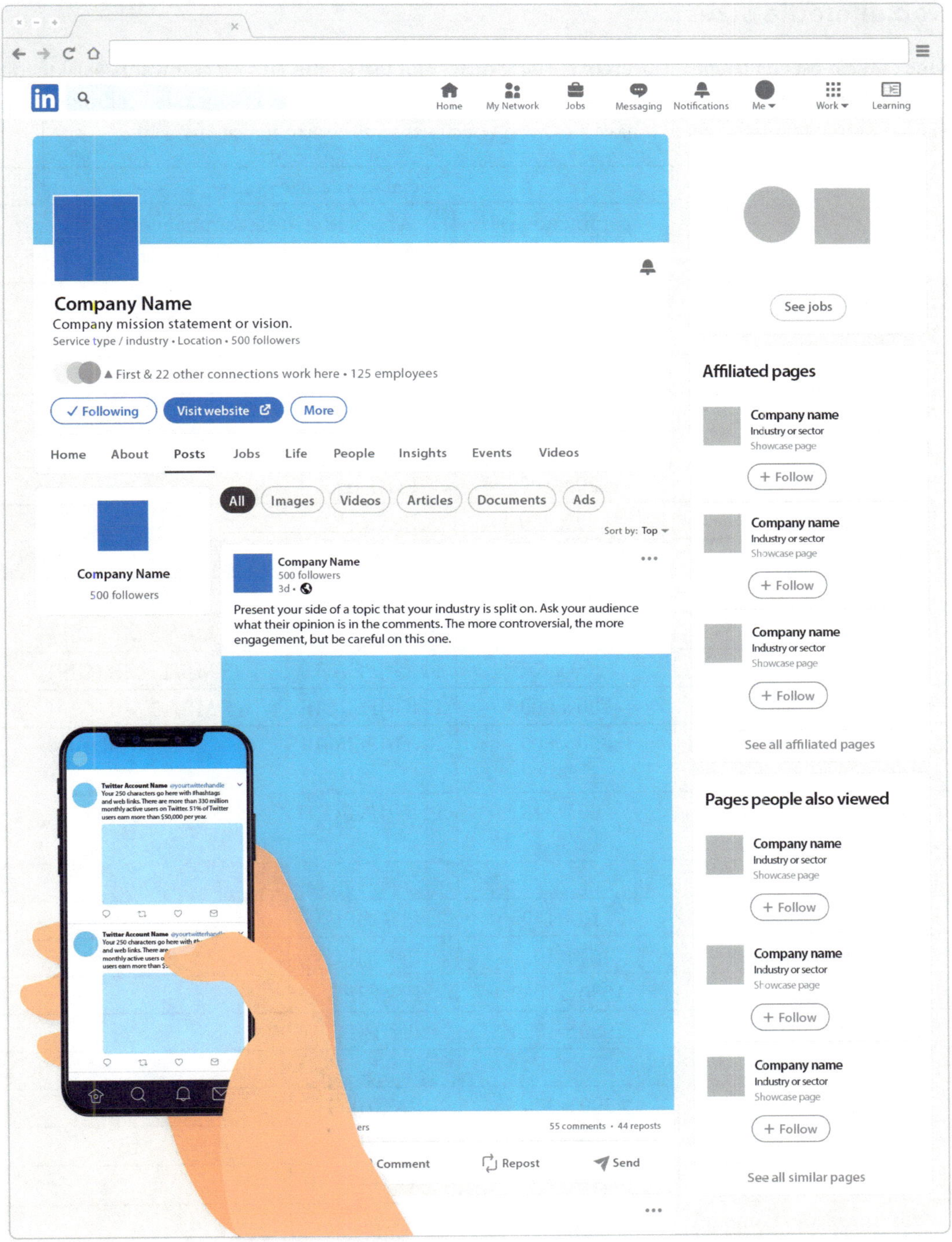

Fig 6.6: A LinkedIn profile page and the accompanying mobile app

Social media sizes

One of the most challenging aspects of creating images for use online, and especially for social media, is considering the sizes required by each platform. In the following table, I've included common image sizes required by platforms that have a focus on business and the strong use of visuals:

	Social media size guide		
	Recommended size	Accepted file formats	Recommended max file size
Facebook			
Profile	180 x 180	PNG/JPG	5 MB
Cover	820 x 312	PNG/JPG	
Shared image	1200 x 630	PNG/JPG	
Shared link with Image	1200 x 628	PNG/JPG	
Event image	1920 x 1005	PNG/JPG	
Fundraiser image	800 x 300	PNG/JPG	
Twitter			
Profile	400 x 400	PNG/JPG/GIF	5 MB/15 MB (GIF)
Header	1500 x 500	PNG/JPG/GIF	5 MB/15 MB (GIF)
Single shared image	1200 x 675	PNG/JPG/GIF	5 MB/15 MB (GIF)
Two shared Images	700 x 800	PNG/JPG/GIF	5 MB/15 MB (GIF)
Carousels (2-6 images) 1:1 aspect ratio	800 x 800	PNG/JPG/GIF	20 MB (total)
Carousels (2-6 Images) 1:91:1 aspect ratio	800 x 418	PNG/JPG/GIF	20 MB (total)
Instagram			
Profile	110 x 110	PNG/JPG	
Photo thumbnails	161 x 161	PNG/JPG	
Photo feed	1080 x 1080	PNG/JPG	
Stories (portrait)	1080 x 1920	PNG/JPG	
LinkedIn			
Company logo	300 x 300	PNG/JPG	4 MB
Company cover photo	1128 x 191	PNG/JPG	4 MB
Shared image or link	1200 x 627	PNG/JPG/GIF	
Main image and company photos (Life tab)	1128 x 376	PNG/JPG	

	Social media size guide		
	Recommended size	Accepted file formats	Recommended max file size
Pinterest			
Profile	165 x 165	PNG/JPG	10 MB
Pin (tall, 2:3 aspect ratio)	900 x 600	PNG/JPG	
Board display (large)	222 x 150	PNG/JPG	
Board display (small)	55 x 55	PNG/JPG	

In this section, we have previewed the principles of the tools and techniques that will be deployed to create our social media projects. We have also reviewed the various platform characteristics and image sizes required for branding your organizations home pages and posting. Next, we will create a web document and its corresponding artboard.

Working with artboards

In this first exercise, we will define document characteristics for a single artboard as a starting point to build the remaining content upon:

1. Go to **File** → **New**. When the **New Document** dialogue appears, click on the **Web** tab at the top of the dialogue to display the presets. Click on the **Web Most Common** thumbnail. Enter `SM24`, an abbreviation of the project name and year, into the **Name** field in the top-right of the dialogue.
2. Change the **Width** to `400 px` and the **Height** to `400 px`. This will match the profile image size on Twitter. Ensure the **Artboards** checkbox is active, **Color Mode** is set to **RGB Color**, **8-bit**, and **Background Contents** is **White**. Click **OK** when done to generate the document.
3. Hover your cursor over the artboard named `Artboard 1` in the **Layers** panel and double-click to open the type entry field. Type `Tw-Profile` and press *Enter* to apply the name change. Notice that the label above the top-left corner of the artboard in the **Image** window has also updated.
4. Next, we will add a branded color to the background. Click on the **New Fill and Adjustment layer** icon (*Figure 6.7, A*) at the bottom of the **Layers** panel and choose **Solid Color** from the list of options. When the **Color Picker** dialogue appears, enter `142` into the **Red** field, `58` into **Green**, and `42` into **Blue** to create a burnt red color. Click **OK**.

5. Go to **File** → **Place Linked**, browse to the `06-Social` folder, and select the file named `WildCo_Logo.ai`. Click **Place** when done. When the dialogue appears, left-click on the page 7 thumbnail, which contains a white version of the logo. Then click **OK** to import the artwork.

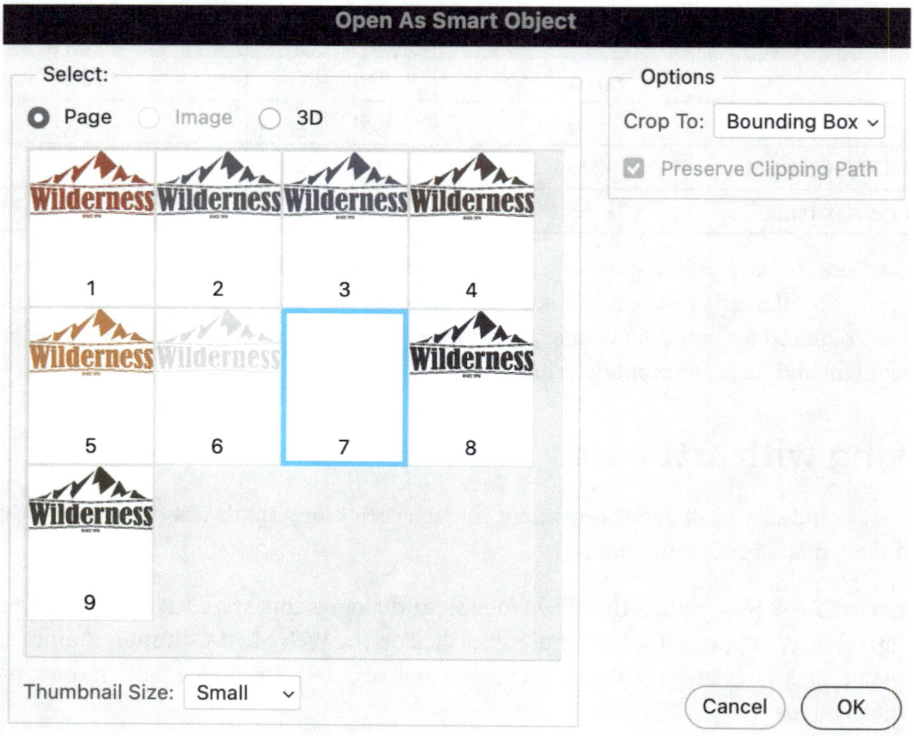

Fig 6.7: Choose the white logo on page 7.

6. When the logo appears, it will be scaled to fit the artboard. Ensure the **Width** and **Height** fields are linked in the **Options** bar, change the **Scale** to `60%`, and click on the **Commit Changes** button in the **Options** bar to finish the import process.

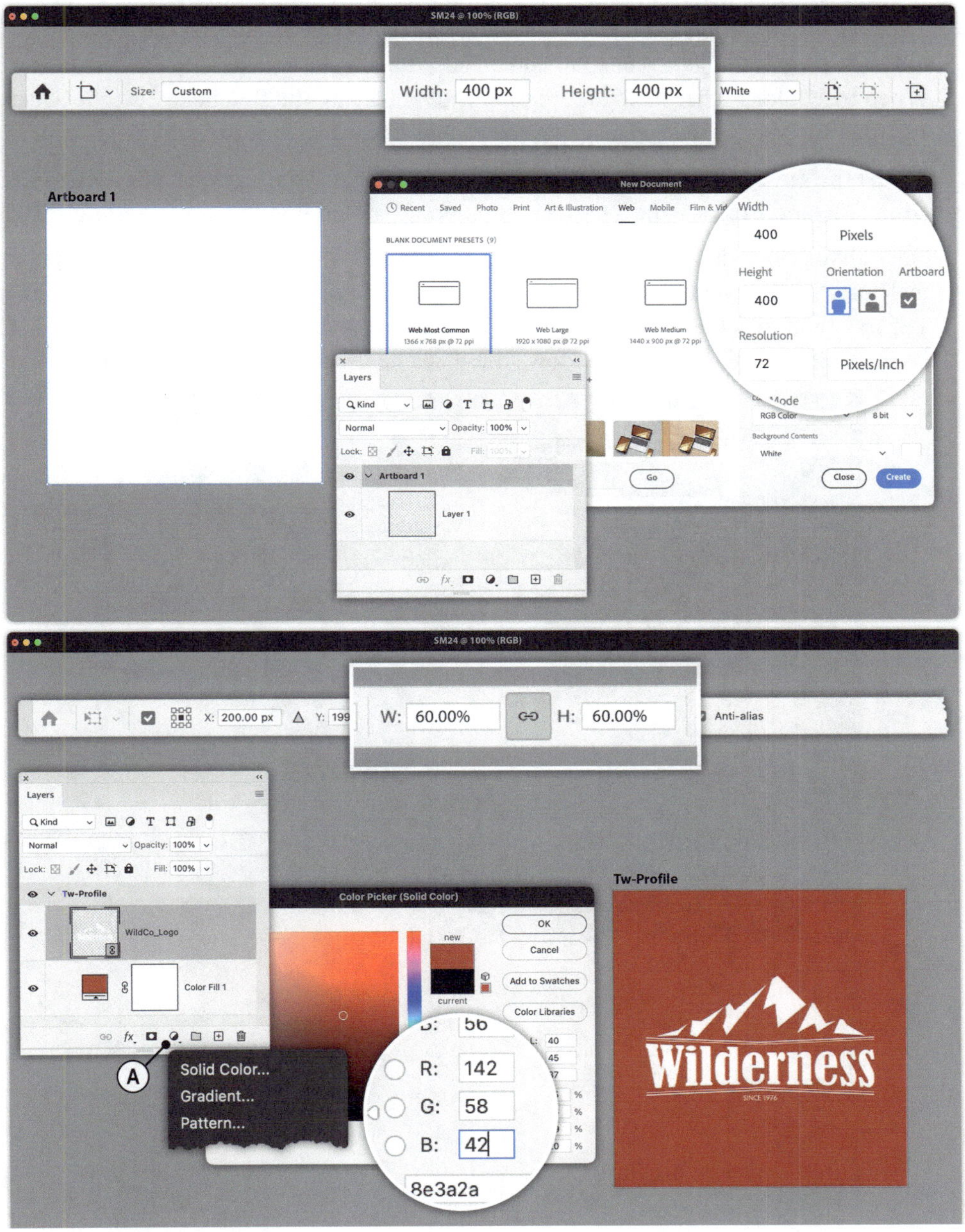

Fig 6.8: Create a Solid Color fill layer containing the brand color as a background

7. With the logo layer still active in **Layers**, click on the **Fx** icon at the bottom of the same panel and choose **Color Overlay** from the list. When the dialogue appears, the overlay setting should be visible. Click on the **Color Picker** icon, and when the **Color Picker** dialogue appears, enter `142` into the **Red** field, `58` into **Green**, and `42` into **Blue** to create a burnt red color. Click **OK** when done to dismiss the **Color Picker**.

8. From the list on the left-hand side of the **Layer Effects** dialogue, click on the plus icon adjacent to **Color Overlay** (*Figure 6.8, A*) to add an additional color. Click on the **Color Picker** icon. When the **Color Picker** dialogue appears, enter `101` into the **Red** field, `39` into **Green**, and `86` into **Blue** to create a deep magenta color. Click **OK** when done to dismiss the **Color Picker**.
9. Repeat the same technique to create a further two colors: a dark green composed of **Red** `65`, **Green** `72`, and **Blue** `43` and a dark blue composed of **Red** `88`, **Green** `90`, and **Blue** `105`.
10. Once all the colors have been added, click on **Drop Shadow** from the list in the **Layer Effects** dialogue. Set the **Opacity** to `30%`, **Angle** to `90`, **Distance** to `0%`, **Spread** to `0%`, and **Size** to `18 px`. Then click **OK** to close the **Layer Effects** dialogue. Turn off the visibility for all **Color Overlay** effects and the **Drop Shadow**. These will be needed on other artboards.

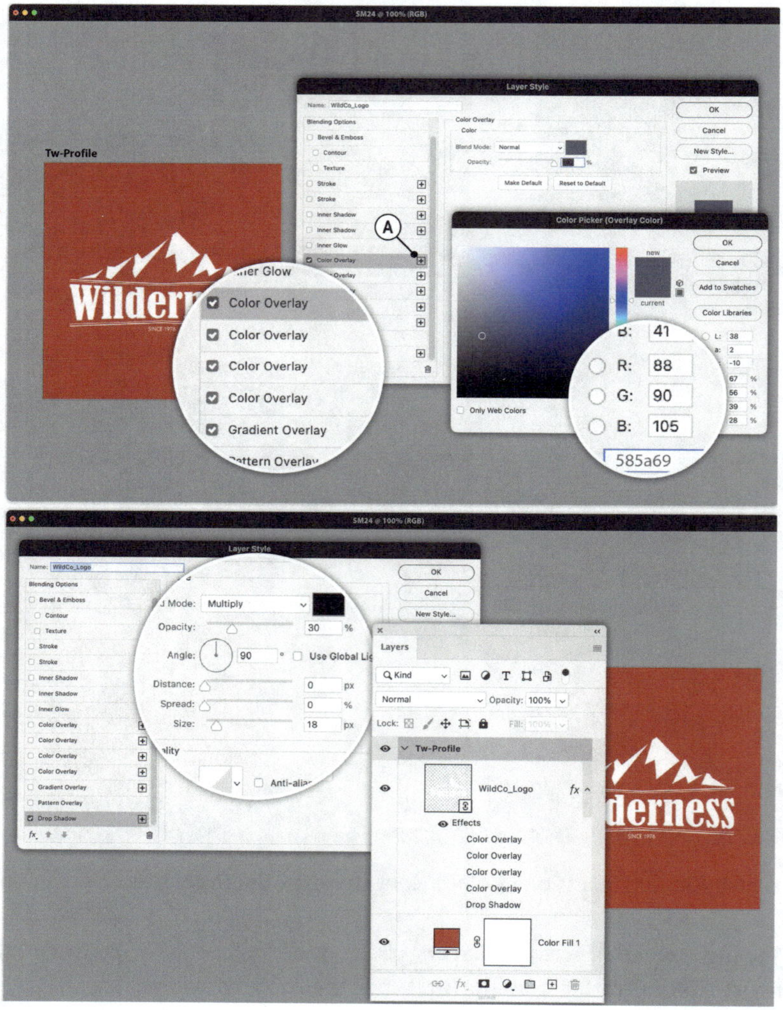

Fig 6.9: Adding multiple color overlays to a layer to change the logo color

Adding a header image

With the first artboard and two editable brand assets created, you will now build on this to create a Twitter header graphic:

1. Switch to the **Artboard** tool by left-clicking on the artboard name `Tw-Profile` located in the top-left corner of the artboard in the **Image** window. You should now see widgets along each side of the artboard, shown as circles with a plus symbol within them. These **Widgets** allow you to copy or duplicate existing artboards. Left-click on the right-hand **Widget** (*Figure 6.9, A*) to create a second artboard.
2. Double-click the artboard name `Artboard-1` in the **Layers** panel to open its type entry field. Enter a new name of `Tw-Header` and press *Enter* to apply the name change. Ensure that the **Artboard** tool is still active. From the **Options** bar, change the **Width** of the active artboard to `1500 px` and the **Height** to `500 px`. Press *Enter* to apply the changes.
3. Go to **File** → **Place Linked**, browse to the `06-Social` folder, and select the file named `Trek-A.jpg`. Click **Place** when done.
4. From **Options**, change the **Scale** to `40%` and **Rotate** to `14%`. Click on the **Commit Changes** button. Reposition the artwork to include as many items from the flat-lay photo as possible within the artboard.

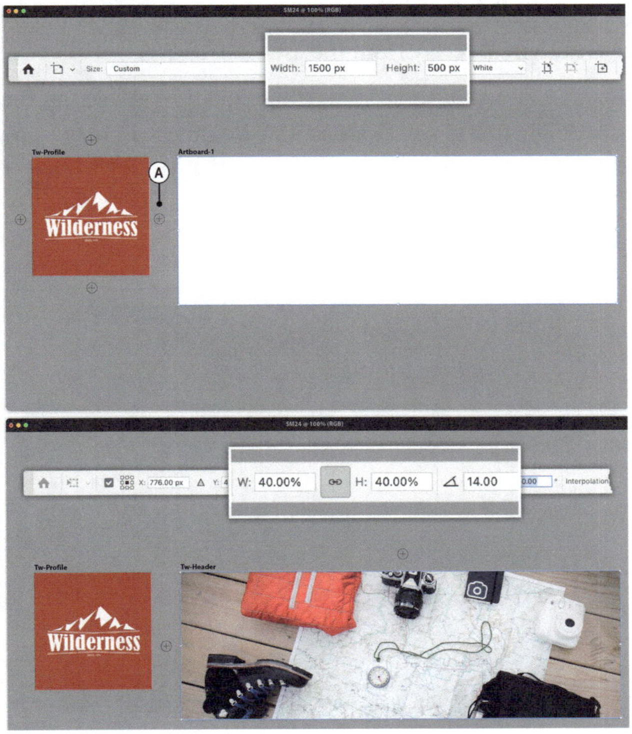

Fig 6.10: Editing the new artboard size to 1500 x 500 pixels and importing and resizing the photo

Creating a tweet template

This type of image will require flexibility built into it to account for different backgrounds, colors, and contrast with the logo. Depending on how many images you post in a tweet will influence the size. Next, you will create a template for a tweet containing a single image:

1. Switch to the **Artboard** tool by left-clicking on the artboard name `Tw-Header`. When the widgets appear along each side of the artboard, left-click on the right-hand **Widget** (*Figure 6.10, A*) to create a third artboard.
2. Double left-click the artboard name `Artboard-1` in **Layers**. Enter a new name of `Tw-1200x675-01` and press *Enter* to apply the name change. Ensure that the **Artboard** tool is still active. From **Options**, change the **Width** of the active artboard to `1200 px` and the **Height** to `675 px`. Press *Enter* to apply the changes.
3. Go to **File** → **Place Linked**, browse to the `06-Social` folder, and select the file named `Trek-B.jpg`. Click **Place** when done.
4. From the **Options** bar, change the **Scale** to `27%` and click on the **Commit Changes** button. Reposition the artwork so that both hikers and the peak of the mountain are visible on the artboard.
5. With the hiking photo still active in the **Layers** panel, press the *D* key to reset the foreground and background colors in the **Tools** panel. This will ensure that when we set the following gradient, black will be active. Click on the **Fx** icon at the bottom of the same panel (*Figure 6.11, A*) and choose **Gradient Overlay** from the list.
6. When the dialogue appears, the gradient setting should be visible. Set **Blend Mode** to **Mutiply**, **Opacity** to `100`, **Angle** to `90`, and **Scale** to `100%`. Choose **Linear** from the **Style** drop-down menu, turn off the **Reverse** checkbox, and activate the **Align with Layer** checkbox.

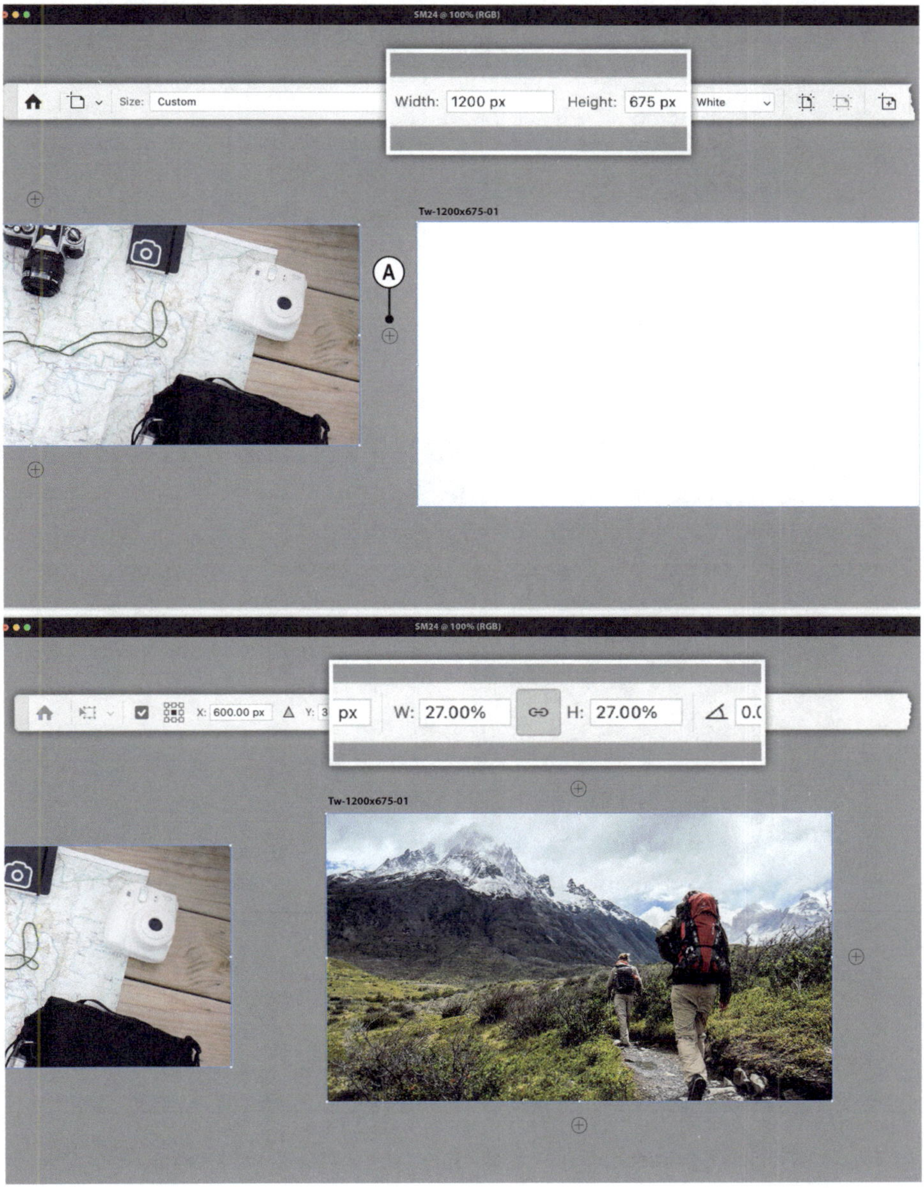

Fig 6.11: Changing the new artboard size to 1200 x 675 and importing and scaling the photo to 27%

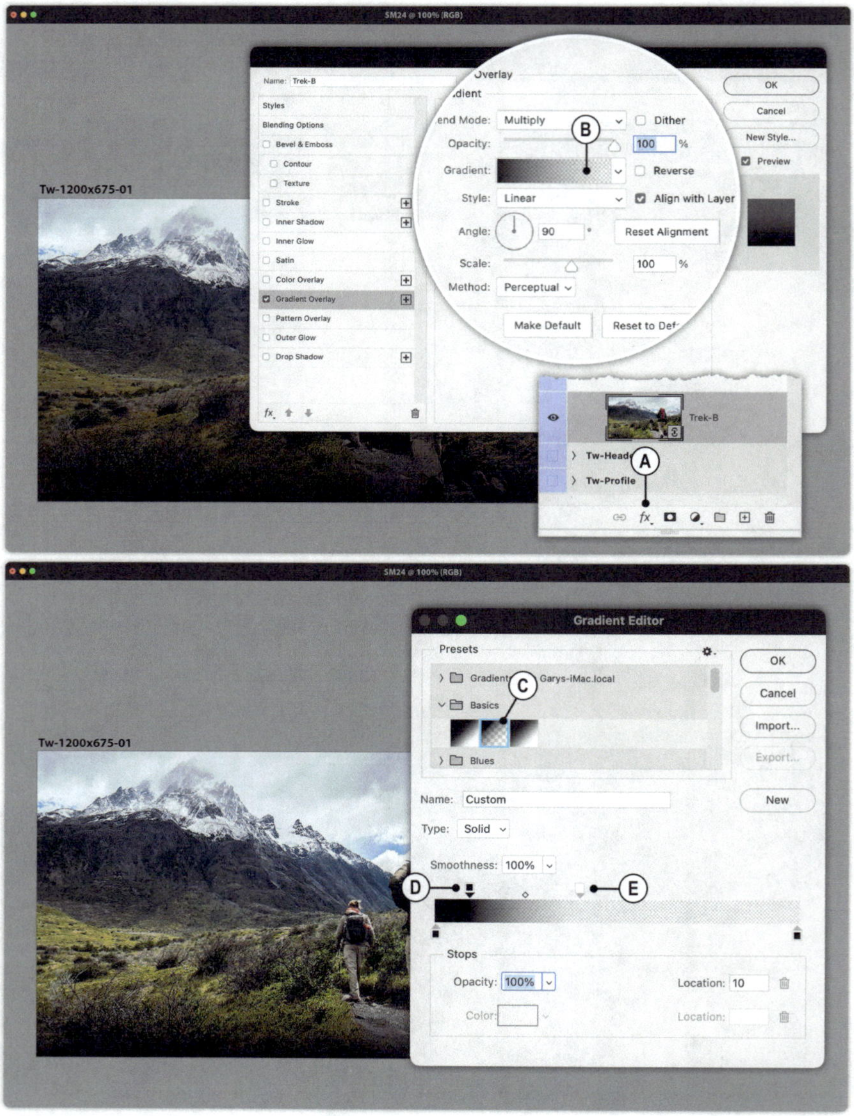

Fig 6.12: Adding a gradient overlay to the photo to help text and logos remain legible

7. Click on the Gradient Preview (*Figure 6.12*, B) to open the editor, expand the `Basics` folder, and click on the gradient named `Foreground to Transparent` (*Figure 6.12*, C). Then, click on the top-left **Transparency Stop** (*Figure 6.12*, D) to make it active. Change the values lower down in the dialogue. Set **Location** to `10%` and **Opacity** to `100%`.

8. Click on the top-right **Transparency Stop** (*Figure 6.12*, E). Change its **Location** to `40%` and **Opacity** to `0%`. This should create a black fade along the bottom of the photo, which will make any text or logo stand out when necessary. Click **OK** to close the editor, and then click on **OK** to close the **Layer Styles** dialogue.

9. Hover your cursor over the layer containing the logo in the **Layers** panel, imported in a previous exercise, which can be found in the Right-click on the layer name and choose `Duplicate Layer` from the list of options. When the **Duplicate layer dialogue** appears, rename the layer `Wildo_Logo 2`, set the **Destination Document** to `SM24.psd` (the file you are editing), and set **Artboard** to `Tw-1200x675-01`. Click **OK** when done.
10. Ensure the newly duplicated layer `Wildo_Logo 2` is active in the **Layers** panel. Then go to **Edit** → **Free Transform** and **Scale** the logo down to `30%` from the **Options** bar. Press *Enter* to apply the changes. Drag the logo to the left-hand side of the artboard. Keep the logo layer active in **Layers**.
11. Go to **File** → **Save** and keep the document open.

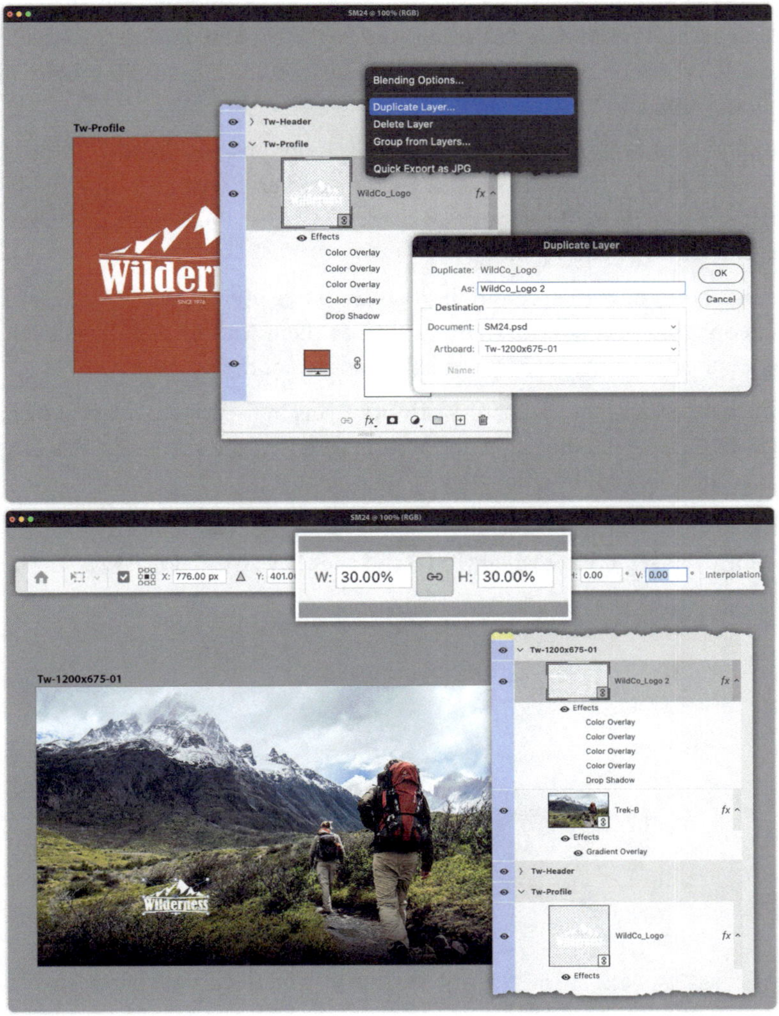

Fig 6.13: Duplicating the logo and reusing it on the third artboard, Tw-1200x675-01

Adding text to the artboard

With the main part of the design comprising of a company logo and an aspirational photo now created, it is now time to add a simple text heading to promote the destination of the holiday. The fonts used in all the exercises in this book can be installed from the Adobe Fonts website. Alternatively, you can use a different font already installed on your hard drive of your choosing. Here is how to add text to the artboard:

1. Switch to the **Horizontal Type** tool by pressing the *T* key. Hover the tool over the left-hand side of the `Tw-1200x675-01` artboard. Left-click and drag to the right to draw a text frame that is approximately half the width of the artboard. Release the left mouse button to generate the text frame, inside of which you will see the active type cursor.
2. Type `Patagonia` into the text frame and highlight all characters in the frame with the **Horizontal Type** tool. From the **Properties** panel, set the **Font** to **Flood Std**, **Size** to `60 pt`, **Leading** to **Auto**, and **Tracking** to `350`.
3. Set the alignment to **Center** from the **Paragraph** options. Set the text **Color** to white by left-clicking on the color swatch to open the **Color Picker**. Enter `255` into the **Red**, **Green**, and **Blue** fields. Click **OK** to apply the color change and close the **Color Picker**. Press *Esc* to apply the text and exit type editing mode.
4. Ensure that both the text layer and the logo are active in the **Layers** panel. From the **Options** bar, click on **Align Horizontal Centers** to align them with one another. Switch to the **Move** tool and reposition them in the lower left-hand side of the artboard.
5. Right-click on each of the artboard **Visibility Icons** in the **Layers** panel and change the color highlight to `Blue` from the list of options. As we add more artboards, this can make it easier to distinguish artboards by color.
6. Go to **File** → **Save**. When the **Save As** dialogue appears, browse to the `06-Social` folder. Ensure that the format is set to **Photoshop (PSD)** and click **Save** when done. Keep the document open.

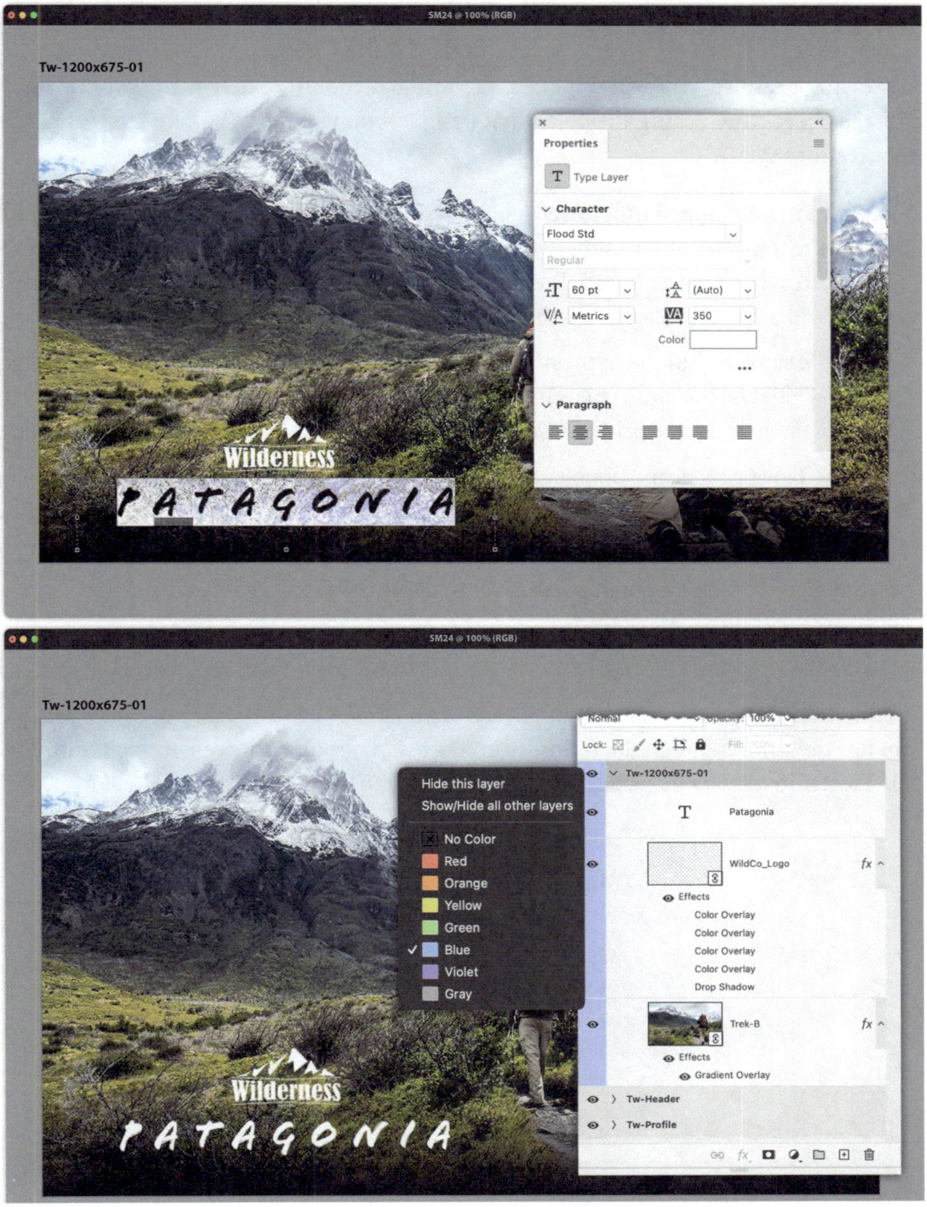

Fig 6.14: Adding text to the artboard and then changing the layer color to blue

In this section, we have added key assets to our social media templates, including an aspirational photo, company logo, brand colors, and text. In the next section, we will use these template designs to create additional designs in varying sizes for other platforms.

Duplicating artboards

In the following exercise, you will duplicate the initial artboards, such as the profile, header, and shared image tweet. Then, using these original designs, you will modify them to create artwork for a different platform:

1. Switch to the **Artboard** tool by left-clicking on the artboard named `Tw-Profile` located outside the top-left corner of the artboard in the **Image** window. You should now see widgets along each side of the artboard. Press *Alt (Windows) Option (macOS)* as you left-click on the bottom widget to duplicate the artboard. The duplicate will now appear under the original.
2. Repeat the same technique of pressing *Alt (Windows) Option (macOS)* and left-clicking on the bottom widget of the two remaining artboards, `Tw-Header` and `Tw-1200x675-01` to duplicate them under the originals. You should now have six artboards in total in the document.
3. Go to the **Layers** panel and double-click the artboard named `Tw-Profile copy` to open the type entry field. Enter a new name of `Fb-Profile` and press *Enter* to apply the name change.
4. Double-click the artboard named `Tw-Header copy` to open the type entry field. Enter a new name of `Fb-Cover` and press *Enter* to apply the name change.
5. Finally, double-click the artboard named `Tw-1200x675-01 copy` to open the type entry field. Enter a new name of `Fb-1200x630-01` and press *Enter* to apply the name change.
6. Right-click on each of the newly duplicated artboards' **Visibility** icons in the **Layers** panel and change the color highlight to **Yellow** from the list of options. Any remaining artboards created for Twitter in the **Layers** panel should be recolored to blue to distinguish them from each other.

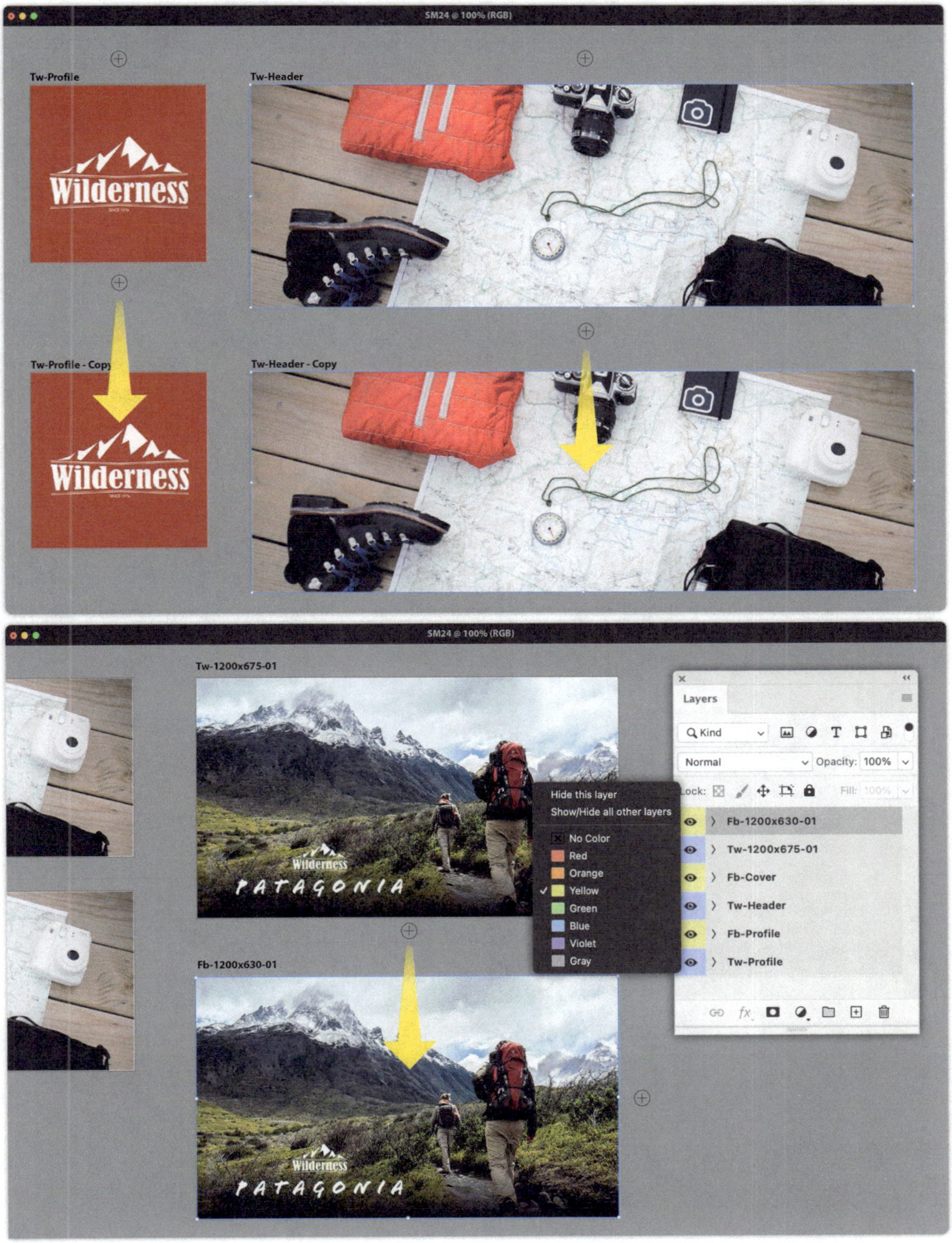

Fig 6.15: Duplicating all three original artboards and renaming and color-coding them yellow

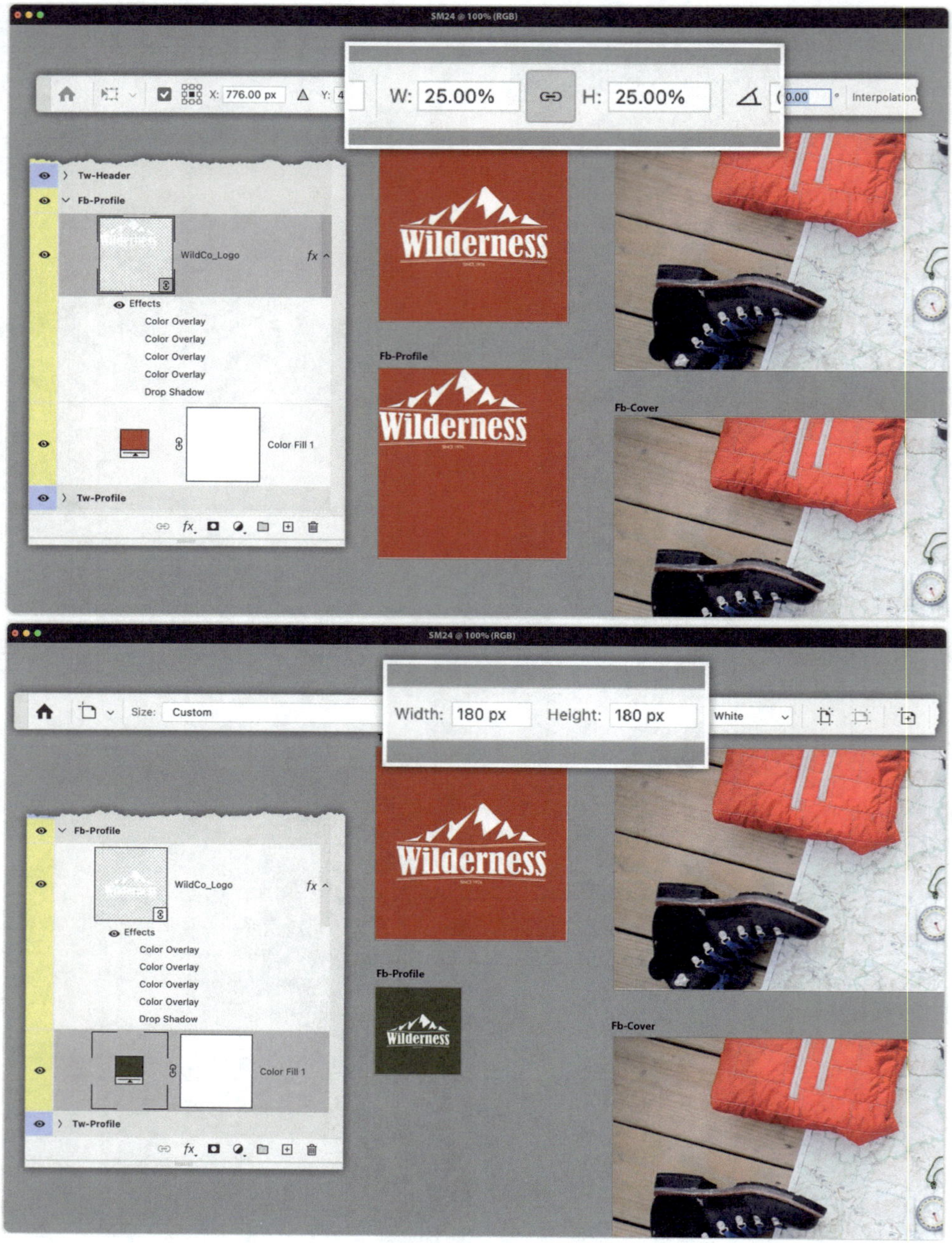

Fig 6.16: Scaling the Facebook logo and artboard and changing the background color

7. Switch to the **Move** tool, left-click on the `WildCo_Logo` layer inside of the `Fb-Profile` artboard, and drag the logo to the top-left corner of the artboard. Go to **Edit** → **Free Transform**. Change the **Scale** of the photo to `25%` and click on the **Commit** button under **Options**.
8. Left-click on the artboard label `Fb-Profile` in the **Image** window to switch to the **Artboard** tool and make the artboard active. From **Options**, change the **Width** of the active artboard to `180 px` and the **Height** to `180 px`. Press *Enter* to apply the changes.
9. Switch to the **Move** tool, left-click on the `WildCo_Logo` layer in the active artboard, and drag the logo to the center of the artboard.
10. Next, left-click on the `Color Fill` layer inside of the newly created `Fb-Profile` artboard. To change the color, double left-click on the layer thumbnail in the **Layers** panel, shown as a swatch. When the **Color Picker** dialogue appears, set **Red** to `65`, **Green** to `72`, and **Blue** to `43` for a dark green color. Click **OK** when done to apply the change.
11. Left-click on the artboard label `Fb-Cover` in the **Image** window to switch to the **Artboard** tool and make the artboard active. From **Options**, change the **Width** of the active artboard to `820 px` and the **Height** to `312 px`. Press *Enter* to apply the changes.
12. Left-click on the photo inside the `Fb-Cover`. Switch to the **Move** tool and then go to **Edit** → **Free Transform**. Change the **Scale** of the photo to `58%` and click on the **Commit** button in the **Options** bar. Reposition the photo as required within the artboard.
13. Left-click on the artboard label `Fb-1200x630-01` in the **Image** window to switch to the **Artboard** tool and make the artboard active. From **Options**, change the artboard **Height** to `630 px` and press *Enter* to apply the change. Reposition the text and logo as required within the artboard.

14. Go to **File** → **Save** when done and keep the document open.

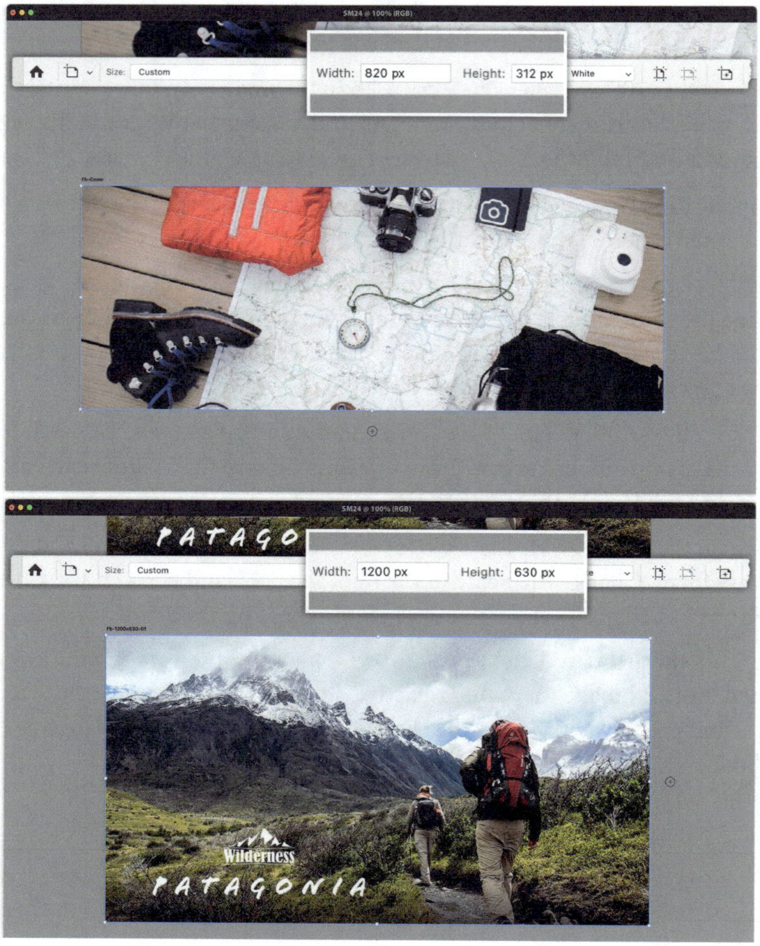

Fig 6.17: The remaining two Facebook artboards resized accordingly

In this section, we have used a variety of tools to add guides to a print file which indicate safe zones, trim lines, and bleed. Guides that can be added with millimeter precision and layout grids that form columns and rows, allowing for more broad methods of measuring the width and height of assets and assist in juxtaposing content. In the next section, we will add images, logos, and text to these templates.

Exporting and scheduling posts

When the demands of social media are time-sensitive, the last thing you will want is to waste valuable time saving artboards as separate files, choosing a directory to save them to, and naming them every time. The following techniques seek to avoid the time-consuming challenge of exporting to the web.

Batch export artboards

Photoshop has provided batch export options for decades, but with the advent of artboards, these long-standing features were unable to process these new multi-page designs. Thankfully, Adobe eventually added a set of scripts that could export all artboards in a single document:

1. With the `SM24` document open, go to **FileExport → Artboards to Files**. When the dialogue appears, click on the **Browse** button, select the `06-Social` folder, and click **Open**. The location will default to the folder the document has been saved to each time.
2. Under **File Name Prefix**, set the current file to `SM24`, which is an abbreviation of "social media 2024." This name will default each time you enter the dialogue box, so it is worth considering saving your files with short names.
3. Under the dialogue, you have a choice of two radio buttons. **Include Overlapping Area** will include artwork from another artboard if they overlap in the **Image** window. This does not increase the size of the exported image. Alternatively, **Artboard Contents Only** will only export visible content inside the artboard. Choose **Artboard Contents Only**.

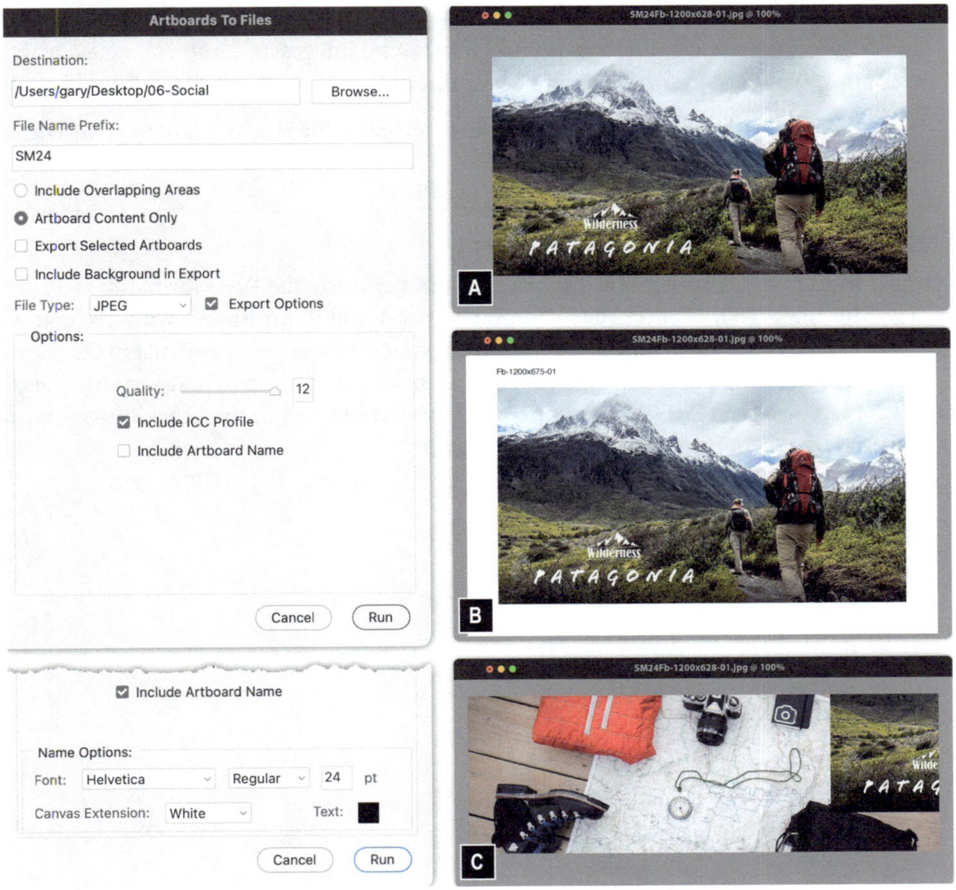

Fig 6.18: (A) Exporting artboard content only, (B) exporting with labels, and (C) the overlapping regions

4. The checkbox **Export Selected Artboards** is useful when you've just made an edit to an artboard and wish to export an updated version, but it is not relevant in our scenario. If you decide to use this feature later, you will need to left-click on the artboard you wish to export before returning to this dialogue box.
5. **Include Background in Export** is useful for artboards containing a standard white background or another color that you wish to include in the exported artwork. In most cases, the background will be hidden by your own artwork and is not relevant. We will leave this deactivated.
6. Under the **File Type** drop-down menu, you can choose from BMP, JPEG, PDF, PSD, Targa, TIFF, PNG-8, and PNG-24. Choose **JPEG**, as the bulk of our artwork contains photographic content. Remember that if you wish to export content containing 256 or fewer colors, such as a logo for a profile, you can use PNG-8 for a smaller file size.
7. Turn on the **Export Options** checkbox. When the options appear, ensure the **Quality** is set to `12`, which is the maximum. Turning on **Include ICC Profile** is helpful when color modes such as Adobe RGB 1998 need to be honored, but this is not the case with our files.
8. You can add a text label to the exported artwork by turning on **Include artboard Name**. Located in the top-left of the image, the canvas of the exported image will be extended to accommodate this feature. Historically, this was useful for proofing images and referencing each asset, but not appropriate for our final artwork. Leave this option deactivated. Click **Run** when done.
9. Once all files have been exported and you have reviewed the results, you can go to **File** → **Save**. Then, close the document.

Which file formats should I use when posting?

If your image contains mostly text and plain colors, try using the PNG format to reduce the file size. This offers more appropriate compression and is built for images with 256 colors or less. Use JPG for continuous tone images, such as photos, where you are managing thousands of colors. You can post animated GIFs to your Facebook timeline up to 8 MB in size, but they should contain less than 20% text and not have grainy content or flashes; these posts may not be approved by Facebook if you try to boost them.

Scheduling posts with Adobe Express

In 2022, Adobe released major updates to Express, an online tool for the creation of web and social media graphics. It's useful for still images such as photos and vectors, as well as videos, that can be resized to work with different platforms. Here is how to schedule posts with Adobe Express:

1. From your web browser, head to `https://express.adobe.com/`, where you may need to log into your Creative Cloud account by clicking on the avatar icon in the top-right of the web page.
2. Once logged in, click on the large, purple plus icon in the top-left of the web page called **Create New**. When the popup menu appears, choose **From your photo** from the list of options.
3. Next, you will be prompted to **Drag & drop an image** or **Browse** for one on your device. Choose whichever option you prefer and browse to the `06-Scil` folder, where the exported images you saved in the previous exercise can be found. Select `SM24Tw-1200x675-01.jpg`.
4. In the following dialogue, you will be prompted to choose a **Canvas Size**, select `Twitter`, and click on **Start with this photo**.
5. You will then be taken to yet another dialogue. This is the **Adobe Express Editor**, where you can apply filters and edit the image. This is not relevant to our image, as all the work has been done in Photoshop. Instead, click on the **Schedule your post to social media** icon, shown as a calendar at the top of the web page.
6. In the **New post** window, you can then compose your post just as you would on Twitter. You have access to emojis and the ability to add URLs and hashtags. Under **Select Channels**, click on **Twitter**.
7. Choose a **Publish date** and **Time** from the corresponding drop-down menus to the right of the interface and click **Schedule**. Your post will then appear in the calendar, where you can left-click on it to edit it. Adobe Express will then automatically post your tweet on the date and time specified.

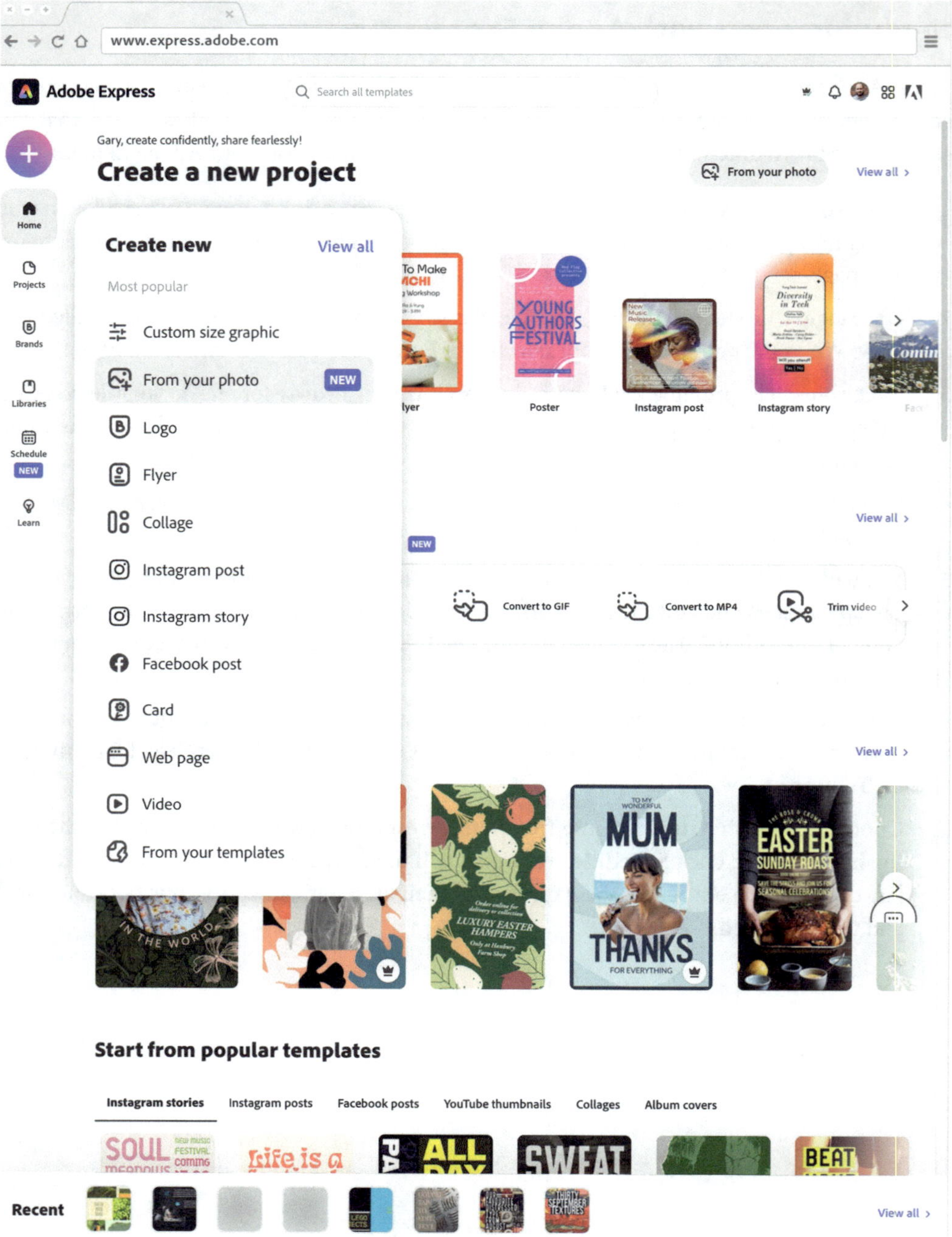

Fig 6.19: Clicking on the purple plus icon to create a new post and selecting From your photo

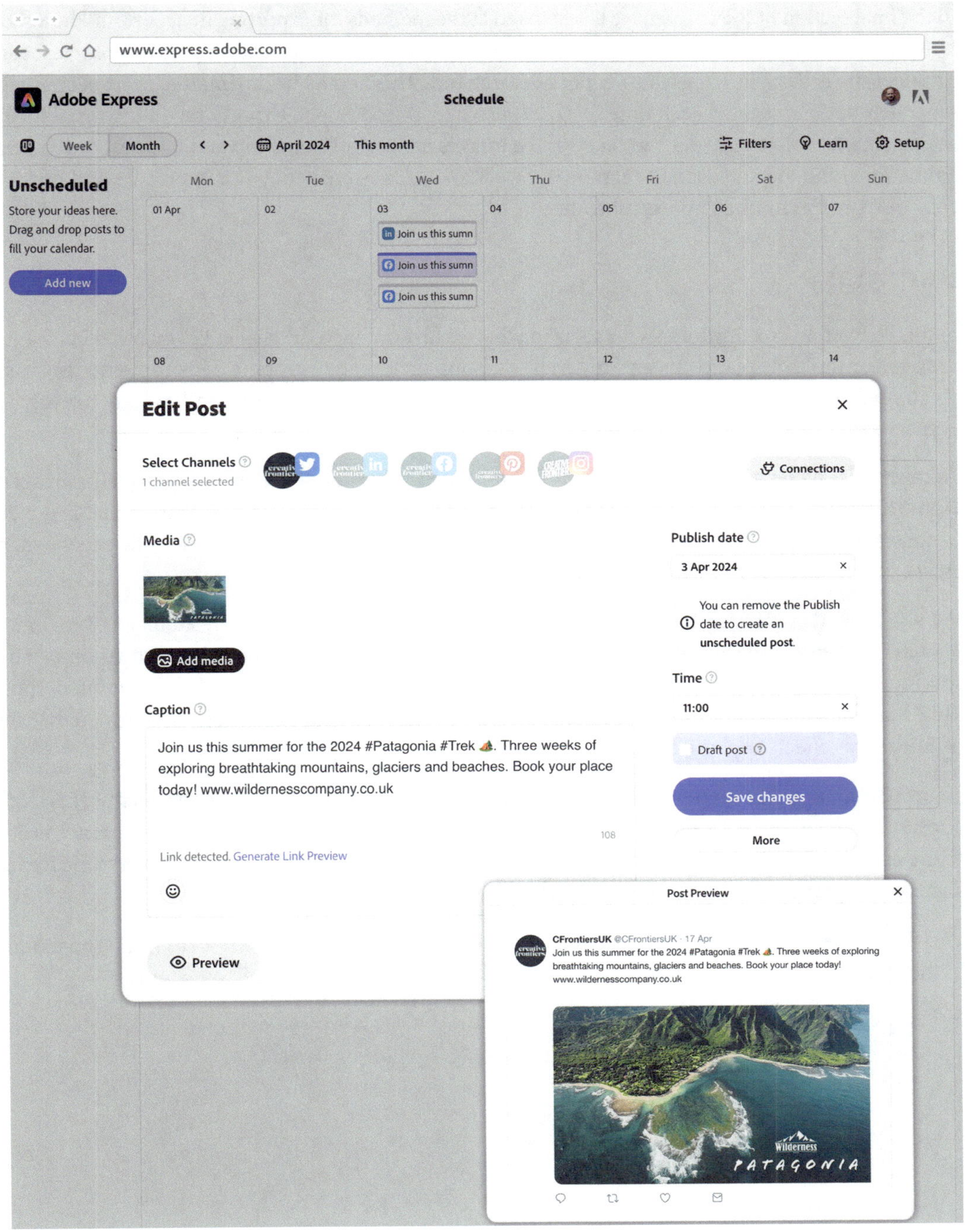

Fig 6.20: Creating, previewing, and scheduling posts in Adobe Express

In the final section of the chapter, we have looked at the methods for exporting images from Photoshop for use on social media platforms. By utilizing scripts for this task, we can batch process every artboard or select the artboards we wish to export beforehand. This avoids us having to export each image separately and name them each time. We have also introduced Adobe Express, an online social media management tool, where you can take source images edited in Photoshop and add responsive text, animations, and videos to adapt them to each platform. Once created, you can prepare and preview your posts in the Adobe Express scheduler.

Summary

In this chapter on creating images for social media, we first outlined the challenges involved in creating content for multiple platforms and different sizes for each type of graphic depending on their use. To compound the issue, the nature of social media often requires us to respond quickly to evolving events so that we can capitalize on public engagement.

To meet this challenge, we looked at features built into Photoshop that deliver high-quality imagery with short project timescales while managing dozens of images with identical content that is subject to constant changes. First, artboards allow us to create a single document with multiple pages, where assets are just a click away and easy to duplicate.

We also looked at infusing brand colors into layers such as logos to provide flexibility and maintain legibility. By applying multiple layer effects, such as color overlays, we can simply turn on or off a specific color. We also applied gradient overlays to background images so that when required, those same logos and text can be made legible against a soft vignette, fading from black to transparent. Each of these layer effects can be edited quickly.

Smart objects, as we have seen in so many chapters, are invaluable for protecting the quality of original photos. These can be replaced with ease for future projects or scaled for different artboards according to the use case. Finally, we used scripts to batch export our social media images to a specific file format and directory, avoiding the need to complete this process manually for each image.

We will continue with the theme of social media in the next chapter, where our focus will be on motion in the form of animated GIFs and videos. Both of these can be created in Photoshop!

7

Creating Animated GIFs and Videos

Photoshop is one of the most powerful image editors around, and since the 2007 release of Creative Suite 3, it has also been possible to import and edit videos. You might be wondering why you would choose to edit videos in Photoshop when there are dedicated applications such as Premier Pro and After Effects. If you edit large projects containing a multitude of assets, it would be prudent to look to Adobe's flagship video editing applications. However, if you need to combine a video clip with some text and an audio file to create a short sequence, then you may find comfort in Photoshop's simplified workflows and familiar tools.

In the late 90s, Photoshop introduced the **History** panel, which provides access to your last 50 document states, rather like an undo panel. Using similar techniques, it became possible to capture layer states that included visibility, position, and opacity. Much like the hand-drawn frame animation of the early 20th century, Photoshop frames could be turned into an animation sequence and saved as a GIF. Animated GIFs might be an "old-timer" file format, but they have survived through the birth and death of Flash. Today, animated GIFs still have a place across the spectrum of social media platforms.

In this chapter, you will utilize familiar tools and techniques to create video and frame animations for use on social media. You'll characterize new documents, work with a timeline to organize and edit your footage, and export files in formats that are suitable for posting online.

You will explore the following topics:

- Creating new motion projects in Photoshop
- Creating animated GIFs
- Working with video and audio in Photoshop
- Creating videos from still images and text
- Exporting animations and video from Photoshop
- Creating new motion projects in Photoshop

Before we create new motion projects, we need to cover two fundamental features to manage the timing and arrangement of **audiovisual** (**AV**) content in Photoshop.

Technical requirements

The project files for this chapter can be found at: `https://github.com/PacktPublishing/Mastering-Adobe-Photoshop-2024/tree/main/Chapter07`

The Timeline panel

A standard workflow in Photoshop involves editing still images where time is of no concern. However, when working with sequences or a set of frames that need to appear on the canvas at a specific time, we need a way of arranging assets accordingly. That's where the aptly named **Timeline** panel comes in. It provides a linear editing system where, on the far left-hand side, we can see the start of the sequence. When dealing with animation frames, they start at frame 1 (shown as **D** in *Figure 7.1*), while a video timeline starts at zero.

You add the first few items you wish to see at the start of the timeline, then keep adding more assets to the right-hand side to build up a sequence. In traditional hand-drawn animation, a sheet of paper would represent one frame, and approximately 24 sheets of paper would provide 1 second of animation. The appearance of each frame can be controlled from the **Layers** panel by changing the visibility, position, opacity, or layer style. Once the appearance of a frame has been altered to your satisfaction, you can add a new frame or delete an active frame (*Figure 7.1*, **C**).

The **Timeline** panel allows you to set a frame delay (*Figure 7.1*, **F**), where the animation pauses before moving on to the next frame. The delay is set to a default of 0, but you can change the delay of the active frame (*Figure 7.1*, **E**) from 0.1 seconds to 5 seconds. This is handy for frames containing logos or titles that you may wish to keep on-screen longer. You can navigate from the current frame to the previous or next frames in the **Timeline** panel using the frame select buttons (*Figure 7.1*, **A**) or preview the animation by pressing the **Play** button.

It is also possible to use the concept of layers in your motion sequences, just as you would with a still image for print. Imagine the scenario of opening titles that contain a background, such as video footage, a still image, or a plain color with text in front of it. This would ideally be achieved with two layers: a background layer containing the color or footage, and then, further along the timeline, a separate layer where text fades in:

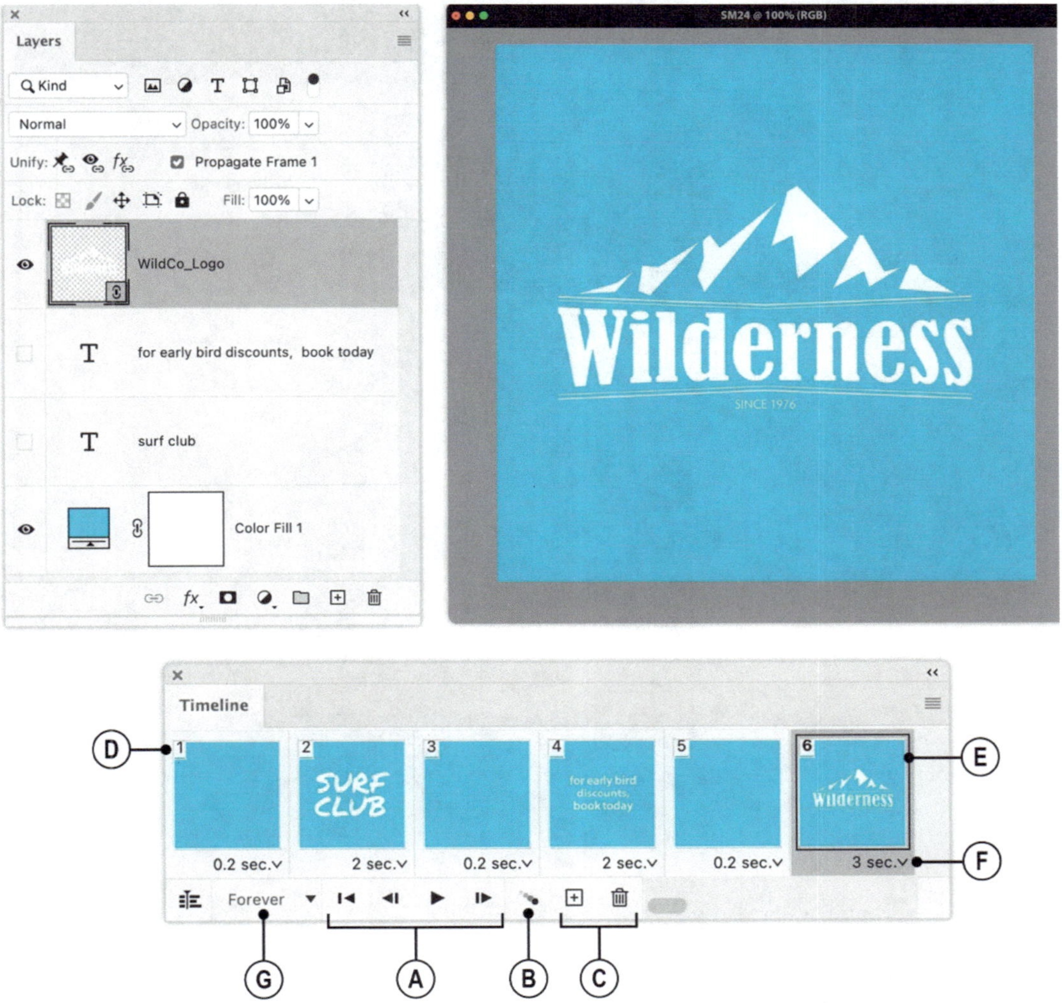

Figure 7.1: Animated GIFs can be created and managed in the Timeline panel

Video groups

In the previous chapter, we used artboards and artboard groups extensively to create several pages of artwork in a single document. When editing video assets in Photoshop, we use video groups, which act rather like regular layer groups, allowing you to store multiple assets within them. The difference with video groups is that they work in conjunction with the **Timeline** panel, where they appear in the same stacking order as the **Layers** panel, allowing you to arrange text layers in front of colored backgrounds to create, for example, a title sequence. These layers are independent of each other in the **Layers** and **Timeline** panels so that they can appear when needed:

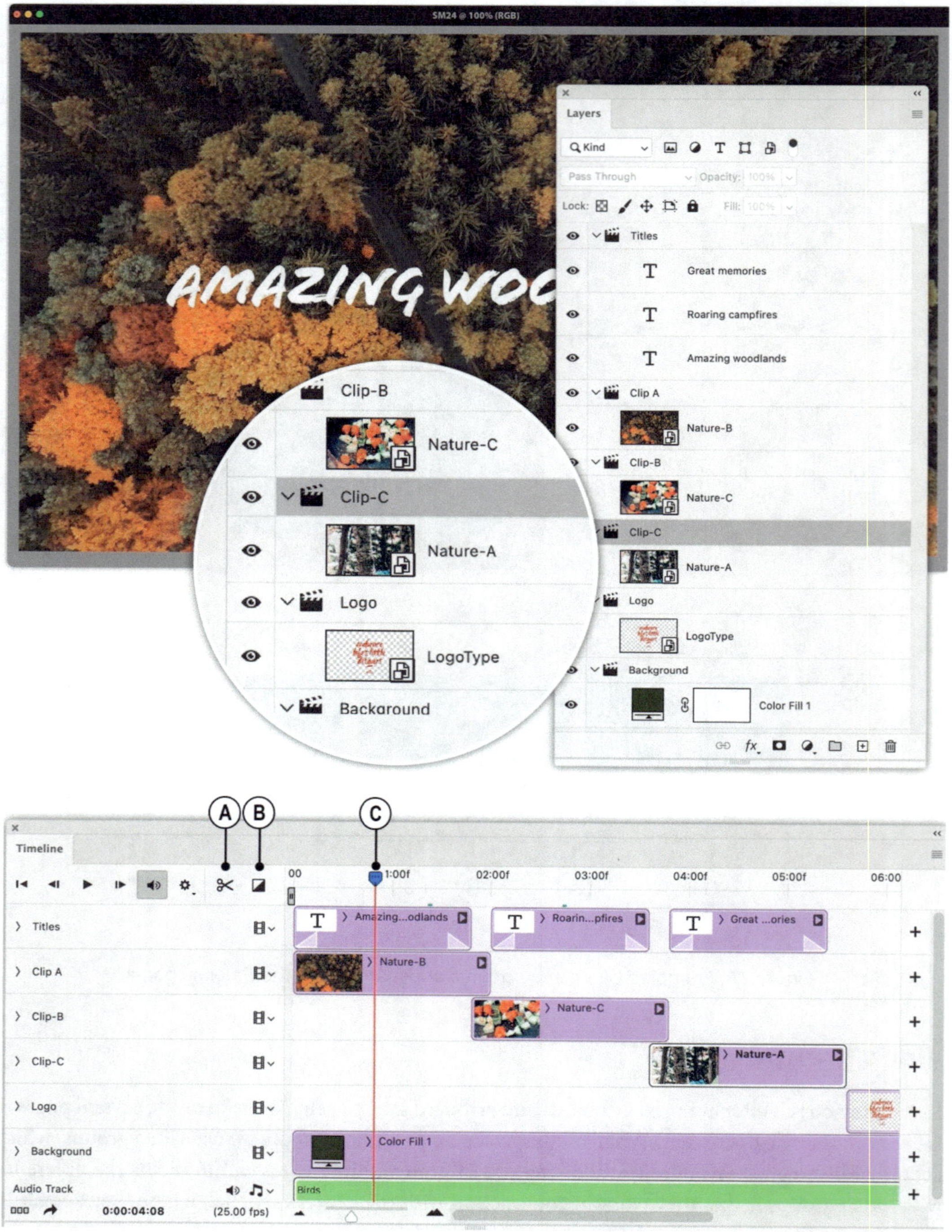

Figure 7.2: A video timeline allows you to add and trim video (A), audio, and transitions (B)

If your video requires several titles that need to appear one at a time, they can be created as separate text layers in a video group named "Titles." This will allow you to control when each text frame appears, the duration for which they will be visible, and when they disappear. At the bottom of the layer stack is a second video group containing the background.

AV file formats accepted by Photoshop

One of the greatest strengths of Photoshop is its ability to work with a wide range of still images, video, sequences, and audio formats. In the following table, I've listed most formats you can import and export when working with motion projects in Photoshop. However, the file formats that I have experienced the best performance from have been highlighted in bold.

As with still image editing, JPEG and PSD cover almost everything you need when importing graphic formats into Photoshop for video projects. In addition, I often use Adobe Illustrator AI, which imports an embedded PDF version of the original artwork.

I've found the balance between quality and file size offered by MOV and MPEG-4 suitable for most Photoshop projects. Bear in mind that in the following exercises, we aim to publish to social media, where the maximum size will be 1,920 x 1,080 pixels and the duration no more than 1 minute.

MP3 audio is abundant and for most online stock sites, it will be the format of choice that you will download in. It provides appropriate quality combined with low data sizes:

Import formats	
Video	.264, 3GP, 3GPP, AVC, AVI , F4V, FLV, **MOV (QuickTime)**, MPE, MPEG-1, **MPEG-4**, MPEG-2, MTS, MXF, R3D, TS, VOB
Audio	AAC, M2A, M4A, MP2, **MP3**
Graphic	WebP, BMP, Cineon, CompuServe GIF, DICOM, HEIF/HEIC, IFF format, **JPEG**, JPEG2000, Large Document Format PSB, Photoshop EPS, **PSD**, Photoshop Raw, Pixar, PNG, Targa, TIFF, **PDF**
Export formats	
Video	DPX, **MOV (QuickTime)**, **MP4**, JPEG2000 (QuickTime)

Video and GIF limitations on social media

Video is one of the best methods for generating higher engagement on social media. Both MOV and MPEG format videos are supported online, with animated GIFs supported on many platforms. The following table provides specifications for posting video files to popular social media platforms:

	Social media video and animation guide
Facebook	
Supported file types	MP4, MOV GIF
Recommended video dimensions	1,280 x 720 pixels
Minimum video dimensions	1,200 pixels wide (portrait/landscape)
Aspect ratio	16:9
Maximum data size	4 GB (8 MB for GIF)
Maximum duration	240 minutes
Twitter	
Supported file types	MP4, MOV GIF
Recommended video dimensions	1,280 x 720 or 720 x 720 pixels
Minimum video dimensions	32 x 32 pixels
Aspect ratio	16:9 or 1:1
Maximum data size	512 MB (5 MB for GIF when uploaded from a smartphone or 15 MB on desktop)
Duration	0.5 – 140 seconds
Instagram	
Supported file types	MP4, MOV
Recommended video dimensions	1,920 x 1080
Minimum video dimensions	1,080 x 1080
Aspect ratio	16:9 or 1:1 or 4:5
Maximum data size	4 GB
Duration	3 – 140 seconds
TikTok	
Supported file types	MP4, MOV GIF
Recommended video dimensions	1,080 x 1,920
Minimum video dimensions	1,080 x 1,080
Aspect ratio	9:16 or 1:1
Maximum data size	287.6 MB
Duration	15 – 60 seconds
YouTube	
Supported file types	AVI, AVI, FLV, MOV, MPEG-1, MPEG-4, MP4, MKV, WMV, 3GPP, WebM, GIF
Recommended video dimensions	1,920 x 1,080
Minimum video dimensions	426 x 240

	Social media video and animation guide
Aspect ratio	9:16 or 4:3
Maximum data size	128 GB
Duration	15 seconds – 12 hours
LinkedIn	
Supported file types	ASF, AVI, FLV, MOV, MPEG-1, MPEG-4, MP4, MKV, WebM
Recommended video dimensions	1,080 x 1,920
Minimum video dimensions	1,080 x 1,080
Aspect ratio	16:9 or 1:1 or 9:16
Maximum data size	5 GB
Duration	3 seconds – 10 minutes
Pinterest	
Supported file types	MP4, MOV, M4V
Aspect ratio	16:9 or 1:1 or 2:3 or 4:5
Maximum data size	2 GB
Duration	6 – 15 minutes

In this section, we reviewed the key tools and features that are used in Photoshop to create and manage motion projects and the file types you can import and export from the application. This section also included a guide on the recommended specifications for posting videos and animated GIFs to popular social media platforms. Next, we will create a new web document for an animation project.

Creating animated GIFs

In this first exercise, we will define document characteristics for a short and simple GIF animation to become familiar with the techniques surrounding frame animation. To maintain a low file size when output, it is prudent to limit the number of colors you use in a GIF animation. An animation containing hundreds of colors will dramatically increase file size.

Defining a new animation document

I've come to think of animation files as containing three crucial elements that could be likened to a theatrical performance. You have the canvas, which is the stage, the cast, which are the individual layers, and the scenes, which is the arrangement of content in the **Timeline** panel. I should point out that I don't get out much! So, the first step is to set up a suitable stage with a new document and canvas:

1. Go to **File** → **New**. When the **New Document** dialog appears, click on the **Web** tab at the top of the dialog to display the presets. Click on the **Web Most Common** thumbnail. Enter `Surf-A` into the **Name** field at the top right-hand side of the dialog.

2. Change **Width** to `1080` px and **Height** to `1080` px. Turn the **Artboards** checkbox off as we only need a single image; then, set **Color Mode** to **RGB Color**, **8-bit** and **Background Contents** to **Transparent**. Click **OK** when you're done to generate the document.
3. Go to **View** → **Guides** → **New Guide**. Add a **Vertical** guide at `540` px, set the guide's **Color** to **Yellow** from the drop-down menu, and click **OK**.
4. Next, head back to **View** → **Guides** → **New Guide**. Add a **Horizontal** guide at `540` px, set the guide's **Color** to **Yellow** from the drop-down menu, and click **OK**. These two guides will help with centering content visually in the canvas:

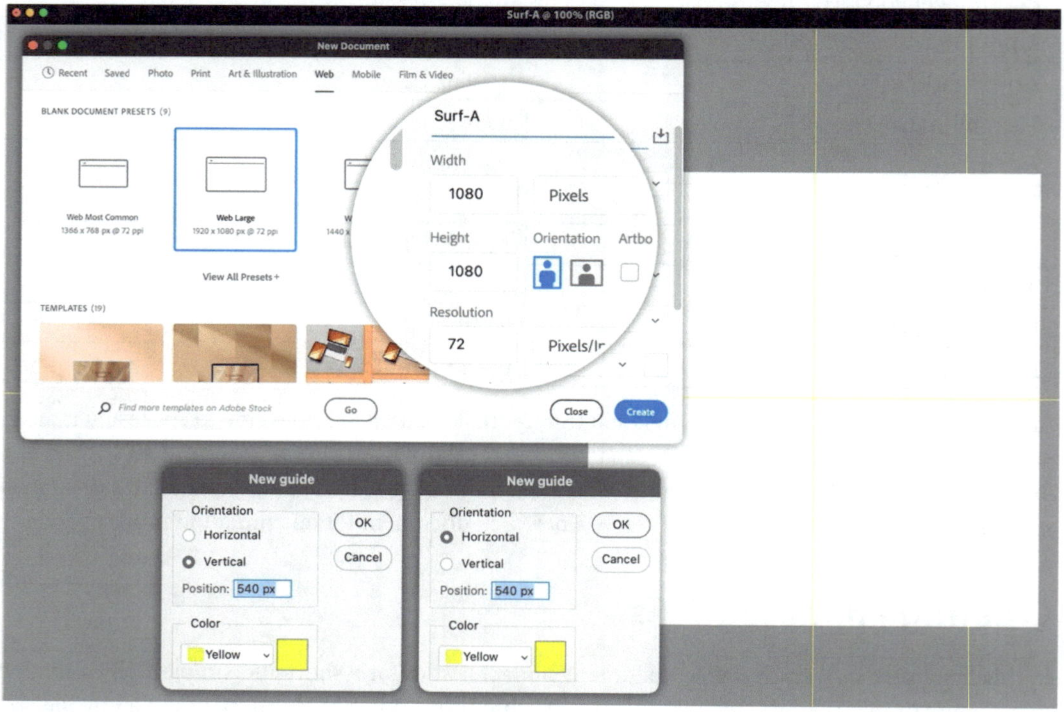

Figure 7.3: Creating a new file with guides added across the center of the canvas

Adding brand colors, logos, and text

Sticking with our theatre theme, next, we need to add the cast in the form of layers:

1. Here, we will add a branded color to the background. Click on the **New Fill and Adjustment layer** icon at the bottom of the **Layers** panel and choose **Solid Color** from the list of options. When the **Color Picker** dialog appears, enter `0db0d9` into the **Hexadecimal** field to create cyan. Click **OK**.

2. Switch to the **Horizontal Type** tool by pressing the *T* key. Hover the tool over the center of the canvas, then left-click and drag to the right to draw a text frame that is slightly smaller than the canvas. Release the left mouse button to generate the text frame, inside of which you will see the active type cursor.
3. Type `SURF CLUB` into the text frame, then highlight all characters in the frame with the **Horizontal Type** tool. From the **Properties** panel, set **Font Size** to **Permanent Marker**, **Size** of `350 pt`, **Leading** to `250 pt`, and **Tracking** to `-20`.
4. Set the alignment to **Centre** from the **Paragraph** options. Set the text's **Color** to white by left-clicking on the color swatch to open the color picker. Enter `ffffff` into the **Hexadecimal** field. Click **OK** to apply the color change and close the color picker:

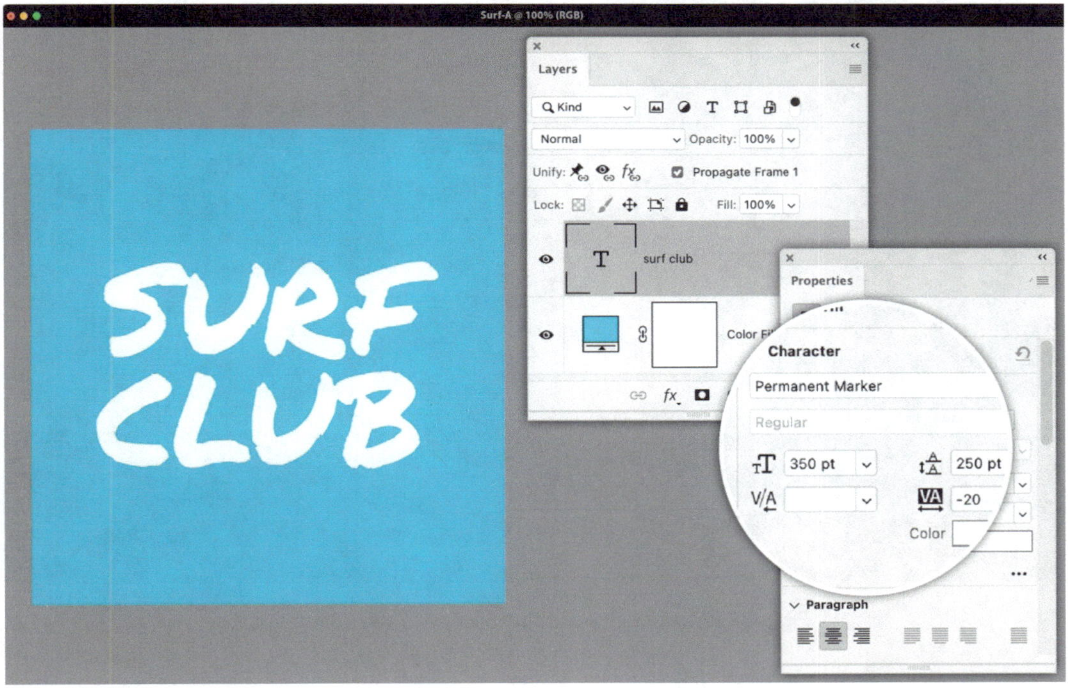

Figure 7.4: Adding a text frame using the Permanent Marker Creative Cloud font

5. With all copies formatted, reduce the size of the text frame so that it is just large enough to show all text. Press *Esc* to apply the text and exit type editing mode. Then, turn the visibility of the text layer you just created off.
6. Hover your cursor over the top-left region of the canvas and left-click and drag to create another text frame that is around the same size as the one you just created.

7. From the **Properties** panel, set **Font** to **Myriad Pro**, **Style** to **Bold**, **Font Size** to `128 pt`, **Leading** to `133 pt`, and **Tracking** to `-25`. Then type, `for early bird discounts, book today` into the text frame.

8. Set the alignment to **Center** from the **Paragraph** options. Set the text's **Color** to white by left-clicking on the color swatch to open the color picker. Enter `ffffff` into the **Hexadecimal** field. Click **OK** to apply the color change and close the color picker. Again, reduce the size of the text frame so that it fits the text. Press *Esc* to apply the text and exit type editing mode. Turn the visibility of the text layer off:

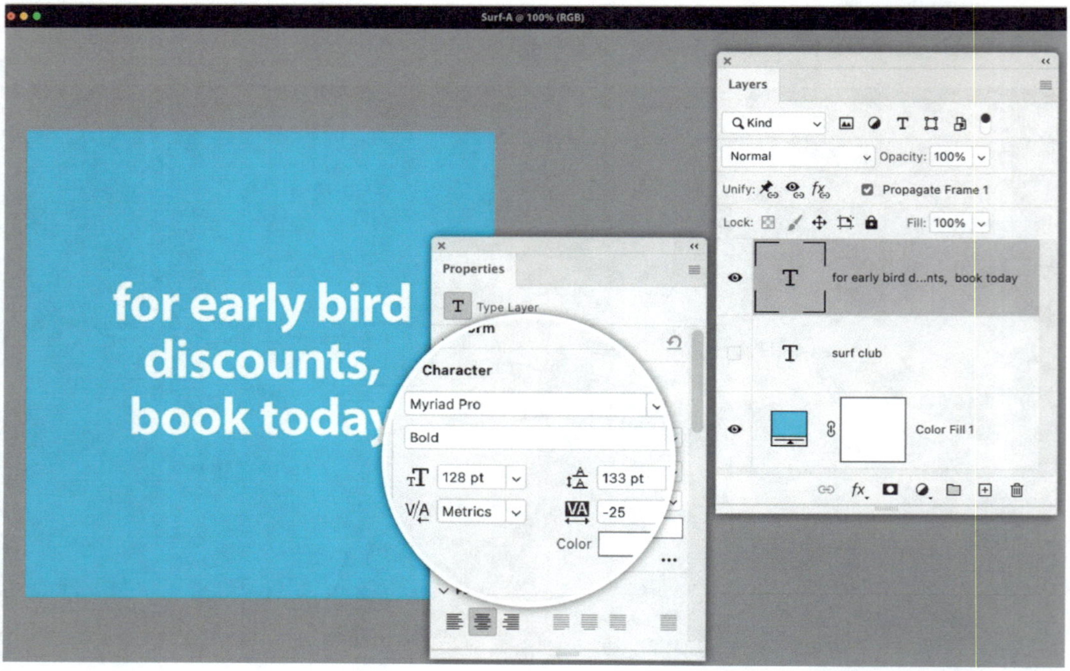

Figure 7.5: Adding a second text frame to the document

9. Go to **File** → **Place Linked**, browse to the `07-Motion` folder, select the `WildCo_Logo.ai` file, and click **Place**. When the dialog appears, left-click on the page 7 thumbnail, which contains a white version of the logo. Then, click **OK** to import the artwork.

10. When the logo appears, it will be scaled to fit the artboard. Ensure the **Width** and **Height** fields are linked in the **Options** bar, then change **Scale** to `150%` and click on the **Commit Changes** button in the **Options** bar to finish the import process.

11. Switch to the **Move** tool and reposition the logo to the center of the canvas using the guides to help you. Turn the visibility of the logo layer off, and then turn the visibility for each text layer on, one at a time, and center them to the canvas visually. When using the align tools, the size of the text frame will be taken into account, often leaving text looking off-center. Once

all the layers have been aligned to the center of the canvas, hide all layers except for the cyan **Color Fill** layer:

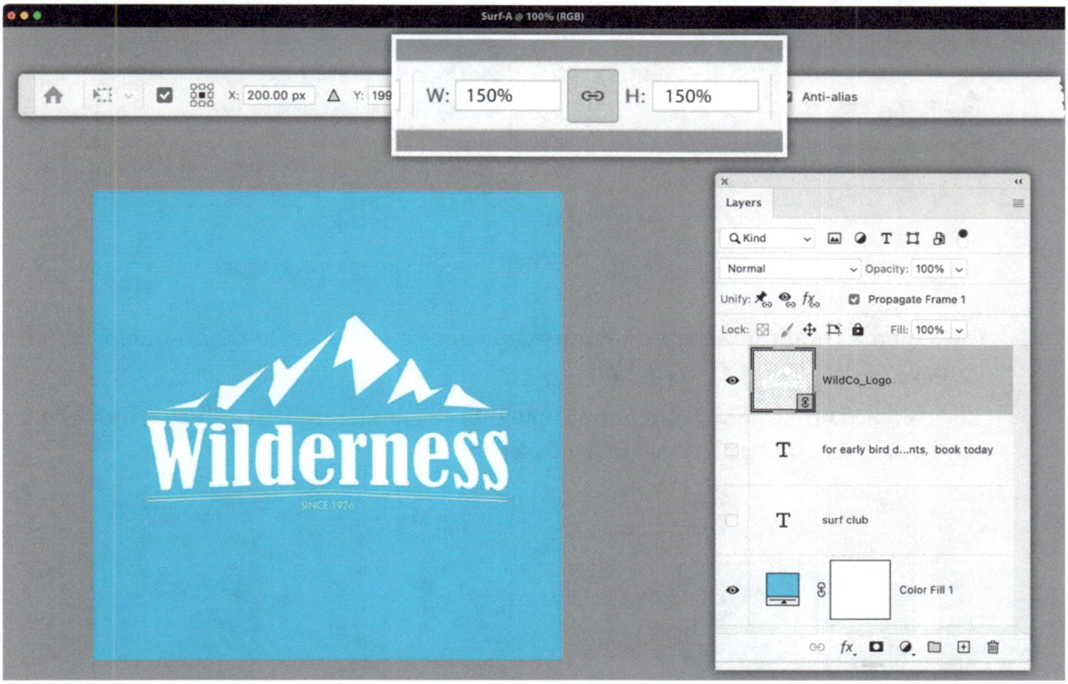

Figure 7.6: Placing a vector logo in the document and increasing the original scale to 150%

Creating frame animations

Act one, scene one! Now, we can start making our animated GIF frames using the **Timeline** panel. We'll start with frame pauses to generate the animation timing:

1. Open the **Timeline** panel by going to **Window** → **Timeline**. It will appear docked at the bottom of the interface. In this position, it takes up far too much room. Undock it by dragging the **Panel** tab containing the **Timeline** panel's name upwards. I suggest placing it adjacent to your canvas.
2. Click on the **Create Frame Animation** button in the **Timeline** panel to get started (**A** in *Figure 7.7*). This will generate the first frame of the animation; it will match the current state of your **Layers** panel. Ensure that the only visible layer is the cyan **Color Fill**.
3. Click on the **Duplicate selected Frame** button at the bottom of the **Timeline** panel (**B** in *Figure 7.7*). Now that we have an additional frame, we can change the appearance of the document canvas through the **Layers** panel. Turn the visibility of the **SURF CLUB** layer on:

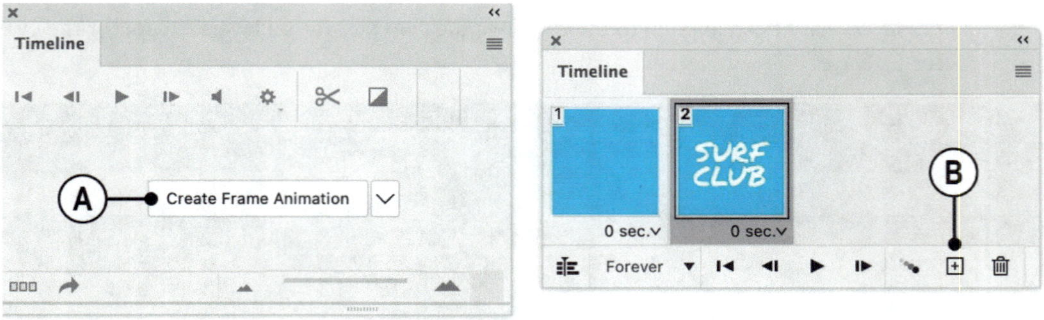

Figure 7.7: Setting the timeline to frame animation to get started

4. Click on the **Duplicate selected Frame** button once more to create a third frame. Turn the visibility of the **SURF CLUB** layer off.
5. Click on the **Duplicate selected Frame** button to create a fourth frame. Turn the visibility of the **for early bird…** text layer on in the **Layers** panel:

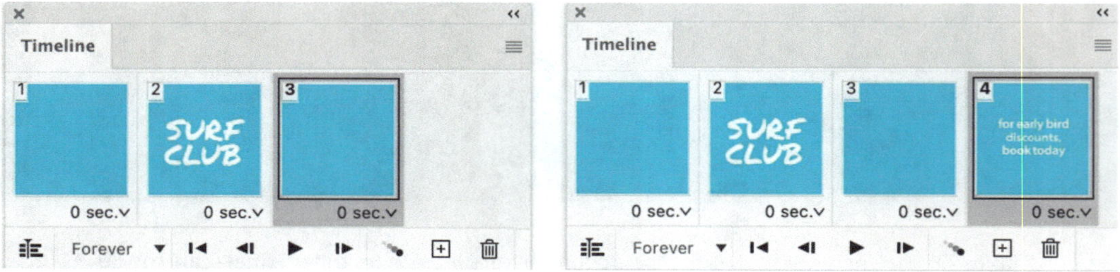

Figure 7.8: Adding new frames and making changes to the Layers panel to build the animation

6. Click on the **Duplicate selected Frame** button once more to create a fifth frame. Turn the visibility of the **for early bird…** layer off.
7. Click on the **Duplicate selected Frame** button to create a sixth frame. Turn the visibility of the **WildCo_Logo** layer off in the **Layers** panel. With that, we've created the required number of frames to generate our animated GIF.
8. Next, left-click on the **Frame 1** thumbnail to make it active. You will notice that the image changes appearance to match the thumbnail. Click on the **Select Frame Delay** drop-down menu under the **Frame 1** thumbnail (**A** in *Figure 7.9*), which currently reads **No delay**. Choose **0.2 sec.** from the list:

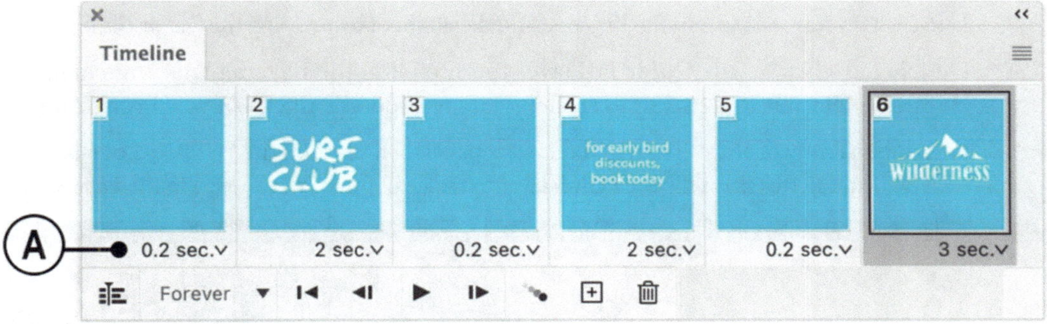

Figure 7.9: The completed six-frame animation, created with frame pauses

9. Left-click on **Frame 3** and **Frame 4** in turn and apply the same edit to pause the frames for **0.2 sec.**.
10. Next, left-click on the **Frame 2** thumbnail to make it active. This will reveal the **SURF CLUB** text. Change **Frame Delay** to **2 sec.** from the list. Then, left-click on **Frame 4** thumbnail to make it active. This will reveal the early bird text. Change its **Frame Delay** to **2 sec.** from the list.
11. Finally, left-click on the **Frame 6** thumbnail to make it active and reveal the logo. Change its **Frame Delay** to **3 sec.** from the list. Then, ensure the **Loop** option is set to **Forever** from the bottom-left corner of the **Timeline** panel.
12. Now, you can sit back and watch your animation by left-clicking on the **Play Animation** button at the bottom of the **Timeline** panel. Press the **Stop Animation** button once you have checked the animation.
13. Go to **File** → **Save**, browse to the `07-Motion` folder, save the file as a PSD file called `Surf-A`, and keep the document open for the next exercise. You will learn how to export animated GIFs at the end of this chapter.

Creating tween animations

Traditional animation required an artist to draw each frame to capture movement, a process that I imagine would have required considerable patience. Similarly, in Photoshop, when we want to create the impression of movement, we need to generate every frame of that animation. Fortunately, we can use a technique called tweening, where we define the start and end of the animation, after which Photoshop generates the frames in between, hence the name tweening! Let's take a look:

1. With the **Surf-A** document still open and active, go to **Image** → **Duplicate**. When the dialog appears, name the duplicate file `MotionSurf-A` and click **OK**.
2. Go to **File** → **Save As**, browse to the `07-Motion` folder and save the document as a PSD file. Then close the original `Surf-A` file.

3. Left-click on frames 2 to 6 in the timeline and delete them by pressing the *Del* or *Backspace* key.
4. Double left-click on the **Color Fill** layer thumbnail in the **Layers** panel and change the **Hexadecimal** value to `32838C` to create a vibrant turquoise. Click **OK** when you're done.
5. Turn the visibility of all layers on in the **Layers** panel. Left-click on the **WildCo-Logo** layer and then *Shift* and left-click on the **Surf Club** layer to make all three layers active in the **Layers** panel:

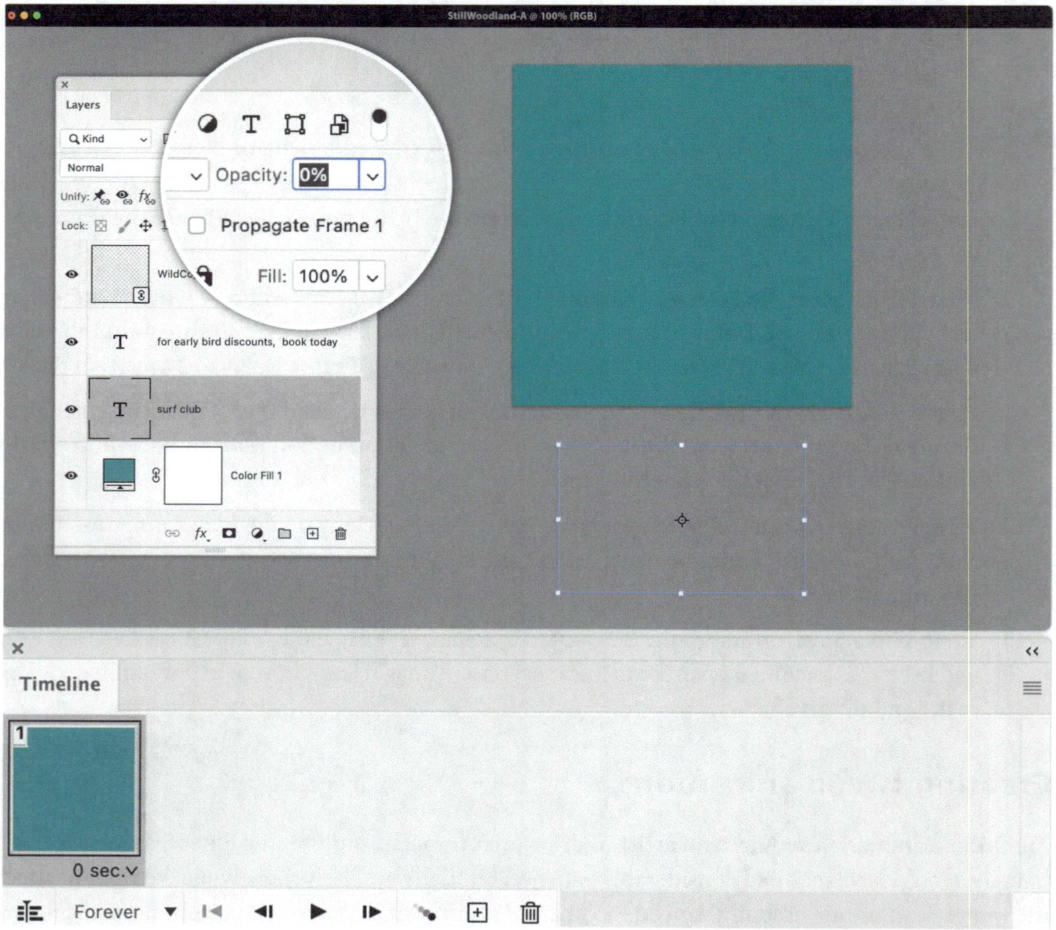

Figure 7.10: Each new keyframe defines the start and end of the final animation

6. Switch to the **Move** tool from the **Options** bar and turn on the **Show Transform Controls** checkbox. Drag all the active layers off the bottom of the canvas until they disappear and hold *Shift* as you do so to prevent the layers from moving horizontally. Then, reduce the **Opacity** value of all active layers to `0%`.
7. Click on the **Duplicate selected Frame** button at the bottom of the **Timeline** panel to create an additional frame.

8. Left-click on the **Surf Club** layer to make it active. Increase the **Surf Club** layer's **Opacity** to `100%`. Then, drag the active layer to the center of the canvas, again holding *Shift* as you do so to prevent the layer from moving horizontally:

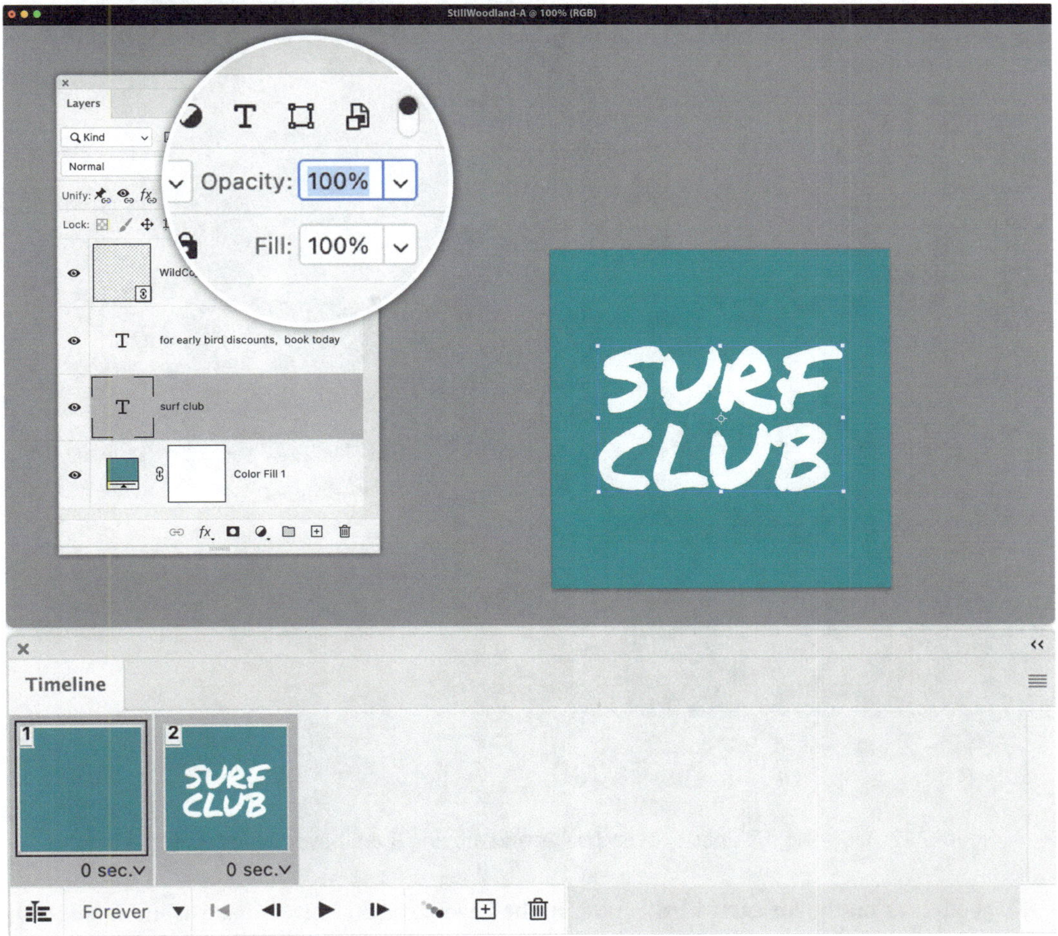

Figure 7.11: Moving each layer back onto the canvas and increasing the opacity

9. Click on the **Duplicate selected Frame** button at the bottom of the **Timeline** panel to create an additional frame.
10. Select the **Surf Club** layer and drag it off the top of the canvas until it disappears, holding *Shift* to prevent the layers from moving horizontally. Then, reduce the layer's **Opacity** to `0%`.
11. Click on the **Duplicate selected Frame** button at the bottom of the **Timeline** panel to create an additional frame:

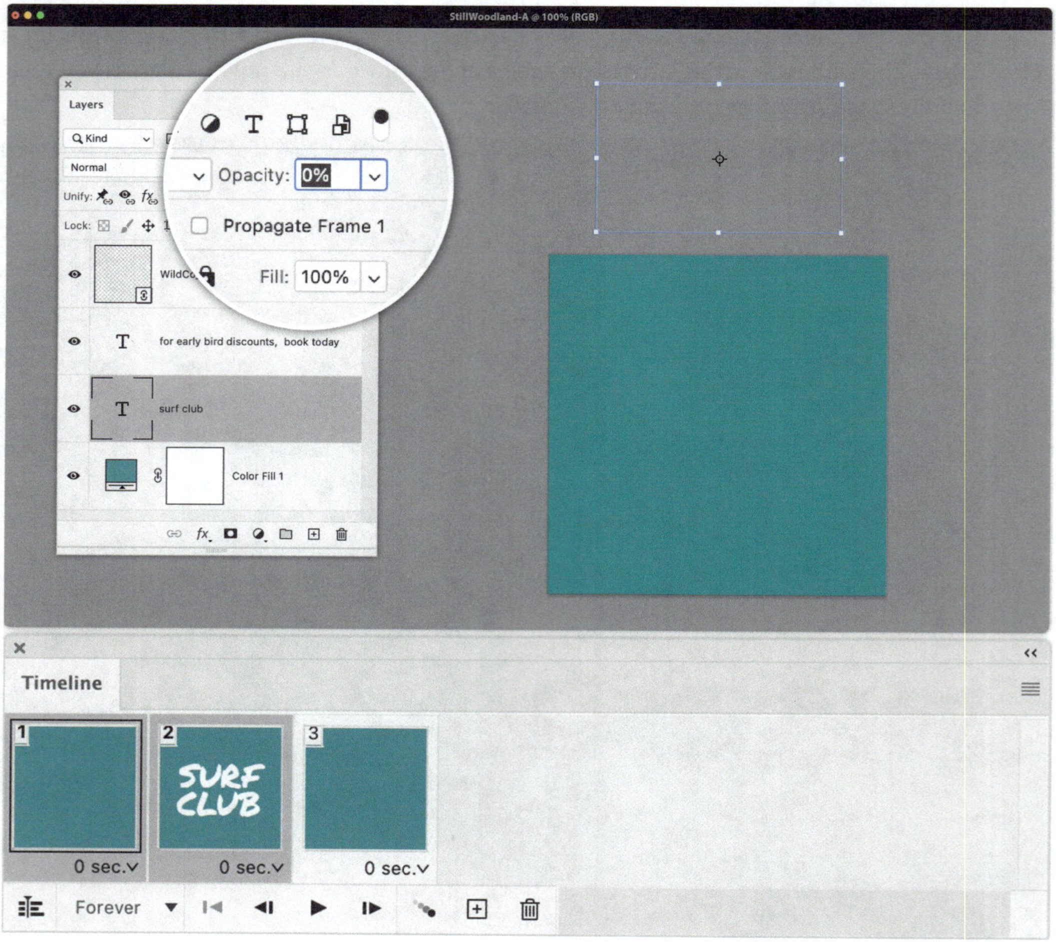

Figure 7.12: Reducing the opacity of each layer and moving them beyond the top of the canvas

12. Left-click on the **for early bird...** layer in the **Layers** panel to make it active and increase the layer's **Opacity** to `100%`. Then, drag the active layer to the center of the canvas, again holding *Shift* as you do so to prevent the layer from moving horizontally.
13. Click on the **Duplicate selected Frame** button at the bottom of the **Timeline** panel to create an additional frame.
14. With the **for early bird...** layer active, drag it off the top of the canvas until it disappears, holding *Shift* to prevent the layers from moving horizontally. Then, reduce the layer's **Opacity** to `0%`.
15. Click on the **Duplicate selected Frame** button at the bottom of the **Timeline** panel to create an additional frame.

16. Left-click on the **WildCo_logo** layer in the **Layers** panel to make it active and increase the layer's **Opacity** to `100%`. Then, drag the active layer to the center of the canvas, again holding *Shift* as you do so to prevent the layer from moving horizontally.
17. Click on the **Duplicate selected Frame** button at the bottom of the **Timeline** panel to create an additional frame.
18. With the **WildCo_logo** layer active, drag it off the top of the canvas until it disappears, holding *Shift* to prevent the layers from moving horizontally. Then, reduce the layers's **Opacity** to `0%`:

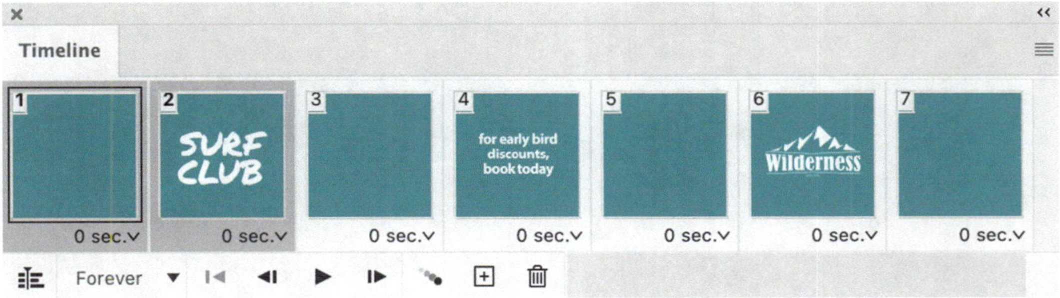

Figure 7.13: With all keyframes created, a pair of frames can be tweened

19. Left-click on **Frame 1** in the **Timeline** panel and then *Shift* and left-click on **Frame 2** to make both frames active. Click on the **Tween animation frames** button from the bottom of the **Timeline** panel.
20. When the dialog appears, set **Tween with** to **Selection**, **Frames to Add** to `5`, include **All Layers**, and leave all the **Parameters** checkboxes active. Click **OK** when you're done to add the additional frames.
21. Left-click on **Frame 7** in the **Timeline** panel and then *Shift* and left-click on **Frame 8** to make both frames active. Click on the **Tween animation frames** button from the bottom of the **Timeline** panel. The settings should be identical to the ones you defined previously. As such, click **OK**.
22. Left-click on **Frame 13** in the **Timeline** panel and then *Shift* and left-click on **Frame 14** to make both frames active. Click on the **Tween animation frames** button and click **OK** when the dialog appears.
23. Left-click on **Frame 19** in the **Timeline** panel and then *Shift* and left-click on **Frame 20** to make both frames active. Click on the **Tween animation frames** button and click **OK** when the dialog appears.
24. Left-click on **Frame 25** in the **Timeline** panel and then *Shift* and left-click on **Frame 26** to make both frames active. Click on the **Tween animation frames** button and click **OK** when the dialog appears.

25. Left-click on **Frame 31** in the **Timeline** panel and then *Shift* and left-click on **Frame 32** to make both frames active. Click on the **Tween animation frames** button and click **OK** when the dialog appears. This completes the tweening process!
26. In turn, select frames 1, 7, 19, and 31 and change the frame delay to **1.0 sec.**. This will allow the text and the logo to pause onscreen before disappearing.
27. Press the **Play** button in the **Timeline** panel to preview the animation and press **Stop** when you're done. Go to **File → Save** and close the document:

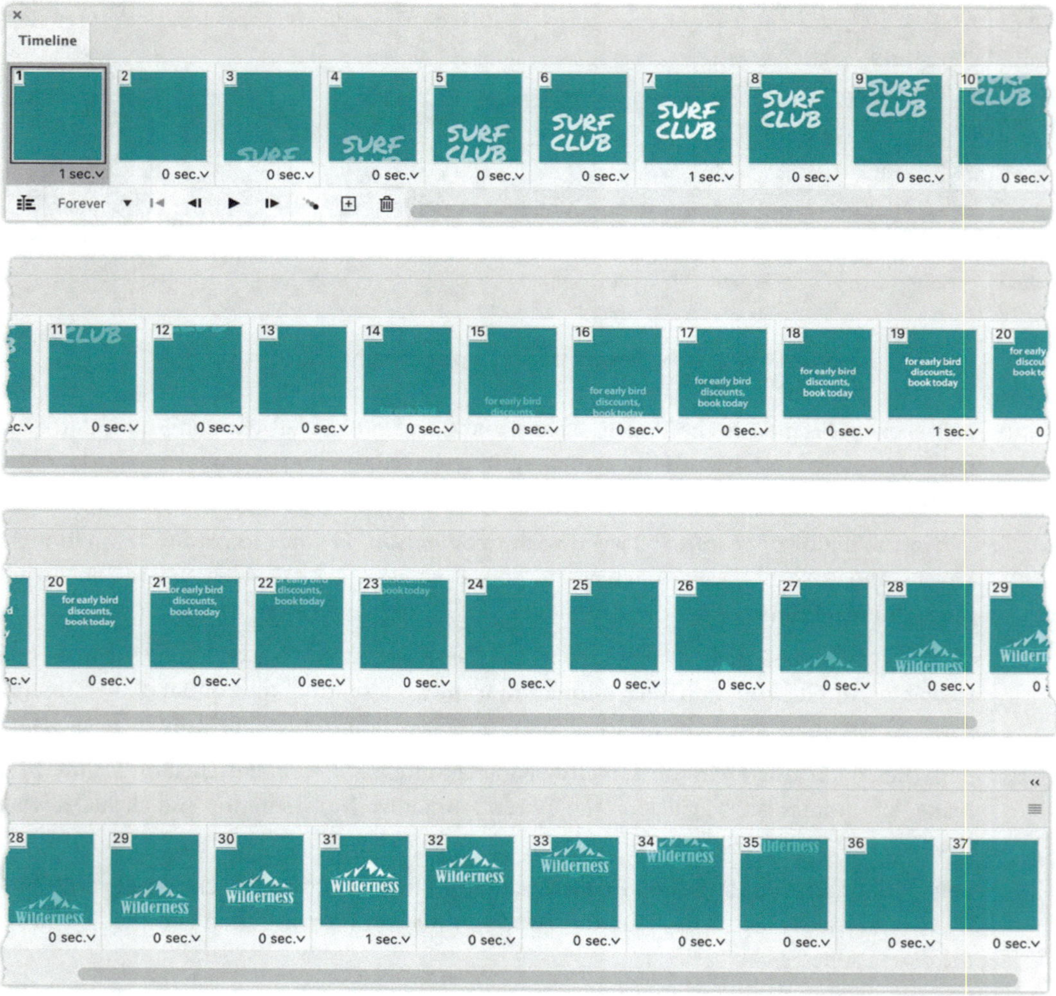

Figure 7.14: Every frame of the animation after tweening

In this section, we explored two types of animated GIF techniques. The first required creating frames and pauses in the form of frame delays. The second technique required us to create keyframes to capture the position and opacity changes. Then, we tasked Photoshop with tweening, a process in which the additional frames are generated, and in doing so, create the final animation. Next, we will create a new video project, where we'll be importing MPEG-4 video and audio.

Working with video and audio in Photoshop

Believe it or not, Photoshop was created by John Knoll to facilitate motion picture special effects, who was working with a company called Industrial Light & Magic. Some 20 years later, Photoshop allowed for editing and rendering of video footage with the launch of Creative Suite 3 in 2007, and its features have strengthened since.

Creating a new document intended for video

The easiest method for creating a PSD intended for video output is to video footage, just as you would a JPG file. Photoshop will then create a document that is based on the source video characteristics, such as size and ratio. However, the footage we are starting with came from an iPhone and you can start with a clean document canvas:

1. Go to **File** → **New**. When the **New Document** dialog appears, click on the **Video** tab at the top of the dialog to display the presets. Click on the **HDTV 1080p** thumbnail. Enter `VideoWoodland-A` into the **Name** field at the top right-hand side of the dialog.
2. This canvas size is larger than those recommended by Twitter and Facebook. However, we can scale down the video size at output time and still post to YouTube at the recommended 1,920 x 1,080-pixel size as the ratio for both sizes is identical. Leave all other settings set to their defaults. Then, click **OK** when you're done to generate the document.
3. Ensure that the **Timeline** panel is visible (**Window** → **Timeline**). You will notice that the **Timeline** panel is empty. Click on the **Create** drop-down menu in the center of the **Timeline** panel (**A** in *Figure 7.9*) and change the timeline option to **Create Video Timeline** from the list to make it visible. Then, click on the **Create Video Timeline** button to generate the timeline:

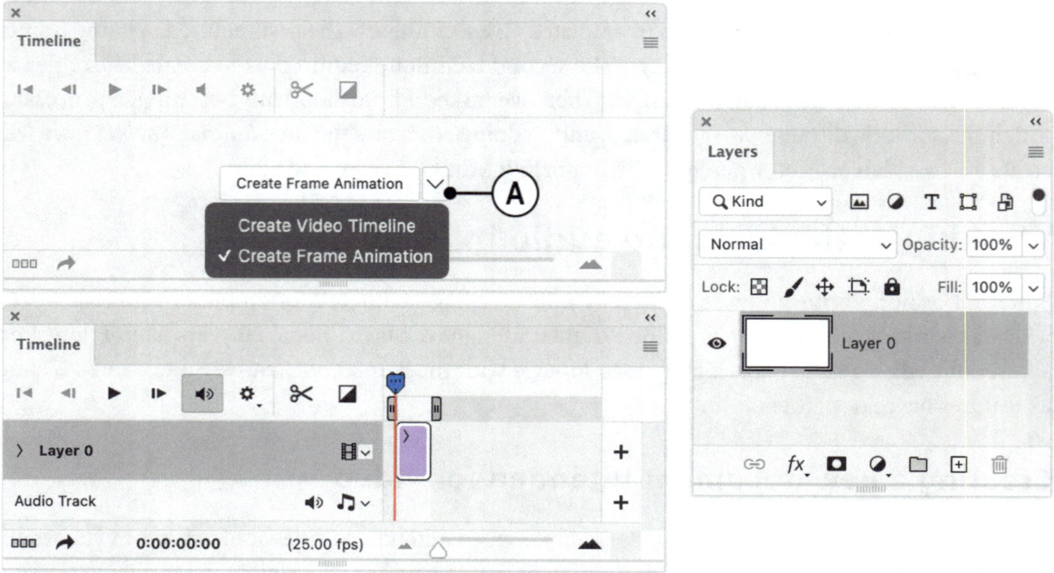

Figure 7.15: Creating a new video timeline to get started

4. This will add one media group containing a generic white background, reflecting the visibility of the **Layers** stack. Click on the **Timeline Panel fly-out** menu, choose **Set Timeline Frame Rate** and **25 frames per second**, and click **OK**.

Adding media to the timeline

You will start by adding footage to the active timeline and then edit its position, duration, and audio settings:

1. Click on the **New Fill and Adjustment layer** icon at the bottom of the **Layers** panel and choose **Solid Color** from the list of options. When the **Color Picker** dialog appears, enter `41472c` into the **Hexadecimal** field to create a dark green. Click **OK**.
2. Left-click on **Layer 0** in the **Layers panel** to make it active and press the *Del* or *Backspace* key to delete the layer, leaving just the color fill you created in the **Layers Stack** area.
3. Go to the **Timeline** panel, click on the **Media** button, shown as a film strip icon, and choose **New video group from clips** from the list of options. This will create a new video group in both the **Layers Panel** and **Timeline Panel** and place the **Color Fill** layer in it.
4. Go to the **Layers** panel, double left-click on the video group's name to open the type entry field, and rename it `Background`. Press *Enter* to apply the name change.
5. Head back to the **Timeline** panel, click on the **Media** button once more, and choose **New video group**. Rename the layer `Footage` using the same technique that you used in the previous step.

6. Click on the **Add media** button adjacent to the **Footage** video group in the **Timeline** panel and choose **Add Media** from the list. Browse to the `07-Motion` folder, select the `Forest_01.mpg` video file, and click **Open** to import the footage:

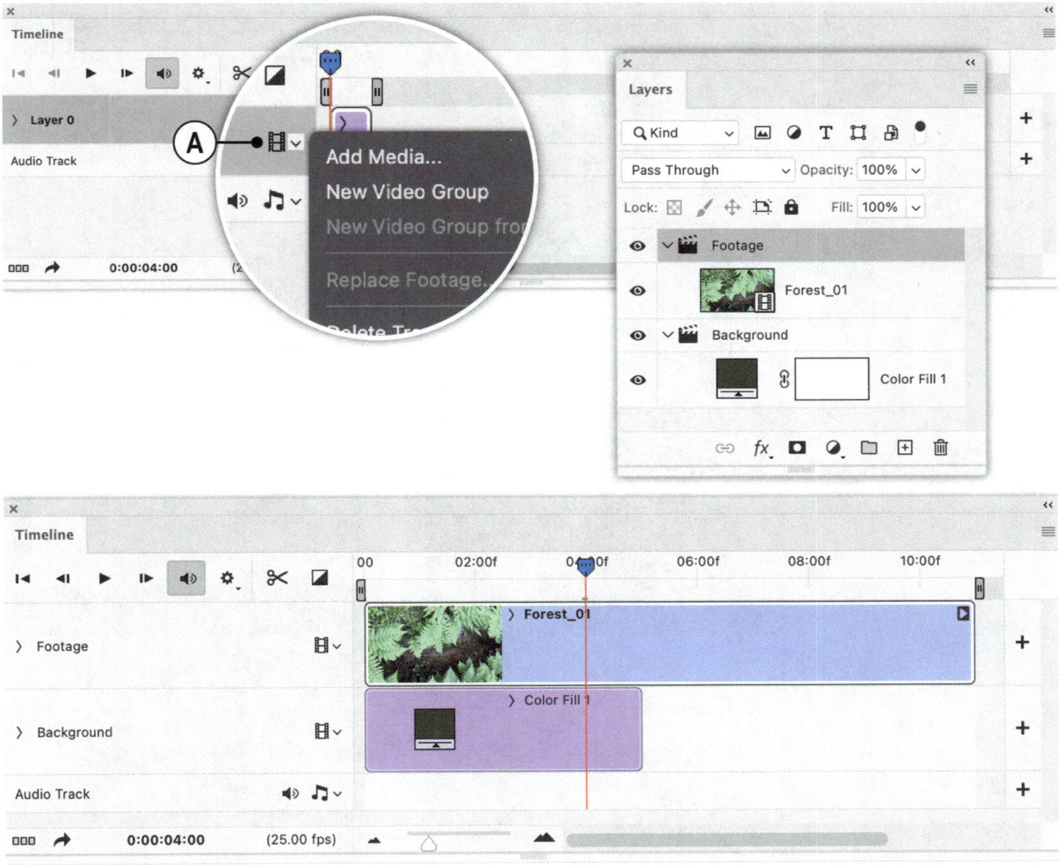

Figure 7.16: Splitting the first video clip and deleting the right-hand side footage

7. If the content in the timeline appears too small or is not entirely visible, try using either the **Zoom out Timeline** or **Zoom in Timeline** icons at the lower left-hand side of the **Timeline** panel, represented as small and large mountain icons, so that the entire sequence can be seen.
8. We do not require the full sequence of 11 seconds and the footage will need to be trimmed. Hover your cursor over the playhead, drag it to **frame 04:00**, and then release the left mouse button. Go to the **Timeline fly-out** menu and choose **Split at Playhead**. This will cut the footage into two sections. Left-click on the right-hand portion and press the *Del* or *Backspace* key to delete the unwanted footage.
9. With the `Forest_01.mpg` footage now positioned accordingly, we need to add the last two pieces of video footage. Ensure the `Forest_01.mpg` file is active in the timeline, click on the

Add media icon in **Video Group 1** in the **Timeline** panel, and choose **Add Media**. Browse to the `07-Motion` folder and select `Forest_02.mpg` and `Forest_03.mpg`. Click **Open** to import the footage; it will appear adjacent to the `Forest_01.mpg` footage:

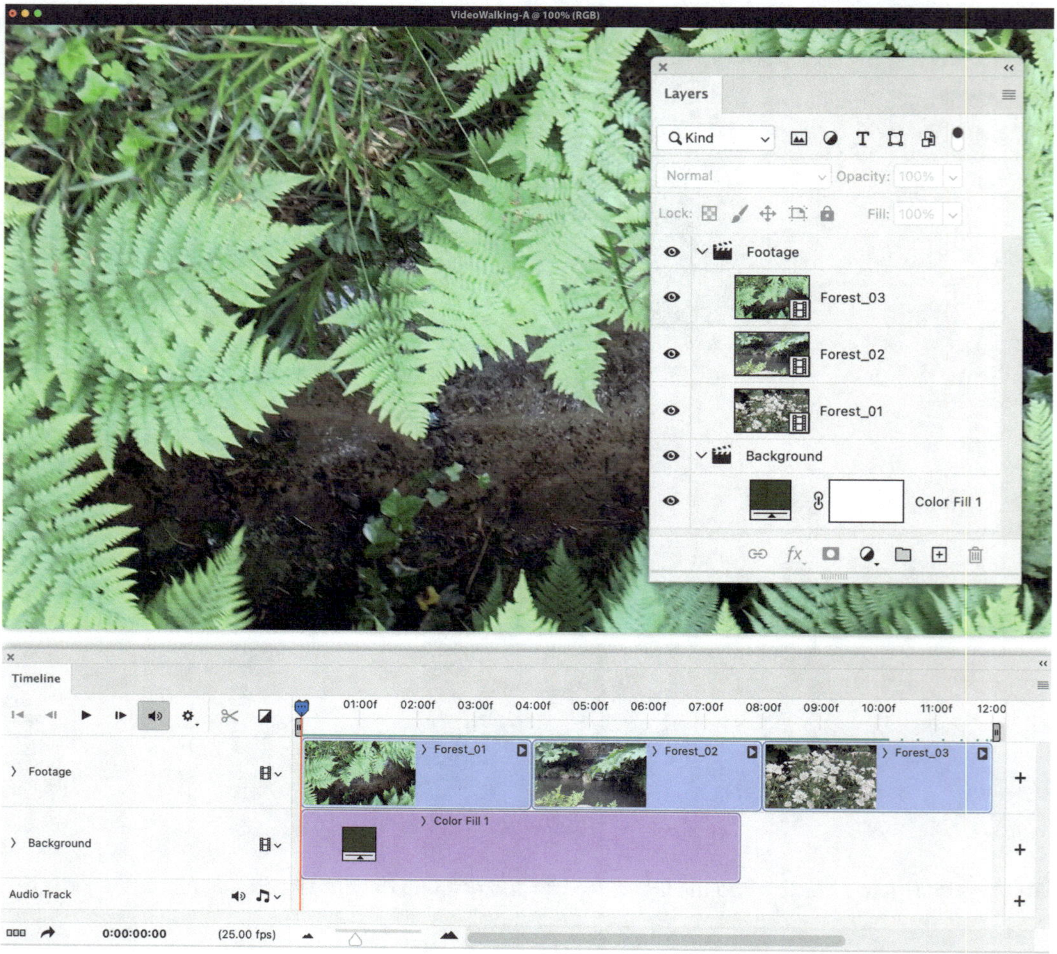

Figure 7.17: Adding the remaining two video clips to the timeline

Applying transitions to footage

Rather than leaving an abrupt cut between each piece of footage, we can fade to a color or between two pieces of footage, referred to as a cross-fade. Let's learn how to do this:

1. Click on the **Transitions** icon (**A** in *Figure 7.12*), located on the top left-hand side of the **Timeline** panel, to reveal the pop-out menu. Transitions in Photoshop can be added by dragging them from the pop-up menu and onto, or between, separate footage.

2. Drag the **Cross Fade** transition icon from the pop-up and over to the region where the `Forest_01.mpg` and `Forest_02.mpg` footage meet, at which point you will see a bold black box appear, indicating you can release the mouse button to add the **Cross Fade** transition. Adding a crossfade will shorten the footage because it must overlap the two pieces of video to be created.
3. Drag a second **Cross Fade** transition from the pop-up and over to the region where the `Forest_02.mpg` and `Forest_03.mpg` footage meet. Release the mouse button when you see the bold black box appear around the two clips.
4. The `Forest_03.mpg` footage will also need a **Fade** transition added to it so that it fades to the background color. Click on the **Transitions** icon and drag the **Fade** transition icon onto the end of the `Forest_03.mpg` clip in the timeline. When the black outline box appears, release the mouse:

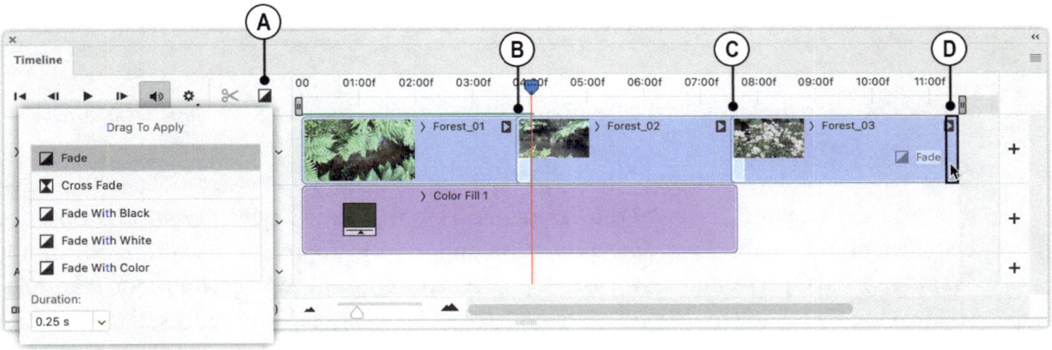

Figure 7.18: Adding Cross Fade transitions between each video clip and fading the last clip

Placing and animating an Adobe Illustrator logo in the timeline

To reinforce the company brand, we will place the logo in the timeline, and then transform and apply transitions to it so that will be animated:

1. Left-click on the **Footage** video group in the **Timeline** panel to make it active and then left-click on the `Forest_03.mpg` clip. This can help prevent new footage from appearing in an undesirable position in the timeline.
2. Go to **File** → **Place Linked**. Browse to the `07-Motion` folder and select `LogoType.ai`. Click **Open** to import the footage; it will appear adjacent to the `Forest_03.mpg` footage.
3. Click on the **Maintain Aspect Ratio** button in the **Options** bar to link the **Width** and **Height** values and then change the scale to `280%`. Click on the **Commit changes** button in the **Options** bar to complete the import process.

4. Right-click on the **LogoType** layer's name in the **Layers** panel and choose **Convert to Smart Object**. This will allow the layer to be animated.
5. Hover your cursor over the end of the **LogoType** clip in the **Timeline** panel to reveal the clip editing icon, then left-click and drag the end of the clip to the 20-frame mark in the timeline:

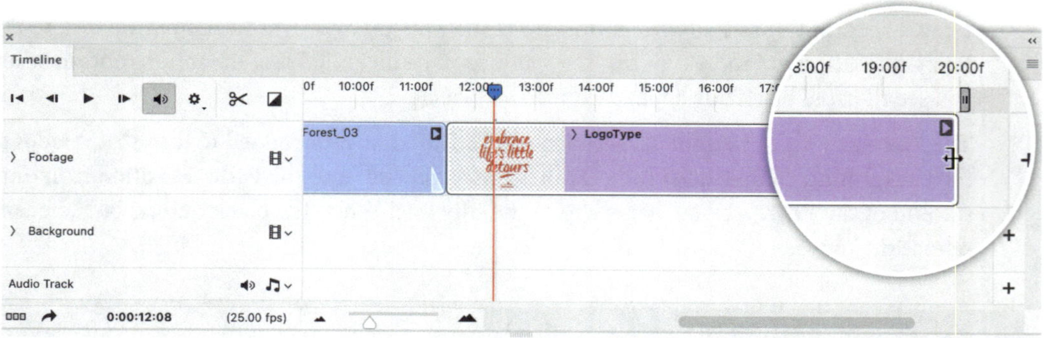

Figure 7.19: Changing the length of the LogoType clip by dragging the end of the clip in the timeline

6. Drag the playhead to the start of the **LogoType** clip. Expand the **Footage** video group toggle in the **Timeline** panel to reveal the **Transform**, **Opacity**, and **Style** animation properties. Left-click on the **Enable keyframe animation** button (**A** in *Figure 7.13*), which is adjacent to **Transform** and **Opacity** and shown as a stopwatch icon. This will add a keyframe for **Transform** (**B** in *Figure 7.13*) and **Opacity** (**C** in *Figure 7.13*) where your playhead resides in the timeline:

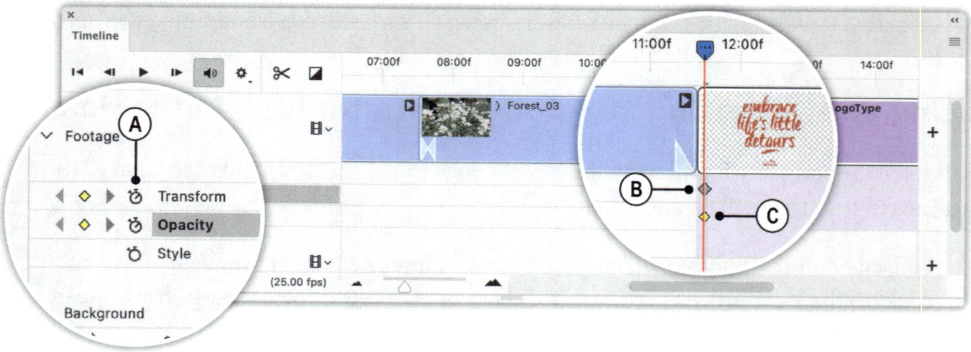

Figure 7.20: The transform, opacity, and style properties of smart objects can be animated

7. Reduce the **Opacity** value of the **LogoType** layer to `0%` from the **Layers** panel. Then, drag the playhead to **Frame 14** and increase **Opacity** to `100%`. This should add a second keyframe.
8. Go to **Edit** → **Free Transform** and, in the **Options** bar, link the **Width** and **Height** values. You will notice that because we turned the **LogoType** layer into a smart object, the scale now reads

100%. Reduce the scale to 75%. Click on the **Commit changes** button in the **Options** bar to apply the edits. This will add a second keyframe under the **Transform** section of the animation properties in the **Timeline** panel.

9. The background is currently transparent behind the logo. Locate the **Color Fill** layer, which can be found in the **Background** video group. Hover your cursor over the end of the clip and drag it to the end of the sequence at **Frame 20**.
10. The **LogoType** clip will also need **Fade** to be added to it. Click on the **Transitions** icon and drag the **Fade** transition icon onto the start of the **LogoType** clip in the timeline. When the black outline box appears, release the mouse.
11. Drag the playhead back to the start of the clip and press **Play**. You should now see the logo appear and zoom smaller into the center of the canvas. Press **Stop** when you have reviewed the animation:

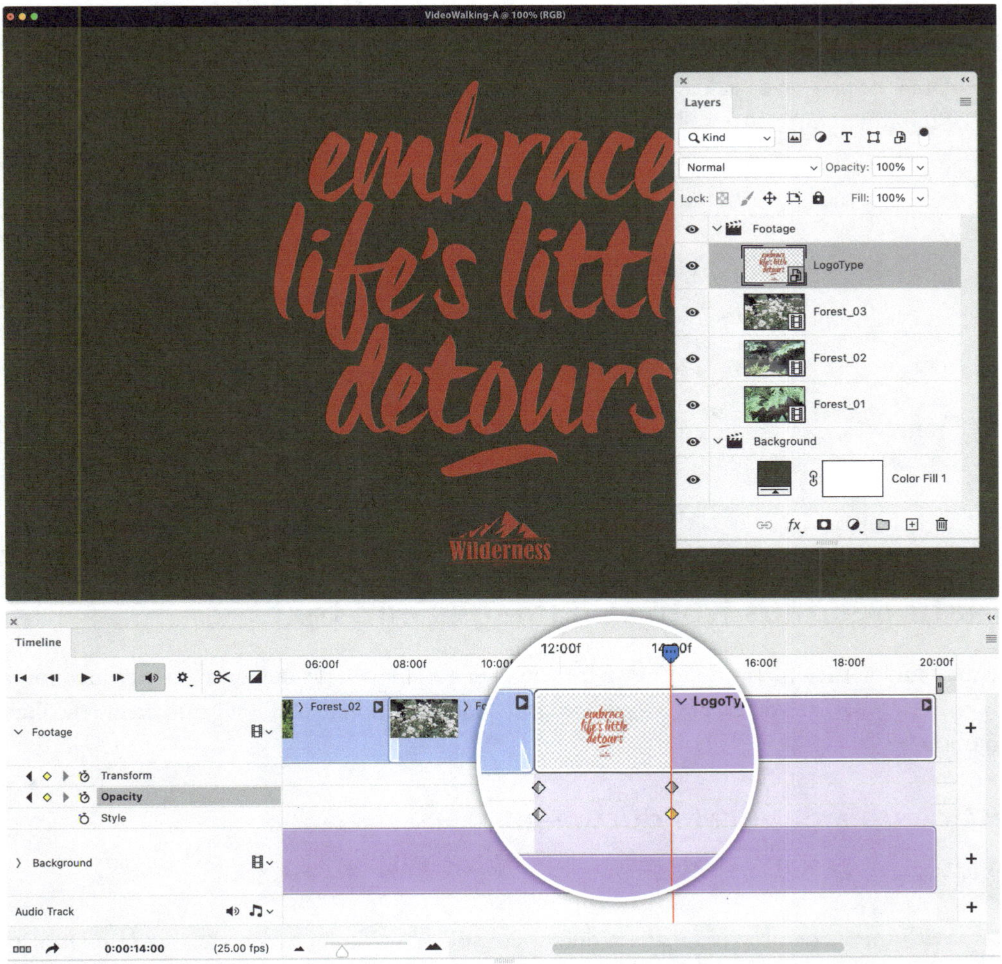

Figure 7.21: Reducing the scale of the logo will automatically add a keyframe

Adding a soundtrack to the timeline

You can add audio files to the timeline, where they can be edited like video clips. This allows you to add a music backing track of your choice to the timeline for dramatic effect:

1. Click on the musical note icon in the lower left-hand side of the **Timeline** panel and choose **Add Audio** from the list of commands. Browse to the `07-Motion` folder and select `Birds.mp3`. Then, click **OK** to import the audio.
2. In the **Timeline** panel, zoom out to find the end of the audio clip. Hover your cursor over the end of the clip to reveal the **Trim** icon, drag it to the left-hand side to the 20-frame mark so that it matches the length of the sequence, and then release the mouse button.
3. Now that we have shortened the audio, we need to fade it out. Right-click on the `Birds.mp3` clip at the bottom of the **Timeline** panel to reveal the **Audio options** pop-up. Change the **Fade Out** value to `1 s`, and then the **Fade Out** value to `1 s`. Click away from the pop-up to make it disappear.
4. Drag the playhead back to the start of the timeline and press **Play** to check the sequence. Press **Stop** when you're done and then go to **File** → **Save**. Keep the document open for the next exercise:

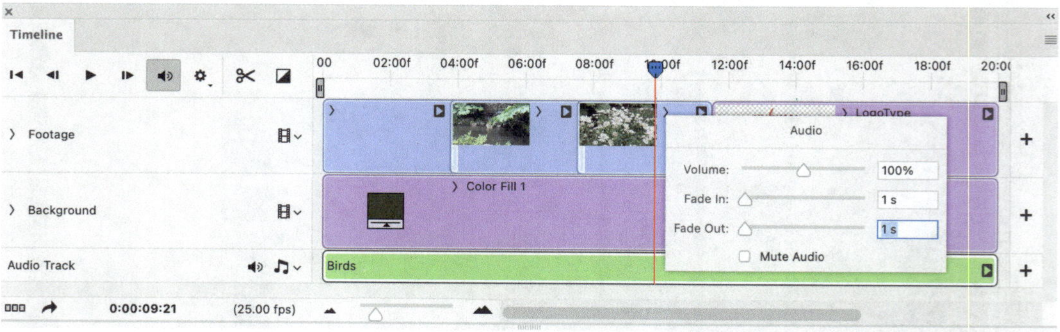

Figure 7.22: Right-clicking audio clips to access the fade-in and fade-out controls

Creating videos from still images and text

You may find yourself in a situation where you need to post videos but are without video footage. This exercise will take you through the process of adding motion to still images to create the illusion of motion.

Setting up a duplicate document

Follow these steps:

1. With the `VideoWoodland-A` document still open and active, go to **Image** → **Duplicate**. When the dialog appears, name the duplicate file `StillWoodland-A` and then click **OK**.

2. Go to **File** → **Save As**, browse to the `07-Motion` folder, and save the document as a PSD file. Then, close the original file – that is, `VideoWoodland-A`.
3. Left-click on each of the MPEG-4 video clips in the timeline and delete them by pressing the *Del* or *Backspace* key.
4. Change the name of the **Footage** video group to `Logo` from the **Layers** panel. Then, click on the **Media** button adjacent to the **Logo** group in the **Timeline** panel and select **New video group**. Change the name of the new group to `Clip-A`:

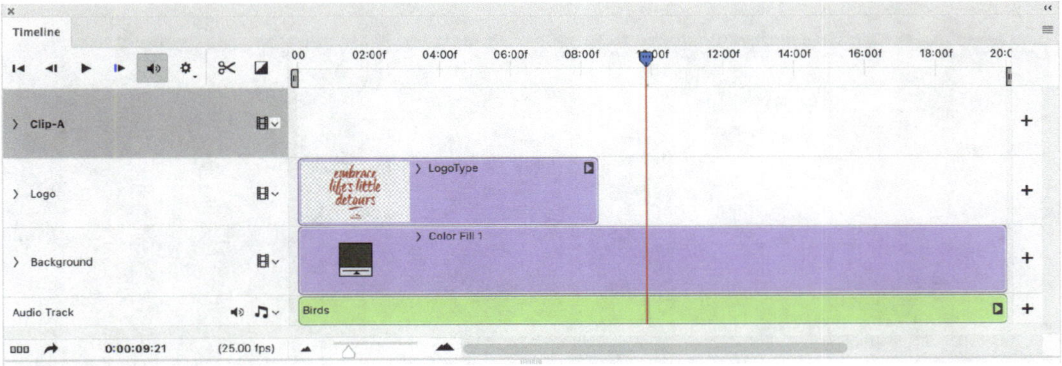

Figure 7.23: Deleting all the unwanted clips in the timeline

Importing and animating an image

You will be animating three still images in total. However, the hard work of animating the images only needs to be done once, after which they can be copied to subsequent clips:

1. Click on the **Media** button adjacent to the **Clip-A** group in the **Timeline** panel and select **Add Media**. Browse to the `07-Motion` folder and select `Nature-1.jpg`. Click **Open** when you're done.
2. Once the images appear in the timeline, right-click on the layers and choose **Convert to Smart Object** to enable animation features.
3. Next, shorten the length of the imported clip so that its duration is `2.0 frame`. Ensure the clip starts at **Frame 0**, the beginning of the timeline.
4. Go to **Edit** → **Free Transform** and link the **Width** and **Height** fields in the **Options** bar. Reduce **Scale** to `41%`. Click on the **Commit** button in the **Options** bar to apply the edits.
5. Drag the playhead to the start of the `Nature-1` clip. Expand the **Clip-A** video group toggle in the **Timeline** panel to reveal the **Transform**, **Opacity**, and **Style** animation properties. Left-click on the **Enable keyframe animation** button adjacent to **Transform**.

6. Drag the playhead to **Frame 2.10**. Go to **Edit** → **Free Transform** and increase **Scale** to `44%`. Click on the **Commit changes** button in the **Options** bar to apply the edits and create a new keyframe. Left-click on the **Enable keyframe animation** button adjacent to **Opacity** to add an opacity keyframe.
7. Drag the playhead to **Frame 2.24**. Go to **Edit** → **Free Transform** and increase **Scale** to `74%` and **Rotation** to `-18`. Click on the **Commit changes** button in the **Options** bar to apply the edits and create a new keyframe. Then, lower the **Opacity** value of the layer to `0%` from the **Layers** panel:

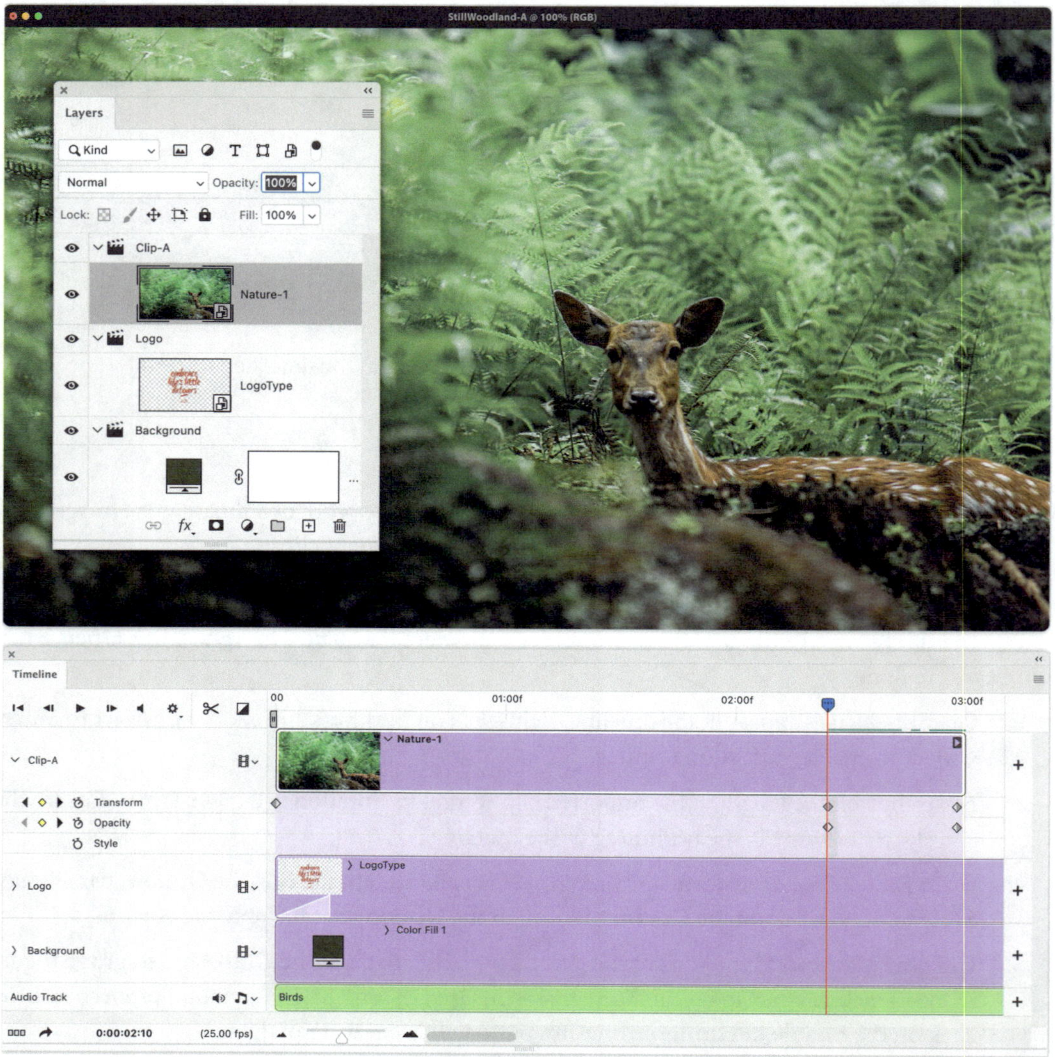

Figure 7.24: Adding scale, rotation, and opacity keyframes to the still image

Copying and pasting keyframes onto the second clip

Now that the hard work of animating the first clip is complete, we will copy and paste the animation onto a new media clip:

1. Left-click on the `Nature-1` clip in the timeline, then go to the **Timeline** panel's flyout menu and choose **Keyframes** → **Select all** from the list of options. Then, return to the same flyout menu once more and choose **Keyframes** → **Copy**. The keyframes should now be highlighted yellow in the timeline.
2. Click on the **Media** button adjacent to the **Logo** group in the **Timeline** panel and select **New video group**. Change the **Name** of the new group to `Clip-B`. This will create a new group under the **Clip-A** group so that when the images transition, they will fade and become visible.
3. Click on the **Media** button adjacent to the **Clip-B** group in the **Timeline** panel and select **Add Media**. Browse to the `07-Motion` folder and select `Nature-2.jpg`. Click **Open** when you're done.
4. Once the images appear in the timeline, right-click on the layers and choose **Convert to Smart Object** to enable animation features. As we did previously, shorten the length of the imported clip so that the duration is `3.0` frames in length.
5. Go to **Edit** → **Free Transform** and link the **Width** and **Height** fields in the **Options** bar. Reduce **Scale** to `41%`. Click on the **Commit changes** button in the **Options** bar to apply the edits.
6. Left-click on the `Nature-2` clip in the timeline, then go to the **Timeline** panel's flyout menu and choose **Keyframes** → **Paste** from the list of options. This will add the same scale, rotation, and opacity transformations.
7. Then, drag the clip so that it starts at **Frame 2.10** in the timeline, at the point where the previous clip begins to rotate and fade:

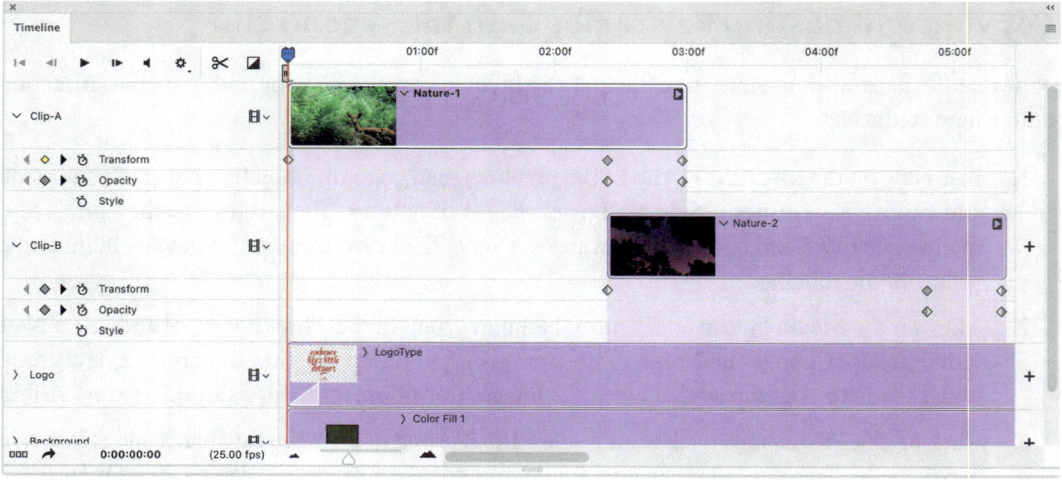

Figure 7.25: Copying and pasting keyframes from the first clip onto the second clip

Copying and pasting keyframes onto the third clip

In the following steps, you will be repeating the same process you went through for the second clip to paste animation keyframes. This will complete the animation for the document:

1. Click on the **Media** button adjacent to the **Logo** group in the **Timeline** panel and select **New video group**. Change the name of the new group to `Clip-C`.
2. Click on the **Media** button adjacent to the **Clip-C** group in the **Timeline** panel and select **Add Media**. Browse to the `07-Motion` folder and select `Nature-3.jpg`. Click **Open** when you're done.
3. Once the images appear in the timeline, right-click on the layers, choose **Convert to Smart Object**, and shorten the clip to `3.0` frames in length.
4. Go to **Edit** → **Free Transform** and link the **Width** and **Height** fields in the **Options** bar. Reduce **Scale** to `41%`. Click on the **Commit changes** button in the **Options** bar to apply the edits:

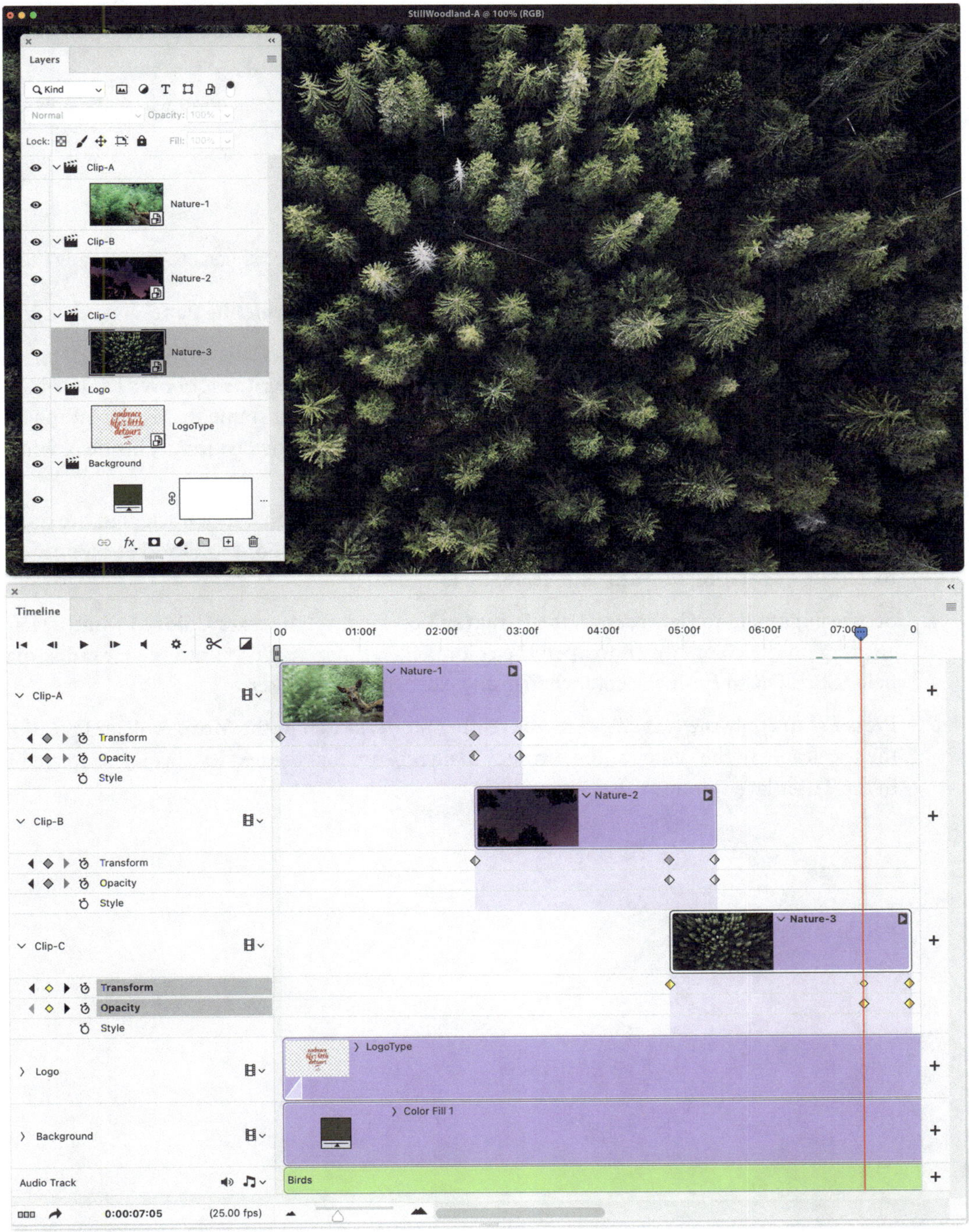

Figure 7.26: Each of the three images with keyframes pasted on clips two and three

5. Left-click on the `Nature-3` clip in the timeline, then go to the **Timeline** panel's flyout menu and choose **Keyframes** → **Paste** from the list of options.
6. Then, drag the clip so that it starts at **Frame 4.20** in the timeline, at the point where the previous clip begins to rotate and fade.

Adding titles to the sequence

Now that the images have been arranged and animated, we can create the title text to accompany them:

1. Click on the **Media** button adjacent to the **Clip A** group in the **Timeline Panel** and select **New video group**. Change the name of the new group to `Titles`.
2. Switch to the **Horizontal Type** tool by pressing the *T* key. Hover the tool over the left-hand side of the canvas. Left-click and drag to the right to draw a text frame that is almost the full width of the canvas. Release the left mouse button to generate the text frame, inside of which you will see the active type cursor.
3. Type `Amazing Woodlands` into the text frame, then highlight all characters in the frame with the **Horizontal Type** tool. From the **Properties** panel, set **Font** to **Flood Std**, **Font Size** to `128 pt`, **Leading** to **Auto**, and **Tracking** to `-25`.
4. Set the alignment to **Centre** from the **Paragraph** options. Set the text's **Color** to white by left-clicking on the color swatch to open the color picker. Enter `ffffff` into the **Hexadecimal** field. Click **OK** to apply the color change and close the color picker.
5. Press *Esc* to apply the text and exit type editing mode, switch to the **Move** tool, and position the text frame in the center of the canvas. Finally, ensure that the text layer you just created is in the **Titles** layer group:

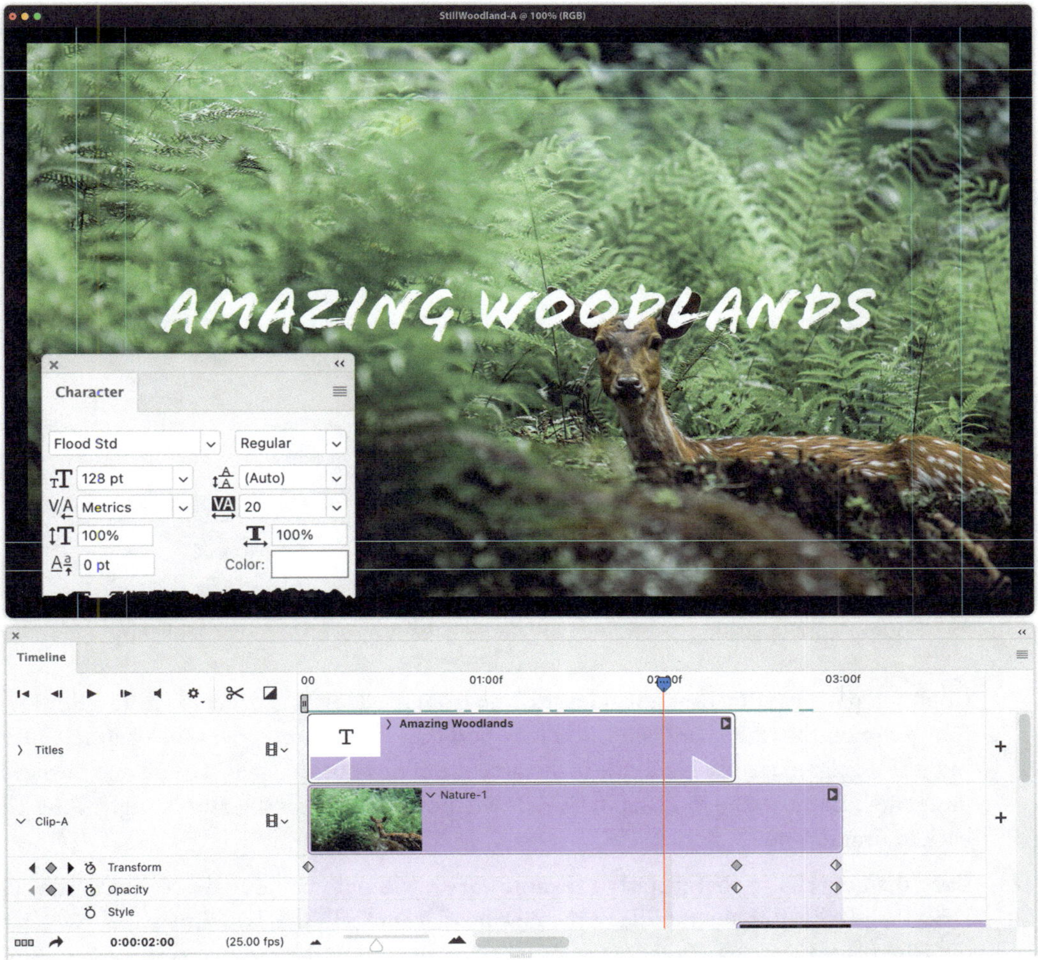

Figure 7.27: Adding a text layer with fades applied to the start and end of the clip

6. In the **Timeline** panel, ensure the **Amazing Woodlands** clip starts at **Frame 00:00** and extends to **Frame 02:10**, ending at the point where the **Nature-A** image begins to rate and fade.
7. From the **Transitions** pop-out menu in the **Timeline** panel, drag a **Fade** transition, lasting `0.25` seconds, onto the start and end of the **Amazing Woodlands** clip.
8. Ensure the **Amazing Woodlands** clip is active in the **Timeline** panel and press *Ctrl* + *C* (Windows) or *Cmd* + *C* (macOS). After, press *Ctrl* + *V* (Windows) or *Cmd* + *V* (macOS) to paste a copy of the clip to the right of the original in the timeline.

9. Drag the new clip so that it starts at **Frame 03:00** and shorten the clip by dragging the end to **Frame 04:20**. Drag the playhead to the middle of the new text layer clip in the **Timeline** panel. Switch to the **Horizontal Type** tool and click on the text in the canvas to enter type editing mode. Replace the current text with `Starry night skies`, press *Esc* to apply the text, and exit type editing mode:

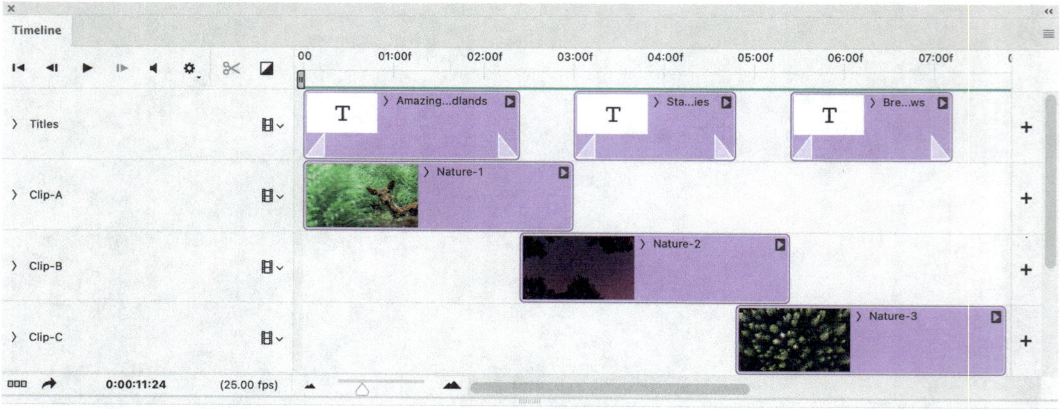

Figure 7.28: Duplicating text frames with fades already applied saves valuable time

10. Copy and paste the **Starry night skies** text clip from the **Timeline** panel to create a third text frame clip on the right-hand side. You may find that Photoshop moves the original **Starry night skies** clip to the left-hand side of the timeline. If that does happen, move it and the newly pasted text frame to the right-hand side. Then, move the start of the **Starry night skies** clip back to **Frame 03:00**.

11. Drag the new clip so that it starts at **Frame 05:10**, without changing the length of the clip. Drag the playhead to the middle of the new text layer clip in the **Timeline** panel. Switch to the **Horizontal Type** tool and double left-click on the text in the canvas to enter type editing mode. Replace the current text with `Breathtaking views`, press *Es* to apply the text, and exit type editing mode.

12. Ensure the **LogoType** clip starts at **Frame 07:20** and ends at **Frame 12:00**. You will also need to drag the green **Color Fill** clip and the **Birds** audio clip endpoints to **Frame 12:00** so that all footage finishes at the same time.

13. Rewind the playhead to the start of the timeline and press **Play** to preview the animation. Press **Stop** when you're done and go to **File** → **Save**:

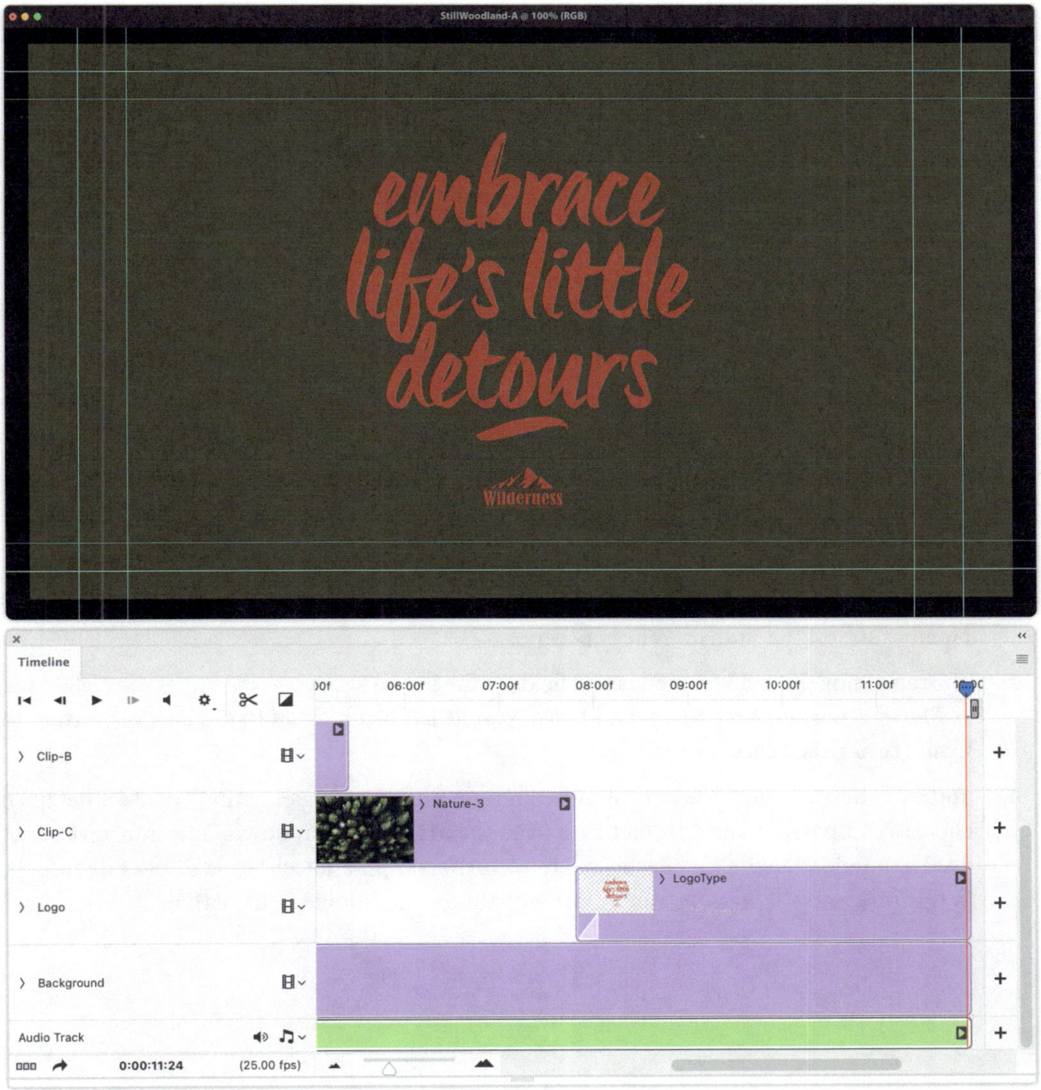

Figure 7.29: The completed sequence

In this section, we created a new document specifically for a video sequence. We set up video groups in the **Layers** and **Timeline** panels to organize our media clips. Then, we imported a series of MPEG-4 video files into the timeline, where they were trimmed and arranged into a sequence. We added cross-fade transitions between the clips to blend them seamlessly. We also added an MP3 audio track to the timeline to accompany the visuals. Next, we'll export the video so that it's ready to be used on YouTube, Twitter, and Facebook.

Exporting animations and video from Photoshop

In this final section, you will export the PSDs using Photoshop's built-in rendering tools. In the case of animated GIF, you have the ancient **Save for Web** dialog, which was renamed to include **(Legacy)** over a decade ago, denoting there are more advanced features available in the application to achieve a similar result. However, **Save for Web (Legacy)** remains the only method for exporting animated GIFs from Photoshop that provides a preview of your file and data size before you export.

Exporting animated GIFs

Having created several animations, it would be a shame to ruin that hard work by exporting GIF animations that will be rejected by social media platforms because the data size is too large, or the looping options are not set to forever. The following workflow will help strike a balance between low file size and high quality:

1. Go to **File** → **Export** → **Save for Web (Legacy).**
2. When the dialog appears, select **GIF** from the **Optimized file format** drop-down menu. Set the number of **Colors** to `16` and choose **Selective** from the **Color reduction algorithm** dropdown. Finally, turn off the **Transparency** checkbox.
3. The remaining drop-down menus and fields in the **Preset** section at the top of the dialog, such as **Matte**, **Amount**, **Web Snap**, and **Lossy**, can be left blank or set to `0`. However, ensure the **Convert to sRGB** checkbox is active.
4. You can choose to include data about copyright and your organization's contact details by choosing **Copyright and Contact Info** from the **Metadata** dropdown. This information will need to be added to the file, ideally before you export from Photoshop via **File** → **File Info**, but in this case, we will press on and export without that additional information:

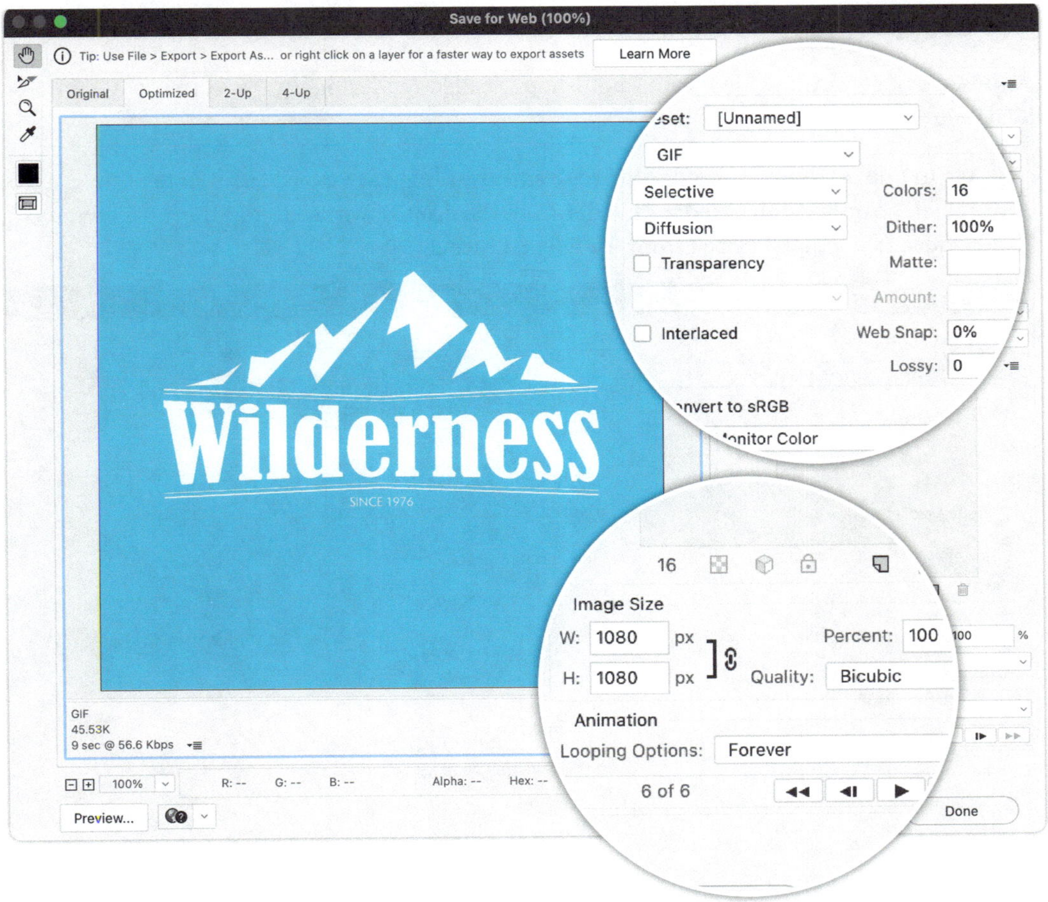

Figure 7.30: The Save for Web (Legacy) dialog remains the best method for exporting GIF animations

5. Under **Image Size**, set the dimensions to their original **Width** of `1080 px` and **Height** of `1080 px`. If you want to experiment with different sizes if the file size is a little large, you can always use the **Percent** field. However, in this example, we will leave the scale at `100%`.
6. Under **Animation settings**, ensure **Looping Options** is set to **Forever**. If you wish to preview the animation one last time before exporting, use the controllers in the same section.
7. With all the settings in place, click **Save** and browse to the `07-Motion` folder, name the file `Surf-A`, and then click on the **Save** button. Photoshop will now generate the animated GIF.
8. Once all the files have been exported and you have reviewed the results, you can go to **File** → **Save**. Then, close the document.

Exporting video

The process of exporting video from Photoshop is called rendering. In this scenario, we'll output video for YouTube:

1. Go to **File** → **Export** → **Render Video**. Name the file `SurfPromo.mp4` in the `07-Motion` folder. Choose **Adobe Media Encoder** from the drop-down menu to export the sequence as a video. Then, select **H.264** from the **Format** menu:

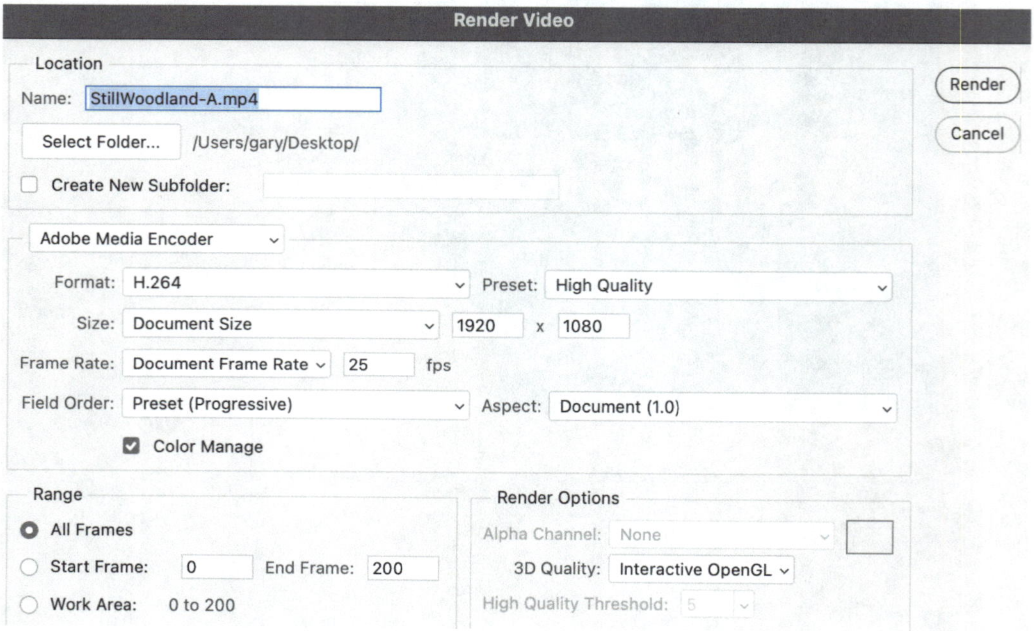

Figure 7.31: You can render video sequences from within Photoshop

2. Ensure that **Frame rate** is set to **25 fps**. Set **Range** to **All Frames**. Click on the **Render** button when you're done.
3. Photoshop will display a progress bar to indicate the rendering task. Once complete, browse the `07-Motion` folder via your operating system and watch the video. On returning to Photoshop, go to **File** → **Save** and close the document.

In this section, we looked at how to export video and animation from Photoshop using two contrasting methods. However, both allow us to create ready-to-post files on a multitude of online platforms. The fact that we can create, edit, and export from Photoshop and thereby avoid using third-party applications is a real plus.

Summary

In this chapter, we have seen the simple yet intuitive features offered by Photoshop for creating and editing motion files.

First, we explored some key concepts related to motion files, namely time, in the form of frames and how they relate to the duration of our animations and videos. We also explored some of the specifications to be aware of when posting videos online, such as maximum file size, duration, and loop settings for animations.

Then, we created new documents to house our motion projects, complete with safe frames and a dedicated timeline for adding assets, all of which can be saved as PSD files. Starting with just a logo and layers that we created from scratch, such as color fills and text layers, we organized them in the **Layers** panel specifically for animating.

We used the **Timeline** panel to capture the current state of a file as individual frames to create simple animations with pauses and loops for GIFs. By turning the layer visibility of layers on or off, we can change the appearance of the animation and capture new frames.

We also used keyframes to capture movement in our animations, allowing us to specify a start and end point. Then, using tweening, we tasked Photoshop with the job of creating individual frames between them to form animation.

For complex motion projects, we turned to video and audio. This is managed in a video timeline, where content is stored in video groups in the **Layers** panel. This allows content to appear in the **Timeline** panel so that it can be arranged and trimmed to the desired duration or have transitions applied to it. We saw how MP3 audio can be added to the timeline, where the volume can be modified or faded where necessary.

Finally, we used two methods for exporting motion files from Photoshop. We exported animated GIFs with a visually led dialog box that accurately previews what the file will look like before exporting, along with the predicted file size. We rendered our timeline to create MPEG-4 and QuickTime video.

In the next chapter, we will dive deep into typography and use a series of layer styles and special effects to bring our copy to life, all while keeping the text editable.

Part 3: Building Visual Components

Not all Photoshop projects start with a stunning stock image or a professional photo shoot. You can create amazing visuals with just the tools and features within the application. This part looks at techniques for creating impactful type effects and custom backdrops with patterns and textures. Finally, by mastering the immense power of Photoshop brushes, you'll complete artwork with your own custom brush tips to create snowflakes, retouch hair, and leverage sampled real brush strokes to create a portrait.

This part has the following chapters:

- *Chapter 8, Bringing Typography to Life with Effects and Styling*
- *Chapter 9, Creating Textures, Patterns, and Backdrops*
- *Chapter 10, Creating and Applying Brushes*

8

Bringing Typography to Life with Effects and Styling

Effects can be used to add a simple drop shadow or stroke outline to make types stand out against a busy background. They can also be combined and even stacked together to create stunning designs such as molten lava or blocks of ice, all of which can be edited and saved for later use in other documents. In this chapter, you will explore a variety of effects and workflows that can bring your designs to life.

We will start by slicing editable types in half with Smart Objects and layer masks. After, we will create a classic paper emboss effect using a single layer group and stacked layer styles that transform the look of any layer added to it.

The most challenging exercise of this chapter will involve creating a faux 3D effect, where the editable type will be distorted to create paper cut-out letters and folds while we keep the type layers editable.

In the second half of this chapter, we will focus on painterly effects, starting with a displacement technique that deforms editable types to create a dripping paint effect. In the final exercise of this chapter, we will recreate spray paint effects using blend modes and a field blur.

We will cover the following topics:

- Understanding typographic terms and principles
- Synchronizing Adobe fonts
- Creating cut and fold effects
- Applying ink and paint effects

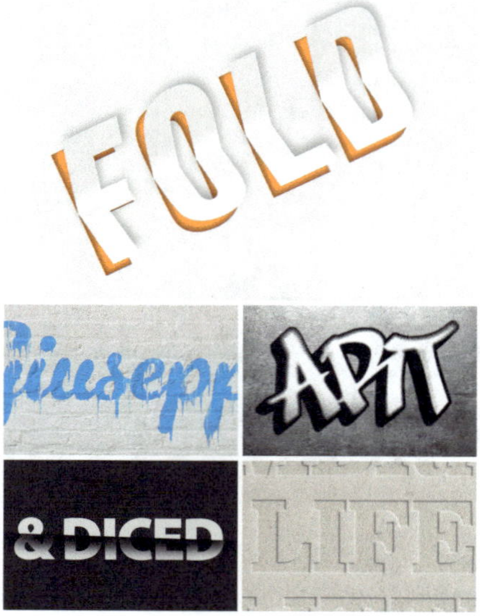

Figure 8.1: Examples of the projects you will undertake in this chapter

Technical requirements

The project files for this chapter can be found at: `https://github.com/PacktPublishing/Mastering-Adobe-Photoshop-2024/tree/main/Chapter08`

Understanding typographic terms and principles

To understand how to achieve effective type formatting, it is necessary to be aware of the various characteristics and terminology. Type characters rest upon an invisible baseline – below it extends descenders, and between the baseline and the top of the lowercase charters where the *x* height resides. The region above the *x* height contains ascenders, such as at the top of the lowercase *k*:

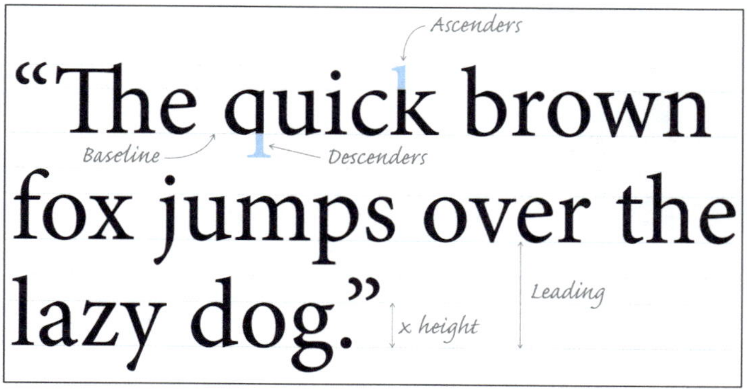

Figure 8.2: Typographic terms that are also utilized in Photoshop

Serif is an accent or embellishment that's found at the end of the main vertical and horizontal portions of some typefaces. Its counterpart, sans serif, which originates from French, meaning without serif, does not contain the same decorative strokes or accents at the main sections of the type:

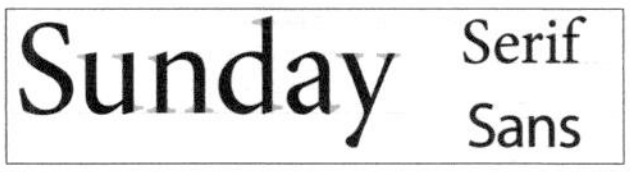

Figure 8.3: A comparison of serif and sans serif typefaces

Typefaces come in a multitude of weights, thicknesses, and styles, all of which control the text's slant or posture. It is common to find several weights in a single font, such as normal, italic, and bold, while some typefaces offer dozens of weights. Some desktop software and web browsers will generate a faux bold when the typeface is unavailable for a given font:

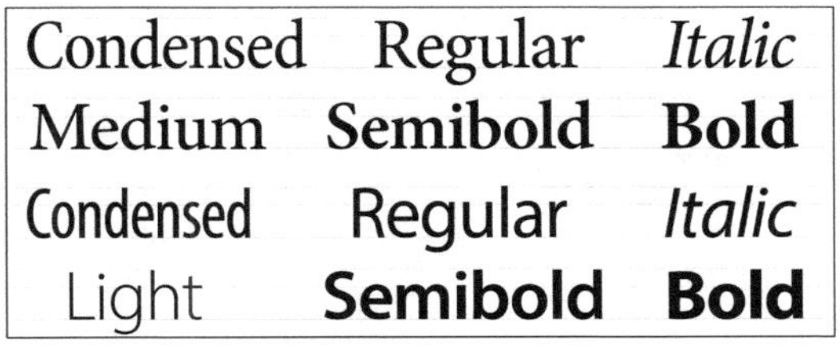

Figure 8.4: Some of the weights or styles that can be found in typefaces

Many of the buttons and features relating to typography throughout Creative Cloud have their origins in fifteenth-century printing presses, which utilized an assortment of metal-type blocks that could be arranged as required. Leading (pronounced LED-ing) defined space between two lines of text, from one baseline to another, and was originally formed of strips of lead that could be inserted between lines of text:

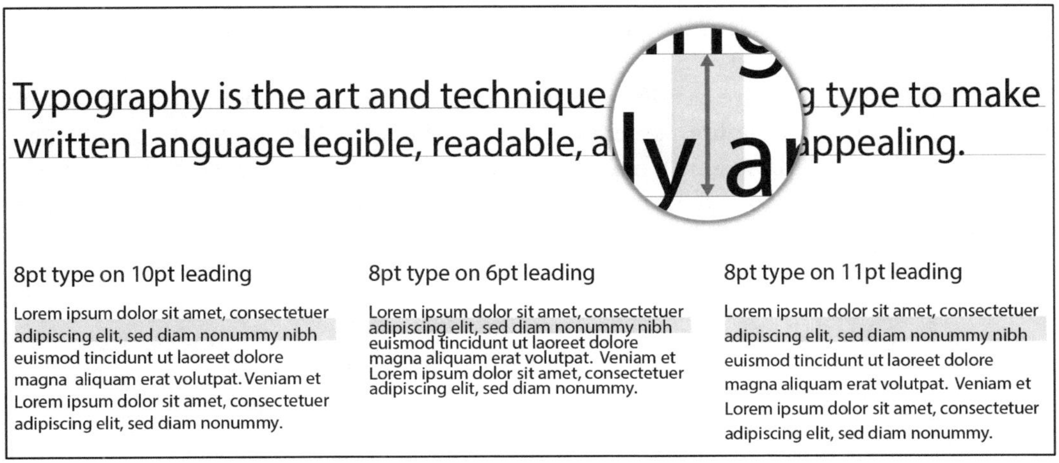

Figure 8.5: Leading controls vertical line spacing

Many of the Creative Cloud applications import or create typefaces at 12 points in size with 14.4 points of leading. Leading that is smaller than the size of the text can result in a cramped appearance. When you alter the size of your text, the leading automatically adjusts to match the size of the characters to maintain appropriate space between each line. This is known as auto-leading. You can increase the size of the leading to provide more space for your text.

Kerning refers to the spacing between a pair of type characters. For example, when the characters *A* and *V* or *W* and *A* are arranged together, this can create unwanted white space between them, which can be mitigated by reducing the kerning value to tighten the space between them.

Tracking in typography refers to the consistent spacing between characters within a word or a line of text. It involves adjusting the overall letter spacing to enhance readability and aesthetic appeal. For example, tracking is used in movie posters to space out the name of a production company to match that of the movie's name:

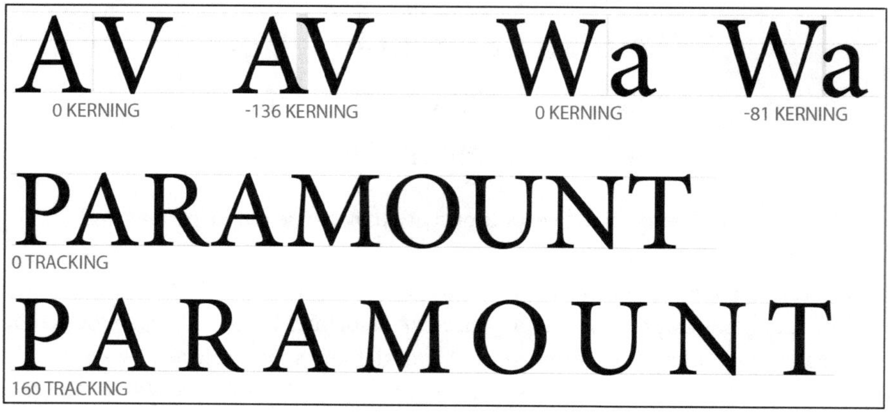

Figure 8.6: Kerning controls the space between a pair of characters, while tracking affects the space between multiple characters and words

All typeface characters rest on a baseline – that is, an invisible line. To move type characters above or below the baseline, you can utilize a feature known as baseline shift. Increasing baseline shift moves characters higher while decreasing it moves characters lower. An appropriate use of baseline shift would be to separate the type from an underline to make text more legible, or to center numerical values between parentheses. Baseline shift can be found in the **Character** panel in Photoshop:

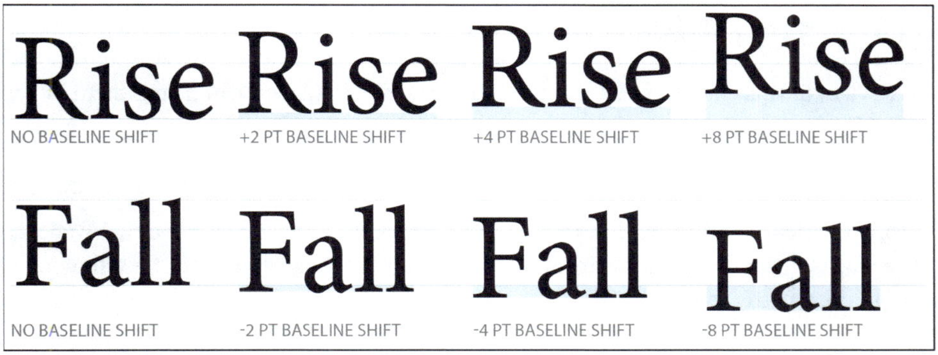

Figure 8.7: Baseline shift moves characters up or down from the line they rest upon

Fonts are composed of hundreds of characters, referred to as glyphs. These range from letters and numbers to symbols and ornaments, such as trademark symbols. You will find several versions of letters that are designed for specific scenarios, such as superscript, where the letters *S* and *T* combine to create 1st. *Figure 8.8* provides a selection of just some of the glyph characters available. These include superscript (**1**), subscript (**2**), fractions (**3**), all small caps (**4**), swash (**5**), ligatures (**6**), discretionary ligatures (**7**), registration mark (**8**), trademark (**9**), math symbols (**10**), and the degree sign (**11**):

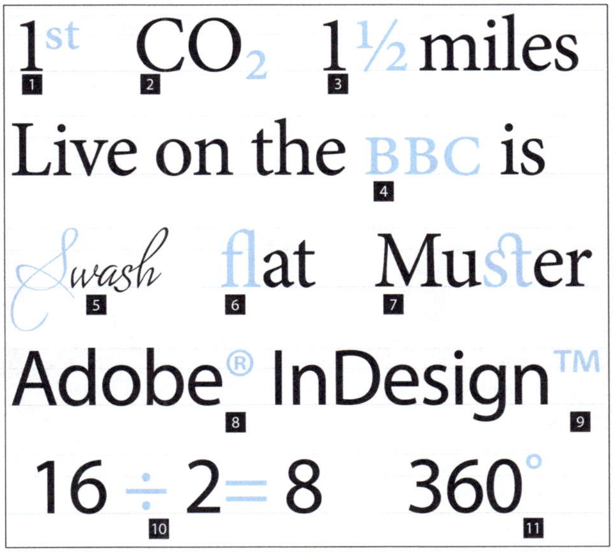

Figure 8.8: Examples of open type characters

In this section, we explored essential typographic terms and principles that will allow you to take granular control of text within Photoshop, and across Creative Cloud. Now that we know how to fine-tune type and white space, it's time to embark on exercises that bring type to life in a variety of visual styles and effects.

Synchronizing Adobe fonts

All the exercises in this chapter utilize fonts from Creative Cloud. You can install them by following these steps:

1. Open your preferred web browser and head to `https://fonts.adobe.com`.
2. Using the **Search all fonts, foundries, and designers** bar in the center of the web page, type the name of the desired font. In this chapter, you will need to install the following fonts to complete the exercises:

    I. Abril Text, Extra Bold,

    II. Nimbus Sans Condensed, Black,

    III. Gelato Luxe, Regular,

    IV. Subway New York SC, and Regular.

3. The search results will preview the closest matches to your query in the form of thumbnails of the font and its name. Click on the appropriate thumbnail to view the corresponding font family page. There, you will find a list of font styles. Click on the **Activate Font** button adjacent to the relevant font:

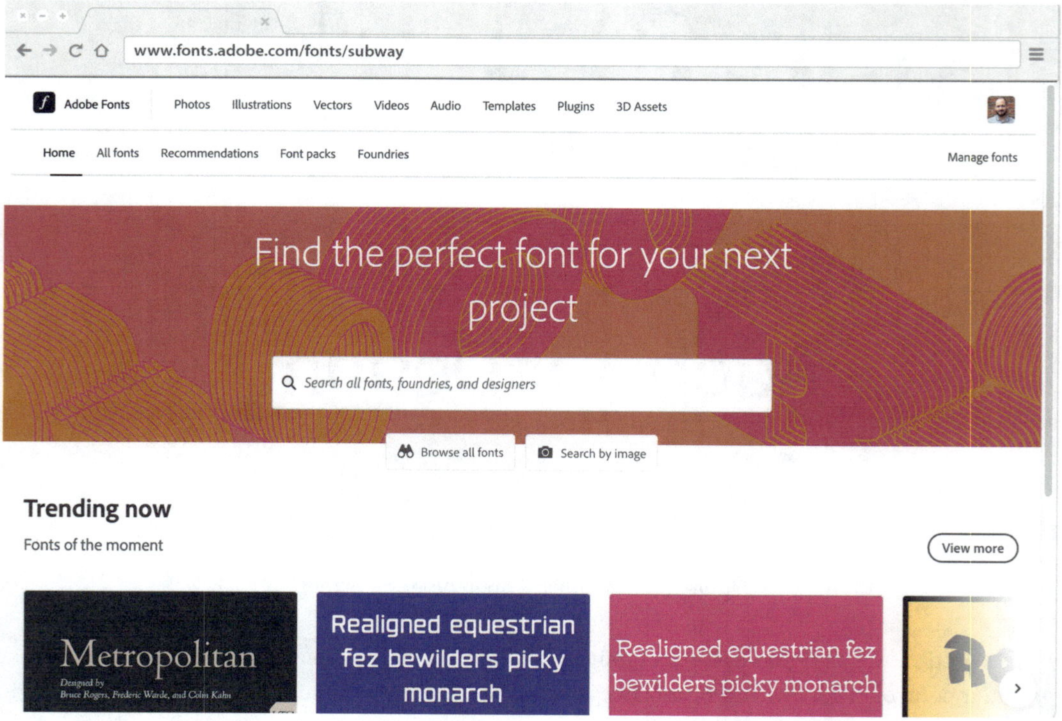

Figure 8.9: Searching for fonts on the Adobe Fonts website

4. Once you've activated the desired fonts, the Creative Cloud desktop app will automatically sync and download them to your computer. This process may take some time, depending on the number and size of the fonts.
5. Once the fonts have finished syncing, you can access and use them within Adobe applications such as Photoshop, Illustrator, and InDesign. The synchronized fonts should appear in the Photoshop font menus.
6. Repeat this process until you have installed all the necessary fonts. You can use similar fonts if you desire, or if you do not have an active internet connection:

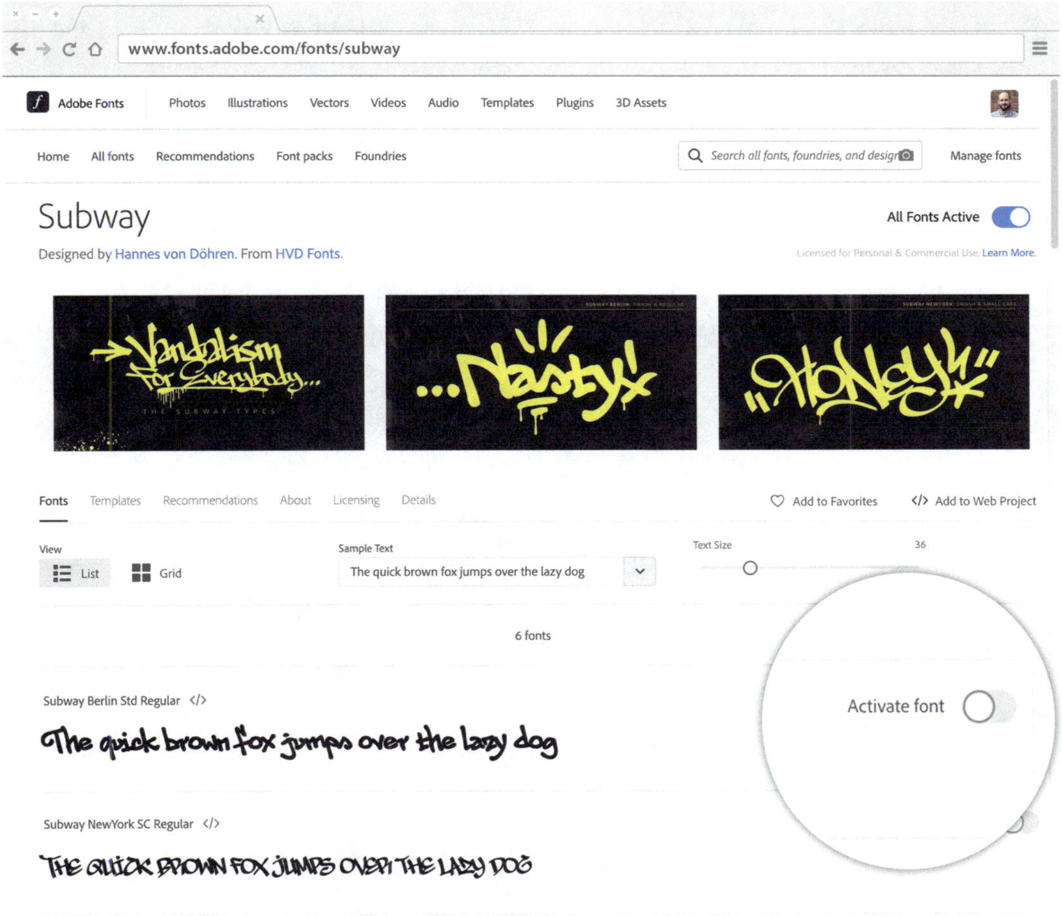

Figure 8.10: Activate one or more fonts to use them in your desktop Adobe apps

In this section, we outlined the steps required to install fonts from Creative Cloud. Although not essential, using the suggested fonts will allow you to better match the look and feel of the artwork you will create in each of the exercises. Next, you will begin by creating a sliced text effect.

Creating cut and fold effects

In the following exercises, you will slice, tear, and cut out text as though it had been applied to paper, all with the power of mart objects and editable types.

Creating sliced text

In the first of our text effect exercises, you will cut an editable text layer in half and apply shadows to the lower half to create the illusion of sliced text running through it:

1. Go to **File** > **Open** and browse to the `08-Text` folder. Select `Background.psd` and then click **Open**.
2. Switch to the **Type** tool from the **Tools** panel and left-click on the center of the canvas to create a point type that is intended for a single line of text. You will now see the type cursor flashing in the canvas. Type `& diced` and then select all the characters with the **Type** tool.
3. Go to the **Properties** panel and set **Font** to **Myriad Pro**, **Style** to **Black**, **Leading** to **Auto**, **Font Size** to `400 pt`, and **Tracking** to `-60`. Then, click on the **Color** preview (*Figure 8.11, A*) to open the color picker, enter `dddddd` into the **Hexadecimal** field, and click **OK**:

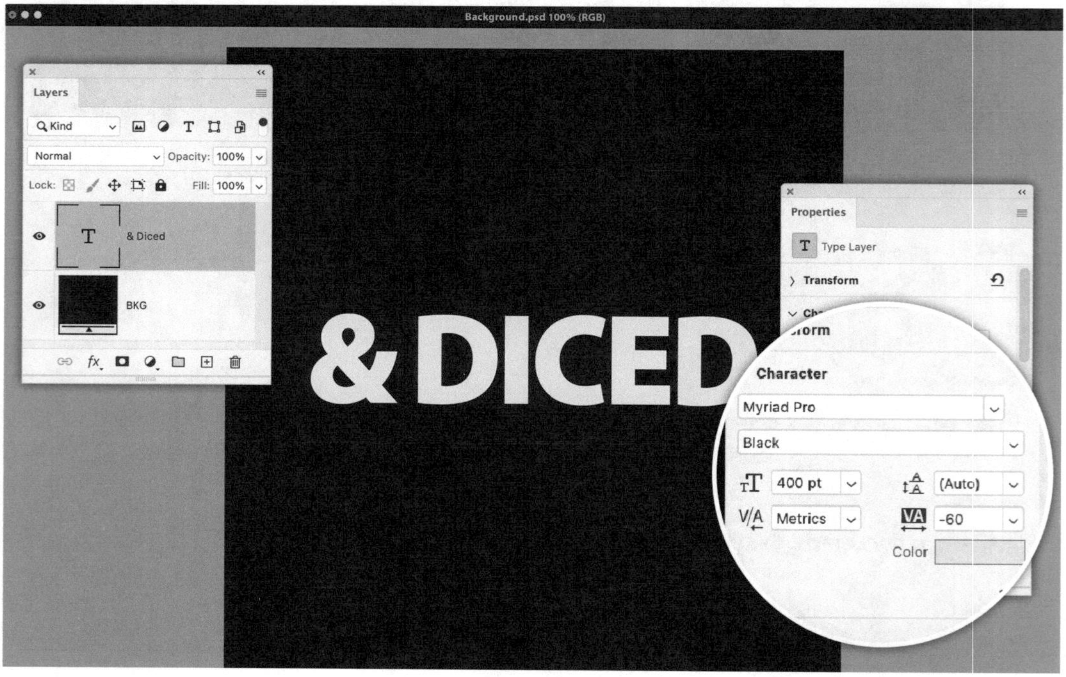

Figure 8.11: The formatted base type layer

4. When you're done, click on the **Commit changes** button in the **Options** bar to add the text layer. Switch to the **Selection** tool, ensure **Smart Guides** is active from **View | Smart Guides**, and drag the text to the center of the canvas.
5. Hover your cursor over the **BKG** layer in the **Layers** panel, then *Shift* and left-click on the layer's name to make it and the text layer active in the **Layers** panel. Right-click on the **BKG** layer's name in the **Layers** panel and choose **Convert to Smart Object** from the list of commands.
6. Then, double left-click on the layer's name and rename it `bottom`. Next, right-click on the layer's name in the **Layers** panel and choose **Duplicate Layer** from the list. In the dialog box that appears, enter a new name of `Top` in the **Duplicate As** field and click **OK**.
7. Go to **File | Save As**, browse to the `08-Type` folder, and save the document as a PSD file before clicking **Save**. Keep the document open:

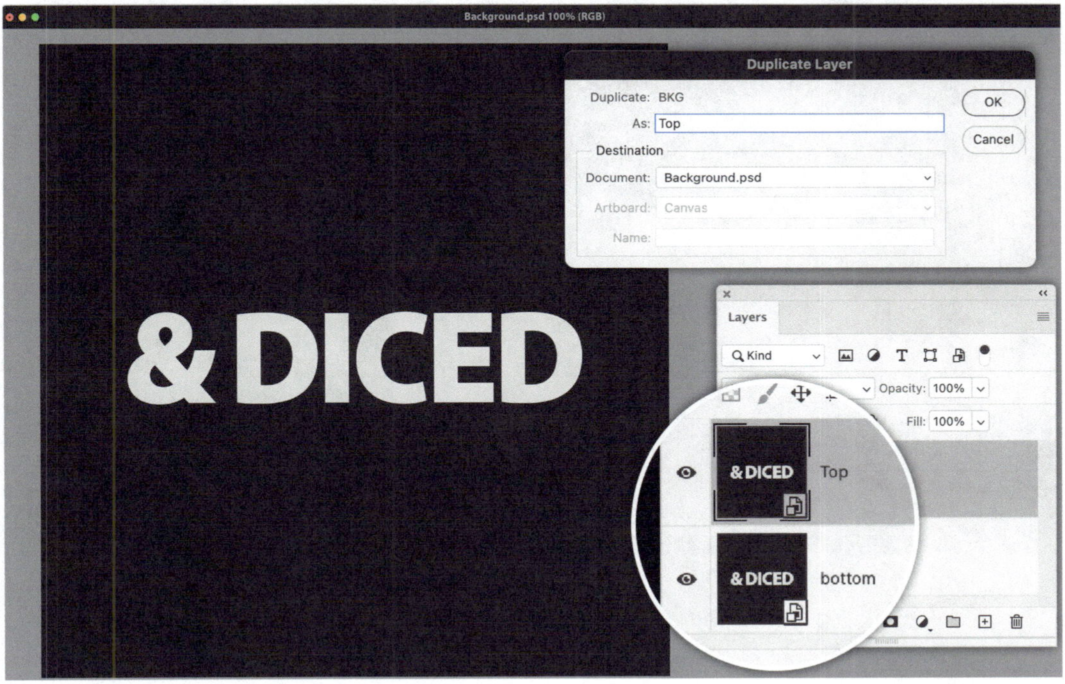

Figure 8.12: Type converted to smart objects

8. Ensure only the **Top** layer is active in the **Layers** panel, then switch to the **Polygonal Lasso** tool from the **Tools** panel. From the **Options** bar, set the selection **Mode** to **New** and **Feather** to `0`. Turn off the bottom layer's visibility in the **Layers** panel.

9. Create a selection that starts outside the top-left corner of the canvas by left-clicking once in that region (see *Figure 8.13, A*). Then, hover your cursor lower down the outer-left edge of the canvas and left-click again (see *Figure 8.13, B*). Hover your cursor over the right-hand side, beyond the canvas, and left-click (see *Figure 8.13, C*). Then, left-click in the top-right corner beyond the canvas (see *Figure 8.13, D*), and finally left-click on the place you first started to generate the selection.
10. With the selection in place, click on the **Add a Mask** button at the bottom of the **Layers** panel (see *Figure 8.13, E*) to hide the bottom region of the layer outside of your selection:

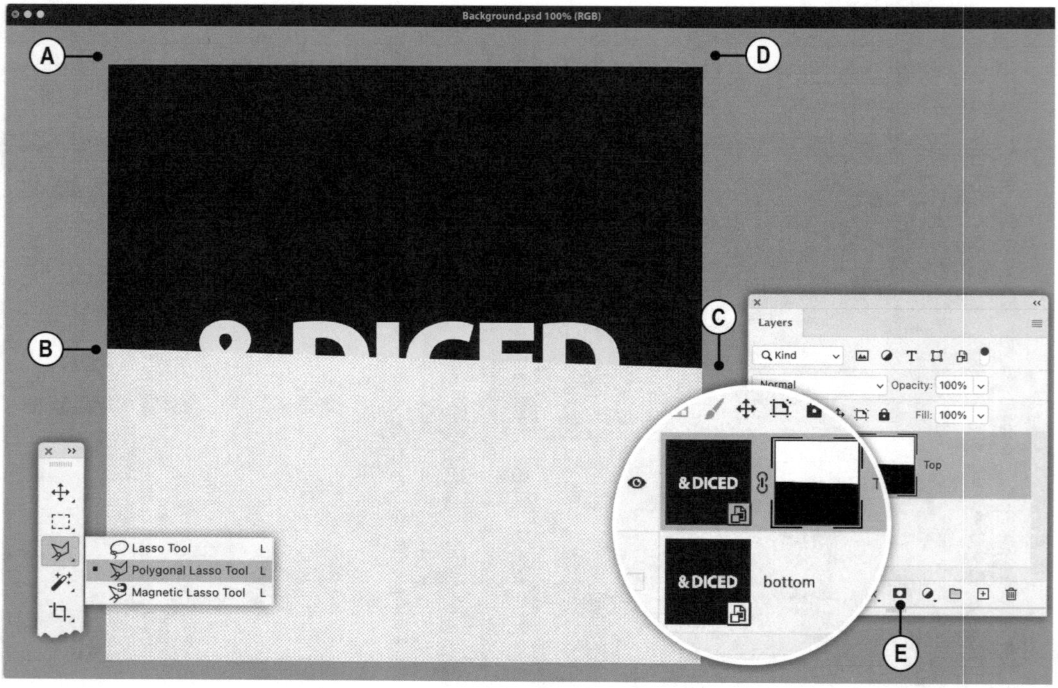

Figure 8.13: The layer mask applied to the top version of the text

11. Left-click on the `bottom` layer to make it active, then turn on the layer's visibility. Then, click on the **New Layer** icon in the **Layers** panel, which will appear immediately above the bottom layer in the stack. Double-click on the new layer's name and change it to `Shadows`. Then, change **Blend Mode** to **Multiply**.
12. Switch to the **Brush** tool by pressing the *B* key. From the **Options** bar, set **Brush Tip** to **Soft Round** and reduce **Opacity** to `30%`. Press the *D* key to reset your colors back to black and white.

13. Hover the **Brush** tool's cursor just beyond the left edge of the bottom half of the text, then drag to the right-hand side to paint a black paint stroke region that finishes just beyond the right edge of the text. Repeat the same technique to darken the shadow as necessary. Go to **File** > **Save** when you're done and close the document:

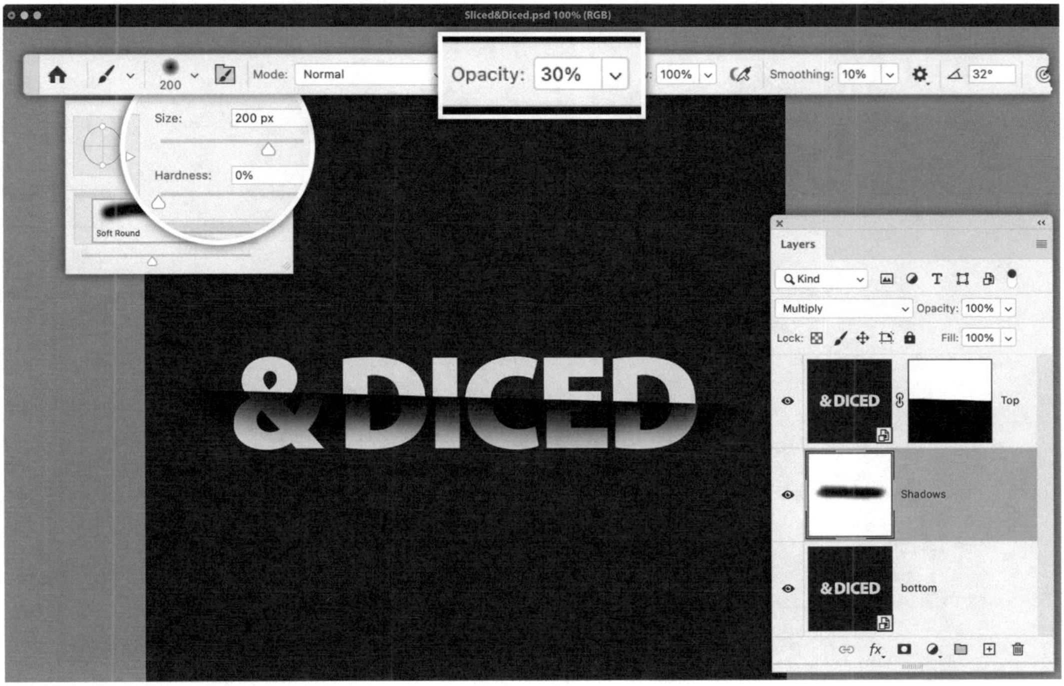

Figure 8.14: Painting with the Brush tool to create the shadow effect across the bottom half

Creating an embossed type

This paper embossing technique is handy for conceptualizing printing effects to demonstrate the final product before it goes to print. Let's get started:

1. Go to **File** | **Open** and browse to the `08-Text` folder. Select `Embossed.jpg` and then click **Open**.
2. Press the *D* key to reset the colors to black and white and then switch to the **Type** tool from the **Tools** panel.
3. Left-click and drag across the canvas to create an area type text frame that occupies a least half the canvas area. Type `Embrace life's little detours` and then select all characters with the **Type** tool.

4. Go to the **Properties** panel and set **Font** to **Abril Text**, **Style** to **Extra Bold**, **Font Size** to `400 pt`, **Leading** to `375 pt`, and **Tracking** to `-20`. Set **Alignment** to **Centered**:

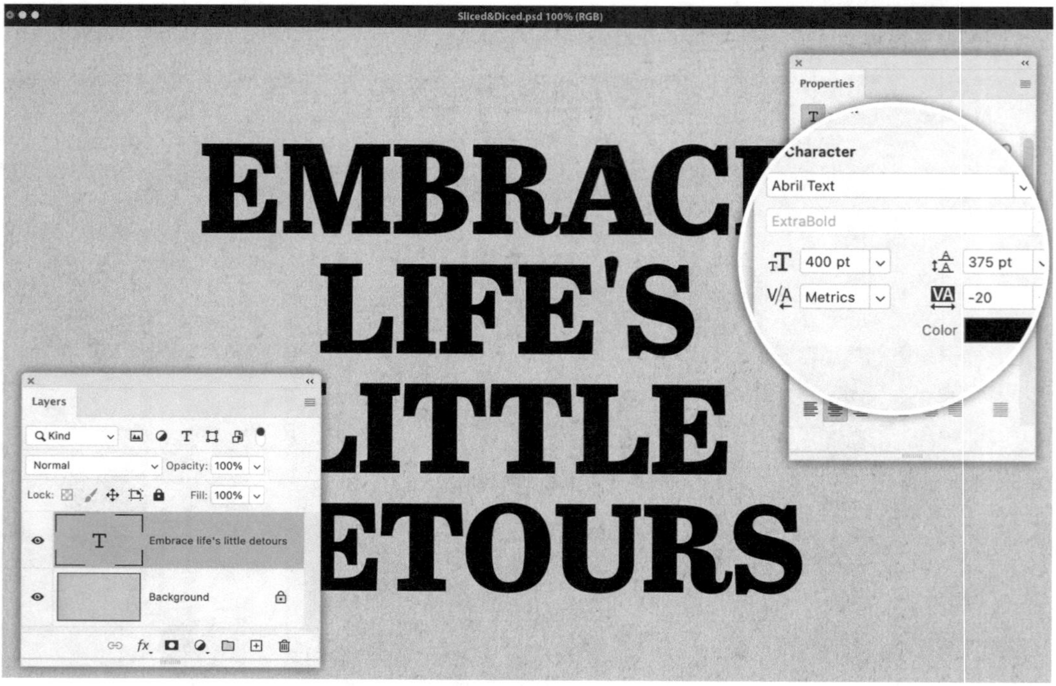

Figure 8.15: The underlying type layer with basic formatting applied

5. Resize the text frame so that one word appears on each line, creating four lines of text. Click on the **Commit changes** button in the **Options** bar to complete the text frame edits.
6. With the text layer still active, press *Ctrl* + *G* (Windows) or *Cmd* + *G* (macOS) to add the text to a new layer group. Rename the layer group `Logotype`.
7. Ensure the layer group is still active in the **Layers** panel, and then click on the **Add a layer style** button at the bottom of the **Layers** panel. From the list of options, click on **Blending Options**. When the dialog appears, reduce **Fill Opacity** to `0%`.
8. Next, click on the **Bevel & Emboss** style from the list on the left-hand side of the dialog to apply the effect and reveal the options. Click on the **Reset to Default** button at the bottom of the emboss settings. Then, set **Style** to **Inner Bevel**, **Technique** to **Smooth**, **Depth** to `90%`, **Direction** to `Down`, **Size** to `8` px, and **Soften** to `2` px.

9. From the **Shading** group of settings lower down, set **Angle** to `40°`, **Altitude** to `40°`, **Highlight Mode Opacity** to `80%`, and **Shadow Mode Opacity** to `65%`:

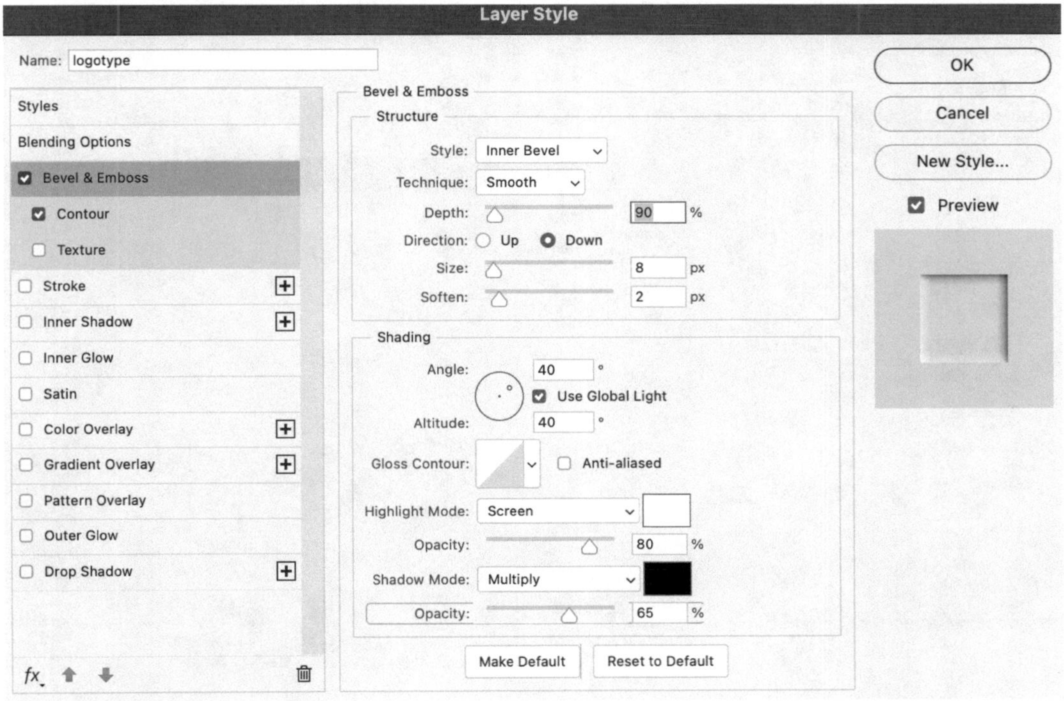

Figure 8.16: Emboss settings

10. Click on the **Contour** subcategory from the list on the left-hand side. When the options appear, click on the **Contour Editor** thumbnail to open the editor. Then, click on the center of the line that appears in the grid to add a new point. Change **Input** to `35%` and **Output** to `55%`. Click **OK** to apply the settings. This will change the shape of the emboss so that it's smoother and shallower:

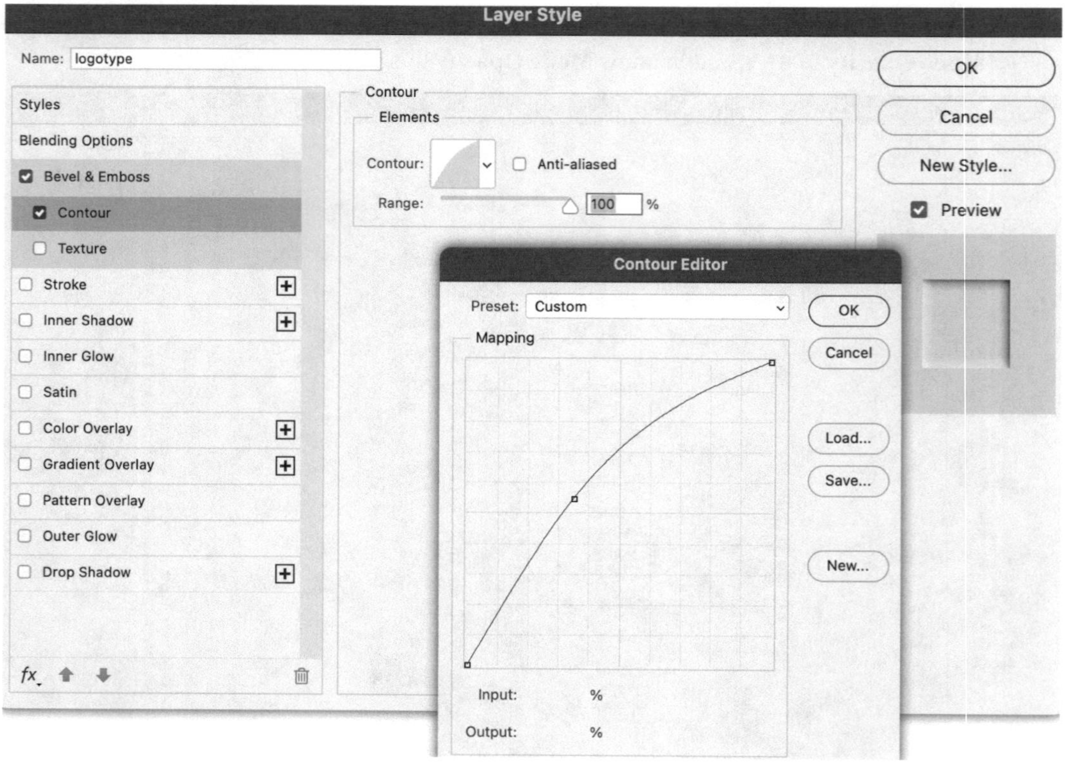

Figure 8.17: Custom contours can be smoothed in the Contour Editor area

11. Next, click on **Color Overlay** from the list on the left-hand side. Change **Blend Mode** to **Color Burn** and **Opacity** to `40%`, and then click on **Set color of overlay** to open the color picker. Hover your cursor over a region away from the text to sample the paper color and click **OK** to close the **Color Picker** dialog. This will darken the embossed region of text subtly to help differentiate it from the other regions of the paper:

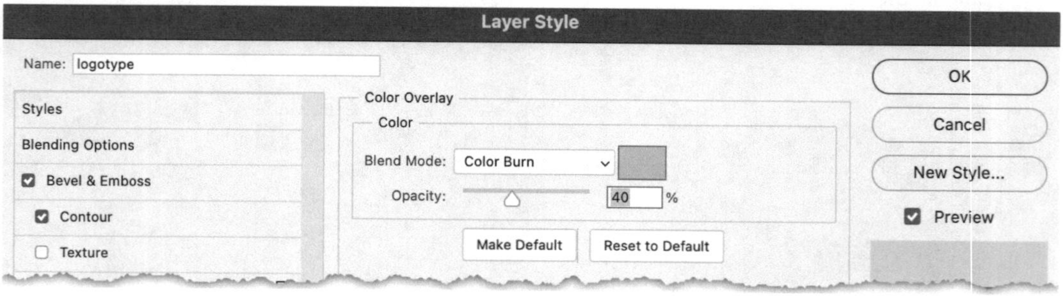

Figure 8.18: Color Overlay helps darken the type characters

12. With the **Layer Style** dialog box still open, click on **Drop Shadow** from the list on the left-hand side. Click on the **Reset to Default** button at the bottom of the emboss settings. Ensure **Blend Mode** is set to **Multiply**, turn off the **Use Global Light** checkbox, and set **Opacity** to `24%`, **Angle** to `-145°`, **Distance** to `5` px, **Spread** to `0%`, and **Size** to `2` px:

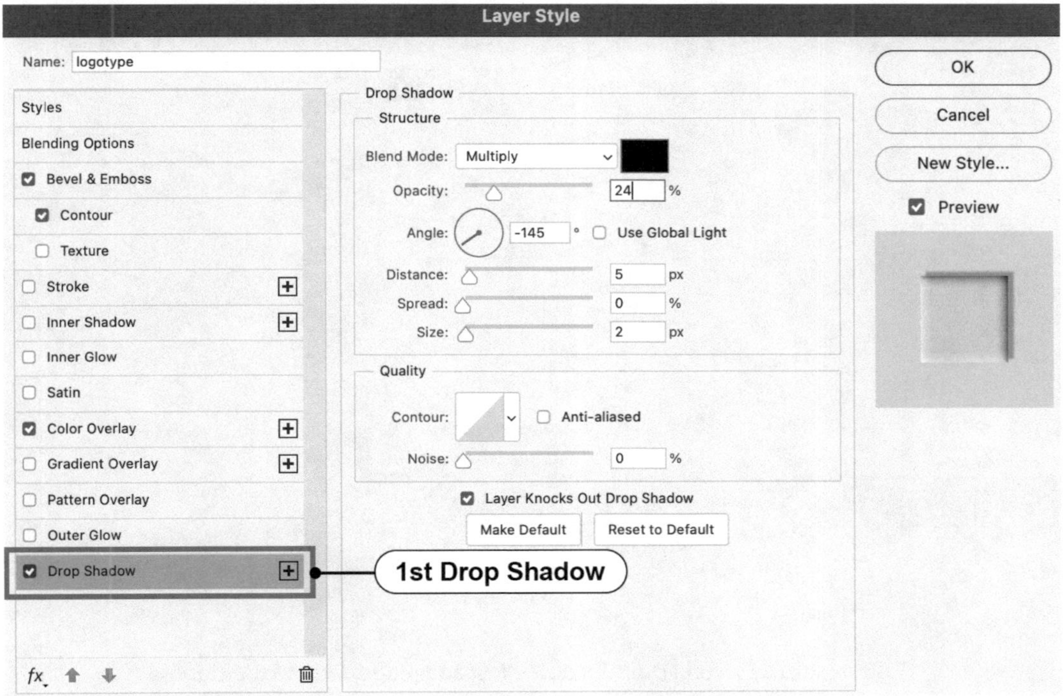

Figure 8.19: The first of four Drop Shadow effects

13. Next, we need to emphasize the shaded regions inside the embossed text. Click on the **Duplicate Style** button, shown as a plus (+) icon, adjacent to the **Drop Shadow** effect you just edited from the list on the left-hand side.

14. Set the newly duplicated **Drop Shadow** options – that is, set **Opacity** to `4%`, **Angle** to `-145°`, **Distance** to `26` px, **Spread** to `0%`, and **Size** to `65` px:

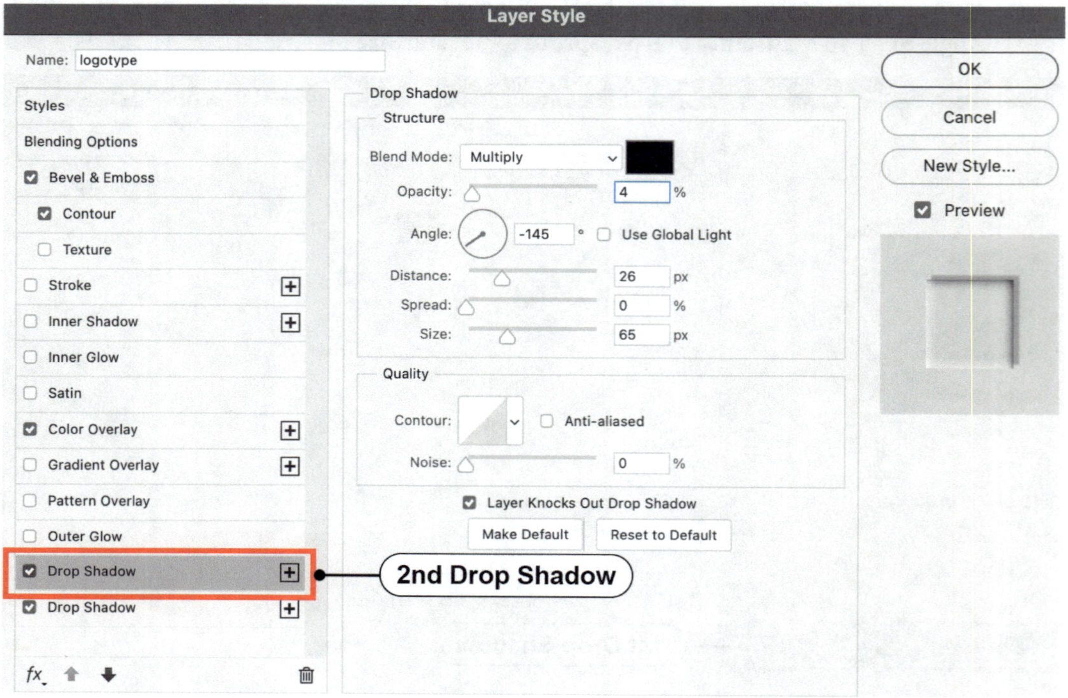

Figure 8.20: The second Drop Shadow effect adds edge detail to the emboss

15. Repeat the same step to add a third **Drop Shadow** effect by clicking on the **Duplicate Style** button adjacent to the one you just added. However, this time, we need to emphasize the highlighted edges.

16. Set the third **Drop Shadow** effect's options – that is, set **Blend Mode** to **Screen**, **Opacity** to `24%`, **Angle** to `40°`, **Distance** to `5` px, **Spread** to `0%`, and **Size** to `4` px:

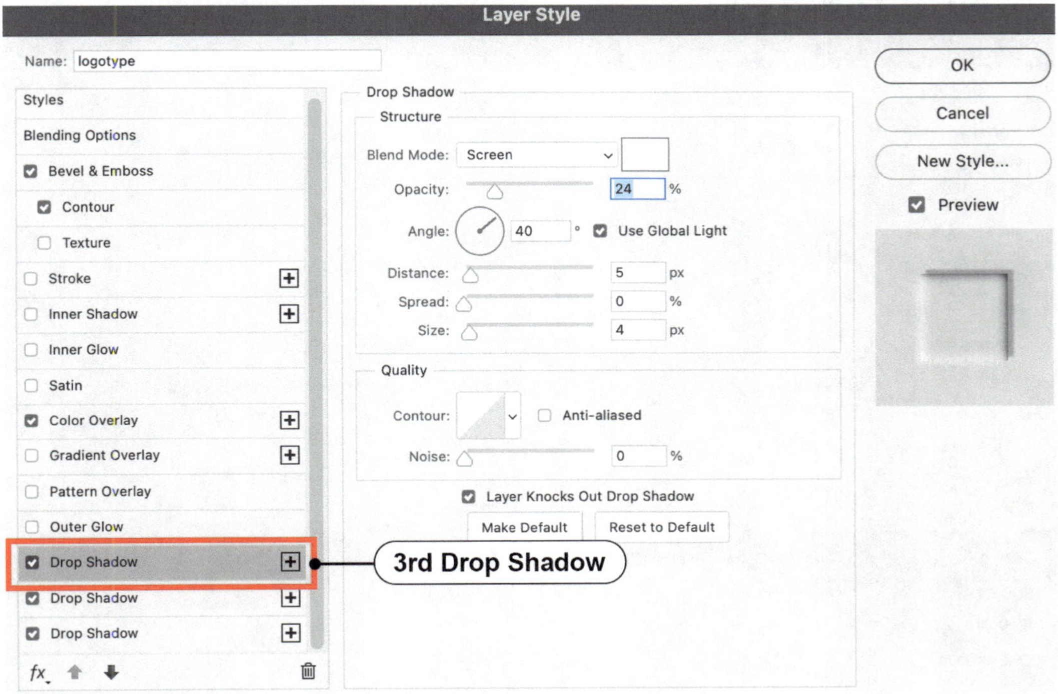

Figure 8.21: The third Drop Shadow effect adapted here to create edge highlights

17. Finally, add a fourth **Drop Shadow** effect by clicking on the **Duplicate Style** button adjacent to the one you just added. This effect will lighten the surface around the text.

18. Set the fourth **Drop Shadow** effect's options – that is, set **Opacity** to `15%`, **Angle** to `40°`, **Distance** to `40` px, **Spread** to `0%`, and **Size** to `40` px. You will be relieved to read that you can now click **OK** to apply all of the effects, close the dialog box, and return to the main Photoshop interface:

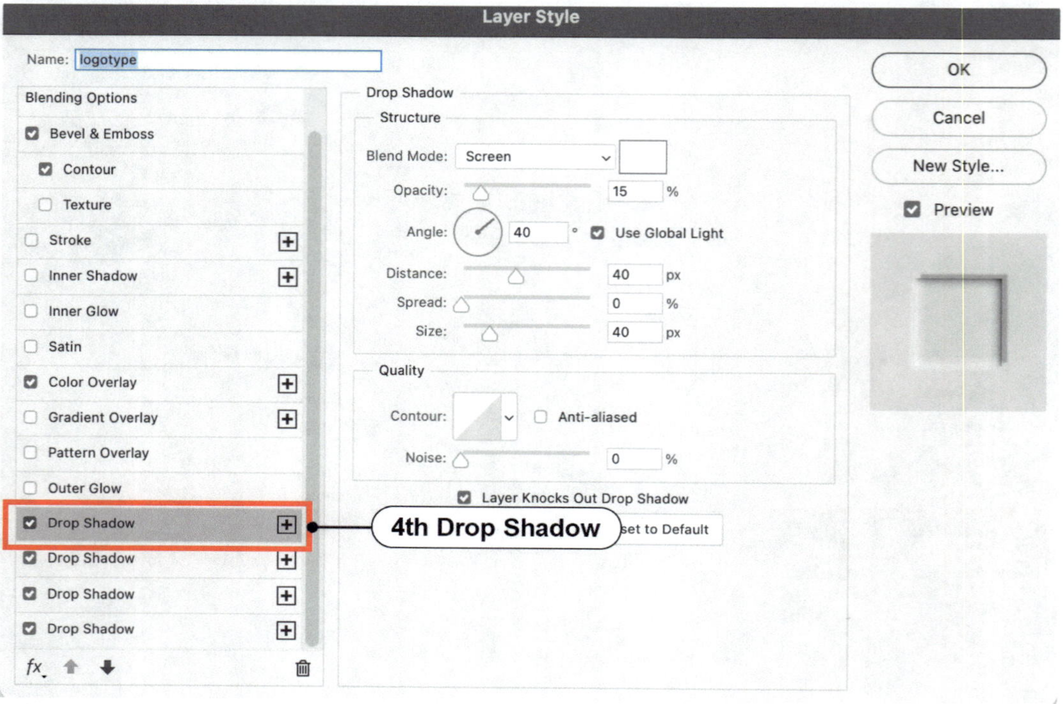

Figure 8.22: The fourth and final Drop Shadow effect used here to lighten the area around the type

19. This technique will allow you to add any content to the **Logotype** layer group, after which it will apply the embossed effect, keeping all text editable. Go to **File | Save**, browse to the `08-Text` folder, and save the document as a PSD file. Close the document when you're done:

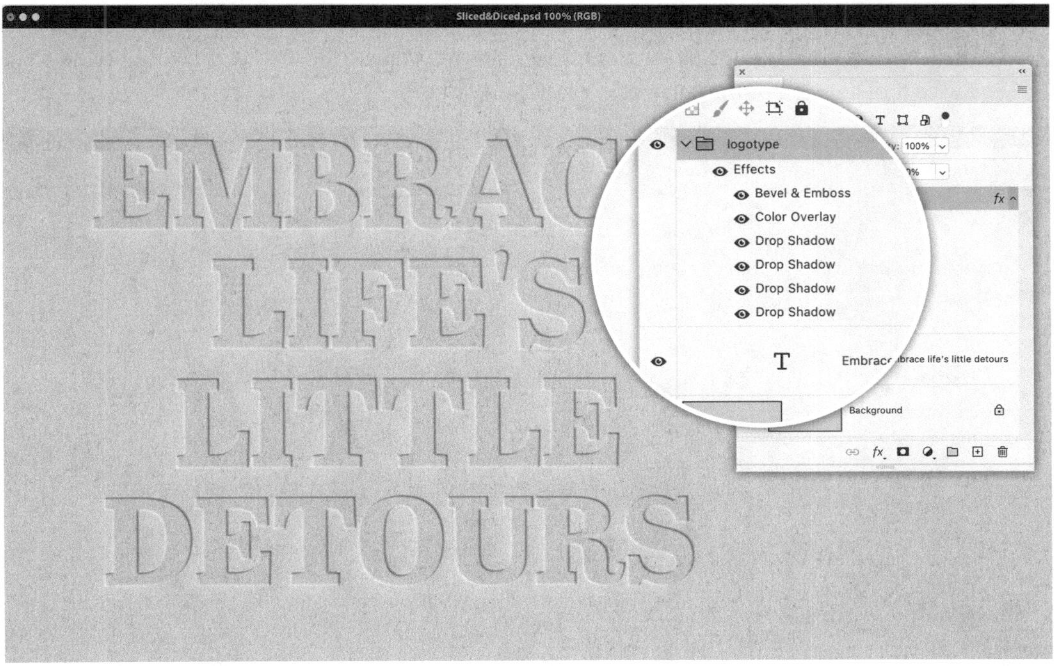

Figure 8.23: The completed embossing effect

Creating cut and fold effects

This 3D text effect is great for grabbing attention in ads or web banners on social media. The technique allows for editable text and doesn't require any 3D tools. Let's take a look:

1. Go to **File** | **Open** and browse to the `08-Text` folder. Select `3DPaper.jpg` and then click **Open**.
2. Press the *D* key to reset the colors to black and white and then switch to the **Type** tool from the **Tools** panel.
3. Left-click and drag across the canvas to create an area type text frame that occupies a least half the canvas area. Type `FOLD` and then select all characters with the **Type** tool.
4. Go to the **Properties** panel and set **Font** to **Nimbus Sans Condensed**, **Style** to **Black**, **Leading** to **Auto**, **Font Size** to `1000 pt`, and **Tracking** to `60`. Lower down the same panel, under **Type Options**, turn on **All Caps**. Click on the **Set text color** thumbnail and enter `fb920a` into the **Hexadecimal** field to set the color to bright orange; then, click **OK**. Finally, set **Alignment** to **Centered** from the **Paragraph** section of the **Properties** panel.

5. Resize the text frame so that it is as small as possible, without hiding any characters. Click on the **Commit changes** button in the **Options** bar to complete the text frame edits. Switch to the **Move** tool and center the text to the canvas:

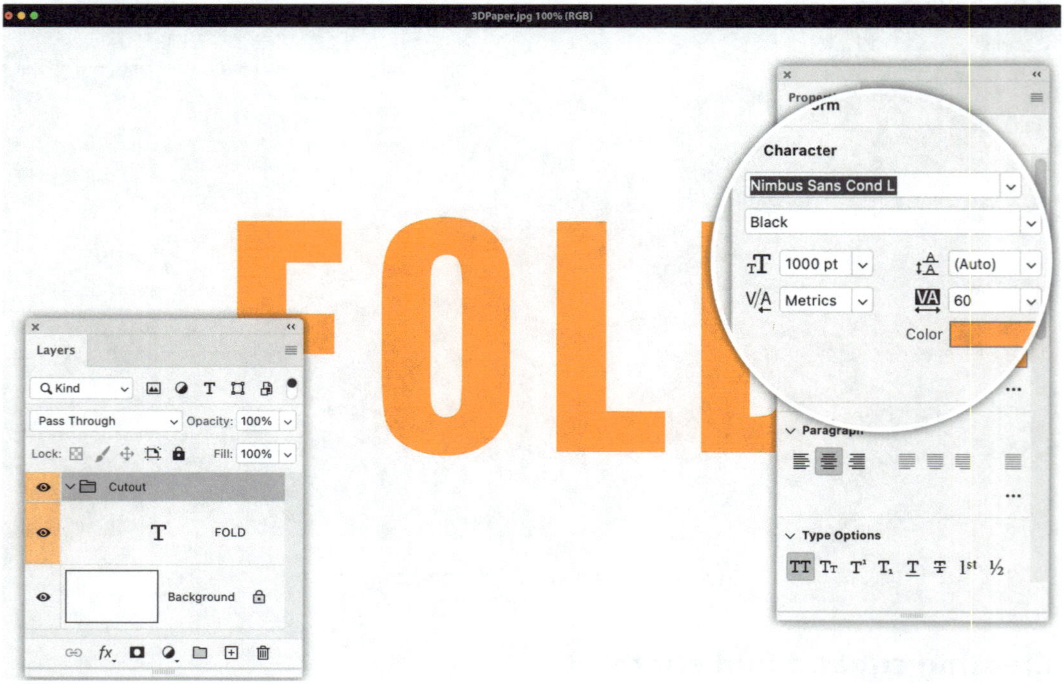

Figure 8.24: The base type layer formatting

6. With the text layer still active, press *Ctrl* + *G* (Windows) or *Cmd* + *G* (macOS) to add the text to a new layer group. Rename the layer group `Cutout`.
7. Ensure that the layer group is still active in the **Layers** panel, and then click on the **Add a layer style** button at the bottom of the **Layers** panel. From the list of options, click on **Inner Shadow**.
8. Click on the **Reset to Default** button at the bottom of the **Inner Shadow** settings. Then, set **Opacity** to `50%`, **Angle** to `-126°`, **Distance** to `13` px, **Spread** to `20%`, and **Size** to `40` px. Click **OK** to apply the effect when you're done:

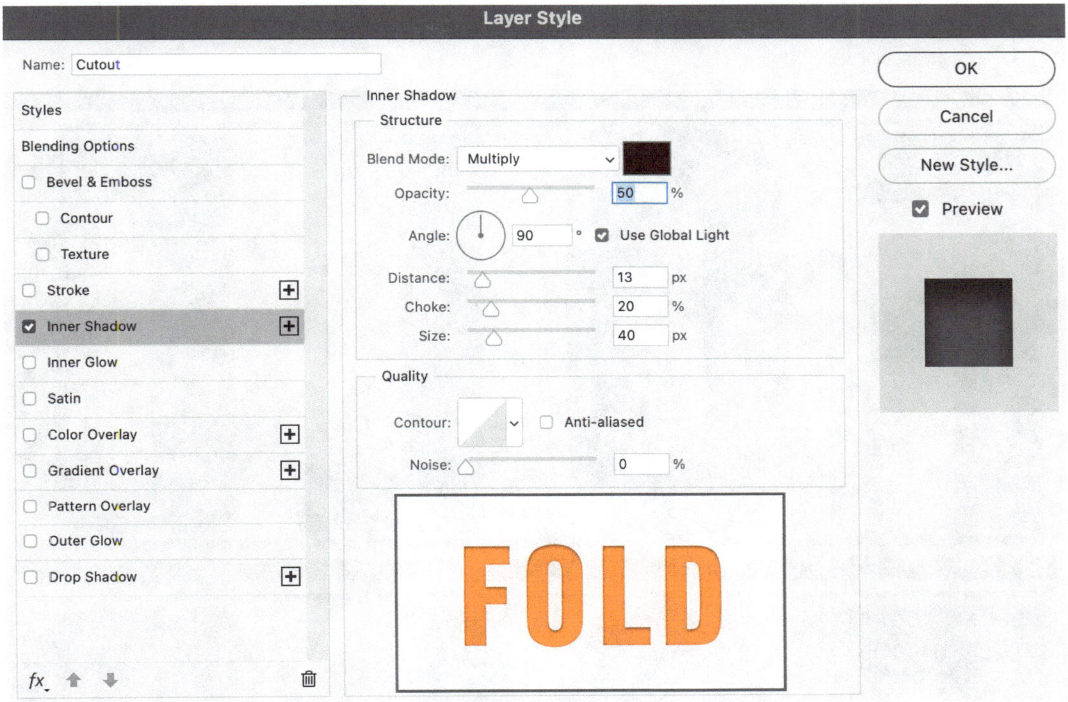

Figure 8.25: Inner shadow settings with the effect shown

9. Duplicate the text frame by dragging the text layer onto the **Create new layer** icon at the bottom of the **Layers** panel. Then, drag the duplicated text layer to the top of the layer stack, and out of the layer group. From the **Properties** panel, click on **Set text color** and change the color of the text to black.
10. Right-click on the text layer name you just edited and choose **Convert to Smart Object** from the list of commands. Rename the layer `Top`. Then, double left-click on the **Top** layer thumbnail to open the contents in a new window.
11. Go to **View | Rulers** if the rules are not visible in the image window. Then, go to **View | Snap** to turn off snapping, which will avoid the guide you are about to add snapping to the center of the canvas. Hover your cursor over the middle of **Horizontal Ruler** and drag a new guide down to the middle of the text, at approximately `365 px`.
12. Switch to the **Crop** tool from the **Tools** panel. From the **Options** bar, set **Mode** to **Ratio** and click on the **Clear** button. Turn off the **Delete cropped pixels** and **Content-Aware** checkboxes. Then, go to **View | Snap** to turn snapping back on. Drag the bottom-middle crop handle up the guide you added in a previous step and click on the **Commit changes** button in the **Options** bar to apply the edit.

13. Go to **File | Save** and close the **Top** document when you're done. This should return you to the master file:

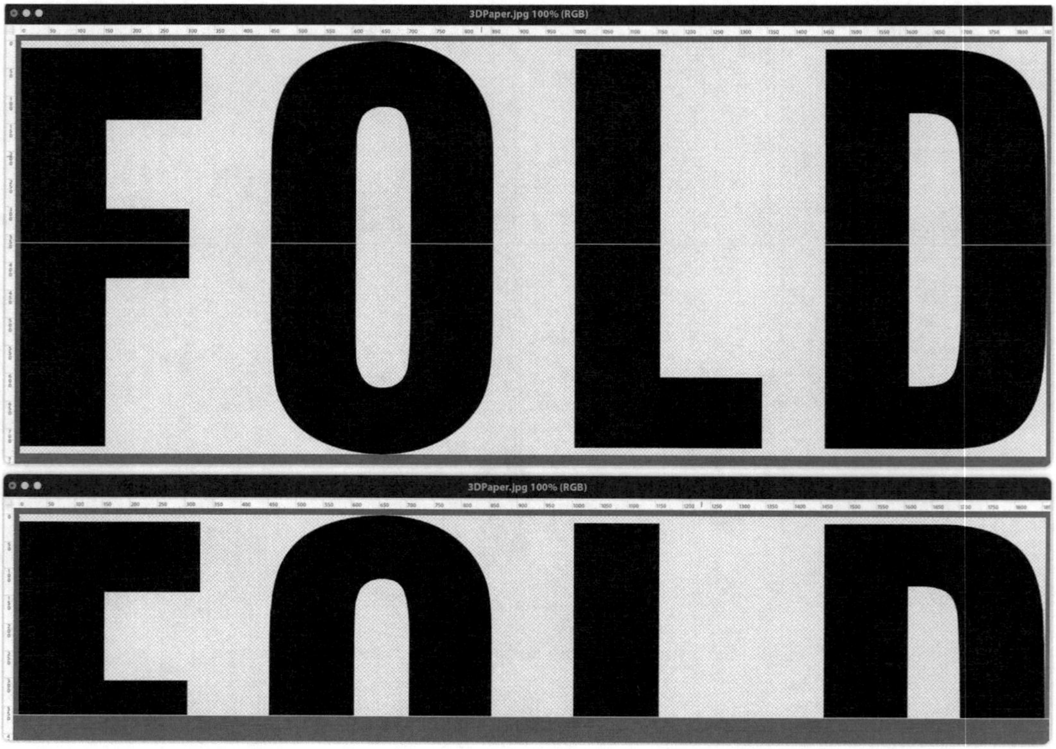

Figure 8.26: Adding guides to the middle of the type and cropping the type in half

14. You will notice that the text has moved because of the crop edit. Switch to the **Move** tool and reposition the cropped text so that it aligns with the top of the original orange text once more.
15. Right-click on the **Top** layer's name, choose **New Smart Object via Copy**, and rename the newly duplicated layer `Bottom`. Then, drag the **Bottom** layer under the **Top** layer in the **Layers** panel.
16. Next, double left-click on the **Bottom** layer's thumbnail to open the contents in a new window. Go to **Image | Reveal All**. Switch to the **Crop** tool, drag the top-middle handle of the crop frame down to the guide, and click on the **Commit** button in the **Options** bar to crop the top half of the text. Go to **File | Save** and close the **Bottom** document when you're done.
17. Left-click on the **Top** layer in the **Layers** panel to make it active. Then, click on the **Add a layer style** button at the bottom of the **Layers** panel. From the list of options, click on **Gradient Overlay** and click on the **Reset to Default** button in the **Gradient Overlay** settings.
18. Set **Bend Mode** to **Normal** and **Opacity** to `100%`, ensure the **Reverse** checkbox is deactivated, and set **Style** to **Linear**, **Angle** to `90°`, **Scale** to `100%`, and **Method** to **Perceptual**.
19. Next, left-click on the **Gradient** thumbnail to open the **Gradient Editor** area. When the dialog appears, expand the **Basic** folder of presets and choose the first preset, named **Foreground to background**.
20. Then, click on the left-hand **Color Stop** to make it active, then change its appearance by clicking on **Change color of selected stop**, the color swatch thumbnail. Enter `ffffff` into the **Hexadecimal** field to make the color stop white.
21. Then, click on the right-hand **Color Stop** to make it active. Click on **Change color of selected stop**. Enter `e8e8e8` into the **Hexadecimal** field to make the color stop a light gray. With the right-hand **Color Stop** still active, set **Location** to `30%`. Click **OK** when you're done. Then, click **OK** in the **Layer Style** dialog box to apply the overlay:

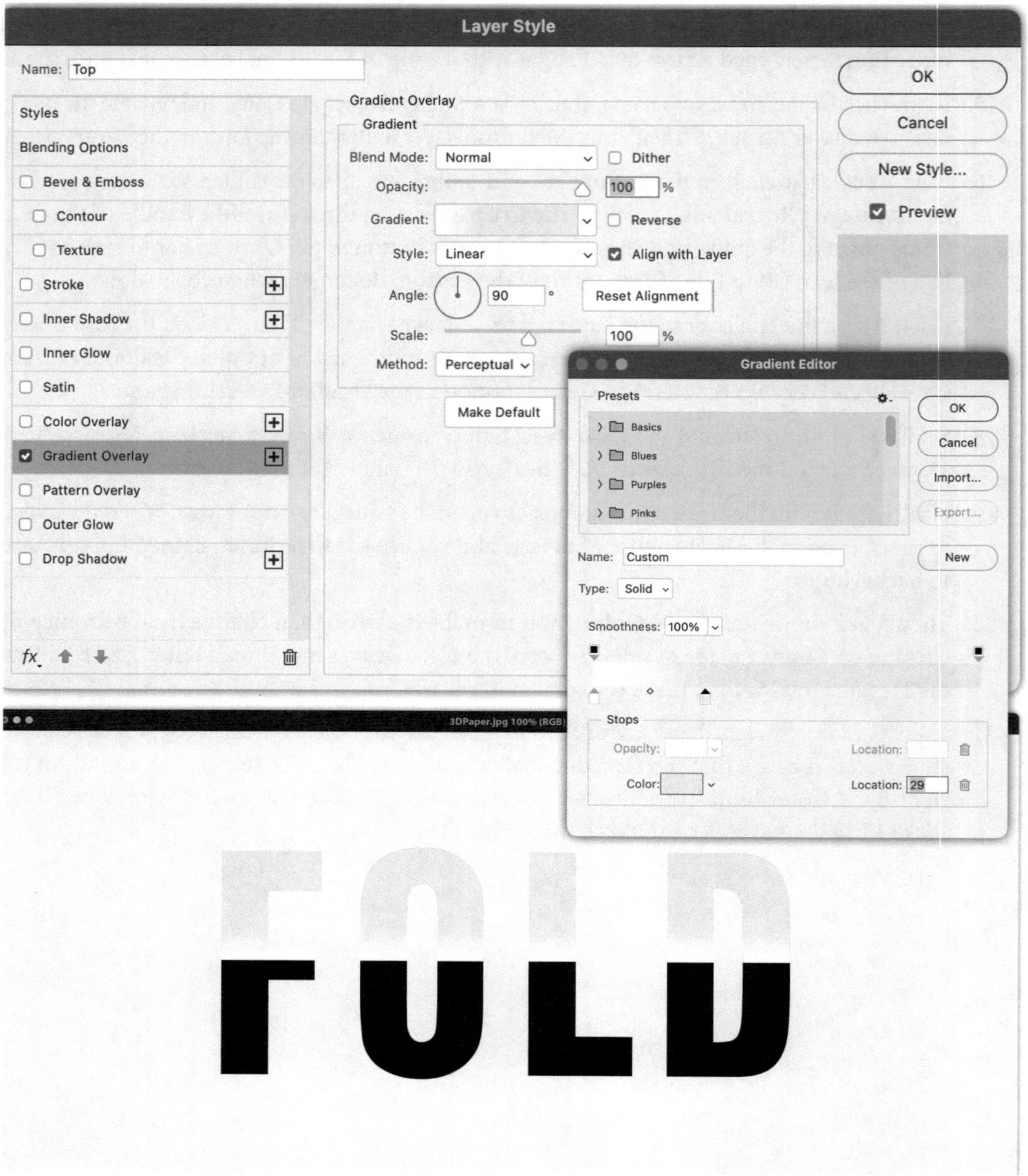

Figure 8.27: Gradient Overlay effects used to create highlights

22. Hover your cursor over the **Fx** icon assigned to the **Top** layer in the **Layers** panel, hold *Alt* (Windows) or *Option* (macOS), and drag the **FX** icon onto the layer named **Bottom** to duplicate the effect:

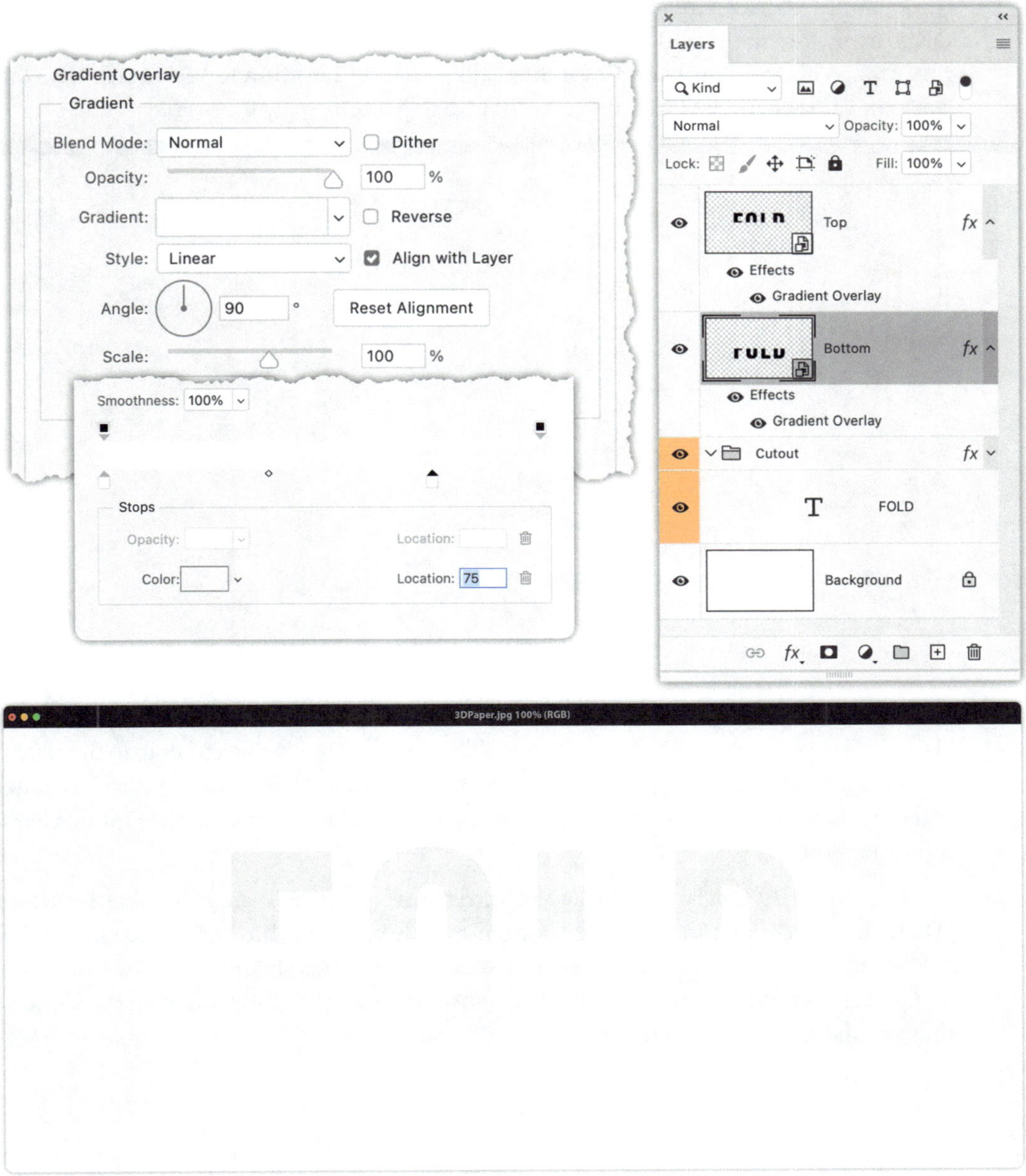

Figure 8.28: The lower-half Gradient Overlay settings

23. Double left-click on the newly duplicated text label, **Gradient Overlay**, that was assigned to the **Bottom** layer in the **Layers** panel to edit it. When the dialog appears, left-click on the **Gradient** thumbnail to open the **Gradient Editor** area.

24. Click on the left-hand **Color Stop** to make it active, then change its color to `fcfcfc`. Click **OK** to apply the change and then click on the right-hand **Color Stop** and change its color to `f2f2f2`. With the right-hand **Color Stop** still active, set **Location** to `75%`. Click **OK** when you're done. Then, click **OK** in the **Layer Style** dialog box to apply the overlay:

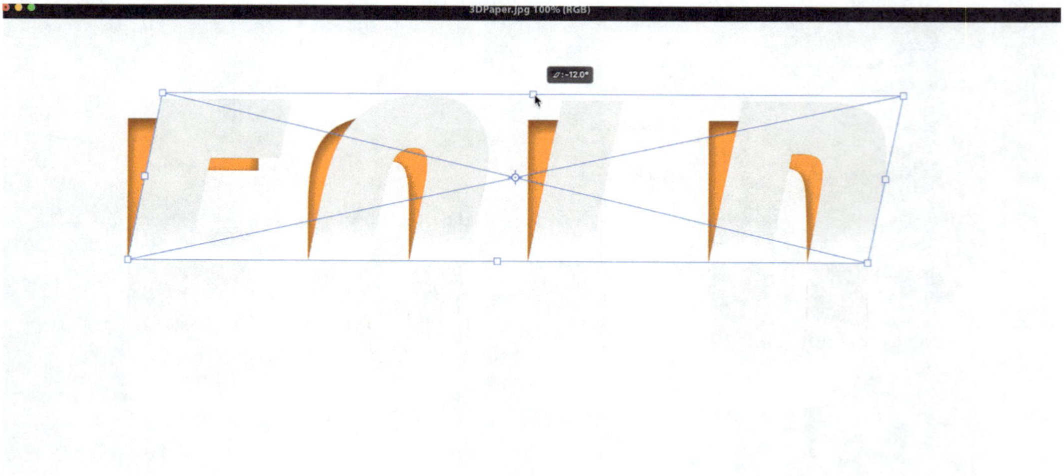

Figure 8.29: The distorted upper-half type characters

25. Left-click on the **Top** layer in the **Layers** panel to make it active. Then, go to **Edit** | **Transform** | **Distort**. Hover your cursor over the top-middle bounding box point and drag to the right to skew by `-12°` and then drag upward to make the text look as though the top edge has moved to the right, and upward slightly. Click on the **Commit changes** button in the **Options** bar to apply the edits.

26. Left-click on the **Bottom** layer in the **Layers** panel to make it active. Then, go to **Edit** | **Transform** | **Distort**. Hover your cursor over the bottom-middle bounding box point, drag to the right to **Skew** by `10°`, and then drag upward to **Skew** by `12°`. This should make the text look as though the bottom edge has moved to the right, and upward slightly. Click on the **Commit changes** button in the **Options** bar to apply the edits:

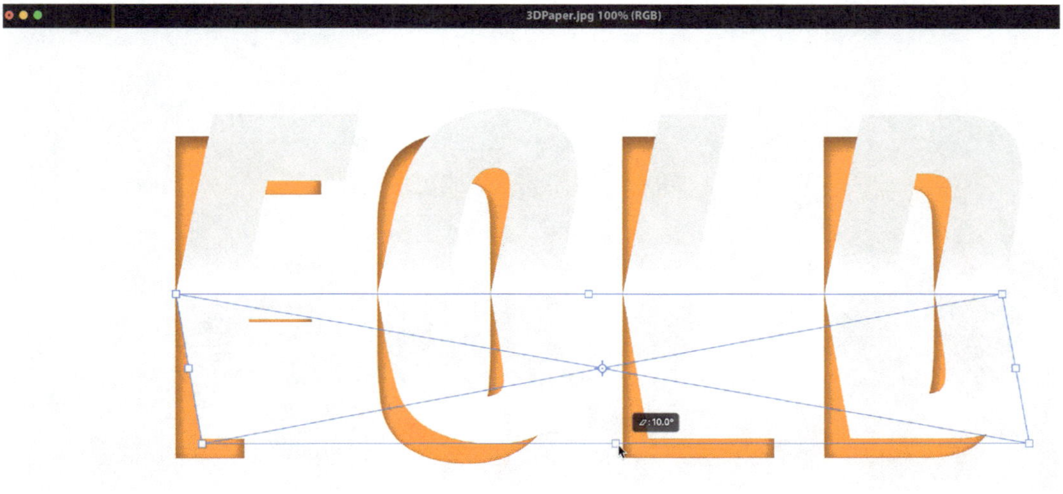

Figure 8.30: The distorted lower-half type characters

27. With the **Bottom** layer still active, hold *Shift* and left-click on the **Top** layer to make both layers active. Then, press *Ctrl* + *G* (Windows) or *Cmd* + *G* (macOS) to add the text to a new layer group. Rename the layer group `Letters`.
28. Right-click on the **Letters** layer group and choose **Duplicate Group** from the list of commands. When the dialog appears, change the **As** field to **Shadows** and click **OK**.
29. Expand the **Shadows** layer group and make both the **Top** and **Bottom** layers active in the **Layers** panel. Right-click on one of the active layer names and choose **Clear Layers Style** from the list. The text needs to be black for the shadow effect.
30. Make the **Top** layer active in the **Shadows** layer group by left-clicking on it. Then, go to **Filter** | **Blur** | **Gaussian Blur**. Set **Radius** to `25` px and click **OK**. Then, left-click on the **Bottom** layer in the **Shadows** layer group to make it active. Finally, go to **Filter** | **Gaussian Blur** to apply the same effect:

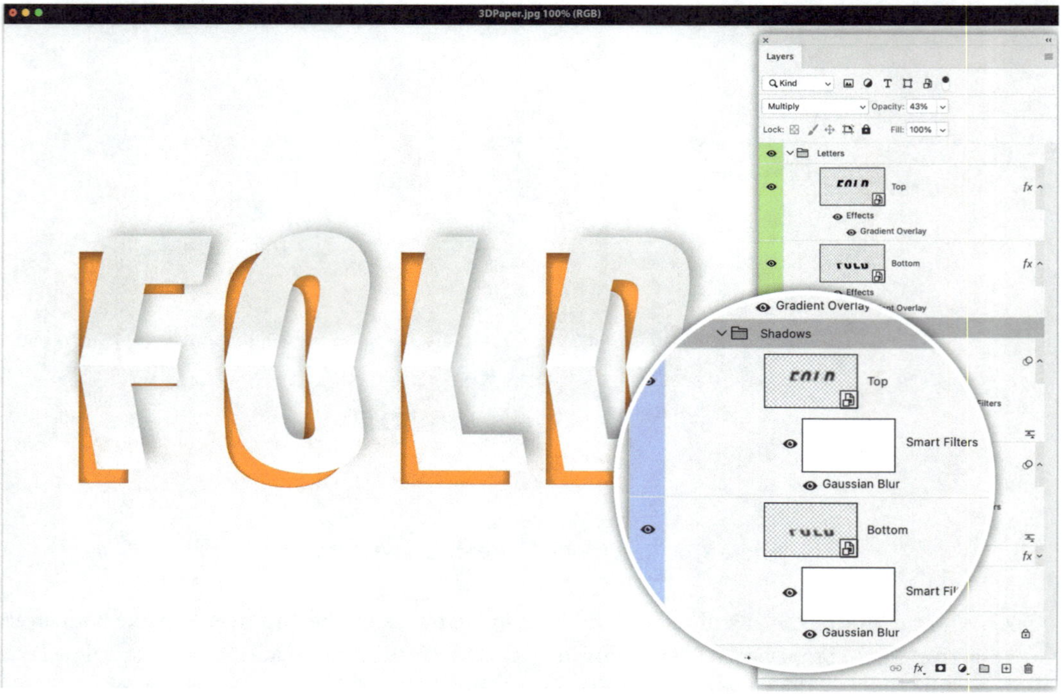

Figure 8.31: Duplicate the text to turn it into type shadows

31. To make this design more flexible, collapse all the layer groups in the stack and make them all active. Then, left-click on the **Letters** group, hold *Shift*, and left-click on the **Cutout** layer. Right-click on any of the active layer group names and choose **Convert to Smart Object** from the list.
32. You can then move, rotate, and scale as necessary. In the example shown here, the **Letters** Smart Object was rotated by `-25°`.

33. Go to **File | Save**, browse to the `08-Text` folder, and save the document as a PSD file. Close the document when you're done:

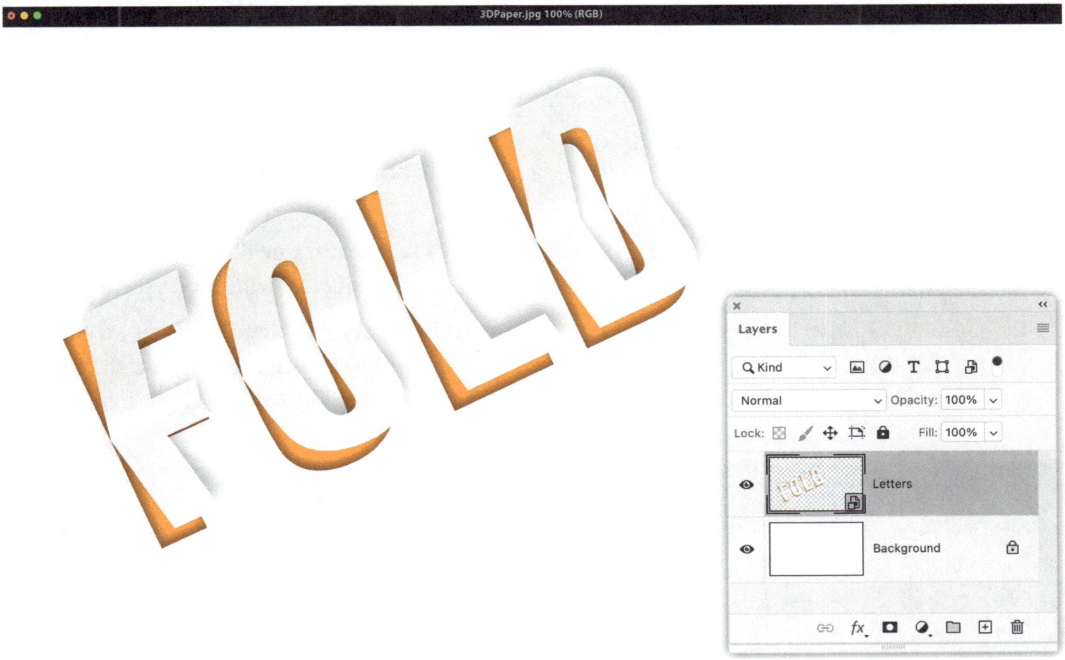

Figure 8.32: The completed faux 3D effects

In this section, we explored a series of effects that create slices, folds, and embosses that can be applied to text. Each technique allows for the text to remain editable using a combination of Smart Objects and layer styles, assigned via layer groups. In the next set of exercises, we will explore painterly effects.

Applying ink and paint effects

Infusing type with painterly effects is always a challenge when translating into a digital context, and something is often lost in the process. However, with a sound knowledge of Photoshop filters and layer styles, you can achieve impressive results.

Creating dripping paint

This technique uses displacement maps to distort editable text, giving the impression of paint dripping in a vertical direction. Let's get started:

1. Go to **File** | **Open** and select `DrippingPaint.jpg` from the `08-Text` folder. Then, click **Open**.
2. Press the *D* key to reset the colors to black and white and then switch to the **Type** tool from the **Tools** panel.
3. Left-click and drag across the canvas to create an area type text frame that occupies a least half the canvas area. Type `Giuseppe's` and then select all characters with the **Type** tool.
4. Go to the **Properties** panel and set **Font** to **Gelato Luxe**, **Style** to **Regular**, **Font Size** to `900 pt`, **Leading** to **Auto**, and **Tracking** to `0`. Set **Alignment** to **Centered**. Click on the **Set text color** thumbnail and enter `26befd` into the **Hexadecimal** field to create a light blue. Finally, click **OK**:

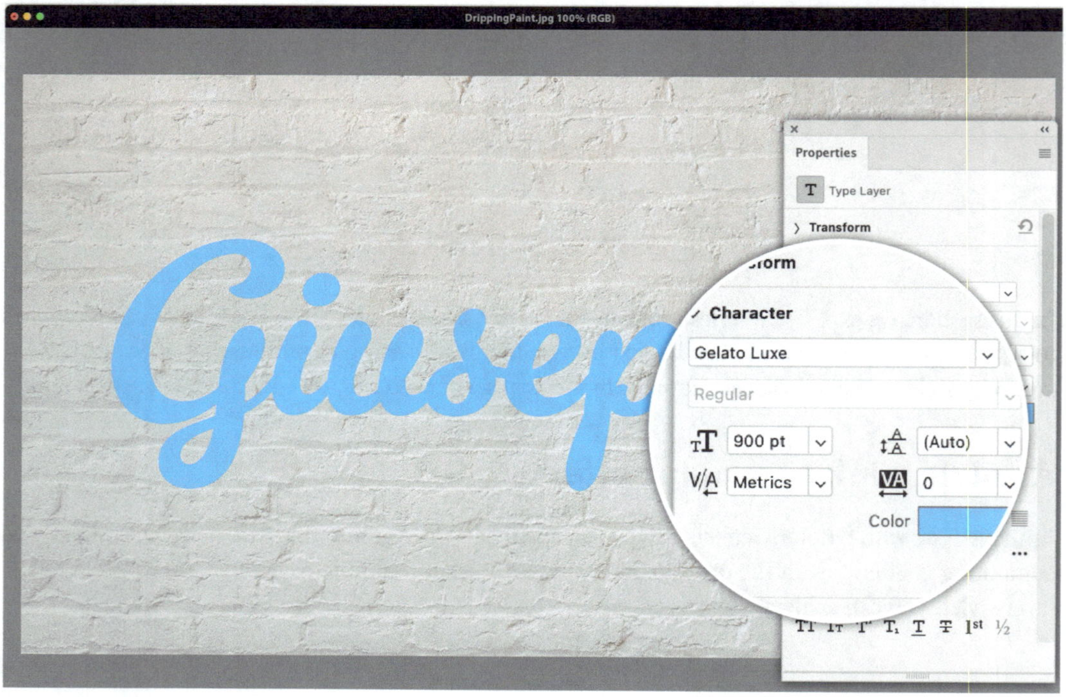

Figure 8.33: The base type formatting when using the Gelato Luxe font

5. Resize the text frame so that it's as small as possible without hiding any characters. Click on the **Commit changes** button in the **Options** bar to complete the text frame edits. Change **Blend Mode** for the text layer to **Linear Burn** to help blend the text in with the white brickwork.
6. Right-click on the text layer's name and choose **Convert to Smart Object** from the list of commands. This will allow the displacement filter to be applied nondestructively as a smart filter.

Creating and applying the paint displacement map

To create the dripping effect, we need to create a displacement map that will pull parts of the text layer down the canvas, imitating paint. Follow these steps:

1. Go to **File | New**. Click on the **Web** text tab at the top of the dialog. Change the name of the document to **PaintDisplace**. Set its **Width** to `3840` px and **Height** to `2160` px, and turn off the **Artboards** checkbox. Set **Background Contents** to **White** and then click on the **Create** button.
2. Right-click on the **Background** layer's name and choose **Convert to Smart Object**. Rename the layer `Texture`.
3. Press the *D* key to reset the **Foreground** and **Background** colors to black and white, respectively. Then, go to **Filter | Render Fibers**. When the dialog appears, set **Variance** to `15` and **Strength** to `6`. Click **OK** when you're done.
4. Next, go to **Image | Adjustment | Levels**. You will notice three numerical fields under the **Input Fields** graph. Enter `50` into the right-hand field to set the white point to increase the contrast, and reduce the amount of black fiber marks. Under the **Output** fields at the bottom, change the white point to `128`. We're doing this because displacement maps affect regions of an image that are black and white when applied, but a mid-tone gray will remain unaffected. Click **OK** when you're done to apply the edit.
5. Next, go to **Filter | Blur | Gaussian Blur**. When the dialog appears, set **Radius** to `5.0` px. Click **OK** when you're done. Double left-click on the **Gaussian Blur Blend Mode** icon, adjacent to the filter name in the **Layers** panel (*Figure 8.34, A*). Change **Blend Mode** to **Darken** and click **OK**.
6. Then, apply a similar edit by going to **Filter | Gaussian Blur**. When the dialog appears, set **Radius** to `1.0` px. Click **OK** when you're done:

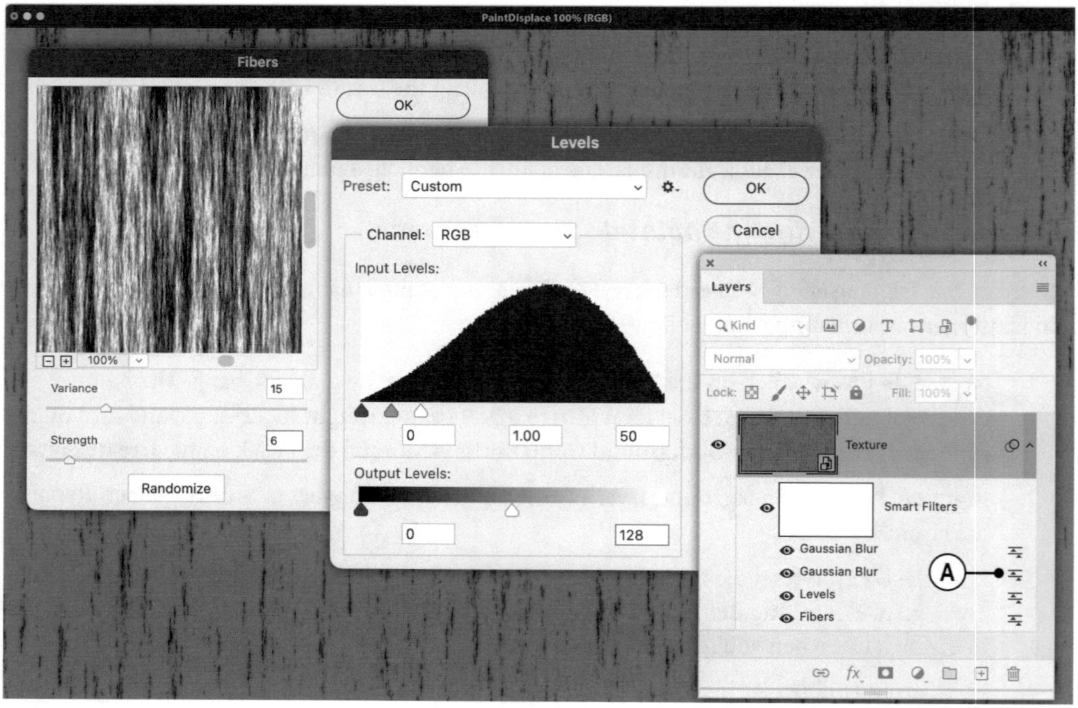

Figure 8.34: Fibers, Levels, and blur effects used to create a displacement map

7. Go to **File** | **Save**, browse to the `08-Text` folder, and save the document as a PSD file. Close the document when you're done.
8. With the `DrippingPaint.jpg` document open and active, ensure that the **Giuseppe's** Smart Object layer is active in the **Layers** panel.
9. Then, go to **Filter** | **Distort** | **Displace**. When the dialog appears, set **Horizontal Scale** to `0` and **Vertical Scale** to `100`. This will ensure that the displacement map pulls pixels in the layer downward only. You can leave the other settings with their defaults. Click **OK** when you're done.
10. You will then be prompted to select an image to use as your displacement map. Choose `PaintDisplace.psd` and click **OK**. This will apply a subtle drag downward to the editable text.
11. You can use the same technique to intensify the effect by going to **Filter** | **Displace**, selecting the same document (`PaintDisplace.psd`), and clicking **OK**. Repeat this as many times as you require. In this example, the displacement was applied five times:

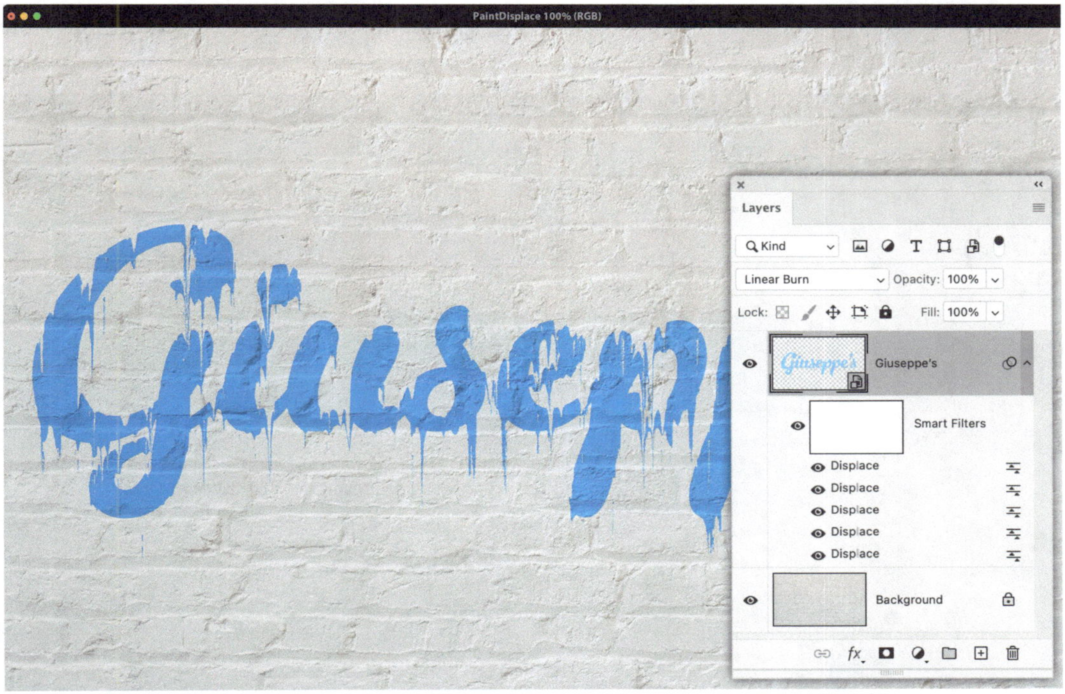

Figure 8.35: The effect of each of the five displacement maps once added

Refining the paint effect

You cannot predict how a displacement filter effect will look before you apply it. In the case of the dripping paint, some portions could be enhanced with a layer mask. Let's do this now:

1. Switch to the **Brush** tool by pressing the *B* key. Click on the **Brush Tip** menu from the **Options** bar. Click on the fly-out menu, shown as a cog icon in the top-right corner of the **Brush Tip** menu, and choose **Legacy** from the list.
2. Expand the **Legacy brush** folder when it appears, then expand the **Default Brushes** folder. Scroll down the list of brushes until you find **Dry Brush**. Left-click on it to make it active and increase its **Size** value to `100` px.
3. Ensure **Opacity** is set to `100%` in the **Options** bar and set black under **Foreground Color** in the **Tools** panel. Left-click on the **Smart Filter** mask in the **Layers** panel that is assigned to the Smart Object you created with your text in it. Then, start to click and drag across the parts of the text in the image window that you wish to reveal.

4. Go to **File | Save**, browse to the `08-Text` folder, and save the document as a PSD file. Close the document when you're done:

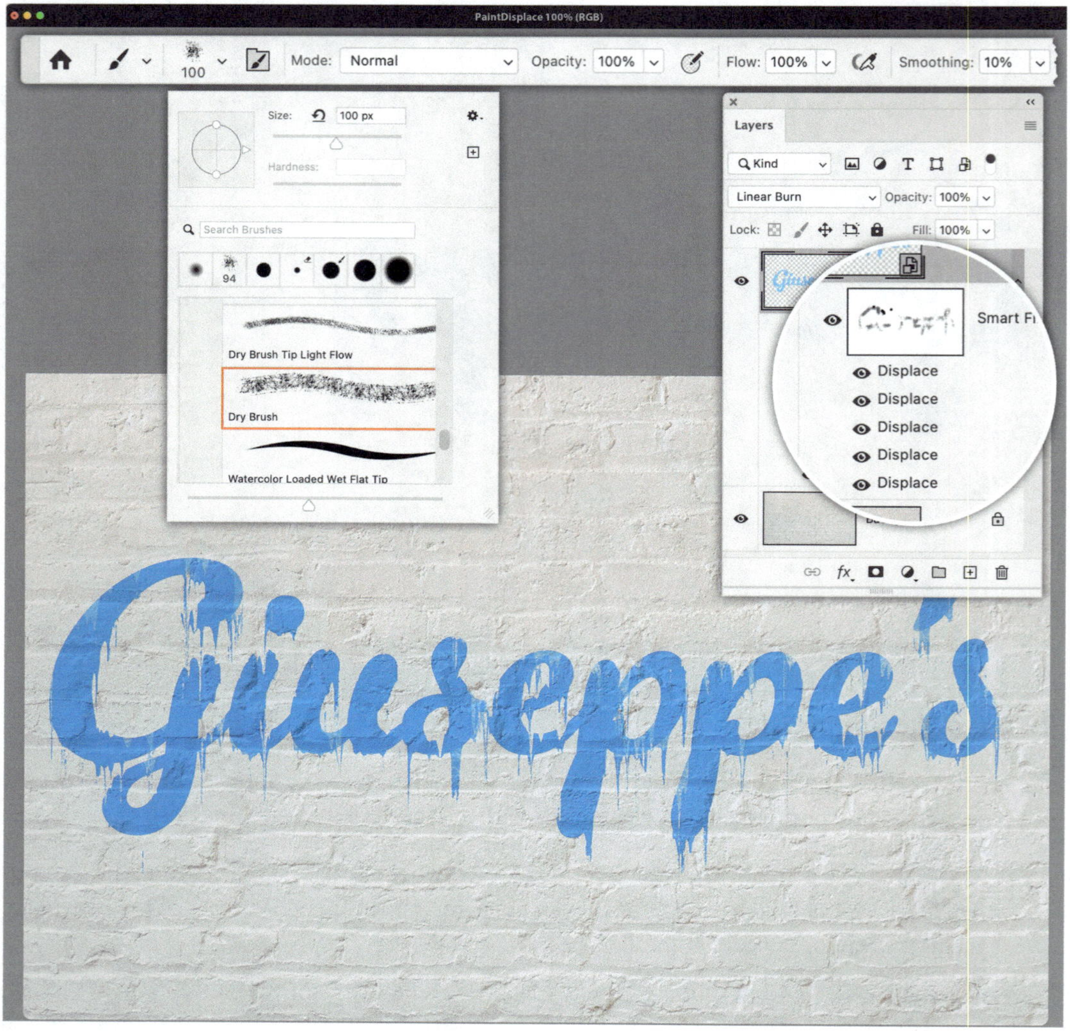

Figure 8.36: Masking out parts of the paint drips with the Brush tool

Creating a graffiti typographic effect

This exercise combines several techniques to create a graffiti street art style, allowing you to consolidate some of the techniques we covered in earlier chapters under a different context. Again, the aim here is flexible, editable type effects.

Formatting the underlying type layer

As with previous exercises, we need to start with a type layer as the basis for our document artwork. Let's get started:

1. Go to **File | Open** and select `StreetArt.jpg` from the `08-Text` folder. Click **Open**.
2. Press the *D* key to reset the colors to black and white and then switch to the **Type** tool from the **Tools** panel:

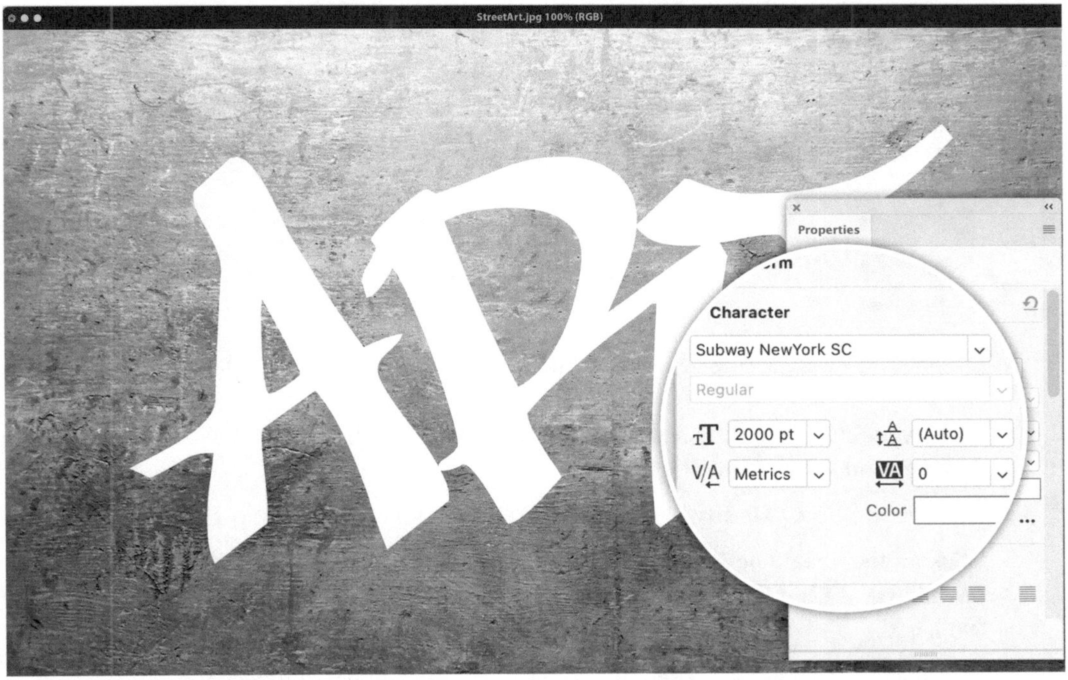

Figure 8.37: The base type formatting, using the Subway NewYork SC font

3. Left-click and drag across the canvas to create an area type text frame that occupies a least half the canvas area. Type `Art` and then select all characters with the **Type** tool.
4. Go to the **Properties** panel and set **Font** to **Subway NewYork SC**, **Style** to **Regular**, **Font Size** to `1000 pt`, **Leading** to `Auto`, and **Tracking** to `0`. Set **Alignment** to **Centered**. Click on the **Set text color** thumbnail, enter `ffffff` into the **Hexadecimal** field to define white text, and click **OK**.
5. We need the text to be `2000 pt`, but Photoshop has a limit regarding the size it can be increased by when entering numerical values. The answer is to go to **Edit | Free Transform**, increase **Scale** to `200%`, and click on the **Commit changes** button in the **Options** bar.

Creating long shadows

In *Chapter 5*, we utilized the **Actions** panel to record repetitive, tedious steps to save valuable time. Here, we will use it to create a long shadow effect:

1. Open the **Actions** panel by going to **Window | Actions**. Then, click on the **Create new set** icon at the bottom of the panel. Name the set `Effects` and click **OK** when you're done.
2. Click on the **Create new action** button at the bottom of the **Actions** panel, name it `Long Shadow`, ensure it is added to the **Effects** set, and click **Record**:

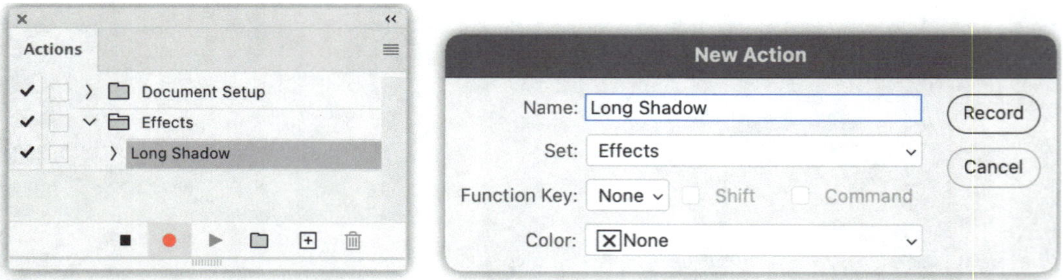

Figure 8.38: Creating a new action to record the long shadow effect

3. Hover your cursor over the **Art** type layer thumbnail and then press *Ctrl* (Windows) or *Cmd* (macOS) and left-click to select the type.
4. Then, go to **Select | Modify | Expand**, set the **Expand By** value to `20` pixels, and click **OK**.
5. Click on the **Create new layer** icon at the bottom of the **Layers** panel. Then, press *Ctrl* + *[* (Windows) or *Cmd* + *[* (macOS) to move the layer down one level in the stack, under the **Art** text layer.
6. Press the *D* key to reset the **Foreground** and **Background** colors, and then press *Alt* + backspace (Windows) or *Option* + backspace (macOS) to fill the selection with black. Then, press *Ctrl* + *D* (Windows) or *Cmd* + *D* (macOS) to deselect.
7. Switch to the **Move** tool, then press the down arrow key once and the left arrow key once to move the layer one pixel down and one pixel to the left.
8. Create a duplicate of the layer by pressing *Ctrl* + *J* (Windows) or *Cmd* + *J* (macOS), then press *Ctrl* + *[* (Windows) or *Cmd* + *[* (macOS). After, press the down arrow key once and the left arrow key to extend the shadow effect.
9. Repeat the previous step a further eight times to generate the shadow effect. In total, you should now have 10 shadow layers. Next, we need to merge them into a single layer by pressing *Alt* + *Shift* + *[* (Windows) or *Option* + *Shift* + *[* (macOS) nine times to select each of them in the layer stack. Then, press *Ctrl* + *E* (Windows) or *Cmd* + *E* (macOS) to merge them.

10. Create a duplicate of the merged shadow layer by pressing *Ctrl* + *J* (Windows) or *Cmd* + *J* (macOS), then press *Ctrl* + *[* (Windows) or *Cmd* + *[* (macOS). Then, press the *Shift* + down arrow key once and the *Shift* + left arrow key to extend the shadow effect 10 pixels down and to the left.
11. Repeat the previous step four times to complete the long shadow effect. Then, press *Ctrl* + *E* (Windows) or *Cmd* + *E* (macOS) to merge them. Rename the newly merged layer `Shadow`.
12. Press *Alt* + *Shift* + *[* (Windows) or *Option* + *Shift* + *[* (macOS) four times to select each of the shadow layers in the layer stack. Then, press *Ctrl* + *E* (Windows) or *Cmd* + *E* (macOS) to merge them.
13. Press the **Stop** button at the bottom of the **Actions** panel to stop recording and then collapse the actions by clicking on the toggle adjacent to the action name **Long Shadow**.
14. With the **Shadow** layer still active in the **Layers** panel, you can test the action you just created by left-clicking on the action's name and then pressing the **Play selection** button at the bottom of the **Actions** panel. This will create a second long shadow effect, building upon the first. You will use both to progress the artwork. Make both shadow layers active in the **Layers** panel and press *Ctrl* + *E* (Windows) or *Cmd* + *E* (macOS) to merge them:

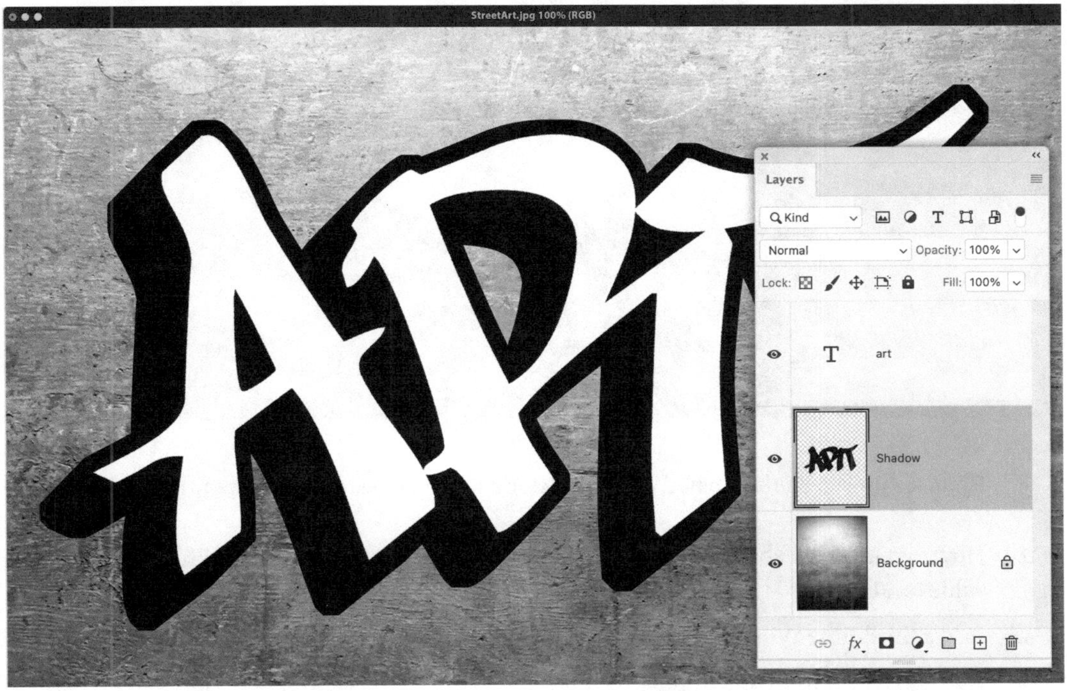

Figure 8.39: The completed long shadow effect

Adding spray paint effects to the text and shadows

Follow the steps given below:

1. Ensure the **Art** type layer is active in the **Layers** panel, then right-click on the layer's name and choose **Convert to Smart Object** from the list of commands. Change the layer's **Blend Mode** to **Dissolve**.
2. With the **Art** layer still active, go to **Filter | Blue Gallery | Field Blur**. When the **Blur Gallery** interface appears, you will see a single **Blur Widget** in the canvas. Drag the first **Blur Widget** above the letter *R*, then change **Blur** to `60 px` from the **Blur Tools** panel:

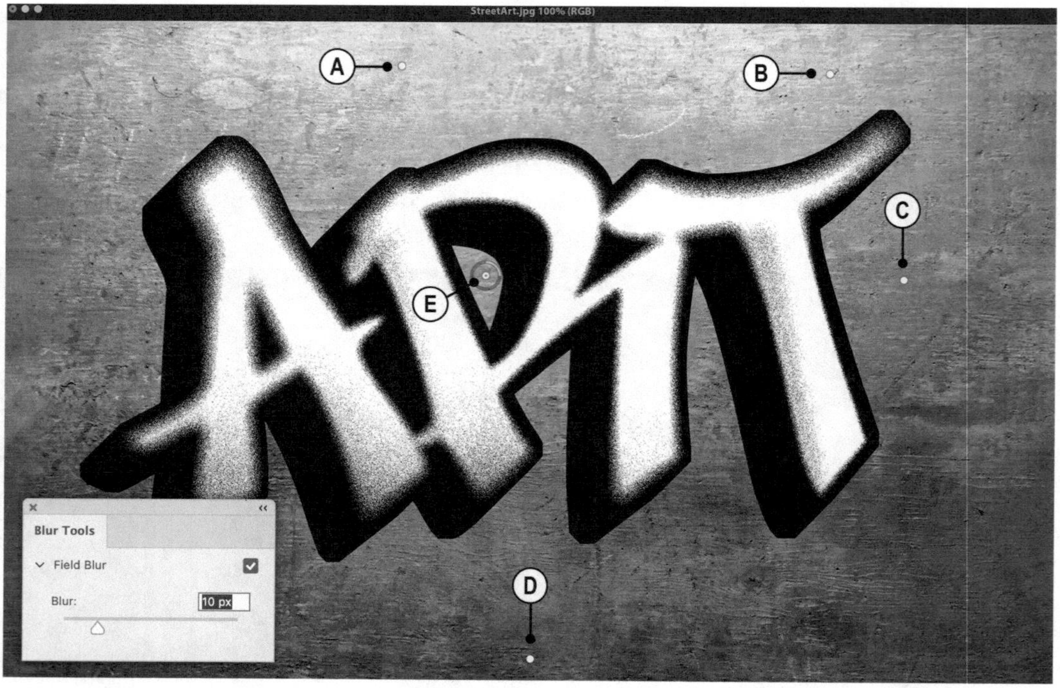

Figure 8.40: Field Blur combined with the Dissolve blend mode to create a spray paint effect

3. Hover your cursor above the letter *T* and left-click to add a second **Blur Widget**. Set the **Blur** value to `50 px`.
4. Add a third **Blur Widget** to the right-hand side of the letter *T* and set the **Blur** value to `5 px`.
5. Add a fourth **Blur Widget** under the middle of all the letters and set the **Blur** value to `35 px`.
6. Finally, add a fifth **Blur Widget** inside the counter of the letter *R* and set the **Blur** value to `10 px`. Turn on the **High Quality** checkbox in the **Options** bar, and then click **OK** to apply the blur edits and close the interface.

7. Left-click on the **Shadow** layer in the **Layers** panel, then right-click on the layer's name and choose **Convert to Smart Object** from the list of commands. Change the layer's **Blend Mode** to **Dissolve**.
8. Next, hover your cursor over the **Smart Filter** mask named **Blur Gallery**, hold *Alt* (Windows) or *Option* (macOS), and then drag the smart filter onto the **Shadow** layer:

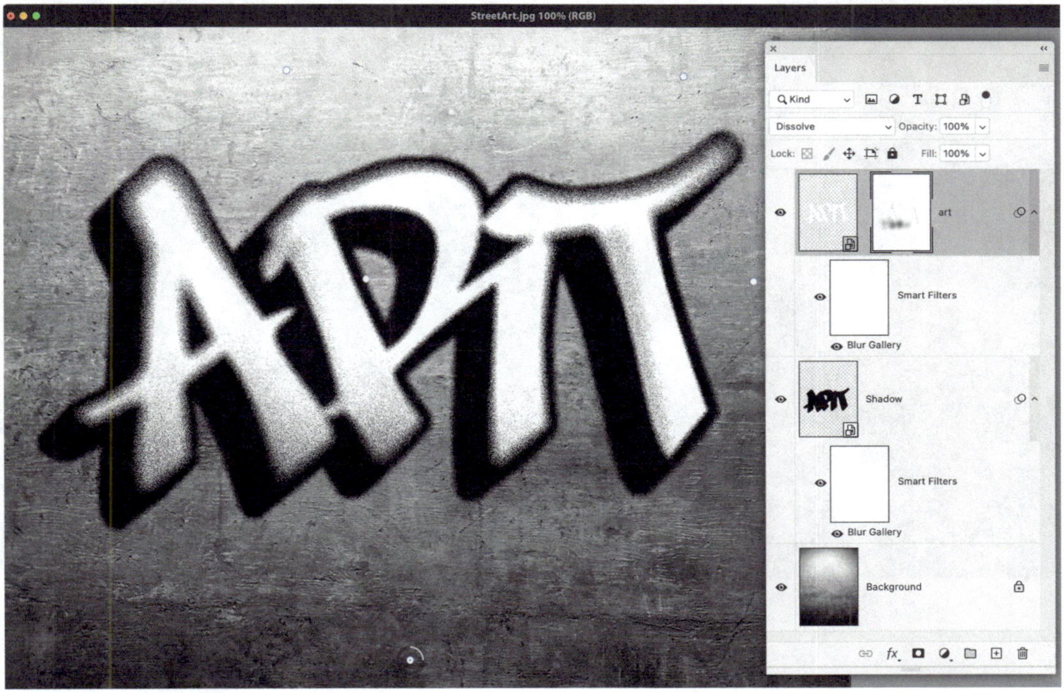

Figure 8.41: The Shadow layer with spray paint effects applied

9. Then, double left-click on the **Blur Gallery** filter name that was assigned to the **Shadow** layer to open **Blur Gallery**. Change all **Blur Widget** values to `8 px` and click **OK** to apply the edits.
10. If you wish to emphasize the spray paint effect on any part of the **Art** text or **Shadow** layer, you can add a layer mask and paint black into the mask. In the example shown, I used a **Soft Round** brush tip with a **Size** value of `600` px, **Hardness** set to `0%`, and **Opacity** set to `30%`. Focus on painting along the ends of the type characters to create a diffused spray paint effect.

11. Go to **File | Save** when you're done to capture all edits, saving it as a PSD file in the `08-Type` folder. Close the document when you're done:

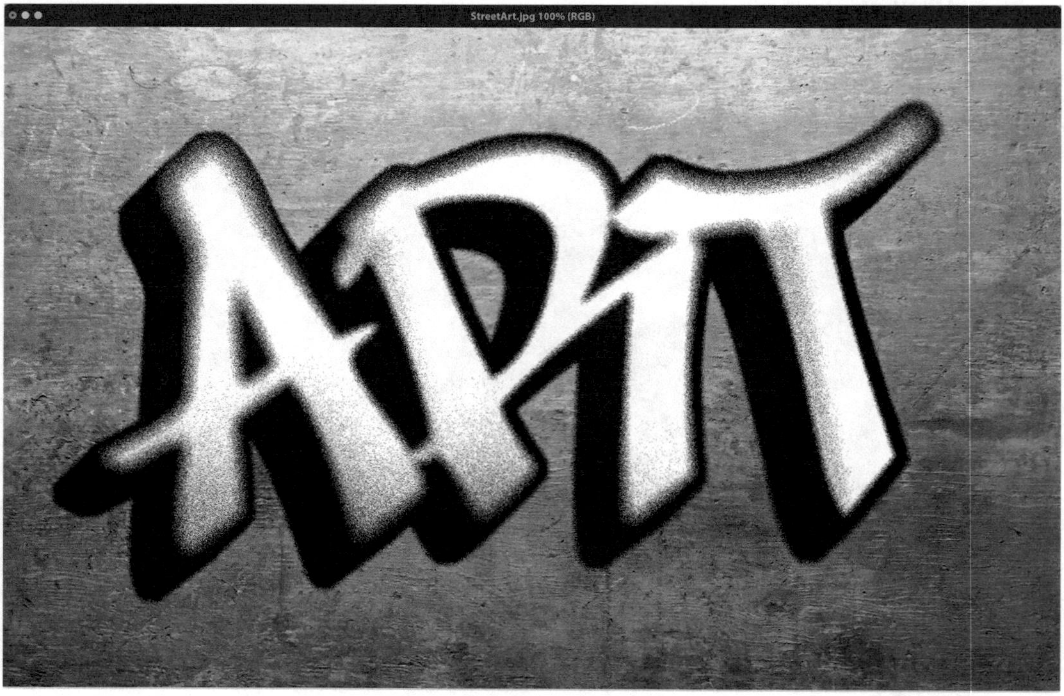

Figure 8.42: The completed graffiti effect

In this section, we used a variety of filters to recreate painterly effects such as spray paint and dripping paint. We also utilized actions to create long shadow effects that can be applied to editable text layers in the future for ease.

Summary

In this chapter, we leveraged Photoshop's powerful layer styles, filters, and effects to create visually arresting type layers. Each used a nondestructive workflow that allows for type to be edited without the need for us to recreate any effects.

First, we converted an editable type layer into a Smart Object, duplicated it, and then, using a layer mask, divided the text into two halves to form a slice effect. This enabled the type to remain editable, with any edits applied to either half automatically updating the other.

Then, we created a classic paper embossed effect with a combination of layer styles. On this occasion, the effects were added to a single layer group, where any content added to the group would be instantly styled with the embossed effects. This technique keeps the styling limited to a single item in the layer stack that can be updated with ease and allows for vector logos and text to be added or removed as required. Once removed from the layer group, the original layer's appearance is reinstated.

After, we explored a faux 3D effect, which started with the primary text layer as a cutout effect. This was then copied and converted into a two-linked Smart Object. Each half was then distorted to create cut-out letters with gradient overlays to create highlights and shadow effects.

Then, we moved on to displacement maps to create a dripping paint effect. Using a combination of a fiber filter, level adjustments, and blur effects, we created a displacement map that was then applied multiple times to vertically distort the type layer to achieve the dripping paint effect. Again, the type and the distortion effects remained editable.

Finally, we looked at a technique for creating spray paint graffiti type by combining the dissolve blend mode with field blur effects.

In the next chapter, we will explore methods for creating interesting backdrops with patterns, gradients, and filter effects.

9

Creating Textures, Patterns, and Backdrops

Sometimes, even an extensive library of stock images can't provide that one special design aesthetic that you're looking for. That's when you can leverage Photoshop's textures, gradients, and patterns to turn a dull image into one that bursts with energy and visual interest.

Textures add a certain feel to a surface, which can be random or consistent, and by using them as a subtle backdrop to your visuals, you can avoid the mundane feel of a solid color. Ranging from natural surfaces such as wood and stone to steel mesh, textures are diverse. In the first section of this chapter, we will look at techniques to create textures from scratch and apply them to an image as a fill, or with a painting tool.

Gradients combine two or more colors, blending them together smoothly, like a sunset that blends a deep blue to warmer orange and red tones on the horizon. Gradients are useful to add emphasis or atmosphere to an image. We will look at techniques to create gradients with a layer style and the **Gradient tool**.

When we think of patterns, wallpaper is often the first thing that springs to mind – a repeating design that contains no discernable joints or edges. In this chapter, we will create patterns with both pixels and vector shapes with the **Pattern Maker**.

You will have the opportunity to integrate backdrops into existing compositions and experiment with a combination of layer styles, painting tools, and filters to create realistic effects such as start fields.

This chapter covers the following topics:

- Creating new textures, gradients, and patterns
- Managing backdrop assets
- Simulating environments with filters and effects

Technical requirements

The project files for this chapter can be found at: `https://github.com/PacktPublishing/Mastering-Adobe-Photoshop-2024/tree/main/Chapter09`

Creating new textures, gradients, and patterns

As with almost all Photoshop projects, creating great-looking visuals starts with high-quality source content. However, when it comes to textures, gradients, and patterns, we have greater flexibility, as they can each be constructed from scratch in the application.

Gradients are almost always generated via layer styles, layer overlays, or the Gradient tool. Textures and patterns can be generated from raster graphics or vector graphics.

Creating a texture from scratch

In the first exercise, we will create background artwork that comprises a texture, then a pattern, and finally, a gradient, using a combination of filters, layer overlays, and blend modes without any source imagery:

1. Go to **File** → **New**, click on the **Web** tab at the top of the dialog. Enter the name `Road`, and then change the document width to `3840 px` and the height to `2160 px`. Turn off the **Artboards** checkbox, and set **Background Contents** to **White**. Then, click on **Create** to generate the file.
2. Then, go to **Edit** → **Fill**; when the dialog appears, choose **50% Gray** from the **Contents** drop-down menu, and then click **OK**. This will fill the layer with a neutral gray that will enhance the filters you will add in later steps.
3. Right-click on the **Background** layer name in the **Layers** panel, and choose **Convert to Smart Object** from the list of commands. Rename the layer `Tarmac`.
4. With the `Tarmac` layer still active, go to **Filter** → **Noise** → **Add Noise**. When the dialog appears, set **Amount** to `340%`, set **Distribution** to **Gaussian**, and turn on the **Monochromatic** checkbox. Click **OK** when done.
5. Next, go to **Filter** → **Pixelate** → **Pointillize**. When the dialog appears, set the **Cell Size** to `30`, and then click **OK** when done.

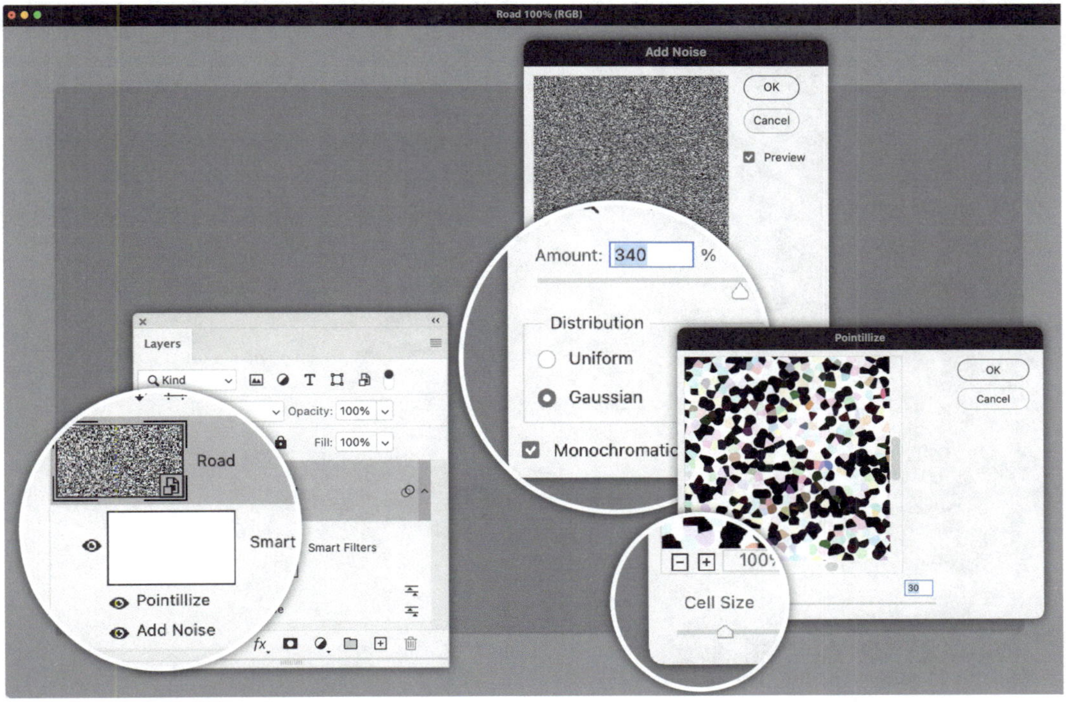

Figure 9.1: The gray layer with the Add Noise and Pointallize filters applied

6. With the `Tarmac` layer still active, go to **Filter** → **Noise** → **Filter Gallery**. When the dialog appears, expand the **Sketch** filters, and left-click on **Reticulation**. Set **Density** to `5`, **Foreground Level** to `45`, and **Background Level** to `5`.
7. Click on the **New Effect layer** icon (**A** in *Figure 9.2*) at the bottom of the dialog to duplicate the first effect, replace it by expanding the **Artistic** filters, and then left-click on **Fresco**. Set **Brush Size** to `2`, **Brush Detail** to `8`, and **Texture** to `1`.

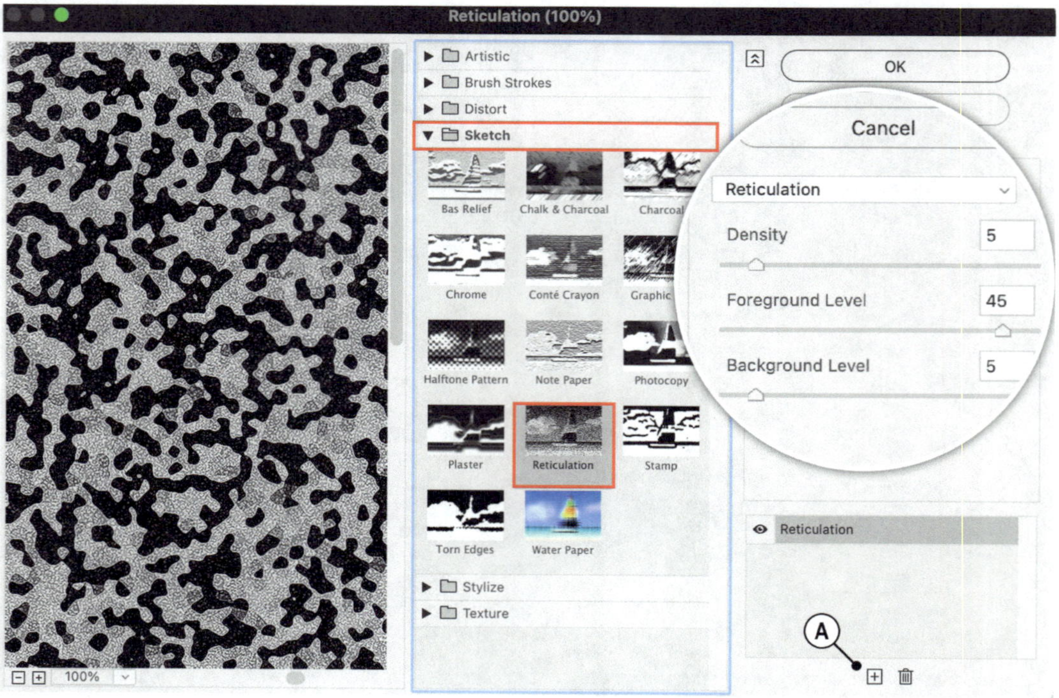

Figure 9.2: Filter Gallery, showing Reticulation settings

8. Duplicate the effect by clicking on the **New Effect layer** icon at the bottom of the dialog. Leave this effect as we need it to emphasize the first version.
9. Click on the **New Effect layer** icon for a third time to duplicate the previous effect, replace it by expanding the **Texture** filters, and then left-click on **Craquelure**. Set **Craquelure Spacing** to `8`, **Crack Depth** to `2`, and **Craquelure Brightness** to `0`. Finally, click **OK** to apply the edits and exit.
10. With the `Tarmac` layer still active, go to **Select** → **All**. Then, go to **View** → **Pattern Preview**. If a warning message appears, click **OK** to proceed to preview mode.

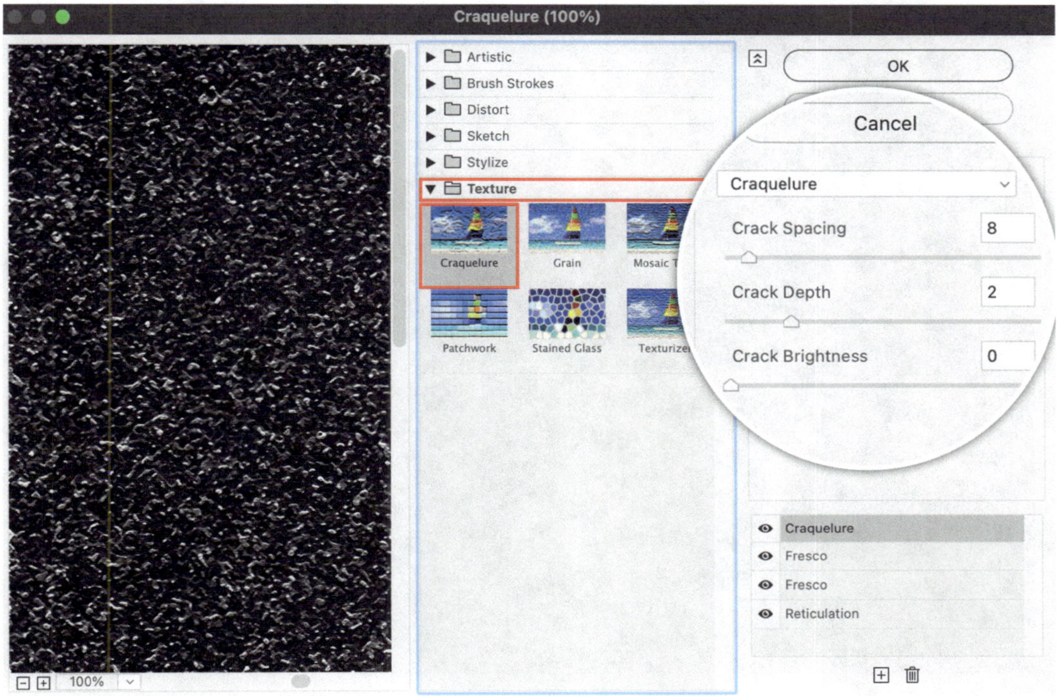

Figure 9.3: The Filter Gallery showing the Craquelure settings

11. Next, open the **Patterns** panel by going to **Window** → **Patterns**. Then, click on the **New Pattern** icon at the bottom of the **Pattern** panel. When the dialog appears, name the pattern `Tarmac`, and click **OK**.
12. Go to **View** → **Pattern Preview** to deactivate the mode, and then go to **Select** → **Deselect**. You now have a saved pattern that can be applied to any document in the future, so let's test it out.

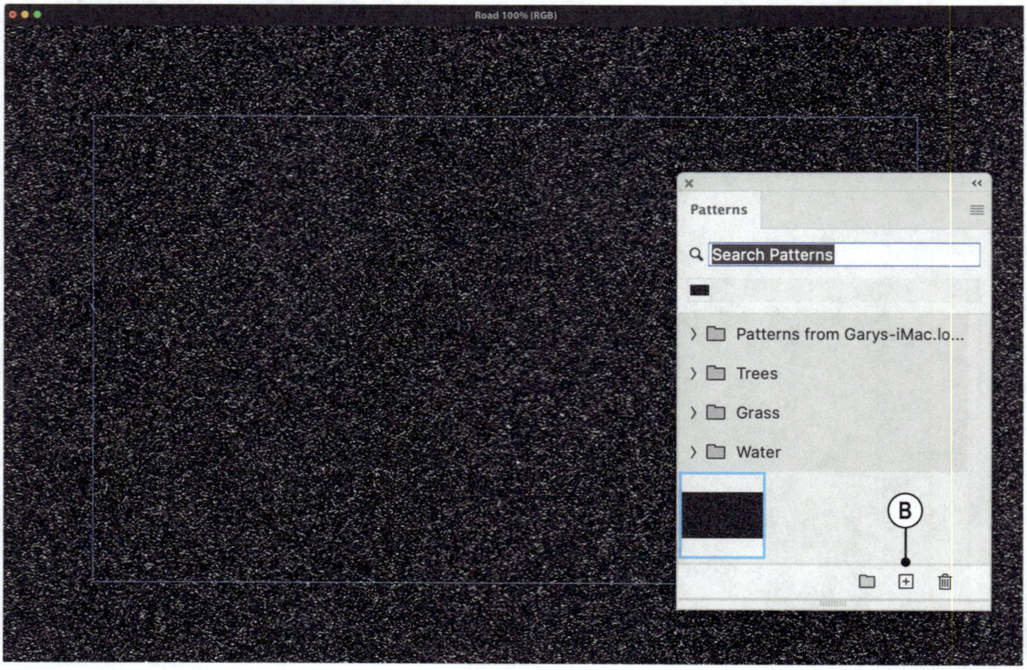

Figure 9.4: The tarmac pattern added to the Patterns panel

13. Head to the **Layers** panel, and click on the **Create new fill or adjustment layer** icon; from the list of options, choose **Pattern**. When the dialog appears, click on the **Pattern picker** thumbnail to reveal the library, and then left-click on the `Tarmac` pattern, which will appear at the bottom of the list. Set **Scale** to `85%`, and then click **OK**.
14. Next, we need to add a highlight across the surface of the tarmac. To achieve this, click on the **Fx** icon at the bottom of the **Layers** panel, and select **Gradient Overlay** from the list of options.
15. When the **Layer Styles** dialog appears, set **Blend Mode** to **Overlay** and **Opacity** to `100%`, turn on the **Align with layer** checkbox, and set **Style** to `Linear`, **Angle** to `75%`, and **Scale** to `125%`.
16. Then, click on the **Gradient Preview** thumbnail to open the **Gradient Editor** dialog. Left-click on the bottom-left **Color** stop, and then left-click on the **Color** thumbnail lower down. Change the **Hexadecimal** value to `646464`, and click **OK**.
17. Left-click on the bottom-right **Color** stop, and left-click on the **Color** thumbnail lower down. Change **Hexadecimal** to `ffffff`, and click **OK**.
18. Between the left and right **Color** stops is a **midpoint**, shown as a diamond symbol. Left-click on it to make it active, and then change the **Location** value to `70%`. Click **OK** to close the **Gradient Editor** dialog, return to **Layer Styles**, and click **OK** to apply the edits and close the dialog.

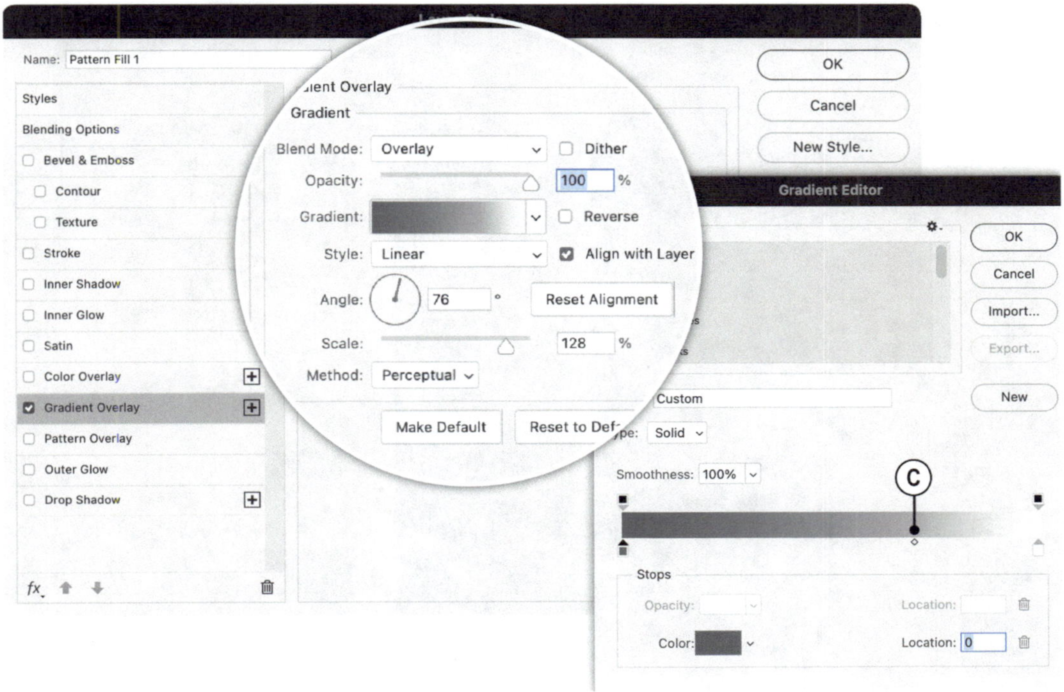

Figure 9.5: Add a gradient overlay

19. Switch to the **Rectangular Marquee** tool from the **Tools** panel. From the **Options Bar**, set the **Selection Mode** to **New**, **Feather** to `0 px`, and **Style** to **Normal**.

20. Hover your cursor approximately 5% into the left edge of the canvas, but above the top of the canvas edge. Click and hold down the left mouse button to drag down and beyond the bottom of the canvas. The **Widget** adjacent to your cursor should inform you that the height of the selection is `2160 px`. Drag across to the right-hand side until the width of the selection reads `160 px`. Then, release the left mouse button to complete the selection.

21. From the **Options** bar, set the **Selection Mode** to **Add**, and then create a second selection of the same size to the right-hand side of the original, leaving a gap of around the same width as the first selection.

22. Head to the bottom of the **Layers** panel, and click on the **Create new fill or adjustment layer** icon; from the list of options, choose **Solid Color**. When the **Color Picker** dialog appears, set **Hexadecimal** to `c2ad20`, creating a deep yellow. Then, click **OK** when done.

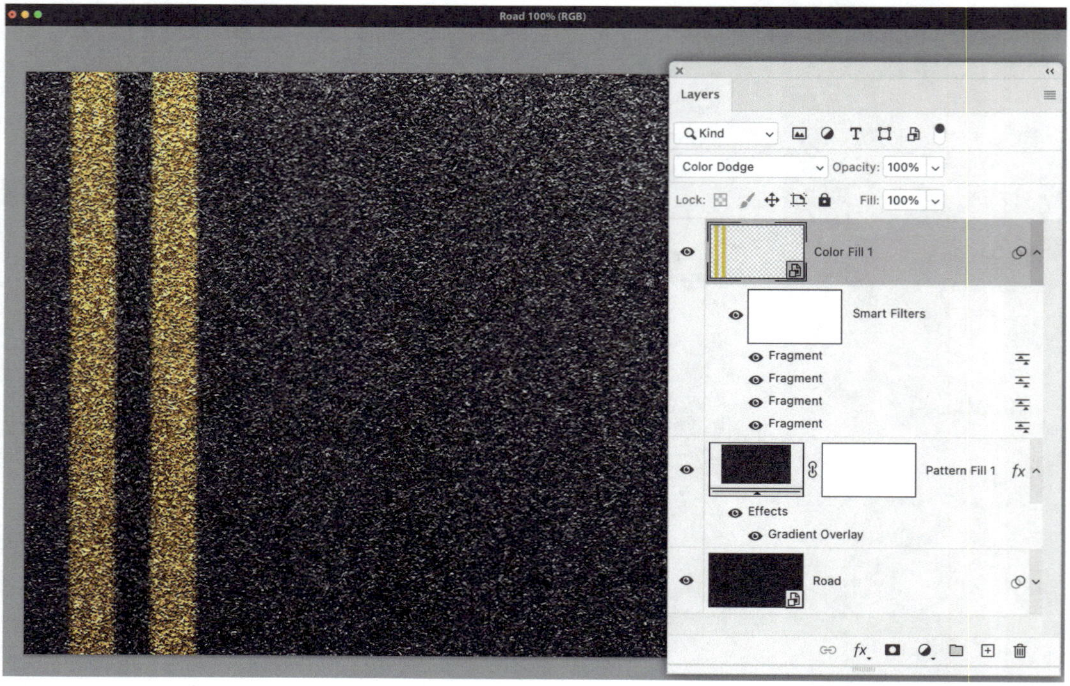

Figure 9.6: The road markings added via a color fill

23. Right-click on the **Color Fill** layer name in the **Layers** panel, and choose **Convert to Smart Object** from the list of commands. Rename the layer `Markings`.
24. To roughen the lines slightly, go to **Filter** → **Pixelate** → **Fragment**. You can enhance the effect by going to **Filter** → **Fragment**, duplicating the effect. Repeat this step until you are happy with the edge details. In our example, the filter was added four times.
25. Finally, change the layer **Blend Mode** to **Color Dodge**, and save the document in the `09-Backdrops` folder as a PSD file. Close the document when done.

This form of backdrop can be used to add text to or, if you work with 3D models, provide the basis for a seamless texture that can be applied to your mesh. If you add editable text to images like this, convert the type layer to a Smart Object and use filters such as **Fragment** or a displacement map to make them look as though they are painted on a road surface.

Creating an atmospheric gradient backdrop

Gradients in Photoshop tend to be applied once, in isolation from one another, like the previous exercise. There are, however, ways that you can apply multiple gradients, overlapping them to achieve interesting effects using the Gradient tool:

1. Go to **File** → **New**, and click on the **Web** tab across the top of the dialog. Enter the name `Atmospherics`, and then change the document width to `3840 px`, and the height to `2160 px`. Turn off the **Artboards** checkbox, and set **Background Contents** to **White**. Then, click on **Create**.
2. Switch to the Gradient tool by pressing *G* to activate the correct group of tools in the **Tools** panel. If the Gradient tool isn't visible, click and long-hold on the active tool, which will be the Paint Bucket tool, to reveal the tool pop-up, and then click on the Gradient tool from the list.
3. From the **Options** bar, change **Gradient Mode** to **Classic gradient**. This will ensure you have access to blend modes, which is crucial for this technique. Click on the **Linear Gradient** button, which is active by default, select `Difference` from the **Blend Mode** menu, and set **Opacity** to `100%`. Turn off the **Reverse** checkbox, but ensure that the **Dither** and **Transparency** checkboxes are active.

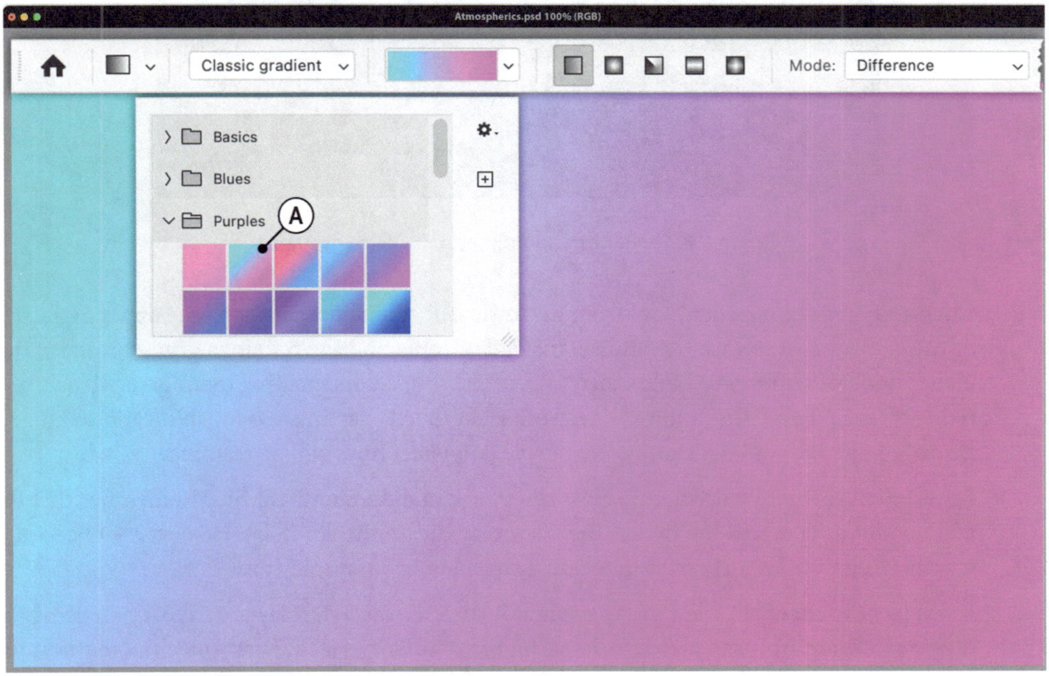

Figure 9.7: The road markings added via a color fill

4. Finally, we need to choose a color for our gradient. Click on the arrow adjacent to the gradient thumbnail in the **Options** bar to view **Gradient Presets**. From the folders that appear, expand **Purples**, and then click on the second thumbnail within that group, named `Purple 2`.
5. With the **Background** layer active, hover your cursor over the top-left corner outside the canvas, click and drag down to the lower-right corner of the canvas, and then release the left mouse button to create the gradient. Now that you have color on the canvas, you can start experimenting.

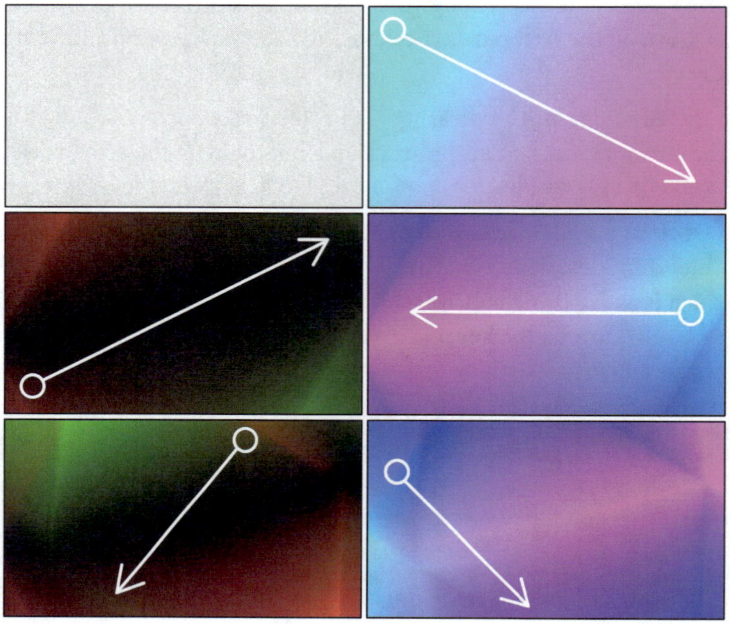

Figure 9.8: The length and direction of each gradient

6. Click and drag the **Gradient** tool from the lower-left side of the canvas to the upper-right side of the canvas, and release the mouse. Instead of replacing the previous gradient, the active blend mode of **Difference** builds on it and inverts the colors, making them green, black, and red. However, if you drag a third time, from right to left, starting and finishing approximately a third of the way into the canvas, the purple and violet hues will be restored.
7. Experiment further by dragging across the image in different directions. Remember that the further you drag across the image, the smoother the gradient will be. However, you can also try dragging over a short distance to add a short but pronounced transition.
8. If you like the effect but want to experiment further, create a new layer and carry on using the same technique. You can also try changing the gradient preset. Save your document in the `09-Backdrops` folder when you have finished.

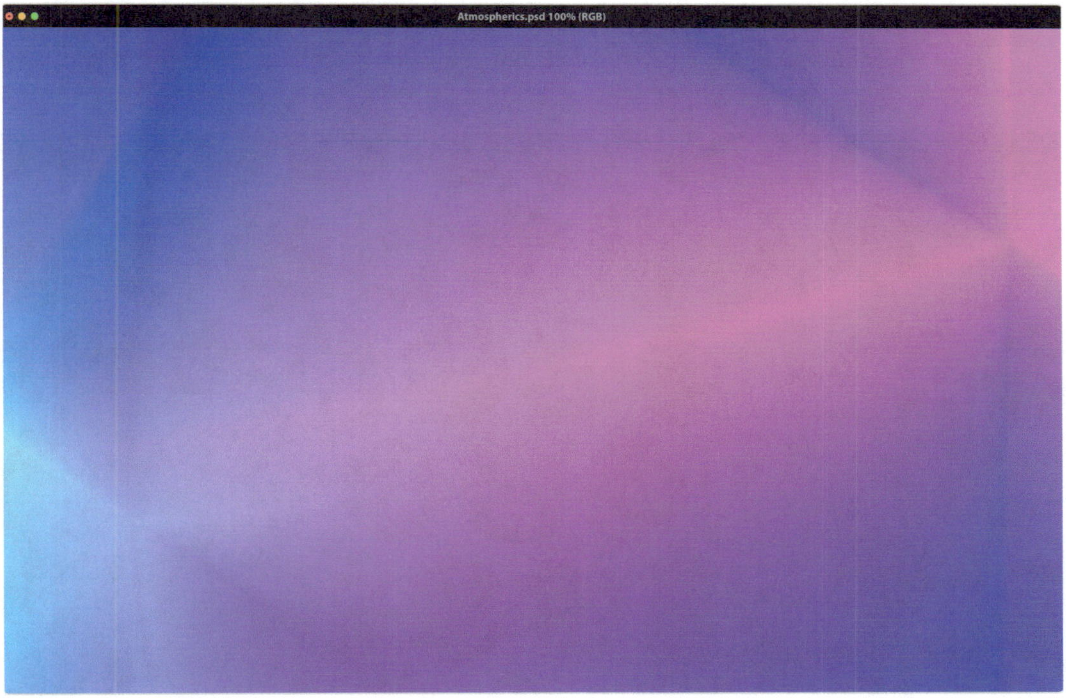

Figure 9.9: The completed gradient backdrop

Creating pop art-inspired artwork with custom patterns

Roy Lichtenstein's pop art is renowned for its imitation of print material, such as comic books, with vivid primary colors, half-tone ink dots, and bold outlines. In this exercise, you will create your own dot patterns and use them to create a pop art-inspired image:

1. Go to **File** → **Open**, and select `Dots.psd` from the `09-Backdrops` folder. This document contains a series of shape layers, containing circles that have been arranged ready to be turned into a pattern and stored in a layer group.
2. Next, go to **Select** → **All**. Then, go to **View** → **Pattern Preview**. If a warning message appears, click **OK** to proceed to preview mode.

3. Next, open the **Patterns** panel by going to **Window** → **Patterns**. Then, click on the **New Pattern** icon at the bottom of the **Pattern** panel. When the dialog appears, name the pattern `Red Dots`, and click **OK**.

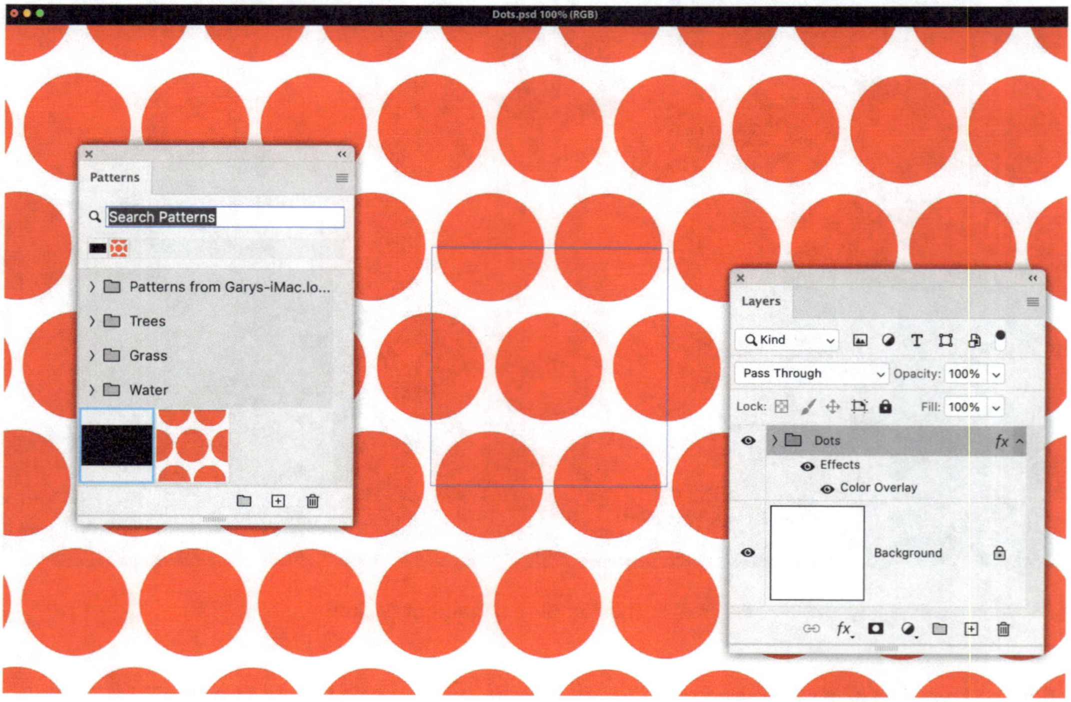

Figure 9.10: The red dotted pattern saved in the Patterns panel

4. Double left-click on the **Color Overlay** effect that is assigned to the **Dots** layer group in the **Layers** panel. When the dialog appears, change the color to a yellow **Hexadecimal** value of `F8E605`. Click **OK** to update the color, and then click **OK** to apply the change to the layer.
5. Then, click on the **New Pattern** icon at the bottom of the **Pattern** panel. When the dialog appears, name the pattern `Yellow Dots`, and click **OK**.
6. Double left-click on the **Color Overlay** effect once more, and change the color to a blue **Hexadecimal** value of `3B86C7`.

7. Once the change has been made to the color overlay, click on the **New Pattern** icon at the bottom of the **Pattern** panel. When the dialog appears, name the pattern `Blue Dots`, and click **OK**.

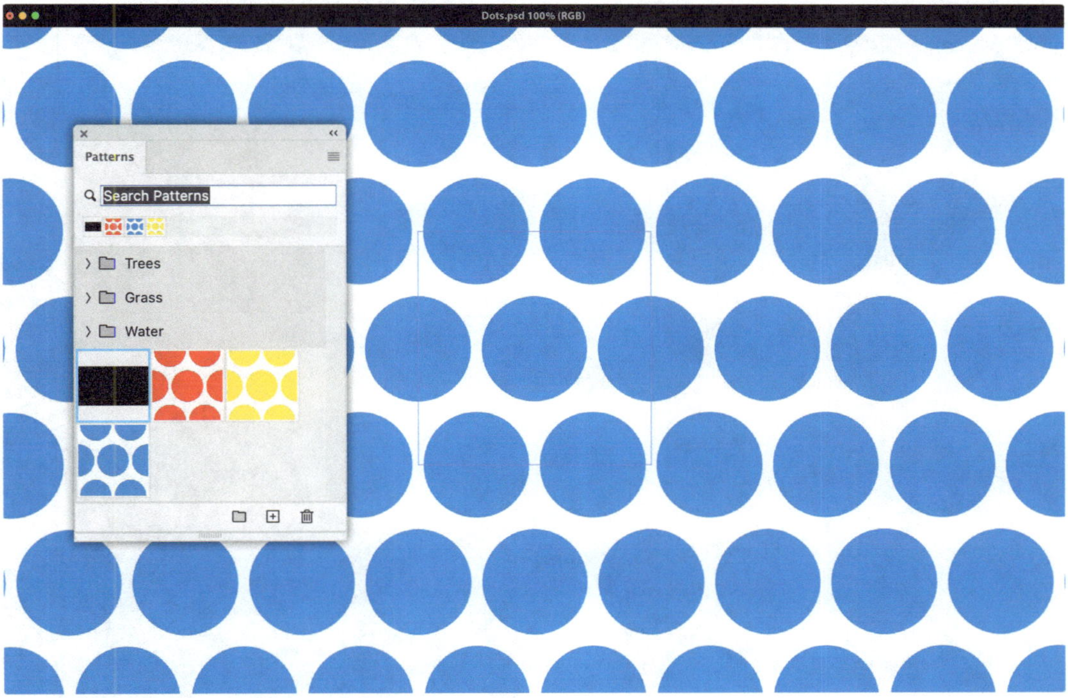

Figure 9.11: The red, yellow, and blue dots saved in the Patterns panel

8. Go to **View** → **Pattern Preview** to deactivate the mode, and then go to **Select** → **Deselect**. Save and close the `Dots.psd` document.
9. Go to **File** → **Open**, and select `PopArt.psd` from the `09-Backdrops` folder. This document contains several shape layers that need the patterns you've just created, applied to the designs.
10. Switch to the Path Selection tool by pressing *A* to activate the correct group of tools in the **Tools** panel. If the Path Selection tool isn't visible, click and long-hold on the active tool, which will be the Direct Selection tool, to reveal the tool pop-out, and then click on the Path Selection tool.

Left-click on the Bang 4 shape layer in the **Layers** panel to make it active. From the **Options** bar, click on the **Fill** icon, and then open the **Set fill type** dialog. Click on the **Pattern** icon to change the fill type, and then choose the `Red Dots` pattern you made earlier, setting **Scale** to `25%`.

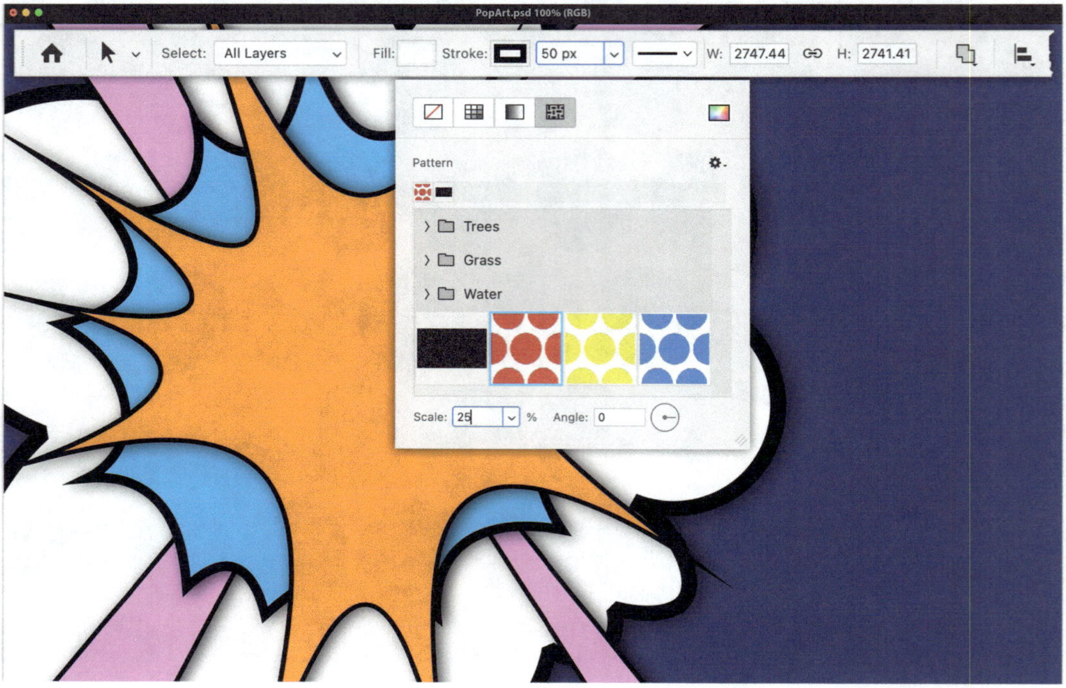

Figure 9.12: The pop-art document without patterns

1. Left-click on the Bang 2 shape layer in the **Layers** panel to make it active. Then, apply the `Blue Dots` pattern you made earlier, again setting the scale of the pattern to `25%`. Feel free to experiment with other shape layers and patterns. Save and close the document when done.

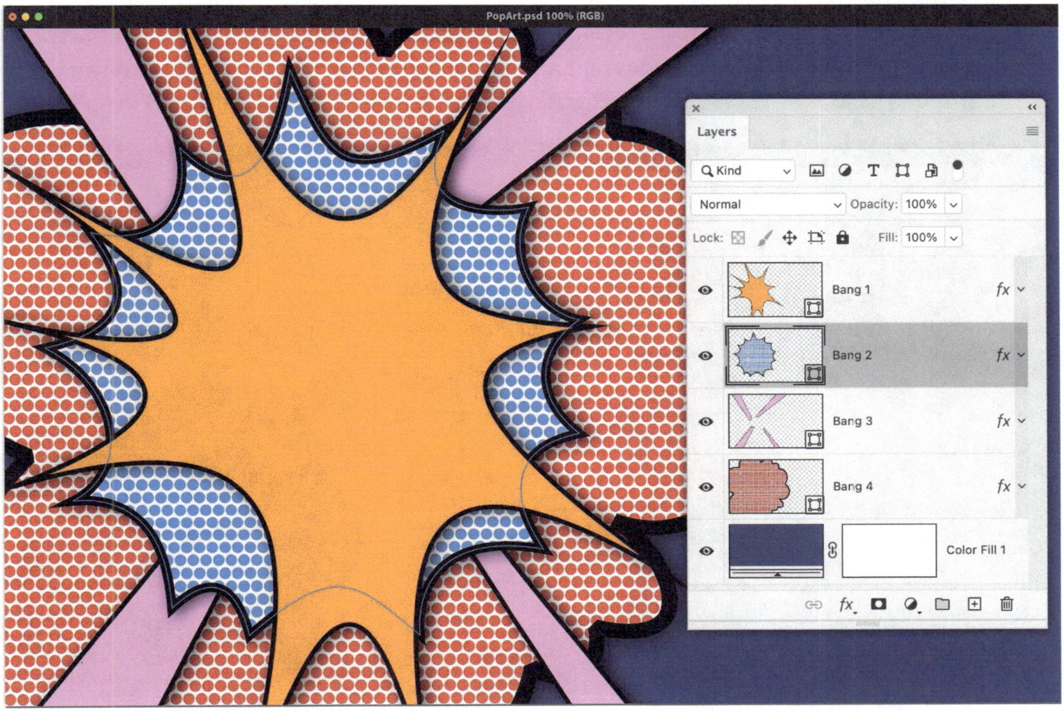

Figure 9.13: The completed pop-art image

In this section, we have looked at techniques to create a texture, patterns, and gradients, using methods such as a painting tool, shape fills, and adjustment layers. In the next section, we will integrate backdrops into project files.

Managing backdrop assets

You don't have to create textures, gradients, and patterns every time you need to utilize them; you can download and import them or store them in Creative Cloud Libraries.

Syncing your assets between devices

Photoshop recently added the ability to sync your user-created brushes, gradients, swatches, styles, shapes, and patterns, making them available wherever you log in with your Creative Cloud account:

1. Go to **Photoshop Preferences** on macOS via **Photoshop** → **Preferences** → **General**, or on Windows, via **Edit** → **Preferences** → **General**. Alternatively, you can press *Ctrl* + *K* (Windows) or *Cmd* + *K* (macOS) to launch the preferences and reveal the **General** settings.

2. Turn on the checkbox for **Preset Syncing** (**A** in *Figure 9.14*), and then click **OK** to exit **Preferences**, at which point you will see a message informing you that your assets will sync to Creative Cloud. This may take a few moments to complete, due to the potential file sizes involved.

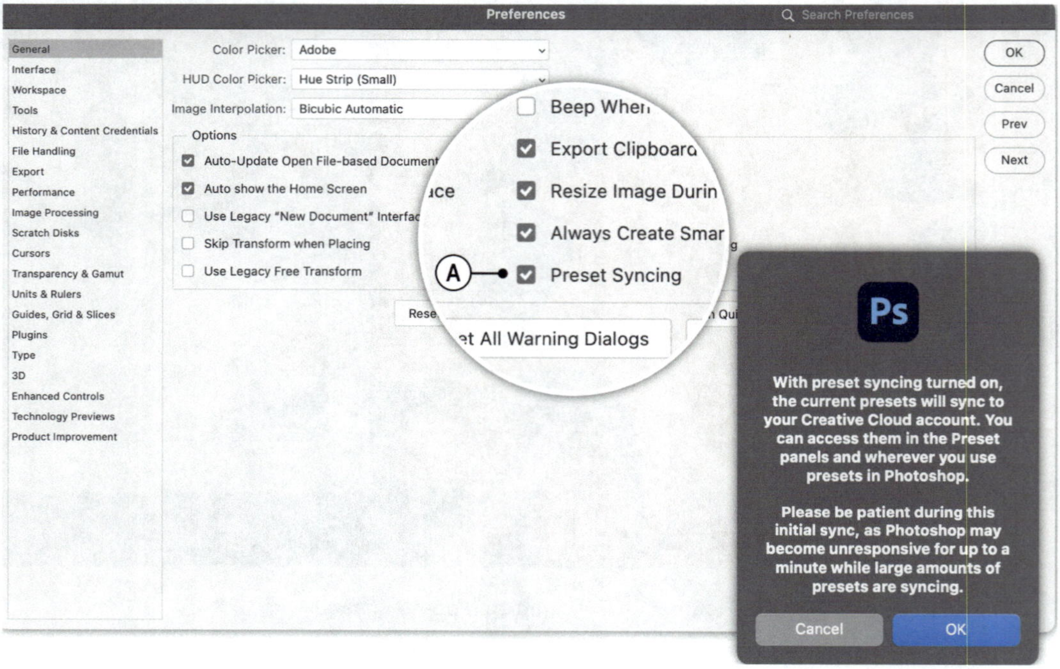

Figure 9.14: Preset syncing in the Preferences dialog

Importing and exporting assets

If you prefer to keep a local backup of assets such as patterns and gradients, you can export them as a file. In the following steps, we will look at exporting patterns, but the process is identical for other asset types:

1. Select the patterns you wish to export in the **Patterns** panel.
2. Click on the **Panel** flyout menu, found at the top right-hand side of the **Patterns** panel. Choose **Export Selected Patterns**.
3. Browse to the folder you wish to export the assets to, and click **Save** when done.
4. To import assets such as patterns, click on the **Patterns** panel's flyout menu. Choose **Import Patterns…**.
5. Browse to the folder where your patterns are stored, select the desired file, and click **Open** when done.

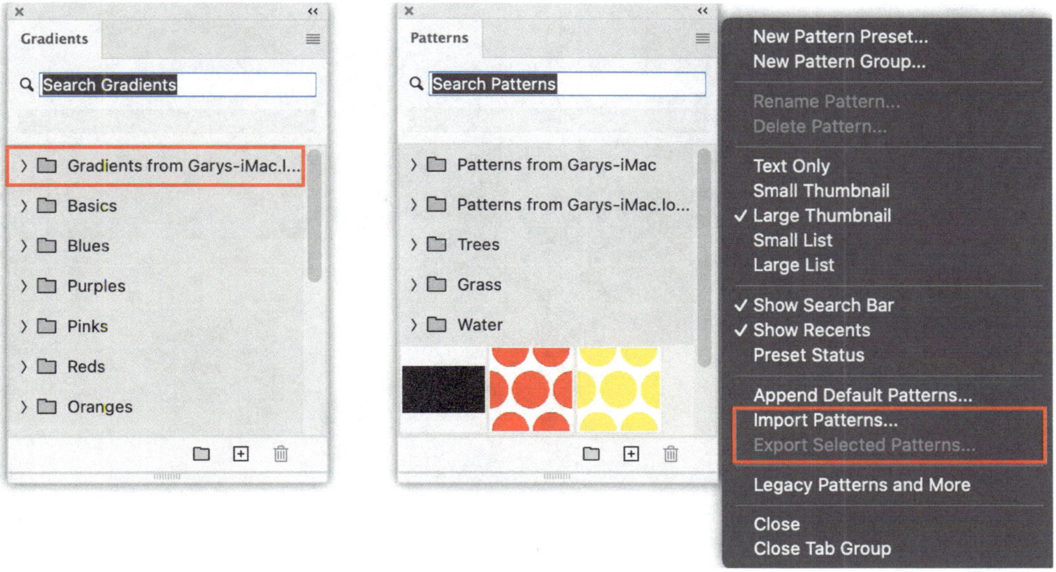

Figure 9.15: Importing and exporting assets such as patterns

In this section, we looked at the process of sharing assets such as patterns, gradients, and swatches on Creative Cloud, making them available to you wherever you log in with your Adobe ID. We also reviewed techniques to import and export assets to a locally stored folder. In the next section, you will create an entire space scene with no source images, using only filters, effects, and painting tools.

Simulating environments with filters and effects

In the last exercise of this chapter, you are going to create a space scene using only filters, effects, and brushes. First, we need to create stars, both large and small, as our backdrop, and then add a nebula with the focal point of a starburst:

1. Go to **File** → **New**, and click on the **Web** tab at the top of the dialog. Enter the name `Atmospherics`, and then change the document width to `1920 px` and the height to `1080 px`. Turn off the **Artboards** checkbox, and set **Background Contents** to **Black**. Then, click on **Create**.
2. With the **Background** layer still active, right-click on the layer name, choose **Convert to Smart Object** from the list of options, and rename the layer `Stars SMALL`.
3. Go to **Filter** → **Noise** → **Add Noise**. When the dialog appears, set **Amount** to `25%` and **Distribution** to **Gaussian**, and then turn on the **Monochromatic** checkbox. Click **OK** when done.
4. Next, go to **Filter** → **Blur** → **Gaussian Blur**. When the dialog appears, set **Amount** to `0.3 px`, and click **OK** when done.

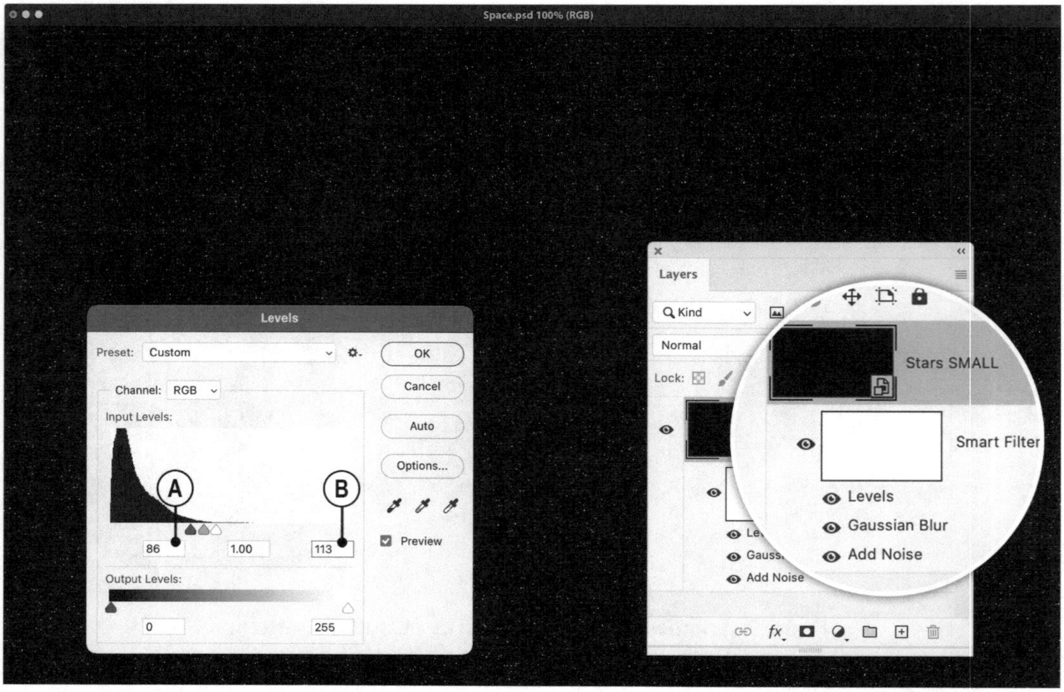

Figure 9.16: Add a noise filter

5. We now need to reduce the number of small stars by going to **Image** → **Adjustment** → **Levels**. When the dialog appears, set **Shadow Input** to `86` (**A** in *Figure 9.16*), **Midtone** to `1.00`, and **Highlight Input** to `113` (**B** in *Figure 9.16*). Then, click **OK**.
6. Drag the Stars SMALL layer onto the **New Layer** icon at the bottom of the **Layers** panel to duplicate it. Rename the layer `Star BUILDER`. Right-click on the Star SMALL **layer visibility** icon, and color-code the layer red to help differentiate it.
7. Double left-click on the **Gaussian Blur** text label, assigned to the newly duplicated Star BUILDER layer in the **Layers** panel. When the dialog appears, increase **Amount** to `1.2 px`, and click **OK** when done.
8. Double left-click on the **Levels** text label assigned to the newly duplicated Star BUILDER layer in the **Layers** panel. Set **Shadow Input** to `51`, **Midtone** to `1.00`, and **Highlight Input** to `57`. Then, click **OK**.
9. With the white portions created that form the basis for our Star BUILDER, we now need to turn them into a selection so that we can add an outer glow to them. Go to **Window** → **Channels**, and hover your cursor over the **RGB** composite thumbnail, which combines all color data in the visible image. Hold *Ctrl* (Windows) or *Cmd* (macOS) as you left-click on the **RGB** thumbnail (**A** in *Figure 9.17*). The selection will now appear around each of the white pixels in the image.

10. Go to the bottom of the **Layers** panel, click on the **New fill or adjustment** layer, and select **Solid color** from the list. When the **Color Picker** dialog appears, choose white by entering `ffffff` into the **Hexadecimal** field, and then click **OK**. Rename the new color fill layer `Stars Large`.
11. Move the Star BUILDER layer up to the top of the **Layers** stack, and hide it by left-clicking on the **layer visibility** icon. You should now have just three layers in the **Layers** panel.

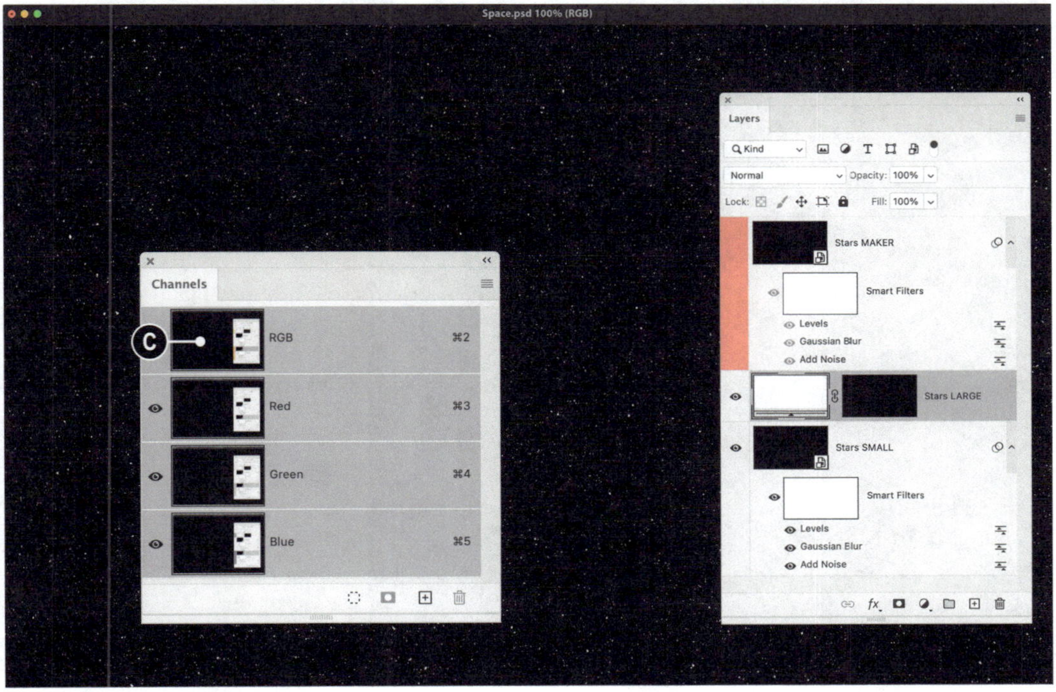

Figure 9.17: Use the Channels panel to select white pixels

12. Left-click on the Stars Large layer to make it active, click on the **Fx** icon at the bottom of the **Layers** panel, and then select `Outer Glow` from the list. When the **Layer Style** dialog box appears, set **Blend Mode** to `Screen`, **Opacity** to `45%`, **Noise** to `0%`, **Spread** to `0%`, **Size** to `16 px`, and **Range** to `29%`. Then, click **OK**.
13. Turn on the **layer visibility** for the Star BUILDER layer, and rename it `Star COLOURS`. Drag the **Levels** adjustment assigned to it onto the **Delete** button at the bottom of the **Layers** panel to remove it.
14. Double left-click on the **Add Noise** filter assigned to the Star COLOURS layer to edit it. When the dialog appears, set **Amount** to `350%` and **Distribution** to **Gaussian**, and turn off the **Monochromatic** checkbox to create random colored noise. Then, click **OK**.

15. Double left-click on the **Gaussian Blur** filter assigned to the Star COLOURS layer to edit it. When the dialog appears, set **Amount** to `1.7 px`, and click **OK** when done. This will blur the noise just enough to recolor the stars in the layers below it in the **Layers** stack.
16. With the Star COLOURS layer still active, change its **Blend Mode** property to `Color` from the **Layers** panel.

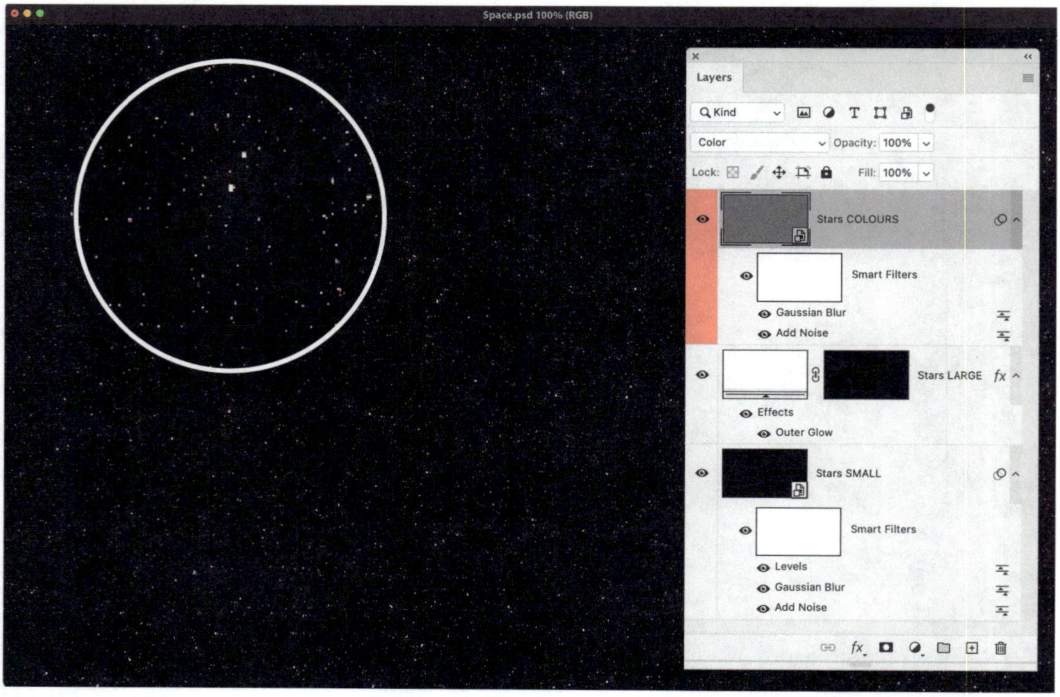

Figure 9.18: The stars with random colors applied

17. Next, go to **Select** → **All Layers** and press *Ctrl* + *G* (Windows) or *Cmd* + *G* (macOS) to add the star layers into a new **Layer** group. Name the new group `Stars`.
18. Add a new layer to the **Layers** panel, and name it `Nebula Clouds`. Go to **Edit** → **Fill**; when the dialog appears, choose **Black** from the **Contents** drop-down menu, and click **OK**. Right-click on the layer name, and choose **Convert to Smart Object** from the list of options.

19. Press the *D* key to reset the **Foreground** and **Background** colors in the **Tools** panel so that the clouds we generate will be grayscale. Go to **Filter** → **Render** → **Clouds**.

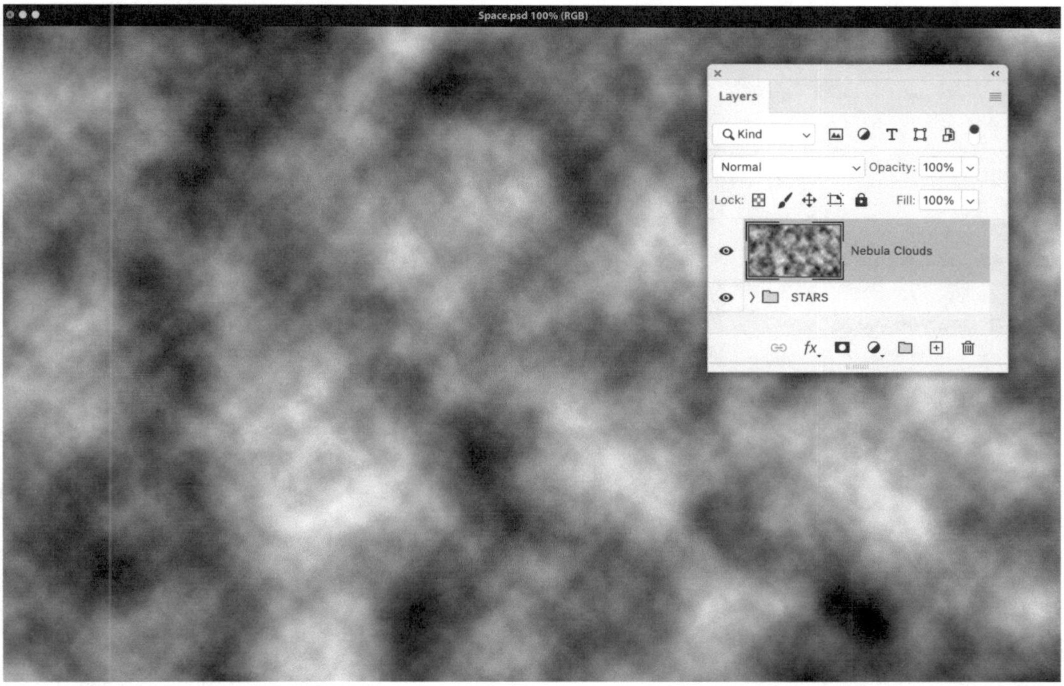

Figure 9.19: The render clouds filter

20. Change the **Blend Mode** property of `Nebula Clouds` to **Color Dodge** from the **Layers** panel. Add another new layer to the **Layers** panel, and name it `Nebula Colour`. Drag it below the `Nebula Clouds` layer in the **Layer** stack.
21. Switch the **Brush** Brush tool by pressing the *B* key. Click on the **Brush Tip** preset menu in the **Option** bar, and select **Soft Round brush** from the list. Ensure **Hardness** is set to `0%` and **Opacity** is set to `10%`.
22. Left-click on the **Foreground Color** swatch in the **Tools** panel to define the brush color. When the dialog appears, enter `25538b` in the **Hexadecimal** field to create a light blue, and click **OK**.
23. Hover your Brush tool cursor over the canvas, and left-click in different areas of the image to reveal the blue-colored clouds. Experiment with the placement of your brush clicks to add a nebula cloud.

24. Try changing the **Foreground Color** swatch to `f43f4c` to create a light red color, and click **OK**. Left-click on random sections of the image with the Brush tool.

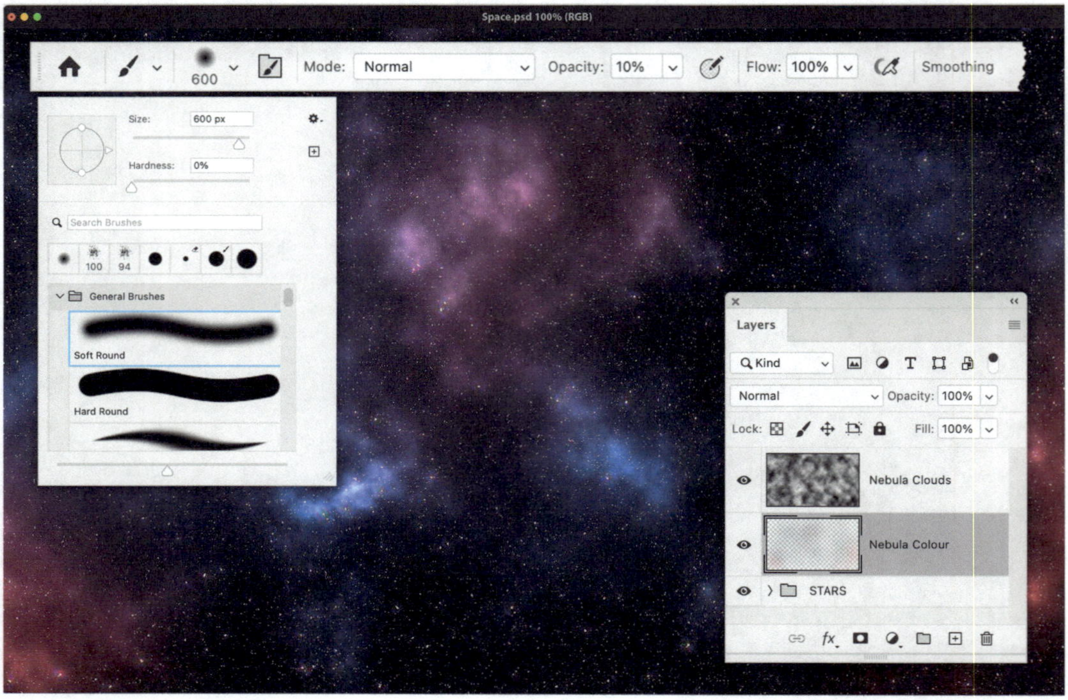

Figure 9.20: Paint blue and red onto the Nebula layer

25. Left-click on the Nebula Cloud layer to make it active. Add another new layer to the **Layers** panel, and name it `Starburst`. Ensure that it is at the top of the **Layer** stack.
26. Go to **Edit** → **Fill**; when the dialog appears, choose **Black** from the **Contents** drop-down menu, and click **OK**.
27. Then, right-click on the layer name, and choose **Convert to Smart Object** from the list of options. Change the **Blend Mode** property of the `Starburst` layer to **Screen** from the **Layers** panel.

28. Go to **Filter** → **Render** → **Lens Flare**. When the dialog appears, select **35mm prime**. Then, hover your cursor over the center of the preview window and left-click to set the center of the canvas as the place it will be added to. We need to create the effect of a star; however, clicking around the edges of the preview creates a flare, like those created by the lens of a camera, which is not required in this scenario. Set **Brightness** to `30%`, and click **OK**.

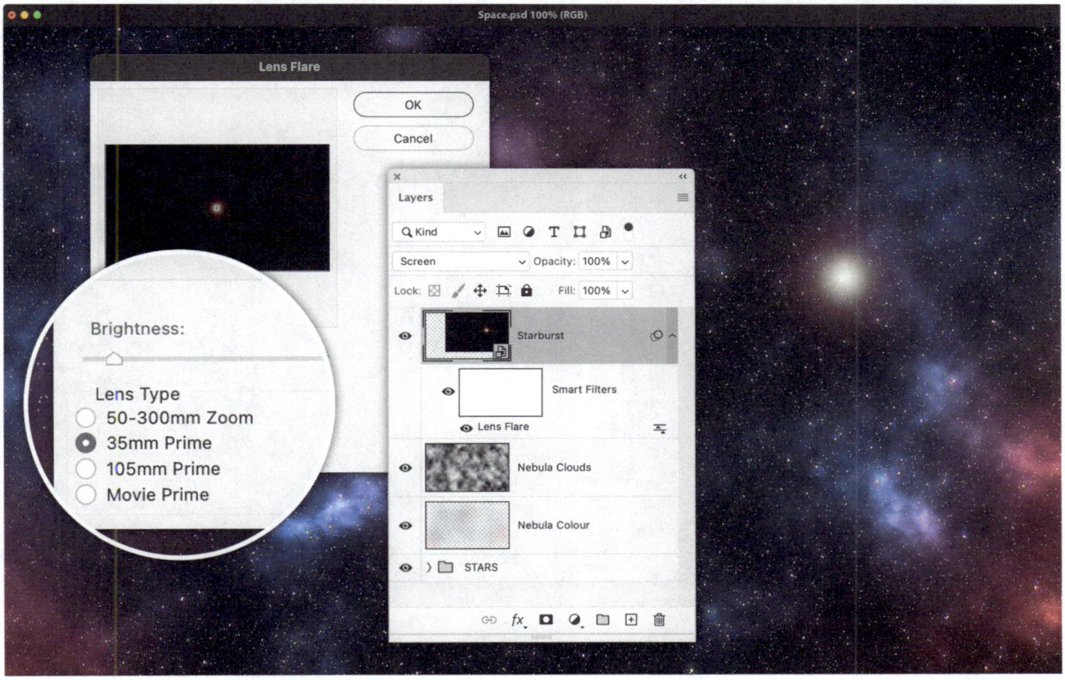

Figure 9.21: The lens flare filter

29. The star will appear in the center of the canvas. You can now move the `Starburst` layer to any part of the image. If you wish to edit the **Lens Flare** properties, simply double-left-click on the **Lens Flare** text label under the `Starburst` layer in the **Layers** panel.

30. Go to **File** → **Save**, browse to the `09-Backdrops` project folder, and save the document as a PSD file. Close the document when done.

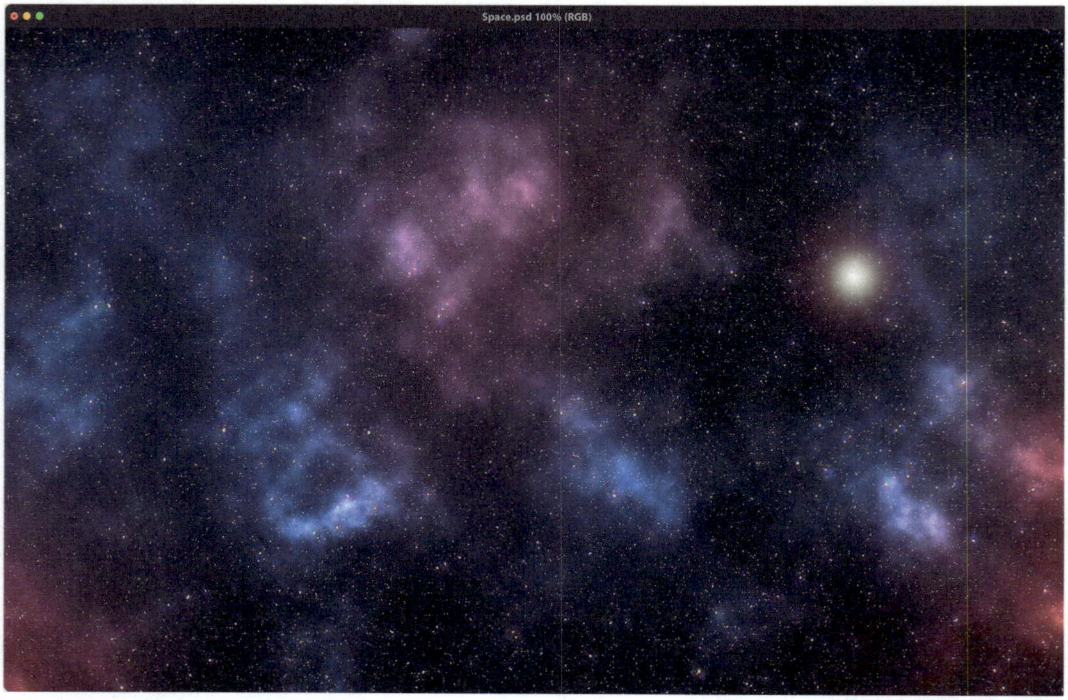

Figure 9.22: The completed space scene

In the final section of this chapter, we have created an entire space scene made from a combination of Photoshop filters, layer styles, blend modes, and the Brush tool, all without the need for source photographs.

Summary

In this chapter, we focused on the creation of backdrops to complement a design, for scenarios where stock images do not meet our needs, or when there is a need to have greater control over content.

The key features to create backdrops were textures, patterns, and gradients, with the help of Photoshops filters and effects. We first experimented with a combination of a texture, patterns, and gradients to create a road surface backdrop. This provided an opportunity to see how each process works within Photoshop.

We then created abstract artwork with the use of the Gradient tool. Changing the blend mode allowed us to combine several gradients to form subtle geometric shapes and lines against a light background.

We then moved on to creating patterns, taking a red dot and turning it into a seamless pattern with the help of Photoshop's **Pattern Preview** feature. These patterns were saved in the **Patterns** panel and used to complete a pop art-inspired image.

We also looked at methods to import, synchronize, and export assets such as patterns, through preference settings, Creative Cloud, and locally stored library files.

Finally, we took all we had learned to create an entire space scene with no original source assets, just the use of filters, effects, and painting tools. We created a star field by adapting a noise filter and created clouds that could be turned into a colorful nebula, by painting with cool and warm colors using the Brush tool. The image was given a focal point with the inclusion of a lens flare effect to create a nearby star.

In the next chapter, we will continue exploring brushes as we examine libraries of brush tips, as well as create our own brush tips and brush effects.

10
Creating and Applying Brushes

Brushes are an integral part of day-to-day editing in Photoshop. Whether it's one of the handful of brush tools themselves, the clone stamp, or healing brush tools, brush tip and style have a profound impact on the results you achieve.

Photoshop ships with an extensive library of brush tips ranging from the default soft and hard round brush tips for general-purpose mark-making to leaf and grass brushes, which are applied randomly to achieve a natural look. With a little adaptation, these brush tips will serve you well. As such, you could be forgiven for just sticking with this default set of brush libraries; however, you can also download and create your own.

The process of creating custom brush tips is relatively quick and simple. As we get started in this chapter, you will first create a flock of birds from custom brush tips from a black and white image. This will allow you to add a focal point to a photo and bring the image to life.

As we progress through the chapter, we'll experiment further by sampling real-world brush marks as source shapes for our Photoshop brush tips. We'll then apply them to more obscure features, such as the Art History Brush tool, to randomizing the size, spacing, color, and angle of each individual brush mark.

By the end of this chapter, you will be able to create, edit, import, and export a brush tip preset, apply brush marks for creative effects, and retouch images by adding snowflakes. In this chapter, you will explore the following topics:

- Creating and managing brush tip presets
- Modifying brush properties
- Applying brushes for creative effect
- Using brushes for retouching

Technical requirements

The project files for this chapter can be found at: `https://github.com/PacktPublishing/Mastering-Adobe-Photoshop-2024/tree/main/Chapter10`

Creating and managing brush tip presets

Most of the brushes you use in Photoshop derive from a single greyscale image. White regions of the source image become transparent, while darker shades of grey become brush marks that you can change the color of as required.

Creating a custom bird brush

Following are the steps for creating a custom bird brush:

1. Go to **File** → **Open** and browse to the `10-Brushes` folder. Select `Flock.jpg` and then click **Open**. The image contains a flock of birds.
2. Right-click on the `Background` layer under **Layers** and choose **Convert to Smart Object** from the list of options. Rename the layer to `Source`.
3. Then go to **Image** → **Adjustments Levels**. Set the **Shadow Input** value to `14` and the **Highlight Input** to `230`. This will turn the background into a bright white. Click **OK** when done.

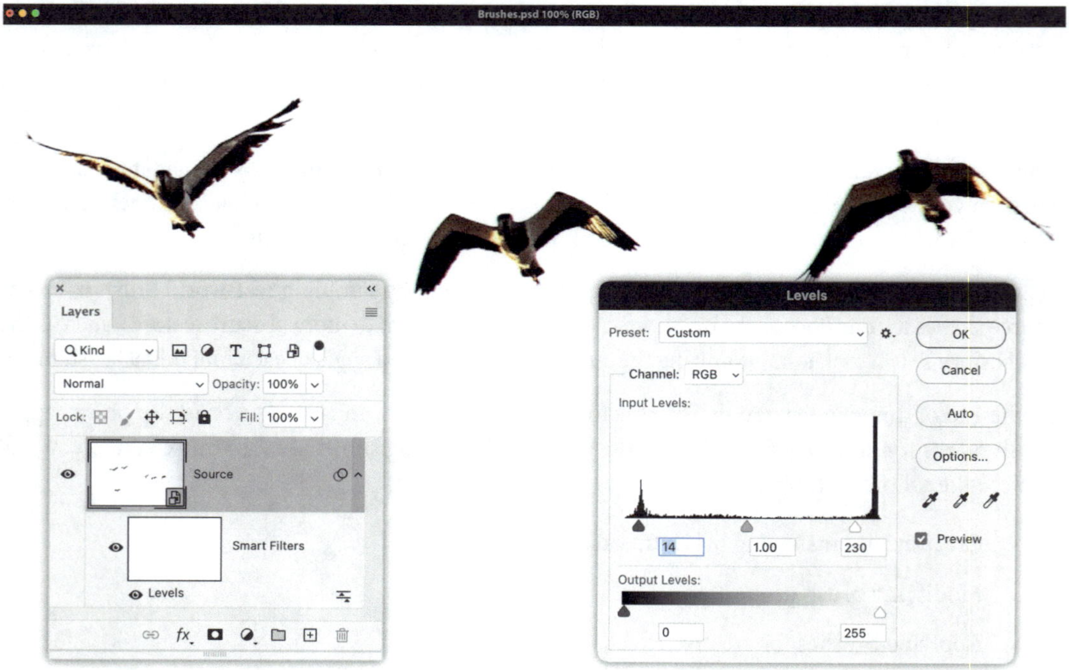

Figure 10.1: Removing any background details to prevent them appearing in the brush tip

4. Switch to the **Rectangular Marquee** tool from the **Tools** panel. Set the selection **Mode** to **New**, **Feather** to `0`, and **Style** to **Normal**. Create a selection around one of the birds in the image, leaving a generous border around it so that when the brush tip is created, it will have a transparent border.
5. Then go to **Edit** → **Define Brush Preset**. When the **Brush Name** dialogue appears, enter the name `bird 1`. Click **OK** when done. The brush preset will now be saved to the **Brushes** panel and is ready to use. Select it from the brush tip pop-up menu when a painting tool is active.

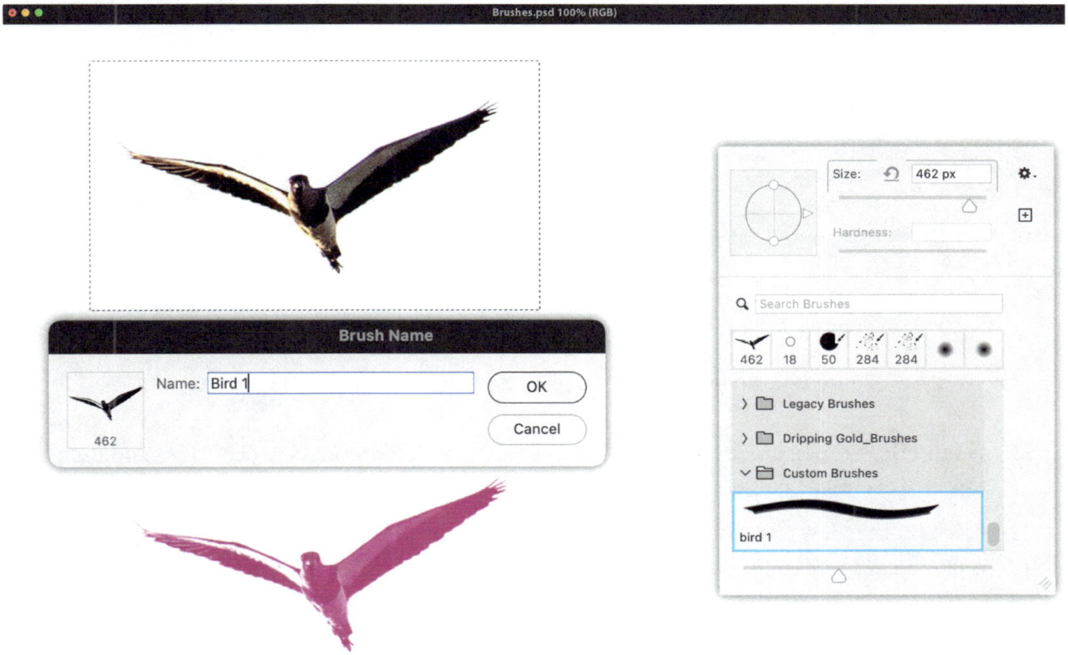

Figure 10.2: The selected artwork captured as a brush tip in Photoshop

6. Switch to the **Rectangular Marquee** tool from the **Tools** panel. Hover your cursor inside the active selection, allowing you to drag it over a different bird with an alternative pose.
7. Then go to **Edit** → **Define Brush Preset**. When the **Brush Name** dialogue appears, name the brush tip `bird 2` and click **OK**.
8. With the **Rectangular Marquee** tool still active, drag the selection over a different bird with a different pose from the previous two.
9. Then go to **Edit** → **Define Brush Preset**. When the **Brush Name** dialogue appears, name the brush tip `bird 3` and click **OK**.
10. Save the document in the `10-Brushes` folder as a PSD file and close the document when done, as it is no longer required.

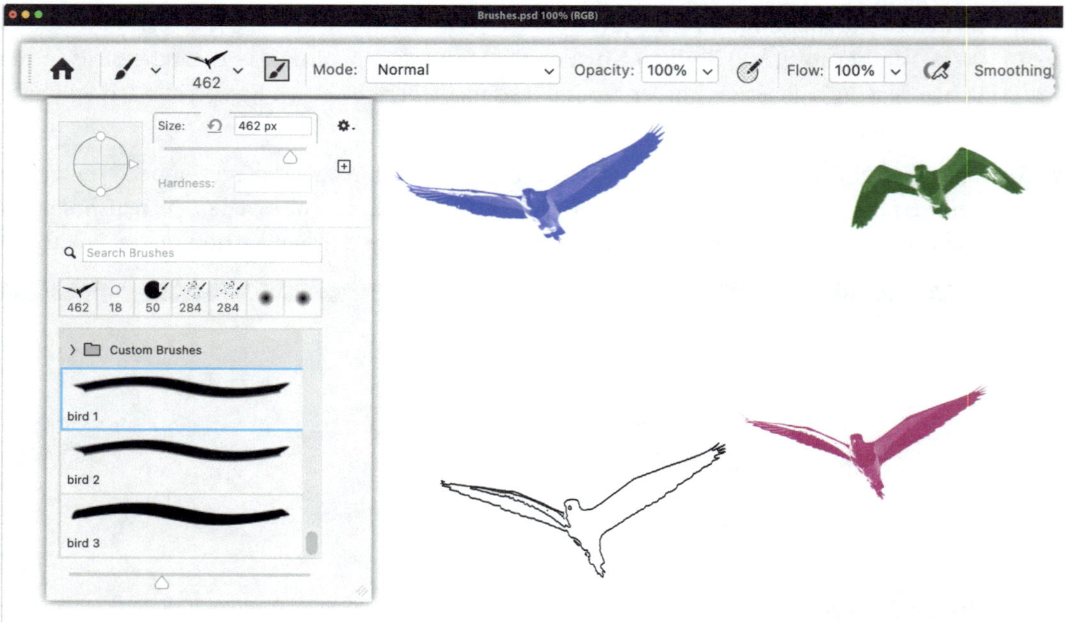

Figure 10.3: An example of the three bird brushes added to Photoshop

11. Go to **File** → **Open** and browse to the `10-Brushes` folder. Select `Lake.jpg` and then click **Open**. This image could benefit from a mid-ground focal point.
12. Click on the **New Layer** icon at the bottom of the **Layers** panel to add a new empty layer and rename it `Birds`.
13. Switch to the **Brush** tool by pressing the *B* key. From **Options**, click on the **Brush tip** menu and scroll down to the bottom of the list where you will find your newest brush tips and folders. Left-click on the `bird 1` brush. Change the **Size** of the brush to approximately `175px`.
14. Hover your cursor over the dark silhouette of the trees that run along the horizon line. Then hold *Alt (Windows) or Option (macOS)* as you left-click in the same region to sample the color of the trees. For reference, this should provide a hexadecimal of `012440`. This color will be ideal to use for the bird brush marks.
15. Hover your cursor in a region approximately 1/3 of the way up the upper right-hand side of the image. Then, left-click once to paint a bird in the sky.

16. Switch to the `bird 2` brush, setting the **Size** to approximately `175px`. Then, left-click to add it to the image in a similar region. Repeat the same step to add 4–6 different birds to the image. Try varying the size of each bird to make some look as though they are positioned further away from the camera.

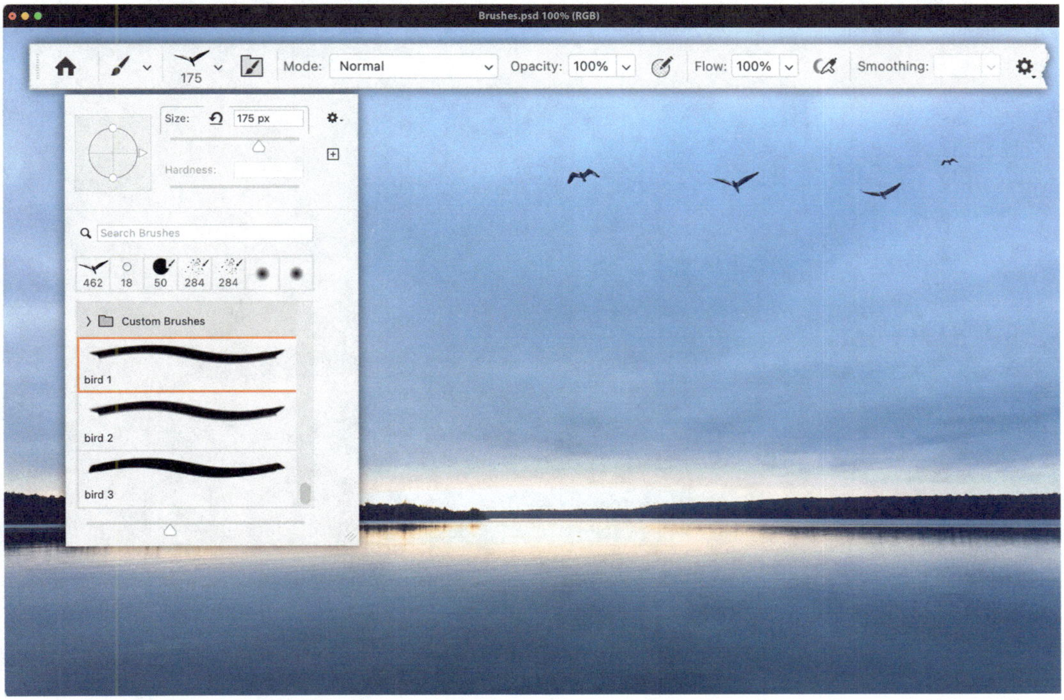

Figure 10.4: The bird brush marks added to the photo

17. Drag the `Birds` layer onto the **New layer** icon at the bottom of the **Layers** panel to duplicate it. Rename the duplicated layer `Reflections`.
18. Go to **Edit** -> **Transform** -> **Flip Vertical**. The duplicated layer should now appear upside down. Switch to the **Move** tool and drag the reflections layer down the image and over the lake.
19. Change the **Blend Mode** of the `Reflections` layer to **Multiply** and reduce the layer **Fill** to `30%`. Reducing the fill will make the layer fainter and in doing so a touch more realistic.

20. Save the image as a PSD in the `10-Brushes` folder and close the document.

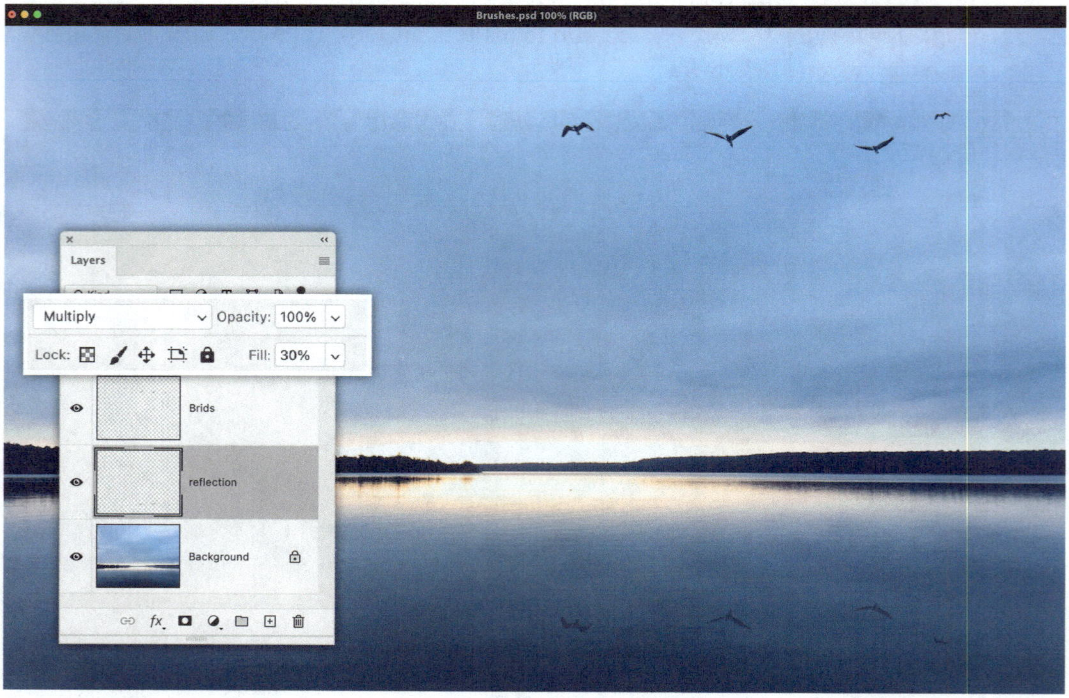

Figure 10.5: The completed image with birds and reflections made from brush marks

In this first section, we looked at the process of capturing image content as a brush tip that can be used for painting. In this scenario, three bird images were painted onto an empty sky to provide a focal point. In the next section, you will create brushes from real-world paint marks.

Modifying brush properties

Hidden away at the bottom of a popup in the **Tools** panel is the **Art History Brush** tool. The first time you experiment with this tool, its default brush settings can be off-putting, to say the least. But with a little experimentation, you can produce interesting results:

1. Go to **File** → **Open** and browse to the `10-Brushes` folder. Select four documents, `Brush-01.jpg`, `Brush-02.jpg`, `Brush-03.jpg`, and `Brush-04.jpg`, then click **Open**.
2. Each image is taken from a series of paint marks I created, captured with my iPhone and then cropped down to size. I applied a **Levels** adjustment to ensure that the white background is pure white (red 255, green 255, blue 255) and the brush has transparent edges. With `Brush-01.jpg` active, go to **Edit** → **Define Brush Preset**. Name it `Brush-1` and click **OK**. Close the document.

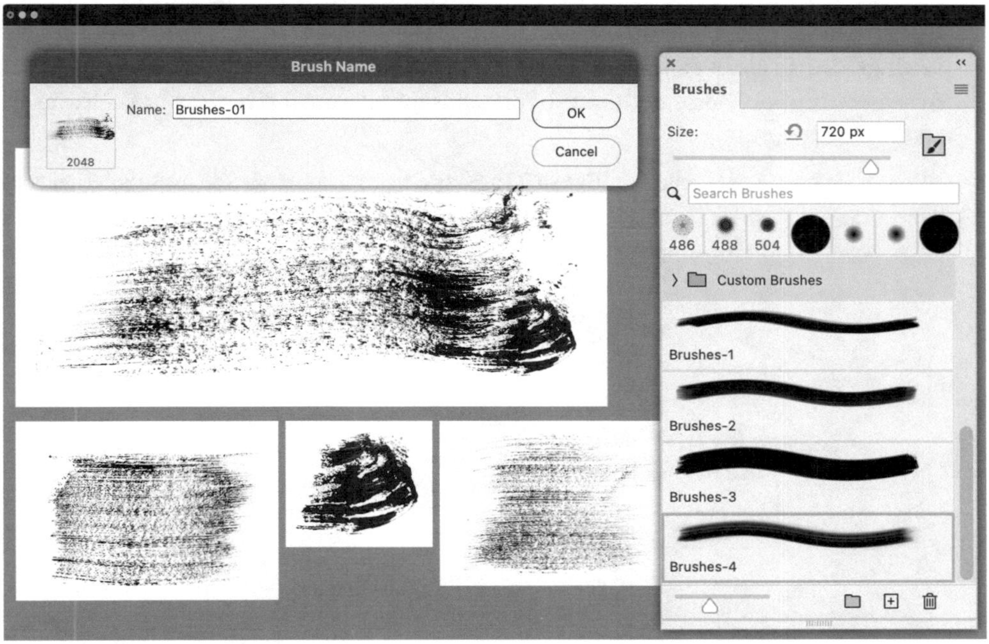

Figure 10.6: Saving real brush marks as digital brush tips in Photoshop

3. Repeat the same step for `Brush-1`, `Brush-2`, `Brush-3`, and `Brush-4`, naming them accordingly. Once complete, close all documents. Go to **File** → **Open** and browse to the `10-Brushes` folder and select `Pattern-Canvas.jpg`. Click **Open**.
4. Go to **Edit** → **Define Pattern**. Name it `Canvas` and click **OK**. Check the pattern has been added by going to **Window** → **Patterns**.
5. Go to **Window** → **Brushes**. The **Brushes** panel lists all default, imported, and user-created brushes in Photoshop. Now that the base shapes for the brushes have been created, they need to be modified and saved as new brushes for the **Art History Brush** tool.

Creating the large Art History Brush

Follow the given steps below:

1. Switch to the **History Brush** tool by pressing the *Y* key. This will most likely activate the **History Brush**. Click and hold the left mouse button on the active tool in the **Tools** panel to reveal the sub-tools popup. Hover over and left-click on **History Brush** tool.
2. From **Options**, set the **Mode** to `Normal`, **Opacity** to `100%`, **Style** to `Dab`, and **Area** to `200%`.

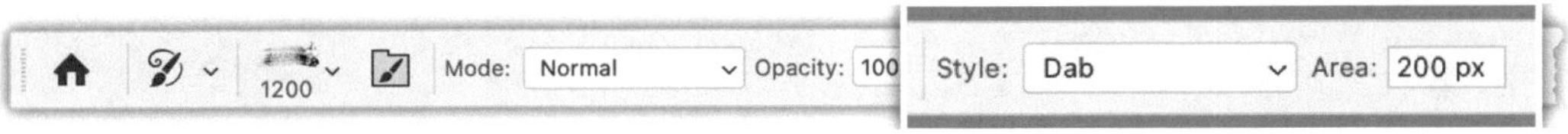

Figure 10.7: The Art History Brush tool options

3. Click on `Brush-1` in the **Brushes** panel to make it active. Then, go to **Window → Brush Settings**. The **Brushes** panel allows you to browse for, activate, and resize a brush tip, but the **Brush Settings** provide a multitude of methods for altering the way the brush leaves marks on the digital canvas.
4. With `Brush-1` active, click on **Brush Tip Shape** from the **Brush Settings** panel on the left-hand side. Set the **Size** to `1200 px`, **Angle** to `0°`, **Roundness** to `100%`, and **Spacing** to `10%`.

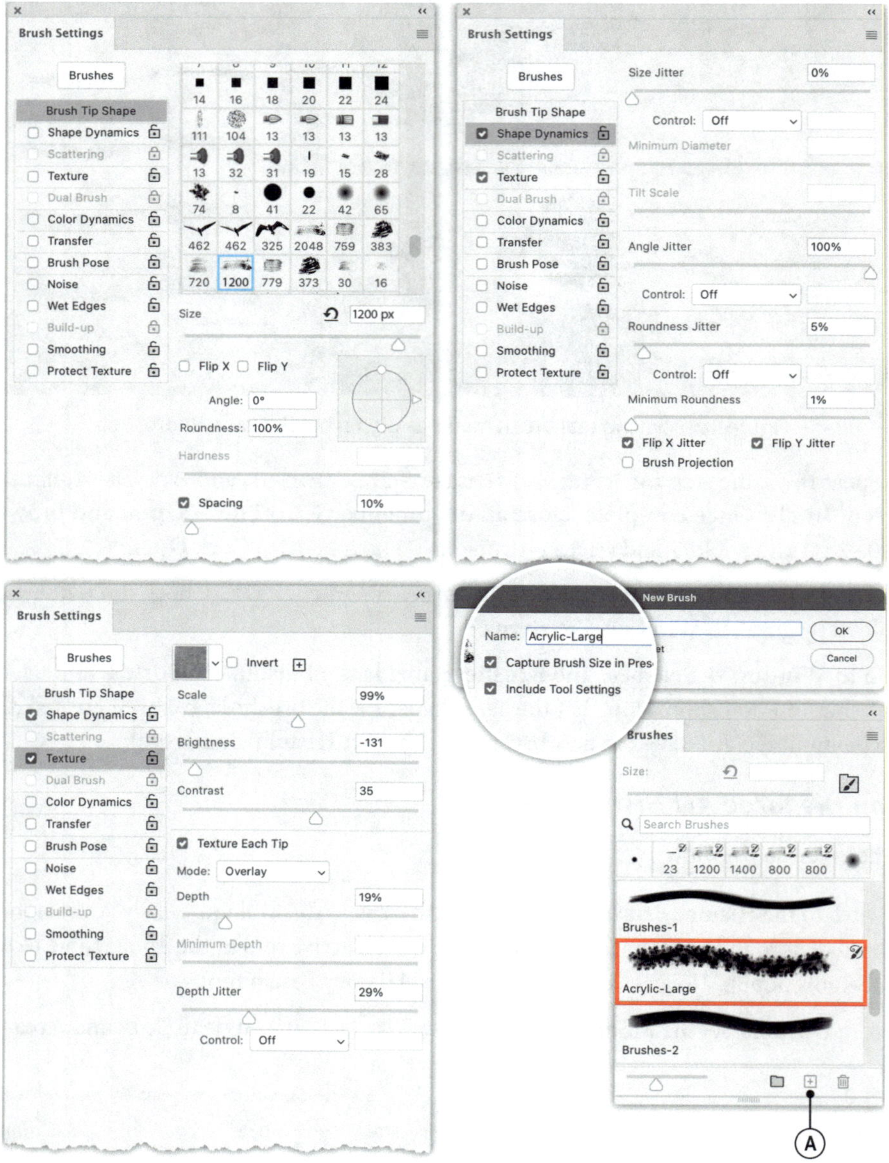

Figure 10.8: Brush-1 used as the basis for a new brush preset named Acrylic-Large

5. Next, click on **Shape Dynamics** from the left-hand list. Set the **Size Jitter** to `0%`, **Angle Jitter** to `100%`, **Roundness Jitter** to `5%`, and **Minimum Roundness** to `1%`. Turn on the **Flip X Jitter** and **Flip Y Jitter** checkboxes but leave **Brush Projection** unchecked. This step will make the brush tip rotate randomly at different angles and stretch the brush tip shape slightly.
6. Next, click on **Texture** from the left-hand list. Click on the **Pattern Picker** thumbnail at the top of the panel. Scroll down to the bottom of the list to find the `Canvas` pattern created in a previous step. Set the **Scale** to `100%`, **Brightness** to `131%`, and **Contrast** to `35%`. Turn on the **Texture Each Tip** checkbox and set the **Mode** to **Overlay**. Set the **Depth** to `19%` and **Depth Jitter** to `29%`. This will add the `Canvas` pattern as a subtle texture to each brush stroke, giving a little added realism and character.
7. Click on the **Create New Brush** icon (*Figure 10.8, A*) at the bottom of the **Brushes** panel to capture the changes as a new preset. Name the brush `Acrylic-Large` and click **OK**.

Creating the medium Art History Brush

To do so, follow the steps given below:

1. Click on `Brush-2` in the **Brushes** panel to make it active. Then, from the **Brush Settings** panel, click on **Brush Tip Shape** from the list on the left-hand side. Set the **Size** to `700 px`, **Angle** to `0°`, **Roundness** to `100%`, and **Spacing** to `26%`.
2. Click on **Shape Dynamics**. Set the **Size Jitter** to `0%`, **Angle Jitter** to `100%`, **Roundness Jitter** to `15%`, and **Minimum Roundness** to `25%`. Turn on the **Flip X Jitter** and **Flip Y Jitter** checkboxes but leave **Brush Projection** unchecked.
3. Click on **Texture** from the left-hand list. Click on the **Pattern Picker** and select the `Canvas` pattern again. Set the **Scale** to `100%`, **Brightness** to `114%`, and **Contrast** to `19%`. Turn on the **Texture Each Tip** checkbox and set the **Mode** to **Overlay**. Set the **Depth** to `100%` and **Depth Jitter** to `50%`.

4. Click on the **Create New Brush** icon, name the brush `Acrylic-Medium`, and click **OK**.

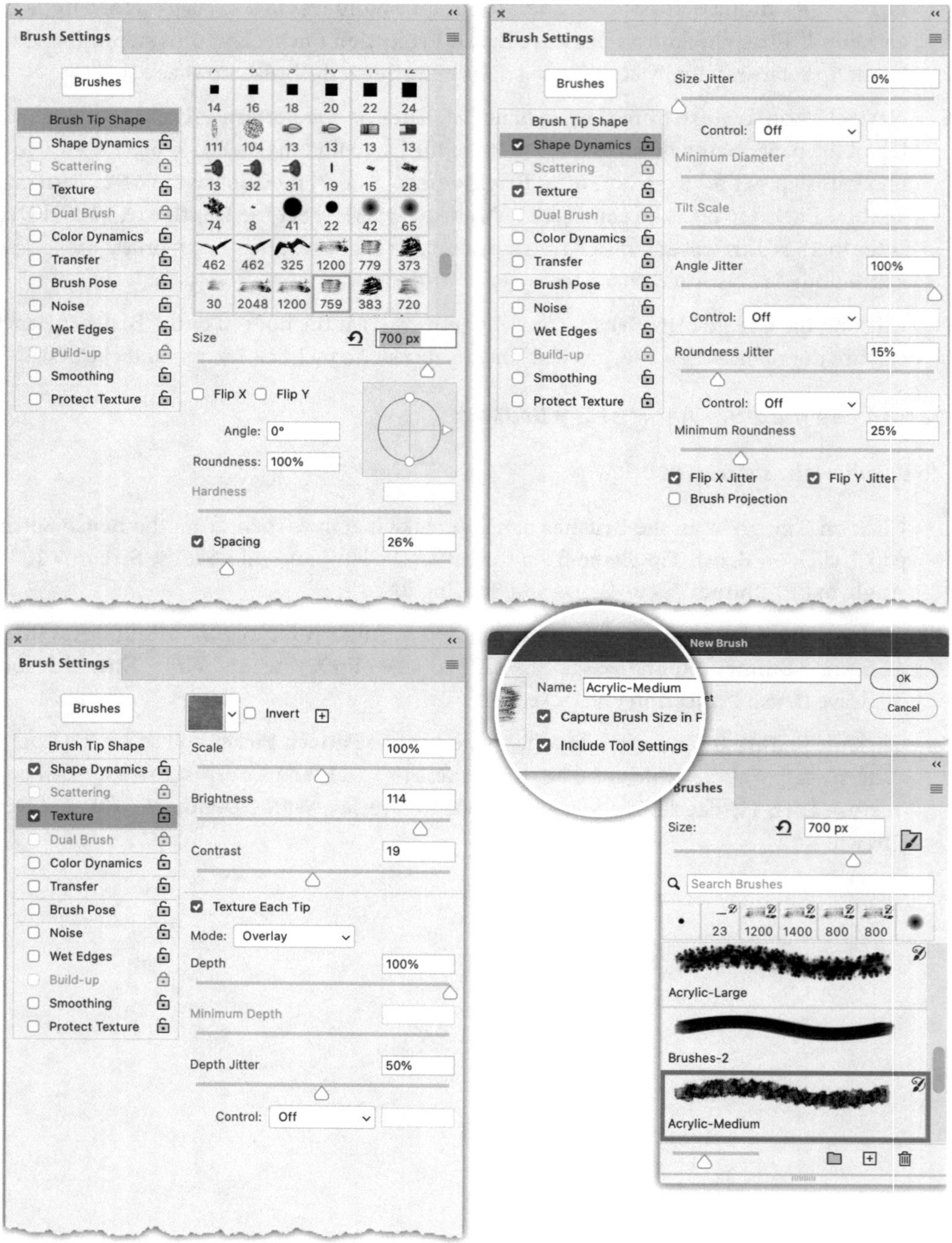

Figure 10.9: Brush-2 used as the basis for a new brush preset named Acrylic-Medium

Creating a small Art History Brush

To do so, follow the steps given below:

1. Click on `Brush-3` in the **Brushes** panel to make it active. Then, from the **Brush Settings** panel, click on **Brush Tip Shape** from the list on the left-hand side. Set the **Size** to `373 px`, **Angle** to `0°`, **Roundness** to `100%`, and **Spacing** to `10%`.
2. Click on **Shape Dynamics** from the list on the left-hand side. Set the **Size Jitter** to `0%`, **Angle Jitter** to `100%`, **Roundness Jitter** to `0%`, and **Minimum Roundness** to `0%`. Turn on the **Flip X Jitter** and **Flip Y Jitter** checkboxes but leave **Brush Projection** unchecked.

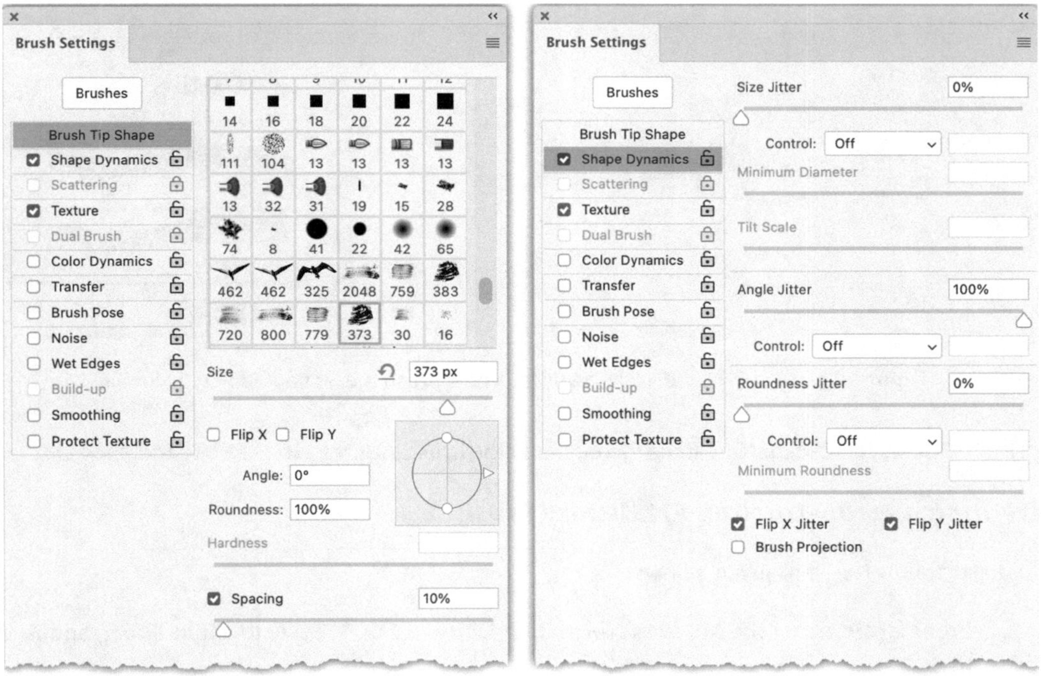

Figure 10.10: Brush-3 tip shape and dynamics

3. Click on **Texture** from the left-hand list. Click on the **Pattern Picker** and select the `Canvas` pattern again. Set the **Scale** to `100%`, **Brightness** to `0%`, and **Contrast** to `14%`. Turn on the **Texture Each Tip** checkbox and set the **Mode** to **Height**. Set the **Depth** to `12%` and **Depth Jitter** to `28%`.

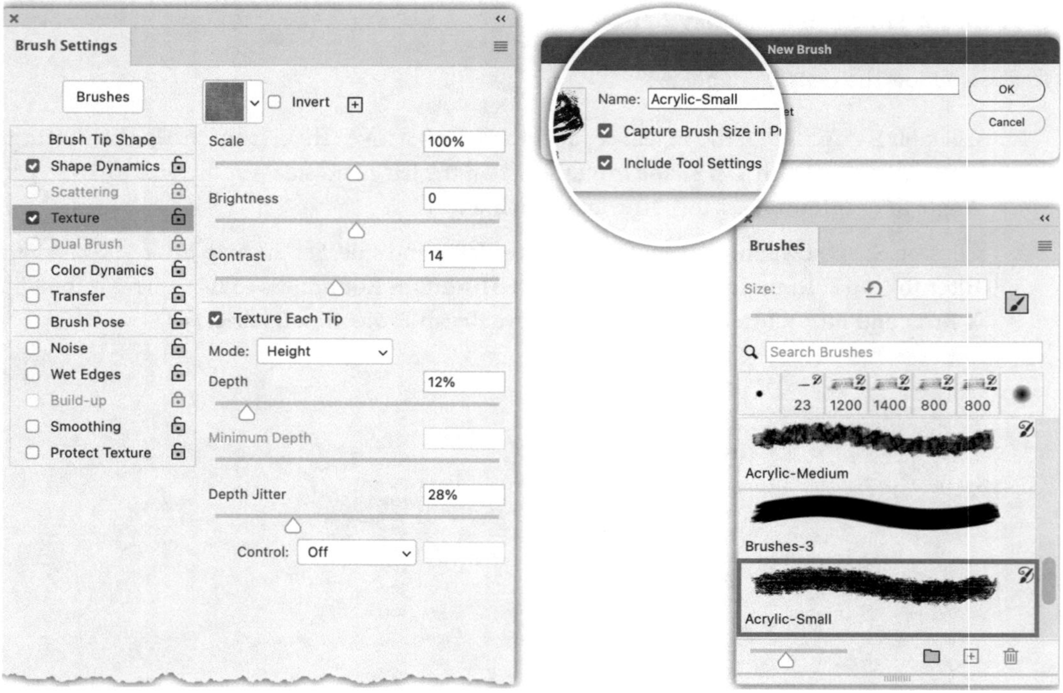

Figure 10.11: Brush-3 used as the basis for a new brush preset named Acrylic-Small

4. Click on the **Create New Brush** icon, name the brush `Acrylic-Small`, and click **OK**.

Creating a reconstruction Art History Brush

To do so, follow the steps given below:

1. From **Options**, set the **Mode** to **Normal**, **Opacity** to `100%`, **Style** to **Tight Short**, and **Area** to `500%`.

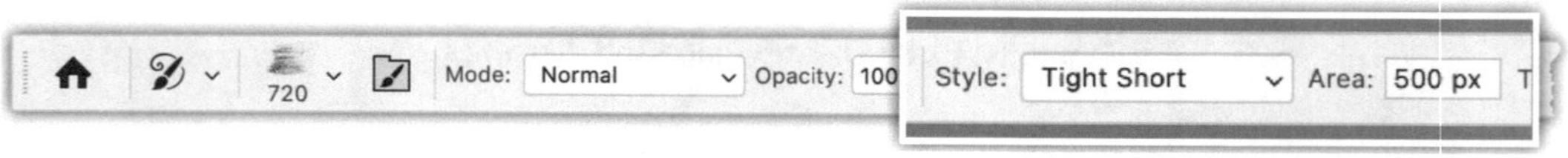

Figure 10.12: The Art History Brush tool options defined for the reconstruction brush preset

2. Click on `Brush-4` in the **Brushes** panel to make it active. Then, from the **Brush Settings** panel, click on **Brush Tip Shape** from the list on the left-hand side. Set the **Size** to `700 px`, **Angle** to `0°`, **Roundness** to `100%`, and **Spacing** to `26%`.

3. Click on **Shape Dynamics** from the list on the left-hand side. Set the **Size Jitter** to `0%`, **Angle Jitter** to `0%`, **Roundness Jitter** to `84%`, and **Minimum Roundness** to `1%`. Turn off the **Flip X Jitter**, **Flip Y Jitter**, and **Brush Projection** checkboxes.

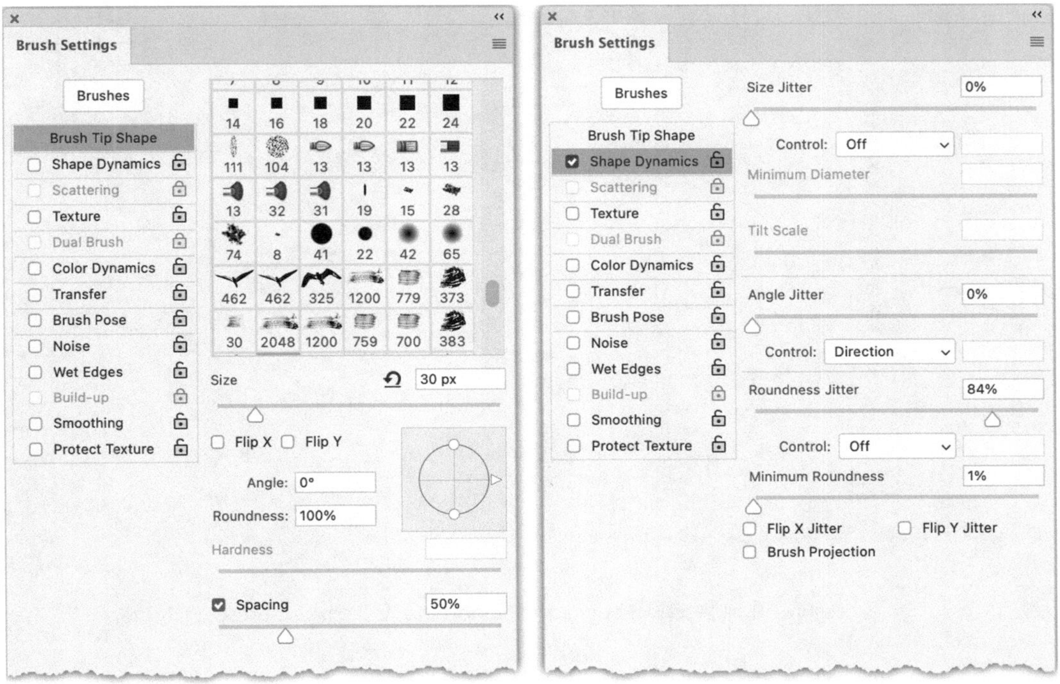

Figure 10.13: Brush-4 tip shape and dynamics

4. Click on **Texture** from the left-hand list. Click on **Pattern Picker** and select the `Canvas` pattern again. Set the **Scale** to `100%`, **Brightness** to `0%`, and **Contrast** to `14%`. Turn on the **Texture Each Tip** checkbox and set the **Mode** to **Overlay**. Set the **Depth** to `12%` and **Depth Jitter** to `28%`.

5. Click on **Transfer** from the left-hand list. Set **Opacity Jitter** to `50%` and **Flow Jitter** to `0%`. Finally, turn on the **Wet Edges** and **Smoothing** checkboxes from the list on the left-hand side, neither of which contain settings to define.

6. Click on the **Create New Brush** icon and name the brush `Acrylic-Reconstruct`. Then, click **OK** to save the final acrylic brush.

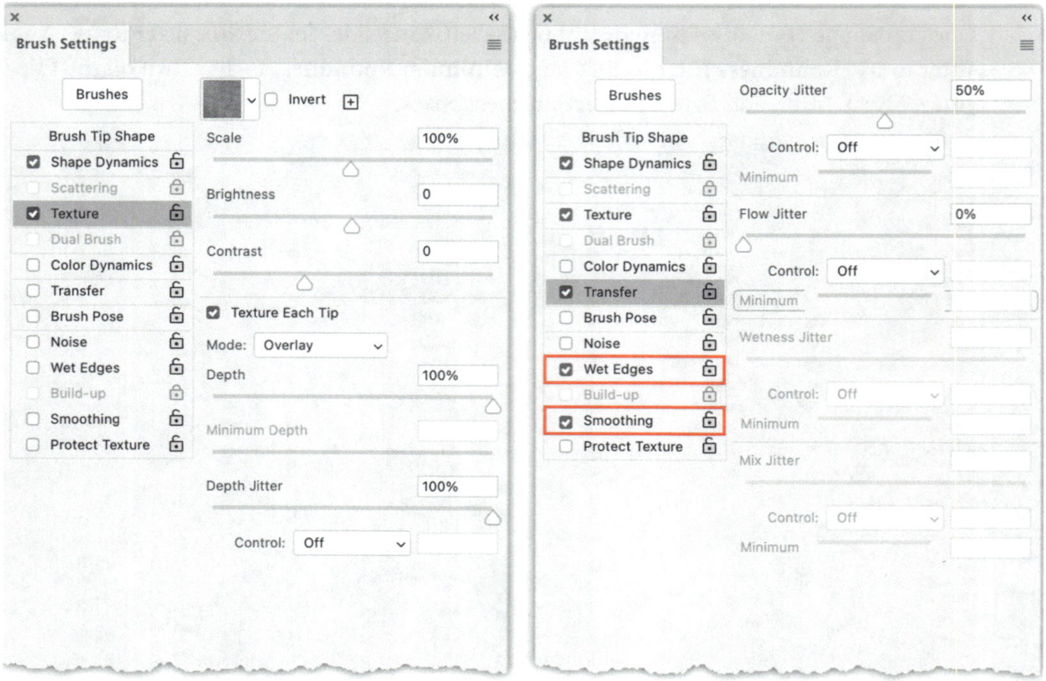

Figure 10.14: Add wet edges and smoothing to the brush preset

Creating and backing up a brush preset group

To do so, follow the steps given below:

1. Click on the **Create a new group** icon at the bottom of the **Brushes** panel. Name the group `Acrylics` and click **OK**.
2. With the new group created, start dragging each of the Art History Brush tool presets into it. This should only include `Acrylic-Large`, `Acrylic-Medium`, `Acrylic-Small`, and `Acrylic-Reconstruct` brush presets.
3. The original brushes, `Brush-1`, `Brush-2`, `Brush-3`, and `Brush-4`, are no longer required and as such can be deleted by left-clicking on them and pressing the **Delete Brush** button at the bottom of the **Brushes** panel.
4. Left-click on the `Acrylics` brush group folder in the **Brushes** panel. Go to the **Brushes** panel fly-out menu and choose **Export selected brushes**. Browse to a folder of your choice, name it `Acrylics`, and choose **Save**.

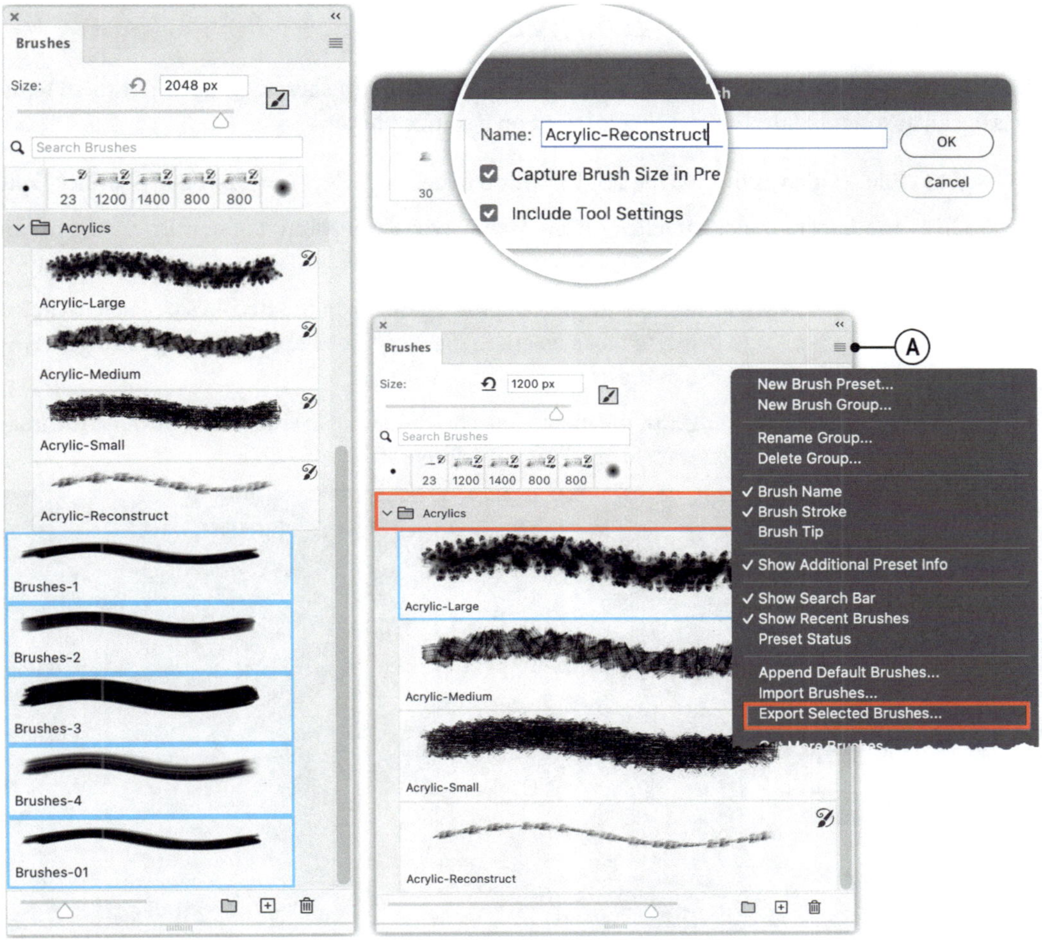

Figure 10.15: Save the new Acrylic-Reconstruct brush preset

In this section of the chapter, we have created and modified brush tips. Starting with real paint marks, we captured the basic form as a brush tip preset. Then, with the Art History Brush tool active, we modified the properties of the brush specifically for that tool. We added shape dynamics that randomly altered the angle of each brush stroke when applied, as well as built a canvas texture into the brush tip itself. In the next section, you will use the brushes to create an abstract portrait image from a photo.

Applying brushes for creative effect

With the real-world brush marks now converted to Photoshop brushes, it's time to put them to use, creating an abstract painterly effect that is based on a source photo:

1. Go to **File** → **Open**, browse to the `10-Brushes` folder, and select `Portrait.jpg`. Click **Open**.
2. Go to the **Layers** panel and click on the **New Layer** icon. Name the new layer `Paint` and ensure it is active.
3. Switch to the **History Brush** tool by pressing the *Y* key. From the **Brushes** panel, left-click on the `Acrylic-Large` brush to make it active. You won't need to edit the tool settings, as they were captured with the brush preset.
4. Starting from the outer edges of the image, left-click and drag in short bursts around the image until the edges have been transformed into brush marks.

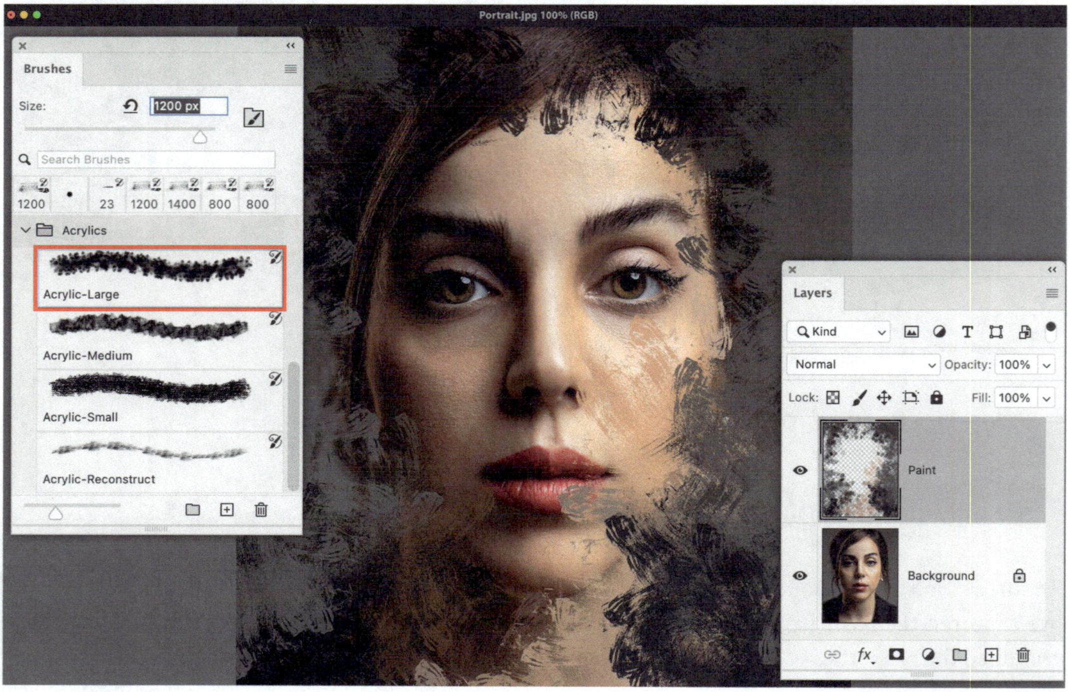

Figure 10.16: Painting from the edges of the image up to the face

> **How the Art History Brush tool works**
>
> By default, the **Art History Brush** tool uses the state of the document when it was opened as a reference for color and structure. As you drag across the image, the original photo is sampled and transformed into paint marks.

5. From the **Brushes** panel, left-click on the `Acrylic-Medium` brush to make it active. Paint over some of the inner brush marks and to add some strokes to the center of the image so that the original photo is concealed in paint. Ensure that you left-click and drag over the image in short bursts to prevent the brush from distorting the color and form too much.

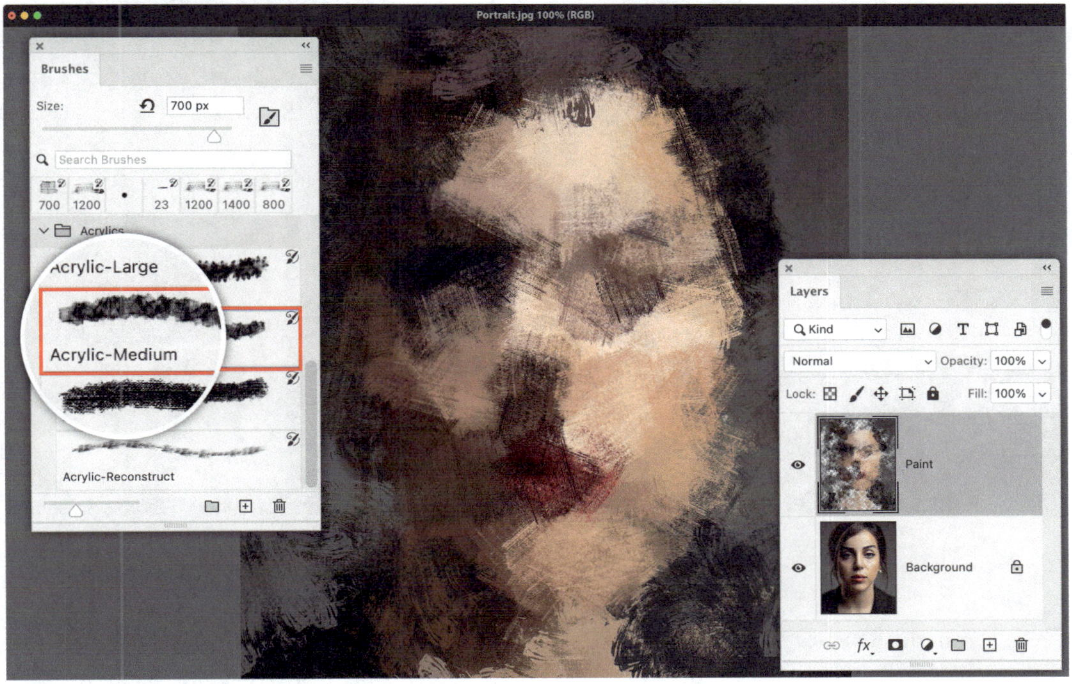

Figure 10.17: Painting over the center of the image to conceal the original photo

6. From the **Brushes** panel, left-click on the `Acrylic-Small` brush to make it active. Reduce the brush size to `125 px`. Focusing on the subject's features only, paint over the eyes, nose, and mouth. This will add some of the structure back into the image.

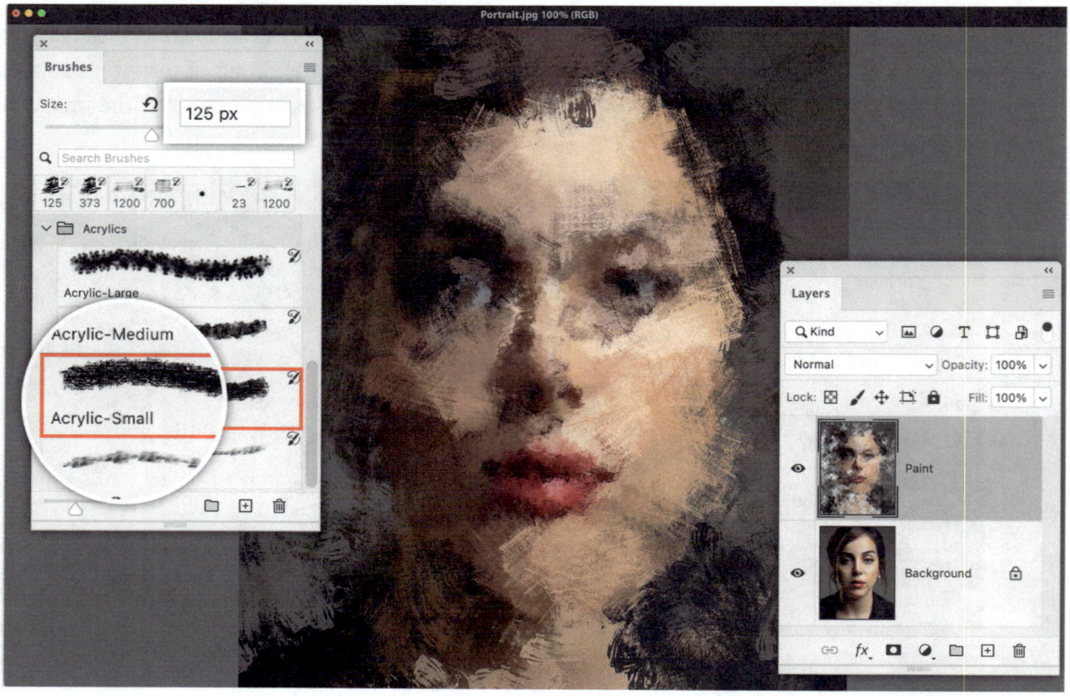

Figure 10.18: Painting over the center of the image to conceal the original photo

7. From the **Brushes** panel, left-click on the `Acrylic-Reconstruct` brush to make it active. This brush will look for contrasting edges, only applying paint strokes along them. In doing so, it restores detail to the painting. Focus your brush strokes on the facial features, as well as the neck and jaw.
8. You may find that some regions will require a little touching up with the `Acrylic-Small` brush to restore the correct colors or paint a clearer jawline for example. By switching back to the `Acrylic-Reconstruct` brush afterward, you will be able to add more definition and tidy the edges once more.

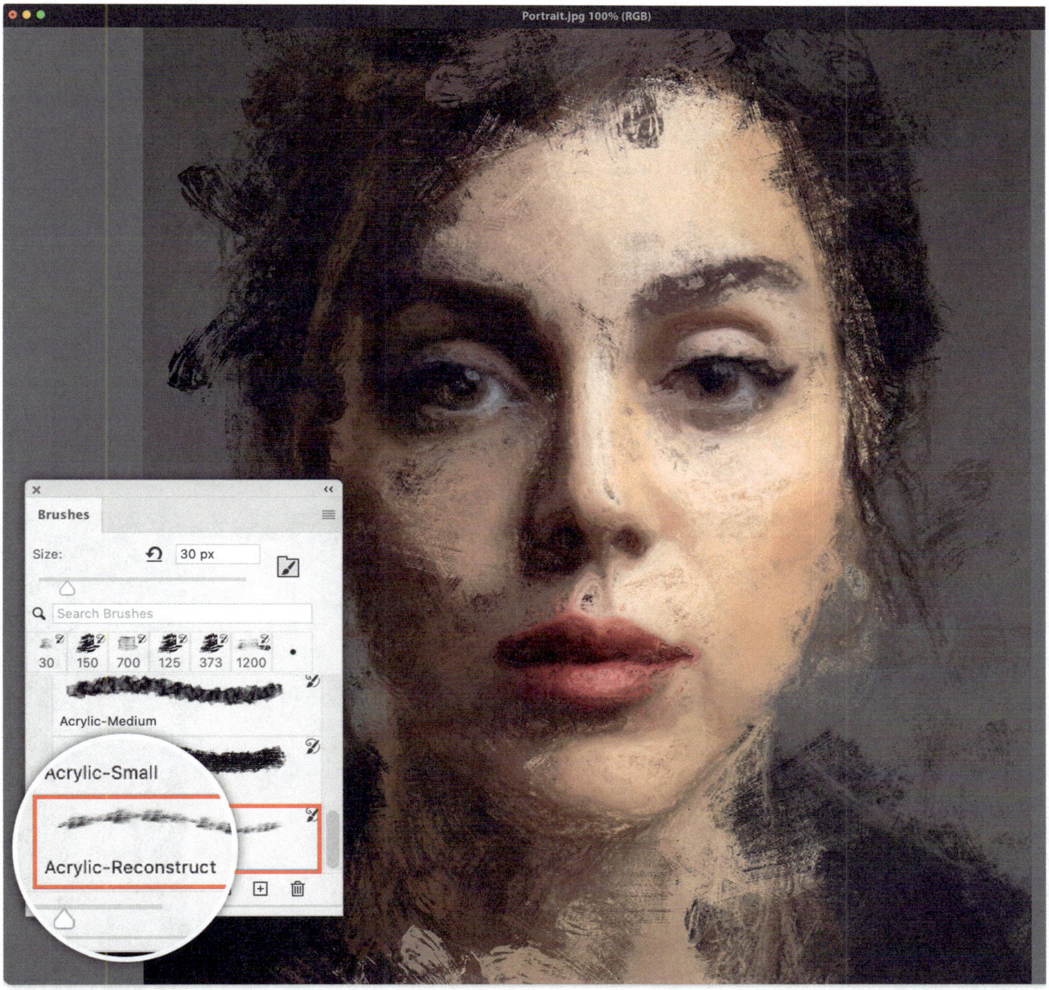

Figure 10.19: The completed image

9. Once completed, save the image as a PSD in the `10-Brushes` folder and then close the document.

In this section, we have applied Art History Brush tool paint marks to a photo to create an abstract art piece. First, we added broad strokes around the edges via lower detail mark-making. Then, as we progressed to the center of the image, the brushes became progressively smaller to capture facial features. We then used a brush to reconstruct fine details and edges, built specifically to paint over regions with contrasting edges in the original photo. Next, you will use brushes for healing and retouching.

Using brushes for retouching

We have already seen the flexibility of brushes in this chapter in terms of adding basic marks or painterly effects to images. However, brushes can also be used for retouching, and in the following exercise, you will create a snowflake brush and a stubble brush.

Creating a snowflake brush

Follow the steps given below:

1. Go to **File** → **Open** and browse to the `10-Brushes` folder. Select `Snow.jpg` and `Winter.jpg` and click **Open**.
2. With the document active, go to **Edit** → **Define Brush Preset**. Name it `Snow` and click **OK**. Then, close the document.

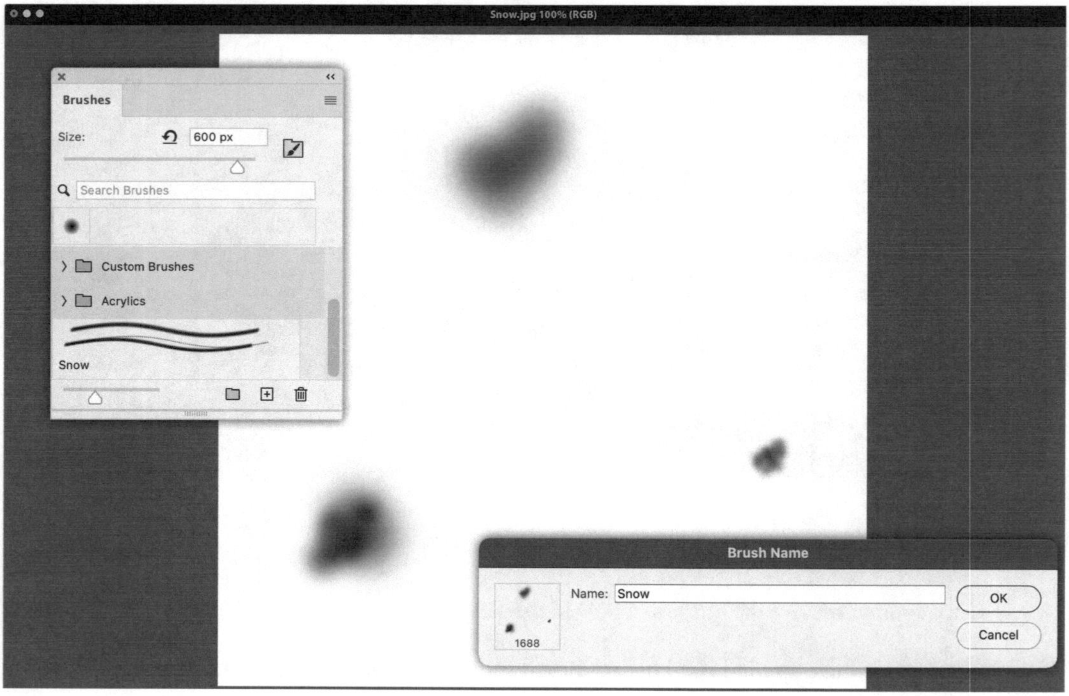

Figure 10.20: The initial snow brush after capturing from an image

3. Click on the `Snow` brush, located at the bottom of the **Brushes** panel to make it active. Then, go to **Window** → **Brush Settings**.

4. Switch to the **Brush** tool from the **Tools** panel. Set the **Blend Mode** to **Normal**, **Opacity** to `100%`, and **Flow** to `85%`.

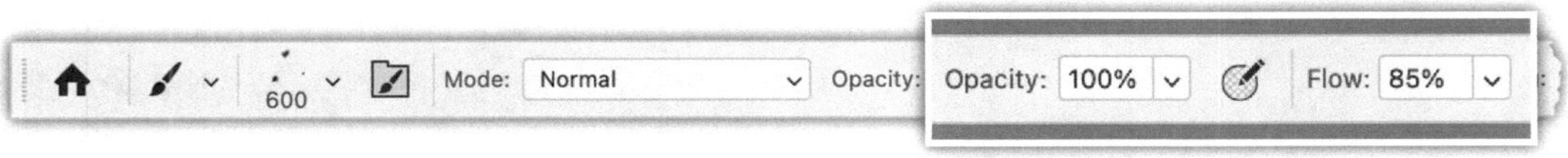

Figure 10.21: The Brush tool options

5. Click on **Brush Tip Shape** from the **Brush Settings** panel from the list on the left-hand side. Set the **Size** to `200 px`, **Angle** to `0°`, **Roundness** to `100%`, and **Spacing** to `60%`.

6. Next, click on **Shape Dynamics** from the left-hand list. Set the **Size Jitter** to `100%`, **Angle Jitter** to `100%`, **Roundness Jitter** to `25%`, and **Minimum Roundness** to `2%`. Turn off the **Flip X Jitter**, **Flip Y Jitter**, and **Brush Projection** checkboxes.

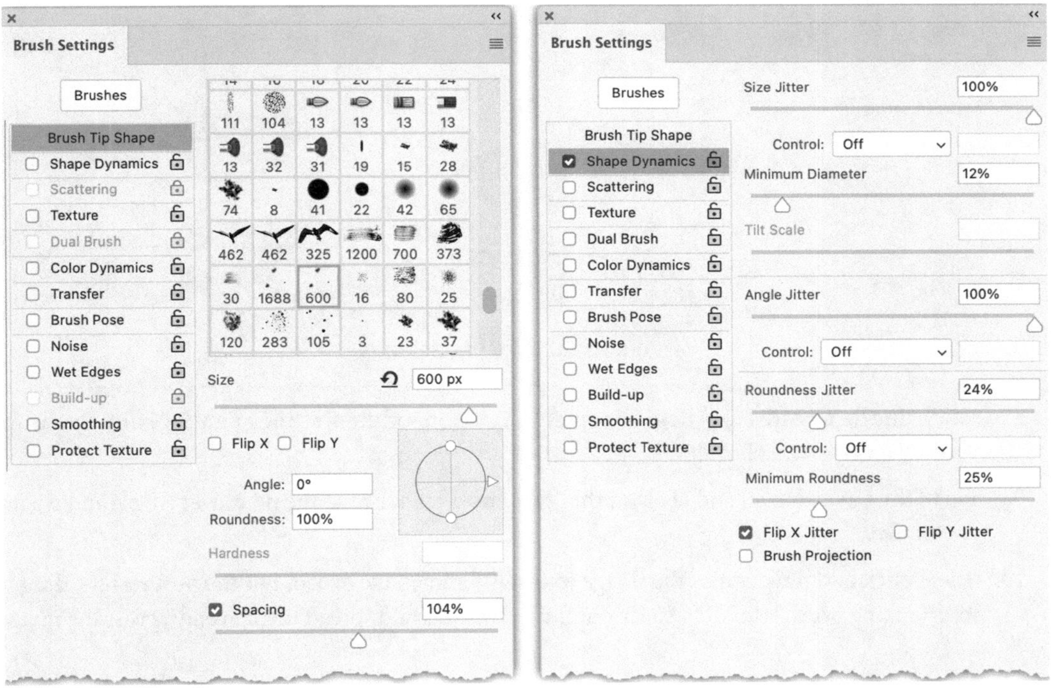

Figure 10.22: The Brush Tip Shape and Shape Dynamics settings

7. Next, click on **Scatter** from the left-hand list. Turn on the **Both Axis** checkbox at the top of the panel and set the **Scatter** value to `1000%`. Set the **Count** to `1` and **Count Jitter** to `0%`. Finally, turn on the **Smoothing** checkbox from the list on the left side.

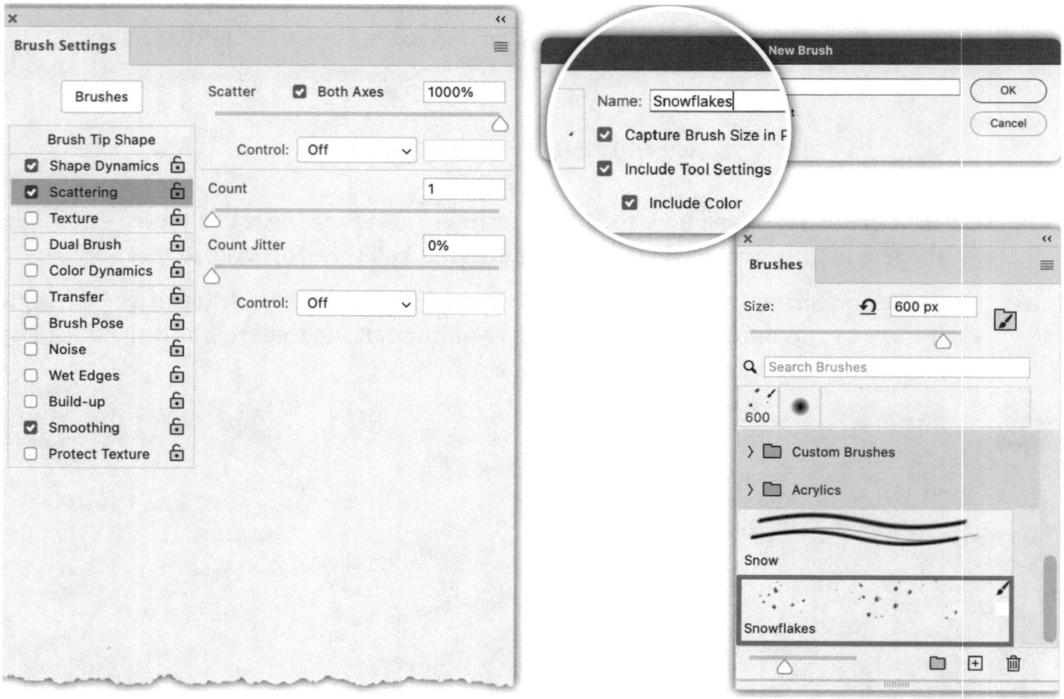

Figure 10.23: Scattering settings

8. Click on the **Create New Brush** icon at the bottom of the **Brushes** panel. Name the brush `Snowflakes` and click **OK**.
9. Go to the **Layers** panel and click on the **New Layer** icon. Name the new layer `Snow` and ensure it is active.
10. Then, click and drag across the image to test the snowflake brush. For the best results, drag in long arching brush strokes to space out the snowflakes and spread them evenly across the image.

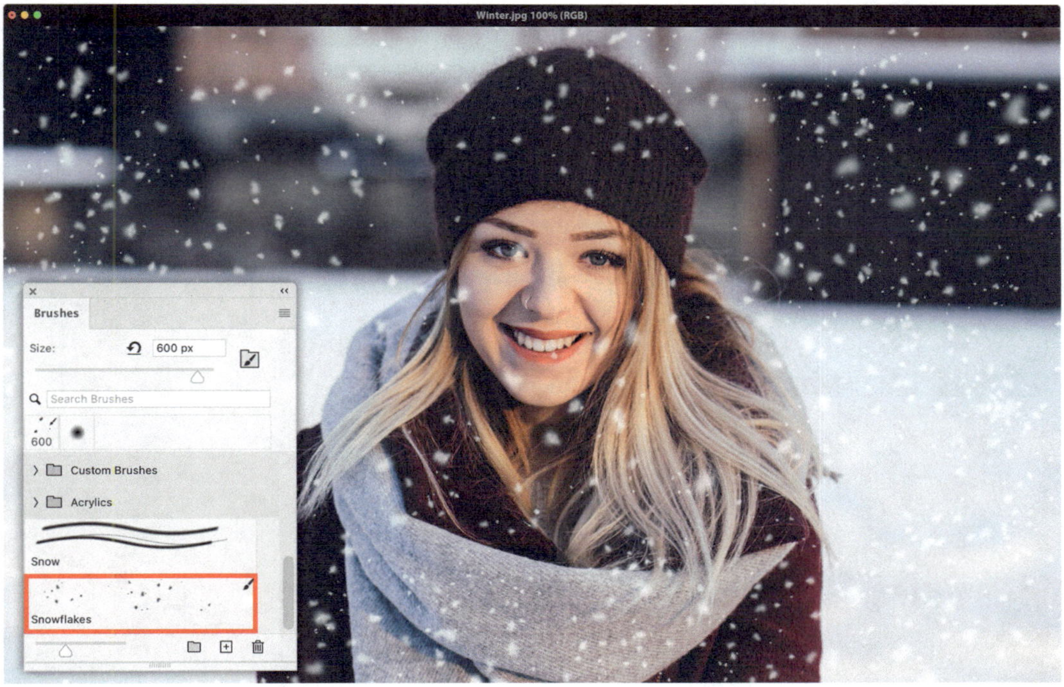

Figure 10.24: The brush mark applied to the original photo

11. Reduce the **Brush Size** to at least half its original size, approximately `300 px`. Then, repeat the same technique of dragging across the image to add finer snowflakes. Try to avoid adding too many snowflakes in front of the subject's face, as we don't want to obscure it.
12. As a final step, the snow would benefit from some motion. Right-click on the `Snow` layer and choose **Convert to Smart Object** from the list of options.
13. Go to **Filter** → **Blur** → **Motion Blur**. Set the **Angle** to `-35°` and the **Distance** to `21 px`. The **Distance** value controls how intense the blur is, as such we don't need to add too much blur to the snowflakes. Click **OK** when done. If you need to edit the snow at any point in the future, you can double-click on the `Snow` layer thumbnail in the **Layers** panel to open the smart object.

14. Once complete, save the image as a PSD in the `10-Brushes` folder and then close the document.

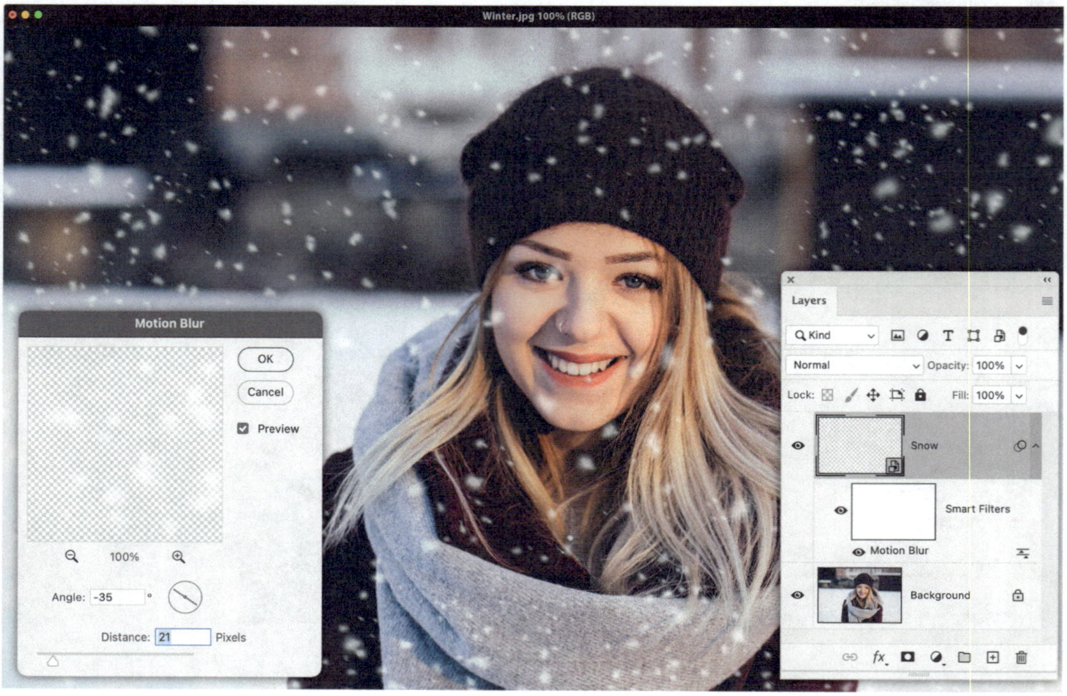

Figure 10.25: The completed snow image

Creating a stubble brush

In the last exercise of this chapter, you will create a brush based on a simple brush stroke representing a hair to fill in the subject's beard:

1. Go to **File** → **Open** and browse to the `10-Brushes` folder. Select `Hair.jpg` and `Barbor.jpg`, then click **Open**.
2. With `Hair.jpg` active, go to **Edit** → **Define Brush Preset**. Name the brush `Single Hair-1` and click **OK**. Close the document.
3. Click on the `Single Hair-1` brush, located at the bottom of the **Brushes** panel, to make it active. Then go to **Window** → **Brush Settings**.

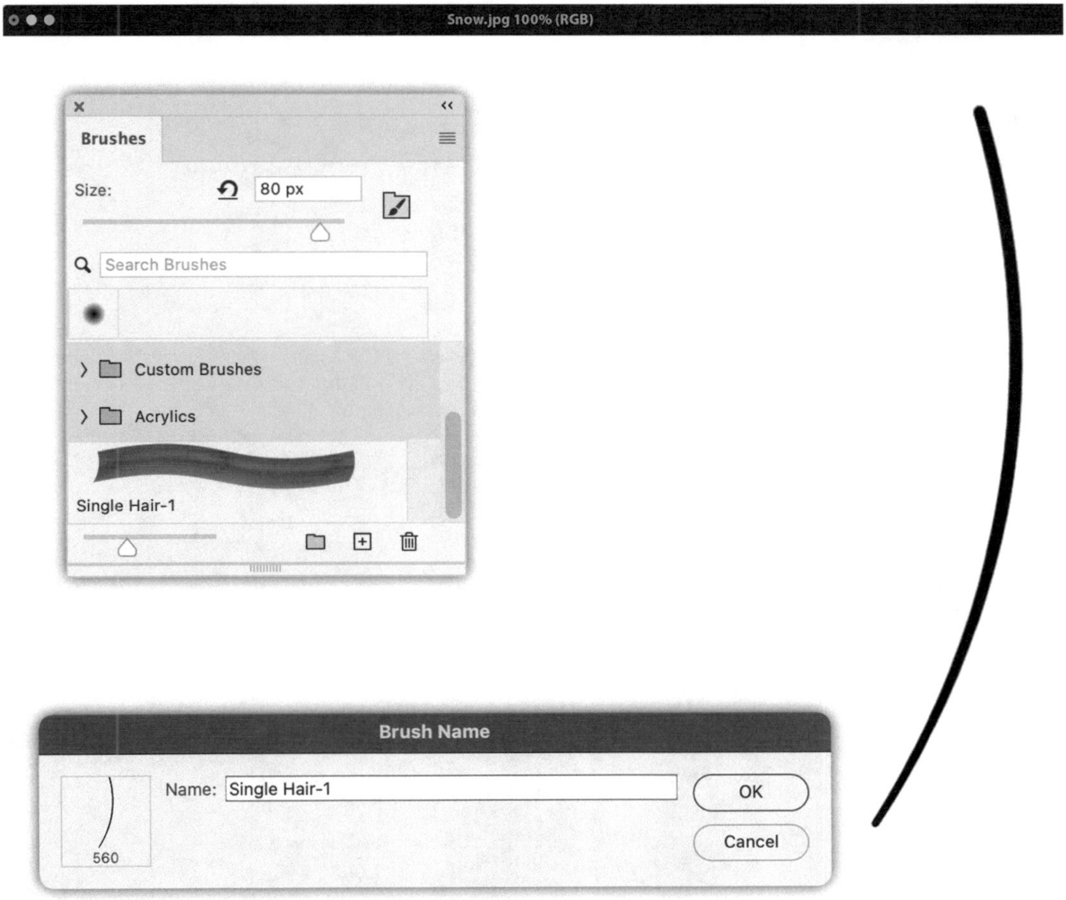

Figure 10.26: The source hair image

4. Click on **Brush Tip Shape** from the **Brush Settings** panel from the list on the left-hand side. Set the **Size** to `80 px`, **Angle** to `86°`, **Roundness** to `100%`, and **Spacing** to `70%`.
5. Next, click on **Shape Dynamics** from the left-hand list. Set the **Size Jitter** to `100%` and **Minimum Diameter** to `2%`. Set the **Angle Jitter** to `7%` and then change the **Control** dropdown to **Initial Direction**. With this specific brush, positioning the angle of the hairs is tricky. I find the direction you start dragging in with the mouse reliable. Set the **Roundness Jitter** to `6%` and **Minimum Roundness** to `1%`. Turn off the **Flip X Jitter**, **Flip Y Jitter**, and **Brush Projection** checkboxes.
6. Next, click on **Scatter** from the left-hand list. Turn on the **Both Axis** checkbox at the top and set the **Scatter** value to `395%`. Finally, turn on the **Smoothing** checkbox from the list on the left.

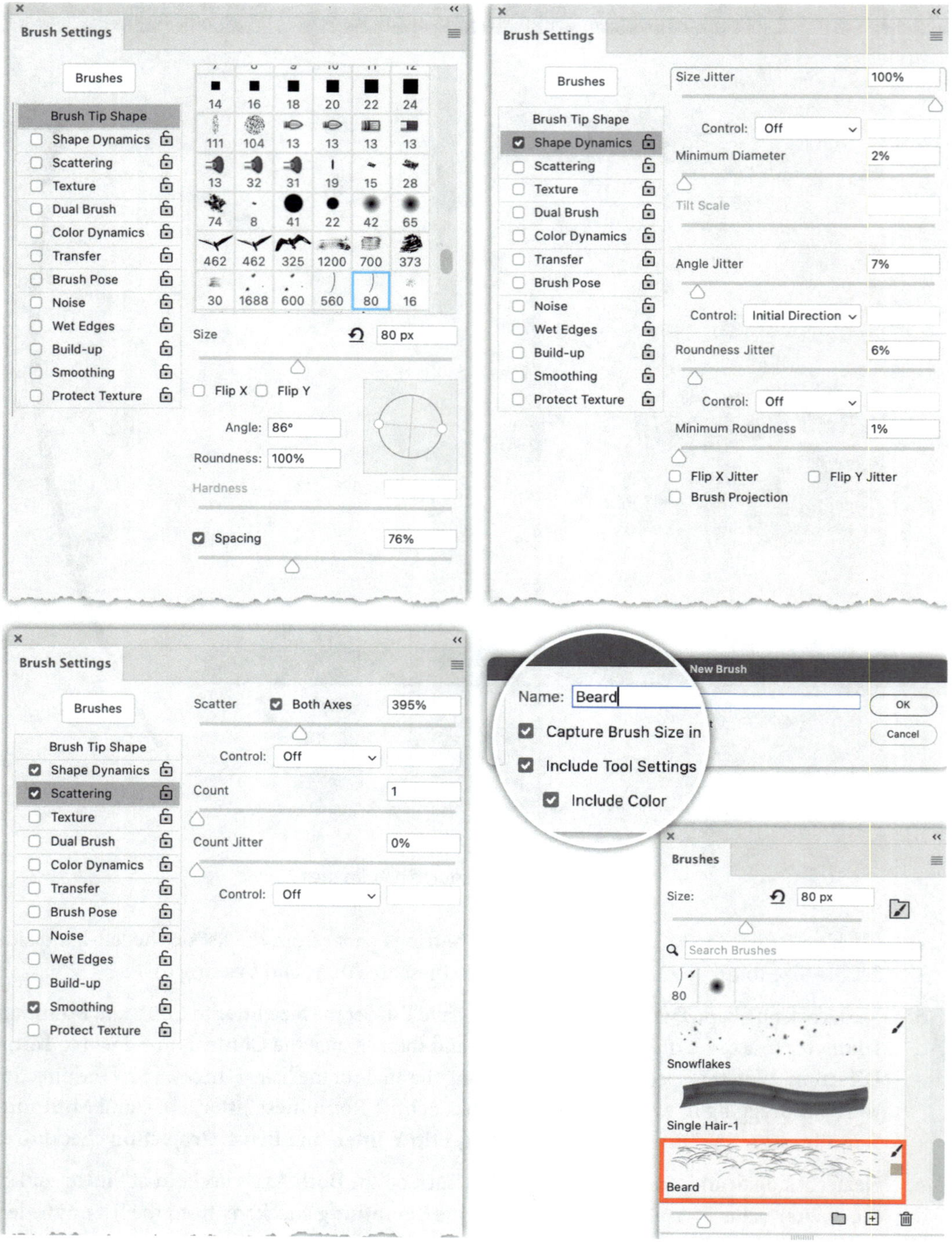

Figure 10.27: The brush settings for the beard brush

7. Click on the **Create New Brush icon** at the bottom of the **Brushes** panel. Name the brush `Beard` and click **OK**.
8. Go to the **Layers** panel and click on the **New Layer** icon. Name the new layer `Hair` and ensure it is active.
9. Switch to the **Brush** tool in the **Tools** panel. From **Options**, set the **Blend Mode** to **Normal**, **Opacity** to `100%`, **Flow** to `100%`, and **Smoothing** to `10%`. Set the **Foreground Color** to a hexadecimal of `987c67` to match some of the colors in the subject's beard.

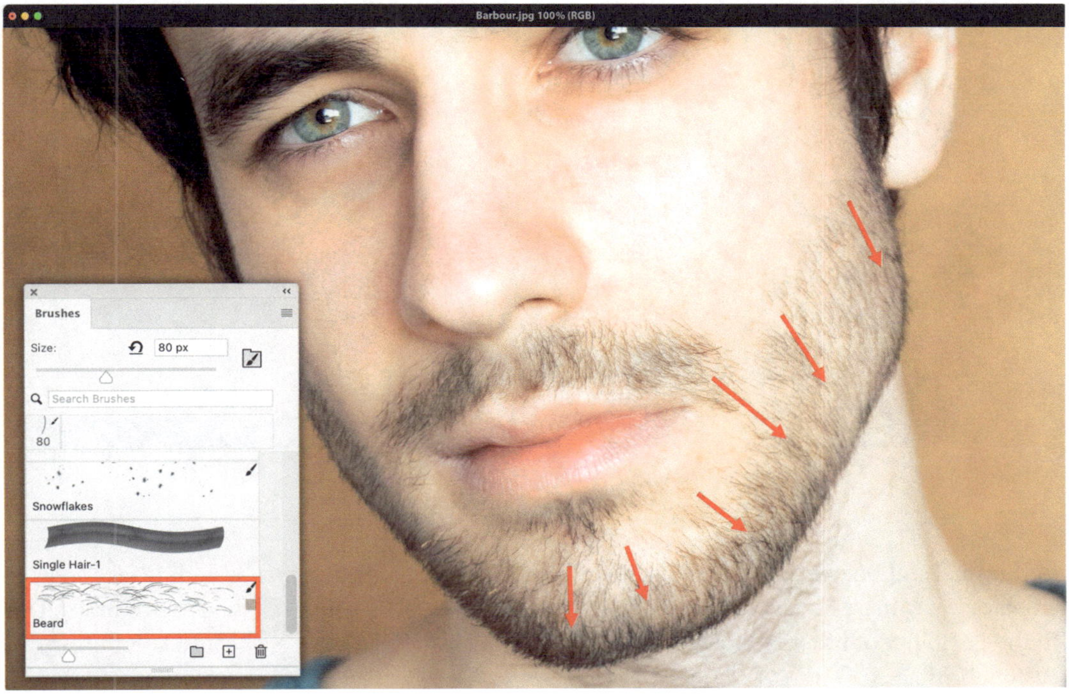

Figure 10.28: Add brush marks over the existing beard

10. Then, click and drag across the man's cheek, ensuring that you drag the mouse downwards in the direction that the hairs point. Vary the colors by changing to a lighter brown, such as `be9d81`. You can also vary the size of the brush to enhance the result, especially for the chin and top lip.
11. As a final step, switch to the **Blur** tool from the middle of the **Tools** panel. From the **Options bar**, set the **Mode** to `Normal`, **Strength** to `50%` and ensure the **Sample All Layers** checkbox turned off. Click and drag across the hair marks where the shot is out of focus so that the painted hairs match those around them in the original photo.

12. Once completed, save the image as a PSD in the `10-Brushes` folder and then close the document.

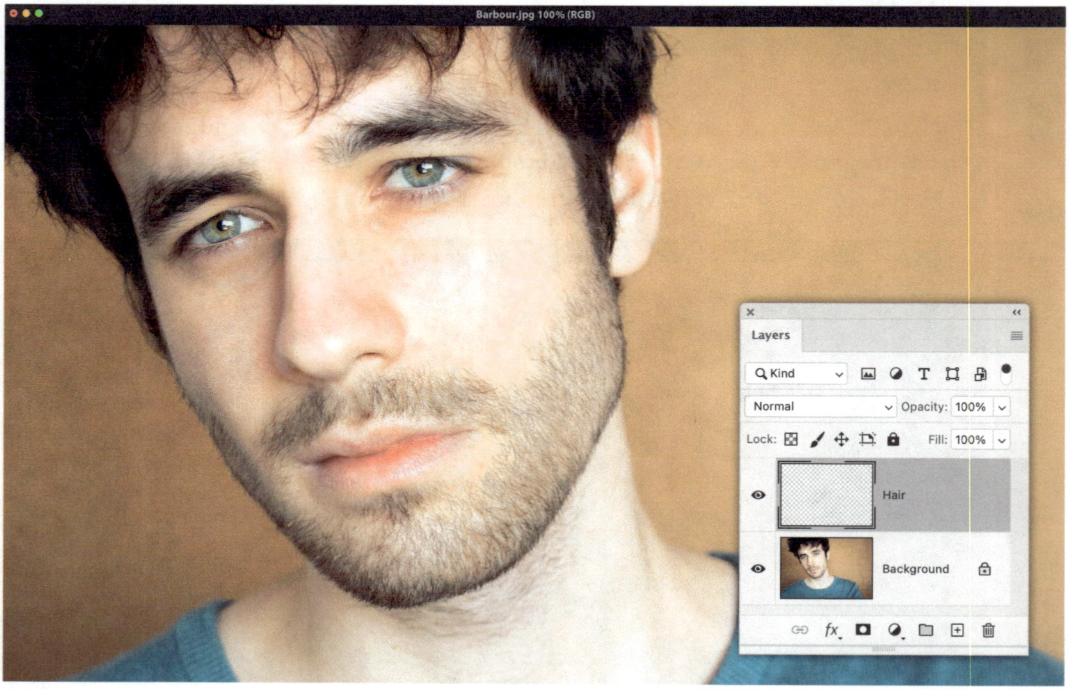

Figure 10.29: The completed image

In this final section, we have used brushes to heal and retouch images, first by adding fake snow to emphasize a wintery scene and then by creating a brush for facial hair to fill in gaps in a beard. Due to the flexibility of brushes, if you can think of a use for them, there's probably a solution with a custom brush.

Summary

In this chapter, we focused on creating and editing custom Photoshop brushes. In the first instance, we captured portions of an existing image within a rectangular selection to create three bird brushes. We saw how a brush is converted into a greyscale image. White portions of the brush act as transparent portions when painting, and anything darker than white applies a color of your choice, selected from the **Color Picker**.

The resulting brushes were then used to paint a small flock of birds in an image to provide a focal point. We sampled colors from the original photo to form dark bird silhouettes on a separate layer and duplicated it to create a mirrored version to create reflections on the lake's surface.

In the second exercise, we captured real-world brush strokes. Once captured as a basic brush tip shape, we then adapted each of them, adding shape dynamics that allowed the brush angle to change randomly when used, as well as a canvas texture to give that paint-on-canvas feel with each stroke. These brushes were then combined with the Art History Brush tool to sample colors from a portrait and then reapplied in dabbed strokes with a painterly effect. As the painted version of the image developed, we utilized a series of smaller brush tips to reconstruct the finer details of the image.

Finally, we created a snowflake brush to emphasize a wintery scene. This brush had shape and position dynamics applied to it so that the snowflakes were sized, rotated, and scattered randomly to achieve a more realistic look.

In the final two chapters, we will start to combine many of the skills covered in this book to take on more challenging projects, starting with image collages.

Part 4: World Building

In the final part of this book, you will put your professional editing skills to the test. You will leverage all your learning to blend multiple assets into a single photomontage. You'll work with collaging techniques, panoramas, and high dynamic range images. Finally, you'll be set two challenges to craft some surrealist compositions. These challenges will test your Photoshop abilities to the limit: the perfect way to consolidate your learning by putting it into practice.

This part has the following chapters:

11
Blending and Collaging Images

Throughout this book, blending or masking has been a constant theme and an essential skill that allows you to hide unwanted content or combine multiple subjects into one composition. In this chapter, we'll be taking that concept a little further.

First, we will take six photographs of a beach landscape and stitch them seamlessly as a panorama, getting Photoshop to do the heavy lifting for us, removing vignettes and transparent edges with **Content-Aware Fill**. You'll also practice your healing and retouching skills as you remove all the tourists from the beach with the **Healing Brush** tool and the **Clone Stamp** tool.

We'll then move on to collaging, where you'll take source images of weathered posters, newsprint, and paint to recreate a portrait. This will involve the use of adjustment layers, smart objects, masks, and brushes.

You'll then have the opportunity to create a double-exposure image, where two photos are blended to form a surreal composition. In the exercise, you'll blend an atmospheric forest scene through the hair of a subject, again using a variety of masking techniques.

Finally, you'll create a **high dynamic range** (**HDR**) image, typically combining three images of the same scene taken at different exposures. The aim is to capture details such as shadows and highlights that would otherwise be lost in a single image. By practicing many of the techniques covered in this book along with montaging workflows, you will acquire all the skills required to tackle the final chapter, the culmination of all learning.

This chapter will require you to download and install Adobe Bridge for the HDR exercises. In a nutshell, Adobe Bridge is a visually focused file browser and asset management tool that can be used alongside your other Adobe applications.

In this chapter, you will explore the following topics:

- Creating seamless panoramas
- Building collages with textures and paint
- Creating double-exposure compositions
- Working with HDR images

Technical requirements

The project files for this chapter can be found at: `https://github.com/PacktPublishing/Mastering-Adobe-Photoshop-2024/tree/main/Chapter11`

Creating seamless panoramas

Photoshop has a very intuitive photo-merging feature that will detect where images should be joined and will even blend the edges of each photo seamlessly for you. Here's how to use it:

1. Head to Adobe Photoshop and go to **File** → **Automate** → **Photomerge** to launch the **Photomerge** image browser.
2. Click on the **Browse** button and select `Coast_01.jpg` to `Coast_06.jpg` (six files in total) from the `11-Blend` folder. Click **Open** when done to add them to **Photomerge**.
3. Set **Layout** mode to **Auto**, which is the default. Then, turn on the checkboxes for **Blend Images Together**, which performs the seamless stitching for us, **Vignette Removal**, to remove darkened edges around each image, and **Content-Aware Fill Transparent Areas**. Click **OK** when done:

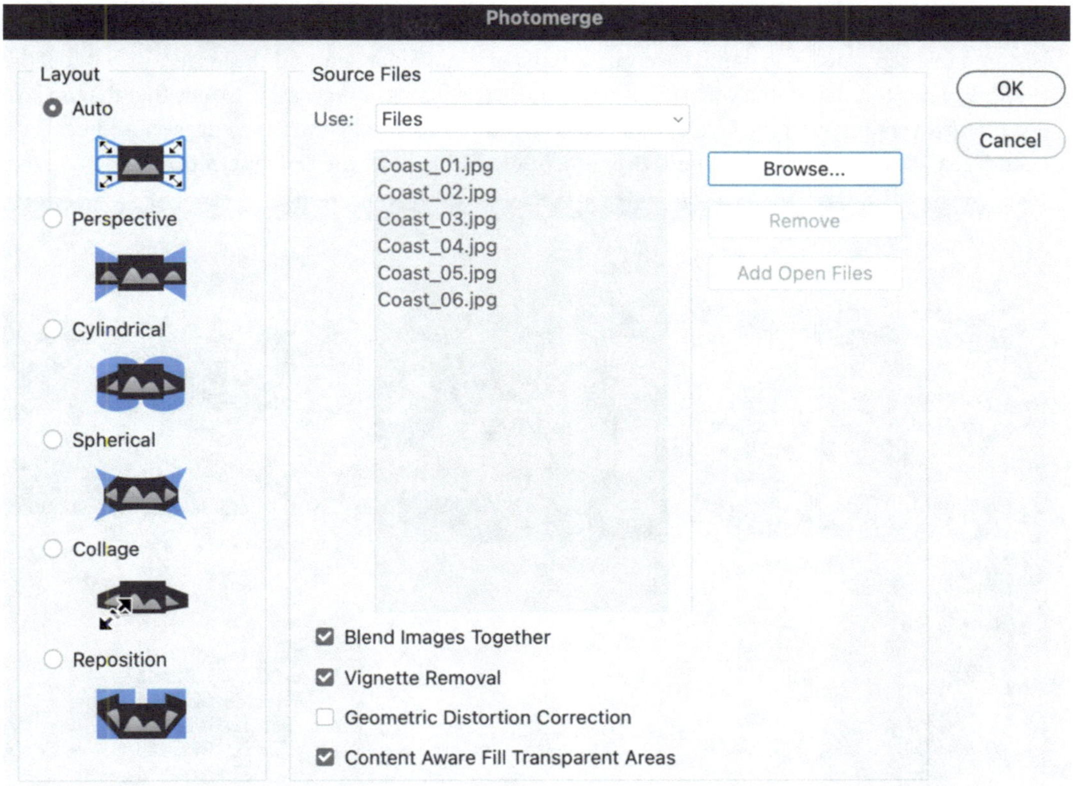

Figure 11.1: Adding images to the Photomerge dialog

Photomerge source options

Geometric Distortion Correction is beneficial when stitching images that contain structures such as buildings and other manufactured subjects. However, focusing on maintaining strong visual lines, **Geometric Distortion Correction** can add considerable time to completing the stitching process. My suggestion is to stitch your images without this feature turned on, and if necessary, repeat the process with the option turned on if the initial panorama lacks the quality you require. Vignettes are a phenomenon that darkens or lightens the edges of an image at the point of capture. For a panorama to be seamless, vignettes must be removed; that's where **Vignette Removal** comes in. We are no strangers to **Content-Aware Fill**, having used it several times in this book. It is common that in the process of stitching and distorting each image to build a panorama, the edges will suffer from an uneven "bow-tie" effect. **Content-Aware Fill** simply fills the transparent regions around the edge of the canvas to provide a full image. Prior to **Content-Aware Fill**, images were often cropped down, which resulted in the loss of large portions of image content.

Photoshop will now open each of the six images and merge them into one new document. Each image is stored in a separate layer, named according to its original file name, and these are stitched together to form a seamless panorama with a series of simple yet effective layer masks. Notice that the top layer is a merged version of all the layers in the panorama. The original panorama edges should have also been filled with the help of **Content-Aware** technology, inside of the active selection:

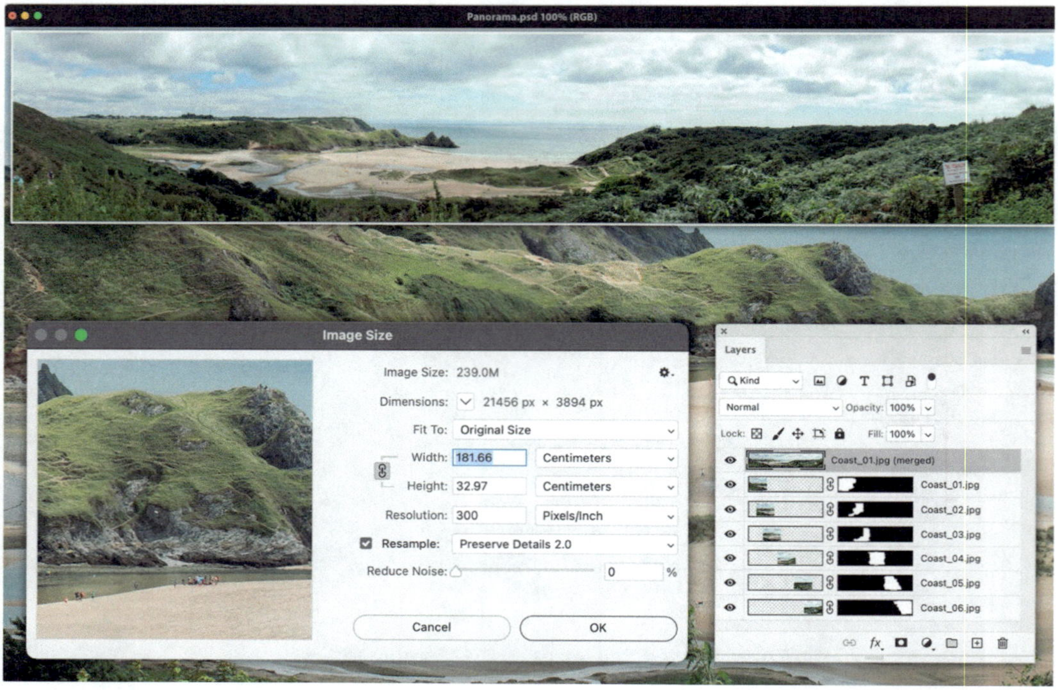

Figure 11.2: The stitched panorama in Photoshop

1. Go to **Select** → **Deselect** and then head to **Layer** → **Flatten Image**. This is one of the few occasions when it is prudent to lose additional layers – in this scenario, layers we cannot see – to reduce file size. After all, this image is 181 cm x 33 cm at a resolution of 300 PPI.
2. Click on the **Create new layer** icon at the bottom of the **Layers** panel and name the layer **Retouch**. Ensure it is active.
3. Go to **File** → **Save**. Name the document `Panorama` as a PSD in the `11-Blend` folder. Click **Save** when done and keep the document open.
4. Switch to the **Spot Healing Brush** tool by pressing the *J* key, then left-click and hold down the left mouse button on the active tool in the **Tools** panel. From the popout, click on the **Spot Healing Brush** tool to make it active.

5. Left-click on the **Brush Tip** menu and set the brush **Size** value to `40 px`. Set the **Type** option to **Content-Aware** and turn on **Sample All Layers**. Ensure that the **Retouch** layer is active in the **Layers** panel:

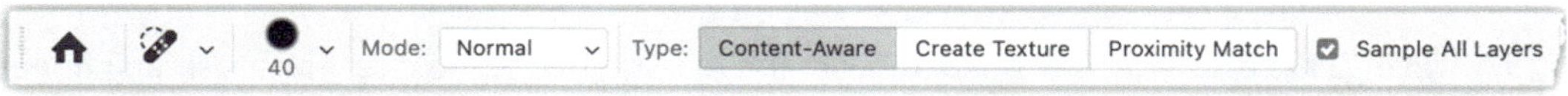

Figure 11.3: The Spot Healing Brush settings in the Options bar

6. Left-click on as many people and brightly colored tents as you can find on the beach to remove them, leaving an almost empty beach scene. Remember to drag across the entire subject as you attempt to remove it; otherwise, Photoshop will tend to smudge the leftover pixels into the surrounding region:

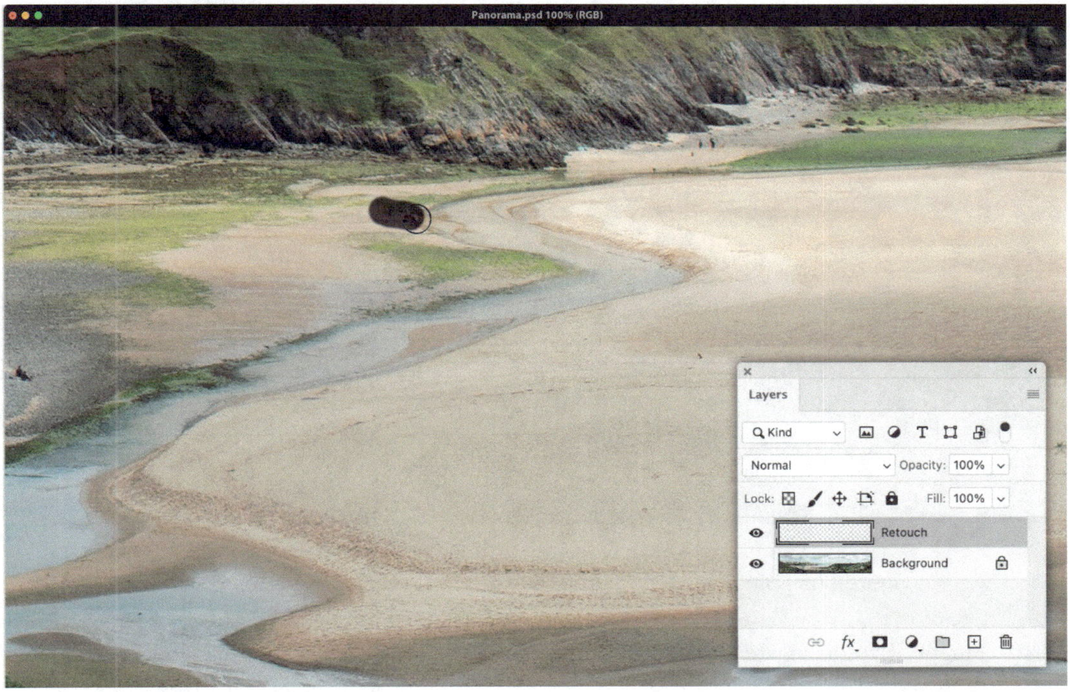

Figure 11.4: Removing distracting elements from the beach

7. Try to avoid retouching several textures at once; for example, where people are standing in front of the river, with a backdrop (texture) of water, the river edge, and sand. The **Spot Healing Brush** tool can struggle to remove the subject and maintain hard lines such as the river edge, often smudging or distorting surrounding pixels. You can instead try the **Clone Stamp** tool. Remove all the tourists on the beach and in the sea.

8. Next, zoom in to the lower-left corner of the panorama where you will find a group of people that need to be concealed as they are distracting. Instead, you might be better served by switching to the **Clone Stamp** tool by pressing the *S* key. Click on the **Brush Tip** menu in the **Options** bar, scroll down the list of brushes, and then you find the **Chalk 60** brush.
9. Change the brush tip **Size** value to `150 px`, then press *Enter* to close the brush tip popout. Set **Mode** to **Normal**, and ensure the **Opacity** and **Flow** options are both set to `100%`. From the sampling settings, turn on the **Aligned** checkbox and set the **Sample** drop-down menu to **Current & Below**:

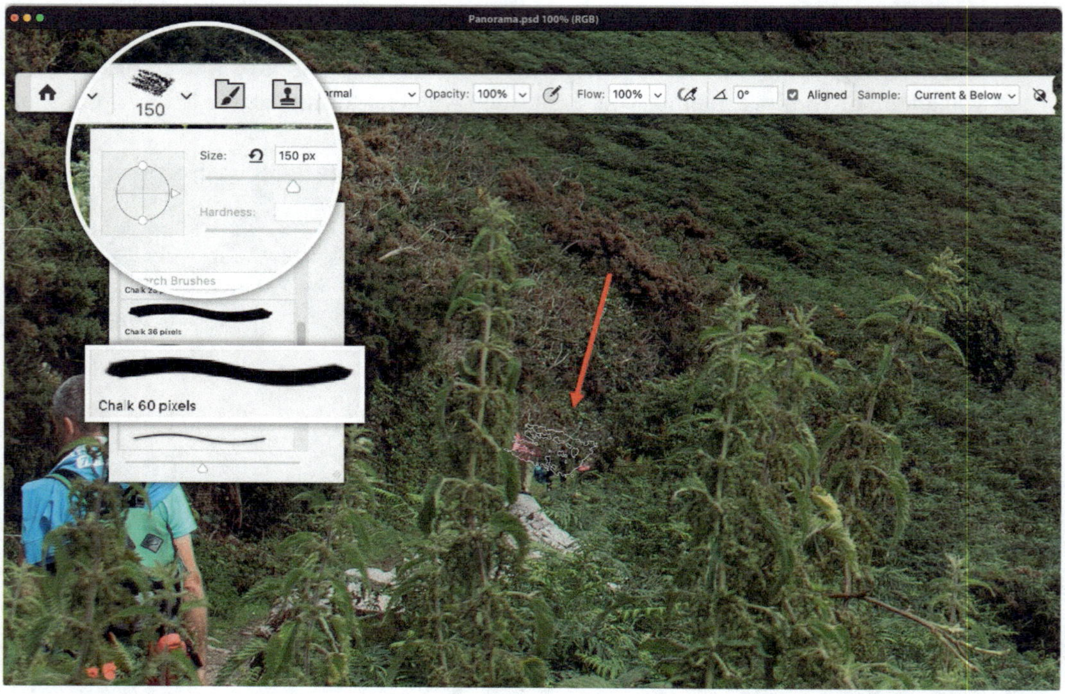

Figure 11.5: Using the Clone Stamp tool to conceal people in the foreground

10. Finally, if you navigate to the right-hand side of the image, you might recognize the sign; we removed it from a similar image in *Chapter 2*. If you want to practice further, try removing the sign in this panorama.
11. When done, go to **File** → **Save** and close the document.

In the first section of this chapter, we used **Photomerge** to combine six images, remove vignettes, and apply automatic layer masks to achieve a seamless panorama. We then applied our knowledge of the **Spot Healing Brush** tool and the **Clone Stamp** tool to remove tourists from the landscape. Next, we'll turn a photo into a collage.

Building collages with texture and paint

In this exercise, you are going to transform a portrait photo into a collage by turning the source image into defined bands of grayscale. These will then be turned into selections, within which will appear our collage artwork.

Posterizing the source photo

1. Go to **File** → **Open**, browse to the `11-Blend` folder, and select `LayeredMan.jpg`. Click **Open** when done.
2. Duplicate the background layer by dragging the layer onto the **New layer** icon at the bottom of the **Layers** panel. Rename the duplicated layer `Subject`. Turn off background layer visibility.
3. With the **Subject** layer active, right-click on the layer name and choose **Convert to Smart Object** from the list of options:

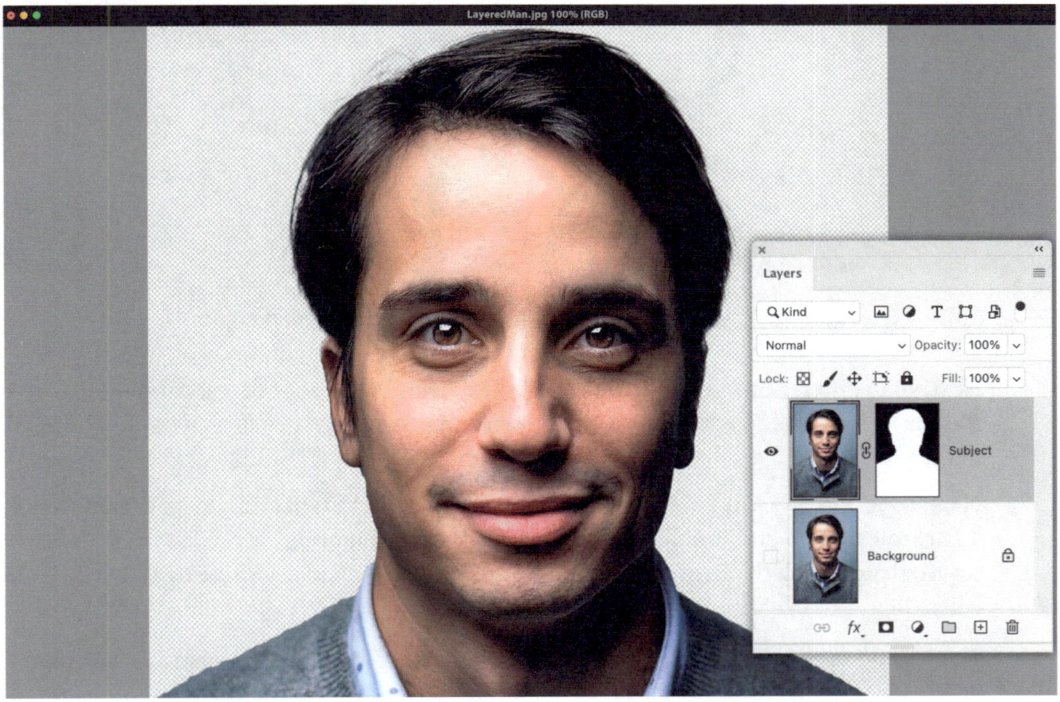

Figure 11.6: Duplicating the background layer and masking the subject

4. Switch to the **Magic Wand** tool and click on **Select Subject** from the **Options** bar. With the selection in place, click on the **Add a mask** button at the bottom of the **Layers** panel to hide the backdrop in the photo.

5. Go to **Image** → **Adjustment** → **Black & White**, and when a dialog appears, click **OK** to apply the default settings:

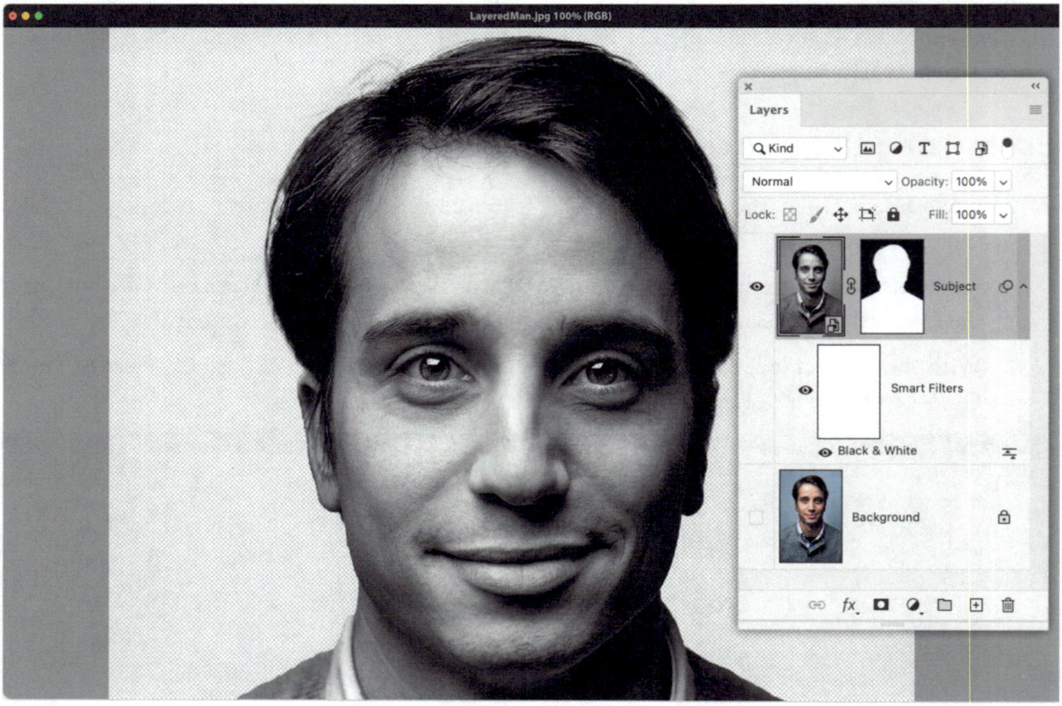

Figure 11.7: Applying a Black & White adjustment as a smart object

6. Next, go to **Filter** → **Sharpen** → **Unsharp Mask**. When a dialog appears, set **Amount** to `100%`, **Radius** to `1.0`, and **Threshold** to `10` before clicking **OK**. This will help emphasize the details in the photo.

7. Next, go to **Filter** → **Oil Paint**. When a dialog appears, set **Stylization** to `7`, **Cleanliness** to `4.3`, **Scale** to `0.7`, and **Bristle Detail** to `10`. Click on the **Lighting** checkbox to make it active, set **Angle** to match the light in the photo at around `133°`, and set **Shine** to `1.3`. Click **OK** when done.

   The settings used here will help make the source artwork feel less like a photo as we progress it. The idea here is the create effects of oil pit marks that are pronounced. Depending on the size of the image you apply this to and the nature of the content, you will need to adapt the settings each time to suit.

8. Next, go to **Image** → **Adjustment** → **Posterize**. This will reduce the number of colors – or, in this case, shades of gray – from a possible 256 to a new amount of our choosing. For this image, we don't need too many levels of grayscale to achieve the desired effect; as such, 4 levels will be sufficient. This will allow us to turn these bands of color into selectable regions more easily in the next exercise.

9. Go to **File** → **Save** and browse to the `11-Blend` folder, saving the file as a PSD. Keep the image open for the next exercise:

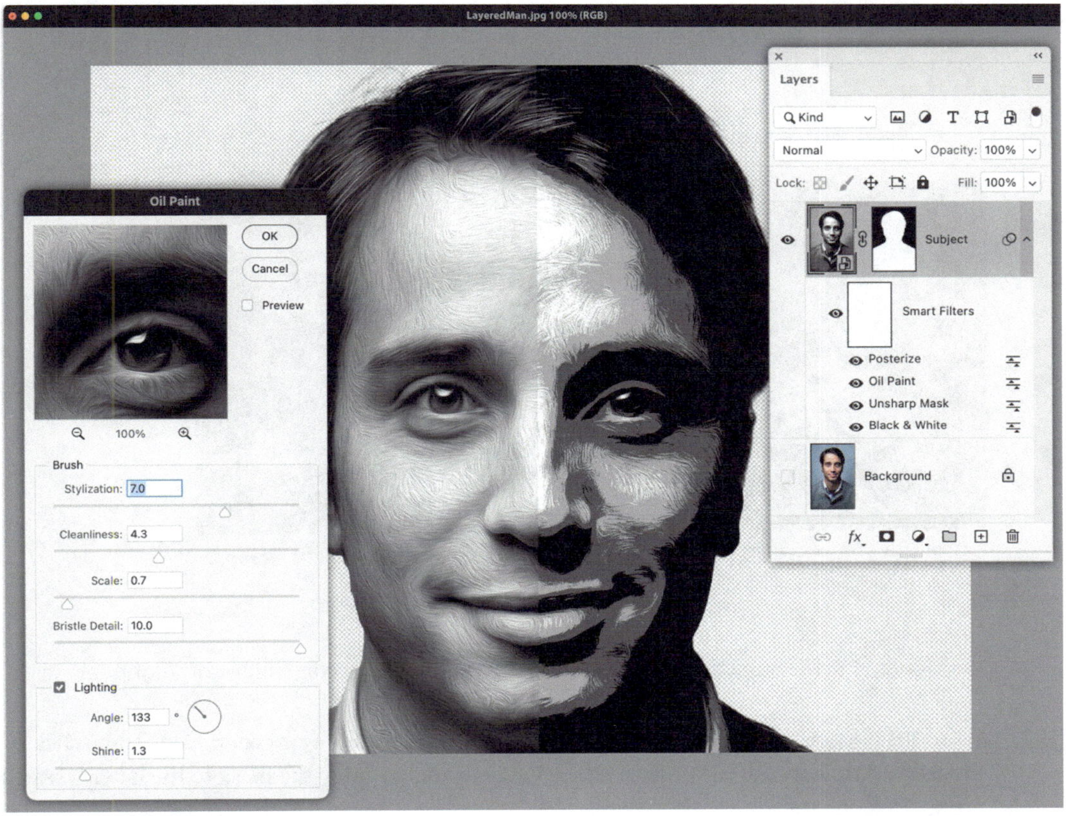

Figure 11.8: Photo with the Oil Paint filter applied (left) and after posterization (right)

Selecting and masking posterized regions

To do so, follow the steps given below:

1. With the **Subject Source** layer active, go to **Select** → **Color Range**.
2. When a dialog appears, hover your cursor over the black region of the subject's hair and left-click to define the selection. To ensure you select only black regions of the image, reduce the **Fuzziness** slider to around `25%`. A preview of the selected pixels will be shown as white in the dialog's preview thumbnail. Click **OK** when done to generate the selection:

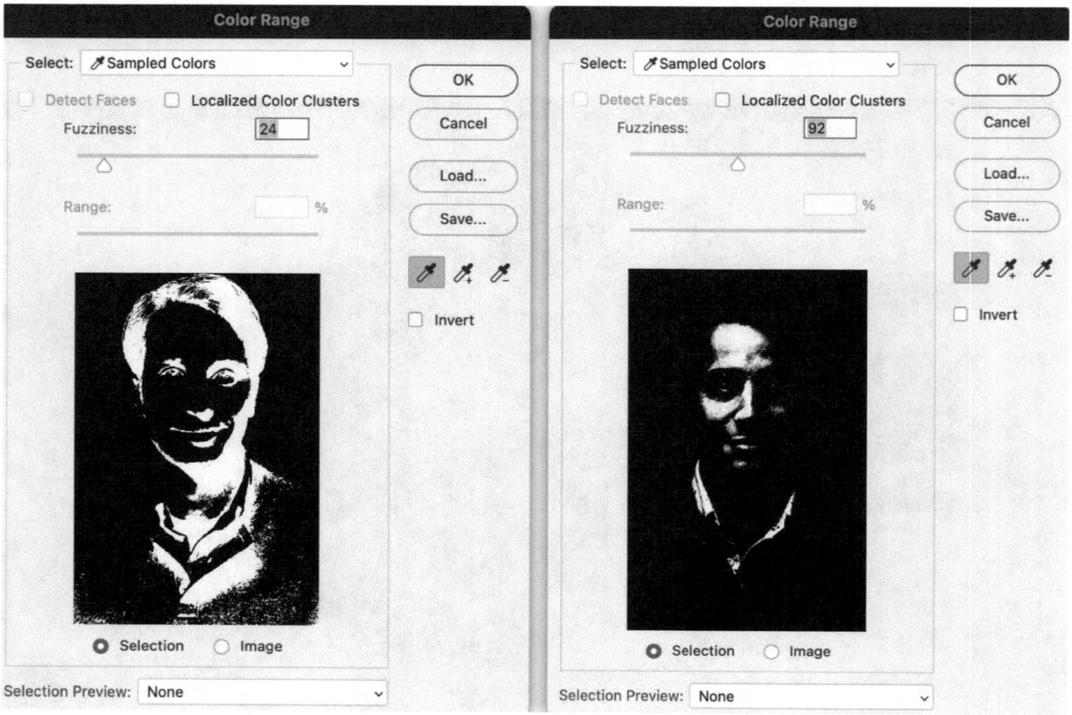

Figure 11.9: First selecting shadow details (left) and then selecting highlights (right)

3. Go to the bottom of the **Layers** panel and click on the **Create a new group** icon. Then, click on the **Add a mask** icon at the bottom of the **Layers** panel to apply the mask to the newly created group. Rename the group `Shadows`.
4. With the **Subject Source** layer active, go to **Select** → **Color Range** and repeat the same technique as before, but this time select the dark gray band of color in the image and adjust the **Fuzziness** slider to suit. In this example, I chose `16`.
5. Select the layer group named **Black** and then click on the **Create a new group** icon to add a new group at the top of the stack. Then, click on the **Add a mask** icon at the bottom of the **Layers** panel to apply the mask to the second group. Rename the group `Dark Gray`.
6. Using the techniques in this exercise, create two more layer groups for light gray and white. You should now have four layer groups named **Shadows**, **Dark Gray**, **Light Gray**, and **Highlights**. To help identify each part, color code the **Shadows** layer group blue, the **Dark Gray** group green, the **Light Gray** group orange, and the **Highlights** group red.
7. Hover your cursor over the **Subject** layer mask thumbnail, hold *Ctrl* (Windows) or *Cmd* (macOS), and left-click to load the mask as a selection. Left-click on the **Create a new group** icon. Then, click on the **Add a mask** icon at the bottom of the **Layers** panel to apply the mask to the newly created group. Rename the group `ALL`.

8. Drag the newly created layer group to the top of the layer stack. Left-click on the layer group named **Highlights**, then press *Shift* and left-click on the layer group named **Shadows** to make all four layer groups active. Then, drag them into the layer group called **ALL**. This will ensure the edges of the subject are neat and tidy once you add textures to them:

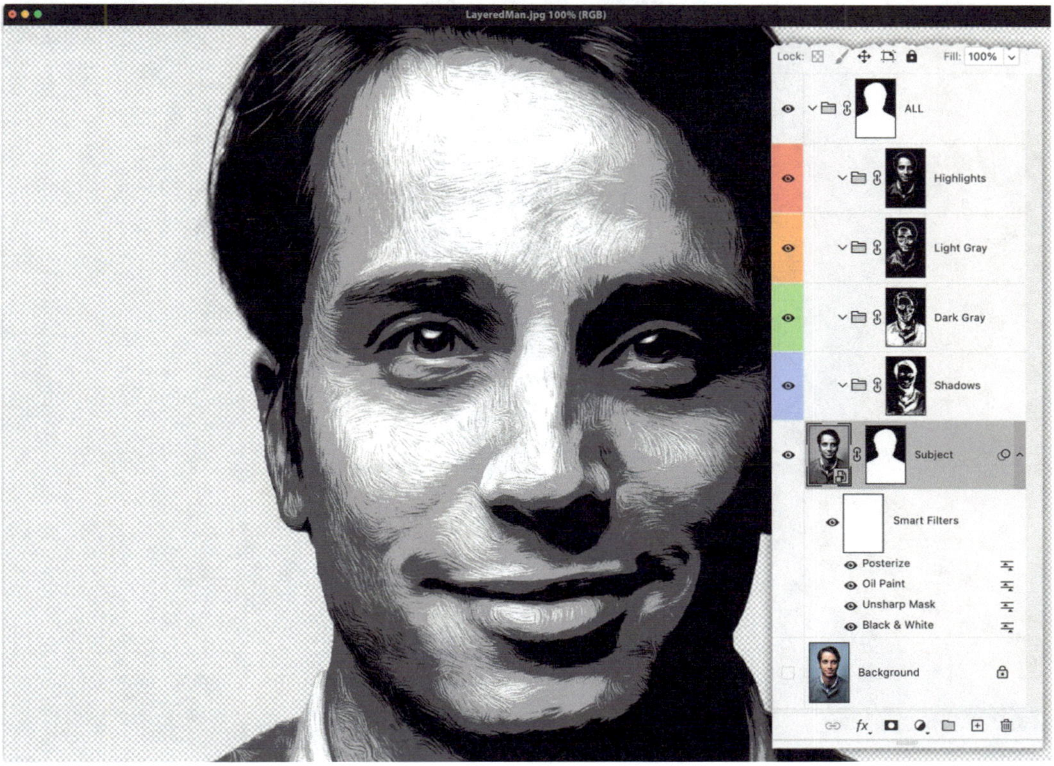

Figure 11.10: From each selection, creating a layer group with an assigned layer mask

Adding texture and paint to the posterized sections

To do so, follow the steps given below:

1. Click on the **Background** layer in the **Layers** panel to make it active. Then, click on the **Create new fill or adjustment layer** icon at the bottom of the **Layers** panel and select **Solid Color** from the list. When the **Color Picker** appears, enter `fcdc00` into the **Hexadecimal** field to create a vivid yellow.

2. Next, go to **File** → **Place Embedded**, browse to the `11-Blend` folder, select `Texture-01.jpg`, then click **Open**. When the image appears, press *Enter* to complete the import. Change the layer **Blend** mode to **Color Burn**:

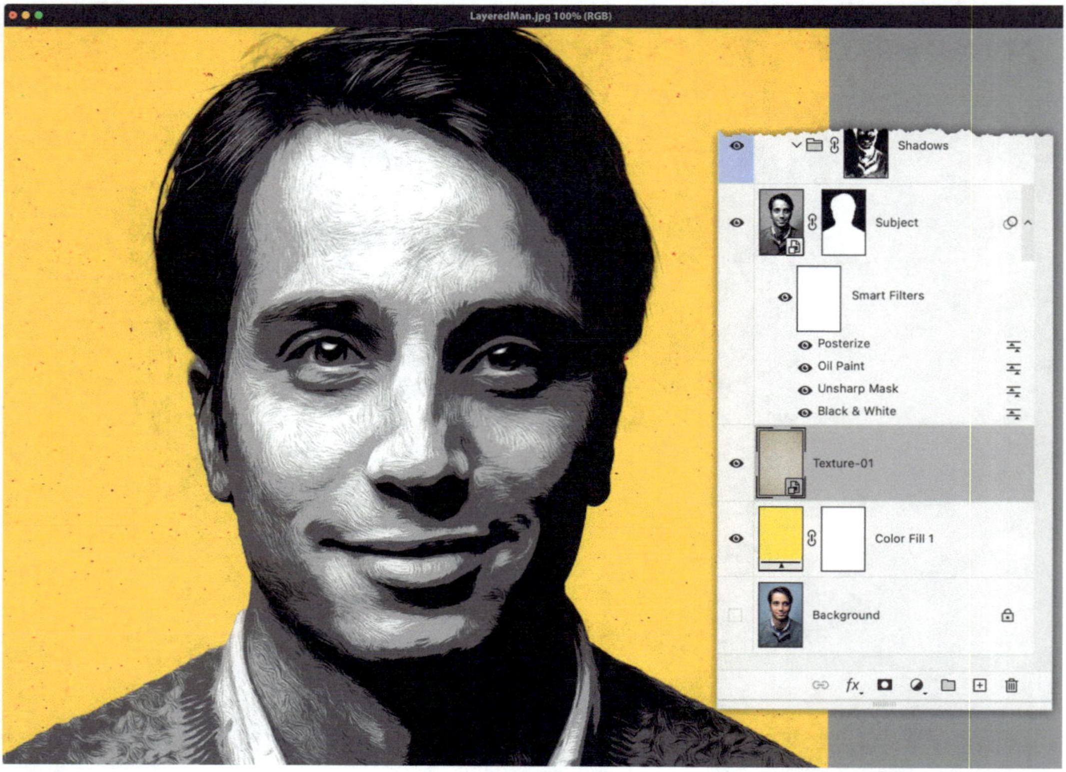

Figure 11.11: Adding a color fill layer and then overlaying the paint spatter texture

3. Left-click on the **Dark Gray** layer group, then go to **File** → **Place Embedded**, browse to the `11-Blend` folder, select `Paint-01.jpg`, and then click **Open**. When an image appears, press *Enter* to complete the import.
4. Ensure the imported artwork is added to the **Dark Gray** layer group by dragging the layer in the **Layers** panel onto the **Dark Gray** layer group folder icon. Switch to the **Move** tool from the **Tools** panel and drag the **Paint-01** layer into a position so that it covers the man:

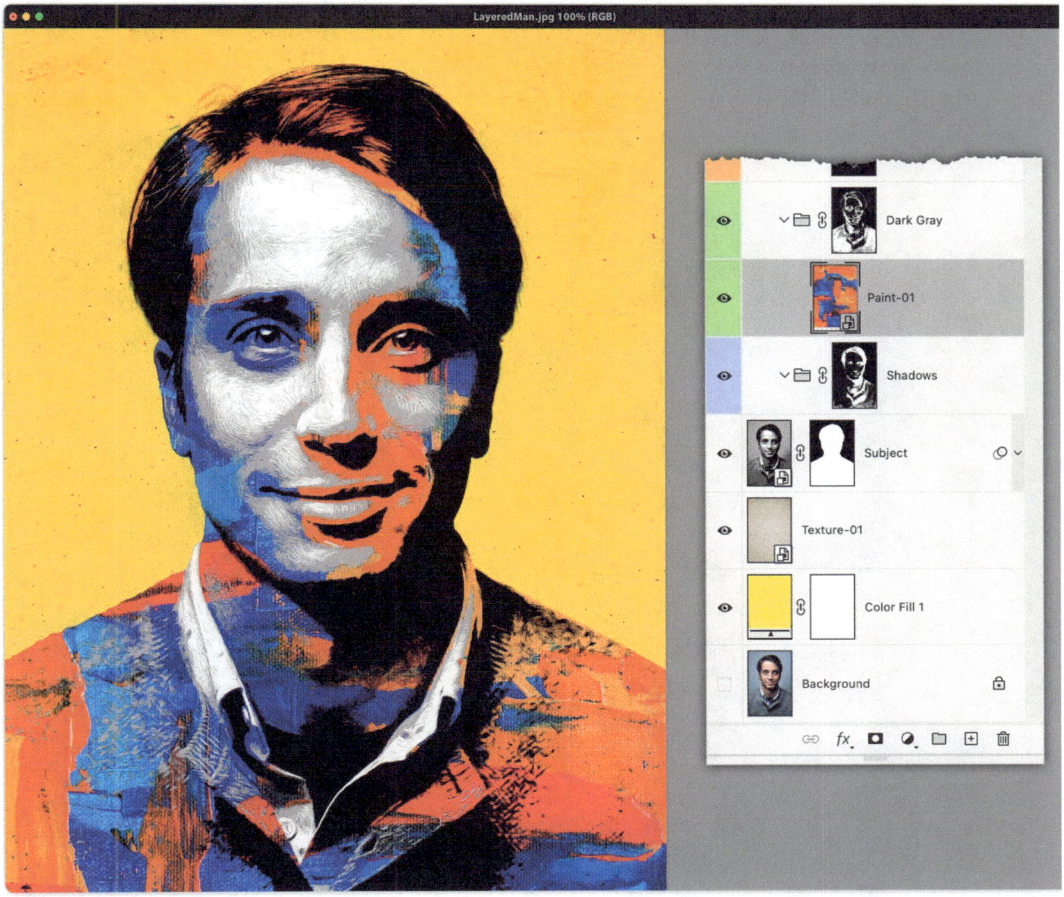

Figure 11.12: Adding the first paint sample to the Dark Gray layer group

5. Left-click on the **Shadows** layer group and repeat the same technique to import `Paint-02.jpg` from the `11-Blend` folder. Ensure the **Scale** value of the layer is `100%`, and reposition the artwork to cover the subject. Drag the imported artwork onto the **Shadow** layer group icon to ensure it is added to the group.

6. With the **Paint-02** layer still active, go to **File** → **Place Embedded**, browse to the `11-Blend` folder, select `Paint-03.jpg`, then click **Open**. Change **Blend** mode to **Multiply**. This will emphasize dark tones:

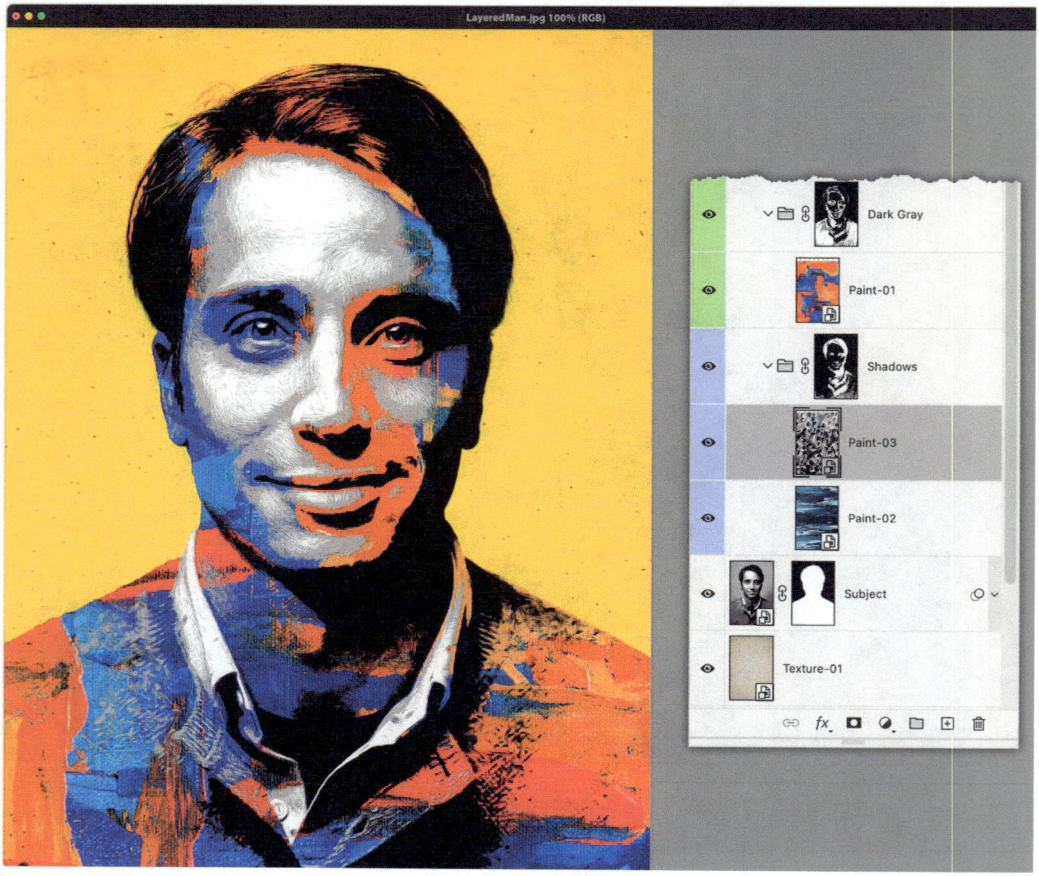

Figure 11.13: Adding two paint images to the Shadows layer group

7. Left-click on the **Light Gray** layer group, go to **File** → **Place Embedded**, browse to the `11-Blend` folder, select `Texture-02.jpg`, then click **Open**. Ensure the **Scale** value of the layer is `100%`, and reposition the artwork to your own preference. Press *Enter* to complete the import.
8. Ensure the imported artwork is added to the **Light Gray** layer group by dragging the layer in the **Layers** panel onto the **Light Gray** layer group folder icon.

9. Left-click on the **Highlights** layer group, go to **File** → **Place Embedded**, browse to the `11-Blend` folder, select `Paint-05.jpg`, then click **Open**. Ensure the **Scale** value of the layer is `65%`, and reposition the artwork so that it covers all white regions of the artwork. Press *Enter* to apply the edits:

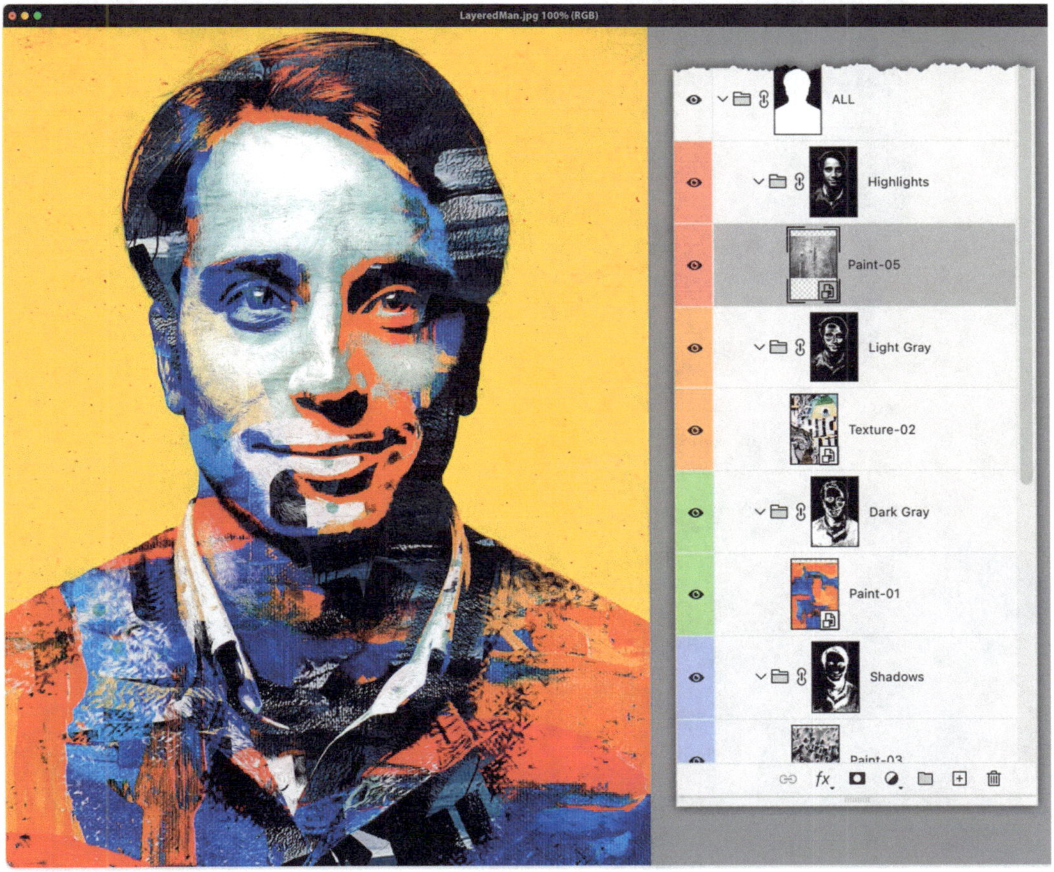

Figure 11.14: Adding the distressed poster photo to the Light Gray layer group

10. Ensure the imported artwork is added to the **Highlights** layer group by dragging the layer in the **Layers** panel onto the **Highlights** layer group folder icon.
11. Left-click on the **Paint-01** layer, go to **File** → **Place Embedded**, browse to the `11-Blend` folder, select `Paint-04.jpg`, then click **Open**.
12. Ensure the **Scale** value of the layer is `60%`, set the **Angle** to `110°`, and reposition the artwork so that it covers the lower section of the image only, with a small portion overlapping the subject's chin. Press *Enter* to apply the edits.

13. Experiment with **Blend** mode to see which is your favorite. I chose **Overlay**, but you can change the appearance drastically with modes such as **Multiply**. Save the document when done:

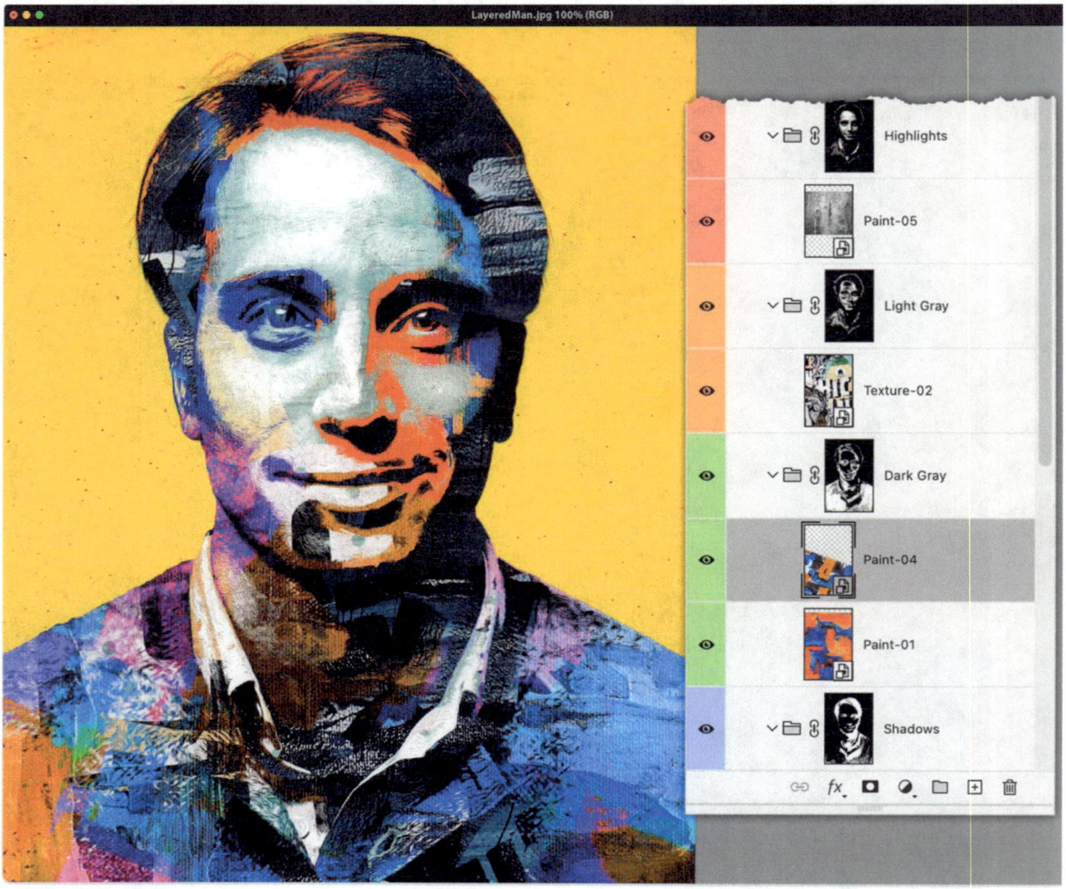

Figure 11.15: The completed collage

In this section, we created accurate selections with the help of **Select Subject**, applied oil-painting brush-stroke effects, and posterized artwork to form four regions: highlights, lighter and darker midtones, and shadows. We turned each region into a selection that we then filled with paint and texture samples to create a colorful collage effect. All of these can be re-edited, replaced, and transformed in a nondestructive workflow. Next, we will take a look at double-exposure effects.

Creating double-exposure compositions

A double exposure was originally achieved in photography by exposing the same frame of film several times to blend different images on a single negative.

Blending unrelated images

You will first create an accurate selection and mask the street image in the shape of the woman's body. Follow these steps:

1. Go to **File** → **Open**, browse to the `11-Blend` folder, select `Exposure-Subject.jpg`, and click on **Open**.
2. Then, go to **File** → **Place Linked**, browse to the `11-Blend` folder, select `Exposure-Street.jpg`, and click on **Place**.
3. When the artwork appears, click on the **Commit** button in the **Options** bar. Turn off the **Exposure-Street** layer visibility and left-click on the **Background** layer in the **Layers** panel to make it active:

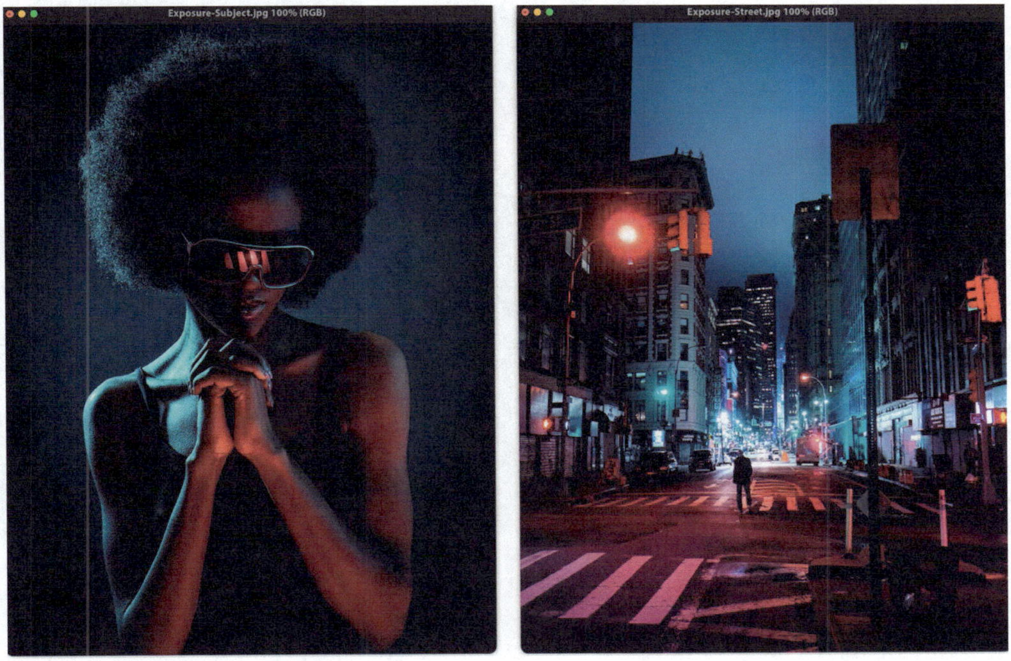

Figure 11.16: The source images will be combined to form a double-exposure effect

4. Press the *W* key to switch to any one of the selection tools, either the **Magic Wand** tool, **Quick Selection** tool, or **Object Selection** tool. From the **Options** bar, left-click on the **Select Subject** button to create a selection of the woman.
5. Next, left-click on the **Exposure-Street** layer to make it active, even though it is hidden, then click on the **Create a new group** icon at the bottom of the **Layers** panel. Ensure the new group is active in the **Layers** panel before clicking on the **Add a mask** icon at the bottom of the **Layers** panel. The selection will now be assigned to the layer group.

6. Rename the layer group `Street`, and then drag the **Exposure-Street** layer into the layer group. In the example shown, the layer group was also color-coded red for clarity by right-clicking on the visibility icon adjacent to the **Exposure-Street** layer:

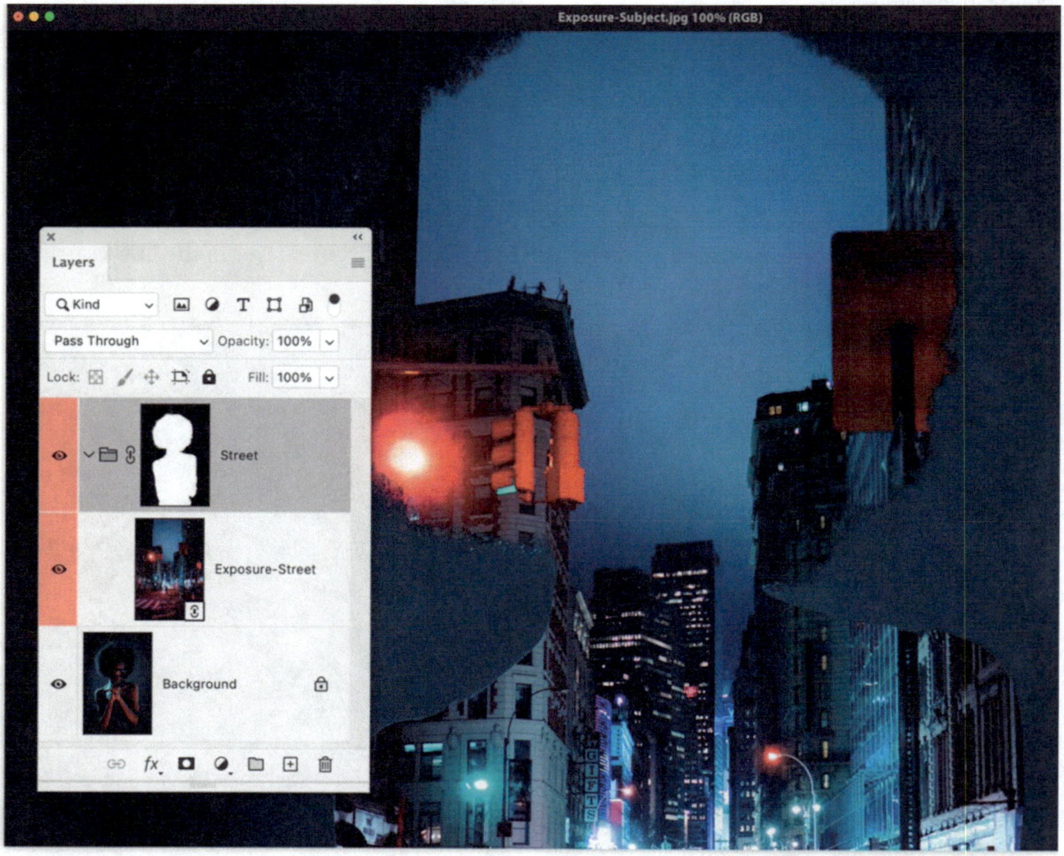

Figure 11.17: Street photo masked in front of the subject

7. Turn on the visibility for the **Exposure-Street** layer. You should now see that the street image is masked. By adding the street image to a layer group with an assigned mask that is the same shape as the woman's silhouette, we can apply a second layer mask, this time to the **Exposure-Street** layer, and edit it without affecting the first mask.
8. Go to **Select** → **Reselect**; this will load the previously created selection of the woman. Then, left-click on the **Background** layer in the **Layers** panel and choose **Layer** → **New** → **Layer via Copy**.
9. When the pasted layer appears above the background in the **Layers** panel, rename it **Overlay**, and drag the layer to the top of the layer stack:

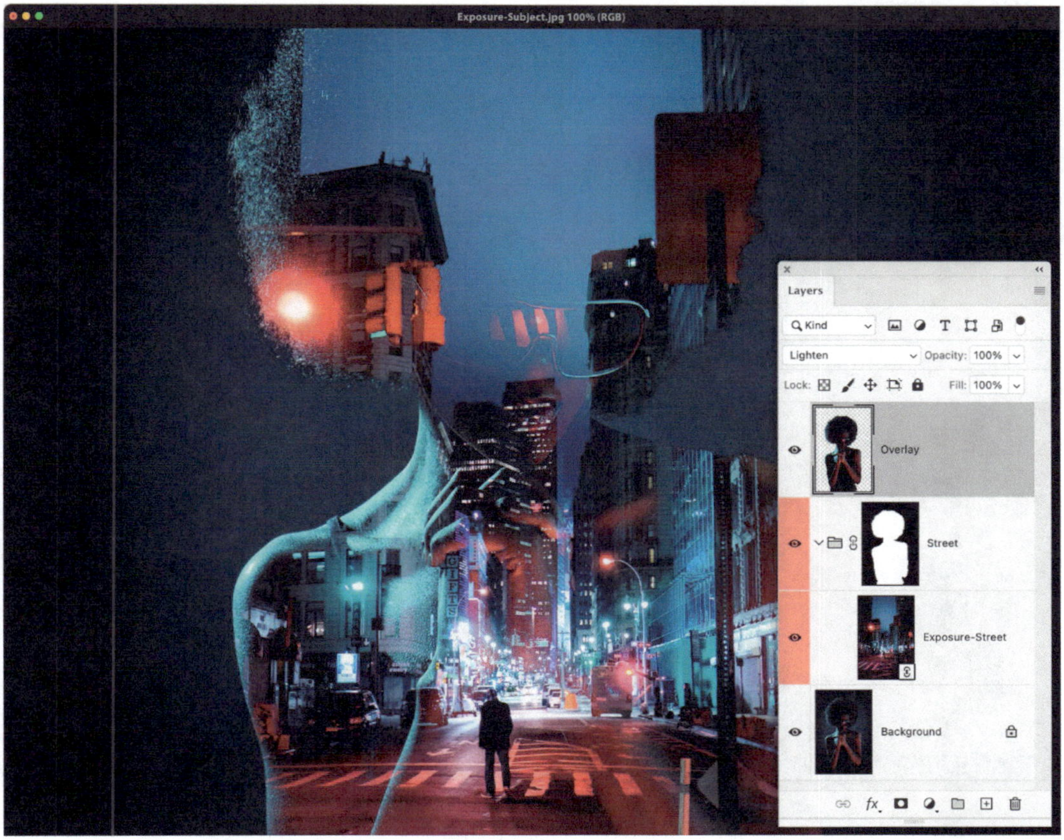

Figure 11.18: Adding a duplicate of the background layer subject to restore vital details

10. Left-click on the **Exposure-Street** layer to make it active, and then click on the **Add a layer mask** icon at the bottom of the **Layers** panel.
11. Switch to the **Brush** tool by pressing the *B* key. In the **Options** bar, click on the **Brush Tip** preset menu and choose the **Soft Round** brush tip:

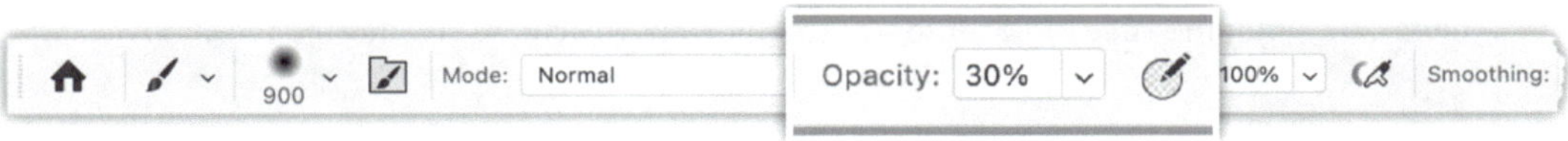

Figure 11.19: The brush settings

12. Set the brush **Size** value to `900 px` and the **Opacity** value to `30%` from the **Options** bar. Press the *D* key to reset the **Foreground** and **Background** colors, and then press the *X* key to switch them so that black is the active color to paint with.

13. Hover your cursor over the region where the woman's face is and drag across it with the **Brush** tool to gradually fade the street image:

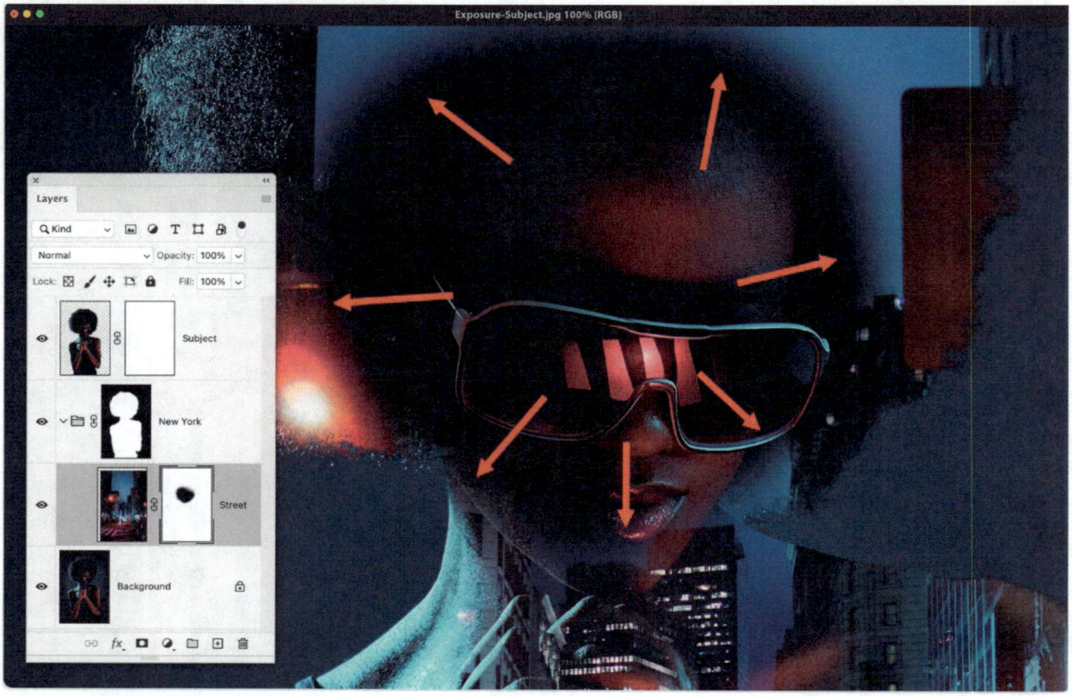

Figure 11.20: Masking the street layer where it covers the woman's face

14. Work from the outside edge of the woman's hair, toward the face, concealing the street image. Ensure that not all parts of the street layer are removed from the top and right-hand side of the woman's hair. You can leave some of the faint glow of the streetlights around the left-hand-side edges of the hair for dramatic effect if you wish.
15. Reduce the **Size** value of the brush tip to `200 px` and then conceal the street image around the region of the woman's chin by painting black in that region with the **Brush** tool. A simple, soft fade along the edge of the chin will be sufficient to achieve the desired look:

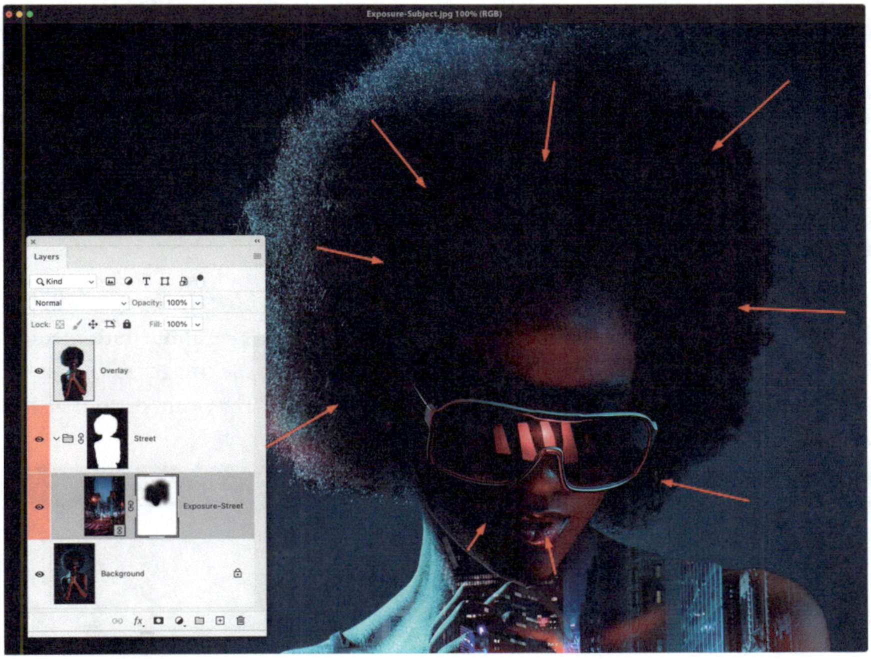

Figure 11.21: Using the Brush tool, concealing sections around the woman's face and hair

16. Once the masking is complete, go to **File** → **Save** and browse to the `11-Blend` folder, saving the image as a PSD with the name `SeeingDouble`. Then, close the document when done:

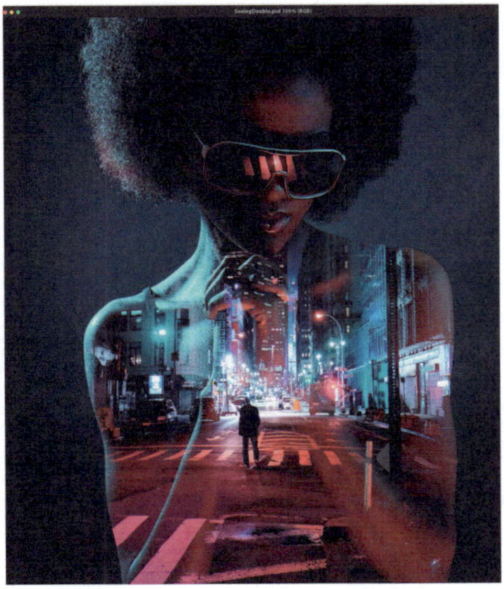

Figure 11.22: The completed image

Blending two exposures of the same image

We first need to merge two separate files using a Photoshop script that creates copies of the documents, combining them in a new file. Follow these steps:

1. Go to **File** → **Scripts** → **Load files into stack**, browse to the `11-Blend` folder, and select `01-Hands.jpg` and `02-Face.jpg`. Leave all checkboxes deactivated and then click on **OK** when done.

   The order of the images listed in the **Load Layers** dialog is how the images will be layered in Photoshop. In this case, we needed the image of the subject's face at the bottom and the shot of the hands in front of the face at the top of the stack. Hence, the images are numbered `01` and `02` so that Photoshop imports them in the order required. They can, of course, be reordered in Photoshop as well:

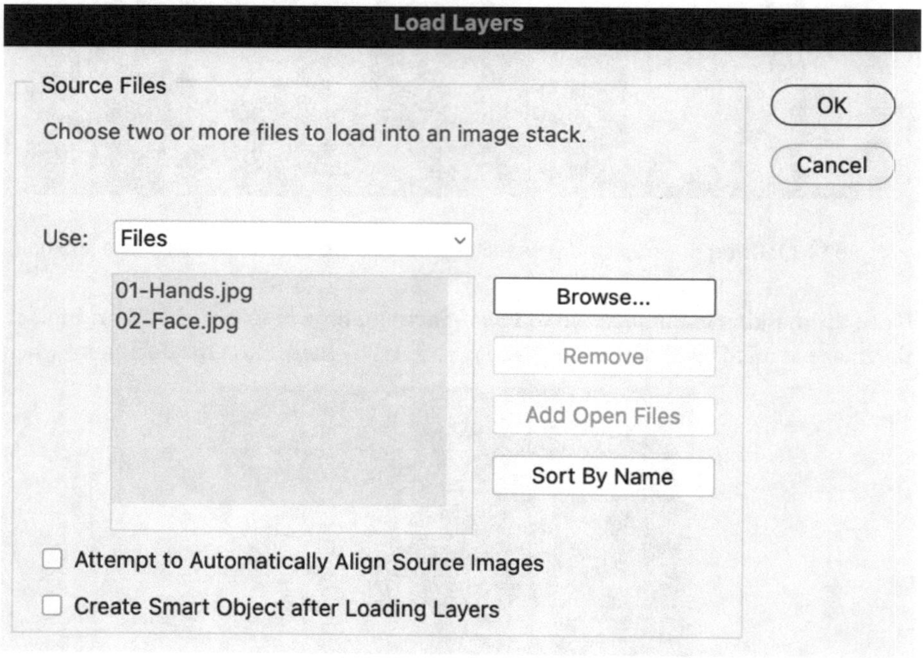

Figure 11.23: Importing both JPG files into a single-layer stack

2. Left-click on the `01-Hands.jpg` layer in the **Layers** panel to make it active. Then, click on the **Add a mask** icon at the bottom of the **Layers** panel to add an empty layer mask, filled with white.

3. Press the *D* key to reset the **Foreground** and **Background** colors back to black and white, then press the *X* key to switch them so that black is the active color to paint with:

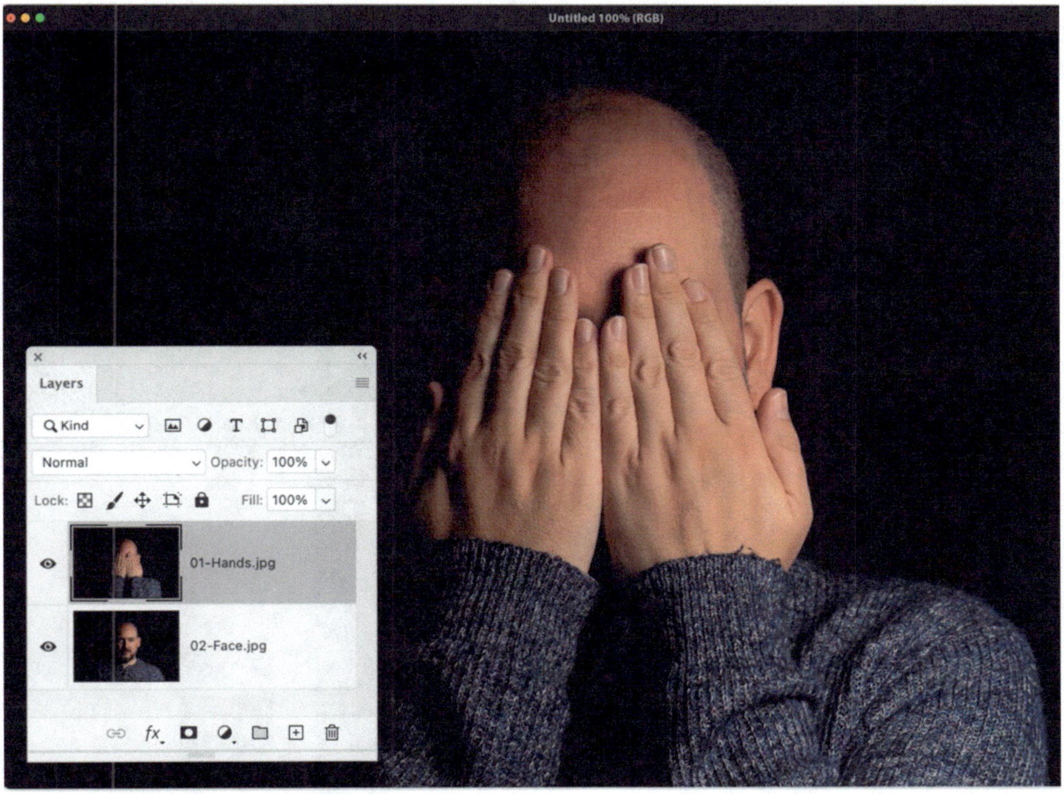

Figure 11.24: The imported images as layers in the stack

4. Switch to the **Brush** tool by pressing the *B* key. In the **Options** bar, click on the **Brush Tip** preset menu and choose the **Soft Round** brush tip:

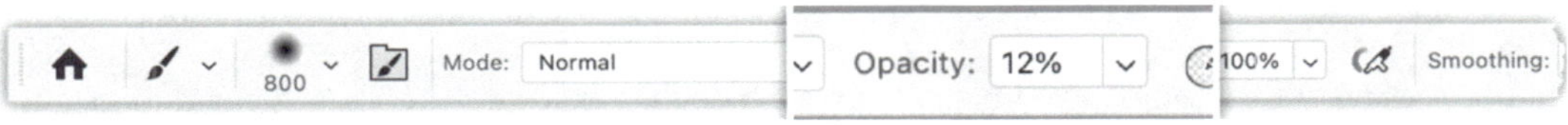

Figure 11.25: The brush settings

5. Set the brush **Size** value to `800 px` and the **Opacity** value to `12%` from the **Options** bar. With this technique, we need to fade the hands very subtly to achieve the desired result, so having the **Opacity** value set low will help restrain the brush marks.

6. Hover the **Brush** tool over the region where the right eye should be and left-click repeatedly, which should make them appear gradually. You will also need to ensure that you leave enough of the hands and fingers visible. You can press *X* to switch the **Foreground** and **Background** colors, painting white to reveal the hands and fingers if you go too far with your masking.
7. Repeat the same technique by hovering the **Brush** tool over the region where the left eye should be and left-click repeatedly to reveal it:

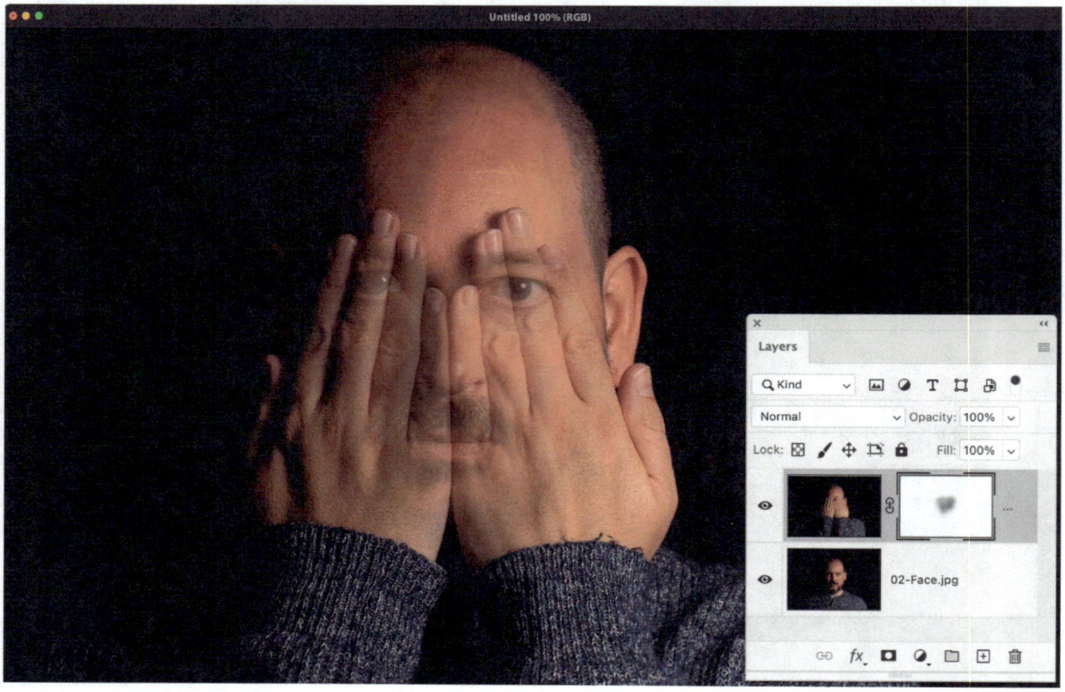

Figure 11.26: The completed image, revealing the face through the hands

8. Once the masking is complete, go to **File** → **Save** and browse to the `11-Blend` folder, saving the image as a PSD with the name `Visions`. Then, close the document when done.

In this section, we combined two images to create a double-exposure effect using blend modes and layer masks. The first mask was applied to a layer group, which allowed us to set an edge for the street layer around the silhouette of the woman's hair and body. The second mask was applied to a specific layer to hide the parts of the street image that obscured the woman's face. In the next section, we will combine five photos to overcome challenging lighting conditions with an HDR image.

Working with HDR images

Single-shot photos with a digital camera can sometimes lack the detail required to show the full luminance range, resulting in deep black shadow areas or blown-out white highlights. HDR images preserve light data closer to that perceived by the human eye. By combining several shots at different bracketed F-stops (exposures), you can create 32-bit images to keep incredible detail in your photographs.

Advice for shooting HDR source images

Although a growing number of DSLRs offer an HDR feature that captures several shots automatically, many cameras still require you to generate an HDR image by taking several shots of the same scene at different exposures, each capturing different light information. The challenge with this is movement, called ghosting, between each shot. To give yourself the best chance of capturing several shots and with minimal ghosting, use a tripod. Keep the aperture setting constant throughout each shot or you will risk altering the depth of field. Use a remote cord, as even pressing the capture button for each shot will move the camera.

Installing Adobe Bridge

Earlier in this chapter, I mentioned that Adobe Bridge will be needed for the HDR exercises. While this isn't strictly accurate, utilizing Adobe Bridge for combining and editing HDR images or digital negatives certainly does make life easier. Here's how to use it:

1. To check if you have **Bridge** installed, go to **File** → **Open with Bridge**. If **Bridge** is not installed, the **Creative Cloud** desktop application will appear and display all the installed apps, along with other apps that you can choose to install, including **Bridge**.
2. Click on the **Install** button adjacent to **Bridge** to begin the process. **Bridge** will transfer to the bit at the top of the dialog, alongside your installed applications and show the progress of the installation:

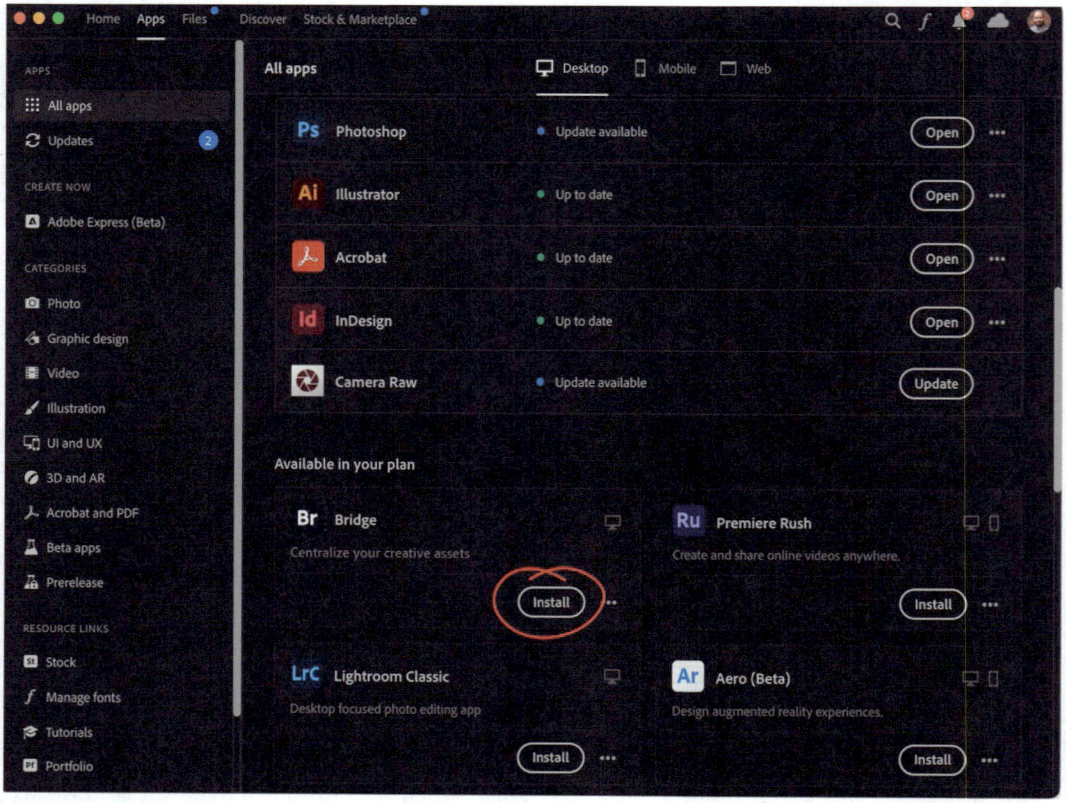

Figure 11.27: Installing Bridge from the Creative Cloud desktop application

3. Once the installation is complete, you can click on the **Open** button in the **Creative Cloud** desktop application dialog. **Bridge** should now appear after a couple of minutes. If you are prompted to install components from other Adobe applications such as **Photoshop**, choose **Yes**.

You may need to be patient as **Bridge** connects to other Adobe applications on the first occasion it is launched. If you intend to use the **Open in Bridge** command found in Photoshop, this may not work until you perform a restart of your computer. Once restarted, **Bridge** should connect accordingly to **Photoshop**.

Creating an HDR image with HDR Pro

You will combine five photos to create a composite of an architectural interior where lighting conditions mean that no one image can capture all the light from shadows to highlights. Here's how to do it:

1. With **Bridge** open and active, click on the **Folder** panel name, in the upper left-hand side of the interface, to display your locally connected drives. The **Folder** panel acts just like a file browser, allowing you to navigate to existing folders. Browse to the `11-Blend` folder. In this example, the project files for this book are stored on my desktop:

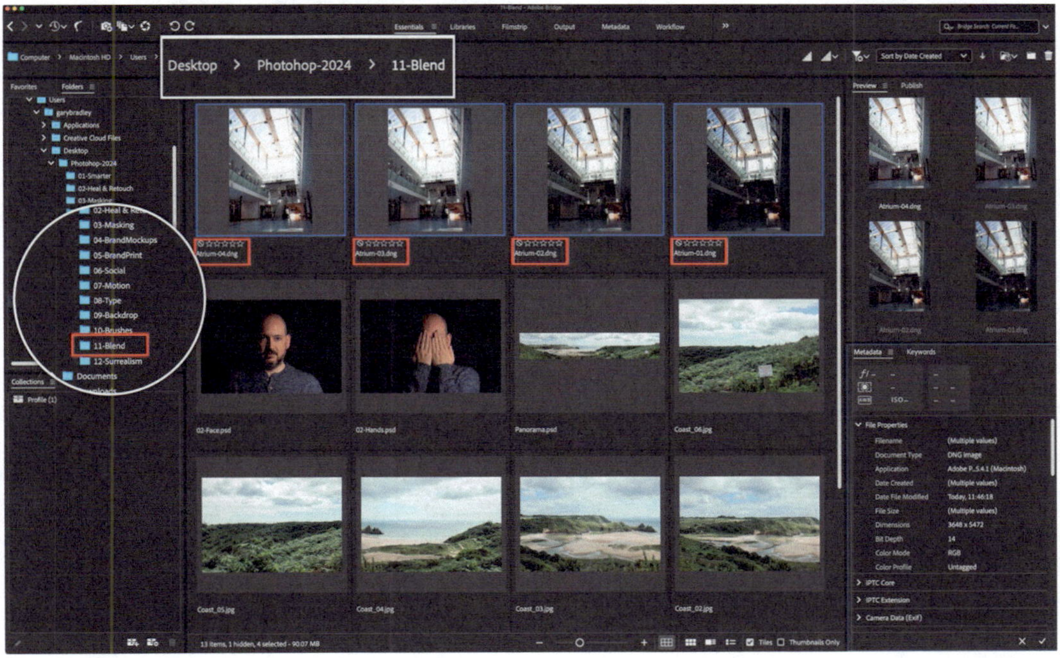

Figure 11.28: Installing Bridge from the Creative Cloud desktop application

2. Once you left-click on the `11-Blend` folder from the **Folder** panel, you will then see the files displayed in the central portion of **Bridge**, called the **Content** panel, the nearest thing to an image window that you would see in Bridge. The **Content** panel is where you interact with your files. Left-click on `Atrium-01.dng` and then press *Shift* and left-click on other atrium images, four in total.

3. This will place a highlight color around each of the active image's thumbnails. Next, right-click on one of the highlighted thumbnails, and from the context menu, choose **Open with Camera Raw**:

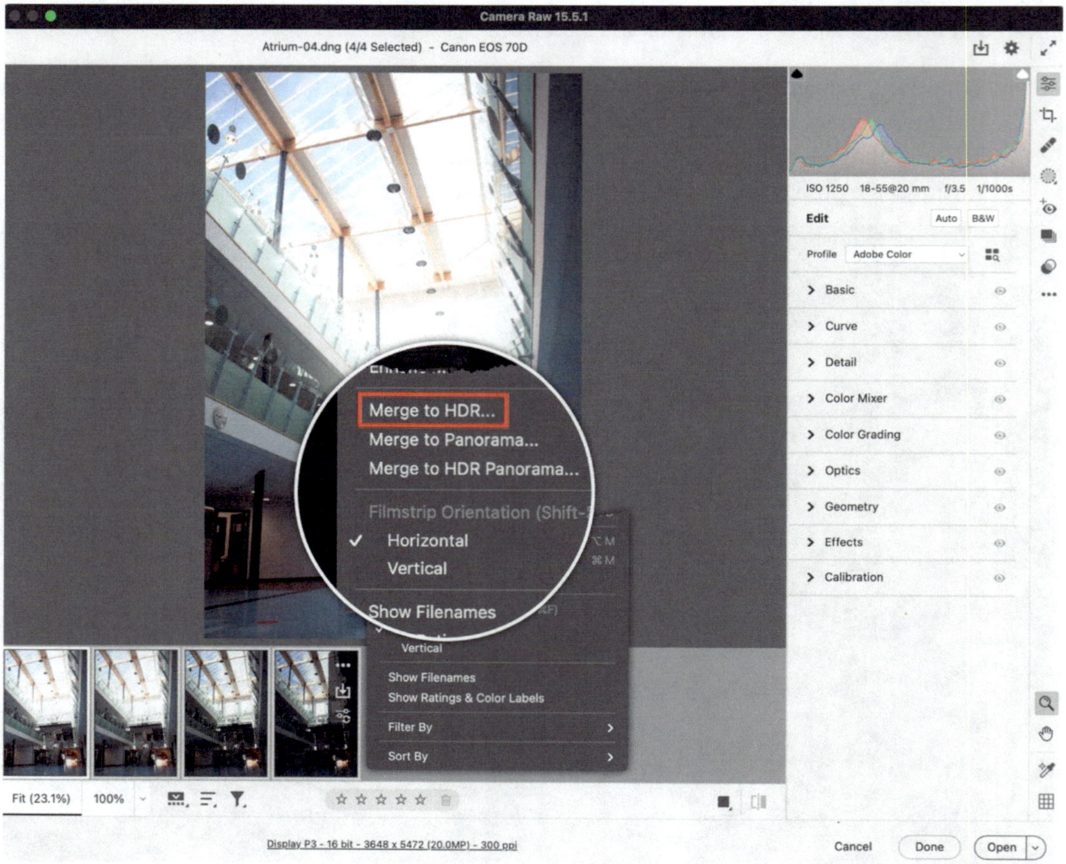

Figure 11.29: The five atrium images open in Camera Raw

4. The images will then appear in **Camera Raw**, shown at the bottom of the interface in the filmstrip, one of which will be shown in the image window. The images now need to be combined into a HDR image.

5. Next you will again need to select all of the photos. Left-click on the far left-hand thumbnail to make it active, then press *Shift* and left-click on the far right-hand thumbnail to select all four images. Hover your cursor over one of the thumbnails to reveal a rollover menu, containing three dots, then click on it and choose **Merge to HDR...**:

6. When the **HDR Pro** dialog appears, turn on the **Align Images** and **Apply Auto Settings** checkboxes and set the **Deghost** dropdown to **Off**. Then, click on the **Merge...** button, at the bottom right-hand side of the dialog.

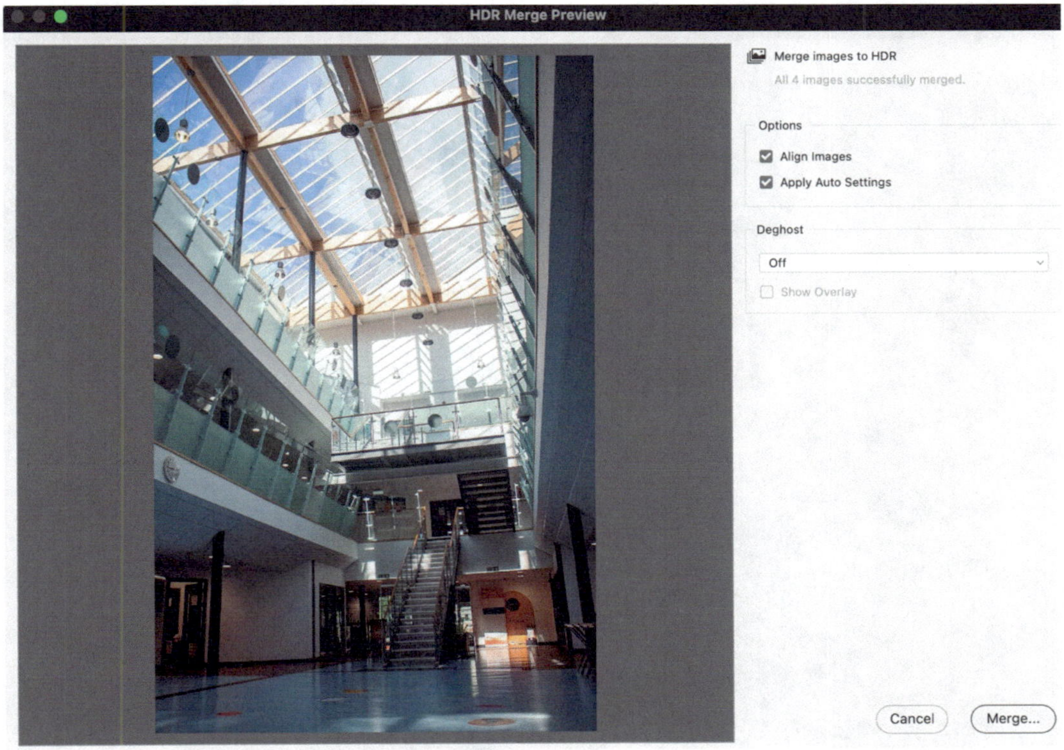

Figure 11.30: The HDR Merge Preview dialog

7. You will then be prompted to save the image as **HDR** in the Digital Negative format (DNG). Save it in the `11-Blend` folder as `Atrium-HDR`.
8. Once the file has been saved, you will be taken back to the **Camera Raw** interface. Click on the **Auto** button (*shown as A in Figure 11.31*) to apply basic color and tonal edits to the image. However, it's likely that you will need to fine-tune the settings further:
9. Click on the **Basic** toggle (*shown as B in Figure 11.31*) to expand the settings. Set **Exposure** to `+0.03`, **Contrast** to `+7`, **Highlights** to `-85`, **Shadows** to `+75`, **Whites** to `+10`, and **Blacks** to `-24`.
10. Leave the **Texture**, **Clarity**, and **Dehaze** sliders set to `0`. Then, set **Vibrance** to `+15` to boost the warmth of the wood beams in the roof, and boost the color intensity slightly by setting **Saturation** to `+3`.

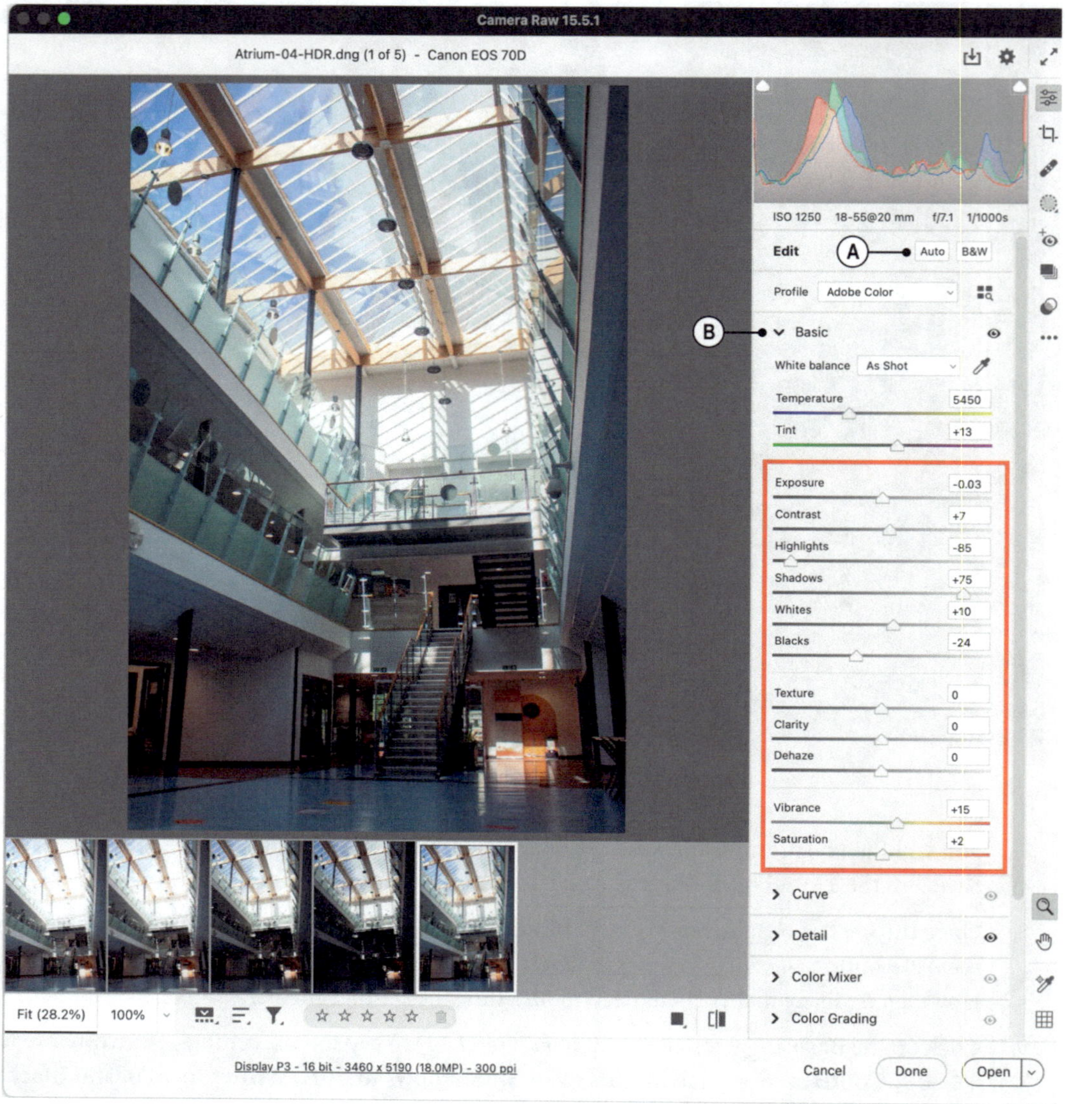

Figure 11.31: The HDR Merge Preview dialog

11. Click on the **Detail** toggle (*shown as C in Figure 11.32*) to expand the settings to reveal sliders for editing sharpening. Set **Sharpening** to `79`. To preview the sharpening in grayscale, hold *Alt* (Windows) or *Option* (macOS) as you drag the slider to the right-hand side.
12. Leave the **Radius** slider set to its default of `1.0`. Then, set the **Details** slider to `50` by again holding *Alt*/*Option* and dragging the slider to the right-hand side to visualize the edit in grayscale.

13. Next, reduce the sharpening effect in regions of low detail by holding *Alt* (Windows) or *Option* (macOS) and dragging the **Masking** slider to `81`. We need edge details such as the handrails to be sharper but want to avoid adding noise to the image on flat surfaces such as walls.

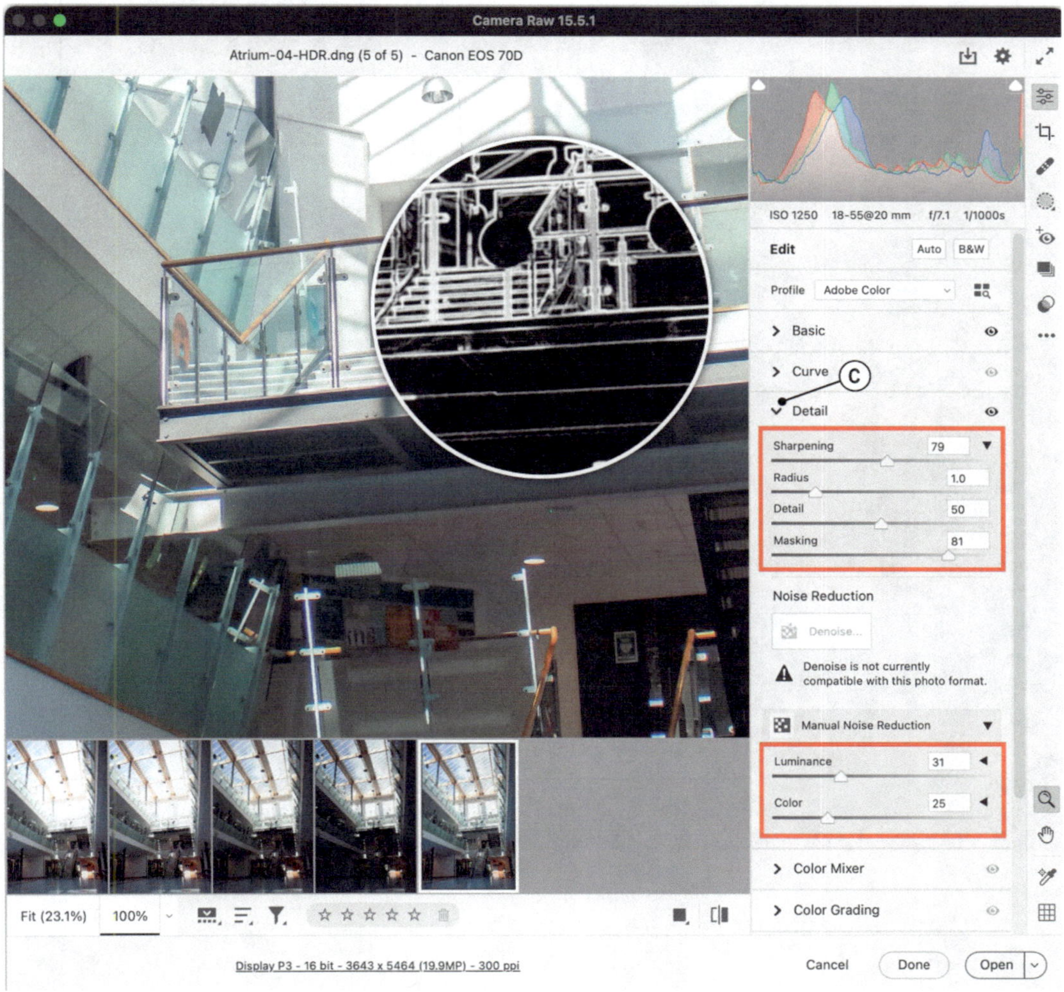

Figure 11.32: Adjust the sharpening options

14. Finally, to reduce the grainy effect of noise that is synonymous with low lighting conditions, expand **Manual Noise Reduction** and set **Luminance** to `31` and **Color** to `25`. This should remove any grayscale noise (**Luminance**) and random colored noise (**Color**) that was present in the image.

15. Next, click on the **Crop Tool** icon (shown as *A* in *Figure 11.33*), located on the right-hand side of the interface. Once the options appear, click on the **Straighten Tool** icon (*B*):

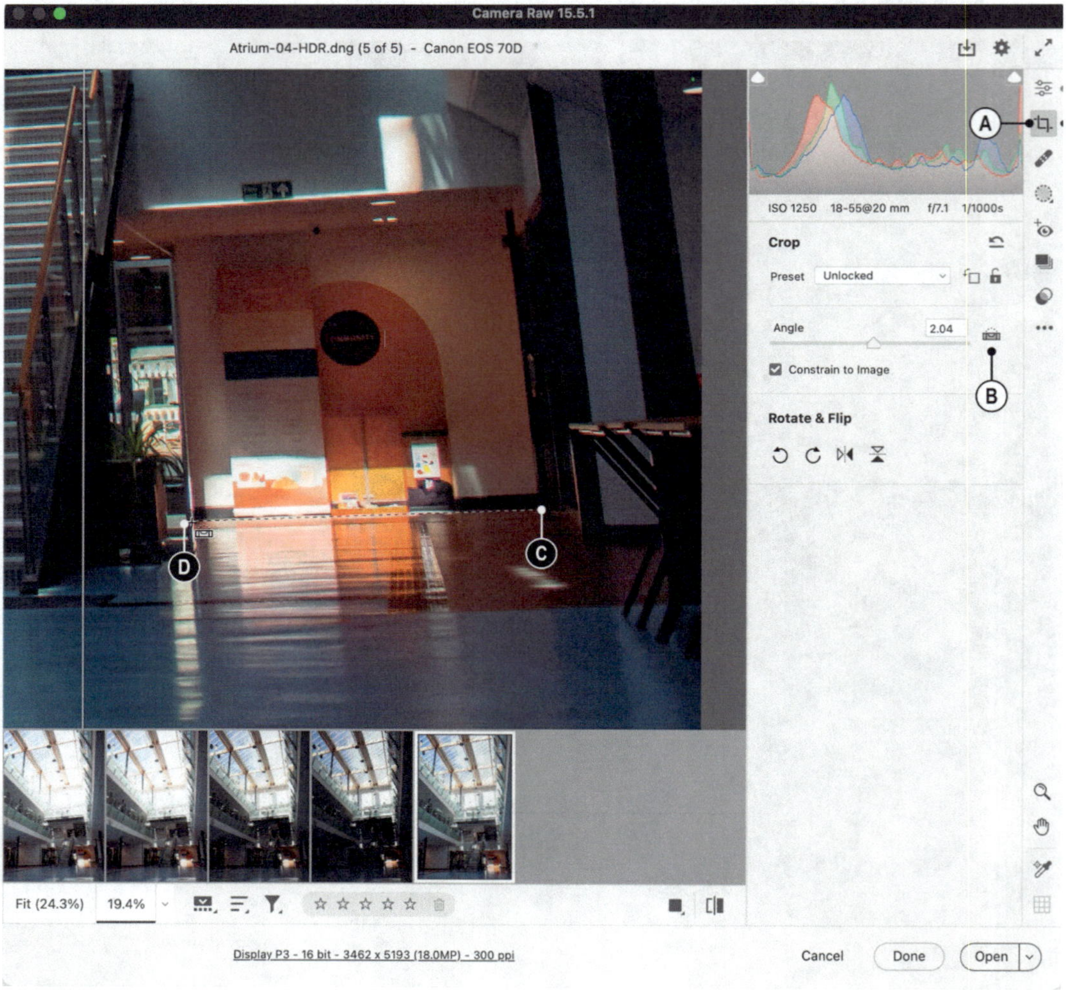

Figure 11.33: Straightening the photo

16. Hover the **Straighten** tool over the right-hand side skirting in the image (*C*), then click and hold the left mouse button down, drag to the far-left edge of the skirting, and release the left mouse button (*D*). By using the skirting in the photo, which should be level, this will straighten the image.

17. Once all the edits have been applied, click **Done** to apply all settings, close **Camera Raw**, and return to **Bridge**:

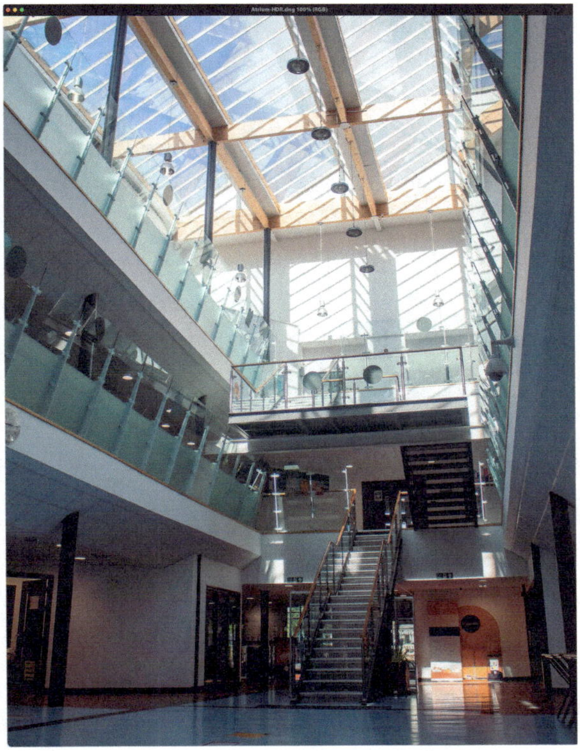

Figure 11.34: The completed HDR image

In the final section of this chapter, we took several images shot at different exposures that on their own would not be adequate, but by combining them as an HDR image, we were able to use the data in all five images. The final composite utilizes a far broader range of luminance levels that successfully capture details in shadows, midtones, and highlights.

Summary

In this chapter, we looked at a variety of techniques for combining multiple images, firstly, as a panorama, where six images of a beach were stitched together seamlessly to form a single image.

We then recapped some of the healing and retouching techniques covered in previous chapters to remove tourists and other distracting elements from a beach using the **Spot Healing Brush** tool and the **Clone Stamp** tool. Photoshop also gave us a helping hand during the stitching process to fill in uneven, empty regions around the edge of the panorama with **Content-Aware Fill**.

We then used two unrelated images to form a double-exposure effect by generating accurate selections and layer masks to overlay the image of an atmospheric nighttime street scene over the figure of a woman.

Using a similar set of techniques, we created an unusual overlay effect, combining two photos: one of my head and shoulders, and another where I held my hands over my face. Once combined and aligned together, we used a layer mask to reveal parts of my eyes, nose, and mouth through my hands.

We then looked at a more artistic method for collaging artwork that combined old posters, paint marks, and newsprint. We created bands of light from the source image and turned them into layer masks, assigned to layer groups; this enabled us to deposit the source print marks and distressed paper images to form a digital collage.

Finally, we overcame the challenge of poorly lit building internals. I took five source images, each captured at a different exposure setting so that we could then combine them as an HDR image. The final artwork used light data from all five images to capture details in shadows and highlights without these being lost.

In the final chapter, we'll create surreal artwork by combining several images with selections, layer masks, and painting tools.

12
Creating Surrealist Artwork

One of the most impressive and undoubtedly challenging aspects of Photoshop is the creation of surreal or abstract compositions. From a house floating in a lightbulb through the vacuum of space to rowing boats gliding through clouds, impossible realities and fantastical illusionary images can look impressive when executed with time and care. The techniques in this chapter are aimed at pushing your Photoshop skills to the limit.

This chapter will approach the creation of surrealistic artwork with two methodologies. Firstly, with little or no budget, I'll show you how to curate and assemble high-quality artwork from stock content. The second approach will focus on planning, capturing, and creating surrealist artwork specifically for the project.

Regardless of the methods you choose to combine separate images to create a montage, lighting is one of the most critical aspects. Done with sophistication and impeccable planning or simply good luck, consistent lighting will make or break a montage – in particular, the direction of highlights and shadows.

I first want to focus on how you can create relatively simple but highly effective surrealist images using techniques we have covered in this book already, allowing you to become comfortable with the types of challenges you will face with this type of work and prepare you for the final project.

In the final project of this book, we will be moving onto our most ambitious challenge yet: combining multiple images through a series of demanding techniques that will take approximately 2 hours to create a visually stunning and professional surrealistic image. To help manage this challenge into more manageable chunks, we will approach the topics in the following sections:

- How to approach a surrealist art project
- Creating simple yet effective surrealist art
- Creating and editing project-specific assets

Technical requirements

The project files for this chapter can be found at: `https://github.com/PacktPublishing/Mastering-Adobe-Photoshop-2024/tree/main/Chapter12`

How to approach a surrealist art project

Surrealist art emerged in the early 20th century as a movement that sought to explore the realms of the subconscious and challenge conventional notions of reality. Influenced by Sigmund Freud's theories on the unconscious mind, surrealist artists aimed to unleash their creative potential through dreamlike imagery, unexpected juxtapositions, and unconventional techniques.

Surrealist art often features bizarre, irrational, and fantastical elements that aim to provoke thought and tap into the viewer's subconscious. It seeks to transcend rationality and embrace the power of imagination, symbolism, and the unexpected. Surrealist artworks evoke a sense of mystery, ambiguity, and psychological depth, inviting viewers to interpret the works in their own subjective and personal ways.

Building these dreamlike, imaginary worlds will require us to implement everything we've learned so far in this book. In previous chapters, we've taken an in–depth look at masking, healing, retouching, and montages. These will be central to a surrealist workflow, as well as time and patience.

Lighting is a key factor in combining separate images. While it is possible to change the hue of an image to match another, if the sum of the parts doesn't contain consistent lighting, it won't hold the viewers' attention. Low–budget projects that rely on completely unrelated stock content will require you to dedicate serious time scouring the web for images containing the subjects and locations you require and lit in similar ways. The alternative is to pay for a photographer to create source images specifically for your project, which comes at a financial cost that is far greater than royalty–free stock content. Alternatively, you could of course shoot the images yourself if you have the capability.

If you resort to stock content, I suggest downloading the watermarked version to test whether the images will combine successfully before you purchase the full–quality image. I can't tell you the number of times my initial feeling about the suitability of an image turned out to be no good when "comped" with the other assets. To create a quick proof of concept, copy and paste each of the images together and juxtapose them in the correct positions in your mock–up. This will indicate if the lighting, angle, and quality meet your needs. You won't know if the resolution of an asset is good enough until you paste it into the composition.

In the first exercise of this chapter, we will combine two stock images using many of the skills learned in previous chapters, such as masks, blend modes, and adjustment layers.

Creating simple yet effective surrealist art

The first exercise uses free stock images that are the best match for a concept I wanted to include of an out-of-place object. In this case, the Moon turns into a balloon that is fastened to a wooden chair. I had to keep my mind open to working very loosely with this concept.

Transferring the moon artwork

This project requires just two pieces of artwork: an image of the moon against a night sky, and a studio image of a chair with a balloon tied to a chair. We'll use the studio image as the "master image" within which the composition will be built. The first step is to transfer the moon into the master file. Here's how to do it:

1. Go to **File** → **Open**, browse to the `12-Surreal` project folder, select `Moon.jpg` and `Balloon.jpg`, then click **Open**.
2. With the `Moon.jpg` document open and active, switch to the **Elliptical Marquee** tool. From the **Options** bar, set the **Selection Mode** setting to **New**, **Feather** to `0 px`, the **Anti-alias** checkbox to **Active**, and **Style** to **Normal**.
3. Left-click and drag across the moon in the photo to create a very basic selection; don't worry about this being accurate. With the selection created and active, go to **Select** → **Transform Selection**.
4. Use the bounding-box frame handles to change the scale of the selection to match the moon. Once complete, click on the **Commit** button in the **Options** bar to update the selection.
5. The **Elliptical Marquee** tool should still be active. From the **Options** bar, click on the **Select and Mask** button to launch the editor.
6. Under the **Global Refinements** section, set **Smooth** to `4%` and **Shift Edges** to approximately `-16`. This will ensure that the edge of the selection is consistent, eradicating any pixelated regions of the original selection and trimming away any green fringe pixels. Click **OK** when done to close the editor and update the selection:

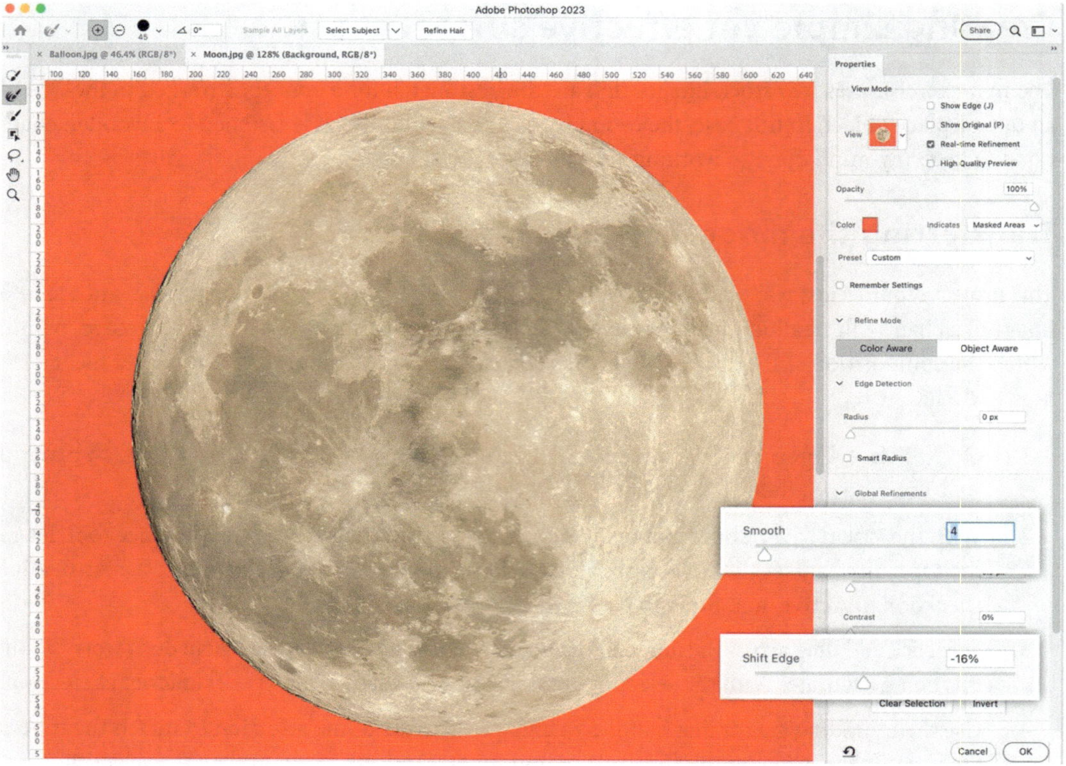

Figure 12.1: The moon contracted selection with a smoother edge

7. From the bottom of the **Layers** panel, ensure the **Background** layer is active, then press *Ctrl* + *J* (Windows) or *Cmd* + *J* (macOS) to create a copy of the selection to a new layer. This is one scenario when we definitely don't need the black background, and as such, a mask is not necessary.
8. Right-click on the newly copied layer name, and from the content menu, choose **Duplicate Layer**. When a dialog appears, enter a new **Name** value of `Moon`, and set the **Destination** option to `Balloon.jpg`. Click **OK** when done.
9. Check that the **Moon** layer has been transferred to the `Balloon.jpg` document, and then close the `Moon.jpg` file without saving changes when prompted:

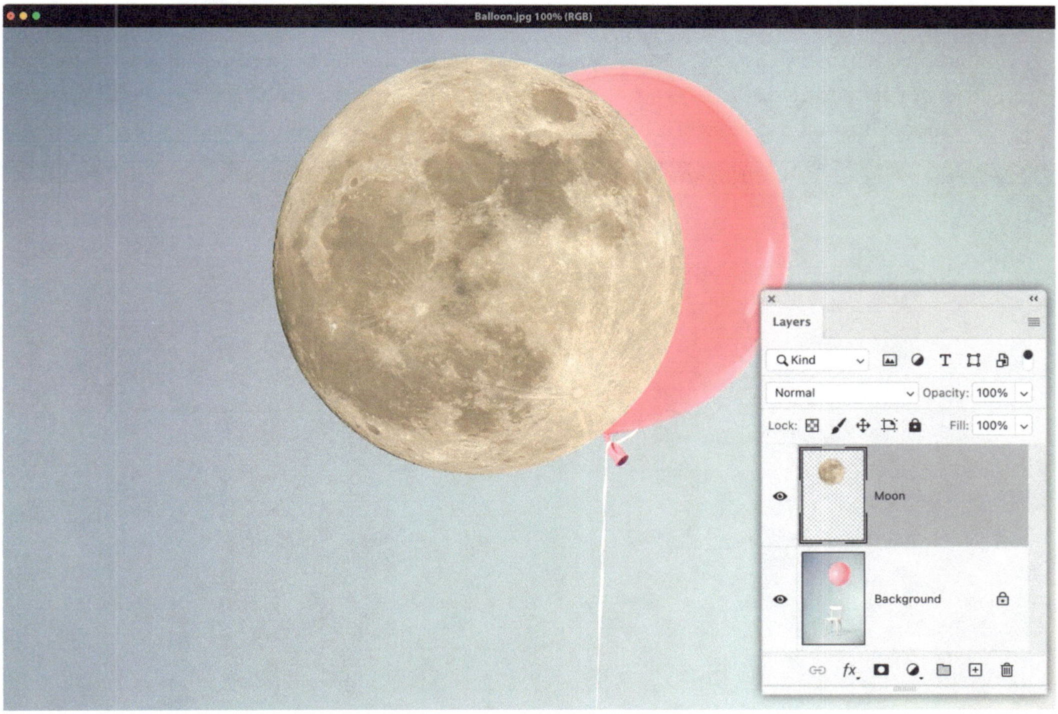

Figure 12.2: The moon image transferred to the master file

10. Next, you will need to scale the size of the moon to be slightly larger than the balloon. To see both the pink balloon and the moon simultaneously, change the **Blend Mode** setting of the moon layer to **Linear Burn**. This blend mode change is only a temporary measure.

Scaling and distorting the moon

Next, you will make the moon match the shape of the balloon as closely as possible. Here are the steps:

1. Go to **Edit** → **Free Transform**. Hover your cursor over the center of the moon, inside the transform frame, and position it centrally to the balloon.
2. Then, making sure that the **Width** and **Height** fields are linked in the **Options** bar, drag opposing corners of the transform frame to scale the moon down in size. Scale the moon so that it is still slightly larger than the balloon. I found that approximately `87%` was appropriate.
3. With the moon scaled accordingly, right-click on the transform frame, and choose **Distort** from the list of modes. Turn off the link between the **Width** and **Height** fields in the **Options** bar for greater flexibility. Pull the bottom-middle transform handle downward so that the moon covers the bottom of the inflated balloon; avoid the region where it is tied in a knot if possible.

4. You will find that the lower half of the balloon will need to be tapered so that the width is narrower than the top half of the moon. To do this, drag the bottom-left and bottom-right transform handles inward toward the center while ensuring the moon remains larger than the balloon. Click on the **Commit** button in the **Options** bar when done to apply the changes:

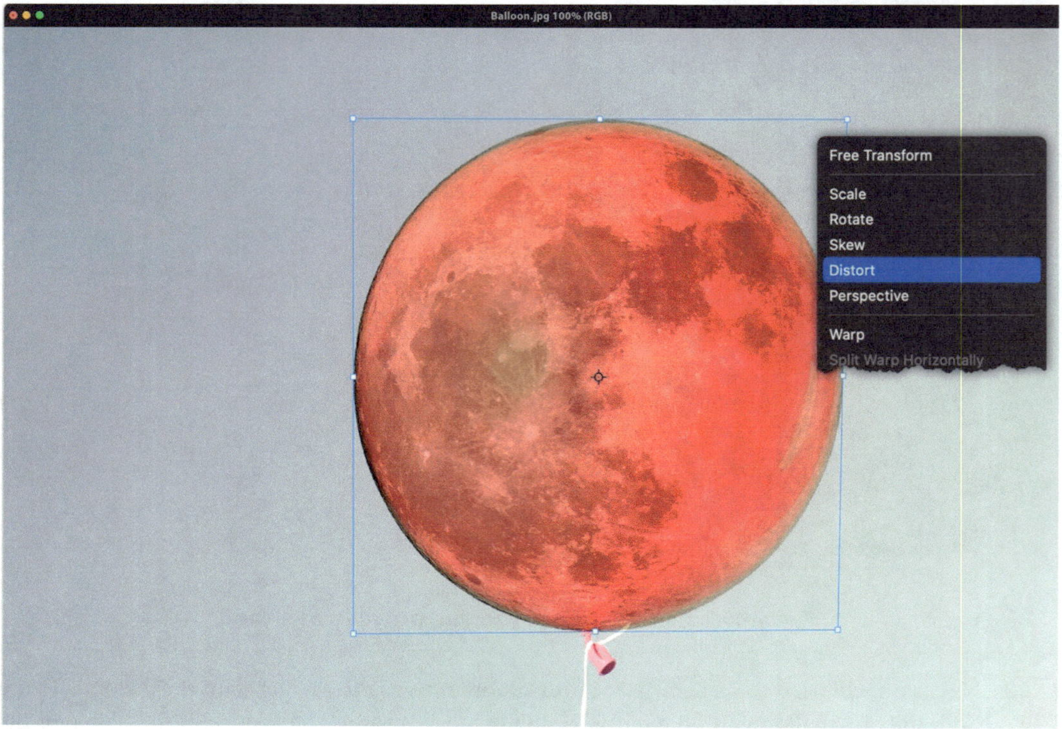

Figure 12.3: Scaling and distorting the moon to be slightly larger than the balloon shape

5. From the **Layers** panel, change the **Blend Mode** setting to **Normal** so that we can see a natural version of the moon artwork. Next, we need to extend the moon image over the ink-knotted region with the **Clone Stamp** tool.
6. Hover your cursor over the **Moon** layer thumbnail in the **Layers** panel, hold *Ctrl* (Windows) or *Cmd* (macOS), and left-click on the thumbnail to select all pixels. Then, go to **Select** → **Inverse**. This will prevent you from adding Clone Stamp marks on the original inflated moon image, preserving the edge details so that you only add Clone Stamp brush marks over the knotted region at the bottom of the balloon.
7. Switch to the **Clone Stamp** tool and set the brush tip to **Soft Round**, at a **Size** value of `35 px`. Ensure the **Sample** drop-down menu is set to **Current**, as we don't want to sample any of the balloon, just the lunar surface of the moon.

8. Start by sampling from a darker region of the lunar surface, remembering to press *Alt* (Windows) or *Option* (macOS), and left-click to set the sample. Ensure the **Moon** layer is targeted and the selection is still active:

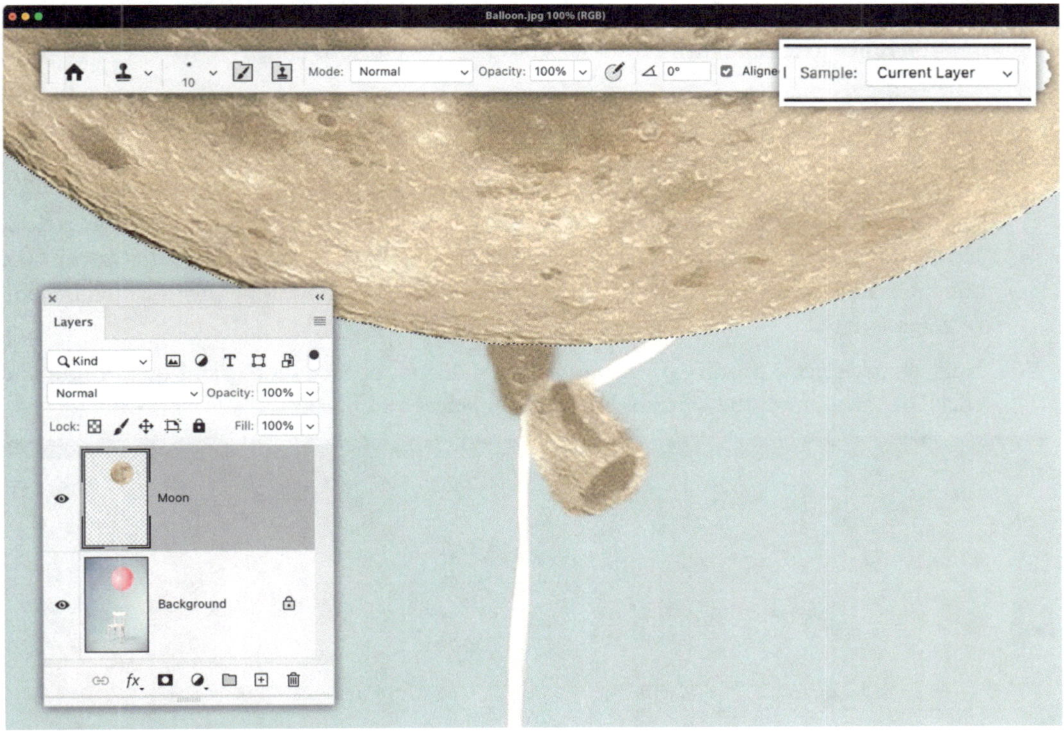

Figure 12.4: Clone Stamp over the balloon knot with samples from the lunar texture

9. Then, hover the brush tip over the top edge of the pink balloon knot and add clone marks to the image. Don't be concerned if you add Clone Stamp brush marks beyond the knot of the balloon; we'll be masking those out later.

10. Working down the rest of the balloon knot, paint light patches of the lunar surface over highlighted regions of the knot, and darker regions of the lunar surface over shadow areas of the knot until off-pink regions have been concealed. Go to **Select** → **Deselect**.

Turning the pink balloon into grayscale

For the montage to work seamlessly, the balloon needs to be grayscale so that highlights and shadows shine through the moon layer, but without appearing pink. Here's how you can achieve this:

1. Switch to the **Rectangular Marquee** selection tool, then from the **Options** bar, set **Mode** to **New Selection**, **Feather** to `0`, and **Style** to **Normal**.

2. Create a selection that includes all of the pink balloon, but don't worry about including the background; we will remove this from the selection later.

3. Next, switch to the **Magic Wand** tool, then from the **Options** bar, set **Mode** to **Subtract Selection** and **Sample Size** to **11 by 11 Average**, to sample an average pixel color of `11 px x 11 px`. Set **Tolerance** to `15` and turn on all checkboxes in the **Options** bar:

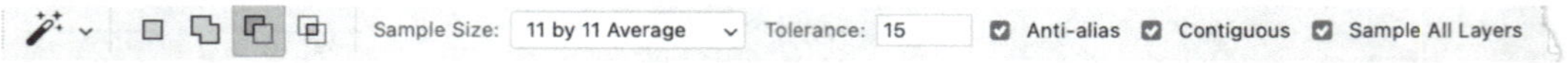

Figure 12.5: Setting the Magic Wand tool to sample colors in the image background

4. Hover the **Magic Wand** tool in the background, then left-click to remove that part of the selection. Repeat the same technique, clicking in the background until only the pink balloon remains selected.

5. Next, go to **Select** → **Modify** → **Expand**. When a dialog appears, set **Expand By** to `1 px` and click **OK**. Then, from the **Options** bar, click on **Select and Mask**:

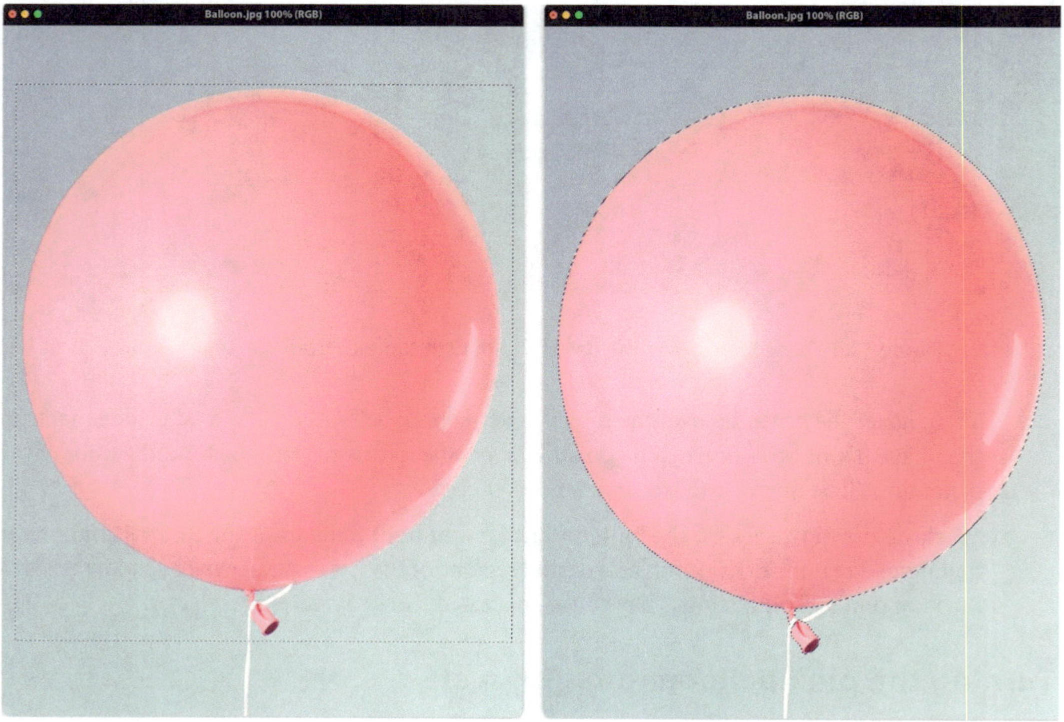

Figure 12.6: The initial rectangular selection (left), then with the background trimmed (right)

6. Click on **Select and Mask** from the **Options** bar to launch the editor. When a dialog appears, go to the **Global Refinements** settings and change the **Smooth** slider to `3` and **Shift Edges** to `+70%`, then click **OK**. This will enlarge the selection slightly to ensure the remaining pink of the balloon has been included in the selection area.
7. Go to **Select** → **Save Selection**. When a dialog appears, ensure the **Document** dropdown is set to `Balloon.jpg`, **Channel** to **New**, and then name the selection **Balloon** before clicking **OK**.
8. Ensure that the **Background** layer is active in the **Layers** panel, and then head to the **Adjustments** panel. Click on the **Black & White** adjustment icon, shown as a box that is half black and half white. This will turn the pink of the balloon into grayscale:

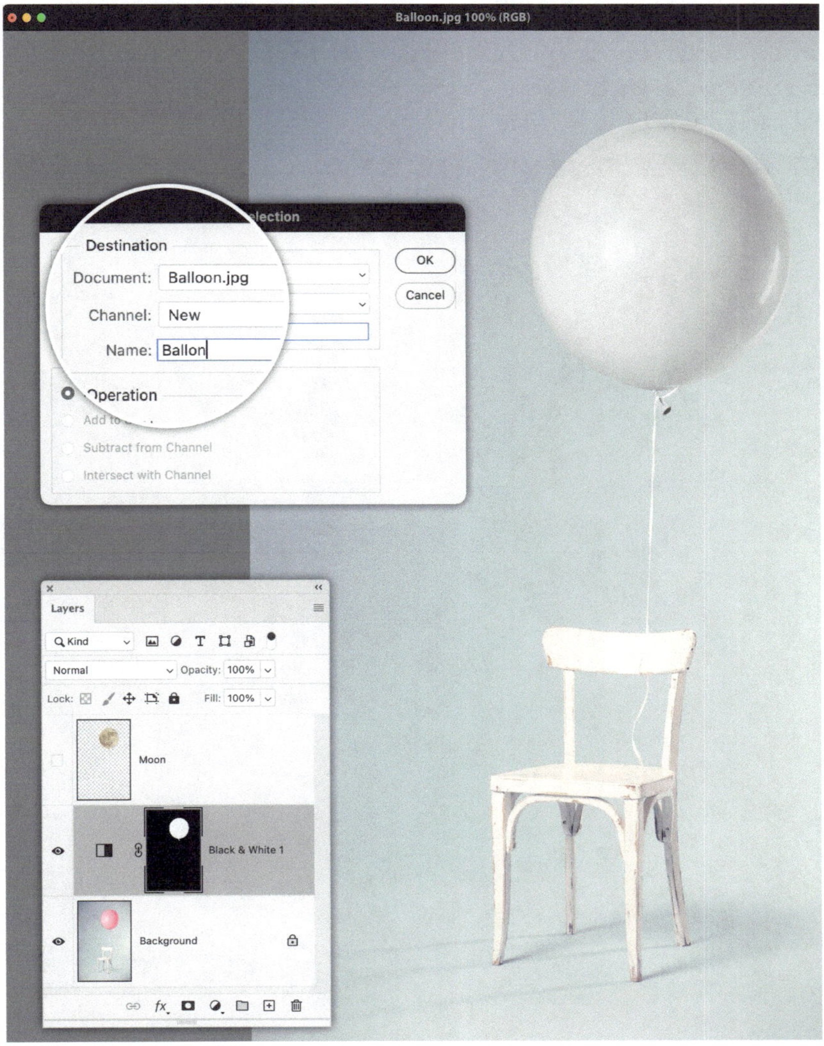

Figure 12.7: Save the active selection

Replacing chair shadows

The moon will affect shadows cast across the chair and floor. The existing floor needs to be replaced, which starts by isolating the chair from the background. Let's proceed:

1. Switch to the **Rectangular Marquee** selection tool, then from the **Options** bar, set **Mode** to **New Selection**, **Feather** to `0`, and **Style** to **Normal**. Then, create a selection that includes all of the chair.
2. Switch to the **Magic Wand** tool, then from the **Options** bar, set **Mode** to **Subtract Selection** and **Sample Size** to **3 by 3 Average**. Set **Tolerance** to `10` and turn on all checkboxes in the **Options** bar, except for **Sample all layers**, which should be deactivated.
3. Ensure the **Background** layer is active in the **Layers** panel. Then, click in the background to remove it from the selection, remembering to exclude portions under the seat where you can see the background (*A–E in Figure 12.8*):

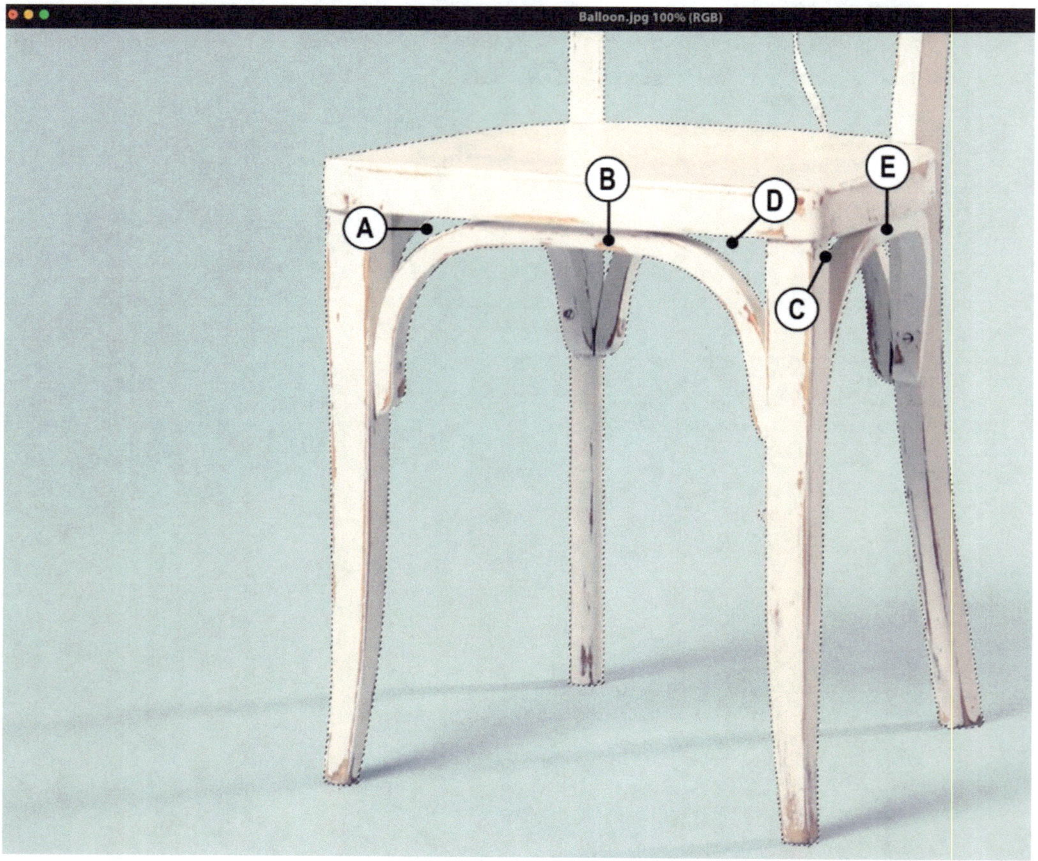

Figure 12.8: Select the background of the image, including portions seen through the chair legs

4. Tidy the selection using any selection tool you prefer, focusing on areas such as shadows under the chair legs, and the ribbon, except where it is tied to the top of the chair. Looking closely at the selection edges around the chair legs, I found that they were very uneven and required the **Polygonal Lasso** tool to create neater straight edges.
5. Once you have completed the refinements of the base selection, click on **Select and Mask** in the **Options** bar. When a dialog appears, go to **Global Refinements** and change the **Smooth** slider to `4`, **Feather** to `2.0 px`, **Contrast** to `52%`, and **Shift Edges** to `-10%`, then click **OK**. This should help smooth uneven edges by feathering them and then tightening them with a higher contrast value:

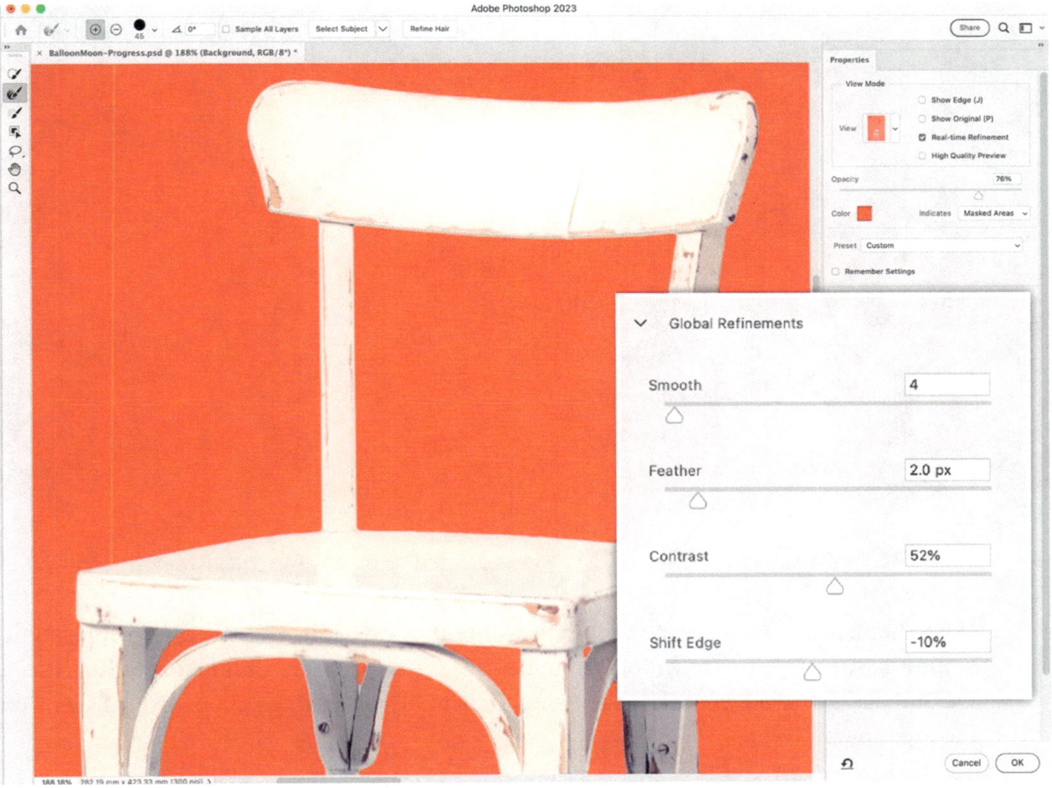

Figure 12.9: The Refine Edge settings applied to the chair selection

6. Go to **Select** → **Save Selection**. When a dialog appears, ensure the **Document** dropdown is set to `Balloon.jpg`, **Channel** to **New**, and then name the selection **Chair** before clicking **OK**.
7. With the selection still active, go to **Layer** → **New** → **Layer Via Copy**. The new layer will appear above the **Background** layer in the **Layers** panel. Rename the new layer **Chair**.
8. Left-click on the **Background** layer in the **Layers** panel to make it active, then hide all other layers in the stack.

9. Switch to the **Polygonal Lasso** tool, then from the **Options** bar, set **Mode** to **New Selection**, **Feather** to `0`, and leave the **Anti-alias** checkbox turned on. Create a selection around all shadows cast by the chair, which should run across the entire width of the image:

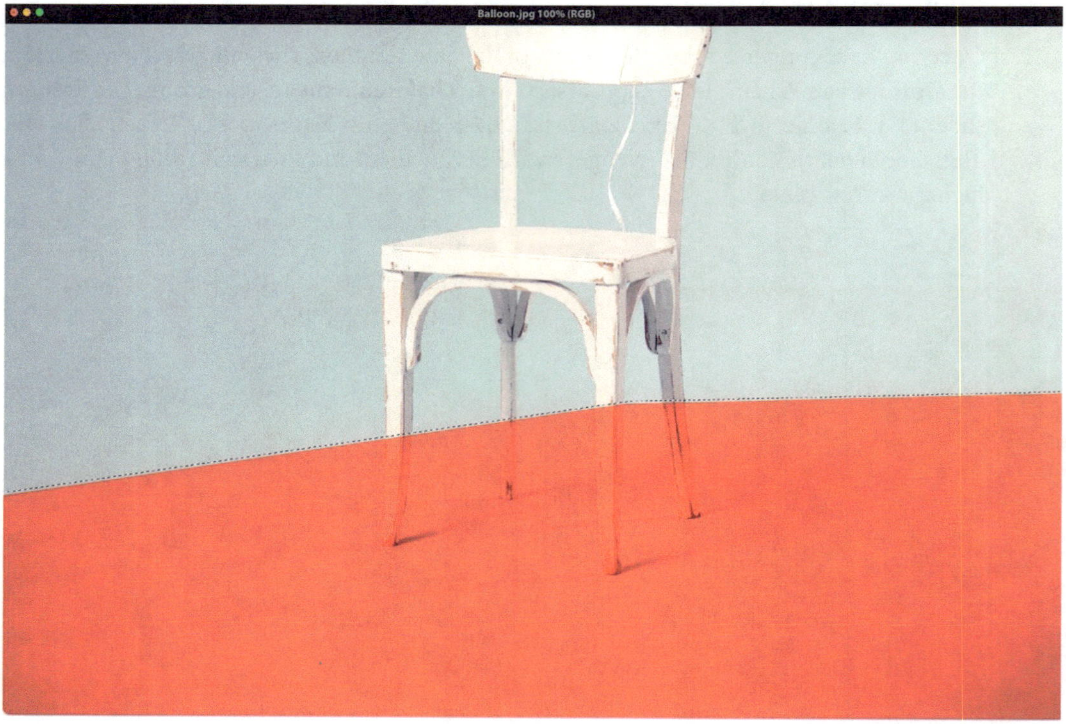

Figure 12.10: Creating a selection of all shadows created by cast by the chair (shown in red)

10. With the selection in place, go to **Edit** → **Content-Aware Fill**. When a dialog appears, set **Sampling Area Options** to **Auto**, then under **Fill Settings**, ensure **Color Adaptation** is set to **Default** and **Rotation Adaptation** to **None**. Under **Output Settings**, choose **New Layer** from the dropdown.
11. The left-hand window displays the sampling area, highlighted in green by default. To achieve the result we are striving for, you will need to switch to the **Sampling Brush** tool from the upper left-hand side of the dialog and remove any green sampling from the chair. This should provide a smooth replacement floor.

12. Click **OK** when done to add the edits into a new layer. Then, rename the newly created layer **Floor** and hide the **Background** layer visibility:

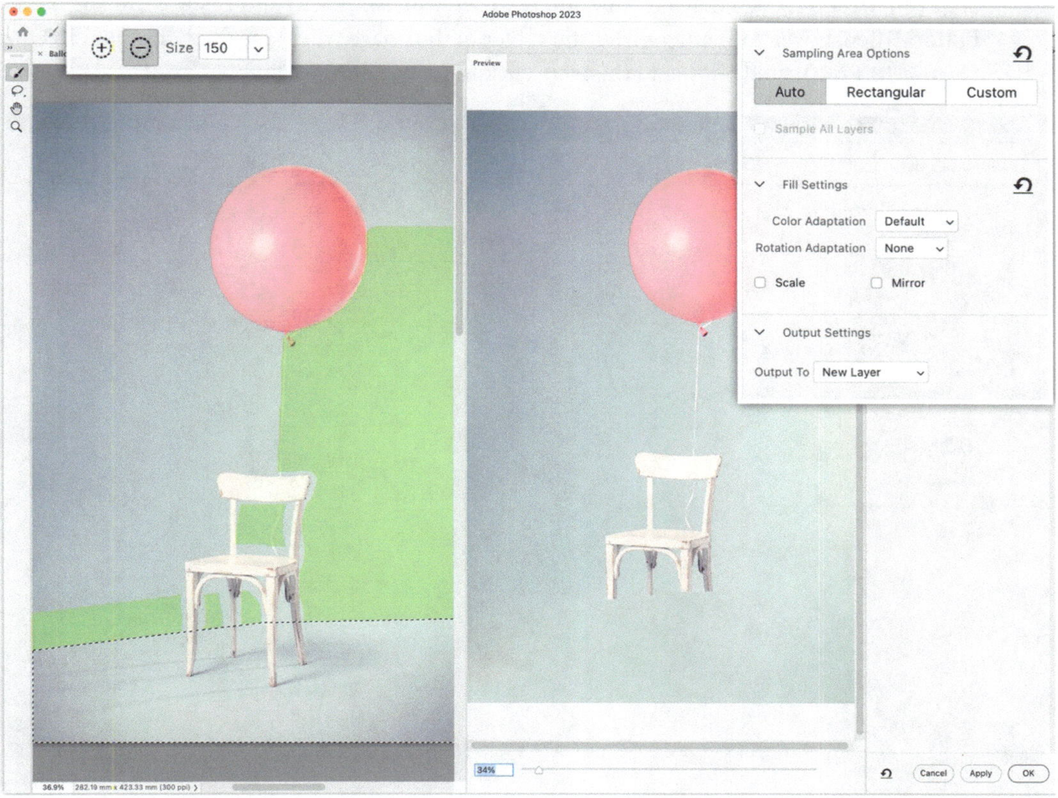

Figure 12.11: Removing sampling from the chair by painting over the green highlights

13. To prevent hard edges from appearing along the new **Floor** layer we added, it might be worth softening the edges with a mask. With the **Floor** layer active, left-click on the **Add a mask** icon at the bottom of the **Layers** panel.
14. Switch to the **Brush** tool, then from the **Options** bar, choose the **Soft Round** brush tip, but increase the **Hardness** value to `30%` to prevent too much of the floor from disappearing. Then, set the brush tip **Size** value to `25 px` and set the **Opacity** value to `100%`.

15. Ensure the **Foreground** and **Background** colors are reset by pressing the *D* key. Hover your cursor over the left edge of the canvas, level with the edge of the floor pixels added in a previous step (*Figure 12.12, A*). Left-click to add a circular brush mark, and release the left mouse button. Then, hover your cursor over the center of the image where the floor changes direction (*Figure 12.12, B*), hold *Shift*, and then left-click to paint a straight line:

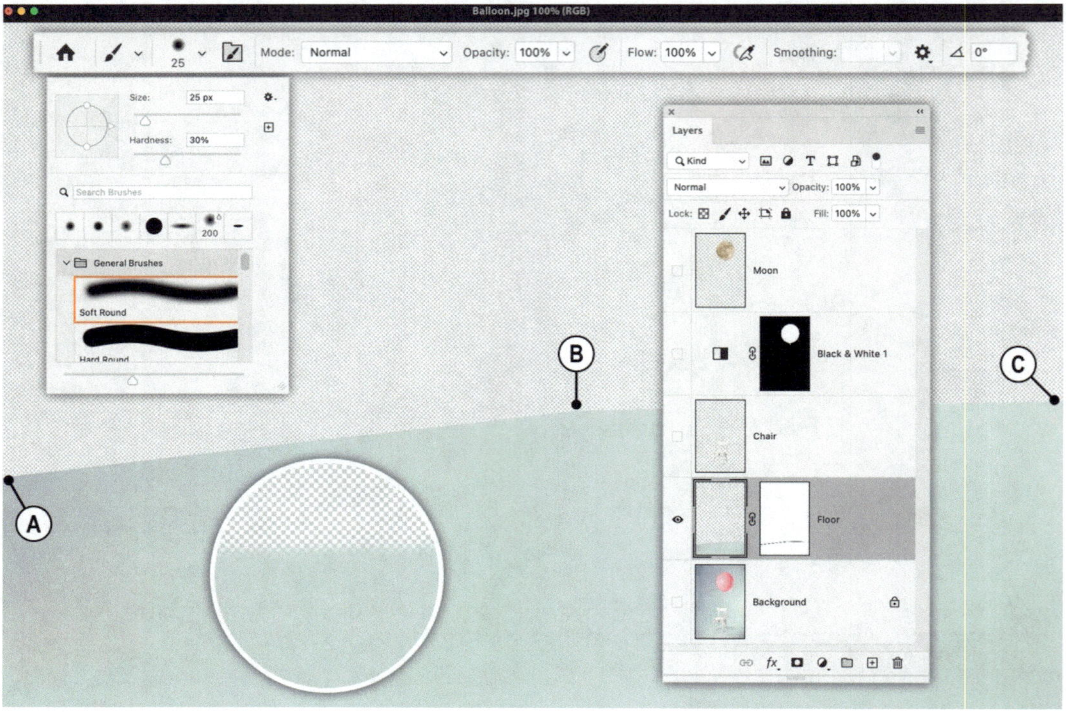

Figure 12.12: Soften the edge of the floor with a layer mask and a sift edge brush tip

16. Repeat the same technique by left-clicking in the same place you previously clicked in the center of the image (*Figure 12.12, B*) and then hover your brush tip cursor over the far-right edge of the floor pixels where it meets the edge of the canvas (*Figure 12.12, C)*, hold *Shift*, and then left-click to paint a second straight line. This should now create a soft edge.

17. With the **Floor** layer active in the **Layers** panel, click on the **Create a new layer** icon at the bottom of the **Layers** panel. Name the new layer **Leg shadows** and then change the **Blend Mode** setting to **Multiply**.

18. Switch to the **Brush** tool, then from the **Options** bar, choose the **Soft Round** brush tip with a **Hardness** value of `30%`. Then, set the brush tip **Size** value to `55 px`. Next, make the brush tip elliptical by dragging the bottom **Roundness** widget close to the center of the brush preview (*Figure 12.13*, *A*). Then, set the **Opacity** value to `70%`:

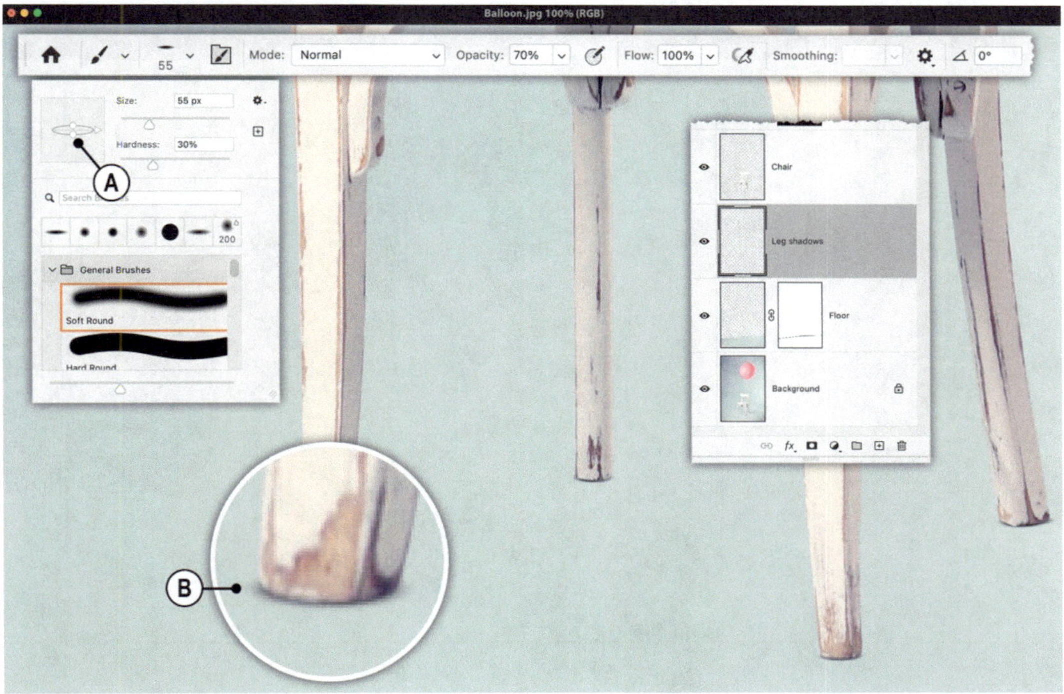

Figure 12.13: Adding shadows under the chair legs to make it look to be in contact with the floor

19. Turn on the **Chair** layer visibility, then left-click on the **Leg shadows** layer once more to make sure it is active. Hover your cursor level with the underside of a chair leg (*Figure 12.13*, *B*) and left-click once to add a pale, soft shadow. I found that left-clicking four times under each leg provided an appropriate shadow.

20. The final step for replacing the original shadows will be to add a shadow cast under the chair from the moon. For this, I created a simple shape in Photoshop to represent a loose interpretation of a shadow in a separate file. Left-click on the **Leg shadows** layer in the **Layers** panel to make sure it is active. Then, go to **File** → **Place Embedded**. Browse to the `12-surreal` folder and select `Seat.psd`. Click **Open**:

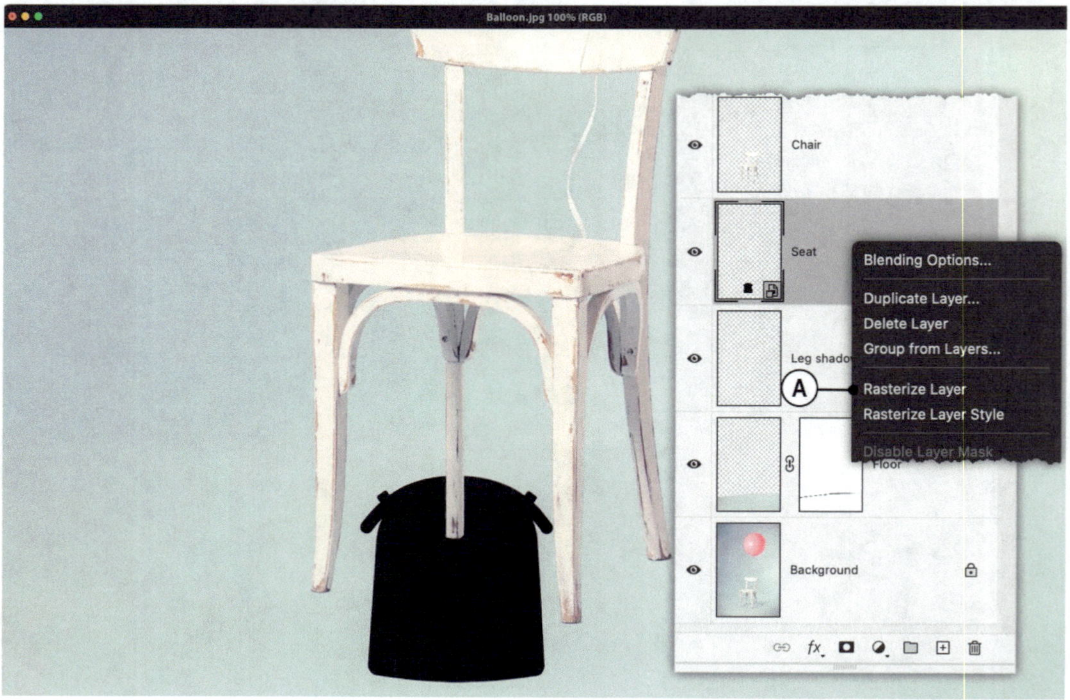

Figure 12.14: Importing the fake seat shadow

21. When the artwork appears in the image window, click on the **Commit** button in the **Options** bar to complete the import process. Right-click on the **Seat** layer in the **Layers** panel and choose **Rasterize Layer** from the list of options (*Figure 12.14, A*).

22. Go to **Select** → **All** to create a selection that includes all content on the canvas. Then, go to **Edit** → **Cut**. Ensure the **Seat** layer is still active, then go to **Filter** → **Vanishing Point**.

23. When a dialog appears, the **Create Plane** tool will already be active by default. Hover your cursor over the outer edge of the left-hand chair leg (*Figure 12.15, A*) and left-click to add a point. Repeat the same technique to complete the grid by adding a point level with the outer corner of each leg (*Figure 12.15, B-D*). Finally, left-click on the first point you added to form a perspective grid:

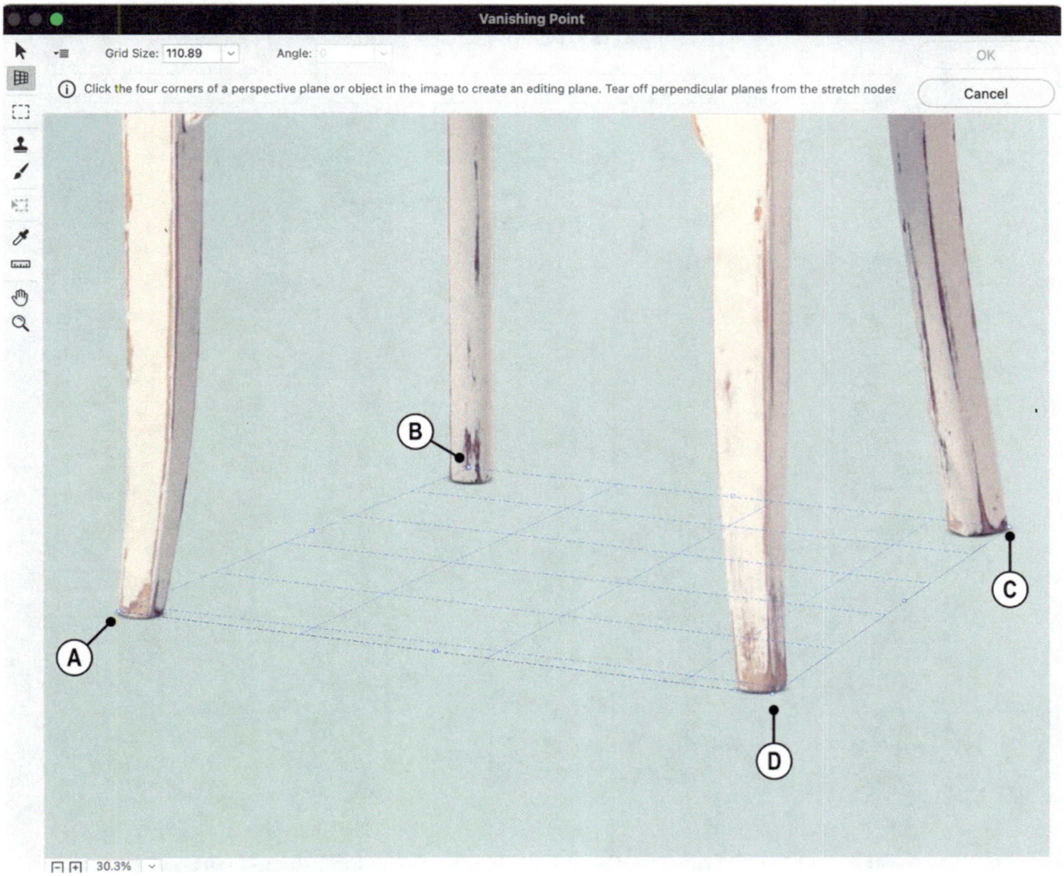

Figure 12.15: Adding a grid point on each of the outer corners of the chair legs (A-D)

24. With the grid now created, it needs to be enlarged to accommodate the entire fake chair shadow image. Hover your cursor over each edge handle on the grid and drag them away from the center of the grid to enlarge it (*Figure 12.16*):

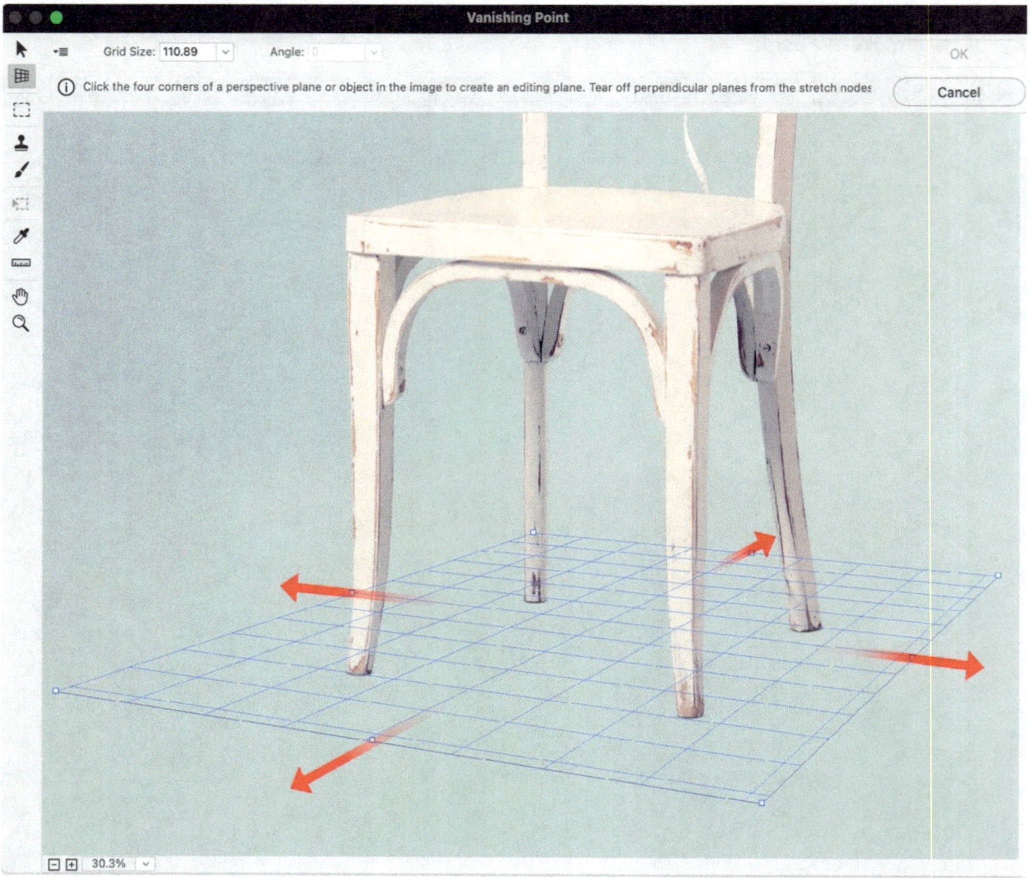

Figure 12.16: Dragging out each edge handle of the grid to increase its size

25. With the grid now in place and at the appropriate size, you can press *Ctrl* + *V* (Windows) or *Cmd* + *V* (macOS) to paste the artwork into the dialog. Remember that the artwork always appears in the top-left corner of the image window, so if you can't see it, you may need to zoom out.

26. Hover your cursor over the pasted seat image, then drag it onto the perspective grid where it will conform to the plane. Once in place, click **OK**:

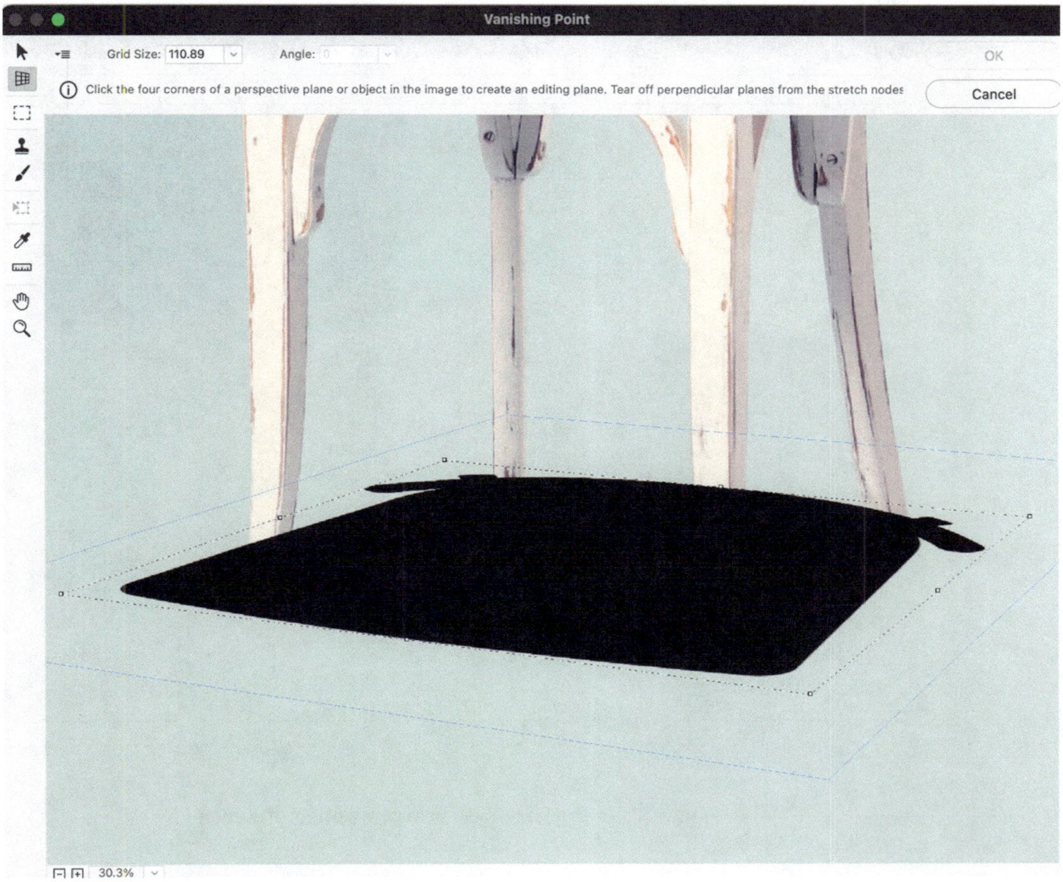

Figure 12.17: Pasting and placing the fake shadow artwork into the grid

27. The artwork will be pasted back into the active layer. Change the **Blend Mode** setting for the seat layer to **Multiply** and reduce the layer **Opacity** value to `12%`.
28. Left-click on the **Chair** layer, then hold *Shift* and left-click on the **Floor** layer to select them both, and any layers between them in the layer stack. Then, press *Ctrl* + *G* (Windows) or *Cmd* + *G* (macOS) to add the selected layers into a new layer group.

29. Rename the layer group `Shadows`. Then, right-click on the layer group visibility icon and choose **Violet** from the list of available colors to tag it with. Then, rename the **Seat** layer `Seat shadow`:

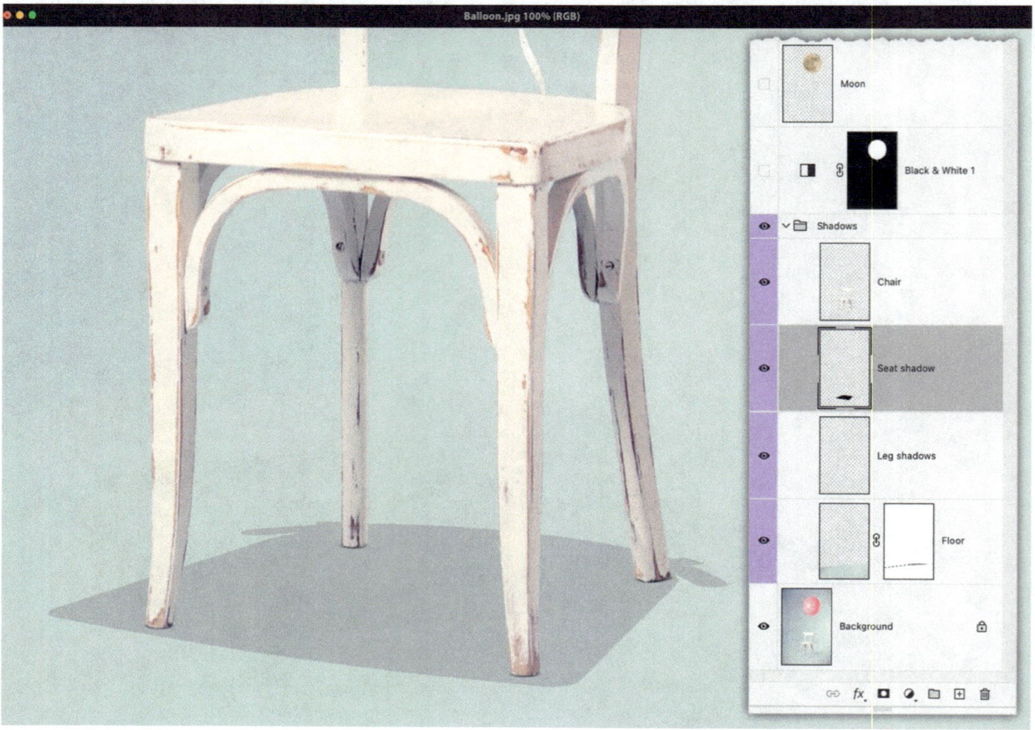

Figure 12.18: The fake shadow in place under the chair

30. Left-click on the **Seat shadow** layer in the **Layers** panel and go to **Filter** → **Blur** → **Gaussian Blur**. Set the **Amount** value to `1.0 px` and click **OK**. This will add a slight blur to the shadow based on the distance from the seat to the floor to make it more realistic.
31. Switch to the **Blur** tool, found in the middle of the **Tools** panel. Set the brush tip to **Soft Round**, **Size** to `100 px`, and **Hardness** to `0 px`, then from the **Options** bar, set the **Strength** value to `75%`. This controls how much blur will be applied as you click and drag over a region.
32. With the **Seat shadow** layer active, hover your cursor over the back-left edge of the shadow and drag over it to increase the softness of the edge (*Figure 12.19*, *A*). Repeat the same step for the back-right portion of the shadow, also labeled *A* in *Figure 12.19*:

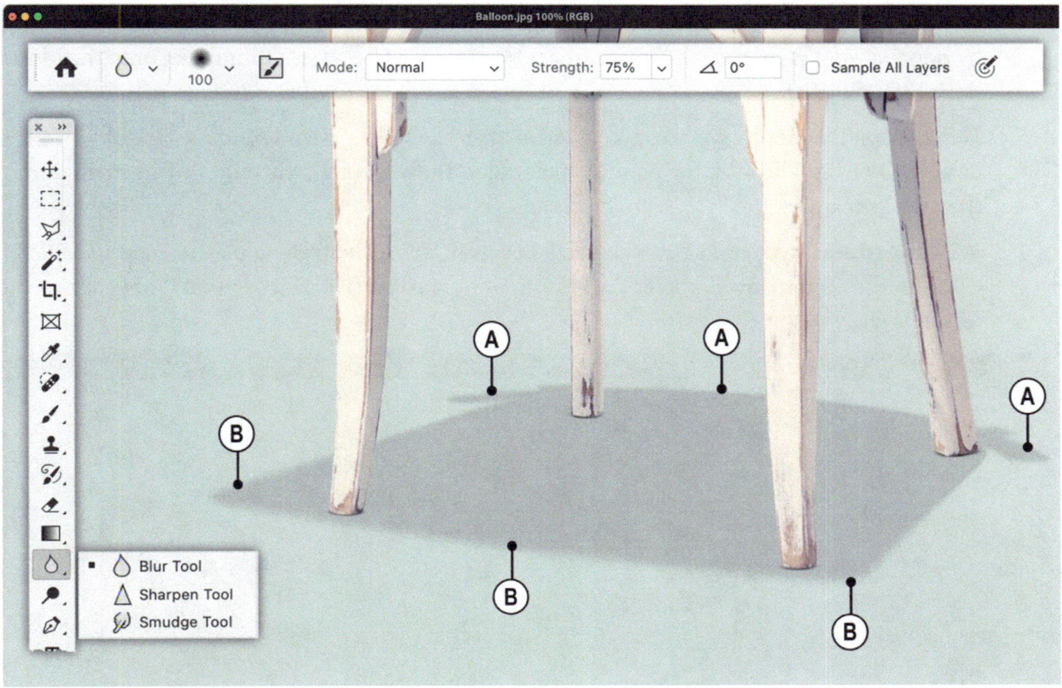

Figure 12.19: Softening the shadow at the back-left and -right edges

33. Next, from the **Options** bar, change the brush **Size** value to `200 px` and set the **Strength** value to `100%`. We'll need to intensify the effect for the next edit.
34. Hover your cursor over the front edge of the shadow (*Figure 12.19*, *B*). Drag repeatedly across the front edge of the shadow with the **Blur** tool, doubling the softness compared to the rear of the shadow.
35. With all the edits complete for the shadows, you can collapse the **Shadows** layer group in the layer stack.

Creating moonlight effects

The final step for our surreal balloon-moon image is to turn the studio shot into a nighttime scene, add highlights to the chair, and emit a glow from the moon. Let's get started:

1. Left-click on the **Moon** layer, then hold *Shift* and left-click on the **Black & White** adjustment layer beneath it to select them both. Then, press *Ctrl* + *G* (Windows) or *Cmd* + *G* (macOS) to add the selected layers into a new layer group. Rename the layer group `Balloon` and color-code it **Yellow**.

2. Hover your cursor over the layer mask assigned to the **Black & White 1** adjustment layer, then, by pressing *Alt* (Windows) or *Option* (macOS), drag the layer mask thumbnail onto the **Moon** layer to duplicate it.
3. Left-click on the **Moon** layer to make it active, then change the **Blend Mode** setting of the **Moon** layer to **Overlay**, allowing the balloon material to show through the moon while maintaining the moon's texture.
4. With the **Moon** layer still active, click on **Levels** in the **Adjustments** panel (*Figure 12.20, A*). Click on the **Clip to layer** icon at the bottom of the **Properties** panel so that it only affects the **Moon** layer:

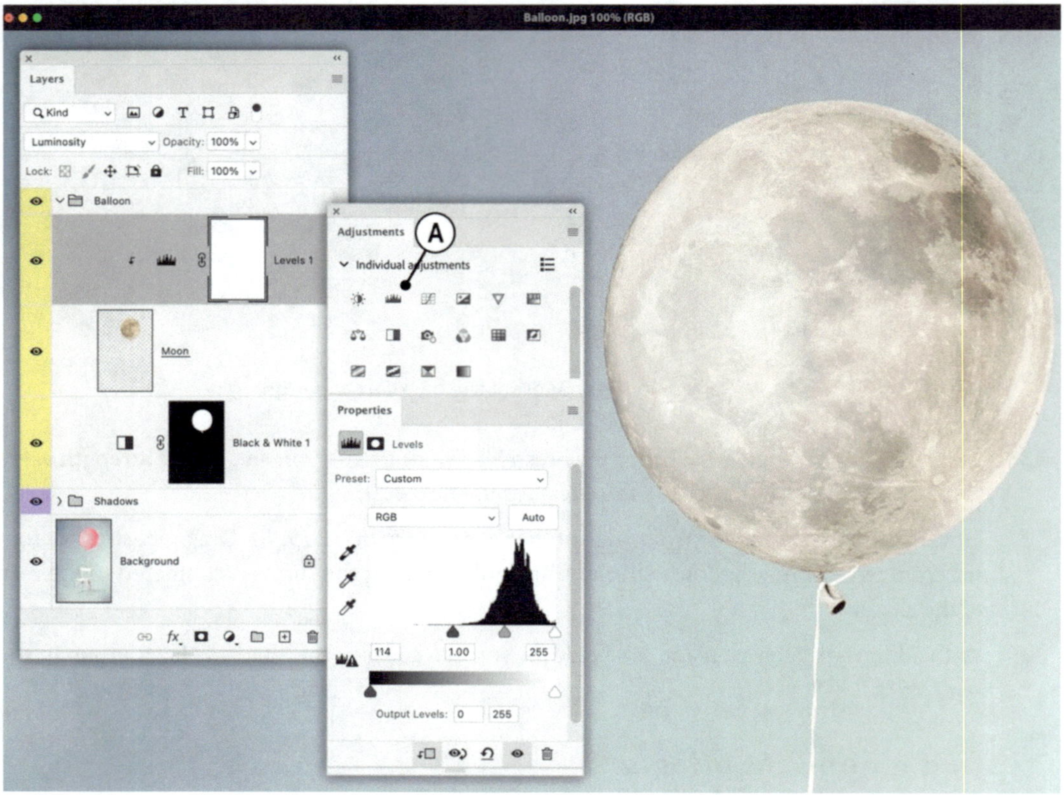

Figure 12.20: Enhancing the contrast of the moon layer with a Levels adjustment

5. Drag the **Black point** slider in the **Levels** settings to an **Input** value of approximately `112`, which should be where the data starts to appear in the graph above in the **Properties** panel. This will enhance the contrast of the layer. Then, change the **Blend Mode** setting of the **Levels** adjustment layer to **Luminosity** so that it affects only the light, not the colors of the moon.

6. Next, click on the **Color Lookup** setting in the **Adjustments** panel. When the **Properties** panel appears, choose `NightFromDay.CUBE` from the **3DLUT File** dropdown (*Figure 12.21, A*).
7. Hover your cursor over the layer mask assigned to the **Black & White 1** adjustment layer, then press *Alt* (Windows) or *Option* (macOS) to drag the layer mask thumbnail onto the **Color Lookup** layer:

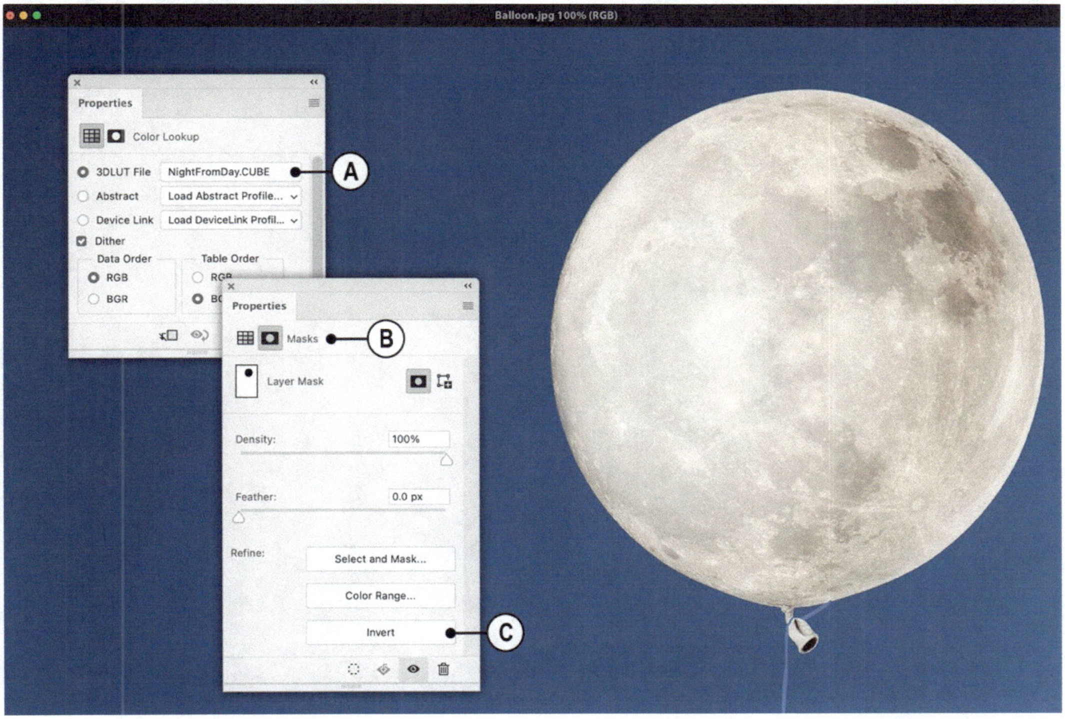

Figure 12:21: Invert the selection

8. Next, click on the **Masks** icon located at the top of the **Properties** panel to reveal masking options (*Figure 12.22, B*). Ensure the **Properties** panel is tall enough to reveal all three buttons at the bottom of the panel. Then, click on the **Invert** button (*Figure 12.22, C*).

9. Ensure the **Color Lookup** adjustment layer resides between the **Shadows** and **Balloon** layer groups in the layer stack. Right-click on the adjustment layer visibility icon and change the layer color tag to **Blue** from the list. Then, finally, change the **Blend Mode** setting of the **Color Lookup** layer to **Multiply**:

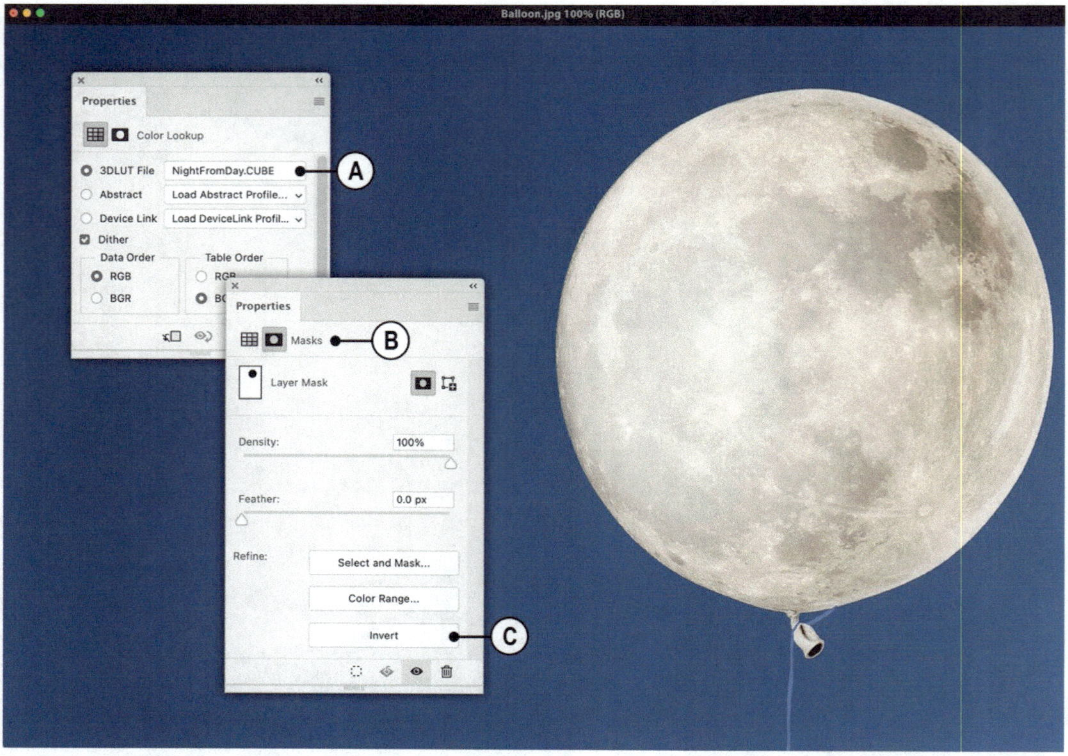

Figure 12.22: Changing the scene from night to day with a Color Lookup adjustment

10. Switch to the **Polygonal Lasso** tool. From the **Options** bar, set the **Selection Mode** setting to **New** and **Feather** to `0 px`. Then, create a selection of the chair backrest, just the front portion of it that faces the camera (*Figure 12.23, A*).

11. Change the **Selection Mode** setting to **Add to Selection**. Then, create a selection of both the chair support fronts that connect the backrest to the base of the chair (*Figure 12.23*, *B*):

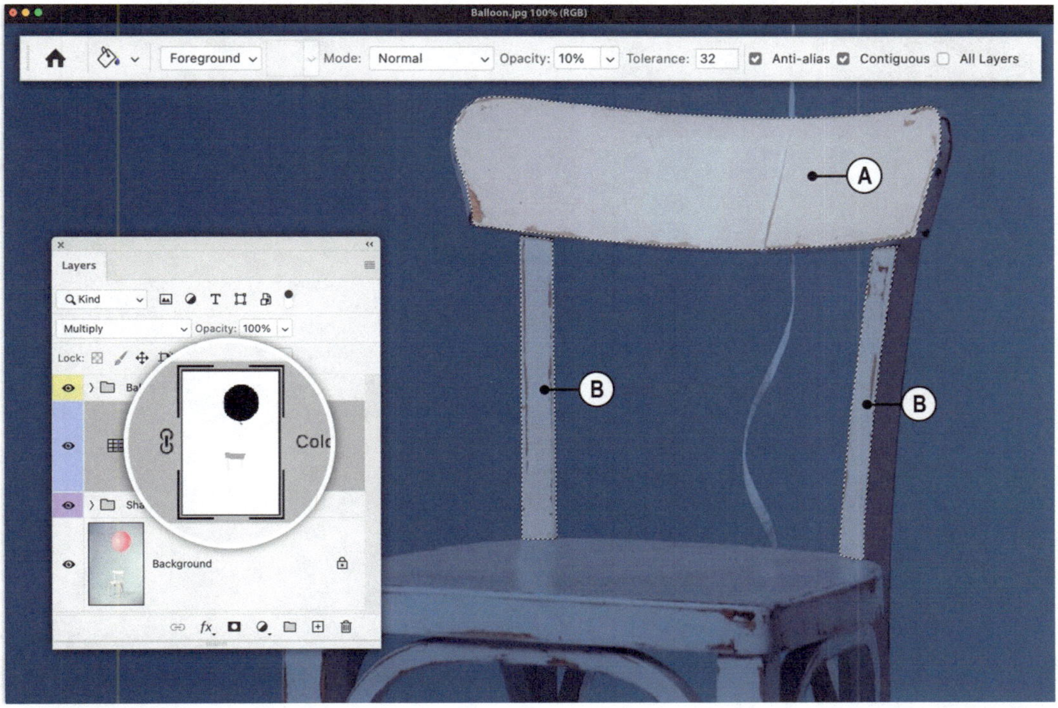

Figure 12.23: Selecting the chair backrest and supports

12. Switch to the **Paint Bucket** tool by pressing the *G* key to activate the correct group of tools, then long hold on the active tool, and from the popout, select the **Paint Bucket** tool.
13. From the **Options** bar, set the selection **Source** drop-down menu to **Foreground**, **Mode** to **Normal**, **Opacity** to `10%`, and **Tolerance** to the default of `32`. Turn on all checkboxes except **All Layers**, which should be deactivated. Press the *D* key to reset the **Foreground** and **Background** colors to their defaults of black and white, with black being the foreground color you will paint with.
14. Hover your cursor over any region inside the active selection and left-click six times. As you do so, you will see the blue hue disappear – in this case, to 40% of the strength it was originally.
15. Go to **Select** → **Save Selection**. Name the new selection **Chair back support** and click **OK**. If you decide to experiment with the strength of the blue, it will be quicker to load the selection. Then, go to **Select** → **Deselect**.
16. Switch to the **Polygonal Lasso** tool. From the **Options** bar, set **Selection Mode** to **New**. Create a selection of the chair seat (*Figure 12.24*, *A*).

17. Switch to the **Paint Bucket** tool. Then, hover your cursor inside the active selection and left-click eight times to reduce the blue hue and brighten the seat as though lit by moonlight. Again, save the selection if you believe it will be of benefit in the future and save time:

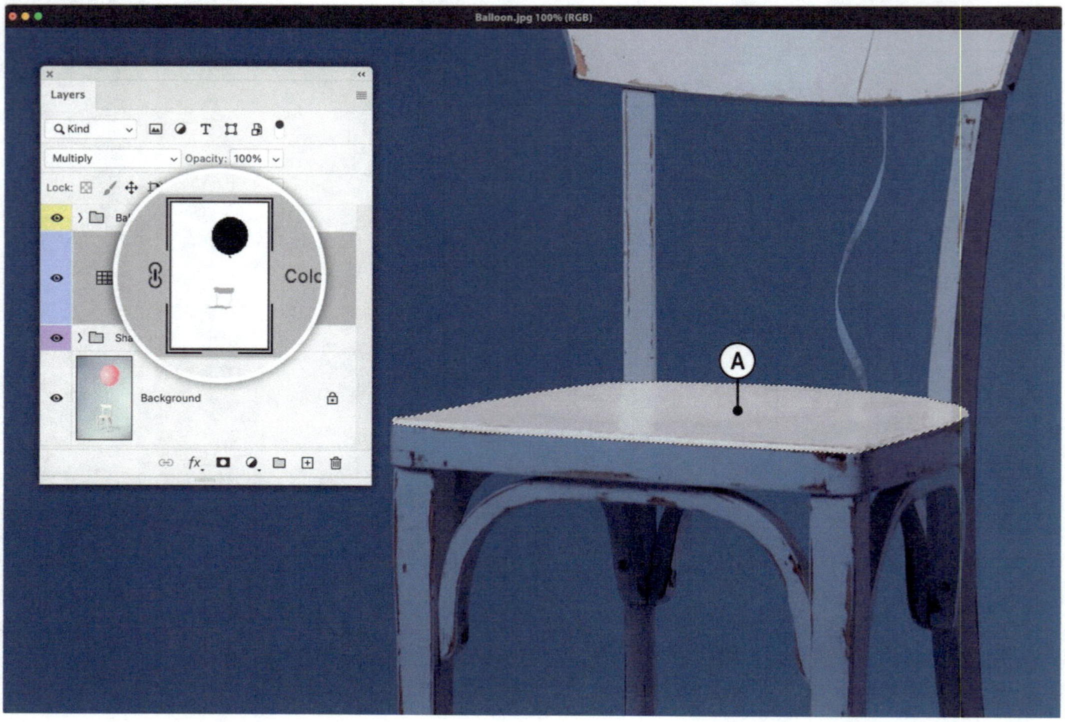

Figure 12.24: Reducing the blue hue on the seat

18. Hide all layers in the **Layers** panel except for the **Background** layer.
19. Switch to the **Polygonal Lasso** tool. Ensure that **Selection Mode** is set to **New**. Create a selection around all the ribbon that ties the balloon to the chair; this will inevitably include some of the background, which you will remove in a later step. Once you have created a selection of one region of the ribbon, make sure you change **Selection Mode** to **Add to Selection**.
20. Now, switch to the **Magic Wand** tool. From the **Options** bar, set **Mode** to **Subtract from selection**, set **Sample Size** to **3 by 3 Average** and **Tolerance** to `10`, and then turn on the **Anti-alias** and **Contiguous** checkboxes.
21. Hover your cursor inside any part of the selection that includes the background color and left-click to remove those portions. Continue this for the entire selection until you are left with just the ribbon selected.

22. Left-click on the **Color lookup** layer mask thumbnail to make it active. Ensure that black is the foreground color in the **Tools** panel. Then, press *Alt + Backspace* (Windows) or *Options + Backspace* (macOS) to remove the blue hue completely from the ribbon.
23. Go to **Select** → **Save Selection**. Name the new selection **Ribbon** and click **OK**. Then, go to **Select** → **Deselect**.
24. Go to **Select** → **Load Selection**. Select **Chair** from the **Channel** drop-down menu and click **OK**. Then, go to **Select** → **Inverse** to select everything in the canvas except the chair.
25. Switch to the **Brush** tool, then from the **Options** bar, choose the **Soft Round** brush tip with a **Hardness** value of `0%`. Then, set the brush tip **Size** value to `50 px`, and the **Opacity** value to `25%`.
26. Ensure black is set as the **Foreground** color to paint with and that the **Color Lookup** adjustment layer mask is active. Then, add paint strokes along the regions of the ribbon where it twists and becomes thinner.
27. Work your way along the entire length of the ribbon to add the blue hue back in where the ribbon twists. When done, go to **Select** → **Deselect**:

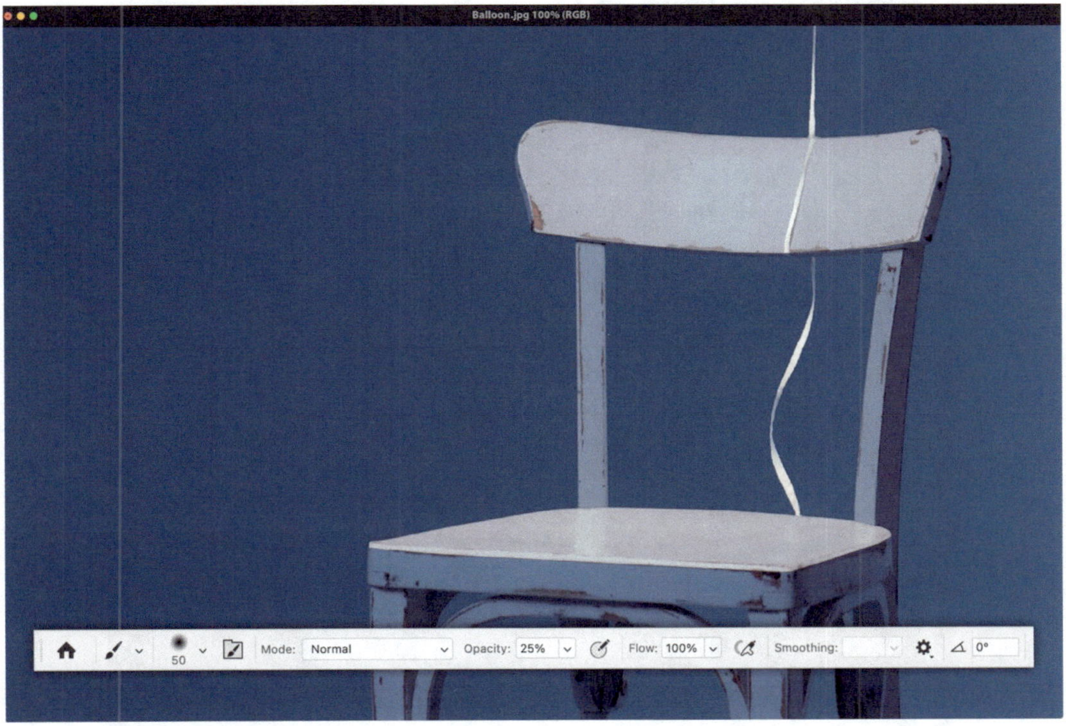

Figure 12.25: Adding a blue hue along the twisted parts of the ribbon for effect

28. As a final touch, left-click on the **Moon** layer to make it active. From the bottom of the **Layers** panel, click on the **Fx** icon and select **Outer Glow** from the list of effects. When a dialog appears, set **Blend Mode** to **Screen**, **Opacity** to `15%`, **Noise** to `0%`, and **Size** to `185 px`. Click **OK** when done.

29. As an optional step, you can make the lighting more dramatic by duplicating the **Color Lookup** adjustment layer and setting the **Fill** value to `50%` at the top of the **Layers** panel.

30. Take a moment to admire all your hard work. Then, go to **File** → **Save**, browse to the `12-Surreal` project folder, save the document as a PSD, and close the document when ready:

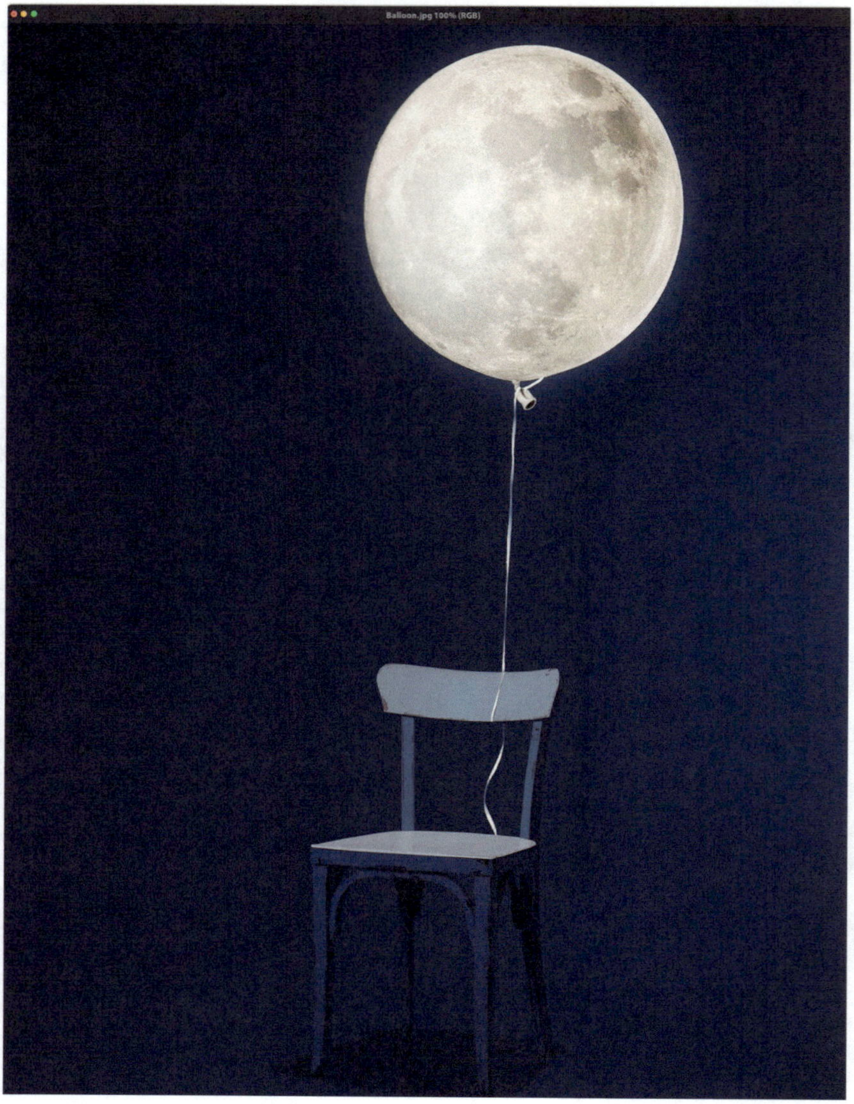

Figure 12.26: The completed project

In the first exercise, we looked at a workflow that incorporated stock images, and the challenges of making the artwork fit our best intentions artistically. In this scenario, just two source images were utilized to create the balloon-moon. Most of the work was spent removing unwanted shadows, whereas if the source image had been created specifically for the project, we would have ensured we had a shot that was lit from the position of the balloon. In the following exercise, we will flip the workflow by using project-specific shots to create an **artificial intelligence** (**AI**)-inspired theme.

Creating and editing project-specific assets

This project is based on an editorial I designed on AI. The three source images have been re-shot for this exercise and feature hands, an iPad, and a combination of both.

Isolating the hands from the shot

The hands for this image have been photographed against the original backdrop and without the iPad present; however, the background needs to be removed. Here's how to do that:

1. Go to **File** → **Open**, browse to the `12-Surreal` project folder, and select `AiIpad.jpg`. Click **Open** when done.
2. Go to **File** → **Place Linked**, browse to the `12-Surreal` project folder, select `Hands.jpg`, and click **Open**. Both images are the same size; as such, you can click on the **Commit** button in the **Options** bar to complete the import process.
3. With the **Hands** layer active, switch to the **Object Selection** tool, and once active, click on **Select Subject** from the **Options** bar to select the hands, while ensuring you don't include the pencil in the selection.
4. You may need to fine-tune the selection to tidy the edge details. I found the **Magnetic Lasso** tool handy for this follow-up step due to the high-contrast background of the photo.

5. Go to **Select → Save Selection**, and when a dialog appears, set **Selection Name** to **Hands** and click **OK**:

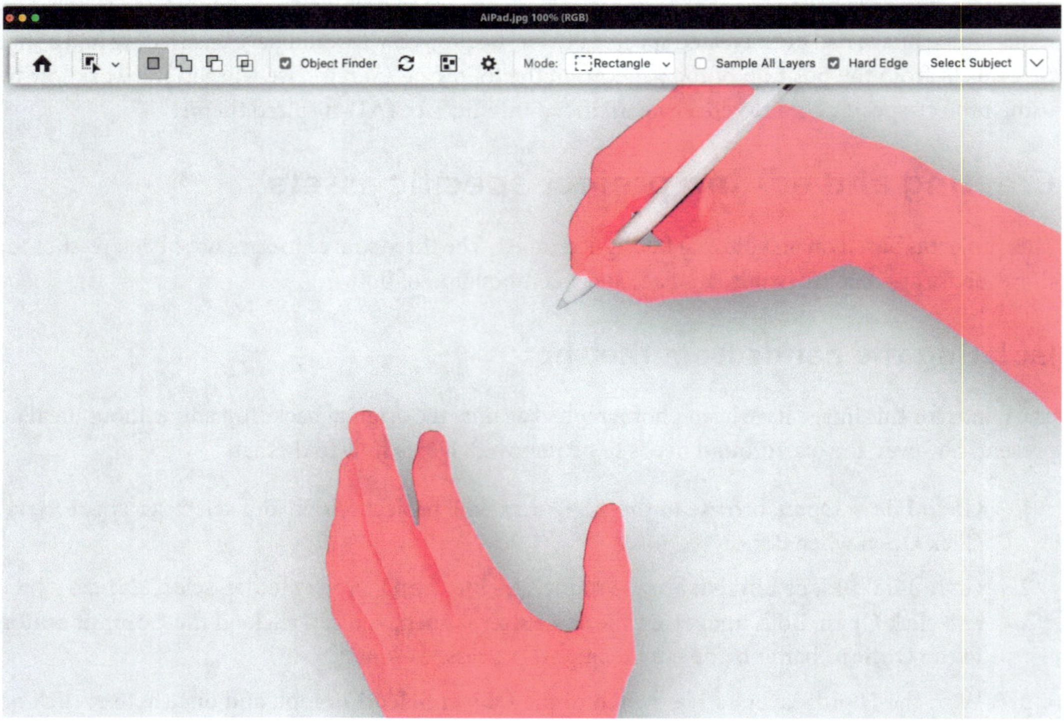

Figure 12.27: Creating a base selection of the hands, then refining its accuracy

6. Next, create a selection of the pencil only. To achieve this, you will probably find it best to start with the **Polygonal Lasso** tool first to match the clean straight lines. Don't worry too much about including the rounded ends of the pencil at either end.
7. With a base selection in place, click on the **Quick Mask** button at the bottom of the **Tools** panel (*Figure 12.28, A*). If you haven't tried it before, it displays selected regions in a light red overlay you can then paint black or white to add and remove sections of the selection.

8. Switch to the **Brush** tool, then choose the **Soft Round** brush tip with a **Hardness** value of `96%` and a brush **Size** value of `15 px`. Hover the brush tip over the drawing end of the pencil; you should find the brush tip is almost an exact match for the rounded end. Ensure the **Foreground** color in the **Tools** panel is white, and left-click once or twice to match the rounded end of the pencil:

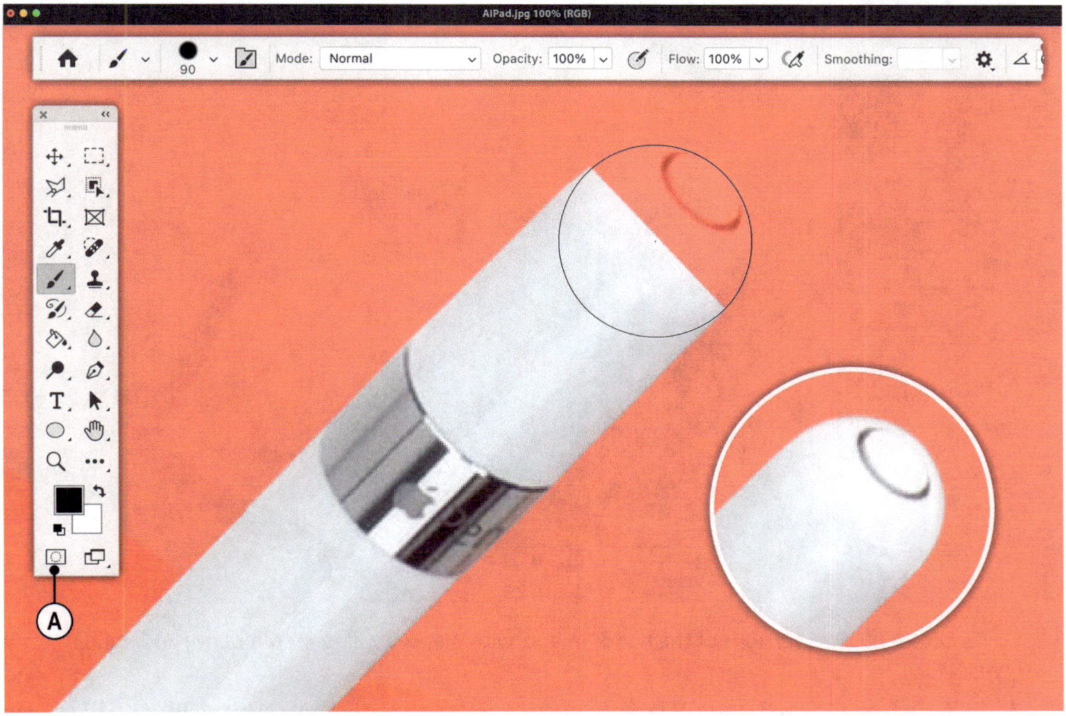

Figure 12.28: Creating a selection of the pencil with the Quick Mask mode

9. Repeat the same technique to add the eraser end of the pencil but increase the brush **Size** value to `90 px`. Again, you may find it takes two to three left clicks to add the entire rounded section.
10. Go to **Select** → **Save Selection**. When a dialog appears, set **Selection Name** to **Pencil** and click **OK**.
11. With the selection still active, create a duplicate of the **Hands** layer by dragging the layer onto the **New Layer** icon at the bottom of the **Layers** panel. Rename the duplicate layer **Pencil** and left-click on the **Add a mask** icon, also at the bottom of the **Layers** panel.

12. Go to **Select → Load Selection**. When a dialog appears, choose **Hands** from the **Channels** drop-down menu at the top of the screen and click **OK**:

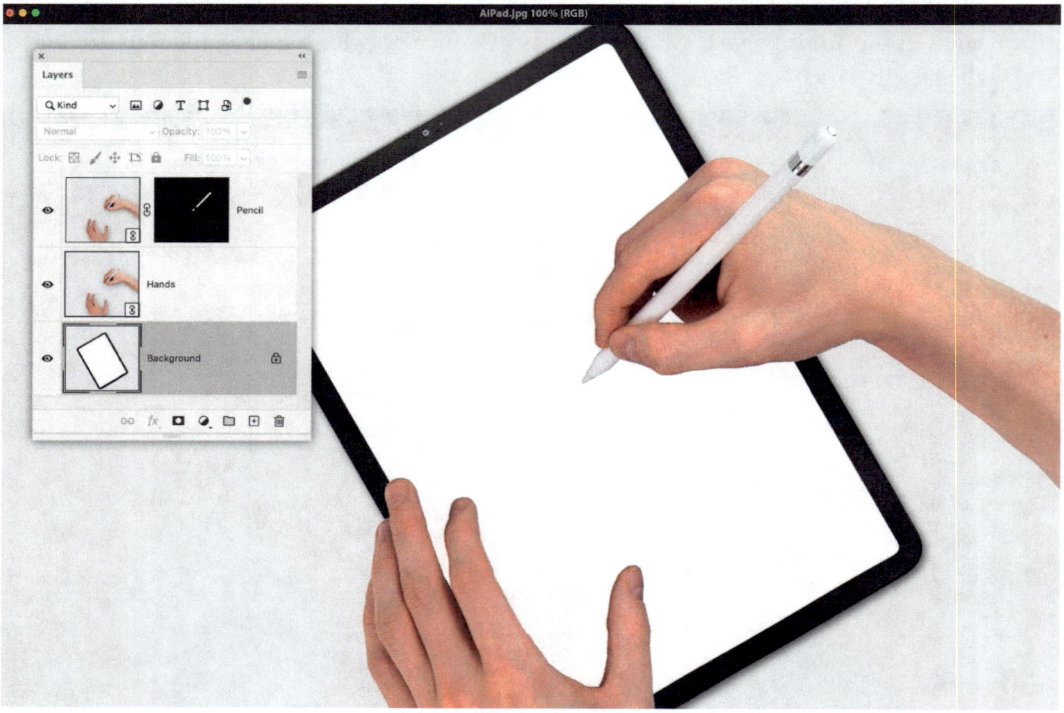

Figure 12.29: Two versions of the hands image, with masks applied for the pencil and hands

13. Left-click on the **Background** layer to make it active, then click on the **New fill or adjustment layer** icon at the bottom of the **Layers** panel. Choose **Solid Color** from the list and set the **Hexadecimal** value to `b6b6b6`, to create a light gray. As we are going to make the original hands disappear at first, we need something to represent the area where they should be; that's the purpose of the fill layer. Rename the fill layer `Guides`.
14. Color-code the layer's **Visibility** column green by right-clicking on the **Visibility** icon in the **Layers** panel.
15. Next, left-click on the **Create a new layer** icon at the bottom of the **Layers** panel. Name the new layer `Thick`. With the layer active, press *Ctrl* + *G* (Windows) or *Cmd* + *G* (macOS) to add it to a new layer group. Rename the layer group `Lines` and set the color of the **Visibility** column to **Red**.

16. Left-click on the **Hands** layer, go to the **Layers** panel fly-out menu, and from the list of options, choose **Create Clipping Layer**. This will make the hands disappear in the image window. Next, we'll add them back in along sweeping brush strokes:

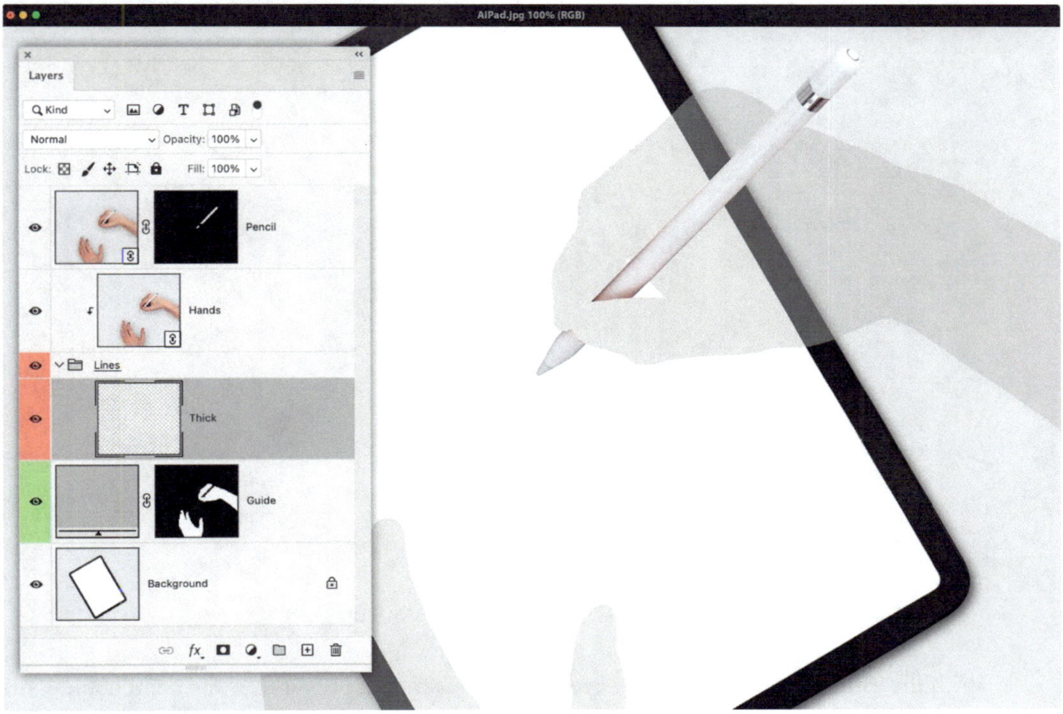

Figure 12.30: Setup layers ready for drawing thick, thin, and fine-painted lines

17. Switch to the **Brush** tool, and then go to **Window** → **Brushes Settings**. We need to create a brush that smooths out hand gestures to create lovely looping brush strokes. Choose the **Hard Round** brush preset from the **Brush Tip** menu in the **Options** bar. Set the **Hardness** value to `85%`.

18. From the **Brush Settings** panel, click on the **Brush Tip Shape** category from the list on the left-hand side. Set the **Size** value to `4 px` and **Spacing** to `1%`. From the list on the left-hand side of the panel, turn on the **Smoothing** checkbox (*Figure 12.31, A*). This will make the **Smoothing** field in the **Options** bar become active. You can then set the **Smoothing** value to `50%`:

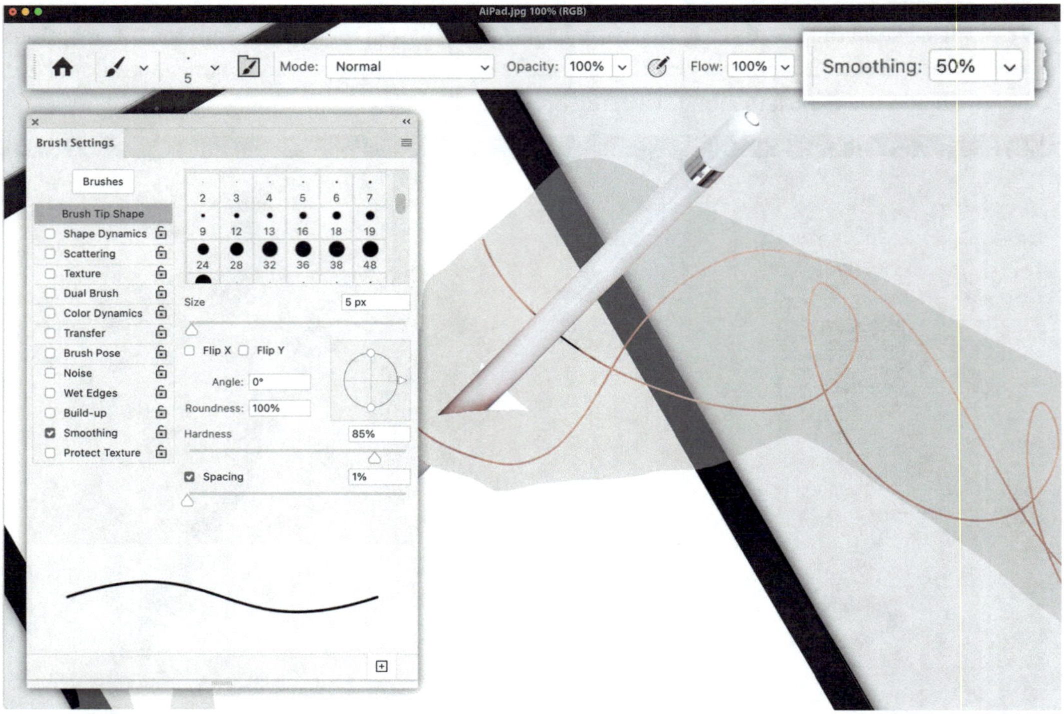

Figure 12.31: Creating a new brush tip

19. With the **Thick** layer active in the **Layers** panel, hover your cursor over the hand holding the pencil, close to a fingertip, and then drag out a long, looping brush stroke along the wrist, staying within the gray region denoted as the hand and beyond the edge of the right-hand side of the canvas. As you do, you will notice the brush stroke is textured with the image of the hand.
20. Repeat this technique for both hands, adding eight to ten brush marks for each hand. We need to give the impression that the hand is made of futuristic cables or nanoparticles.

21. Once you have established some baselines for the hands, you can then add two loose brush strokes that veer away from the hand to make it seem as though they are forming toward the fingertips:

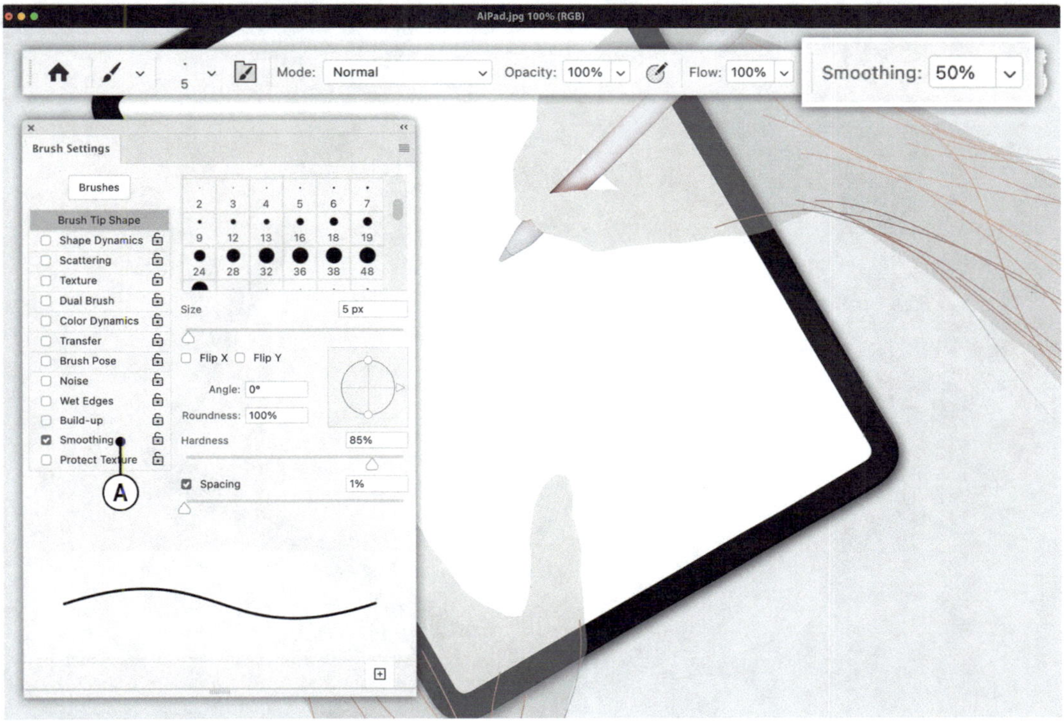

Figure 12.32: Building up loose brush-stroke lines

22. Left-click on the **Create a new layer** icon at the bottom of the **Layers** panel. The new layer should appear immediately above the **Thick** layer in the stack. Rename the new layer `Thin`.

23. Change the brush tip **Size** value to `3 px`. With this layer of thin lines, we need to keep most of the brush marks within the gray guide region of the hands. Try to follow the contour of where you believe fingers are, creating long looping lines. Create some lines that follow the edge of the hands and wrists to give it more form and structure.

24. Add more lines that estimate the regions where the nails would be and the curve of the fingers. All of this will help give the lines a 3D feel when added together:

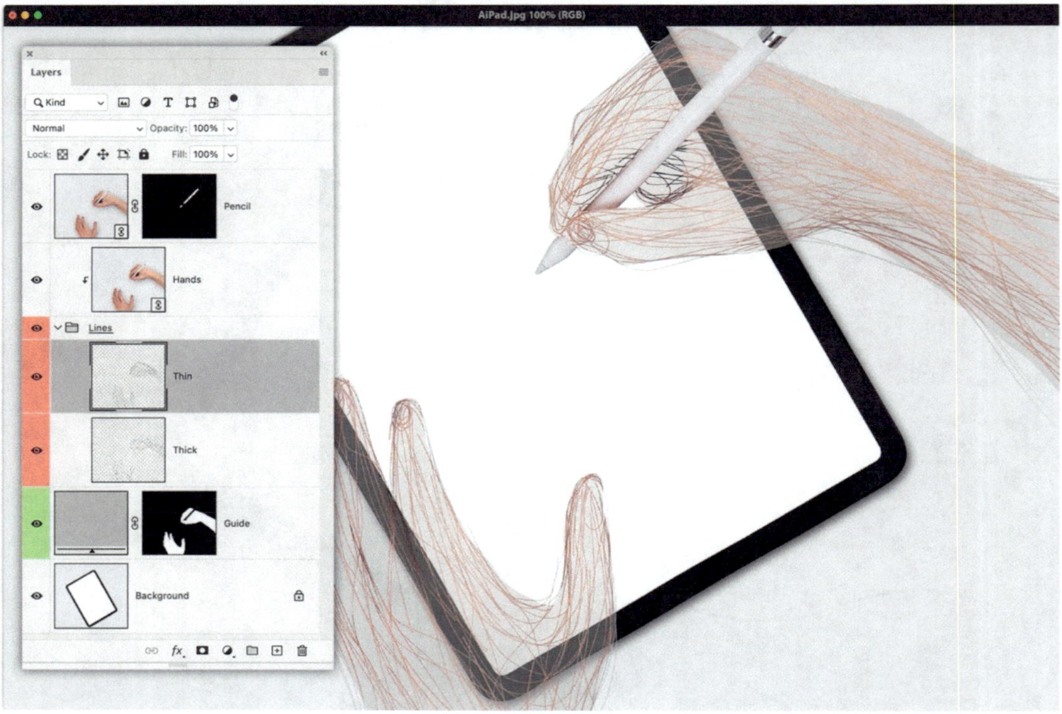

Figure 12.33: Adding thin details to the hands

25. Left-click on the **Create a new layer** icon at the bottom of the **Layers** panel. The new layer should appear immediately above the **Thin** layer in the stack. Rename the new layer **Fine**.
26. It's painstaking work, so if you wish, I have also included a document called `FineDetails.psd` in the `12-Surreal` project folder. You can import it into the master file.
27. If you want to do this the hard way, but with your own brush marks, proceed to scribble in the rest of the details. To keep a neater edge for your scribble lines, go to **Select** → **Load Selection**, and when a dialog appears, choose **Hands** from the **Channels** drop-down menu and click **OK**.
28. Left-click on the **Add a mask** icon, also at the bottom of the **Layers** panel. Then, left-click on the image thumbnail for the **Fine** layer to ensure you are painting on the layer and not on the mask.

29. Set the brush tip **Size** value to `1 px`, then lower the **Smoothing** value in the **Options** bar to `15%`. Keep the scribble lines compact near the fingertips, but as you work down the wrist to the arm, loosen the lines to make them look as though they are untangling:

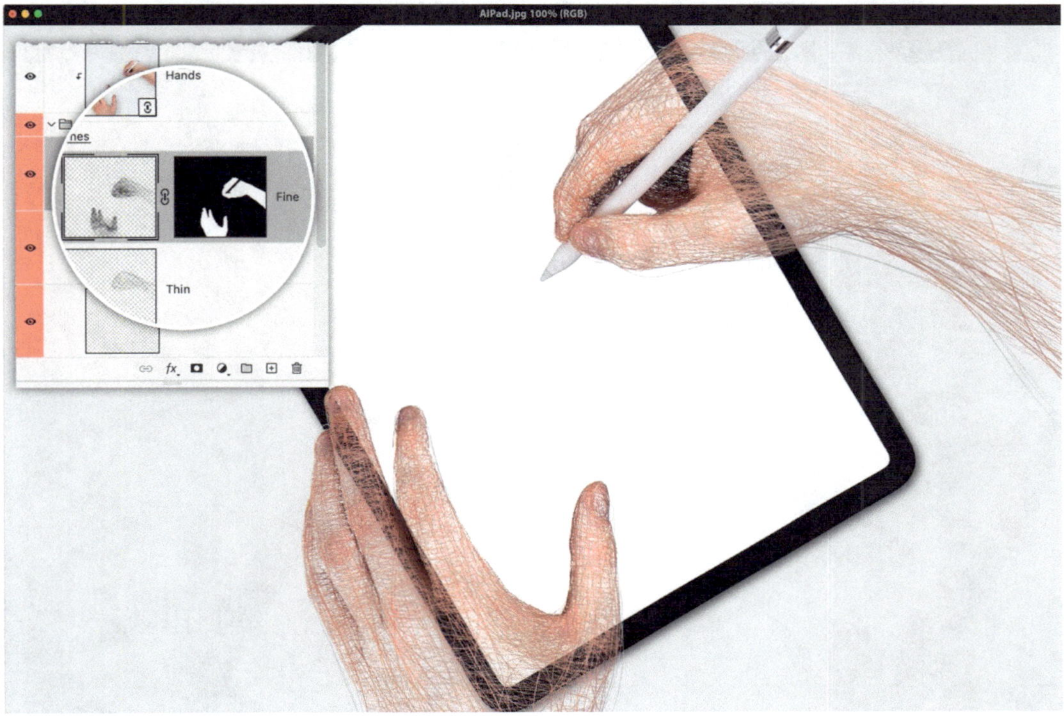

Figure 12.34: Filling in the details along the fingers and knuckles

30. Left-click on the **Hands** layer in the **Layers** panel; then click on the **Create a new layer** icon at the bottom of the **Layers** panel. The new layer should appear immediately above the **Hands** layer in the stack. Rename the new layer **Dots**.

31. From the **Brush Settings** panel, under **Brush Tip Shape**, set the brush tip **Size** value to `4 px` and increase the **Spacing** value to `470%`. This will create a dotted brush-stroke appearance when applied.

32. These brush strokes need to be applied from the wrist and down the arm, toward the edge of the canvas to add a digital element to the lines. Left-click in the **Foreground** swatch in the **Tools** panel and enter `9e6e62` into the **Hexadecimal** field to create a dark brown color. Apply dotted brush marks in long, weaving lines down the arm:

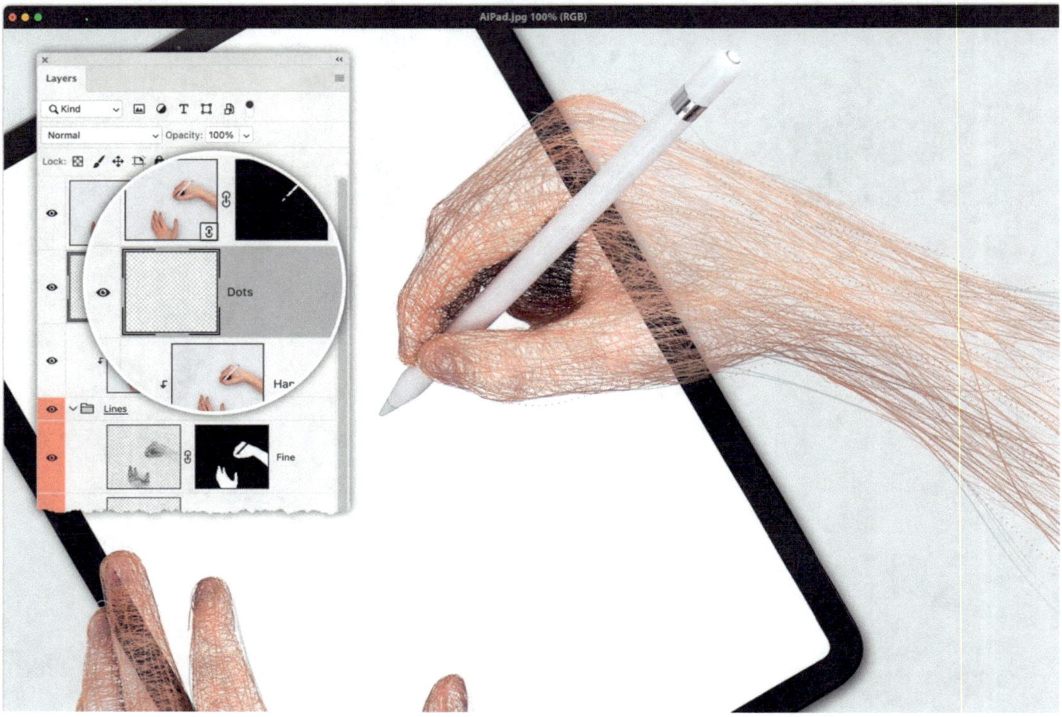

Figure 12.35: Adding dotted lines along the wrist

33. The screen on the iPad needs to be replaced. Hide the gray color fill layer named **Guide**. Then, left-click on the **Background** layer in the **Layers** panel, go to **File** → **Place Linked**, browse to the `12-Surreal` project folder, and select `ScreenArt.jpg`. Click **Open** when done.

34. When the artwork appears in the image window, click on the **Reference Point** checkbox to activate it, and then pin the top-center point on the reference grid. Hover your cursor over the transform frame in the image window and reposition the artwork so that the top-center point of the transform frame is in the same place as the iPad camera.

35. From the **Options** bar, change the **Scale** value to `43%` and then enter `-30°` into the **Angle** field. This should center the image over the iPad screen. Click on the **Commit** button in the **Options** bar to complete the import process:

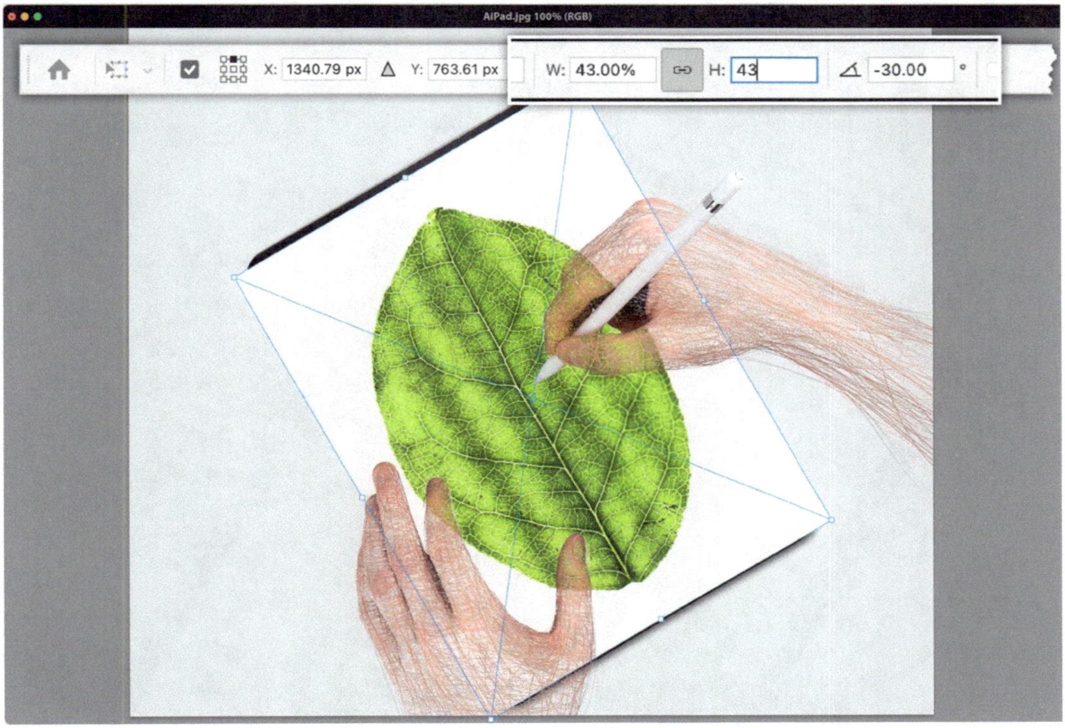

Figure 12.36: Add the screen art image

36. Hide the layer you just imported and left-click on the **Background** layer. Switch to the **Magic Wand** tool, and from the **Options** bar, set the **Tolerance** value to `10` and turn off the **Sample All Layers** checkbox. Hover your cursor over the white screen of the iPad and left-click to select it.

37. Turn on the layer visibility for the **ScreenArt** layer and make it active. Then, click on **Add a Mask** icon from the bottom of the **Layers** panel.

38. To add depth to the screen, click on the **Fx** icon at the bottom of the **Layers** panel, and from the list of options, choose **Inner Shadow**. Set the **Opacity** value to `46%`, **Angle** to `117°`, **Distance** to `11 px`, **Choke** to `0%`, and **Size** to `35 px`. Click **OK** when done to apply the effect:

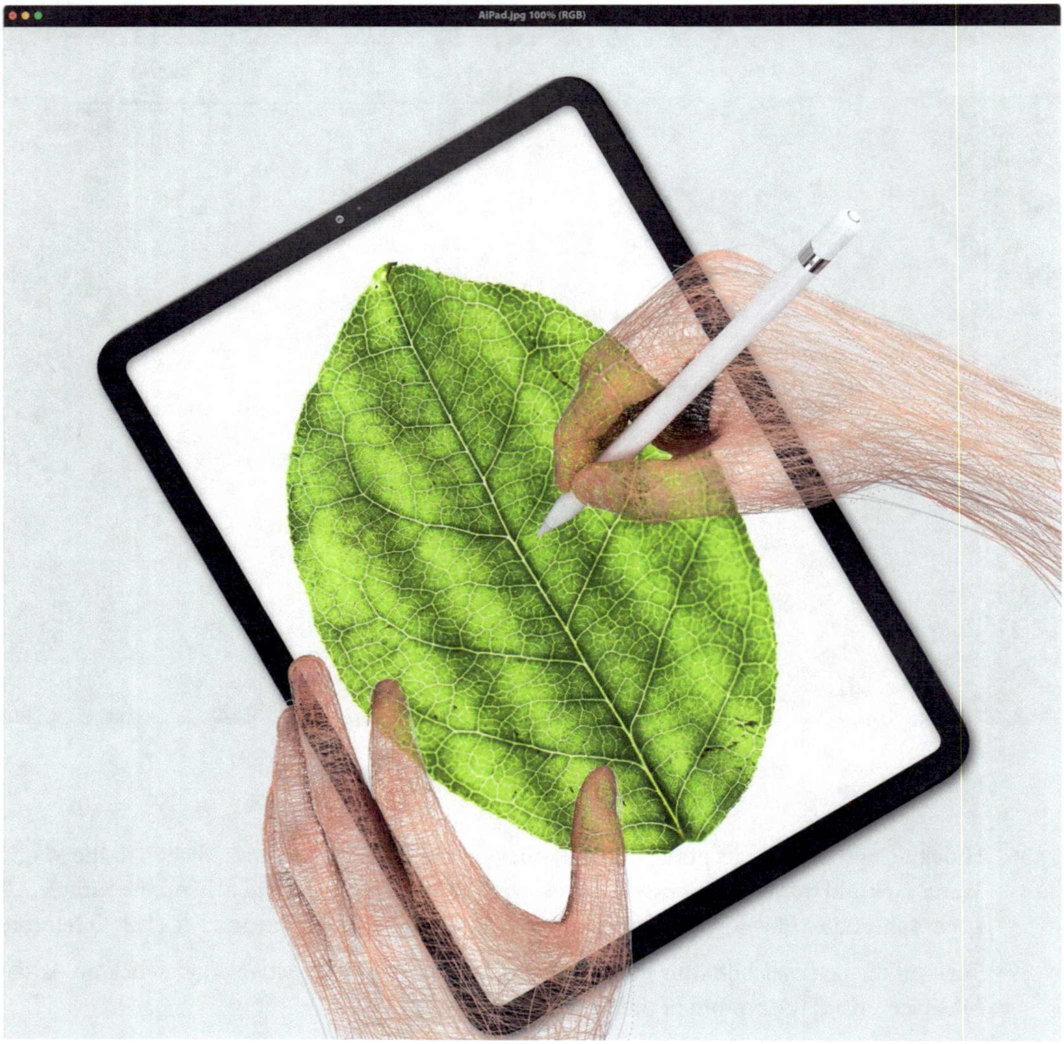

Figure 12.37: The completed image

39. You can now go to **File** → **Save**, browse to the `12-Surreal` project folder, and save the document as `AiPad.psd`. Close the document when done.

In the second half of this chapter on surrealism, we used images of an iPad Pro and hands, shot specifically for this project. This enabled us to have more control over the editing process and achieve the exact look we were aiming for without compromising with unrelated stock images. We used clipping masks as the method for turning the hands into wire-like fibers from a series of layers filled with custom brush marks.

Summary

In this final chapter, we looked at two techniques for creating surrealist images. The first used a set of curated stock images to turn the moon into a balloon that was tied to a chair. We replaced the original shadows on the floor and painstakingly replaced them with our own. We saw how most of the work involved correcting unwanted details from those stock images.

In the second surrealist project, we started with a series of studio shots taken specifically for the project. Each image was carefully set up to work with each other through post-production editing in Photoshop. We combined a shot of an iPad Pro against a white background, then superimposed a shot of hands, one holding an Apple Pencil. We then used a series of layers to reveal the hands with a clipping-mask technique. This gave the impression of the hands forming from fine cables that assembled at the fingers where the hand was holding the pencil. In this exercise, most of the work involved painting hundreds of lines with custom brush tips to achieve the desired effect.

Congratulations! You've completed the final exercises in this book. It's my hope that you will now have a better understanding of how to approach a multitude of Photoshop challenges across print, web, and screen projects. In addition, you should have greater confidence to choose an appropriate tool for each task and manipulate it to suit your needs, along with other facets of the Photoshop editing environment.

Of course, we never truly stop learning, just as Photoshop never ceases to evolve. You'll no doubt find, as I have over the years, that it's only when you undertake your own projects with a different set of challenges that you truly push your abilities to the limit and discover things that you didn't know about yourself, and not just Photoshop. Keep practicing, and good luck. I hope you find the same sense of fun and fulfillment that I have over the years using Photoshop.

Index

A

H

I

J

K

L

M

S

T

V

Z

Other Books You May Enjoy

If you enjoyed this book, you may be interested in these other books by Packt:

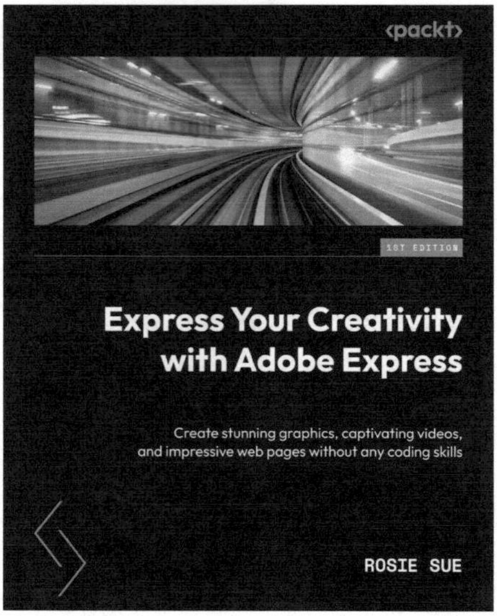

Express Your Creativity with Adobe Express

Rosie Sue

ISBN: 978-1-80323-774-9

- Learn how to create stunning social media graphics without having any prior design skills.
- Repurpose graphic content and convert them to animations.
- Create a beautiful responsive web page or marketing splash page, without coding knowledge.
- Create once and repurpose the content in different aspect ratios for all the social media platforms.

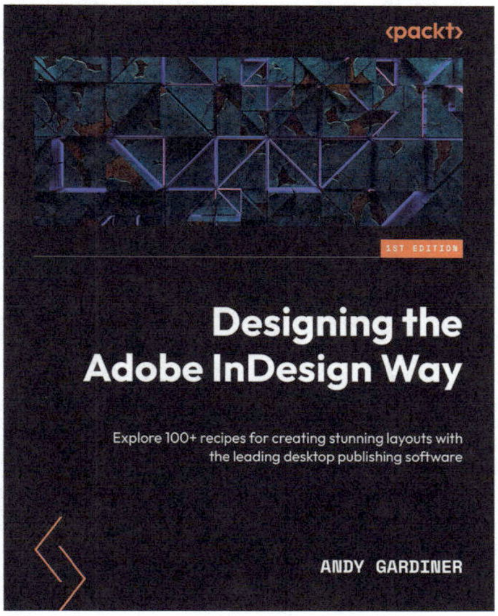

Designing the Adobe InDesign Way

Andy Gardiner

ISBN: 978-1-80107-443-8

- Navigate and customize the InDesign interface.
- Understand how to set up new documents for different types of content.
- Explore how to add and adjust content within your documents.
- Discover a range of tools to speed up your workflow and make you more efficient.
- Check your documents for errors and make the required corrections.
- Share your document output in different formats based on specific requirements.

Packt is searching for authors like you

If you're interested in becoming an author for Packt, please visit `authors.packtpub.com` and apply today. We have worked with thousands of developers and tech professionals, just like you, to help them share their insight with the global tech community. You can make a general application, apply for a specific hot topic that we are recruiting an author for, or submit your own idea.

Hello!

I'm Gary Bradley, author of *Mastering Adobe Photoshop 2024,* I really hope you enjoyed reading this book and found it useful for enhancing your digital editing skills and Photoshop Knowledge.

It would really help us (and other potential readers!) if you could leave a review on Amazon sharing any of the projects covered in the book.

Go to the link below or scan the QR code to leave your review:

`https://packt.link/r/1838822011`

Your review will help us to understand what's worked well in this book, and what could be improved upon for future editions, so it really is appreciated.

Best wishes,

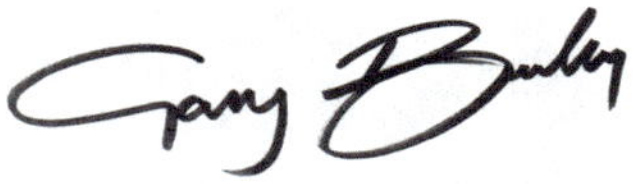

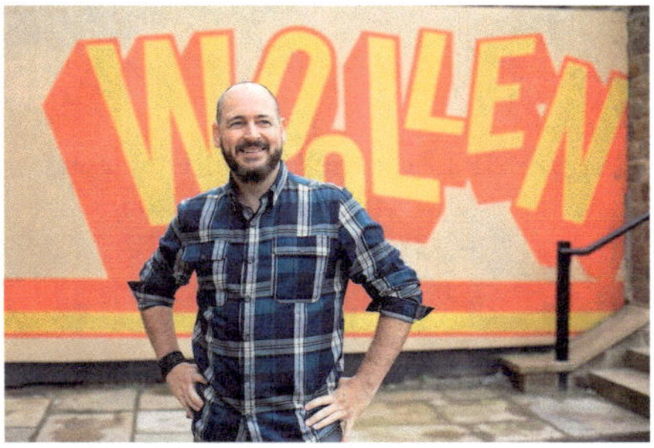

Download a free PDF copy of this book

Thanks for purchasing this book!

Do you like to read on the go but are unable to carry your print books everywhere?

Is your eBook purchase not compatible with the device of your choice?

Don't worry, now with every Packt book you get a DRM-free PDF version of that book at no cost.

Read anywhere, any place, on any device. Search, copy, and paste code from your favorite technical books directly into your application.

The perks don't stop there, you can get exclusive access to discounts, newsletters, and great free content in your inbox daily

Follow these simple steps to get the benefits:

1. Scan the QR code or visit the link below

`https://packt.link/free-ebook/9781838822019`

2. Submit your proof of purchase
3. That's it! We'll send your free PDF and other benefits to your email directly

Made in the USA
Columbia, SC
28 February 2024

32360743R00250